INTRODUCTION

THE real biography of Proust, that is to say, the history of his spiritual or intellectual life is to be found neither in his correspondence nor in the impressions garnered by his friends, but in *A la recherche du temps perdu* which he describes as 'le livre où j'ai mis le meilleur de ma pensée et de ma vie même'. I do not propose, therefore, in this study which is an attempt to interpret Proust's great novel, to discuss the external facts of his life. Indeed, these can be very briefly summarized because Proust, until the eve of his death in November 1922, was almost unknown to the general public.

The son of the distinguished physician, Professor Adrien Proust, Marcel was born at Auteuil, in 1871, at his uncle's house. His mother, a retiring lady, was a Jewess whose adoring love for her son was fully reciprocated by Marcel and is wonderfully expressed in those pages of his novel devoted to his studies of the narrator's grandmother and mother, both of whom reflect the character of Mme Proust. At the age of nine, Marcel contracted asthma, which resisted every form of treatment. As he remarks somewhere in *A la recherche du temps perdu*, the confirmed invalid learns how to compromise with the malady which, like an unwelcome guest, has elected a domicile in his body. This is exactly what Proust did all his life, though it must have been torture for one so passionately sensitive to natural beauty to be obliged, because of his asthmatic seizures, to dread the scent of flowers and trees in blossom. Illness, too, interfered with his studies at the lycée Condorcet and later, at the Sorbonne where, after a half-hearted attempt to study law, he turned in relief to philosophy. It was here that Proust, like so many of his fellow-students, came under the spell of Henri Bergson, who was subsequently related to him by marriage. As we shall observe, Proust discovered in Bergsonism an almost complete equivalent of his own attitude to life. One must always remember, however, that Proust was a novelist and not a metaphysician and, in the course of this study, I will try to show

the precise nature and extent of his affinities with Bergson whose
conception of reality so closely resembles his own.

Even as a schoolboy, Marcel had frequented the society of the
aristocratic Faubourg Saint-Germain and soon became a familiar
figure in the fashionable *salons* of the nineties. With Fernand
Gregh, Daniel Halévy, Léon Blum and others whose names have
since become famous, he helped to found an esoteric review,
Le Banquet, which was short-lived. By the end of the century,
he was known to a very limited circle as the 'Horatio' who
contributed articles to *Le Figaro* on the *salons* of the period.
In 1896, he published a booklet, *Portraits de peintres*, and
in the same year, a collection of articles and studies. Most of
them had already appeared in *Le Banquet* or in the Symbolist
organ, *La Revue Blanche*. They appeared under the title of *Les
Plaisirs et les Jours* and contained little to distinguish the author
from a dozen other young Parisians of talent. In 1900, he
wrote for *Le Mercure* an article on Ruskin. In 1904, Proust
translated *The Bible of Amiens* and, in 1906, *Sesame and Lilies*.
These were prefaced by two admirable studies, later revised
and included in the volume entitled *Pastiches et Mélanges* (1919).
Most of Proust's early articles and reviews were assembled
and republished by his brother in *Chroniques* (1927) which
contains also two brief but pregnant essays on the style of
Flaubert and Baudelaire.

The death of his mother, in 1905, was a grievous blow which
altered the tenor of Proust's life. Very soon, for this reason and
also because of his increasing bad health, he practically deserted
fashionable society, retiring to his celebrated cork-insulated
flat in the Boulevard Haussmann. Here Marcel embarked on
his 'recherche du temps perdu': his attempt to obtain a vision
of his real past, of his life as he had really experienced it in the
depths of his consciousness.

In 1913, he submitted for publication the first fruits of his
meditations, *Du côté de chez Swann.* Refused by three firms, it was
accepted at the author's expense, by Grasset. Proust's friends
wrote laudatory articles, proclaiming his genius. But the professional critics, except for Paul Souday of *Le Temps* who appreciated
its originality, preserved a stubborn silence in regard to this

first volume of Proust's novel. In June 1914, La Nouvelle Revue Française printed an extract from the unpublished *Le côté de Guermantes*. However, of the small group who had read *Swann* the majority remembered it as a queer, esoteric novel by an author who wrote in an alambicated style. Thanks to Jacques Rivière, who read Proust's first volume in a German prison camp, La Nouvelle Revue Française undertook to publish *A l'ombre des jeunes filles en fleurs*, which just managed to win the Goncourt Prize in November 1919. A bitter polemic arose. It was considered scandalous that the award should go to a wealthy dilettante, an habitué of the Ritz, a member of the Jockey Club who had spent the war-years in a nursing-home, whilst his rival, Dorgelès, was a demobilized fighting soldier. Proust had originally contemplated a work of three volumes, but these rapidly expanded, with *Le côté de Guermantes* and *Sodome et Gomorrhe*, into nine and, finally, into sixteen volumes. *La Prisonnière*, *Albertine disparue* and *Le temps retrouvé* were published after the author's death, at the age of fifty-one, from pneumonia.

By this time, of course, the gossip-writers of the flimsier literary journals were busy spinning a web of inaccuracies round the personality of the dead novelist and his *Correspondance générale*, edited by his brother, Dr Robert Proust, and Paul Brach, was eagerly awaited. It began to appear in 1930, and with Proust's own letters, those of his correspondents and various tributes, ran to six volumes. Even Proust's greatest admirers, if they were honest, had to admit a feeling of disappointment not unlike that described by the author himself when he first perused the letters of Flaubert. In an essay on Flaubert's style, he notes with pained surprise, how inferior is the language of the *Correspondance* to that of *Madame Bovary*. Readers of Proust's own letters who are familiar with the marvellous prose of *A la recherche du temps perdu* will have experienced an even greater sense of bewilderment.

The explanation of this disparity is to be found, I think, in one of the few distinguished passages which relieve the wearisome chronicle of Proust's domestic woes. 'Une œuvre', he remarks, 'vaut cependant mieux que nous-même.' The truth is

that these letters so piously collected and given to the world by
the author's brother can in no sense be called 'une œuvre', a
work of art. They are worth, not more than the writer, but very
much less both in style and in matter. No one will question
their value to the biographer. But the critic would do well to
read them after and not before he begins to interpret Proust's
great novel. Otherwise, his vision of *A la recherche du temps
perdu* is apt to be obscured. Echoes of Proust's *style parlé*, the
style of the letters, will mar his enjoyment of that unique creation, the style of Proust the artist. Buffon's famous saying: 'Le
style est de l'homme même' is only true if we do not isolate it
from its context, remembering that he was referring only to
'les ouvrages bien écrits' of an author, not to hurriedly penned
notes like those of Proust's *Correspondance* where the man, not
the creative artist, unfolds in a garrulous repetitive style which
is sometimes a dreadful *pastiche* of his full-dress manner, the
litany of his real and imaginary domestic troubles, the *kyrielle*
of his exaggerated enthusiasms and susceptibilities. All this
resembles the tuning-up of an orchestra in a dusty theatre
on rehearsal morning, with its discordant accompaniment of
wailing fiddles, gossiping charwomen and hammering stage-
hands. Occasionally, however, the hubbub is cleft by a pure,
sustained note, auguring the beauty that will be disclosed when
the curtain rises on the first performance. Such, for instance, is
the passage from a letter written in 1904:

Car si on cherche ce qui fait la beauté absolue de certaines choses,
des fables de La Fontaine, des comédies de Molière, on voit que ce
n'est pas la profondeur, ou telle ou telle autre vertu qui semble
éminente. Non, c'est une espèce de fondu, d'unité transparente où
toutes les choses, perdant leur premier aspect de choses, sont venues
se ranger les unes à côté des autres dans une espèce d'ordre, pénétrées
de la même lumière, vues les unes dans les autres, sans un seul mot
qui reste en dehors, qui soit resté réfractaire à cette assimilation...ce
qu'on appelle le Vernis des maîtres.

Yet, how rarely in these letters is Proust really himself; how
seldom does he live up to the golden counsel which Mme de
Sévigné addressed to all letter-writers: 'Soyez *vous* et non
autrui: votre lettre doit m'ouvrir votre âme et non votre biblio-

thèque!' But letter-writing for this unique woman was an art: Proust's art was the creation of novels. In the *Correspondance* there is hardly a trace of a conscious desire to write like an artist, to open his soul which was the soul of a man for whom art was the greatest thing in life. If at moments he writes finely in a letter, you are certain to rediscover the passage, beautifully refashioned and cunningly woven into the fabric of his creative work. A curious and typical instance is the letter, never printed because stolen from its owner, Mme de Noailles, in which Marcel described the death of his mother. This was inserted almost textually, according to Mme de Noailles, in the chapter of *Le côté de Guermantes* where Marcel narrates the illness and death of his grandmother. Then, the artist was stronger than the bereaved son. For a moment, in fact, the Proust of the *Correspondance*, the middle-aged, querulous invalid, moved aside in order to make way for the true Proust whose soul was in art and not in trivialities like unsold carpets, oil shares and doors that let in draughts.

Chapter I

DU CÔTÉ DE CHEZ SWANN

A la recherche du temps perdu is essentially the history of a vocation, or as Proust tells us, of an invisible vocation. At the outset, we must grasp this fact which is not, however, explicitly stated until the sixth volume. Otherwise, Proust's novel will seem formless and labyrinthine as it appeared, in fact, to his early critics whose incomprehension, now apt to strike us as a sign of congenital obtuseness, was on the contrary, very natural. One can sympathize, for instance, with the publisher, Humblot, when, after reading the opening pages of *Du côté de chez Swann*, he wrote to the author's friend, Louis de Robert: 'Cher Ami, je suis peut-être bouché à l'émeri mais je ne puis comprendre qu'un monsieur puisse employer trente pages a décrire comment il se tourne et se retourne dans son lit avant de trouver le sommeil.' And, to judge from much that has since been written about Proust by various critics, there are still Humblots whose minds are hermetically stoppered by a fundamental misunderstanding of this writer's main objective. What they fail to recognize is that *A la recherche du temps perdu* is not simply the reconstruction by the narrator, Marcel, of his past life. Indissolubly fused with this history is the narrative of Marcel's gradual spiritual evolution, the story of how his mind, by a progressive extension in breadth and depth, finally acquired that consciousness of existence which distinguishes the attitude or vision of the artist from that of other men. The narrator, therefore, who is about to unfold his bilateral history is the Marcel who has at last realized himself because he has discovered his predestined vocation—art. And in *A la recherche du temps perdu* we shall follow the contours and sinuosities of a mind, revealed to us at various levels, in the moving, ever-changing stream of the narrator's consciousness, reflecting at one moment the relatively superficial picturesque notations of a *mondain*, at another, the profound and disturbing impressions, visible only to the great artist, which represent the penetration of life into the deepest regions of the soul.

Nothing of this, of course, could be perceived by M. Humblot as he yawned over the opening pages of *Du côté de chez Swann*, though perhaps if his mind had been less rigidly ligatured by custom and prejudice, he might have discerned in these pages something more than the turnings and tossings of a gentleman afflicted by insomnia. For in this prelude is symbolized, I feel, or at least prefigured, if only roughly, Proust's dynamic scheme.

Picture, then, the Marcel of middle age, snuffing out his bedside candle and, book gently sliding from nerveless fingers, plunging into sleep only to be awakened half an hour later by the thought that it is time to go to sleep. Now, perhaps you may imagine, as everyone does before reading Proust, that going to sleep or not being able to go to sleep are experiences so trivial that there is really nothing to be said about them. In these pages, a past-master in the art of pleasant disillusionment removes the scales from your eyes and, through the medium of Marcel's narrative, discreetly suggests that the commonest acts of everyday life, if refracted in the artist's vision, are pregnant with intense and dramatic interest. To awaken, to emerge from sleep, one begins to realize, is to witness the enactment of a miracle play staged by a superhuman dramatist: its theme is the miraculous recovery of the sleeper's identity, the resurrection from a region which knows not Time or Space, of the individual self. Or perhaps it may be, as in the case of Marcel, the rescue by those unrecognized heroes, Memory and Habit, of a self hopelessly lost in the primeval, mysterious country in which man originally groped his way towards intelligence. This, it seems to me, is the miracle portrayed by Proust in Marcel's account of his dreams and awakenings, dreams of childish terrors, of adolescent, erotic hallucinations, of reversions to a mere cave-man sentiment of existence. Observe, too, the process of his return to full consciousness, the slow, inevitable, yet astonishing, recovery of the self called Marcel. During some fleeting instants the panic-stricken mind is completely disoriented whilst the memory of the body, says Proust, the memory of its ribs, shoulders and legs, anticipating thought, but only by a fraction, remembers the position of the bed, the windows, the doors. But what doors, windows and bed? Is it Marcel the small boy, on holiday at Combray, about to awaken in his little room with the marble mantelshelf and the urn-shaped lamp of Bohemian glass? Or is it the Marcel of many years later who has just dozed off before dinner at Mme de Saint-Loup's country-house at Tansonville? In these few seconds of uncertainty, a panorama flashes across the screen of his half-conscious mind, revealing a confusion of memory-pictures—images of different rooms he had inhabited at various seasons and sites of his psychological existence. And the Marcel now lying suspended between sleep and waking in his Paris flat had experienced, in all of those rooms, the same frantic efforts of a self fighting to recover its mislaid individuality, its particular niche in the world of things. This panorama reminds him, also, of the sleepless hours he passed in strange rooms where, even after his eyes had noted the exact shape and position of every object, the mind was still distressed until Habit intervened to rob surrounding objects of their unfriendliness and he was no longer convinced of 'l'hostilité des rideaux violets et de l'insolente indifférence de la pendule qui jacassait tout haut comme si je n'eusse pas été là'.[1]

Already, as I have suggested, the author has begun to prefigure to some extent the general scheme of his novel. Marcel, now thoroughly awake, continues to review the cortège of his memories.

Mais j'avais beau savoir que je n'étais pas dans les demeures dont l'ignorance du réveil m'avait en un instant sinon présenté l'image distincte, du moins fait croire la présence possible, le branle était donné a ma mémoire; généralement je ne cherchais pas à me rendormir tout de suite; je passais la plus grande partie de la nuit à me rappeler notre vie d'autrefois, à Combray chez ma grand'tante, à Balbec, à Paris, à Doncières, à Venise, ailleurs encore, à me rappeler les lieux, les personnes que j'y avais connues, ce que j'avais vu d'elles, ce qu'on m'avait raconté.[2]

Some of the leading threads in Proust's design are already visible and will emerge more clearly in the succeeding pages of

---

[1] *Swann*, I, 18. [2] *Swann*, I, 19.

this volume. Certain ideas, so far only faintly adumbrated, will take definite shape and indicate the importance of the role which they are to play in the narrative. One is undoubtedly the idea of Time which, as Marcel has just shown us, can sometimes be completely dislocated, for example, when we drop off to sleep after a night of insomnia and, on awaking, reveal a total ignorance of solar time. It is the same, too, with his idea of Space and the relation of his body to the rest of the spatial universe. And, again, there is Memory, especially the involuntary memory which must figure largely in Marcel's story along with Habit, that 'amenageuse habile' which does so much for our peace of mind and yet, as we shall discover, is a perfidious and dangerous companion, obscuring from us the reality of our self and of the external world. Dreams, too, one suspects, will have a place in Marcel's history for is there not, in the mechanism of the dreaming mind, a gigantic parody and reflection of what imagination may create in the waking mind under the influence of passion?

Indeed, as Marcel begins the history of his life, these ideas or themes rapidly acquire substance and form. They are woven by the Marcel who has at last discovered his vocation into the narrative of his childhood. In this he is not guilty of any anachronism because these impressions and ideas, though now communicated and for the first time rendered visible, constitute an original and integral part of Marcel's childhood, of existence as it was truly felt and intensely lived by him in the very depths of his being. Time and again, as his narrative will reveal, some intuition, the instinct of the artist as yet unconscious of his vocation, warned the boy Marcel to turn his mind inwards upon these precious sensations and impressions that gave him such unaccountable delight. Impatiently, however, he turned away to seek happiness elsewhere, in the impressions or sensations made upon his mind by its superficial, material contacts with things and people. Of the disillusionment and suffering that resulted from his persistence in this false attitude to reality Marcel will have much to tell us later in this 'histoire d'une vocation invisible'.

In this first volume of *Du côté de chez Swann*, the artist Marcel, reconstructs or, to use a more fluid and therefore more appropriate word, recomposes his childhood. It is summer in Combray, the village in Champagne where every year his family spend their holidays with Marcel's grand-aunt, his grandfather's cousin. Upstairs, in this house overlooking the rue Saint-Jacques is her daughter, Léonie, an eccentric widowed *malade imaginaire* whose maid, Françoise, is to occupy an important place in Marcel's history because, after the death of his aunt Léonie, she goes to Paris as servant to his parents. Yet Combray is anything but a village: it materializes, or rather incarnates, the beauty and moral stability of provincial France, the indestructible virtues, often unintelligible and annoying to foreigners, of the French people. Now, the places of our childhood are always sadly unrecognizable when we revisit them after the absence of years. The mind of the child receives the imprint of only a few impressions, but these are profoundly graven in the depths of its consciousness, in what Proust will later allude to as 'le livre intérieur'. So there exists in Marcel's memory a chart of a special kind on which are recorded impressions, partly material but largely intangible and spiritual, of certain objects which he instantly believed to be unique, treasuring them on that account. There are certain features of Combray which appear in strong and permanent relief, vibrating in a shimmering, mysterious atmosphere composed of exciting colours, sounds and smells. All of us possess such a chart, visible only to ourselves, for we cannot show it to others. Cartography of this kind is an art which is the property of the happy few, like Proust. And since all great art is essentially the revelation of human spiritual identities that had otherwise remained for ever invisible, we observe with mounting astonishment and delight that, in many respects, the chart which Marcel now interprets resembles our own. Such is the supreme function of art.

Let us glance at the salient features on Marcel's chart of Combray. To begin with, his grand-aunt's house defies all the rules of architecture, if not also the law of gravity. Downstairs are the dining-room and the tiny *salon* from which can be seen only a bit of garden-path, the part, in fact, which interests Marcel for reasons to be later divulged. Here, too, are the bottom treads of the staircase, apparently divided by space from the top-floor where a glassed door leads by way of a short corridor to the boy's room. That door is also very important because, nearly every evening about seven o'clock, Marcel's mother comes through it to kiss him good night. When she fails to come, it is sheer desolation. Therefore, at Combray it is always seven in the evening. This, you may object, is very odd, just as odd as the fragmentary house of Marcel's grand-aunt. But Proust would be surprised at your surprise.

A vrai dire [says Marcel] j'aurais pu répondre à qui m'eût interrogé que Combray comprenait encore autre chose et existait à d'autres heures. Mais comme ce que je m'en serais rappelé m'eût été fourni seulement par la mémoire volontaire, la mémoire de l'intelligence, et comme les renseignements qu'elle donne sur le passé ne conservent rien de lui, je n'aurais jamais eu envie de songer à ce reste de Combray.[1]

Here Proust enunciates for the first time a belief which was to be one of the fundamental tenets of his artistic creed. Its influence in shaping the grand design of *A la recherche du temps perdu* simply cannot be overestimated. The recollections that are so easily collected by the voluntary memory, the impressions picked up by the intelligence and arranged in chronological order give us a false map of our past. The real past consists of quite different impressions, in fact of those truly felt emotions and sensations which Marcel is even now busily engaged in communicating to us through the medium of an incomparable style. Observe, however, that at this particular phase in his work of recomposition, he is by no means certain that it lies within even the power of art to recover the impressions so profoundly imprinted in one's subconscious. 'Tout cela était en réalité mort pour moi. Mort à jamais? C'était possible.'

In a charming image inspired by a Celtic superstition, Proust compares such memories to souls held captive in an animal or in some inanimate object like a tree or stone, until one day somebody who loved them in life, passes by and they begin to tremble with excitement, sending out their mute and urgent

---

[1] *Swann*, I, 68.

appeal. The moment such recognition comes, their captivity is over. So, thinks Marcel, it is with his past.

Il en est ainsi de notre passé. C'est peine perdue que nous cherchions à l'évoquer, tous les efforts de notre intelligence sont inutiles. Il est caché hors de son domaine et de sa portée, en quelque objet matériel (en la sensation que nous donnerait cet objet matériel), que nous ne soupçonnons pas. Cet objet, il dépend du hasard que nous le rencontrions avant de mourir, ou que nous ne le rencontrions pas.[1]

His grand-aunt's villa; Aunt Léonie's apartment; the church of Saint-Hilaire; the optician's in the Grand' Place with its little weather-house in the shop-window; the divergent roads that lead, one to Méséglise, the other in the direction of the Guermantes estate and château; Montjouvain where the timid music-teacher and organist, M. Vinteuil lives with his gawky, boyish-looking daughter; Charles Swann's country-house at Tansonville—these are arresting features on Marcel's chart of Combray, the principal sites of his childhood life in the spring or summer season. Do not expect, however, a narrative subservient to the demarcations established artificially in Time by the makers of calendars for, although largely concerned at this stage with life in Combray, Marcel's narrative follows the contours and directions of his thoughts and is liable therefore, at any moment, to carry you swiftly to Paris and, in general, to pay small heed to chronological niceties.

In his grand-aunt's house are Marcel's parents, his beloved grandmother, Mme Bathilde Amédée, his grandfather, who quickly disappears from the scene, his grandmother's sisters, Flora and Céline whose amusing conversations reflect the essential spirit of everything that Combray stands for in France. The boy, an only child surrounded by grown-ups, is delicate and, because of his extreme sensibility, a source of anxiety to his mother and grandmother who steel themselves not to respond too often to his inordinate desire for affection. In every family there evolves, experimentally, a system of education shaped by local circumstances, by the character of the parents and by the temperament of the child for whom it is intended. In Marcel's family it is tacitly accepted that the actions most

[1] *Swann*, I, 69.

severely frowned upon are precisely those to which he is most
addicted, 'celles dont je comprends maintenant', he says, 'que
leur caractère commun est qu'on y tombe en cédant à une
impulsion nerveuse'. No one, of course, ever definitely alluded
to the cause of such actions since that, he subtly remarks, would
have been to infer, perhaps, that they were excusable. One of
the most beautiful and touching incidents in this first volume
and one which was destined to leave an indelible trace on
Marcel's emotional life, relates to this aspect of his upbringing.
Proust devotes to it some of the most sensitive pages he ever
wrote and, from time to time, we catch its echo in the chapters
dealing with Marcel's sentimental evolution.

A frequent visitor is Charles Swann to whom we shall be
properly introduced in a moment. Meanwhile, he is simply the
unwitting cause, at every visit, of a small boy's secret desolation.
In this superb Proustian collection of word-paintings, each of
which interprets a state of soul, you will discover several
Désolations du soir, all, I think, deriving from the original we
are about to contemplate. For when Marcel hears Swann's ring
at the garden-gate he is filled with a sick apprehension that his
mother will be prevented from coming upstairs; that he will
have to be content to say good night before the others. How
well Proust understands the gulf which separates the mind of
the grown-up from that of the child! Poor Marcel knows almost
by heart the ritual that announces his torture. Grandfather
remarks casually with 'unconscious ferocity' that the child
looks peaky and ought to go to bed, since dinner, in any case,
will be later that evening. Father, with equally careless brutality
cordially agrees and, as Marcel clings to his mother, showering
desperate kisses on her, he interrupts: 'Mais non, voyons,
laisse-là ta mère, vous vous êtes assez dit bonsoir comme cela,
ces manifestations sont ridicules. Allons, monte!' And the
small boy, like one ascending the steps of a scaffold, mounts the
accursed stairs, literally, *à contre-cœur*.

But on one particular evening, when the family are dining,
Marcel conceives a desperate scheme. Calling Françoise, he
asks her to hand to his mother at table a note begging her to

[1] *Swann*, I, 45.

speak to him about a serious matter which cannot be mentioned
in his note. But Françoise has nothing to report, on her return,
save that there is no answer, the terrible, stereotyped and
universal 'il n'y a pas de réponse', which as Proust reveals, with
his divine flair for the general human truth implicit in this little
incident, is an inevitable prelude to unwritten drama. Having
burnt his boats, Marcel is filled with a strange felicity and in
his little night-shirt, creeps to the landing, to begin his patient
vigil at the head of the stairs, determined at the cost of no matter
what punishment to waylay his mother on her way up to bed.
Nothing can be worse than the anguish of being deprived of his
viaticum, his good night kiss. From the garden he can hear
the tinkle of the bell that announces the departure of Swann,
a few desultory words, and then his mother's light footsteps on
the stairs. The shadow thrown by her candle grows bigger and
Marcel dashes forward to embrace her. His mother's first look
of astonishment swiftly changes into one of extreme displeasure.
She does not say a word and this is terrible because Marcel
knows that for more venial sins, he has often been sent to
Coventry for days. Suddenly, another shadow looms up and his
mother whispers to him furiously to go to bed at once. It is
too late. His father, candle in hand, his head swathed in a violet
and pink cashmere shawl as a precaution against neuralgia,
stands before them, like some patriarch of the Old Testament.
Tall, aloof, he listens to his wife's explanation and then, to their
stupefaction, with the gesture of Abraham telling Sarah she
must depart for the land of Isaac, laughs at his wife's consternation, airily waving aside her protests that it is bad for the boy to
encourage such habits.

'Mais il ne s'agit pas d'habituer', dit mon père en haussant les
épaules, 'tu vois bien que ce petit a du chagrin, il a l'air désolé, cet
enfant; voyons, nous ne sommes pas des bourreaux! Puisqu'il y a deux
lits dans sa chambre, dis donc à Françoise de te préparer le grand lit
et couche pour cette nuit auprès de lui. Allons, bon soir, moi qui ne
suis pas si nerveux que vous, je vais me coucher.'[1]

So Marcel spends the night in his room with his mother who
hushes his sobbings by reading him to sleep from *François le*

_____
[1] *Swann*, i, 58.

Champi: one of the most blessed nights in his life and also the saddest for, intuitively, he is aware that another furrow has been graven in the heart of his beloved *maman*. And the Marcel who now looks back on his past tells us how often he has relived the emotions of that night:

Mais depuis peu de temps, je recommence à très bien percevoir si je prête l'oreille, les sanglots que j'eus la force de contenir devant mon père et qui n'éclatèrent que quand je me retrouvai seul avec maman. En réalité, ils n'ont jamais cessé; et c'est seulement parce que la vie se tait maintenant davantage autour de moi que je les entends de nouveau, comme ces cloches de couvents que couvrent si bien les bruits de la ville pendant le jour qu'on les croirait arrêtées mais qui se remettent à sonner dans le silence du soir.[1]

What of Charles, the unconscious instrument of this emotional cataclysm? Proust, in projecting his character begins at once to employ that multilateral approach the effect of which is to lend to his great creations not only volume but the appearance of developing before our eyes. They are more dynamic than the creations of his predecessors in the novel. This method or technique originates, it would seem, in Proust's inveterate distrust of the analysing intelligence and its perceptions. Character, for Proust as for Bergson, is a synthesis of the individual's memories and is, therefore, in a continual state of change. No doubt, in certain moments of spiritual stress, the fundamental elements composing the individual self will surge upwards in a volcanic upheaval, breaking through the crust of acquired habits of behaviour and speech which constitute its superficial personality. Yet such volcanic upheavals, Proust would probably tell us, are very rare and in any case not often visible to the external observer. Nothing, in fact, is more difficult to observe than the truth about a person's character and, since most people have a very undeveloped faculty of perception which seldom penetrates below the surface and, moreover, since no two people ever perceive in the same way, an individual is apt to have as many characters as he has friends or enemies. The business of the novelist, therefore, if one may judge from Proust's own achievements, is to present characters in such a way as to reveal these

[1] *Swann*, I, 59.

complexities and obstacles which prevent one individual from knowing the true personality of another. The novelist must observe and project his characters at various descending levels of their *moi* and from different angles. This is the method he now adopts in presenting Swann who is shown to us here as he is seen by Marcel's family. His grand-aunts, who knew Swann's father, still think of the son as an agreeable young flibbertigibbet of no very assured position whose occasional gifts of fruit or Asti Spumanti are received as natural tokens of his gratitude and respect, meriting at best the most oblique and invisible of acknowledgements. If someone observes the name of Charles Swann in the *Figaro* amongst the guests invited by Princess Léon, Flora and Céline will smile to each other knowingly and remark to no one in particular: 'une princesse du demi-monde!' To them Swann is still a gay young fellow, an impression amply corroborated by his absurd marriage to the notorious *cocotte*, Odette de Crécy. Of the drama that led to this marriage they know nothing at all, though Marcel will shortly relate it in 'Un amour de Swann'. Charles, who rarely alludes, and then, apologetically, to his fashionable relationships, is known in the Faubourg Saint-Germain as a wealthy art connoisseur, gifted with exquisite tact and much sought after for his charming conversation and perfect manners. The *habitué* of the best *salons*, the intimate of *grands seigneurs* like the duc de Guermantes and his exclusive brother, the baron de Charlus, Swann is a popular member of the Jockey Club and the confidant of royalty. In his pocket-book as he now sits chatting with Flora and Céline is an invitation to Buckingham Palace. So Proust, by his multilateral approach, begins to expose the character of Swann, the truth about whom gradually presents itself to Marcel when he sees Charles Swann through the eyes of his grand-aunts, his grandfather, his grand-uncle Adolphe, the Verdurins, the Guermantes, through the anonymous informant, perhaps Charlus, who gave him the details of Swann's unhappy passion for Odette and, finally, through his own contacts. How difficult it is to 'know' anyone! The reality is constantly modified according to the changing site of the observer and the changing nature of the personality under observation. To Marcel, the little boy, it

seems at the moment that if Swann knew about his escapade on
the stairs, he would smile with pitying contempt for such
babyish weakness. But, as he learns afterwards, Charles Swann
is the one person who would, on the contrary, understand and
sympathize. To Marcel, the schoolboy, who falls in love with
Gilberte Swann, her father will be an Olympian figure whom it
is almost sacrilege to examine, much less to criticize. But this
is to anticipate Marcel's story.

In his Combray narrative, Marcel inserts the account of
a wonderful experience which did not occur, indeed, until many
years later. But most decidedly this is its proper context since
it describes the resurrection of a fragment of Marcel's life at
Combray. Part of his *moi*, of his being, long buried in the
oblivion of the unconscious, is now recovered, living and intact,
by a miracle. Such miracles, says Proust, happen when a chance
sensation, a perfume, a sound, a taste, analogous to the one
which long ago imposed the authentic seal of reality on a certain
experience, revives that reality. Marcel made such a discovery
in Paris, in his parent's apartment. He came home, one day,
cold and discouraged by the emptiness of life. His mother
insisted on his drinking a cup of tea and handed him one of those
shell-shaped little sponge-cakes which the French call *madeleines*.
This Marcel dipped in his tea and tasted. Suddenly, he was
invaded by an inexplicable sensation of joy which had apparently
no rational connection with the pleasure derived from eating the
cake.

J'avais cessé de me sentir médiocre, contingent, mortel. D'où
avait pu me venir cette puissante joie? Je sentais qu'elle était liée au
goût du thé et du gâteau, mais qu'elle le dépassait infiniment. Il est
clair que la vérité que je cherche n'est pas en lui, mais en moi.....Je
pose la tasse et me tourne vers mon esprit. C'est à lui de trouver la
vérité. Mais comment? Grave incertitude, toutes les fois que l'esprit
se sent dépassé par lui-même, quand lui, le chercheur, est tout ensemble le pays obscur où il doit chercher et où tout son bagage ne lui
sert de rien. Chercher? pas seulement: créer.[1]

Now, in language that astonishes by its lucidity, Proust
describes this first search for vanished time, Marcel's first

---

[1] *Swann*, I, 70.

sincere though incomplete effort to bring into clear consciousness and thus intellectualize that instant of real experience, the
existence of which is now so curiously presented to his awareness.

Je demande à mon esprit un effort de plus, de ramener encore une
fois la sensation qui s'enfuit. Et pour que rien ne brise l'élan dont il va
tâcher de la ressaisir, j'écarte tout obstacle, toute idée étrangère,
j'abrite mes oreilles et mon attention contre les bruits de la chambre
voisine.[1]

Ten times Marcel tries to grasp that elusive state of soul and
to rescue it from the magic cave of the subconscious. Then, when
about to yield to the cowardly advice of what most of us call
reason or common sense which suggests that he should just
drink his tea and forget the whole affair, patience is rewarded
and suddenly the memory surges up in all its beauty. It is
Sunday morning in Combray when Marcel's aunt Léonie used
to give him a morsel of her *madeleine* dipped in an infusion of
lime-tree flowers before he went to Mass. A train of subsidiary
and attendant recollections now slides into his conscious mind.
The various images that compose the Combray of his childhood
begin to form a pattern, as Marcel says, like those little Japanese
paper flowers which open out in a bowl of water. Here is his
grand-aunt's old grey house, Léonie's apartment, the *pavillon*
built on for his parents and looking out on the garden, the
square, the church, the streets, Swann's garden at Tansonville
with its gay flower-beds, the water-lilies in the little river
Vivonne—all marvellously emerge from a vanished past in
Marcel's cup of lime-blossom tea. But why did this memory
bring him such ineffable joy? Marcel confesses that he ought to
have explored this problem, so as to find out the mysterious
cause of his felicity. As we shall see, he did not make this
discovery until many years later and with it ended his 'recherche
du temps perdu'.

There is a maxim often quoted which I sometimes think
would reveal a larger truth were it transposed so as to read: *si
jeunesse pouvait, si vieillesse savait*. After all, is it not the child
who knows but cannot express the real beauty of the external
world? There is an essence, generated by an immediate contact

[1] *Swann*, I, 71.

of the child's mind with the familiar objects of its perception, which is poetry in the virtual state, awaiting creation. And so at every instant of existence the world is deprived of incalculable beauty, destined never to be materialized in language, music, painting or stone, like the soul of an unborn child which is doomed never to assume corporeal shape or substance. Not always. From time to time there emerges a creator, like Proust, who possesses the magic power of retaining and distilling into words the divine and fragrant essence secreted, as a state of soul, in the impressions of his childhood. And, more frequently than in any other section of his great work this unique power is supremely, though not by any means exclusively, illustrated in *Du côté de chez Swann*. Here are two selections from a treasury that offers an embarrassing *foison* of riches. The first is the passage revealing Aunt Léonie's room as it appeared to the unclouded vision of a small boy's consciousness.

C'étaient de ces chambres de province qui, — de même qu'en certains pays des parties entières de l'air ou de la mer sont illuminées ou parfumées par des myriades de protozoaires que nous ne voyons pas, — nous enchantent des mille odeurs qu'y dégagent les vertus, la sagesse, les habitudes, toute une vie secrète, invisible, surabondante et morale que l'atmosphère y tient en suspens; odeurs naturelles encore, certes, et couleur du temps comme celles de la campagne voisine, mais déjà casanières, humaines et renfermées, gelée exquise industrieuse et limpide des fruits de l'année qui ont quitté le verger pour l'armoire; saisonnières, mais mobilières et domestiques, corrigeant le piquant de la gelée blanche par la douceur du pain chaud, oisives et ponctuelles comme une horloge de village, flâneuses et rangées, insoucieuses et prévoyantes, lingères, matinales, dévotes, heureuses d'une paix qui n'apporte qu'un surcroît d'anxiété et d'un prosaïsme qui sert de grand réservoir de poésie à celui qui la traverse sans y avoir vécu. L'air y était saturé de la fine fleur d'un silence si nourricier, si succulent que je ne m'y avançais qu'avec une sorte de gourmandise, surtout par ces premiers matins encore froids de la semaine de Pâques où je le goûtais mieux parce que je venais seulement d'arriver à Combray: avant que j'entrasse souhaiter le bonjour à ma tante on me faisait attendre un instant, dans la première pièce où le soleil, d'hiver encore, était venu se mettre au chaud devant le feu, déjà allumé entre les deux briques et qui badigeonnait toute la chambre d'une odeur de suie, en faisant comme un de ces grands 'devants de four' de campagne, ou de ces manteaux de cheminée de châteaux, sous lesquels on souhaite que se déclarent dehors la pluie, la neige, même quelque catastrophe diluvienne pour ajouter au confort de la réclusion la poésie de l'hivernage....[1]

[They were the kind of rooms to be found in the provinces and which—just as in certain countries whole stretches of the air or sea are illuminated or perfumed by myriads of protozoa which we do not see—enchant us with the thousand smells emanating from the virtues, the wisdom, the habits, from a whole secret, invisible and moral existence suspended in their atmosphere; smells that are still, no doubt, natural and weather-tinted like those of the neighbouring countryside, but already home-loving, human and snug, the exquisite and limpid jelly patiently extracted from all the fruits of the year that have left the orchard for the store-room, seasonal but movable and domestic, offsetting the sting of hoarfrost by the sweetness of fresh-baked bread, idle and punctual like a village clock, nonchalant and re-liable, careless and provident, suggesting linen-closets, early mornings and piety, enjoying a peace which carries with it only extra anxiety and an uneventful happiness which offers a plentiful store of poetry to anyone who passes through it without having lived in this atmos-phere. The air of those rooms was impregnated with the quintessence of a silence so nourishing, so succulent, that I never went into them without a kind of greedy anticipation, especially in those early, still chilly days of Easter when I tasted it more enjoyably because I had just arrived in Combray: before I could go in to say good morning to my aunt they used to make me wait a moment in the front room where the sun, wintry as yet, had come to warm itself at the fire, burning already between its two bricks, plastering the whole room with a sooty odour, turning it into something like one of those rustic cowled oven-fronts, or one of those ingle-nooks in country-houses, esconced in which one hopes it will rain or snow outside, even that some terrific deluge will come down, thus adding to the comfort of being indoors the romantic sensation of being safe in winter-quarters....]

A few pages farther on, we light upon compacted perfections when Marcel, in language appropriate to the celebration of such a renaissance, reveals the original sensations and emotions evoked in him by the church of Saint-Hilaire at Combray, by its ancient porch, its storied windows and flagstoned choir, that 'pavage spirituel' beneath which is housed the noble dust of

[1] *Swann*, I, 76.

innumerable abbots of Combray; above all, by the ubiquitous steeple of Saint-Hilaire. For, as he tells us, if every part of this venerable edifice seems to him unique because it is pervaded by a kind of thought, it is in its steeple that Combray church acquires full consciousness of itself and appears to affirm its individuality.

Quand, après la messe, on entrait dire à Théodore d'apporter une brioche plus grosse que d'habitude parce que nos cousins avaient profité du beau temps pour venir de Thiberzy déjeuner avec nous, on avait devant soi le clocher qui, doré et cuit lui-même comme une plus grande brioche bénie, avec des écailles et des égouttements gommeux de soleil, piquait sa pointe aigue dans le ciel bleu. Et le soir, quand je rentrais de promenade et pensais au moment où il faudrait tout à l'heure dire bonsoir à ma mère et ne plus la voir, il était au contraire si doux, dans la journée finissante, qu'il avait l'air d'être posé et enfoncé comme un coussin de velours brun sur le ciel pali qui avait cédé sous sa pression, s'était creusé légèrement pour lui faire sa place et refluait sur ses bords; et les cris des oiseaux qui tournaient autour de lui semblaient accroître son silence, élancer encore sa flèche et lui donner quelque chose d'ineffable.[1]

[When, after Mass, we used to go into Theodore's and tell him to bring a larger tea-cake than usual because our cousins had taken advantage of the fine weather to come over from Thiberzy to lunch with us, we had in front of us the steeple which, baked golden-brown itself like a larger, hallowed tea-cake, with gummy scales and droplets of sunshine, poked its sharp point into the blue sky. And in the evening, when I came back from my walk and was thinking that I should very soon have to say good night to my mother and not see her any more, the steeple was on the contrary so kindly, at the close of day, that it looked as if it had been placed and thrust like a brown velvet cushion against the pale sky which had yielded under its pressure, had hollowed slightly so as to make room for it and was flowing back over its edges; and the cries of the birds that wheeled round it seemed to amplify its silence, to prolong the uprush of its spire and to invest it with an ineffable quality.]

If, as M. Benda suggests, it is a serious fault for a novelist to be 'à ses heures' a poet, then I fear Proust is an unregenerate offender. However, one may admire the writings of M. Benda —in which so much is admirable—without being obliged to

---

[1] *Swann*, i, 97.

accept his rather stringent conception of the novelist's art. On the other hand, *Du côté du chez Swann* is by no means exclusively the narrative by a sensitive interpreter of the profoundly poetic impressions deposited in Marcel's inmost soul by his life in Combray. Nothing, indeed, could be farther from the truth than to picture his boyhood and adolescence as a perpetual 'rêve intérieur'. Frequent though they are, these flashes of immediate consciousness are intermittent. They constitute, as Proust always maintains, the most real, because most intensely felt, part of Marcel's childhood; but they are interwoven with a mass of other impressions that are less profound and touched with a different, less ethereal beauty. Always in Marcel's narrative we shall be confronted by this interpretation of a self observed at various levels and from changing sites of observation.

There are many old saws and wise maxims which really ought to be overhauled from time to time and, in some cases perhaps, discarded. One which I can no longer take at its face value is Walpole's saying that 'the world is a comedy to those that think, a tragedy to those that feel'. One must read Proust to realize the fundamental inaccuracy of this typically eighteenth-century observation, for he shows us, as indeed everyone may discover who examines his own thoughts and feelings, that profound sensibility is just as often a source of joy as of suffering; and that to those who really think and do not merely receive surface impressions of things and people the world is apt to be, not a comedy, but a tragedy or at any rate a spectacle pregnant with serious significance. The truth which is everywhere reflected in *A la recherche du temps perdu* is that the world, for Proust as for many great artists, is a much more complicated and dynamic organism than one might be led to believe from Walpole's trite remark. The mind of the individual who observes it is not to be conceived as dominated alternatively by the faculties of feeling and thinking: it is an ever changing stream of interfused states of consciousness. We must not therefore expect, in the universe about to be presented in Marcel's narrative, the clear-cut psychological demarcations established by the classic dramatists and carried over by their admirers into the traditional novel of analysis.

Proust, in portraying the extreme sensibility of Marcel the child interprets this complexity. For, although bedtime can be so often invested by sensibility with the genuine emotional atmosphere of tragedy, the very same faculty, in the daytime, reveals to him an exciting suite of joyous and beautiful images or sensations; whether he is rambling alone in the woods round Roussainville, strolling with his parents out Guermantes' way, reading in the garden the novels of his idol, Bergotte, on golden summer afternoons, visiting Aunt Léonie's apartment before Mass or just watching Françoise, in the kitchen, engaged in the entrancing business of dishing up the evening meal. On the whole, this Combray world is sunny and beautiful because, as Marcel knows, bad weather in summertime is not really bad weather. It is just a passing ill humour, not to be taken seriously.

L'été, le mauvais temps n'est qu'une humeur passagère, super-ficielle, du beau temps sous-jacent et fixe, bien différent du beau temps instable et fluide de l'hiver et qui, au contraire, installé sur la terre où il s'est solidifié en denses feuillages sur lesquels la pluie peut s'égoutter sans compromettre la résistance de leur permanente joie, a hissé pour toute la saison, jusque dans les rues du village, aux murs des maisons et des jardins, ses pavillons de soie violette ou blanche.[1]

To the casual outsider, Combray is a sleepy little *bourg* where nothing ever happens and Marcel's domestic environment is that of a typically solid French bourgeois family on holiday with their typically provincial aunts and cousins. And so they are— to the objective spectator. To Marcel, however, life at Combray is a succession of lovely and eventful days, marred sometimes by the approaching hour of seven when he will enter that zone of sadness which separates the exultant happiness of a walk along the banks of the Vivonne from the lonely night. But the days are crowded with little dramatic incidents, rich in comedy and vastly instructive to an alert and insatiably inquisitive mind. As Proust's narrative reveals, our knowledge of the psychological laws that determine human actions is not to be gained so much from the impressive examples constructed by the historian or dramatist as by watching, for instance, the

[1] *Swann*, I, 220.

behaviour of an Aunt Léonie, a Françoise or by overhearing
one's parents discussing the odd conduct of a M. Legrandin or,
better still, by listening to M. Legrandin himself.

Léonie is what the French, who respect the classic origins
of their language, call 'une vieille maniaque', very different
therefore from her English equivalent. She is a harmless,
amusing rather queer old lady who lives in a continual state of
intense suppressed excitement. Having taken to her bed after
the death of her beloved Octave, she enjoys all the pleasures of
bad health with few of its distressing and painful symptoms.
No one quite knows, indeed, what ails her: no one dares, on the
other hand, even to breathe such a doubt. The curious thing
about Léonie is that she never sleeps. This is such an accepted
fact in the family circle that it is no longer regarded as a phenomenon so that Marcel, like Descartes, has acquired a profound
distrust of the evidence offered to his mind by his senses. They,
for example, when he tiptoes into Aunt Léonie's room and sees
a recumbent figure with closed eyes emitting sounds which in
anyone else would be snores, would probably try to tell him
that the old woman is asleep, though of course this is nonsense.
She is resting or meditating with her eyes shut. Léonie's day
does not have twenty-four hours: it is divided into the pepsin
hour, the Vichy-water hour, the hour of Vespers, of the curé's
visit, the really interesting hour marking the arrival of her
chief intelligencer, Eulalie, a devout spinster who brings all the
gossip about the section of Combray invisible from Léonie's
window in the rue Saint-Jacques. If, as upon the occasion
divertingly re-created for us by Proust, the curé's hour should
clash with Eulalie's, a remarkable psychological comedy is
enacted, portraying a veritable tangle of conflicting emotions
and desires. For the curé, good soul, is a local historian, a mine
of inaccurate and picturesque etymologies, a fanatical and pitiless toponymist to whom Léonie is constrained to listen with
barely concealed weariness, anxiously signalling the while to
Eulalie not to leave before the departure of her silver-haired
and innocent tormentor. When Eulalie has emptied her sack of
gossipy odds and ends the curtain rises on another comedy. This
is the presentation of the tip, the coin which Eulalie never fails

to accept but with elaborate reluctance, mock embarrassment and annoyance. This is a ritual so that, if one day Eulalie seems less reluctant and, especially, less vexed than usual, Aunt Léonie is heard to remark in some puzzlement: 'Je ne sais pas ce qu'avait Eulalie; je lui ai pourtant donné la même chose que d'habitude, elle n'avait pas l'air contente.'[1]

A jealous, disapproving silent observer of these antics is Françoise, Aunt Léonie's servant. But when Eulalie has gone, Françoise, having satisfied herself by a peep through the chink in the curtains that the front door is closed behind the intruder, launches invariably into a muttered diatribe, loud enough for her mistress to hear, against the departed Eulalie whose name, however, is never uttered. Watch how Proust with his instinct for the unique, inevitable and revelatory phrase, captures her attitude:

'Les personnes flatteuses savent se faire bien venir et ramasser les pépettes; mais patience, le bon Dieu les punit toutes par un beau jour', disait-elle avec le regard latéral et l'insinuation de Joas pensant exclusivement à Athalie quand il dit: '*Le bonheur des méchants comme un torrent s'écoule.*'[2]

Here, incidentally, is the first of those amusing and ingenious Racinian transpositions which never fail to illuminate their new and unexpected context and, very often, in certain painful situations exercise a beneficial and disarming influence on the reader.

Marcel always thinks of Françoise and the simple little rustic church of Saint-André-des-Champs at Roussainville as incarnating the attributes, good and bad, of the French peasant. For there stands in the porch of Saint-André-des-Champs a saint who could have been modelled on a younger Françoise or on any of the peasant girls of the region who dart in from the fields to shelter from a thunderstorm. Note in this passage the perfect trilogy of epithets which, like a nimbus, lights up the moral countenance of the artist's subject, the French peasant.

Non plus appliquée à la pierre comme ces petits anges, mais détachée du porche, d'une stature plus qu'humaine, debout sur un socle comme sur un tabouret qui lui évitât de poser ses pieds sur le sol

[1] *Swann*, I, 156.   [2] *Swann*, I, 158.

humide, une sainte avait les joues pleines, le sein ferme et qui gonflait
la draperie comme une grappe mûre dans un sac de crin, le front
étroit, le nez court et mutin, les prunelles enfoncées, l'air valide,
insensible et courageux des paysannes de la contrée.[1]

The insensibility, the cruelty of Françoise towards anybody
outside her own family or her employer's, is a continual enigma
to Marcel until he gradually learns that human nature, the
moment we observe in depth, presents an inexplicable mixture
of cruelty and kindness; that the vices and virtues, contrary to
the traditional belief so profusely and marvellously illustrated
in the paintings of the Italian masters, are not apportioned to
separate individuals but lavishly and carelessly showered by the
Creator upon all and sundry. I imagine also that, boy-like,
Marcel is apt to confuse the perfume of his beloved Françoise's
admirable roast chicken with the odour of her virtues. In any
case, he is constantly and rudely shaken by undeniable examples
of her callousness, one of which particularly disturbs him.
Françoise will allow no other servant to attend her mistress or
to cook for the family. But, as she is overworked, a kitchen girl
is hired who very soon begins to show signs of approaching
maternity, resembling as Swann points out, one of Giotto's
symbolic Virtues and thereafter referred to by the family as
'La Charité de Giotto'. This wretched girl is surreptitiously
harried from pillar to post by Françoise whose virtuous contempt
is equalled only by her astonishment that any young man could
have been so depraved as to seek the favours of this ill-favoured
creature. One night, shortly after her accouchement, La Charité
is seized with violent gripes. The doctor is not accessible but,
fearing these attacks, he had left a medical book open at the
page describing the expected symptoms and their treatment.
Marcel's mother tells Françoise to fetch this book and since, at
the end of an hour, she has not yet returned, he is sent down to
the kitchen to make inquiries. There he discovers Françoise
avidly reading the clinical description of the girl's symptoms,
wailing piteously at each new one mentioned, punctuating her
sobs with invocations to the Holy Virgin. Yet, when she is
obliged to pass from the abstract contemplation of this fascinating

[1] *Swann*, I, 219.

malady to the business of alleviating its effects on the wretched patient, all Françoise's compassion vanishes and, furious at having to lose her sleep, she vents her ill-will, once the family is out of earshot, in a flood of muttered abuse and frightful sarcasms. But if her little grandson has a cold, Françoise will set out at night even when she herself is ill, to see if her help is required, trudging the ten miles back to Combray before dawn to be in time for Léonie's *lever*.

I use the word deliberately for, says Proust, if you want to form a real impression of the mechanism of the daily life at court in the reign of Louis XIV you need go no farther than Léonie's apartment at Combray. In the eyes of Françoise, this old lady, the owner of several prosperous farms, is a potentate whose every gesture must be furtively scrutinized, every word carefully weighed. Now, as Marcel instinctively divines, Aunt Léonie lives in two worlds. One is visible to the casual observer who sees merely an eccentric old hypochondriac fussing over her medicine bottles, excessively devout, inordinately curious about the smallest item of Combray news, spending hours in bed with her interminable games of patience. Léonie has also a secret and dramatic inner world where, for instance, the house catches fire and all are consumed in the flames except herself who is miraculously spared to serve as an example of Christian fortitude to the rest of Combray. For this intrepid Léonie, bravely disregarding her bodily ills, gets up, drags herself to church and to the cemetery, a spectacular and admired figure in sombre black, the ideal of a mourner, an example to all who observe. I hope I am wrong, but one gathers from this narrative that the innocent card game of patience is apt in Proust's view, by over-stimulating the imagination, to encourage in solitary old ladies a mild tendency to schizophrenia. Léonie, who loves to think periodically that she is being robbed by Eulalie, or more often, by Françoise, holds lengthy conversations with herself. Now these are not what critics describe as 'monologues intérieurs' when they want to define the peculiar technique of certain modern novelists. They are duologues between a triumphant Léonie and a Françoise caught *in flagrante delicto*, but only after a prolonged and subtle investigation of the crime by a master-mind. These dramatic confession scenes, where Léonie assumes the implacable role of a judge confronting a broken and stammering culprit, are frequently overheard by Françoise. And sometimes Léonie, tiring of what Marcel calls 'spectacles dans un lit', stages the real thing. To Françoise she confides her suspicions of Eulalie, to the latter her doubts on the honesty of Françoise who lives in the house and, therefore, is the natural target of Léonie's innuendoes and oblique, dark accusations. As a result, Françoise watches the old lady with extraordinary attention, trying to decipher the meaning of her silences, her passing frowns, her equivocal phrases exactly like a courtier at Versailles in the reign of the Great Louis. Very logically, Marcel's parents interpret this behaviour as the expression of Françoise's growing hatred of the tyrannical Léonie only to discover, however, at her death many years later how wrong was their diagnosis.

Pendant les quinze jours que dura la dernière maladie de ma tante, Françoise ne la quitta pas un instant, ne se déshabilla pas, ne laissa personne lui donner aucun soin, et ne quitta pas son corps que quand il fut enterré. Alors nous comprîmes que cette sorte de crainte où Françoise avait vécu des mauvaises paroles, des soupçons, des colères de ma tante avait développé chez elle un sentiment que nous avions pris pour de la haine et qui était de la vénération et de l'amour. Sa véritable maîtresse, aux décisions impossibles à prévoir, aux ruses difficiles à déjouer, au bon cœur facile à fléchir, sa souveraine, son mystérieux et tout-puissant monarque n'était plus. A côté d'elle nous comptions pour peu de chose. Il était loin le temps où quand nous avions commencé à passer nos vacances à Combray, nous possédions autant de prestige que ma tante aux yeux de Françoise.[1]

[During the fortnight of my aunt's last illness, Françoise did not leave her for an instant, never undressed, refused to let anyone do the smallest thing for her and did not leave her body till it was buried. Then we understood that the sort of fear in which Françoise had lived of my aunt's hard words, suspicions and outbursts of anger had developed in her a feeling which we had mistaken for hatred and was veneration and love. Her real mistress, she of the absolutely unpredictable decisions, baffling ruses, the kind, so easily softened heart, her sovereign, her mysterious and all-puissant monarch was no more.

[1] *Swann*, I, 221.

Compared with her we were of very little account. Distant was that time when, on first coming to spend our holiday at Combray, we used to possess as much prestige as my aunt in the eyes of Françoise.]

This conclusion is worth noting because it is not only typical of Proust's method of presenting a situation but reflects a view of human nature which will be frequently demonstrated in Marcel's narrative. Where another novelist might well have remained content to end this Léonie-Françoise episode upon a note of high comedy, of comedy, that is to say, which provokes general reflections on human nature, such is not Proust's notion of completeness. *A la recherche du temps perdu* is not, as has sometimes been ineptly asserted, a book of memoirs or an autobiography. It is a novel where, therefore, no incident can exist *in vacuo* but must always form an integral if minor element in the general evolving design of the work of art. We have not finished with Léonie simply because she is dead and in her grave; this we shall observe in discussing the volumes entitled *Albertine disparue*. And, in prolonging the situation in order to reveal how inaccurate were the impressions made by Françoise on Marcel's parents, Proust also had a larger purpose in mind. The vast majority of us, he tacitly suggests, go through life wearing invisible blinkers, to employ Bergson's striking metaphor, so that our vision, like Sam Weller's, is extremely limited —Proust would say—by our intelligence.

In this Combray chapter where Proust so truly reflects the quality and evolution of Marcel's adolescent mind, there are two characteristics which he seems to accentuate. One is, of course, the boy's instinctive belief in the uniqueness of certain things, the conviction that certain objects that leave a special trace on his consciousness possess an intrinsic and individual beauty of which there is no equivalent. The other is a belief that older people are what they seem to be or what they say they are. How Marcel came to lose both these beliefs will emerge progressively from his narrative for this is one of its principal themes. Meanwhile, in the pages introducing M. Legrandin, Proust shows us how Marcel first realized that in any individual whom we know well there may reside two completely different personalities, one of whom may be as invisible to himself as it remained so long to his friends. Proust seizes the occasion to exercise his remarkable talent for psychological analysis, not, it is true, in great depth because Legrandin is a relatively minor character, but on the plane of comedy which naturally precludes exploration on a grand, introspective scale. Nevertheless, operating on this level, Proust displays a freshness of approach, an acuity of perceptiveness which, reinforced by his incomparable sensitiveness to the qualities latent in simple words, place him in a class by himself. In his brief study of Legrandin we can detect one of the secrets of Proust's originality as a novelist of manners. I mean his uncanny gift for reflecting, not so much the physical traits of a character as for rendering immediately audible, nay visible, the latter's intonations or mode of utterance. When Proust is engaged in communicating the behaviour of people in society, what they say is nearly always instructive or amusing; but what is really illuminating is their way of saying it, for then the true and hidden personality becomes visible through the screen of banalities known as conversation.

M. Legrandin is by profession a talented civil engineer though his spiritual vocation, he would have us know, is art and, in particular, poetry. He has in fact two or three slim volumes to his credit and his literary reputation is steadily advancing. Mme Amédée, Marcel's grandmother, professes not the smallest knowledge of art. She possesses, however, an instinctive dislike of any deviation from the simplicity and truth of nature. So, whilst admiring the naturalness and informality of Legrandin's dress and manner, she thinks it a pity that these qualities are not reflected in his conversation. Legrandin talks well, too well, like a book. But in common with the family she regards him as 'le type de l'homme d'élite prenant la vie de la façon la plus noble et la plus délicate'.[1] Still, she is surprised at Legrandin's excessive detestation of the aristocracy and at his violent tirades against snobbery, in his view the sin for which there is no remission. Marcel's grandmother is so utterly devoid of any social ambitions that she simply cannot understand why anyone should waste his breath fulminating against such an absurd and incomprehensible mania. Besides, Legrandin's vociferous

[1] *Swann*, I, 101.

republicanism is not, perhaps, in the best of taste because his
sister is married to M. de Cambremer, a nobleman who has
a château close to Balbec, a seaside resort in Lower Normandy.

One evening, Marcel's father joins the family in Léonie's
apartment, bringing exciting news. Apparently, in some mysterious way, he must have offended Legrandin for the latter,
who was in the company of an elderly châtelaine of the region,
barely returned his salute gazing, as Marcel observed, over his
father's head at some invisible and distant point on the horizon.
This, however, is put down to imagination or perhaps to the distraction of a poet busy with other less mundane thoughts. And,
in fact, Legrandin greets them next day with outstretched hand
and, for Marcel, a quotation from Paul Desjardins. But another
incident shows beyond doubt that their original impression was
correct. Outside church, after morning Mass, the family witness
the spectacle of a transformed Legrandin, wreathed in syco-
phantic smiles, bowing deeply as he is presented to the wife of
an important local squire. Watching his antics, Marcel has his
first intuition of the existence of a Legrandin very different from
the proud and intransigent Jacobin, or from the poet whose
conversation he so much admires because of the speaker's
obvious contempt for things that are not of the spirit. This
other earthy and possibly gross Legrandin, certainly in no way
reminiscent of the Ariel Legrandin, is revealed to him in the
movements of the latter's ridiculous and fleshy rump. But let
Proust tell it in his own language:

La figure de Legrandin exprimait une animation, un zèle extra-
ordinaires; il fit un profond salut avec un renversement secondaire
en arrière, qui ramena brusquement son dos au-delà de la position de
départ et qu'avait dû lui apprendre le mari de sa sœur, Mme de Cambremer. Ce redressement rapide fit refluer en une sorte d'onde
fougueuse et musclée la croupe de Legrandin que je ne supposais pas
si charnue; et je ne sais pourquoi ce flot tout charnel, sans expression
de spiritualité et qu'un empressement plein de bassesse fouettait en
tempête, éveillèrent tout d'un coup dans mon esprit la possibilité d'un
Legrandin tout différent de celui que nous connaissions.[1]

[On Legrandin's face there was an expression of extraordinary
animation and zeal. He made a deep bow—taught him no doubt by the

[1] *Swann*, I, 181–2.

husband of his sister, Madame de Cambremer—with a secondary, backward jerk which carried his shoulders beyond their original position.
This rapid, straightening movement produced a kind of agitated, muscular ripple in Legrandin's rump which was fleshier than I had imagined;
and I don't know why this undulation of pure matter, this entirely carnal
surge devoid of any spiritual expression whatever and lashed into a
tempest by his servile eagerness to please, evoked suddenly in my mind
the possibility of a Legrandin quite different from the one we knew.]

Read, too, on the same page, the marvellous analysis of the
'cut indirect' as practised by a virtuoso in snobbery, by the type
of snob who wants to make the best of two social worlds,
sidling past Marcel's family with a secret twinkling, blue glance
of connivance in extreme contrast to the impassive expression
of the section of his features visible to his exalted companions.
Marcel, dining next evening with Legrandin sees his intuition
confirmed as the result of an idle question. He asks his host if
he knows the Guermantes, thereby innocently probing a deep
and ulcerated wound. It is not Legrandin's words, however,
that reveal him as 'un Saint Sébastien du snobisme'. It is, as
the following passage so admirably divulges, Legrandin's way
of saying that he does not know the Guermantes, though the
dream of his life is to be presented to the Guermantes:

'Non, je ne les connais pas' dit-il, mais au lieu de donner à un
renseignement aussi simple à une réponse aussi peu surprenante le ton
naturel et courant qui convenait, il le débita en appuyant sur les mots,
en s'inclinant, en saluant de la tête, à la fois avec l'insistance qu'on
apporte, pour être cru, à une affirmation invraisemblable — comme si
ce fait qu'il ne connût pas les Guermantes ne pouvait être l'effet que
d'un hasard singulier — et aussi avec l'emphase de quelqu'un qui, ne
pouvant pas taire une situation qui lui est pénible, préfère la proclamer
pour donner aux autres l'idée que l'aveu qu'il fait ne lui cause aucun
embarras, est facile, agréable, spontané, que la situation elle-même —
l'absence de relations avec les Guermantes, — pourrait bien avoir été
non pas subie, mais voulue par lui, résulter de quelque tradition de
famille, principe de morale ou vœu mystique lui interdisant nommé-
ment la fréquentation des Guermantes. 'Non,' reprit-il, expliquant
par ses paroles sa propre intonation, 'non, je ne les connais pas, je
n'ai jamais voulu, j'ai toujours tenu à sauvegarder ma pleine indépendance; au fond je suis une tête jacobine, vous le savez.'[1]

[1] *Swann*, I, 185-6.

['No, I don't know them' he said, but instead of using the natural everyday tone appropriate to such a simple piece of information, to a reply so very unremarkable, he enunciated it with special emphasis on each word, leaning forward and nodding, not only in the convincing, insistent manner of one who is making an improbable statement—as if the fact of his not knowing the Guermantes could only derive from some strange freak of chance—but also with the pomposity of someone who, finding it impossible to keep quiet about a situation painful to himself, prefers to proclaim it openly in order to give others the impression that the confession he is making causes him no embarrassment at all, is in fact, easy, agreeable, spontaneous; that the situation itself—his not knowing the Guermantes—might very well not have been imposed on him by circumstances but be of his own seeking, resulting from some family tradition, moral principle or mystic vow making it impossible for Legrandin to call on the Guermantes. 'No,' he continued, explaining by his words the intonation he had given them, 'no, I don't know them, I've never wanted to; I've always made a point of guarding my complete independence; at heart, you know, I'm a bit of a Jacobin.']

The Marcel who is dining in the moonlight with Legrandin, unlike the Marcel who is reviewing this scene, cannot of course grasp all its nuances. But his common sense tells him that Legrandin is not quite truthful when he claims that old churches, pictures, a handful of favourite books, moonlight and youth are the only things he cares for. Marcel knows that he cares very much for the aristocracy and what they would think about his bourgeois friends. He is a snob. Is he not also a hypocrite? For Legrandin continues, just as before, to fulminate against snobbery and to profess his contempt for the nobility, to the amusement of Marcel's mother and the annoyance of his father. Marcel the narrator, with his larger knowledge of the human mind, points out that Legrandin is quite sincere in these protestations. He does not know he is a snob because no man sees his passions objectively. Our passions do not influence us directly, but indirectly, through the imagination which, as Marcel now realizes, substitutes for our original and crude motives, secondary motives of a much more pleasant aspect. Legrandin's snobbery never tells him crudely that he ought to visit duchesses.

Il chargeait l'imagination de Legrandin de lui faire apparaître cette duchesse comme parée de toutes les grâces. Legrandin se rapprochait de la duchesse, s'estimant de céder à cet attrait de l'esprit et de la vertu qu'ignorent les infâmes snobs.[1]

Only to the external observer who cannot see the intermediary operation of Legrandin's imagination does the latter appear as a common-or-garden snob. This is subtly and truly observed but it does not explain away the essential and reprehensible trait in the character of the snob—the fact that he is ashamed of his friends whilst still clinging to their friendship. This point of view, however, is also appreciated by Proust because he shows us Society as represented by Marcel's father avenging itself by ridicule on the snob, Legrandin. At the same time, like the clever novelist he is, Proust begins already to prepare the stage for future events. Marcel's father who is thinking of sending his boy with Mme Amédée for two months to Balbec, perfectly aware that Legrandin's aristocratic relatives have a château there, maliciously asks him if he knows anyone in those parts whom he might introduce to his mother-in-law. Thoroughly alarmed, the elusive Legrandin takes refuge in the inaccessible regions of poetry.

J'ai des amis partout où il y a des groupes d'arbres blessés, mais non vaincus, qui se sont rapprochés pour implorer ensemble avec une obstination pathétique un ciel inclément qui n'a pas de pitié pour eux.[2]

But his implacable examiner is not so easily shaken off and at every subsequent interview renews his interrogation whilst the wretched Legrandin racks his brains for fresh reasons why Balbec is the one place in France to which Marcel should not be sent for his summer holidays. But, to the end, nothing will induce him to admit that he has a sister living two miles from Balbec. Here is a delightfully humorous and original situation admirably exploited by Proust whose eye once again roves beyond the immediate present. We shall of course make the closer acquaintance of Balbec and Mme de Cambremer but we shall also observe, in the chapters dealing with Marcel and Albertine, the survival, in the former, though expressed in a very different way, of his father's implacable tenacity.

---

[1] *Swann*, I, 188.   [2] *Swann*, I, 191.

Two incidents in this Combray narrative might suggest that
even when a child is blest with admirable parents like Marcel's
for whom the basic elements of a sound upbringing are truth-
fulness and candour, occasions arise when it is imprudent to
practise these excellent qualities. Marcel has a school comrade,
Bloch, who is at once recognized by his grandfather, a connoisseur in such matters, as a Jew. Not that he has any objection
to Jews: it is merely that their reticence about their racial
origins strikes him as excessively humorous, justifying the
greatest wariness in one's dealings with them. Therefore, having
contrived by a subtle interrogation, to discover that Bloch, as he
had suspected, is a member of the chosen tribe, the old man, as
is his invariable custom, when one of Marcel's Jewish friends
come to the house, gleefully hums the airs though not the
words from Halévy's *La Juive* to the profound embarrassment
of his grandson, terrified lest the visitor recognize the text:
'De ce timide Israëlite, Quoi! vous guidez ici les pas.' I do not
think that Bloch would have been in the least disconcerted for,
older than Marcel, he is possessed of unlimited assurance.
Bloch has reached the disillusioned period of adolescence, the
age of sweeping and devastating judgements on literature and
life; of a vast contempt for the so-called classics, for grossly
overrated writers like Racine and Corneille or 'sinistres brutes'
such as Musset or Vigny; the age of immense enthusiasms for
the new writers like Leconte de Lisle; of cynical generalizations
on women accompanied, naturally, by an immeasurable scorn
for the ridiculous habits and virtues of the bourgeoisie. All the
familiar symptoms of adolescence are to be found in their most
rabid form in Marcel's new comrade. Certainly, his parents
would have preferred another companion for their boy though
they wisely keep their opinions as far as possible to themselves.
His father, however, says quite bluntly that in his view Bloch
is an idiot and, to be quite fair, what is one to think of a lad
who replies, when asked whether it is raining: 'Monsieur, je
ne puis absolument vous dire s'il a plu. Je vis si résolument en
dehors des contingences physiques que mes sens ne prennent
pas la peine de me les notifier.' This is not what leads, however,

---

[1] *Swann*, I, 135–6.

to the temporary disappearance of Bloch: it is Marcel's impulsive habit of taking his parents into his confidence. For his comrade swears that he has learned on unimpeachable authority that Marcel's grand-aunt, in her youth, had led a very dissipated life and, indeed, had been publicly kept by at least three wealthy lovers. When Marcel ingenuously passes on this information to his horrified papa and mamma young Bloch, on his next visit, is shown the door and to Marcel's surprise is slightly cold towards him at their next meeting. Bloch will turn up again on many occasions and, oddly enough, we shall observe that he has not essentially changed. There is in Bloch's character a uniformity that distinguishes him from most of Proust's creations. Some of his enthusiasms and exaggerations will of course disappear or be toned down with age, yet his character, in developing, will not reveal new or unsuspected aspects. He is, in short, much more of a type than, for example, even Mme Verdurin or Brichot.

But Marcel relates another of his impulsive confidences which has serious consequences. It concerns his grand-uncle, Adolphe, and is the reason why this dear old bachelor, a retired officer, no longer spends his summer holidays at Combray. Once or twice a month, after lunch, it was Marcel's custom to visit the old gentleman in his Second Empire Paris flat. Now, Adolphe has a weakness for pretty *cocottes* and actresses so that some days are taboo for the purpose of family visits. This rule dates back to an unfortunate occasion when grand-uncle Adolphe's brother had been obliged to speak to him very severely about his habit of introducing his stage countesses to the lady members of the family. By accident, once, Marcel called on one of the wrong days and was ushered by a rather stupid man-servant into the presence of a somewhat flustered grand-uncle Adolphe and of a ravishingly beautiful and vivacious lady in pink. Marcel was old enough to guess that she must be one of those mysterious *cocottes* to whom his parents in private conversation sometimes alluded, invariably with amusement. He is vaguely disappointed to find that she is not very different from his mother's friends and certainly does not possess the theatrical appearance of his favourite actresses, Bernhardt, La

Berma, Madeleine Brohan or Jeanne Samary; for Marcel, in his small way, also collects actresses. In any case, she is absolutely charming so that before his grand-uncle gently pushes him off to school he rushes forward and kisses her hand, to the vociferous delight of the lady in pink. That evening, bursting with excitement, he recounts his visit in minute detail to his parents. There is a stormy interview between them and Adolphe. A few days later, Marcel sees his grand-uncle passing in an open carriage, but instead of saluting him, looks the other way because, he explains, a banal gesture like raising his hat seemed so utterly inadequate to express his seething remorse, grief and gratitude. Adolphe, unfortunately, concludes that the boy is obeying his parents' orders and for this non-existent offence he never forgives them, dying many years later without their ever having seen him. As for the ravishing lady in pink, though Marcel does not discover her identity until long afterwards, she is Odette de Crécy, recently married to Charles Swann. And that is why, although Swann still occasionally drops in to pass the time of day with Marcel's father and grandfather, the family do not call on Mme Swann at Tansonville where, according to Combray scandal, there are fine goings-on between Odette and her husband's old friend, M. de Charlus. [1]

The prevailing mood of this Combray chapter is best conveyed, I think, in Mallarmé's 'le vierge, le vivace et le bel aujourd'hui', that line where lies ensnared the very spirit of youth, the exaltation aroused by sheer joy of living which Marcel, as he strides through the woods and fields round Combray can only express by shouting, singing and threshing the bushes with his stick. Yet something tells him that it is not enough, in the presence of such divine beauty, just to make appreciative noises, admiring gestures or to leap with excitement and ejaculate *zut! zut!* 'Mais en même temps', he says, 'je sentis que mon devoir eût été de ne pas m'en tenir à ces mots opaques et de tâcher de voir plus clair dans mon ravissement.' This is not his first inkling of the precious truth that for the artist an experience is complete only when by an intellectual effort he has understood and translated into words or some other

[1] *Swann*, I, 224.

medium, the unique quality of his sensations. Marcel realizes
this from the serenity that invaded him once when he wrote
down his impressions of the charming ballet danced for his
entertainment by the steeples of Martinville and Vieuxvicq
against the background of a twilight sky as he rattled along the
winding roads in Dr Percepied's dog-cart. He did not profoundly explore those impressions, yet somehow, by the act of
transmuting them into language, Marcel experienced a sense
of inner completeness, of spiritual satisfaction. How often will
he regret, in after life, his failure to repeat that intellectual
exercise, his lethargy and passive acceptance of mere sensuous
enjoyment, his apostasy to art now gloriously purged, however,
by the author of this Combray chapter.

To interpret the sensations inspired in Marcel by Combray
and its environs, Proust ravages the treasure-rooms of all the
arts for the metaphor or simile which will translate his impressions and thus stamp them for ever on the reader's mind.
Who can ever forget the opening words of that passage where
he describes the little field-path at Tansonville?[1]

Je le trouvai tout bourdonnant de l'odeur des aubépines. La haie
formait comme une suite de chapelles qui disparaissaient sous la
jonchée de leurs fleurs amoncelées en reposoir; au-dessous d'elles, le
soleil posait à terre un quadrillage de clarté, comme s'il venait de
traverser une verrière; leur parfum s'étendait aussi onctueux, aussi
délimité en sa forme que si j'eusse été devant l'autel de la Vierge, et
les fleurs, aussi parées, tenaient chacune d'un air distrait son étincelant
bouquet d'étamines, fines et rayonnantes nervures de style flamboyant
comme celles qui à l'église ajouraient la rampe du jubé ou les meneaux
du vitrail et qui s'épanouissaient en blanche chair de fleur de fraisier.
Combien naïves et paysannes en comparaison sembleraient les églan-
tines qui, dans quelques semaines, monteraient elles aussi en plein
soleil le même chemin rustique, en la soie unie de leur corsage
rougissant qu'un souffle défait.

This command of imagery, this talent for expressing one
form of beauty in terms of another gives Proust a unique place
in French prose literature, superior even to that occupied by
Chateaubriand. In his view, it is only the metaphor that can
lend eternity to style. In *Du côté de chez Swann* transposition is

---

[1] *Swann*, I, 199, 200.

already employed with superlative effect but tentatively, as if the
author were experimenting with a device the nature of which he
defines later in his description of the work of the impressionist
painter, Elstir.[1]

Mais les rares moments où l'on voit la nature telle qu'elle est,
poétiquement, c'était de ceux-là qu'était faite l'œuvre d'Elstir. Une
de ses métaphores les plus fréquentes dans les marines qu'il avait
près de lui en ce moment était justement celle qui comparait la terre
à la mer supprimant entre elles toute démarcation.

In *Du côté de chez Swann,* Proust employs this device of transposition, half-humorously, for example, when he attributes to
the snob and dilettante, Legrandin, the following deliberately
precious impressions.

'Il y a dans les nuages ce soir des violets et des bleus bien beaux,
n'est-ce pas, mon compagnon,' dit-il à mon père, 'un bleu surtout plus
floral qu'aérien, un bleu de cinéraire, qui surprend dans le ciel. Et
ce petit nuage rose n'a-t-il pas aussi un teint de fleur, d'œillet ou
d'hydrangéa? Il n'y a guère que dans la Manche, entre Normandie et
Bretagne, que j'ai pu faïré de plus riches observations sur cette sorte
de règne végétal de l'atmosphère. Là-bas près de Balbec, près de ces
lieux sauvages, il y a une petite baie d'une douceur charmante où le
coucher du soleil du pays d'Auge, le coucher de soleil rouge et or que
je suis loin de dédaigner, d'ailleurs, est sans caractère, insignifiant;
mais dans cette atmosphère humide et douce s'épanouissent le soir en
quelques instants de ces bouquets célestes, bleus et roses, qui sont
incomparables et qui mettent souvent des heures à se faner. D'autres
s'effeuillent tout de suite et c'est alors plus beau encore de voir le
ciel entier que jonche la dispersion d'innombrables pétales soufrés ou
roses.'[2]

['There are some very lovely violet and blue tints in the clouds
this evening aren't there, my friend,' he said to my father, 'a blue,
especially, that is more flower-like than aerial, a cineraria blue, surprising to find in the sky. And just look at that little pink cloud!
Don't you think it, too, has the tint of a flower, of a carnation or
hydrangea? Only perhaps on the Channel coast, between Normandy
and Brittany do I remember having observed richer specimens of
what one might call this vegetable kingdom of the atmosphere. Down
yonder, near Balbec, near those wild regions, there is a charmingly
sweet little bay where the sunset of the Auge district, the red and

[1] *JF.* ii, 124.   [2] *Swann*, i, 189.

gold sunset which, incidentally, I am very far from despising, possesses no character; is insignificant. But in that humid, soft atmosphere, suddenly, in the evening, some of these heavenly posies unfold
their blue and pink blossoms; they are incomparable and often take
hours to fade. Others fall at once and then it is even lovelier still to
see the whole sky strewn with innumerable, drifting sulphur or pink
petals.']

This, if you like, is a Proustian pastiche of Proust. Not so the
lovely description of the water-lilies in the Vivonne, a charming
example of transposition, by which the artist expresses the
beauty of flowers in terms of water and sky.

A woodland fragrance pervades the early chapters of the novel.
It filters into the little church in Combray where young Marcel
has his first vision of the duchesse de Guermantes. Here Proust
illustrates that phenomenon called by Stendhal 'crystallization',
that process by which the poet or lover invests the object of his
admiration with all the romantic perfection of his dreams. True,
there is a moment when Marcel is surprised and disconcerted
to see only a lady with a red face over a mauve cravat. But this
image is quickly transfigured when he places the duchess in the
ambience that is really hers, the ambience of history, of that gallant
feudal age storied in the stained-glass windows of Combray
church and bathed in the amethyst tints of the name Guermantes.

Et aussitôt je l'aimai, car s'il peut quelquefois suffire pour que nous
aimions une femme qu'elle nous regarde avec mépris comme j'avais
cru qu'avait fait Mlle Swann et que nous pensions qu'elle ne pourra
jamais nous appartenir, quelquefois aussi il peut suffire qu'elle nous
regarde avec bonté comme faisait Mme de Guermantes et que nous
pensions qu'elle pourra nous appartenir. Ses yeux bleuissaient comme
une pervenche impossible à cueillir et que pourtant elle m'eût dédiée;
et le soleil menacé par un nuage, mais dardant encore de toute sa force
sur la place et dans la sacristie, donnait une carnation de géranium
aux tapis rouges qu'on y avait étendus par terre pour la solennité et
sur lesquels s'avançait en souriant Mme de Guermantes, et ajoutait
à leur lainage un velouté rose, un épiderme de lumière, cette sorte
de tendresse, de sérieuse douceur dans la pompe et dans la joie qui
caractérisent certaines pages de Lohengrin, certaines peintures de
Carpaccio, et qui font comprendre que Baudelaire ait pu appliquer au
son de la trompette l'épithète de délicieux.[1]

[1] *Swann*, I, 255–6.

[And immediately, I fell in love with her because, if sometimes, for us to fall in love with a woman, it is enough that she should despise us as I had thought Mlle Swann did me and for us to think she can never be ours, sometimes, too, she may only have to bestow upon us a kindly look, as Mme de Guermantes was doing, for us to think she may be ours some day. Into her eyes crept the blue of a periwinkle-flower, impossible to pluck, yet seemingly dedicated by her to me; and the sun, threatened by a cloud, beating down, however, with all its strength on the Square and into the sacristy, suffused with a geranium hue the red carpets laid down for the wedding-ceremony and across which Mme de Guermantes was smilingly advancing, enhancing their fleeciness with a velvety pink, a film of luminosity, with that sort of tenderness, of sweet seriousness mingled with pomp and joyfulness which characterize certain pages of Lohengrin, certain paintings by Carpaccio and make us understand why Baudelaire applies the epithet 'delicious' to the sound of the trumpet.]

That confusion of exaltations generated in the adolescent soul by *la joie de vivre*, by the absorption through the eager senses of nature's essence and beauty, by the stirring of vague sexual desires is wonderfully interpreted in Marcel's narrative of his solitary rambles out Méséglise way. Mysteriously, his love of woman is completely interfused with his passionate love of Roussainville or Méséglise so that the imaginary peasant girl whom he longs to hold in his arms must be a peasant girl from Roussainville or Méséglise: any other encounter, it seems, would constitute a kind of emotional anachronism. This state of soul is beautifully and clearly revealed in Proust's words:

C'est qu'aussi — comme il arrive dans ces moments de rêverie au milieu de la nature où l'action de l'habitude était suspendue, nos notions abstraites des choses mises de côté, nous croyons d'une foi profonde, à l'originalité, à la vie individuelle du lieu où nous nous trouvons — la passante qu'appelait mon désir me semblait être non un exemplaire quelconque de ce type général: la femme, mais un produit nécessaire et naturel de ce sol. Car en ce temps-là tout ce qui n'était pas moi, la terre et les êtres, me paraissait plus précieux, plus important, doué d'une existence plus réelle que cela ne paraît aux hommes faits. Et la terre et les êtres je ne les séparais pas.[1]

Proust does not fall into the error of confusing this Marcel of the tumultuous, incoherent desires with the boy who, not

[1] *Swann,* I, 226.

long before, had fallen in love one lovely summer's afternoon
with little Gilberte Swann at Tansonville beside a hawthorn
hedge in bloom. In this scene also, youth, desire and natural
beauty are presented in their inevitable trinity but in a different
emotional atmosphere, in the climate of first love where desire,
purified of its sensuality, has the spiritual quality of a longing
for happiness that is intangible and unattainable. Before his
first vision of Gilberte, Marcel had created a picture of her
formed of impressions communicated to him by Swann and
glorified by an imagination stimulated by memories of Bergotte's
novels. For Gilberte, he learns from her father, is Bergotte's
little friend who accompanies him on visits to the cathedrals
of Normandy and L'Île de France and every day enjoys the
unique privilege of listening to Bergotte's conversation. She
is, therefore, a creature who moves in an almost separate
world from ordinary mortals. So, when Marcel catches his first
glimpse of Gilberte through a screen of may-blossom, in an
immense garden or pleasaunce gay with wallflowers, jasmine,
pansies and verbenas, his soul almost leaps out of his eyes to
meet hers. It is a brief encounter, his father and grandfather
having moved on, yet long enough to capture an unforgettable
impression of a girl flushed with the sun, with fair, almost
coppery hair and eyes of heavenly blue. As he stands transfixed,
she looks down and sideways at his companions, then turns upon
Marcel a glance which plainly reveals her indifference and disdain.
And suddenly with no change of expression save a faint and slyly
contemptuous smile, Gilberte raises her hand in a rude, deliberately insolent gesture which fills him with rage and despair since
it leaves no possible doubts concerning her opinion of his person
and his company. Yet, even whilst seized with a crazy impulse
to pay her back in kind, to shout at her that she is grotesque,
ugly, hateful and repellent, Marcel knows that she is the most
beautiful creature he has ever seen. He has fallen in love:

Cependant, je m'éloignais, emportant pour toujours comme premier
type d'un bonheur inaccessible aux enfants de mon espèce de par des
lois naturelles impossibles à transgresser, l'image d'une petite fille
rousse, à la peau semée de taches roses, qui tenait une bêche et qui
riait en laissant filer sur moi de longs regards sournois et inexpressifs.

Et déjà le charme dont son nom avait encensé cette place sous les épines roses où il avait été entendu ensemble par elle et par moi, allait gagner, enduire, embaumer, tout ce qui l'approchait, ses grands-parents que les miens avaient eu l'ineffable bonheur de connaître, la sublime profession d'agent de change, le douleureux quartier des Champs-Elysées qu'elle habitait à Paris.[1]

The lovely serenity reflected in the prevailing tone of this Combray narrative is fractured, near its close, by a strange and ugly incident which at the moment appears to leave no durable imprint on Marcel's mind yet is destined to have a profound influence on his emotional life. At Montjouvain, near Combray on the road to Méséglise lives a music-teacher, M. Vinteuil. His wife is dead and all his affections are centred on his daughter, a robust clumsy-looking girl whom he treats, however, as if she were a delicate child, fussing over her shawls and wraps, to the amusement of the Combray ladies. But it is kindly amusement. Everyone loves Vinteuil, with his old-fashioned prudishness and morbid fear of wounding anyone's susceptibilities, his excessive timidity and utter selflessness. The rumour goes that he is a composer although, when Marcel's parents beg him to play one of his own pieces, he invariably whisks the score from the piano wondering audibly who could have put it there. Marcel knows how the music got there because the Vinteuil house is built at the bottom of a slope, so that one day, lying under a bush, he is able to look right into the *salon* not a yard away. As his parents are about to enter, he can see Vinteuil hesitatingly take the music from his pocket, lay it open on the piano and then, when his visitors arrive, whisk it away into a corner, fearful lest they might imagine they had been invited only to hear his compositions. Years later, the autumn of Aunt Léonie's death, Marcel happens one sultry day to fall asleep on that very spot under the bushes and, on awakening, finds himself again in the role of unseen though involuntary spectator. What he sees on this occasion is terribly different from the little comedy I have just described.

Vinteuil is dead, of grief, caused by his daughter's infatuation for a woman older than herself and of evil repute, who had

[1] *Swann*, i, 206-7.

settled in their house before her father's death. The old man, in
his desperate anxiety to protect his child's reputation told all
Combray that her friend was a superior person with a heart of
gold, gifted with a remarkable talent for music. Some, like old
Dr Percepied, sniggered behind Vinteuil's back. Others like
Marcel's mother felt sad as they waited for the approaching
spiritual and physical *débâcle*. There is no need to reproduce the
scene witnessed by Marcel or the conversation he overheard
between these two Lesbians, except to remark that it took place
shortly after Vinteuil's death. His photograph, indeed, lies on
the table, placed there by Mlle Vinteuil's friend from a sadistic
desire to profane, in this symbolic fashion, the memory of the
dead man whom she loathed and despised.

The horrible incident, naturally, leaves only an obscure
impression on the mind of Marcel to whom sexual immorality
is thus for the first time manifested in one of its rarest and most
unnatural forms. Proust explains or justifies its intrusion at
this juncture on two grounds. The first is that the memory of
this scene is to play a most important part in the evolution of
Marcel's history. The other reason is that, many years later,
the incident helps Marcel to form an original idea of sadism
and thus, as I gather from his analysis of this idea, to view the
problem of evil in a new perspective. Now, even those who
have never read Proust know that he devotes unusual attention
to the study and interpretation of Lesbianism, homosexuality
and in a minor degree, to the kindred vice of sadism. I should
like to make it clear, at once, that considering the vast scope
of *A la recherche du temps perdu* and the fact that it is a detailed
and illuminating survey of numerous human passions, vices,
manias, foibles and virtues, the three particular vices to which
I have alluded cannot really be said to occupy an inordinate
place in the author's general scheme. The Proustian approach
to these abnormal aspects of human behaviour varies considerably, depending upon the manner and modality of their
expression. For even sadism, as will be revealed in another
context, can sometimes be, not frightful, but simply absurd. In
Mlle Vinteuil, it is neither frightful nor absurd but pitiful.
Looking back on that Montjouvain incident, Marcel cannot see

in the desperate attempts of this unnatural daughter to extract
a diabolic, voluptuous sensation from the profanation of paternal
love, the reflection of a fundamentally evil soul. With profound
wisdom and tolerance, he remarks that did she not in her heart
secretly revere the memory of her father, if she were not by
nature sentimental and virtuous, Mlle Vinteuil would not find
a sacrilegious pleasure in defiling these virtues. In the very act
of abandoning herself to her sadistic impulses she cannot help
betraying in every word gesture and intonation her striking
resemblance to the father she is trying so hard not to resemble.
This is not a clever paradox, an attempt to explain away vice
and evil by subtle dialectic. Proust's attitude is, I think, that
vice and evil are terrible realities; yet the irremediably vicious
people are not the Mlle Vinteuils who think that evil is a rare
or extraordinary state of mind, the source of a mysterious and
unholy pleasure. There is a more appalling, permanent and
universal form of sadism though it does not bear this name. It
is the cruelty which takes the form of indifference to the sufferings we cause in others. And that, as we shall discover, is
to be one of the master themes of Proust's novel because it
plays an enormously more important role in the general scheme
of things than the sadism of a Mlle Vinteuil or a M. de Charlus.
'Un amour de Swann' discloses an order of sensations and
ideas very different, on the whole, from those we have met
in the Combray volume. Some, indeed, regard it as a kind of
hors d'œuvre compromising, therefore, the unity of Proust's work
of art. My own view is that, on the contrary, *A la recherche du
temps perdu* would be incomplete without this episode which,
although it concerns events that took place before Marcel's birth,
forms a necessary prelude to the narrative of his love for
Gilberte and his social relations with the Swanns, Verdurins
and Guermantes. Above all, however, the story of Swann's
jealous passion for Odette which is related, on hearsay, by
Marcel is an indispensable preliminary to the narrative of his
own tragic love for Albertine. The two dramas, although each
has a solution deriving from the individual character of the
protagonist and evolves, therefore, on a different intellectual
plane, must be viewed as an ensemble, as constituent elements

of Proust's searching inquiry into the problem of jealousy.
What emerges in this second volume of *Du côté de chez Swann*
is Proust's interpretation of adult passion, of its genesis and
development in the soul of an experienced *mondain*, a man
sensitive to certain artistic values, capable of moments of rare
delicacy and, also, of 'une certaine muflerie' or caddishness.
Here again, the author takes up the challenge implied in Stendhal's phrase and, with incredible richness of notation, describes
the crystallization of love, elaborating a motif which by its
sweet brevity, seems to echo the *petite phrase de Vinteuil*. For
the pathetic little Montjouvain music-teacher was a composer the
full extent of whose genius has not yet been revealed to the
world, though connoisseurs like Charles Swann are beginning
to perceive in the fragment called *La sonate de Vinteuil* the work
of a great creative artist. Observant Stendhalians will discern in
Proust's narrative of Swann's love, passages that recall their
favourite novelist. These are not, however, imitations but the
original interpretations of a state of soul which Stendhal never
completely explored. That was not for lack of talent. It was
because he distrusted the Romantic attitude, the language of
Chateaubriand, the imagery of the Romantic and their constant
'retour à soi' preferring the clarity, the restraint and simplicity
of the seventeenth-century idiom. Proust, who belonged to a
later generation and, what is immensely more important, had a
much larger conception of what he used to call 'l'acte intellectuel'
than Stendhal or any of his great predecessors, was able to
enjoy the best of several worlds of art. From his greater perspective, he was able to appreciate all their qualities and limitations. Moreover, he is nearly always conscious of his own
originality as an observer of human nature.

Thus, to the exploration of the strange, complex effects of
love on Swann, Proust brings a vision unclouded by passion.
He stands on the plane only attained by Marcel after he has
found his vocation, after the sufferings inflicted on him by love;
for, as Proust always infers, the act of artistic creation is the
translation of really lived and felt experience into its intellectual
equivalent, the communication through the medium of an inevitable style of passions and emotions which must be relived

integrally if art is to fulfil its essential purpose of recomposing life. That is why Proust's interpretation of Swann's infatuation for Odette offers a greater illusion of reality than even Stendhal's portrayal of Mosca's hopeless passion for Sanseverina or Julien Sorel's lust for domination. Stendhal often allowed his vivid memories of his personal experience to obscure the lucidity of his creative vision. This never occurs in Proust.

On the hour that Charles Swann observes in his mistress, Odette de Crécy, a resemblance to Botticelli's Zephora the curtain rises on a drama which is universal and eternal because its theme is jealous love. Yet it is a drama that never repeats itself because the characters, the action, the milieu never combine to form the same design. Prévost, for example, narrates in *Manon Lescaut* the tragic passion inspired in a man of breeding and education by a courtesan, yet nothing could less resemble, despite this general similarity of circumstances, the infatuation of Charles Swann for the *cocotte* Odette. Swann is not a Des Grieux haunted by the intermittent conciousness that, in sacrificing all for love, he has been faithless to the other Des Grieux, the gentleman and scholar who was destined for a noble and dignified vocation. In Swann's relations with Odette the problem of spiritual or intellectual incompatibility can hardly be said to constitute a case of conscience. The question of social incompatibility does on the other hand complicate Swann's existence and it is only when he can no longer bear the tortures of jealousy that he marries the woman whose infidelities, real and imagined, nearly drive him out of his senses.

It is hard to discern the figure of the real Manon since we must perforce view her always through the tinted and distorting screen of her romantic chevalier's idolatrous adoration. Odette is presented, in typical Proustian fashion, from a variety of changing points of view. We surprise her in various moods and situations, reflecting in every new speech gesture and intonation the charm, the shallowness, the amorality of her little *cocotte's* mind. We see her first through the eyes of Swann, in the first, Botticelli stage of his infatuation, fragile and sweetly feminine, surrounded by her orchids and chrysanthemums in her expensive chocolate-box of a house, prattling nonsense over the tea-cups, or else with her arms clinging round her lover's neck, looking up at him with the expression that makes men wish they had led a cleaner life, evoking Swann's latent chivalry and tenderness. Only later does he begin to suspect that the expression of lassitude in Odette's drawn features and in her wistful, beautiful eyes may signify nothing at all or perhaps merely that her butterfly thoughts are settling on questions of new frocks, smart restaurants or on the engrossing problem of how to catch up with the latest form of 'le chic'. In so far as she can love anyone, however, she does at this stage love Charles because he is new, rich, elegant, intriguing and absurdly courteous. Besides, with his monocle, he is 'frightfully distinguished looking'. Moved by that strange madness which makes lovers afraid lest the very monotony of their happiness may finally quench the exciting glow of their romantiç passion, Charles sometimes dashes off a letter full of phrases simulating disappointment, anger, jealousy, simply for the joy of receiving her frightened little note: 'Ma main tremble si fort que je peux à peine écrire.' He little imagines that soon there will come an hour when all his feigned emotions will be transfigured into torturing realities.

There are very few pages in this history of Swann's love and jealousy for Odette de Crécy which do not illuminate the profound truth condensed in Proust's maxim that 'l'art recompose exactement la vie'. Many novelists of genius have interpreted the theme of jealous love in the grand, passionate manner of the classic dramatists but I cannot think of any novel which so faithfully re-creates the gradual dramatic process of the upheaval produced by love in the psychological life of a Charles Swann who, despite his informed and genuine taste for the fine arts, might be described as 'l'homme sensuel moyen'. Swann is a man of naturally phlegmatic temperament, conservative in his habits, essentially bonhomous, viewing human nature with a critical and intelligent disillusionment. What distinguishes him from the majority of fashionable Parisian clubmen is his reputation as a connoisseur of the arts, especially of painting, though to describe him as an enthusiast would be to employ a very strong expression. Swann's keen appreciation of artistic beauty is always tempered by a Faubourg Saint-Germain and ingrained horror of exaggeration in any form.

Only with this general impression in mind can one gauge the nature of the evolution or revolution the progress of which is so marvellously communicated in Proust's 'Un amour de Swann'. Viewed in retrospect, Swann's pleasant, tolerant, half-bored attitude towards Odette may first be said to have crystallized into love as the result of an unexpected interruption of an accepted state of things. Such, I think, is the implication of the scene describing the arrival of Charles at the Verdurin party only to find that Odette has already left. Read the passage that follows with its description of Charles frantically searching all the fashionable restaurants of the boulevards and then, when all hope has vanished, suddenly perceiving her as the gaslights are being extinguished, moving in the gloom towards her carriage. This, surely, is the dawn of love, the first whisper of that 'grand souffle d'agitation' inseparable from love, which begins by ruffling the habitual sang-froid of Charles Swann and with remarkable swiftness acquires the tempestuous, cataclysmic force of a grand passion.

Proust, by introducing us to the Verdurins at this early stage, is not just roughing out the design of the vast fresco of Parisian manners and morals in which he will accord a generous and important place to the Verdurins and Guermantes. It is in the Verdurin *salon* that Charles first experiences the anxiety of love and the first tormenting sting of jealousy. Here, also, Proust reveals in Marcel's account of Swann's early and happy relations with Odette, that remarkable alteration effected by love in a man's habitual outlook and mode of life which is so well expressed in Stendhal's remark: 'l'amour est la plus forte des passions. Dans les autres, les désirs doivent s'accomoder aux réalités; ici ce sont les réalités qui s'empressent de se modeler aux désirs.' Proust shows us Charles Swann, the intimate of the duc de Chartres, of the duc de Luxembourg, of the Guermantes, in short, of a society as remote from the Verdurin *salon* as Mars is from the earth, introduced by Odette into a milieu where the prevailing cult is Music, the atmosphere Bohemian, the tone *avant-garde*, the artists and professional men all deliberately jolly and 'off-duty'. Everything, however, is organized and controlled by the hostess, whose loudly proclaimed contempt for the *salons* of the aristocracy camouflages an obsessing ambition to compose, with the elements now at her disposal, an original and exclusive *salon* with Mme Verdurin as its Egeria. What could more strikingly demonstrate the alchemy of love than these impressions of Swann happily installed as one of the Verdurin 'clan', listening without a grimace to the appalling puns of Dr Cottard, a rising young physician but in all else the type of imbecile designated in English by the second and sixth letters of our alphabet; conversing amiably with Mme Cottard, the typical little bourgeoise with social ambitions for her husband; indulgently amused by the eccentricities of the painter, 'Monsieur Biche' as he is humorously known to his intimates; courteously attentive to the stammerings of the archivist Saniette, the recognized butt of the Verdurins. How charmingly natural and unaffected, he reflects, are these people, how much more intelligent than the habitués of any *salon* in the Faubourg Saint-Germain!

One of the classic symptoms of love is blindness and of course Charles is blind to the defects of Odette, privately described by Mme Verdurin as 'une cruche'. But he is also blind, which is much more serious, to the growing coldness of the Verdurins who begin to suspect beneath his apparent dullness the potential renegade, whose independence threatens what Proust calls the 'moral unity' of their *salon*. The truth is that Swann, on the contrary, is the most loyal and passionate of their devotees, sincerely admiring the magnanimity, the artistic taste and the simplicity of Mme Verdurin. Yet a sense of natural delicacy and of intellectual honesty prevents him from acquiescing in certain of her opinions which he knows to be grotesquely inaccurate. The immediate cause, then, of his descent from paradise through a purgatory of mingled doubts and reassurances into the infernal regions of hatred and jealousy is a dinner given by the Verdurins in honour of two new guests, the pedantic Sorbonne professor, Brichot, and Saniette's snob brother-in-law, Forcheville, who is invited by Odette. Swann's jealousy, if one scrutinizes this episode, will be seen to derive from Mme

Verdurin's jealous alarm concerning her salon, the fear lest Charles may secede, taking with him Odette. Swann has long known Forcheville though they move in different circles but it is only now, watching his easy conquest of Mme Verdurin listening to his completely insincere praise of her exhibits that Forcheville strikes him as a cad. 'Immonde' is the word he uses when Odette asks his opinion of this good-looking bounder who appears to be making such a favourable impression on the company. Swann experiences now his first pang of jealousy and because of an incident which he does not reflect upon until some days later, sees Odette in a new light. Forcheville, to the amusement of the Verdurins, has just administered to poor Saniette a most terrible tongue-lashing, reducing the wretched archivist to supplications and almost to tears. Swann, shocked by this display of bad manners, turns to look at Odette. On her face is an expression he has never seen before:

Odette avait assisté impassible à cette scène, mais quand la porte se fut refermée sur Saniette, faisant descendre en quelque sorte de pluieurs crans l'expression habituelle de son visage, pour pouvoir se trouver dans la bassesse, de plain-pied avec Forcheville, elle avait brillanté ses prunelles d'un sourire sournois de félicitations pour l'audace qu'il avait eue, d'ironie pour celui qui en avait été victime; elle lui avait jeté un regard de complicité dans le mal, qui voulait bien dire: 'voilà une exécution; ou je ne m'y connais pas. Avez-vous vu son air penaud, il en pleurait.'[1]

Before the end of dinner, Mme Verdurin has passed sentence on the unconscious Charles though, had he known it, there was a moment, over coffee, when his Grand Inquisitor might have been placated by a tactful word or smile. Instead, annoyed at Odette's manner towards Forcheville and astonished at Mme Verdurin's malicious and ridiculous description of his friends the La Trémoïlle, whom of course she has never met, Charles mortally offends his hostess by refusing to take her seriously. On the way home, Odette is curt and ill-tempered whilst the Verdurins resolve to do everything possible to detach her from Swann, 'le raté, le petit individu envieux de tout ce qui est grand'.

[1] *Swann*, II, 89.

The conception of jealous love imaged in Racine's superb line, *C'est Vénus toute entière à sa proie attachée,* reflects an outlook on life typical of a classic dramatist whose art is *par excellence* the interpretation of brief, intense and critical states of soul. Proust, as a novelist whose object is to recompose and communicate the history of Swann's passion for Odette, necessarily operates on a different plane from Racine. Nevertheless, he finally reveals a phase in Swann's emotional life where his love and jealousy acquire the intense and dramatic quality of an obsession. On the other hand, Proust is a novelist who can scarcely be described as a psychologist of the Cartesian school. He shows us therefore, what Racine does not reveal; the activities of that human instinct for self-preservation without which jealous love must always inevitably result in suicide, madness or murder.

What is the Proustian conception of jealousy that emerges from this remarkable narrative? In its early stages, Swann's jealousy might be described as an anxiety to establish the truth about certain impressions seized by his surface intelligence. The fact which Proust apparently wants to throw into relief is that Charles, at this period, is only beginning to suspect the existence of a part of Odette's life which is not just a logical prolongation of the part visible to him. Whilst Swann is happily in love, Proust suggests, the character of Odette and her life present a uniformity which quickly disintegrates, however, under the influence of jealousy. But jealousy is largely a malady of the imagination and Swann is not by habit an imaginative person. Proust's object, then, is to reveal the process of interaction whereby this dormant faculty, awakened by jealousy, develops its power of transfiguring reality to such a degree as to exercise a continual revivifying influence on his jealousy.

At first, since Charles is accustomed to view human nature in the light of his critical, reasoning intelligence, his peace of mind is only disturbed by puzzling incidents which do not somehow fit into his idea of Odette. This mental picture, formed of his perceptions of a true, loving and naturally kind Odette, excludes the possibility of acts such as one might associate with a woman of deceitful character, in short, the classic type of kept woman who enjoys making a cuckold of the man from whom she accepts money. Never for an instant does Swann conceive of Odette as 'une femme entretenue'. Certain incidents, however, irritate his curiosity like unsolved mathematical problems. They are concrete incidents, for instance, Odette's insistence one night that he should leave at eleven because she says she is tired. This episode, recounted by Proust, lights up that indeterminate psychological zone where intellectual curiosity is almost, yet not quite transformed into jealousy. Just after midnight, Swann, intrigued by Odette's behaviour, takes a cab to a spot near her house, and stealthily approaches her window. She has not retired because the light streams through the shutters and he can hear the subdued murmur of voices. Swann's dominant emotion, however, is not that of jealousy but of intellectual satisfaction. The problem has been solved. Odette is there with her unknown lover: it is the classic well-made play with the classic dénouement. Charles, remembering her horror of jealous lovers who spy on their mistresses, hesitates to make his presence known. But he finally raps on the shutters crying out breezily: 'Ne vous dérangez pas, je passais par là, j'ai vu de la lumière, j'ai voulu savoir si vous n'étiez pas souffrante.' The window is opened, the shutters thrown back and two old gentlemen stare out in astonishment at this queer, nocturnal visitor. But there are other incidents which present no clear-cut explanation. Why did Odette, for example, fail to open the door when he called that afternoon before his usual time although she admitted that she had heard his ring? But she must also have heard him knocking on her bedroom window? And why, during the conversation that ensued was she so nervous and anxious to detain him? Had this anxiety anything to do with the sound he heard of the front door opening then shutting and of a carriage driving off as if someone had called and been told Odette was not at home? This problem is only partially solved by the letter addressed to Forcheville which Odette gives him with others to post, the letter Charles takes home and reads through its transparent envelope. Its ending is formally polite yet in the text is an apology for not having received Forcheville because her uncle has called and there is also an allusion to a cigarette-case he left on his last visit.

In language which materializes the delicate nuances of Swann's sentiments, emotions and thoughts without, however, ceasing to present them in a process of uninterrupted change, Proust interprets the dynamic alternation and growth of Swann's love and jealousy. One perceives now how admirable was his choice of an Odette as the object of Charles's grand passion. There is, after all, a limit to the influence exercised by the imagination on jealousy which battens, no doubt, on imaginings yet requires a substratum or core of reality. The invisible life of a *cocotte*, the hours she spends outside her lover's society, can furnish an abundance of material facts designed to employ the imagination of a lover and torture his sensibility. Moreover, as Charles has fallen from grace with the Verdurins, this unknown tract of Odette's existence, this *terra incognita* which he now proceeds to explore, quickly enlarges its contours. He still frequents the Verdurins because of Odette. But it is only to realize with despair and impotent fury that his room is preferred to his company. Read that wonderful description of the scene where the Verdurins drive off without Swann who has just overheard their whispered plans for a picnic next day at Chatou, without him. In a few pages Proust contrives to render almost palpable the state of soul of a deserted and madly jealous lover, consumed with loathing for the 'entremetteuse', Mme Verdurin and with an Olympian contempt for her friends and their common little minds; striding through the solitary avenues of the Bois, working off his despair and fury in a stream of invective, talking loudly to himself in a high unnatural voice which reflects, as Proust subtly observes, the artificiality of the speaker's words, chosen by Swann not so much to express his thoughts as to assuage his anger. Curiously, too, as will be apparent later, this new and astonishing Charles Swann employs, to vent his jealous spleen, the vocabulary and the intonations of that irascible megalomaniac, his closest friend, the baron de Charlus. Listen to him as he excoriates the absent Verdurins:

'Quelle gaîté fétide!' disait-il en donnant à sa bouche une expression de dégoût si forte qu'il avait lui-même la sensation musculaire de sa grimace jusque dans son cou révulsé contre le col de sa chemise. 'Et comment une créature dont le visage est fait à l'image de Dieu, peut-elle trouver matière à rire dans ces plaisanteries nauséabondes? Toute narine un peu délicate se détournerait avec horreur pour ne pas se laisser offusquer par de tels relents....J'habite à trop de milliers de mètres au-dessus des bas-fonds où clapotent de tels sales papotages, pour que je puisse être éclaboussé par les plaisanteries d'une Verdurin', s'écria-t-il, en relevant la tête, en redressant fièrement son corps en arrière. 'Dieu m'est témoin que j'ai sincèrement voulu tirer Odette de là et l'élever dans une atmosphère plus noble et plus pure.'[1]

['What foetid humour!' he said, letting his mouth twist into such a violent expression of disgust that he himself felt the muscular sensation produced by his grimace down where the contracted neck-sinews were chafed by his collar. 'And how can a creature fashioned in the image of the Almighty find anything to laugh at in such revolting jokes. Anyone possessing the slightest delicacy would turn away in horror so as not to let her nostrils be offended by these stenches....I inhabit a plane too many leagues above the murky depths where these bawling gossip-mongers spatter forth their dirt for me to be sullied by the witticisms of a Verdurin', he shouted, raising his head and proudly throwing back his shoulders. 'God is my witness that I have sincerely tried to get Odette out of there and to bring her up in a nobler, purer atmosphere.']

There is a remark by that amusing rascal Dr Bartholo in *Le Barbier de Séville* which exactly reflects the mind of a jealous lover: 'Quelle rage a-t-on d'apprendre ce qu'on craint de savoir!' Now that Charles has broken with the Verdurins, his jealous imagination roves over a larger zone so that nearly every conversation with Odette is an *interrogatoire* in disguise whilst she is driven to improvise half-truths or lies, often inventing incidents to keep him quiet, too stupid to realize that these are much more damning in her lover's eyes than the fact she tries to conceal. With his amazing flair for the impression or scene that condenses a general truth, Proust keeps our attention always focused on the essential cause of Swann's tragedy, his hopeless unremitting effort to fix his mind on the image reflected in his love for Odette and avert it from that other image painted by his jealousy. Odette holds him now, less by her coquetry, than by her growing impatience and her indifference to his existence. The moments to which Swann clings

---

[1] *Swann*, II, 102–3.

pathetically are those he spends with the Odette who reminds
him of the old happy days, in her little drawing-room, under
the lamplight, busy with her tea-cups, arranging flowers, with
that expression he adores of frank and charming goodness,
scolding him for not going on with his book on Vermeer,
urging him to write to his friends, and complaining that one of
his coachmen has been impolite. How admirably Proust accentuates the importance to Charles of these trivialities, his delight,
for instance, when he can say to a friend who notices that his
usual coachman is not on the box: 'Oh! sapristi non! je te dirai,
je ne peux pas prendre Lorédan quand je vais rue La Pérouse.
Odette n'aime pas que je prenne Lorédan, elle ne le trouve pas
bien pour moi; enfin que veux-tu, les femmes, tu sais.'[1] But so
often, on the other hand, a word, a name crops up reviving
Swann's irresistible desire to learn what he fears to know, im-
pelling him sometimes to pretend to suspect Odette of conduct
which his reason tells him to be incredible yet, as on one terrible
occasion, proves to be true, when Odette, forced to swear on the
image of Notre-Dame-de-Laghet, admits having once or twice
had Sapphic relations with a stranger in the Île-du-Bois. This
awful moment, when Charles enters a new circle of his Inferno,
is not interpreted by Proust as a turning-point in the drama of
Swann's jealousy. With his profound insight, he suggests that
in certain psychological as well as physical traumas, nature provides her own anæsthetic. So I construe the following passage:

Mais il avait tellement pris l'habitude de trouver la vie intéressante
— d'admirer les curieuses découvertes qu'on peut y faire — que tout
en souffrant au point de croire qu'il ne pourrait pas supporter longtemps une pareille douleur, il se disait: 'La vie est vraiment étonnante
et réserve de belles surprises; en somme le vice est quelque chose de
plus répandu qu'on ne croit. Voilà une femme en qui j'avais confiance,
qui a l'air si simple, si honnête, en tous cas, si même elle était légère,
qui semblait bien normale et saine dans ses goûts: sur une dénonciation
invraisemblable, je l'interroge et le peu qu'elle m'avoue révèle bien
plus que ce qu'on eût pu soupçonner.'[2]

Not even this revelation, which so terribly alters Swann's vision
of the past and casts its shadow on the future, can cure him of

---

[1] *Swann*, ii, 150.   [2] *Swann*, ii, 213.

his infatuation for Odette. There is no anger or revulsion in
his feelings towards her, only pity as he reflects upon what he
has heard about her childhood. His love is now an incurable
malady which is so much a part of his thought, his life, his daily
habits that it cannot be eradicated without destroying Swann
himself: 'comme on dit en chirugie, son amour n'était plus
opérable'.

As if to let us gauge the width and depth of the social chasm
which divides the world of Odette from Swann's familiar universe, the novelist suddenly takes us to the *salon* of Mme de
Saint-Euverte in the Faubourg Saint-Germain. A musical recital
is in progress and Oriane, then princesse des Laumes, later
duchesse de Guermantes, has just entered unobtrusively. This
is a surprise appearance, staged by Oriane who is conscious of
the honour she is conferring on her hostess. Therefore, with
the talent of the practised actress, she has effaced herself timidly
in the background awaiting the inevitable delighted exclamations of Mme de Saint-Euverte. Proust, all through *A la
recherche du temps perdu*, will retain this motif. Fashionable
society is a theatre where every word and gesture is studied.
Only by the decodes of the trained observer is it possible to
distinguish the truth from its admirable but false imitation.
Simpletons accuse Proust of snobbery, failing to observe the
consummate art with which he explains what Saint Simon calls
'la mécanique' of society life and interprets its essential vanity,
egoism and elegant cruelty. His work offers probably the
truest picture and the most devastating criticism of fashionable
mœurs yet presented by a French novelist, not excluding even
Balzac. Its uniqueness is largely due to the intensity of what
Proust himself, in reference to the art of the novelist, calls the
artist's 'pouvoir réfléchissant', the faculty of ceasing to live for
himself and using his personality as a mirror in which life is
reflected. That is why, in the Guermantes and Charlus episodes,
the spectacle of Parisian high society from the end of last century
to the First World War is re-created with such astonishing
reality. Proust invents for our benefit a new optical instrument
with which to observe life—his incomparable style. Consider,

---

[1] *Swann*, II, 133.

for instance, this interpretation of Swann's sensation as he
stands in the vast hall of Mme de Saint-Euverte's town house.
Owing to his marriage with Odette, he has been very little in
society and now, for the first time, Charles realizes what he had
never before noticed, the elaborate mechanism of the fashionable
world—'la meute éparse, magnifique et désœuvrée de grands
valets de pied qui dormaient çà et là sur des banquettes et qui,
soulevant leur nobles profils aigus de lévriers, se dressèrent,
et, rassemblés, formèrent le cercle autour de lui'.[1] Proust loves
these transpositions, these humorous incongruities which force
the reader out of the rut of his familiar observation, shifting him
to a site from which he obtains a new and more illuminating
view of reality:

A quelques pas, un grand gaillard en livrée rêvait, immobile,
sculptural, inutile, comme ce guerrier purement décoratif qu'on voit
dans les tableaux les plus tumultueux de Mantegna, songer, appuyé
sur son bouclier, tandis qu'on se précipite et qu'on s'égorge à côté de
lui; détaché du groupe de ses camarades qui s'empressaient autour de
Swann, il semblait aussi résolu à se désintéresser de cette scène, qu'il
suivait vaguement de ses yeux glauques et cruels, que si c'eût été le
massacre des Innocents ou le martyre de saint Jacques.[2]

This is only a prelude to the larger spectacle which will be
disclosed in *Le côté de Guermantes* and in other volumes.
Proust's real object here is to introduce the master theme of
À la recherche du temps perdu: the relationship between art and
reality. Charles Swann, in the early, halcyon days of his love
for Odette, heard, one evening at the Verdurins, a fragment of
Vinteuil's sonata. Ever since, 'la petite phrase de Vinteuil' has
become indissolubly linked with sweet memories of Odette.
And simultaneously with his need for her love there was born
in Swann another need, the desire to know and understand music.
Now, at Mme de Saint-Euverte's recital, listening to the *Sonate
de Vinteuil*, he recaptures through the medium of the little
phrase, the 'specific and volatile essence' of experiences the
reality of which only now invades his consciousness: the scent
of the chrysanthemums Odette threw into his carriage, her

---

[1] *Swann*, ii, 153.   [2] *Swann*, ii, 154.

anxious, pleading look, the icy spring showers as he drove home
from the rue La Pérouse, the hundred tiny circumstances which
elude the tentacles of one's voluntary memory. Swann's present
suffering is thereby rendered almost unbearable for he knows
now that Odette's love for him is dead. But, gradually, Vinteuil's phrase communicates its secret and divine message of
sympathy and yields its profound truth. Vinteuil, this unknown
brother in suffering, has created out of the sadness of his life
a vision of immortal beauty and wisdom. With the intuition
of genius, a great artist has penetrated beneath the apparent
discord of existence and captured its uninterrupted, inner
melody. Such, it would seem, is the truth beautifully expressed
by Proust in these words:

> C'est que la petite phrase au contraire, quelque opinion qu'elle pût
> avoir sur la brève durée de ces états de l'âme, y voyait quelque chose,
> non pas comme faisaient tous ces gens, de moins sérieux que la vie
> positive, mais au contraire de si supérieur à elle que seul il valait la
> peine d'être exprimé. Ces charmes d'une tristesse intime, c'était eux
> qu'elle essayait d'imiter, de recréer, et jusqu'à leur essence qui est
> pourtant d'être incommunicables et de sembler frivoles à tout autre qu'à
> celui qui les éprouve, la petite phrase l'avait captée, rendue visible.[1]

> [What happened was that, on the contrary, the little phrase, what-
> ever it might think about the ephemeral quality of these states of soul,
> perceived in them, not as did all these people, something less serious
> than our real, everyday existence but, on the contrary, something so
> superior to it as to be alone worth while expressing. What it was trying
> to imitate and re-create was those charms fraught with intimate sadness
> whose very essence which consists, however, in being incommunicable
> and in appearing trivial to any but him who experiences it—had been
> snared and rendered visible by the little phrase.]

Nothing can now rob Charles of this divine consolation. He
is no longer alone in his suffering, for when he reflects on his
lost happiness and on his actual sorrows, Vinteuil's phrase seems
to whisper: 'Qu'est-ce que cela, tout cela n'est rien.' Is this
illusion or reality? Is Swann's idea of the relation between art
and life not just a dream and is art itself not just a beautiful lie
and the world it reveals only a mirage?

[1] *Swann*, II, 188.

Peut-être est-ce le néant qui est le vrai et tout notre rêve est-il inexistant, mais alors nous sentons qu'il faudra que ces phrases musicales, ces notions qui existent par rapport à lui, ne soient rien non plus. Nous périrons mais nous avons pour ôtages ces captives divines qui suivront notre chance. Et la mort avec elles a quelque chose de moins amer, de moins inglorieux, peut-être de moins probable.[1]

This second part of *Du côté de chez Swann* ends on a note that might suggest that Charles, after all, has been cured of his malady, his passion for Odette who has gone away with the Verdurins and Forcheville on a Mediterranean cruise which has already lasted almost a year. But we know that on her return, Swann's irresistible longing will also return and with it a renaissance of his jealousy.

[1] *Swann*, II, 191.

Chapter II

A L'OMBRE DES JEUNES FILLES EN FLEURS

THE third part of *Du côté de chez Swann* which Proust calls
Noms de pays: le Nom belongs, properly, to the volumes entitled
A l'ombre des jeunes filles en fleurs. In the first place, it is here that
Marcel resumes the interrupted narrative of his early youth and,
whilst the physical milieu is still Paris, we are now back in the
spiritual climate of Combray which is very different from that of
'Un amour de Swann'. Proust, although he continues to expand
his huge fresco of Parisian social *mœurs*, never allows this to
obscure our vision of Marcel's evolving psychological life. The
novelist, operating from alternating levels of his consciousness,
yet so cleverly as to produce an illusion of simultaneity, contrives
to interpret the evolution of Marcel's adolescent love for Gilberte in such a way as to reveal how intimately it is synchronized
with and enmeshed in the larger, and therefore more superficially
perceived representation of a whole society in process of change.
At the same time, as is suggested, I feel, in the title: *Noms de
pays: Le Nom*, Proust is also opening up a theme to which he
will frequently return in this history of a vocation. For the
moment it may be designated, very simply, as the theme of
imagination and reality or rather of the relation between imagination and reality. This theme, which Proust begins to illustrate
in his pages on the magic of Names, will be more forcefully
orchestrated in the narrative of Marcel's first love. Only then,
really, does life give him the first sharp intimation that the external world perceived by his five senses will never resemble the
lovely and harmonious inner world constructed by his imagination.
Words, Marcel observes, offer us a clear, workmanlike, yet
not very illuminating, image of things. Names, on the contrary,
express that which is individual for us in things and people.
And, to judge from the enchantment which names possess for

this highly imaginative youth, one might add that they are infinitely more elastic or spacious than mere words. For example, within the cadre of the name, Balbec, once completely occupied by primeval Nature, Marcel contrives to insert with the greatest of ease, an epoch of civilization. This requires, perhaps, some explanation. Before he strayed into the Elysian Fields where he lost his heart to Gilberte Swann, Marcel's imagination was largely focused on Balbec, a little fishing hamlet situated on the towering cliffs near Finistère, 'le dernier campement de pêcheurs' according to the eloquent and elusive Legrandin, 'pareils à tous les pêcheurs qui ont vécu depuis le commencement du monde, en face des royaumes éternels des brouillards de la mer et des ombres'. To Marcel, in Paris, listening to the howling of February winds, nothing appears more desirable than the spectacle of a storm at sea, with the full fury of the Atlantic unleashed against the protecting cliffs of Balbec. An allusion by Swann, however, to the quaint little Norman Gothic church of Balbec, so curiously reminiscent of Persian art, modifies this primitive vision, thus bringing it into juxtaposition with the cadre of historical time, in a delightful alliance of nature and art.

But one day, Marcel's father proposed an Easter holiday in Northern Italy and a new dream comes into being. In this second vision an eternal spring reigns in a country of majestic cities and of landscapes recalling the perspectives of Angelico's paintings where the golden fields are bright with lilies and anemones. So Marcel poring alternately over the time-table of the *État* which contains the marvellous 1.22 p.m. train to Balbec and over the guide books describing the treasures of Florence, Parma, Pisa and Venice, surrenders himself blissfully to the enchantment of Names. After all, the existence of concrete facts like trains is a pretty substantial bridge between imagination and reality, a promise that dreams will come true. And when one's father calmly announces that it is possible to stay at Venice from 20 to 29 April and still reach Florence for Easter morning, the existence of miracles becomes a possibility, to say the least. As Marcel very reasonably argues, his father's very simple words had lifted two dream cities not just out of abstract Space but out of imaginary Time. However, if you are still sceptical about the magic of Names you must read what Marcel sees in the names of the Norman villages where the 1.22 p.m. train from the Gare St-Lazare halts on its way to Balbec; or else the enchantment crystallized in Florence or Parma. Unfortunately, the excitement caused by these 'désincarnations' brings on a severe recurrence of Marcel's suffocating asthmatic fits so that, Balbec and Venice having been ruled out, he has to be content, during his convalescence, to drag his tired feet along the dusty walks of the Champs Elysées, tagging behind Françoise. Thus, one day, watching an excited group of schoolgirls playing rounders, Marcel hears the magic name Gilberte, sees Gilberte and is eventually drawn casually into the radiant and mysterious world inhabited by Gilberte.

As Marcel recomposes the history of his first love there emerges from the intricate Proustian embroidery of glosses and annotations, a general design closely resembling the simple emotional pattern traced by the medieval French poets. Unconsciously, in exploring the psychology of adolescent love, Proust discloses the elements which identify it with 'l'amour courtois' of the Middle Ages, the traits which by their persistent survival lend such a perennial charm and springtime freshness to every authentic story of first love. Chronologically, no doubt, 'Un amour de Swann' ought to have preceded the Combray narrative; yet note how effectively it now throws into relief, by contrast, the quality of Marcel's adolescent love, its purity unclouded by jealousy or sensual desire, the love that is spun from youth's romantic dreams of beauty and mystery. Inevitably, since Proust is not re-creating an immobile state of soul but the dynamic and fluid process of life itself, there arrives a phase in Marcel's relations with Gilberte when he vaguely suspects that love might generate sufferings of a more poignant quality. But his first love is not a tragic experience like Swann's. It is a cult resembling 'l'amour courtois'. A humble, devoted slave, Marcel invests the immature, indifferent and unconsciously cruel schoolgirl, Gilberte, with the attributes of a feudal 'belle dame sans merci'. His is the exaltation of a heart pledged to service, cherishing its own suffering with a melancholy joy. Finally, in a spirit of supreme abnegation, he sternly denies himself the intoxicating but fatal pleasures of Gilberte's society, apparently in the forlorn hope that by some miracle she will relent and, touched at last by the constancy of her 'fin amant', declare her love for him; or else, as he tries to convince himself, that his own love will die of inanition.

In re-creating the fugitive sensations and emotional nuances which compose the tissue of this young lover's existence, Proust subordinates his intuition for essentials to a remarkable penchant and talent for minute analysis. The distinctive qualities of adolescent love are always subtly accentuated: its non-possessiveness, humility and unshakable faith. Gilberte may be unkind, gloating even with unconscious brutality on the fact that tomorrow there will be no rounders in the Champs Elysées because Mamma is taking her to a concert or arranging a party which Marcel will not attend. But this cannot destroy Marcel's belief that for her he is not just anyone, that he is at least a friend and so different from others. As the older and wiser Marcel observes, his boyish love was a love *for* Gilberte and not dependent, therefore, for its existence on the changing moods of Gilberte. No doubt, for a long time, Marcel hopes that he may be mistaken and that, perhaps, his love will be returned. Yet, on the whole, his state of mind is one of resignation. It is enough to enjoy the inestimable privilege of loving Gilberte, of being singled out to play on her side, to own the neck down which she rams snowballs on wintry days; to be able, in short, to adore Gilberte. Love, it is said, laughs at locksmiths. Marcel, I imagine, would have been more grateful if love could have laughed at the meteorologists. Every day, just after lunch, he anxiously watches the iron tracery of his balustrade—love's substitute for a barometer—for the absence or appearance of that shadow on the stone parapet which will decide whether this to be a day or just another period of weary waiting for the sun to come out with Gilberte on the Champs Elysées. No one can interpret better than Proust the new and tremendous role assumed in the life of a young man in love by weather and, for that matter, by the hundred other elements, hitherto unperceived, which ordinary people take for granted in their humdrum lives. What is a Zoroastrian's cult of Ormuzd compared with

Marcel's fervent sun-worship as his fearful eyes follow the fadings and darkenings of the shadow on the balcony?

Un instant après, le balcon était pâle et réfléchissant comme une eau matinale, et mille reflets de la ferronnerie de son treillage étaient venus s'y poser. Un souffle de vent les dispersait, la pierre s'était de nouveau assombrie, mais, comme apprivoisés, ils revenaient; elle recommençait imperceptiblement à blanchir et par un de ces crescendos continus comme ceux qui, en musique, à la fin d'une Ouverture, mènent une seule note jusqu'au fortissimo suprême en la faisant passer rapidement par tous les degrés intermédiaires, je la voyais atteindre à cet or inaltérable et fixe des beaux jours, sur lequel l'ombre découpée de l'appui ouvragé de la balustrade se détachait en noir comme une végétation capricieuse, avec une ténuité dans la délinéation des moindres détails qui semblait trahir une conscience appliquée, une satisfaction d'artiste, et avec un tel relief, un tel velours dans le repos de ses masses sombres et heureuses qu'en vérité ces reflets larges et feuillus qui reposaient sur ce lac de soleil semblaient savoir qu'ils étaient des gages de calme et de bonheur.[1]

[A moment afterwards, the balcony was as pale and reflective as a pool at early morn and a thousand images of its iron lattice-work had alighted upon its surface. These were scattered by a breath of wind. Once again, the stone darkened but, as if they had been tamed, the reflections came back; imperceptibly, it began to whiten once more and as in one of those uninterrupted crescendos which, in music, at the close of an overture lift a single note to the supreme fortissimo by making it swiftly traverse all the intermediate stages, I saw the stone acquire that fixed unalterable gold of settled fine weather against which the clear-cut shadow of the wrought-iron railing of the balustrade was blackly silhouetted like some capricious vegetation, with a delicacy in the tracery of its smallest details that seemed to betray a conscious application, an artist's satisfaction, and with such a volume of relief, such a velvety quality in the restfulness of its sombre and happy mass effects that, in truth, those broad and leafy reflections resting upon that lake of sunshine seemed aware that they were pledges of tranquillity and happiness.]

Yet even the sun can be less fickle than woman, and there are awful days when the sunshine seems to laugh at the desolate Marcel forlornly scanning the distant horizon for the appearance of that dancing feather on the hat of Gilberte's governess. There are also red-letter days in the unique calendar of youthful love;

---

[1] *Swann*, II, 257–8.

the day for instance, when Gilberte calls him by his Christian name and the triumphal afternoon when she regally squanders fifty centimes on a precious agate, the colour of her eyes, and gives it to Marcel as a souvenir. Even so, as Proust observes with his usual ruthless integrity, young Marcel could not possibly, at that moment, know the real extent of his happiness, the true nature of his sensations. The passage is significant because it reflects a typically Proustian conception of reality.

Mais au moment même, je ne pouvais apprécier la valeur de ces plaisirs nouveaux. Ils n'étaient pas donnés par la fillette que j'aimais, au moi qui l'aimait, mais par l'autre, par celle avec qui je jouais, à cet autre moi qui ne possédait ni le souvenir de la vraie Gilberte, ni le cœur indisponible qui seul aurait pu savoir le prix d'un bonheur, parce que seul il l'avait désiré. Même après être rentré à la maison je ne les goûtais pas, car, chaque jour, la nécessité qui me faisait espérer que le lendemain j'aurais la contemplation exacte, calme, heureuse de Gilberte, qu'elle m'avouerait enfin son amour, en m'expliquant pour quelles raisons elle avait dû me la cacher jusqu'ici, cette même nécessité me forçait à tenir le passé pour rien, à ne jamais regarder que devant moi, à considérer les petits avantages qu'elle m'avait donnés non pas en eux-mêmes et comme s'ils se suffisaient, mais comme des échelons nouveaux où poser le pied, qui allaient me permettre de faire un pas de plus en avant et d'atteindre enfin le bonheur que je n'avais pas encore rencontré.[1]

[But at the actual moment I could not appreciate the value of these new pleasures. They were not given by the little girl I loved to the 'me' who loved her, but by the other, the one with whom I used to play, to that other 'me' who possessed neither the memory of the real Gilberte, nor the unchangeable heart which alone could have known the value of a happiness desired by itself alone. Even after I got home I did not taste these pleasures because, every day, the necessity which made me hope that on the morrow I should be able to obtain a clear, calm and happy vision of Gilberte, that she would finally confess her love explaining why up till now, she had been obliged to hide it from me, that very necessity forced me to dismiss the past as of no account, to keep my eyes ever fixed in front of me, to consider the little preferences she had shown me, not in themselves and as self-sufficient, but as fresh rungs on which to place my feet, enabling me to progress one step further towards the final attainment of that happiness I had not yet encountered.]

[1] *Swann*, II, 268.

Though, as I remarked, non-possessiveness is a distinctive trait of the adolescent lover this does not exclude the desire to sink his personality and whole life in the mysterious unknown of the loved one's being and existence. Such is Marcel's longing except in the foolish moments when he dreams of a paradise where Gilberte might share his life, helping him with his literary work. For literature, represented at this stage largely by Bergotte, occupies a place in Marcel's thoughts, particularly since he received from Gilberte one of the Master's brochures on Racine, tied with mauve ribbons and sealed with white wax. This he treasures with the agate marble as a *gage d'amour*, a proof of Gilberte's essential kindness, a sign that she is not quite indifferent.

Proust now indicates a change that occurs in Marcel's sentiments. The beauty of Bergotte's writings, the material beauty of the agate, he discovers, are independent of Gilberte and existed before his love. It is therefore, he means, an illusion to think that because these perfect and beautiful things once belonged to her, she will one day grant him the happiness which they have the power to confer. Very gradually, Marcel becomes conscious of the reality of Gilberte's feelings towards him: it is he who loves whilst she remains indifferent. And so, in his first act of renunciation, he tells her that their friendship must be completely recast, on a new basis. What she makes of this cryptic announcement we do not know.

Resigned to the inevitable, to this 'ordre nouveau' which has taught him the existence of external realities impervious to the influence of imagination, Marcel is now resolved to penetrate the unknown world inhabited by Gilberte. Charles Swann, who strides elegantly into the park occasionally to fetch Gilberte, buying a chair-ticket just like any ordinary person, is invested by Marcel with an almost divine prestige. He imitates Swann's trick of rubbing his eyes and stroking his nose until his exasperated father remarks: 'Cet enfant est idiot, il deviendra affreux!' But his son's only regret is that he is not bald like M. Swann. Odette, naturally, shares in this apotheosis and it is a source of great disappointment to Marcel that his mother refuses to dress like Mme Swann or exchange Françoise for

a governess like the Swann's governess. The names Gilberte
and Swann acquire a magic individuality and so does the Swann's
house, their street, the Allée des Acacias where Gilberte's
mother, one of the queens of fashion, may be seen, either hurrying
on foot like a common mortal or else sweeping past in her
luxurious victoria, a vision of floating veils, mauve parasol, high-
stepping horses, enormous coachman and on the seat beside him
with folded arms, her little groom or as he was then known, 'le
tigre'. Marcel does not know Mme Swann. But his parents have
met her although they never call. For this their son makes amends
by taking up his regular station, on fine days, in the Allée des
Acacias in the hope of seeing Mme Swann, who has some difficulty
in restraining a smile at the spectacle of this odd youngster doffing
his hat with a gesture usually reserved for royalty and to the large
amusement of the passers-by. It is perhaps as well that Marcel
does not hear the comments of the clubmen who remember
Mme Swann as Odette de Crécy, the well-known *cocotte*. The
volume closes with a few charming pages on the Bois as it used
to be in Marcel's early youth and as it is now when he writes
down his memories, after revisiting the Allée des Acacias.

Au lieu des belles robes dans lesquelles Mme Swann avait l'air
d'une reine, des tuniques gréco-saxonnes relevaient avec les plis des
Tanagra, et quelquefois dans le style du Directoire des chiffons liberty
semés de fleurs comme un papier peint. Sur la tête des messieurs qui
auraient pu se promener avec Mme Swann dans l'allée de la Reine-
Marguerite, je ne trouvais pas le chapeau gris d'autrefois, ni même un
autre. Ils sortaient nu-tête. Et toutes ces parties nouvelles du spectacle, je n'avais plus de croyance à y introduire pour leur donner la
consistance, l'unité, l'existence; elles passaient éparses devant moi, au
hasard, sans vérité, ne contenant en elles aucune beauté que mes yeux
eussent pu essayer comme autrefois de composer. C'était des femmes
quelconques, en l'élégance desquelles je n'avais aucune foi et dont les
toilettes me semblaient sans importance. Mais quand disparaît une
croyance, il lui survit — et de plus en plus vivace pour masquer le
manque de la puissance que nous avons perdue de donner de la réalité
à des choses nouvelles — un attachement fétichiste aux anciennes
qu'elle avait animées, comme si c'était en elles et non en nous que le
divin résidait et si notre incrédulité actuelle avait une cause contingente,
la mort des Dieux.

<hr>

[1] *Swann*, II, 297–8.

[Instead of the beautiful dresses which made Mme Swann look like a queen, Graeco-Saxon tunics, pleated à la Tanagra or sometimes, cut in the Directoire style, accentuated the flowered wall-paper design of the Liberty chiffons. On the heads of the gentlemen who might have been strolling with Mme Swann in the Allée de la Reine-Marguerite I no longer saw the old-time grey 'toppers' nor indeed any hat at all. They went out bare-headed. And whilst observing all these new components of the spectacle, I no longer needed to introduce any element of make-believe in order to lend them consistency, unity and existence; they filed past before me in a desultory, haphazard, meaningless fashion devoid of any beauty which my eyes might, as in the old days, have tried to re-create. They were merely women in whose elegance I did not believe and whose dresses seemed to me unimportant. But when a belief disappears, there survives—and with ever-increasing vigour so as to conceal our impotence to invest new things with reality—a fetishistic attachment to the old ones which they had animated, as though the divinity had resided in them and not in ourselves and as if our present unbelief had a contingent cause—the death of the Gods.]

At the outset, one can detect in the first volume of *A l'ombre des jeunes filles en fleurs* a distinct change of tone in the narrative which reflects, increasingly, the perceptions of a mind turned outwards so as to embrace a larger zone of observation. Even so, whilst the perspective extends to include a fascinating and detailed panorama of bourgeois *mœurs*, our attention is never distracted from the central figure, Marcel, and the evolving pattern of his love for Gilberte. At times, therefore, we shall light on pages which reveal his introspective efforts to analyse his sentiments and understand their true nature: *voir clair dans son cœur* is the expression which Marivaux used to employ to describe this process. But these attempts are never very prolonged and they do not take Marcel into the deep and disturbing regions of his consciousness. This is probably because the mind of an adolescent lover is oriented rather towards the immediate present or future than towards the past and tends on the whole to exclude unpleasant memories. Besides, Marcel's remarkably vivid imagination, even though it has already come into sharp conflict with external realities, is still by far the most powerful of his faculties. Time and again, as we shall observe, his imagination is destined to clash with experience, losing many valued

illusions. But time and again, also, imagination makes good
these losses, creating fresh armies of illusions, forging ahead,
undaunted, and inspired by the faith that its objective which
is happiness or peace of mind, lies just beyond the horizon. To
Marcel, at this stage, happiness is like love, something that is
to say, external to himself, a goal that can be attained by the
removal of certain external obstacles or by a rearrangement of
his existing environment. Is not this precisely his present state
of mind as he reflects on his relations with Gilberte? In his
latest bout with experience one must no doubt record a success
for reality, but only a temporary success. For Marcel, in accepting the fact of Gilberte's indifference, has only suffered
a momentary setback. *On recule pour mieux sauter.* Happiness,
therefore, is now represented by the image of a Marcel en-
sconced in the bosom of the Swann family, the confidant of the
Swanns and the dearest friend of their daughter. Now, as it
happens, that is exactly what comes to pass. Yet, somehow,
Marcel's happiness is still as remote as ever.

Charles, married to Odette, still clings to his vision of Odette-
Zephora, though he has no illusions about her intelligence.
Marriage has greatly changed his outlook on life. He is now
a proud father and an attentive husband, absurdly pleased with
his wife's social success, of her beauty and reputation as one of
the most elegantly dressed women in Paris. Yet Odette's callers
are relatively very small fry, the wives of professional men and
of politicians. And though Mme Swann is beginning to build
up round Bergotte the beginnings of a kind of *salon*, she is
ostracized by the wives of respectable and solid bourgeois like
Marcel's father and of Swann's Jockey Club intimates. It will
take a war to jolt the social kaleidoscope into a picture which
shows the Faubourg Saint-Germain and Odette's *salon* in the
same focus. Occasionally, Charles Swann dreams of a future in
which the duchesse de Guermantes will receive Odette and
speak gently to Gilberte about her father and their old friendship. But it is only a dream, because he knows that Faubourg
Saint-Germain society has been recently shocked by a series of
scandals. Women of apparently unimpeachable social position,
on whom everyone called, had suddenly been unmasked as former

courtesans or English spies. And, whilst Odette's anglomania is a mere affectation of smartness, she certainly qualifies by her past for inclusion in the other category of 'femmes brûlées'. Meanwhile, Charles is perfectly happy as he observes, with uxorious pride, the results of what Marcel's mother humorously describes as Mme Swann's marauding expeditions into the territories of the neighbouring unsubdued tribes. He is naïvely elated at her latest capture, Mme Bontemps, the wife of a 'sous-chef de cabinet'. Often, too, when one of his Faubourg Saint-Germain friends calls to see Charles, his wife's guests experience the agreeable thrill of meeting their first duke or prince. Here is an impression of one of these miniature comedies:

> Dans l'entrebaillement d'une tenture, une tête se montrait céré-moniusement déférente, feignant par plaisanterie la peur de déranger: c'était Swann. 'Odette, le Prince d'Agrigente qui est avec moi dans mon cabinet demande s'il pourrait venir vous présenter ses hommages. Que dois-je aller lui répondre?' 'Mais que je serai enchantée' disait Odette avec satisfaction sans se départir d'un calme qui lui était d'autant plus facile qu'elle avait toujours, même comme cocotte, reçu des hommes élégants.[1]

Swann, in spite of the growing number of the trophies brought back by Odette from her forays, occasionally takes a hand himself in the composition of her *salon* rather in the manner of a retired 'cordon bleu' who drops into his own kitchen to experiment with new and amusing gastronomic combinations. To those who knew him at the height of his Jockey Club phase, Charles is now a 'vulgaire esbroufeur' certainly not to be invited for example by Marcel's parents to dine with the ex-ambassador, Norpois.

As this study develops we shall have many opportunities to observe and comment on the art with which Proust creates his superb pictures of aristocratic and upper-class *mœurs*. In this art, even after Balzac, Proust is a great master chiefly, I think, because he never ventures outside the zone of his personal experience. In this connection, I am always reminded of Marcel's anecdote about the famous actor whose admiring friends used to ask him where on earth he found his old-fashioned hats. 'Je ne les trouve pas, je les garde', was his invariable retort. So it is with these marvellously convincing Proustian re-creations: Marcel's family circle; the dinner-party in honour of Norpois; Odette's *salons*: the Guermantes milieu; the Verdurin 'clan'; the Grand Hôtel de Balbec; the impressions of garrison life at Doncières; the receptions of the Prince de Guermantes. They possess the authentic *cachet* of really lived experiences. I do not wish to imply for one moment that their component elements are autobiographical. Proust quite rightly warns us again and again how futile it is to examine his work in such a light. What is certain, however, is that Proust, like the actor with his hats, retained his memories of the impressions made upon his consciousness by the various social milieus which he frequented. Moreover, since he was a great artist, he retained only the significant traits that reflect the individuality of the particular human aggregation which he wanted to resuscitate: the turn of phrase, the smile, the intonation, the passing mode of dress or of polite behaviour. Above all else, he possesses the art of presenting these things as they existed, that is to say in a process of continual though almost imperceptible transition and of interfusion. It has often been objected that his recompositions leave out the social elements that matter most, the common people and the lower middle classes. That is on the whole true but it is a reproach which is really an unintentional tribute to the integrity of a novelist for whom the recomposition by art of real life meant something very different from the mechanical business of reconstructing by second-hand 'documentation' the manners and morals of a vanished period of civilization. Here, as in every aspect of his work, Proust is a great and serious artist whose mind received impressions at an unusual depth, who only wrote of what he knew, in short, only of experience which he assimilated and rendered individual or Proustian by what he used to call 'l'acte intellectuel'. And that, as I hope to show, is also unique.

Described by Proust, therefore, a dinner-party given by Marcel's parents in honour of the marquis de Norpois holds the quintessence of half a dozen volumes of memoirs. Listening to Norpois, the typical diplomat, 'négatif, routinier, conservateur', we are back in the atmosphere that pervaded the world of international politics in the two decades preceding 1914. It was the era when peace or war depended on the result of a conversation between two elegant, white-spatted, urbane old gentlemen strolling in the gardens of the Tuileries or of the Kursaal at Wiesbaden. Yet Proust very cleverly suggests, through the behaviour of the diplomat's audience, the two generations represented by Marcel and his parents, that the epoch incarnated in Norpois is already obsolescent. Their profound belief in the ex-ambassador's wisdom is tempered by respectful amusement at the old-world formality of his periods and vocabulary: 'coutumier du fait'; 'il serait peu séant'; 'leur tailler des croupières'. Norpois is a moment of French civilization seized in its passage *en route* for oblivion. We surprise it in his gestures, silences, his preteritions, his swift decodings of the casual, apparently meaningless word, for example, the expression, *affinités* pronounced by King Théodose at an official banquet, a word destined on the morrow and for many years afterwards, to provide material for endless commentaries in the chancellories of Europe.

In re-creating the past, however, Proust never interrupts the history of Marcel's psychological evolution. Norpois often dines with the Swanns and Gilberte. He smiles indulgently, therefore, when Marcel confesses his passionate admiration for Mme Swann and her daughter. And when Norpois promises to inform them of Marcel's admiration the latter has to check an impulsive desire to kiss the frail white hand of this benefactor. Too impulsive and too passionate. Instinctively alarmed by a disproportionate expression of emotion which may, perhaps, conceal some dubious motive, the old diplomat mentally registers the firm resolve not to mention this peculiarly exalted youth's name to the Swanns. And so it is in an idle moment before dinner that Cottard, Odette's doctor tells her of Marcel's sentiments towards her family.

Cottard is called in to treat a severe recurrence of Marcel's malady although his excellent advice is at first ignored by his parents until, as a last resort, they follow the treatment prescribed by this brilliant diagnostician. The reason for their original failure to take Cottard seriously is that, by nature a timid person, he has adopted for professional ends an impenetrable mask of impassiveness and of brutal autocracy. Marcel recovers and because miracles do sometimes happen in love he receives his first letter from Gilberte. Perhaps, in retrospect, the miracle may have been due to his mother's tactful intervention. Now, the universe is transfigured because Gilberte has invited him, with her parents' consent to come to her parties twice a week. Soon he is a favoured guest, 'le grand crack' as Odette the anglomaniac puts it, smiled on even by the Olympian Swann who, to his unspeakable distress, had been doubtful whether after his letter to Gilberte, this lad ought to be allowed to play with his daughter. Marcel is now, on the contrary, welcomed for his excellent influence on Gilberte and Proust, having forged this link between the two households, sets to work in earnest upon his amazingly life-like representation of the Swann milieu.

The Swanns belong to a social class inferior to the Faubourg Saint-Germain yet, as Marcel puts it,

supérieure à ce qui n'est pas du faubourg Saint-Germain et qui avait ceci de particulier que déjà dégagée du monde des riches, elle était la richesse encore, mais la richesse devenue ductile, obéissant à une destination, à une pensée artistique, l'argent malléable, poétiquement ciselé et qui sait sourire.... [1]

Odette incarnates what in this particular class and period was most ephemeral and perhaps most charming—its craze for elegant luxury, downy comfort, masses of flowers, prettily gowned women and expensive inessentials. With her floating silks, Watteau-like *robes d'intérieur*, her multitudes of cushions, her taffetas, *crêpe de Chines*, velvets, her profusion of jewelled lucky charms, amulets, brooches and bangles, Odette expresses the ideal of a generation whose men demanded clinging femininity in their women and, with the *rentes* steady as rocks at five per cent, could afford to foot the dressmakers' bills. 'Elle était entourée de sa toilette comme de l'appareil délicat et spiritualisé d'une civilisation.' Proust, like Marcel, appreciates the superficiality of this passing moment in French history. As

[1] *JF.* I, 193.

an artist, however, he perceived its beauty and, like the prince de Sagan, paid homage. Here is one tribute. Picture Odette with her mauve silk parasol unfurled walking in the Bois accompanied by Charles and Marcel. Swann draws her attention to a gentleman on horseback who is about to raise his hat.

Et, en effet, le prince, faisant comme dans une apothéose de théâtre, de cirque, ou dans un tableau ancien faire front à son cheval dans une magnifique apothéose, adressait à Odette un grand salut théâtral et comme allégorique où s'amplifiait toute la chevaleresque courteoisie du grand seigneur inclinant son respect devant la Femme, fût-elle incarnée en une femme que sa mère ou sa sœur ne pourraient pas fréquenter.[1]

But apart from its fashion parades, it is on the whole an indoor society except for a few ultra-modern women who, to Odette's contemptuous amusement, play golf and are clad in 'swetters'. Proust seems to remember it most vividly in the autumnal dusk of an October afternoon when Odette, a devotee of 'le five o'clock tea' was to be found in her drawing-room surrounded by tiers of softly tinted chrysanthemums, beautiful in snowy *crêpe de Chine*, waiting for Mme Bontemps, Mme Cottard, Mme Verdurin and her other callers. There is a suggestion of Proust's own nostalgia in these lines:

Mais j'étais touché parce que ces chrysanthèmes avaient moins d'éphémère, que de relativement durable par rapport à ces tons aussi roses et aussi cuivrés que le soleil couché exalte si somptueusement dans la brume des fins d'après-midi de novembre et qu'après les avoir aperçus avant que j'entrasse chez Mme Swann, s'éteignant dans le ciel je retrouvais prolongés, transposés dans la palette enflammée des fleurs comme des feux arrachés par un grand coloriste à l'instabilité de l'atmosphère et du soleil, afin qu'ils vinssent orner une demeure humaine, ils m'invitaient, ces chrysanthèmes, et malgré toute ma tristesse à goûter avidement pendant cette heure du thé les plaisirs si courts de novembre dont ils faisaient flamboyer près de moi la splendeur intime et mystérieuse.[2]

Note, however, that this passage occurs towards the end of the volume and reflects the twilight of Marcel's love for Gilberte, the disillusionment of the 'fin amant' who has begun to suspect, it would seem, that the romantic charm of a *princesse*

---

[1] *JF.* I, 194. [2] *JF.* I, 154.

lointaine exists only so long as she remains *lointaine*. Of this we shall have more to say. Meanwhile, let us turn to the pages devoted to Mme Swann's afternoon teas where Proust's gently malicious humour and his astonishing talent for mimicry are delightfully in the ascendant. It is as if he suddenly opens the drawing-room door, releasing a flood of feminine small talk; the cattinesses of Mme Verdurin, the anecdotes of Mme Bontemps about the latest stupidity of 'la ministresse', the preciosities of Mme Cottard, one of Proust's most amusing lesser characters. Incidentally, I can never understand why Marcel refers to her as 'cette petite bourgeoise peu aimable'. Kind-hearted, though pedantic to an absurd degree, employing always 'un langage noble pour les petites choses', Mme Cottard is an inexhaustible fount of joyous ineptitudes. Listen to this reincarnation of a 'précieuse ridicule' telling Odette about her servant problems.

'Et puis j'ai eu une crise dans ma domesticité mâle. Sans être plus qu'une autre, très imbue de mon autorité, j'ai dû, pour faire un exemple renvoyer mon Vatel qui, je crois, cherchait d'ailleurs une place plus lucrative. Mais son départ a failli entraîner la démission de tout le ministère. Ma femme de chambre ne voulait pas rester non plus, il a y eu des scènes homériques. Malgré tout, j'ai tenu ferme le gouvernail et c'est une véritable leçon de choses qui n'aura pas été perdue pour moi.'[1]

In approaching a novel which has only existed for twenty years the critic is bound to be haunted by the ghosts who walk the cemeteries of literary history. This is a prudent and a wholesome fear which may easily, I think, become a sterilizing obsession. There is, after all, a middle way between the uninformed enthusiasm of the amateur who mistakes superficial novelty for genius and the intransigent attitude of certain specialists who refuse to consider a work under half a century old. I appreciate the hesitation of the mature and therefore somewhat disillusioned literary critic who resists the temptation to express in public his admiration for a recent work. But when he discovers at each successive rereading, corroboration and reinforcement of his original astonished delight it becomes almost a duty to share it with others. Such has been my own experience with Proust. It

[1] *JF.* i, 155.

seems to me that, in creating *A la recherche du temps perdu*, he
mastered a secret which has eluded the greatest of his predecessors. Without ever compromising the unity of his novel, that
is to say, whilst never allowing it to lose that individual quality
which distinguishes a novel from an essay, a treatise or a collection of maxims, Proust has poured and fused into the narrative
of Marcel's life, into this 'histoire d'une vocation' the material
for a hundred essays, books of maxims and memoirs. It is a
talent so extremely rare that I cannot recall a single other
example of its successful exercise, though it is distressingly
easy, on the other hand, to point to writers, even of genius such
as Goethe, Rousseau and Voltaire who have failed to achieve
this fusion. The history of the novel reveals many such failures,
works where the stream of the narrative trickles into nothingness, blocked by huge congelations of ideas on philosophy, art,
literature and life. Everything is there except the illusion which
only the born novelist can impart, the illusion that we are
watching the evolution of a human existence.

Observe, on the contrary, how subtly Proust obtains this
homogeneity to which I allude: it is continuously illustrated in
his work. Persistently suggested, the theme of imagination and
its relation to reality is ever held before our eyes. Marcel now
sees Gilberte in her domestic environment and gradually begins
to perceive that whenever her parents' wishes conflict with her
own immediate desires she can be a very different person from
the ethereal creature of an imagination stimulated by love. But
such disturbing impressions are short-lived. On the other hand,
his first meeting, at a luncheon party given by Odette, with
Bergotte, the famous novelist produces a violent commotion in
his mind. Perhaps he ought to have been prepared for something
of the kind after Norpois's discourging comments on his Martinville impressions. For the ambassador, after reading this maiden
essay at self-expression, and learning of Marcel's enthusiasm for
Bergotte, to whom he attributed the defects of the youngster's
style, had launched into a devastating criticism of the great
novelist's writings and personal habits. Norpois did not, however, manage to shake Marcel's faith in Bergotte; only in his
own talents.

At lunch, seated beside a young, thick-set little man with a goatee and a nose shaped like a snail's shell, Marcel hears from Odette that his neighbour is Bergotte, his idol, 'le doux Chantre' whom he had always visualized as a languorous old gentleman, in short, as the author of the divine prose-poems which first enchanted him at Combray. When he hears Bergotte talk, listening to his emphatic, monotonous and pretentious conversation, the fissure that had suddenly opened between imagination and reality yawns like an unbridgable chasm.

Now Proust, in the most natural and disarming fashion, proceeds to reveal the formation of Marcel's new and complicated impressions of Bergotte and, at the same time, his own thoughts on the subject of the work of art and its relation to the artist; on the difference between the author's spoken and written style; the problem offered by the apparent contradiction between a writer's private vices and the high morality of the theses he defends in his books. Here are pages filled with wisdom. Yet always we are conscious that this is a luncheon party at Swanns: the living presence of Odette, Charles, Marcel and Gilberte is visibly and audibly advertised in the play of phrase and movement. More important still, the general design of these Proustian views on art and literature prolongs the complex, intimate pattern of Marcel's changing sentiments as he listens to the conversation of Bergotte and compares his new emotions with those evoked by the novelist's writings and by Norpois' malicious gossip about Bergotte's shameful love affair and allegedly sordid behaviour in money matters. On Norpois himself a new light is thrown by Swann's revelations. The diplomat now appears as a passionate figure of romance who used to travel twice a week from Italy to Paris in order to spend three hours with his mistress. Elaborated by Proust, this account of a youth's first meeting with his favourite author takes on that quality of universal significance which only very great novelists can extract from things. Marcel, having received one more lesson from life on the difference between the world of the imagination and of reality, receives yet another still on the complexity of reality itself. Which is the real Bergotte: the author of the books that interpret with obvious anxiety the problem of evil, or the man who can be seen at the theatre in company which seems to brand him as an impudent and cynical humbug? Or is it the Bergotte who is now so genuinely and sympathetically interested in Marcel's illness, telling him that he must not worry, because an invalid has leisure to enjoy the pleasures of the intelligence, and listening with such tact and kindness to his views on La Berma's acting in *Phèdre*? Or, again, is the real Bergotte the man with whom he now drives off and who suddenly utters the following malevolent remark on Swann?:

'Quelqu'un qui aurait besoin d'un bon médecin c'est notre ami Swann,' dit Bergotte. Et comme je demandais s'il était malade. 'Hé bien! c'est l'homme qui a épousé une fille, qui avale par jour cinquante couleuvres de femmes qui ne veulent pas recevoir la sienne, ou d'hommes qui ont couché avec elle. On les voit qui lui tordent la bouche. Regardez un jour le sourcil circonflexe qu'il a quand il rentre, pour voir qui il a chez lui.'[1]

Here, one might think, is the perfect conclusion to this episode. But in the art of projecting a scene as in the style of a great artist we must always reckon with that unpredictable quality which is the *cachet* of genius. Proust deems the episode complete only when Marcel arrives home and excitedly relates his good fortune. Naturally his parents, indoctrinated by Norpois, regard their son's meeting with the 'decadent' Bergotte as another proof that he should never have been allowed to frequent the Swanns. But when Marcel casually mentions that according to the Swanns, Bergotte had expressed a high opinion of his intelligence, there is a charming *coup de théâtre*.

'Ah!...Il a dit qu'il te trouvait intelligent,' dit ma mère. 'Cela me fait plaisir parce que c'est un homme de talent.'
'Comment! il a dit cela?' reprit mon père. 'Je ne nie en rien sa valeur littéraire devant laquelle tout le monde s'incline, seulement c'est ennuyeux qu'il ait cette existence peu honorable dont a parlé à mots couverts le père Norpois,' ajouta-t-il sans s'apercevoir que devant la vertu souveraine des mots magiques que je venais de prononcer la dépravation des mœurs de Bergotte ne pouvait guère lutter plus longtemps que la fausseté de son jugement.
'Oh! mon ami,' interrompit maman, 'rien ne prouve que ce soit vrai. On dit tant de choses. D'ailleurs, M. de Norpois est tout ce

[1] *JF.* I, 132.

qu'il y a de plus gentil, mais il n'est pas toujours très bienveillant, surtout pour les gens qui ne sont pas de son bord.'

'C'est vrai, je l'avais aussi remarqué,' répondit ma mère.[1]

The tempo of Marcel's sentimental education is accelerated by the fact that Gilberte unconsciously looks on him as a tacit ally of her parents when, as is now very often the case, the latter have occasion to reprimand her. On the other hand, Marcel commits the supreme blunder of begging her anxiously to tell him what he has done to deserve her coldness, asking like the foolish Dr Bartholo with Rosine, what he ought to do to please her. The inevitable quarrel occurs when Odette, after a sharp altercation conducted in English, to the embarrassment of Marcel who does not know that language, forces Gilberte to give up a dance in order to keep her guest company. Marcel resolves therefore to impose on himself what the narrator calls 'une cure de détachment psychique et d'isolement', in other words, to let his love die a slow death from inanition, by arranging never to call on Gilberte when she is at home and never accept invitations to her *goûters*. This is an extremely painful process which affords Proust, incidentally, the occasion for many a lingering and subtle analysis of the victim's sentiments. At these moments one cannot help remarking an echo of Marivaux, especially in the minute dissection of Marcel's anxiety when New Year's Day comes and goes with no greeting from Gilberte. Here is a typical Marivaux passage rearranged and modernized by Proust:

> Quand on aime, l'amour est trop grand pour pouvoir être contenu tout entier en nous; il irradie vers la personne aimée, rencontre en elle une surface qui l'arrête, le force à revenir vers son point de départ et c'est ce choc en retour de notre propre tendresse que nous appelons les sentiments de l'autre et qui nous charme plus qu'à l'aller, parce que nous ne reconnaissons pas qu'elle vient de nous.[2]

Proust, with his usual tact, knows just when to terminate such auscultations. Considering, finally, that his cure has lasted long enough and that the time has come to discover whether his prestige with Gilberte has been increased by his heroic abstentions, Marcel sells an old Chinese vase inherited from Aunt

[1] *JF.* I, 135.   [2] *JF.* I, 166.

Léonie and, now the delighted possessor of ten thousand francs, sets out for the Swanns, just before dinner. As Marcel drives down the rue de Berri, clutching the money with which to buy endless bouquets for Gilberte, he observes her walking in the dusk with a young man. Proust now reveals, in slow motion, the procession of images conjured up by despair, resulting in the lingering demise of Marcel's first love, the suicide as he calls it, of the self who loved Gilberte. The reason he now gives in his letters for refusing her invitations is an allusion to some mysterious misunderstanding about which Gilberte seems exasperatingly incurious. So their little notes are now tinged with nostalgic references to the past. It is a familiar tone which might be expressed in the formula: 'La vie a pu nous séparer, elle ne pourra nous faire oublier les bonnes heures qui nous seront toujours chères.' As the older Marcel sagely observes, there is nothing quite so delicate or so tender as the correspondence between friends who no longer want to see each other.

The Marcel who sets out with his grandmother for Balbec, two years after he first wandered into the Elysian Fields of first love, is now relatively heart free. Not entirely so, because love memories, like any other memories, have a disconcerting trick of suddenly leaping out of oblivion, evoked by a sensation, by the scent of a wood fire, of a rain-laden breeze, by the stuffy odour of a closed room, by the chance repetition of a name or phrase, of sensations felt long ago, unheeded by our careless surface intelligence, yet recorded by our subconscious. Here Proust recurs, as he will do so often again, to an idea adumbrated in the Combray pages. The best and the most important part of our memory would seem to lie outside ourselves, in objects that evoke sensations common to the present and the past. Yet it is really inside ourselves though hidden from our ordinary perceptions in the oblivion of the subconscious mind, an oblivion which, however, is only temporary and extremely precious. Thanks to the mechanism of the unconscious memory —set in motion by a chance word, a perfume, a touch, a flash of light—we are able, miraculously, to become once again the self we were, to relive the emotional experience of that self just as Marcel, in Balbec, hearing the words 'directeur au

ministère des postes' will experience a brief revival of the suffering
inflicted on the boy who was so hopelessly in love with Gilberte.
From the moment Marcel departs in the company of his
grandmother and Françoise for Balbec on the magic 1.22 p.m.
train from the Gare St-Lazare, there is a perceptible change in
the rhythm of the narrative, reflecting that sense of adventure,
that expectation of vague delights not unmingled with apprehension which, in youth, is inseparable from any major break
with routine. In Marcel's case the excitement is magnified and
complicated because this hypersensitive invalid has never before
left his family. Now, for the first time, he realizes the possibility
of an existence lacking the presence of his mother who is about
to leave for the country near Paris with her husband. Therefore,
to Marcel's desolate eyes, the Gare St-Lazare acquires a new
and strange individuality. I will quote a passage which is a
typical illustration of Proust's amazing talent for transfiguring
the ordinary things of daily life and thus illuminating their
essence. Here then, is the Gare St-Lazare divested of what
'Realists' call the real; transformed by the genius of an artist
into something apocalyptic and eternal:

> Malheureusement ces lieux merveilleux que sont les gares, d'où
> l'on part pour une destination éloignée, sont aussi des lieux tragiques,
> car si le miracle s'y accomplit grâce auquel les pays qui n'avaient
> encore d'existence que dans notre pensée vont être ceux au milieu
> desquels nous vivrons, pour cette raison même il faut renoncer au
> sortir de la salle d'attente à retrouver la chambre familière où l'on
> était il y a un instant encore. Il faut laisser toute espérance de rentrer
> coucher chez soi, une fois qu'on s'est décidé à pénétrer dans l'antre
> empesté par où l'on accède au mystère, dans un de ces grands ateliers
> vitrés, comme celui de Saint-Lazare où j'allais chercher le train de
> Balbec, et qui déployait au-dessus de la ville éventrée un de ces
> immenses ciels crus et gros de menaces, amoncelés de drame, pareils
> à certains ciels, d'une modernité presque parisienne, de Mantegna ou
> de Véronèse, et sous lequel ne pouvait s'accomplir que quelque acte
> terrible et solennel comme un départ en chemin de fer ou l'érection
> de la Croix.[1]

> [Unfortunately, those marvellous places called railway-stations
> whence one sets out for some far-off destination are tragic places also,

[1] JF. i, 197-8.

for if in their precincts is enacted the miracle whereby regions that
had as yet no existence save in our thought are about to become those
in which we are going to live, for that very reason we must abandon,
on emerging from the waiting-room, the familiar apartment which
housed us but a moment ago. We must renounce all hope of returning
home to sleep once we have decided to penetrate into that evil-
smelling cavern which gives access to the mystery, into one of those
huge glassed-in hangars, like that of Saint-Lazare, where I went to
get the Balbec train and which unfurled over the eviscerated city one
of those immense, crude skies, heavy with threatening masses of
drama, like certain sky-paintings, almost Parisian in their modernity,
by Mantegna or Veronese, under which only some terrible and solemn
act could be in process of accomplishment, such as a departure by
train or the Elevation of the Cross.]

In the vocabulary of the literary critic there is an expression
'the creative imagination' which is so abstract as to be often
almost meaningless. Taken literally, it hardly makes sense, for
it is impossible to conceive an uncreative imagination: the
imagination is, surely, the faculty which creates pictures or
concrete images. Still, when we are told that a novelist has
a powerful creative imagination, we know vaguely that he possesses, to an intense degree, the power to create fictitious individuals, situations and milieux. If he is Balzac, his creative
imagination attains a kind of hallucinatory intensity which is
communicated to the reader. Hypnotized by the magic of art,
one believes in the reality of the author's creations, however
monstrous they would appear in the cadre of ordinary existence.
Now, this is *par excellence* the creative imagination of the dramatist, whether he writes plays or novels. It is not, on the whole,
a definition that can be applied to Proust. Exceptionally, no
doubt, he creates situations which are even more imaginative
than anything created by Balzac or Stendhal. Marcel, for instance, when he is tortured by jealous suspicions of Albertine
will keep her a virtual prisoner for almost a year in his Paris
flat. We shall encounter, too, certain situations involving the
baron de Charlus that possess an almost hallucinatory quality.
Nevertheless, such is not the characteristic trend of Proust's
imagination which operates most naturally and effectively when
it transfigures the banal realities of life; dissociating them from

the cadre lent to them by our practical, everyday intelligence; surrounding them with images which illuminate their hidden beauty and significance. The Proustian imagination is not essentially dramatic and though intensely active, is not primarily a Balzacian faculty, working at high tension in the act of continuous fabulation, of inventing critical situations which shall force his characters to reveal the secret recesses of their souls in a series of volcanic upheavals. However, it is only by studying Marcel's narrative that we shall be able to understand the rôle played by the imagination in the creation of Proust's great work.

Adolescence is essentially the age of imagination and for Proust it is the truly formative period of our life, the only period, indeed when we really learn anything, because it is the time when we pay least attention to the perceptions of our intelligence. Spontaneity, movement, uninterrupted re-creation, the essential qualities of life yet never so clearly visible as in life's springtime—these are the qualities which Proust now captures and reveals to us in Marcel's narrative. And with the great artist's intuitive sense of perfect harmony, he chooses for his setting the restless and immemorial ocean whose iridescent moods reflect the ever-changing emotions, sensations, desires and images of adolescent consciousness. The creative imagination of Proust, I have suggested, is never so completely realized as when it transfigures the ordinary situations and happenings of life. Read, for example, Marcel's account of his railway journey to Balbec and you will observe the surprising proliferation that takes place when an apparently banal event is refracted in the prism of Proust's imaginative and intelligent mind; then communicated in the rhythmic pulsations of his incomparable style. He does not need to invoke the aid of sensational or dramatic contingencies. Proust instinctively extracts the drama, invisible to others, yet latent in the little, everyday experiences of life. To prevent a recurrence of Marcel's attacks, his doctor has ordered alcohol before the journey so as to produce a beneficent and necessary euphoria. But he knows from Combray days about his grandmother's ingrained horror of intoxicating liquors. On the other hand, Marcel cannot bear the thought of her watching him in one of his asthmatic seizures, powerless to help, tortured by pity for his distress. So he prefers to go to the bar in the train and absorb several glasses of cognac. In an admirable page which exactly interprets the nuances of pathos and humour inherent in every situation of this nature, Proust shows us a Marcel, exhilarated and talkative, floating in a rosy alcoholic cloud whilst his poor grandmother who can already see the boy tottering on the slippery ramp that leads to dipsomania, sits with averted eyes, answering in monosyllables or tries to forget her sorrows in the fascinating letters of Mme de Sévigné.

The same alchemy transfigures the episode of the night journey, for Marcel travels alone to Balbec where his grandmother, who is spending two days with friends, will rejoin him next morning. I am not alluding to the passage describing his first impressions of the sky and silent countryside at dawn glimpsed alternately from one window then from another as the train changes direction, though here we have the notations of a superb painter in words. Even more admirable is Proust's interpretation of Marcel's exalted state of soul as he perceives, during a brief halt, moving towards the standing train from a little croft beside a rushing torrent, a magnificent peasant girl, such as he had dreamed of at Combray, carrying pitchers of milk and coffee for the bleary-eyed travellers.

Empourpré des reflets du matin, son visage était plus rose que le ciel. Je ressentis devant elle ce désir de vivre qui renaît en nous chaque fois que nous prenons de nouveau conscience de la beauté et du bonheur. . Nous oublions toujours qu'ils sont individuels et, leur substituant dans notre esprit un type de convention que nous formons en faisant une sorte de moyenne entre les différents visages qui nous ont plu, entre les plaisirs que nous avons connus, nous n'avons que des images abstraites qui sont languissantes et fades parce qu'il leur manque précisément ce caractère d'une chose nouvelle, différente de ce que nous avons connu, ce caractère qui est propre à la beauté et au bonheur. Et nous portons sur la vie un jugement pessimiste et que nous supposons juste, car nous avons cru y faire entrer en ligne de compte le bonheur et la beauté, quand nous les avons omis et remplacés par des synthèses où d'eux il n'y a pas un seul atome.[1]

[Flushed by the glowing dawn, her face was pinker than the sky. I felt on beholding her that desire to live which is reborn in us every time we experience a new consciousness of beauty and happiness. We always forget that they are individual and, mentally replacing them with a conventional type which we form by striking a sort of mean amongst the different faces that have pleased us, amongst the pleasures we have known, we obtain only abstract images which are lifeless and insipid precisely because they lack that characteristic immanent in every-thing new, different from anything we have known, that characteristic which is peculiar to beauty and happiness. And we pass a pessimistic verdict on life and imagine it to be accurate, thinking we have allowed for happiness and beauty when in fact we have left them out, inserting in their place syntheses which contain not a single atom of them.]

Balbec church, viewed on an August morning, sharing the sunlight that illuminates the local Savings Bank, the café op-posite, the office of the omnibus company, is sadly different from Marcel's cherished vision. Its steeple does not look down upon tempestuous seas because this is Balbec-le-vieux, situated about fifteen miles from the ocean. Gazing at the figures sculptured in its ancient porch, at the famous Virgin mentioned by Swann, resolutely summoning up all his memories and desires, Marcel tries hard to superimpose imagination on reality. But they refuse to coincide and so, with an increasing sentiment of spiritual deflation, he rejoins his grandmother and sets out for the Grand Hôtel of Balbec-on-sea. And since life, that con-scientious artist, has an infallible flair for harmonious ensembles Marcel discovers his grandmother sitting alone at the station. Françoise, who had been sent on in advance to prepare for their arrival, has been directed to the wrong train by Mme Amédée and is now rattling along the line to Bordeaux.

We shall make closer acquaintance with the intimate geo-graphy of the Grand Hôtel de Balbec and with the intricate protocol that regulates existence in a typical and fashionable French *plage*. Meanwhile, Proust directs our attention to the mingled emotions of Marcel, to his homesickness, apprehension, loneliness and sense of humiliation as he sits in the vast foyer, listening in an agony of shame and abysmal inferiority to his grandmother discussing in a falsetto, unnatural voice the price of the rooms. Who has not in extreme youth gone through this ordeal, now exfoliated by Proust? Who does not remember, because such experiences are timeless and universal, Marcel's awful feeling that he is a solitary object of hostility, contempt and derision, that everyone from the insolently bored reception-clerk down to the smallest and most impertinent lift-boy is wondering why on earth these cads ever thought of coming to the Grand Hôtel; that at any moment an outraged staff will hurl them into the street with every circumstance of ignominy?

Tandis que j'entendais ma grand'mère sans se froisser qu'il l'écoutât son chapeau sur la tête et tout en sifflotant, lui demander sur une intonation artificielle: 'Et quels sont...vos prix?...Oh! beau-coup trop élevés pour mon petit budget', attendant sur une banquette, je me réfugiais au plus profond de moi-même, je m'efforçais d'émigrer dans des pensées éternelles, de ne laisser rien de moi, rien de vivant, à la surface de mon corps — insensibilisée comme l'est celle des animaux qui par inhibition font les morts quand on les blesse, — afin de ne pas trop souffrir dans ce lieu où mon manque total d'habitude m'était rendu plus sensible encore par la vue de celle que semblait en avoir au même moment, une dame élégante à qui le directeur témoi-gnait son respect en prenant des familiarités avec le petit chien dont elle était suivie, le jeune gandin qui, la plume au chapeau, rentrait en demandant 's'il y avait des lettres', tous ces gens pour qui c'était regagner leur home que de gravir les degrés en faux marbre.[1]

[Whilst I heard my grandmother, who betrayed no annoyance at his listening to her with his hat on his head and whistling softly mean-while, ask him in an artificial tone of voice 'And what are...your charges?...Oh! much too high for my little budget', waiting on a bench, I took refuge in the innermost depths of my being, trying to emigrate to a kingdom of eternal thoughts, to leave nothing of myself, nothing living, on the surface of my body—desensitized like that of certain animals which, by inhibition, sham death when wounded—so as not to suffer in this place, my complete lack of familiarity with which was impressed upon me even more acutely by the familiarity with it that seemed to be evinced at the same moment by a fashionable lady to whom the manager showed his respect by taking liberties with her little dog, the young 'blood' with the feather in his hat who came in asking 'Any letters for me', all these people for whom climbing the imitation marble stairs meant going home.]

[1] *JF.* 1, 214.

In middle age we are prone to forget that social existence for a very young man is an alarming succession of journeys into new worlds of the spirit. Proust, it is evident, vividly remembers what it means for the adolescent male to be wrenched from his secure, familiar domestic surroundings and cast, 'naked and alone', into an unknown and probably hostile world. This purgatory is a refined torture for Marcel whose already quivering sensibility is aggravated by his physical malaise. With typical insight, Proust notes and illustrates all the symptoms: Marcel's pathetic, ingratiating attempts to strike up a conversation with the stonily unresponsive lift-boy; his hopeless envy of the elect, the great ones who stroll up to the desk, idly swinging their tennis-rackets, loudly voicing their desires or complaints; the second prolonged station in the unfriendly hotel bedroom where every object mutely protests at this unwarranted intrusion upon its privacy; the pungent odour of vetiver that penetrates, almost viscerally, into his inmost being and, at last, the unspeakable, overwhelming relief when, demoralized by loneliness, apprehension and a recurrence of his suffocations, he throws himself, sobbing, into his grandmother's protecting arms. All this, of course, sounds very 'French', most un-English, and I well remember, indeed, some twenty years ago noting in an unfortunately ephemeral review, appetizingly entitled *Realism*, the scorn aroused in the breast of one of our most talented novelists by this scene and the firm, house-matronly way in which she dealt with Marcel and his grandmother and their sentimental nonsense. Nevertheless, I still think that this is one of the most human and most sensitively communicated incidents in Marcel's account of his adolescent tribulations.

In this first Balbec episode which is fully related in the second volume of *A l'ombre des jeunes filles en fleurs*, Proust brings into the foreground Mme Amédée, the wonderful old lady who incarnates along with her daughter and Françoise, the finest and most enduring qualities of the French. She is the type of cultured bourgeoise, so common in real life yet seldom honoured in literature any more than is the good bread of France in the annals of French cookery. Only after she is dead does Marcel, in the act of stooping to unbutton his shoes, realize, in a blinding

flash of illumination, everything his grandmother meant to him
as a boy, her untiring devotion to the invalid grandson, her
intransigent common sense, her intolerance of humbug, her
delicacy of feeling and infallible natural taste. In the atmosphere
of vulgar and noisy pretentiousness which pervades establish-
ments like the Grand Hôtel, Marcel's grandmother shines out
like a Vermeer in a bazaar. We glimpse her stealing towards
the beach with her umbrella and the *Lettres* of Mme de Sévigné,
to escape the marquise de Villeparisis who also respects and
understands her old friend's desire for privacy. How charmingly
Proust describes their inevitable meeting.

A la fin nous aussi, nous eûmes une relation, malgré mais par ma
grand'mère, car elle et Mme de Villeparisis tombèrent un matin l'une
sur l'autre dans une porte et furent obligées de s'aborder non sans
échanger au préalable des gestes de surprise, d'hésitation, exécuter des
mouvements de recul, de doute et enfin des protestations de politesse et
de joie comme dans certaines pièces de Molière où deux acteurs mono-
loguant depuis longtemps chacun de son côté à quelques pas l'un de
l'autre, sont censés ne pas s'être vus encore, et tout à coup s'aper-
çoivent, n'en peuvent croire leurs yeux, entrecoupent leurs propos,
finalement parlent ensemble, le chœur ayant suivi le dialogue et se
jettent dans les bras l'un de l'autre, Mme de Villeparisis par discrétion
voulut au bout d'un instant quitter ma grand'mère qui au contraire,
préféra la retenir jusqu'au déjeuner, désirant apprendre comment elle
faisait pour avoir son courrier plus tôt que nous et de bonnes grillades
(car Mme de Villeparisis, très gourmande, goûtait fort peu la cuisine
de l'hôtel où l'on nous servait des repas que ma grand'mere citant
toujours Mme de Sévigné prétendait être 'd'une magnificence à mourir
de faim').[1]

[Finally, we also made a social contact, in spite of but through my
grandmother, for she and Mme de Villeparisis ran across each other
in a doorway and were obliged to accost each other, not without having
first exchanged gestures of surprise, of hesitation, executed movements of withdrawal, of doubt and finally broken into polite and joyous
protestations as in certain plays by Molière where two actors each of
whom in his particular corner, a few feet away from the other, has
been engaged for some time in a monologue, are supposed not yet to
have seen each other, and suddenly catching sight of each other, cannot
believe their eyes, interrupt their speech, finally enter into conversation, the chorus meanwhile having sustained the dialogue, and throw

[1] *JF.* I, 241.

themselves into each other's arms. Tactfully, after a moment, Mme de Villeparisis made as if to leave my grandmother who preferred, on the other hand, to keep her till lunch, being anxious to know how she managed to get her letters before us and such nice grilled dishes. (For Mme de Villeparisis, who took a keen interest in her food, had a low opinion of the hotel restaurant where they served us meals which, according to my grandmother who still quoted Mme de Sévigné, were 'sumptuous to the point of starvation'.)⌉

One remembers this old lady best, perhaps, as Marcel will ever remember her, that first terrible evening at Balbec in her old dressing-gown, the familiar guardian of his sleepless hours, the grandmother who rose uncomplainingly at any hour when Marcel's painful attacks forced him to tap on the party-wall, the grandmother whose life was so wrapped up in his welfare that the knowledge of her own approaching death was nothing compared to the thought of his loneliness. Their relationship is reflected very beautifully in the following conversation:

Une fois je lui dis: — 'Sans toi je ne pourrai pas vivre.' — 'Mais il ne faut pas,' me répondit-elle d'une voix troublée. 'Il faut nous faire un cœur plus dur que ça. Sans cela, que deviendrais-tu si je partais en voyage? J'espère au contraire que tu serais très raisonnable et très heureux.'

'Je saurais être raisonnable si tu partais pour quelques jours, mais je compterais les heures.'

'Mais si je partais pour des mois'.... (A cette seule idée mon cœur se serrait), 'pour des années...pour....'

Nous nous taisions tous les deux. Nous n'osions pas nous regarder. Pourtant je souffrais plus de son angoisse que de la mienne. Aussi je m' approchai de la fenêtre et distinctement je lui dis en détournant les yeux:

'Tu sais comme je suis un être d'habitudes. Les premiers jours où je viens d'être séparé des gens que j'aime le plus, je suis malheureux. Mais tout en les aimant toujours autant, je m'accoutume, ma vie devient calme, douce; je supporterais d'être séparé d'eux, des mois, des années....'

Je dus me taire et regarder tout à fait par la fenêtre. Ma grand'mère sortit un instant de la chambre. Mais le lendemain je me mis à parler de philosophie, sur le ton le plus indifférent, en m'arrangeant cependant pour que ma grand'mère fît attention à mes paroles, je dis que c'était curieux, qu'après les dernières découvertes de la science, le matérialisme semblait ruiné, et que le plus probable était encore l'éternité des âmes et leur future réunion.[1]

[1] *JF.* II, 28.

[Once I said to her: 'Without you I could not live.' 'But you must not say that', she replied, in a worried voice. 'We must be pluckier than that. Otherwise what would become of you if I went on a journey? I hope, however, that you would be very sensible and very happy.'

'I could manage to be sensible if you went off for a few days, but I should count the hours.'

'But if I went away for some months'.... (At the mere idea I felt a tugging at my heart-strings) 'for some years...for....'

We both fell silent. We did not dare to look at each other. Yet I suffered more because of her anguish than from my own. So I approached the window and said to her distinctly, with averted eyes.

'You know what a creature of habit I am. The first day when I've just been separated from the people I love most, I am unhappy. But whilst still loving them just as much, I get accustomed to missing them, my life becomes calm, smooth; I could stand being parted from them for months, years....'

I had to stop speaking and look straight out of the window. My grandmother left the room for a moment. But next day I began to talk about philosophy in the most casual tone, taking care however that my grandmother should pay attention to my words. I said it was curious that, after the latest discoveries of science, materialism seemed to have collapsed, and that what was again most probable was the immortality of our souls and their future reunion.]

It is a pity that the word, humanism, originally coined by the men of the Renaissance to express their profound interest in human nature should have acquired its present restricted and academic zone of currency. For Proust, in the most generous connotation of the term, is a humanist. This does not mean that he was obsessed by that 'souci de l'humain' of which in recent years we have heard so much from French novelists some of whom, unfortunately, tend to regard themselves as writers with a 'message', the exact purport of which is often obscure. There is nothing evangelical about Proust's humanism which is expressed, as is strikingly evident in these two volumes we are now discussing, in a variety of modes and tones, nowhere more gravely, however, than in the passages describing the immense and profound tenderness that links Marcel to his grandmother. Yet it would be wrong to give the impression that Proust's absorbing and sympathetic interest in human beings ever takes the form of a 'souci de l'humain', of an anxiety concerning the spiritual and material welfare of humanity. His humanism is not a cult of Humanity, a vast pity for Humanity but an intense desire to know human nature. His only 'souci' is to discover, by scrutinizing and decoding the puzzling impressions of individual behaviour recorded by his consciousness and by studying the workings of his own mind, the ciphers or keys we call psychological laws. His attitude is sometimes disillusioned or humorously satirical but it is not the attitude of a cynic or of a reformer. Perhaps one might best describe it as the enlightened tolerance of an extremely truthful observer whose astonishing acuity of perception is reinforced by his natural habit of sympathy, by the faculty of entering into the minds of others and of seeing the world through their eyes. This trait we usually take for granted in the great masters of fiction. But we have only to examine their novels to realize the inaccuracy of our supposition. The prejudices or preferences of Stendhal, Flaubert and Zola, to mention only three instances, are very definitely reflected in their approach to certain social types and classes. Proust has remarkably few prejudices and, in any case, rarely allows them to obscure his vision of human nature.

But, as Marcel's narrative suggests, it is not enough to possess a natural faculty for entering into the thoughts and feelings of others. Like every faculty of the mind it must be sedulously cultivated, which entails a process of trial and error, representing—if I interpret Proust correctly—an important and necessary phase of Marcel's progress towards his vocation since it is a faculty only found to perfection in the mature artist. During his adolescent stage, indeed, Marcel's natural tendency to put himself in the other person's shoes, as the saying goes, only accentuates his feeling of inferiority and distorts his judgement. However, since the narrator is Marcel the experienced artist, we are able to observe, simultaneously, the formation of the erroneous impressions shaped and coloured by the imagination of youth and the gradual emergence of other, very different impressions furnished by his intimate contacts with people and things. That the latter may often turn out to be equally unreal is a theme which interests Proust very deeply because, as he shows, one must always reckon with the force of Habit which is apt to interpose a veil between our consciousness and reality.

In youth there is always tomorrow morning, the transformation effected by a new day in the climate of the adolescent soul. Stand behind Marcel, for example, and note what happens when on the morning after his first desolate night in Balbec he looks out from his bedroom window.

A tous moments, tenant à la main la serviette raide et empesée où était écrit le nom de l'hôtel et avec laquelle je faisais d'inutiles efforts pour me sécher, je retournais près de la fenêtre jeter encore un regard sur ce vaste cirque éblouissant et montagneux et sur les sommets neigeux de ses vagues en pierre d'émeraude çà et là polie et translucide, lesquelles avec une placide violence et un froncement léonin, laissaient s'accomplir et dévaler l'écroulement de leurs pentes auxquelles le soleil ajoutait un sourire sans visage. Fenêtre à laquelle je devais ensuite me mettre chaque matin comme au carreau d'une diligence dans laquelle on a dormi, pour voir si pendant la nuit s'est rapprochée ou éloignée une chaîne désirée, — ici ces collines de la mer qui avant de revenir vers nous en dansant, peuvent reculer si loin que souvent ce n'était qu'après une longue plaine sablonneuse que j'apercevais à une grande distance leurs premières ondulations, dans un lointain transparent, vaporeux et bleuâtre comme ces glaciers qu'on voit au fond des tableaux des primitifs toscans. D'autres fois c'était tout près de moi que le soleil riait sur ces flots d'un vert aussi tendre que celui que conserve aux prairies alpestres (dans les montagnes où le soleil s'étale çà et là comme un géant qui en descendrait gaiement, par bonds inégaux, les pentes), moins l'humidité du sol que la liquide mobilité de la lumière. Au reste, dans cette brèche que la plage et les flots pratiquaient au milieu du reste du monde pour y faire passer, pour y accumuler la lumière, c'est elle surtout, selon la direction d'où elle vient et que suit notre œil, c'est elle qui déplace et situe les vallonnements de la mer.[1]

[At every other moment, holding in my hand the stiff, starched towel that bore the name of the hotel and with which I was making futile attempts to dry myself, I went back close to the window for one more look at that vast, dazzling, mountainous amphitheatre and at the snowy crests of its waves, polished here and there and translucent as an emerald—waves that, with a placid violence and leonine frown, assented to the disintegration of their tumbling slopes to which the sun contributed an expressionless smile. This was the window at which

[1] *JF.* i, 222–3.

later, every morning, I was to take up my position, as if behind the
window of the stage-coach in which one has slept, to see whether,
during the night, some longed-for range of mountains has come closer
or receded—in this case those hills of the ocean which, before coming
dancing back to us, might withdraw so far that often it was only
across a long sandy plain that, a great distance away, I perceived their
first undulations, in a remoteness transparent, vaporous and bluish
like those glaciers one sees in the background of paintings by the
Tuscan Primitives. At other times, it was quite close to me that the
sun laughed upon those waves of a green as delicate as that which, on
Alpine meadows is preserved (in the mountains where the sun displays
himself here and there like some giant gaily descending their slopes
in erratic bounds), not so much by the humidity of the soil as by the
liquid mobility of the light. Besides, in that breach which the shore
and the waves open up in the midst of the rest of the world so as to
allow the light either to get through or to accumulate, it is, above all,
the light, according to the direction from which it comes and which
our eye follows, it is the light that displaces and situates the undulations
of the ocean.]

But this is only one of the seascapes which illuminate, like
Proust's gorgeous, impressionistic sky-paintings these Balbec
pages. Here, as we have already noted in the Combray volume,
his interpretation of natural beauty is not direct but oblique and
metaphoric. In the passage just quoted, the sea is expressed in
geographic terms, as a vast and mountainous landscape. However, in the account of Marcel's visit to the great artist, Elstir
we shall find an even more striking instance of this technique,
illustrated by a different metaphor.

In Marcel's amusing impressions of Balbec society we have
a preview of the more elaborate panorama he will reveal
in the narrative of his second visit. In addition to the usual
cosmopolitans and Parisians who frequent fashionable seaside
resorts, the tired business men with their overdressed actress-
mistresses, the weedy, spoilt sons of wealthy industrialists and
crooked politicians, there are to be found at Balbec regional
groups of mixed provenance. Chief amongst these is the legal
clique headed by the *premier président* from Caen, the *bâtonnier*
from Cherbourg, the distinguished notary from Le Mans. In
a number of alert and deftly arranged scenes, Proust throws into
comic relief their snobbery, naïve vulgarity and provincial dis-

trust of the stranger who does not fit into their narrow and traditional conception of what constitutes 'la bonne société'. As *fonctionnaires* and staunch Republicans they loudly proclaim their contempt of the decadent *nobles* until the *bâtonnier*, to the ill-concealed chagrin and envy of his colleagues is invited by the *de* Cambremers to lunch at their château. In a few lines, Proust captures what Diderot used to call 'l'âme du moment':

'Eh bien, j'espère que vous vous mettez bien, que vous êtes un homme chic,' lui dit le soir la femme du premier président. 'Chic? pourquoi?' demanda le bâtonnier, dissimulant sa joie sous un étonnement exagéré. 'A cause de mes invités?' dit-il, en sentant qu'il était incapable de feindre plus longtemps. 'Mais qu'est-ce que ça a de chic d'avoir des amis à déjeuner. Faut bien qu'ils déjeunent quelque part!'
'Mais si, c'est chic! C'était bien les *de* Cambremer, n'est-ce pas? Je les ai bien reconnus. C'est une marquise. Et authentique. Pas par les femmes?'
'Oh! c'est une femme bien simple, elle est charmante, on ne fait pas moins de façons. Je pensais que vous alliez venir, je vous faisais des signes...je vous aurais présenté!' dit-il en corrigeant par une légère ironie l'énormité de cette proposition comme Assuérus quand il dit à Esther: 'Faut-il de mes états vous donner la moitié!' 'Non, non, non, non, non nous restons cachés comme l'humble violette....'[1]

So far Marcel's grandmother has eluded her old school friend, the marquise de Villeparisis which is most disappointing because already his feudal and romantic dreams have been revived by the sight of Mlle de Stermaria, the pale, beautiful and aloof daughter of a Breton nobleman who sometimes lunches at the hotel. Introduced by Mme de Villeparisis, Marcel thinks that he might be invited to the Stermaria château and in his reveries he can visualize himself strolling at twilight with Mlle de Stermaria, in a landscape of purple heath and twisted oaks, listening to the lapping waves. The lady vanishes, however, before Mme de Villeparisis takes Marcel and his grandmother under her wing. This is to prove an event of capital importance in Marcel's life. Mme de Villeparisis is the aunt of the duchesse de Guermantes and of the baron de Charlus, the grand-aunt, too, of the marquis de Saint-Loup, all of whose destinies are to be

[1] *JF.* I, 235.

intertwined with Marcel's. Proust now introduces Charlus and Saint-Loup, two of his most interesting creations. Marcel does not know it but he has already met the former, of whom he had a first glimpse in Swann's garden at Tansonville. Charlus was the man with the protruding eyes staring at him with peculiar fixity. Just after his arrival at Balbec, Marcel encountered the same person again at closer quarters:

Le lendemain du jour où Robert m'avait ainsi parlé de son oncle tout en l'attendant, vainement du reste, comme je passais seul devant le casino en rentrant à l'hôtel, j'eus la sensation d'être regardé par quelqu'un qui n'était pas loin de moi. Je tournai la tête et j'aperçus un homme d'une quarantaine d'années très grand et assez gros, avec des moustaches très noires, et qui, tout en frappant nerveusement son pantalon avec une badine, fixait sur moi des yeux dilatés par l'attention. Par moment, ils étaient percés en tous sens par des regards d'une extrême activité comme en ont seuls devant une personne qu'ils ne connaissent pas des hommes à qui, pour un motif quelconque, elle inspire des pensées qui ne viendraient pas à tout autre, — par exemple des fous ou des espions. Il lança sur moi une suprême œillade à la fois hardie, prudente, rapide et profonde, comme un dernier coup que l'on tire au moment de prendre la fuite, et après avoir regardé tout autour de lui, prenant soudain un air distrait et hautain, par un brusque revirement de toute sa personne il se tourna vers une affiche dans la lecture de laquelle il s'absorba, en fredonnant un air et en arrangeant la rose mousseuse qui pendait à sa boutonnière.[1]

Through his grandmother's chance meeting with her old school friend, the marquise de Villeparisis, Marcel again encounters Charlus, her nephew. Again, the predominant impression is disturbing and enigmatic. The baron remains aloofly silent but Marcel cannot escape that searching, inquisitorial glance which reminds him of a detective on a secret mission and yet, because he is amongst friends, temporarily off duty. The young man is still further mystified when Charlus, who has hitherto completely ignored him, suddenly invites him to bring his grandmother to tea in Mme de Villeparisis's apartment. Consider Marcel's stupefaction when, the same evening, on their arrival, the baron, paying not the slightest attention to his greeting, abruptly addresses his grandmother: 'Ah! c'est une très bonne idée que vous avez eue de venir, n'est-ce pas, ma tante?' And when the literal and honest Marcel reminds Charlus of his invitation the latter blandly ignores him except for a vague, contemptuous smile eloquently expressing his opinion of such bourgeois tactlessness. On Marcel's grandmother, however, Charlus lavishes all the deference and charm of the *grand seigneur* who is also a sensitive, informed connoisseur of art and letters. Marcel's first impressions are confirmed, however, as he studies the baron. The expression is enigmatic, even severe: yet the eyes betray the presence of something dangerous, perhaps not altogether sane.

Mais ce visage, auquel une légère couche de poudre donnait un peu l'aspect d'un visage de théâtre, M. de Charlus avait beau en fermer hermétiquement l'expression, les yeux étaient comme une lézarde, comme une meurtrière que seule il n'avait pu boucher et par laquelle, selon le point où on était placé par rapport à lui, on se sentait brusquement croisé du reflet de quelque engin intérieur qui semblait n'avoir rien de rassurant, même pour celui qui, sans en être absolument maître, le porterait en soi, à l'état d'équilibre instable et toujours sur le point d'éclater; et l'expression circonspecte et incessamment inquiète de ces yeux, avec toute la fatigue qui, autour d'eux, jusqu'à un cerne descendu très bas, en résultait pour le visage, si bien composé et arrangé qu'il fût, faisait penser à quelque incognito, à quelque déguisement d'un homme puissant en danger, ou seulement d'un individu dangereux, mais tragique.[1]

[It was useless, however, for M. de Charlus to attempt to seal hermetically the expression of that face to which a slight dusting of powder lent a faintly theatrical air. The eyes produced the impression of a crevice, the one embrasure he had not been able to shutter and through which, according to one's position in relation to him, one suddenly felt oneself in the beam projected by some secret weapon which boded no good even for him who, whilst not absolutely its master, carried it within himself, in a state of precarious equilibrium and always on the verge of explosion; and the circumspect, incessantly anxious expression of those eyes, with the dark rings beneath them and the general air of weariness they lent to his face despite its studied composure, made one think of some *incognito*, of some disguise assumed by a powerful man in danger, or merely by a dangerous but tragic individual.]

[1] *JF.* ii, 58.

No other character is so elaborately introduced as Charlus and, as the action of the novel unfolds, we understand the reason. Somewhere Proust uses the expression 'l'atmosphère close du roman' inferring, possibly, that the novelist, in transferring the persons of real life to the more limited cadre of the work of art, must allow for an inevitable change of perspective. Diderot used to insist on this fact when he contrasted the truth of life with 'le vrai de la scène'. Proust, with his delicate sense of proportion, knew how difficult it is to bring into the enclosed atmosphere of the novel a figure of the stature of Charlus who seems, even in real life, abnormal and perhaps monstrous. Therefore, from the moment of the baron's first entrance Proust insinuates to the reader that this character is not to be measured by ordinary standards. Intellectually, morally and physically, Charlus is an arresting and disturbing person, greater than life-size, the sort of man whose behaviour and appearance will always attract notice even on the occasions, as we shall see, when the baron, in pursuit of his ignoble pleasures, would prefer to remain incognito and to merge in the crowd. Up till now, Marcel has not formed any intimate friendships. Bloch, who will shortly reappear, is not quite in this category. Several times, Marcel has observed in the company of Mme de Villeparisis a tall young man slightly his senior, incredibly elegant and handsome, monocled, fair-haired and continually in movement:

A cause de son 'chic', de son impertinence de jeune 'lion', à cause de son extraordinaire beauté surtout, certains lui trouvaient même un air efféminé, mais sans le lui reprocher car on savait combien il était viril et qu'il aimait passionément les femmes. C'était le neveu de Mme de Villeparisis duquel elle nous avait parlé. Je fus ravi de penser que j'allais le connaître pendant quelques semaines et sûr qu'il me donnerait toute son affection. Il traversa rapidement l'hôtel dans toute sa largeur, semblant poursuivre son monocle qui voltigeait devant lui comme un papillon.... Une voiture à deux chevaux l'attendait devant la porte; et tandis que son monocle reprenait ses ébats sur la route ensoleillée, avec l'élégance et la maîtrise qu'un grand pianiste trouve le moyen de montrer dans le trait le plus simple, où il ne semblait pas possible qu'il sût se montrer supérieur à un exécutant de deuxième ordre, le neveu de Mme de Villeparisis prenant les guides que lui passa le cocher, s'assit à côté de lui et tout en décachetant une lettre que le directeur de l'hôtel lui remit, fit partir les bêtes.[1]

[Because of his 'chic', because he had the insolent manner of the typical young 'blood', above all, because of his extraordinary beauty, some even thought he looked effeminate but without mentioning it to his face, for it was well known how very manly he was and how passionately fond of women. He was that nephew of Mme de Villeparisis she had spoken to us about. I was delighted to think that I was going to have his company for a few weeks and sure that he would be extremely cordial to me. He strode rapidly across the whole width of the hotel floor, apparently in pursuit of his monocle which fluttered before him like a butterfly.... A carriage with two horse was waiting for him in front of the door; and whilst his monocle resumed its dance on the sunny road, with the elegance and mastery which a great pianist contrives somehow to display in the simplest movement, where it did not seem that he could reveal his superiority over a second-rate performer, Mme de Villeparisis' nephew, taking up the reins handed to him by the coachman, sat down beside him and, whilst opening a letter which he had received from the hotel-manager, started up his horses.]

Despite frequent meetings in the foyer, however, Saint-Loup evinces no desire to make the acquaintance of Marcel and Mme Amédée. The former, rather piqued, puts him down as the type of arrogant and insolent young aristocrat who despises the bourgeoisie. This impression is not removed when they are finally introduced by Mme de Villeparisis:

Il sembla ne pas entendre qu'on lui nommait quelqu'un, aucun muscle de son visage ne bougea; ses yeux où ne brilla la plus faible lueur de sympathie humaine, montrèrent seulement dans l'insensibilité, dans l'inanité du regard, une exagération à défaut de laquelle, rien ne les eût différenciés de miroirs sans vie. Puis fixant sur moi ces yeux durs comme s'il eût voulu se renseigner sur moi, avant de me rendre mon salut, par un brusque déclenchement qui sembla plutôt dû à un réflexe musculaire qu'à un acte de volonté, mettant entre lui et moi le plus grand intervalle possible, allongea le bras dans toute sa longueur, et me tendit la main, à distance. Je crus qu'il s'agissait au moins d'un duel, quand le lendemain il me fit passer sa carte.[2]

To Marcel's amazement, he discovers that this extraordinary performance means absolutely nothing: it is merely a fashionable

---

[1] *JF.* II, 29.   [2] *JF.* II, 32.

habit inculcated in Saint-Loup since childhood like his other
Guermantes habit of insisting on being introduced at once to
the relatives of his friends. Robert talks literature with Marcel,
expresses a great desire to become one of his close friends and
reveals himself as an ardent democrat, a passionate admirer of
Proudhon, in short, an intellectual imbued with a profound
contempt for the Faubourg Saint-Germain.

Proust now accentuates a delicate trait in Marcel's character
and one which discreetly reminds us that his narrative is the
history of a vocation. When Robert speaks with delight of
'notre amitié', Marcel feels a sense of embarrassment and even
of sadness. Imbued with his grandmother's admirable honesty,
he wonders whether the joy he experiences in Robert's company
is really friendship. Is it not rather the pleasure of the artist
who notes in every gesture and intonation of Saint-Loup the
survival of history, the survival of the past in the present? 'A
retrouver toujours en lui cet être antérieur, séculaire, cet
aristocrate que Robert aspirait justement à ne pas être j'éprouvais
une vive joie, mais d'intelligence.' How exquisitely Proust
defines the essential quality of friendship which is not merely
a subordination of one's interests to a comrade, but a relationship sometimes almost excluding the consciousness of a separate
individuality, excluding certainly the attitude of critical analysis
which Marcel is so distressed to perceive in himself. Here
Proust adumbrates a conception of the artist's duty to his art
which is more fully and austerely expressed in *Le temps retrouvé*
where he tells us that the great artist cannot experience the
simple joys that life holds for other men, for such is the price
exacted by art from her disciples, the sacrifice implied in the
artist's dedication of himself to his vocation. Robert and Marcel
become, however, inseparable comrades and the latter, ignoring
the admonitions of his artistic conscience which tells him that he
ought to seek his pleasures in meditation, sets out gaily with
Saint-Loup every evening to dine at the fashionable restaurant
of Rivebelle.

Whilst it is impossible to define in a few words the original
creative faculty of a great artist, there is a phrase employed by
Marcel with his friend in the restaurant at Rivebelle, bathed in

the tinted haze of euphoria produced by innumerable glasses of champagne and light port which gives us the formula, so to speak, of the Proustian imaginative system. Exalted by an inner and heroic sense of irresistible power, enthroned on the summit of the world, listening beatifically to the voluptuous strains of Viennese waltzes, letting his fancy play idly over this paradise of bright lights, pretty faces, gay frocks, gleaming crystal and silver, Marcel glances down with lordly commiseration at the elderly and sober diners who cannot see the beautiful visions that float into his imagination because, he says, 'ils n'avaient pas pratiqué dans les choses un sectionnement qui nous débarrasse de leur apparence coutumière et nous permet d'apercevoir des analogies'. To them, Rivebelle restaurant is just a restaurant. To Marcel, at the moment, it is a fairy spectacle. Rivebelle, to mention only one of his brilliant 'analogies', is a harmonious allegorical, astral system. The tables are planets around which one can perceive not merely hurrying waiters, but an incessant, rhythmic and orderly revolution obeying some mysterious law of attraction, whilst in the background two necromancers, who might indeed be mistaken for a couple of horrible old hags at the cash-desk, work out their astrological computations. These half-dozen pages on Rivebelle furnish the essentials for a whole treatise on the psychology of adolescent intoxication which, as Marcel correctly observes, realizes for a few brief and glorious hours 'l'idéalisme subjectif, le phénoménisme pur'.[1]

This is the period of Marcel's first emancipation, the flowering season of his juvenile, immaterial hopes and desires. His unhappy infatuation for Gilberte is now forgotten. Carefree as a colt, he lives in an exciting whirl of fresh and delightful sensations which pursue him into his room with its cincture of glassed book-cases where, as he rests for an obligatory hour before adorning himself for Rivebelle or the casino, he can idly gaze at the marvellous reflected panorama of sea and evening sky. Sometimes, it is true, uneasy prickings of the conscience suggest that he ought to explore these fleeting perceptions and extract from them an essential and durable meaning and beauty. But he brushes them aside. With a mind turned eagerly outwards

[1] *JF.* II, 102.

in search of fresh contacts with the external world he lives on
the plane of immediate action, the plane of youth. Yet one of
these admonitions he finds it hard to abolish from his memory.
Once, out driving with Mme de Villeparisis, Marcel perceived
a little clump of trees which, for no apparent reason, seemed to
beckon to him urgently and despairingly, trying to arrest his
attention as if to warn him that they had a secret message
which he must pause long enough to understand, otherwise a
part of himself would vanish into oblivion. But Marcel did not
stop and somehow, the thought still distresses him.

Proust now reintroduces Bloch, whom Saint-Loup also knows
but does not really like, though admiring him for his intellectual gifts. Otherwise, there could be no greater contrast than
that presented by these two types: Bloch, the renegade Jew
whom we now overhear on the beach, loudly complaining that
Balbec is a second rue d'Aboukir, and the elegant cavalry cadet,
Saint-Loup, the scion of the noblest and most ancient families in
France. Bloch is a Jew, with the well-known physical features of
his race. But, since none of Proust's important characters is quite
static, Bloch is a Jew in process of physical transformation. By
the end of the novel he will have become that anonymous Semitic
type which, in Paris, is almost indistinguishable from the Frenchman until some political or social cataclysm like the Dreyfus case
directs attention to racial attributes which the Jew himself has
forgotten or discarded. At Balbec, however, Bloch is still in
the chrysalis stage and is accompanied, moreover, by a sort of
mobile ghetto—his family and a swarm of their friends. Marcel
describes them as 'une colonie juive...plus pittoresque qu'
agréable'. They compose a homogeneous group avoided by the
French visitors—the local nobility represented by the Cambremers; the legal clique headed by the *premier président* from
Caen, shunned, too, by the well-to-do tradesmen and their
daughters, 'fières, moqueuses et françaises comme les statues de
Reims'. What a contrast with Bloch's ill-mannered sisters and
their over-dressed escorts in dinner-jackets and glossy patent-
leather shoes! Bloch himself emphasizes this discordant note.
Saint-Loup admires him as the brilliant student who came out
first in the *concours général*. But Marcel observes with amusement

the struggle between Robert's traditional prejudices and his intellectual ideals when Bloch displays one of his typically Jewish moods—tactless, assertive and pedantic. Proust, in his description of the dinner-party at the Blochs, presents an amusing but cruelly faithful picture of *mœurs* in a Jewish household where, however, the only orthodox Jew is Bloch's uncle, Nissim Bernard, the family butt, a colossal liar and, as events reveal, a sexual pervert. Indeed, there is little to distinguish Bloch père and his unpleasant daughters from any other vulgar *nouveaux-riches* except the young Bloch's overbearing manner to his sisters and their submissive admiration. Bloch's complex nature is, however, subtly analysed and portrayed. His bad manners, his unpardonable attempts to sow discord between Marcel and Robert, his theatrical fits of remorse and protestations of undying friendship are not portrayed as symptoms of deep-seated egoism or malice. They are the reflexes of an intelligent, ardent young man capable of real generosity but extremely sensitive to the rebuffs which Bloch, as a Jew, has encountered in society. Proust notes with his uncanny perspicacity a typical Bloch expression which is also a defensive reflex; 'Cela n'a d'ailleurs aucune espèce d'importance', a phrase to be heard with many variants in the conversation of all susceptible people, but always to protect their *amour-propre*. Here Bloch employs it when he discovers that the correct pronunciation of *lift* is not, as he had always thought, *laïft*. We observe it again when, in Mme de Villeparisis' *salon*, he knocks over a costly Chinese vase: 'Cela ne présente aucune importance car je ne me suis pas mouillé.' Sometimes, as Proust notes with his profound humanity and insight, the phrase may camouflage the quality of a despair that can lead to suicide. With Bloch, however, it is never a tragic reflex. As in so many Jews, it is simply one of the components of the armour he has acquired to protect his *amour-propre*, the impertinent aggressiveness which in society so frequently evokes repulsion but just as often intimidates, or even commands respect. Bloch possesses a trait, not by any means exclusively Jewish: the irritating habit of attributing to others one's own defects. Thus, in order to camouflage his own snobbery Bloch insists that Marcel, because he likes the company of Saint-Loup, must therefore be a snob: 'Est-ce par goût de t'élever vers la noblesse — une noblesse très à coté, du reste — mais tu es demeuré naïf — que tu fréquentes Saint-Loup-en-Bray? Tu dois être en train de traverser une jolie crise de snobisme. Dis-moi, es-tu snob? Oui, n'est-ce pas?'

Such rudeness is characteristic of Bloch. Luckily for us it does not revolt Marcel, who observes with interest and amusement Saint-Loup's furious reaction to Bloch's *gaffes* and later on, Albertine's instinctive dislike. He is the type of Jew whom women immediately detest, sensing beneath his superficial, mocking courtesy a profound contempt for their intellectual inferiority coupled with a proclivity for aimless maliciousness. Marcel on the other hand, can appreciate the occasional flashes of talent in Bloch's conversation the tone of which is either insufferably literary and precious, or else slangy in the deliberately stupid manner of those callow intellectuals who, in order to display their familiarity with the great writers, talk about 'la mère Sand', 'le bonhomme Hugo' or 'ce coco de Virgile'.

Why is Marcel not repelled by the pedantry, rudeness and mendacity of his comrade who derives, moreover, an almost hysterical pleasure from lying and later, when afraid of being found out, from confessing with tears to his lies? Marcel is incapable of rancour and tolerates Bloch for a curious but interesting reason. The Combray breed, which produced 'des êtres absolument intacts' like his mother and grandmother, seems almost extinct. Therefore, says Marcel, the choice lies between two species—the honest but insensitive brutes who show in every word and intonation that they are not in the least interested in your life, and the others who are, like Bloch, interested in your doings, charming in your company yet quite capable, afterwards, of a cruel jest at your expense. Marcel, on reflection, observes: 'Je crois que c'est la dernière sorte d'hommes dont je préfère, sinon la valeur morale, du moins la société.'[1] This La Rochefoucauld aspect of Proust will repay meditation; otherwise it is easy to go astray in *A la recherche du temps perdu* and to misunderstand the attitude to life reflected in his novel.

Proust now fulfils the promise tentatively held out in the

[1] *JF.* II, 45.

title of these volumes and re-creates the sensations, emotions and thoughts of the Marcel who pursues romance in the sunlit orchard of 'les jeunes filles en fleurs'. To read these pages is to marvel at the apparently inexhaustible resources of the novelist's art; for Proust, by the magic of his prose, succeeds in communicating an experience which is so diaphonous and spiritual that its most direct expression is usually through the medium of music or great lyric poetry.

Youth, without doubt, can pursue romance in any place and under any skies because romance possesses a climate and a landscape of its own where there are always flowers and it is always spring. Proust, however, takes no chances so that Marcel sees his 'jeunes filles en fleurs', Albertine, Andrée, Rosemonde, Gisèle, enveloped in a perpetual haze of delightful and confusing sensations, of blue skies, scented turf, golden sands, sunlit, dancing seas and the beauty of Elstir's paintings. The fragrance, laughter, spontaneity, the fleeting candour of youth and of its desires are recaptured in the pages describing Marcel's early contacts with the little group. The crystal purity of tone is broken only at the close of *A l'ombre des jeunes filles en fleurs* by the alarmed and strident trilling of Albertine's electric bell when, scared and annoyed at Marcel's ardent but clumsy attempts to kiss her, she is obliged to ring for the chambermaid.

'La rêverie de l'amour ne peut pas se noter', wrote Stendhal despairingly. Yet this is precisely what Proust has achieved in a hundred pages of brilliant notations. Albertine and her charming friends dance into the zone of Marcel's consciousness like some graceful, open-air ballet on the sea-wall at Balbec, silhouetted against the yellow sands, the blue ocean and the cirrus clouds of a summer sky.

Marcel's first impressions and sentiments are hopelessly confused. Excited by this vision of lovely nymphs, of smiling, mocking eyes and supple, harmonious and fluid movements, he watches them stream along the breakwater, chattering, leaping, laughing at the expostulations of the sluggish bourgeois who skip aside to avoid being swept along by their irresistible *élan*. A little shocked at their unladylike behaviour, Marcel cannot repress a grandmotherly sense of disapproval: they must be the

kind of girls who frequent stadiums, probably the young mistresses of professional racing cyclists. One in particular, a tall
blonde, arouses his interest. But when he catches the glance of
a dark-haired damsel with a black *polo* tilted over her eyes, hers
is the image that stands out in his reveries when, later, he has
time to collect his memories. Yet, although Marcel haunts the
shore at all hours, only occasionally does he catch sight of the
elusive, tantalizing 'jeunes filles en fleurs' and always silhouetted
against the sea.

Elles étaient du bonheur inconnu et possible de la vie, un exemplaire
si délicieux et en si parfait état, que c'était presque pour des raisons
intellectuelles que j'étais désespéré de peur de ne pourvoir faire dans
des conditions uniques, ne laissant aucune place à l'erreur possible,
l'expérience de ce que nous offre de plus mystérieux la beauté qu'on
désire et qu'on se console de ne posséder jamais, en demandant du
plaisir — comme Swann avait toujours refusé de faire, avant Odette
— à des femmes qu'on n'a pas désirées, si bien qu'on meurt sans avoir
jamais su ce qu'était cet autre plaisir.[1]

In a most indirect and unexpected way, however, Marcel's
dream comes true. He is not only introduced to the little group
but accepted as one of their friends. One evening in the restaurant at Rivebelle, Marcel and Robert see the great painter,
Elstir and, with many misgivings, write him a little note expressing their admiration for his art and respectfully begging
the honour of his acquaintance. Elstir invites Marcel to his
studio but, completely obsessed by his feverish search, the latter
does not take advantage of the invitation until, one day, scolded
by his grandmother for his discourtesy, he sets out for the
studio. As he is looking at the master's paintings, the young
girl with the black *polo* and the bicycle looks in to say good day
to Elstir who casually informs the bemused Marcel, after the
elusive visitor has vanished, that she is Albertine Simonet and
that she and her friends often come to see him. For Marcel,
now, only one thing matters. Under some pretext, Elstir must
be lured outside for a walk on the beach where, almost certainly,
they will meet the little band. The painter agrees, but asks
permission to put the final touches on a water-colour whilst his

guest, outwardly calm, seethes with exasperated impatience. They go for their stroll, but there is not a sign of the quarry on the horizon. Suddenly, as the two men are entering an avenue leading to the studio, the girls appear, moving towards them. An introduction is now inevitable, yet precisely for this reason, Marcel finds himself in a curiously reluctant mood. As he lingers before the shop-window of an antique dealer, feigning an incredible interest in its contents, positive that in an instant Elstir will call him forward, Marcel can see himself going through all the motions, pointing to himself with a look of interrogation and pleased surprise, then trotting forward submissively to be introduced. Observe how Proust analyses these typically Proustian emotions, which Marcel is to experience all his life.

La certitude de la présentation à ces jeunes filles avait eu pour résultat, non seulement de me faire a leur égard, jouer, mais éprouver, l'indifférence. Désormais inévitable, le plaisir de les connaître fut comprimé, réduit, me parut plus petit que celui de causer avec Saint-Loup, de dîner avec ma grand'mere, de faire dans les environs des excursions que je regretterais d'être probablement, par le fait de relations avec des personnes qui devaient peu s'intéresser aux monuments historiques, contraint de négliger. D'ailleurs ce qui diminuait le plaisir que j'allais avoir, ce n'était pas seulement l'imminence mais l'incohérence de sa réalisation. Des lois aussi précises que celles de l'hydrostatique, maintiennent la superposition des images que nous formons dans un ordre fixe que la proximité de l'événement bouleverse. Elstir allait m'appeler. Ce n'était pas du tout de cette façon que je m'etais souvent, sur la plage, dans ma chambre, figuré que je connaîtrais ces jeunes filles.[1]

[The result of my certainty that I was going to be introduced to these girls was not merely to make me simulate but to feel indifference towards them. Inevitable now, the pleasure of making their acquaintance was compressed, diminished and seemed to me less important than that of chatting with Saint-Loup, of dining with my grandmother, of excursions in the vicinity which I should probably be sorry to have to give up because of my relations with people hardly likely to be interested in historic buildings. Besides, what lessened the pleasure I was going to have was not just the imminence but the incoherence of its realization. Laws as precise as those of hydrostatics maintain the superposition of the images we form in a

fixed order which is upset by the imminence of the event. Elstir was
going to call me. That wasn't at all the way I had often, on the beach, in
my room, imagined that I would make the acquaintance of these girls.]

But Elstir does not call him and the girls vanish. Marcel,
however, persuades the painter to give a party and to invite
Albertine. Once again the phenomenon is repeated. Just before
the great moment, the barometer of Marcel's desire registers
a sudden fall. With the certainty that he is to meet the girl whom
his imagination has invested with the charm of the unknown,
Marcel's expectation of pleasure rapidly diminishes and he dawdles
over a chocolate éclair, anxiously questioning an old gentleman
about the traditional fairs of the Norman region. But the introduction does take place because, as Proust explains in an amusing
mock dialogue, the will always calmly ignores the objections proposed by the sensibility and the intelligence. Now, however, we
have the inevitable clash between reality and imagination. This
Albertine is almost unrecognizable from the naiad of the beach.

Il y avait bien une jeune fille assise, en robe de soie, nu-tête, mais
de laquelle je ne retrouvais pas l'entité que j'avais extraite d'une jeune
cycliste coiffée d'un polo, le long de la mer.[1]

Only by subtracting everything contributed by his imagination
and desires can Marcel realize that this is Albertine.

Pour commencer je trouvai à Albertine l'air assez intimidé à la place
d'implacable; elle me sembla plus comme il faut que mal élevée à en
juger par les épithètes de 'elle a un mauvais genre', 'elle a un drôle
de genre' qu'elle appliqua à toutes les jeunes filles dont je lui parlai;
elle avait enfin comme point de mire du visage une tempe assez
enflammée et peu agréable a voir, et non plus le regard singulier
auquel j'avais toujours repensé jusque-là.[2]

But Marcel is to know a dozen different Albertines, all different
according to the tints of his passing desires, the changing temperatures and climates of his soul. Marcel's dreams of love and
beauty, however, are not yet by any means projected on Albertine. His desires weave like bees in a rose garden at swarming
time over Andrée, Gisèle, Rosemonde and her other companions,
though perhaps it is misleading to pronounce the word 'desires'
in such a context. Marcel's relations with the 'jeunes filles en

[1] *JF.* II, 154–5.   [2] *JF.* II, 157.

fleurs' betray no trace of physical desire. The pleasure he derives from their society is that of the artist and this is accentuated in all Proust's impressions of these charming rendezvous on the thyme-scented cliffs, in the little farms behind Balbec, in the coppice where they play at hunt the slipper or gravely discuss the essay subject set for Gisèle's *baccalauréat* examination. As Marcel basks in the sunshine, marvelling at the swiftly changing nuances of colour, light and expression on the charming, eager faces of these schoolgirls, listening with a musician's sensitive perception to the Périgord intonations of Andrée or the tone that betrays Rosemonde's Northern ancestry, noting with a premonitory twinge the physical or moral trait which an- nounces the woman who will be so different from the 'jeune fille en fleur'—Marcel, who is so convinced that he will never be an artist, is already preparing himself for his destined voca- tion. Moreover, since his errant fancy strays from Andrée to Rosemonde and from Rosemonde to Albertine, according to the quantity of mystery which each in turn seem to possess, his sentiments cannot be described as those of a lover. They are best expressed by himself:

Et ainsi l'espoir du plaisir que je retrouverais avec une jeune fille nouvelle venant d'une autre jeune fille par qui je l'avais connue, la plus récente était alors comme une de ces variétés de roses qu'on obtient grâce à une rose d'une autre espèce. Et remontant de corolle en corolle dans cette chaîne de fleurs, le plaisir d'en connaître une différente me faisait retourner vers celle à qui je la devais avec une reconnaissance mêlée d'autant de désir que mon espoir nouveau.[1]

Marcel reflects, meanwhile, with remorse that he is neglecting Saint-Loup. On the other hand, analysing this case of conscience, he arrives at a typically Proustian conclusion. The obligations of friendship must always interfere with the functions and duties of the artist. Artistic creation is a turning inwards of the mind and can only be carried out in solitude. The con- versations of friendship, on the contrary, represent an opposite direction of the artist's thoughts, an interruption of his artistic development, which is purely internal. Friendship entails a focusing of Marcel's intelligence on the ethical aspects of his

[1] *JF.* II, 172.

relations with his comrade, on the debt, for example, which he
owes to Robert whose unfailing sympathy and consideration
do so much to sweeten his existence. Yet, even if he may not
possess the artist's creative gifts, Marcel is uneasily conscious
of a duty he owes himself, in short, the duty to realize himself
by following the natural, introspective trend of his mind. What
then of the hours he spends with the little group?

Près de ces jeunes filles au contraire si le plaisir que je goûtais était
égoiste, du moins n'était-il pas basé sur le mensonge qui cherche à nous
faire croire que nous ne sommes pas irrémédiablement seuls et qui
quand nous causons avec un autre nous empêche de nous avouer que
ce n'est plus nous qui parlons, que nous nous modelons alors à la
ressemblance des étrangers et non d'un moi qui diffère d'eux. Les
paroles qui s'échangeaient entre les jeunes filles de la petite bande et
moi étaient peu intéressantes, rares d'ailleurs, coupées de ma part de
longs silences. Cela ne m'empêchait pas de prendre à les écouter
autant de plaisir qu'à les regarder, a découvrir dans la voix de chacune
d'elles un tableau vivement coloré. C'est avec délices que j'écoutais
leur pépiement. Aimer aide à discerner, à différencier.[1]

The days shorten and it will soon be time to return to Paris.
Albertine, in her aunt's absence, is obliged to spend one night
in the Grand Hotel. She is suffering from a cold and has to retire
early but she invites Marcel to come and talk to her while she
has dinner in bed. Not unreasonably, he immediately changes
his opinion of Albertine and of love which no longer presents
itself as the purely subjective emotion his experience of Gilberte
had taught him to imagine. In a turmoil of excitement, he enters
Albertine's room.

La mer, que j'apercevais à côté de Maineville, le ciel où la lune
n'était pas encore montée au zénith, tout cela semblait plus léger
à porter que des plumes pour les globes de mes prunelles qu'entre
mes paupières je sentais dilatés, résistants, prêts à soulever bien
d'autres fardeaux, toutes les montagnes du monde sur leur surface
délicate. Leur orbe ne se trouvait plus suffisamment rempli par la
sphère même de l'horizon. Et tout ce que la nature eût pu m'apporter
de vie m'eût semblé bien mince, les souffles de la mer m'eussent paru
bien courts pour l'immense aspiration qui soulevait ma poitrine. Je
me penchai vers Albertine pour l'embrasser.[2]

[1] *JF.* ii, 187.   [2] *JF.* ii, 209.

These atomic reserves of energy are, however, superfluous. To the stupefaction of our amateur Don Juan, the lady is extremely alarmed, shocked and angry, threatening to ring for the servants, a threat which Marcel refuses to take seriously until to his intense bewilderment it is vigorously translated into action.

In the volumes dealing with Marcel's love for Albertine, he will, of course, bombard us with his impressions of this enigmatic young woman. And that is precisely the trouble. When a lover tries to tell us about the girl he is passionately in love with, her character always seems enigmatic, since her personality is always reflected on the screen of the narrator's subjective and inchoate emotions and sensations. At present, however, Marcel is not in love. It is, therefore, interesting to observe his impressions of Albertine though, naturally, these are based on rather superficial, incomplete perceptions, reinforced, no doubt, by what he has learned from Andrée and the other girls. Albertine is an orphan, entirely dependent upon her aunt, Mme Bontemps. Yet she has many friends whose parents share their daughters' admiration of her frankness, unselfishness, imperturbable good humour and common sense. She has, nevertheless, one defect which should be noted because of its important repercussions on Marcel's life. It is the habit of what Proust calls 'l'utilisation multiple d'une seule action' and really derives from Albertine's natural kindness. For example, if her aunt insists on her niece's attending some boring social function the latter consents out of consideration for Mme Bontemps. But, having received a cordial welcome, Albertine, in order to make her hostess happy, tells her that she has long been looking forward to this pleasure and is so glad she has been at last allowed to accompany her aunt. At the same party, she may meet a friend who has been very unhappy. To cheer her up, Albertine explains that having learned of her trouble, knowing that her friend was also to be a guest, she specially arranged to be near her and in fact has come for no other reason. After his rebuff, Marcel penitently begs forgiveness and Albertine, who never bears grudges, lets him off with a severe warning not to repeat the offence. She never mentions the incident to anyone. But Marcel is told that their relations must be henceforth those of good comrades. Though still unable

to understand why Albertine invited him in the first place to come
to her room, Marcel reverses his former views on her character
and morality.

To round off this commentary, I should like to remark,
briefly, on that part of Marcel's narrative which concerns the
painter, Elstir. Although he fills the useful role of intermediary
between his young friend and the little band, this is obviously
not the chief reason for his presence. Proust employs, like
Albertine, though for very different motives, 'le système des
fins multiples'. In Marcel's progress towards his vocation, he
makes friends with two great artists: the novelist, Bergotte,
and the painter, Elstir. Vinteuil also contributes to his æsthetic
formation but posthumously, through the medium of the famous
septet. When Marcel talks to Bergotte, the latter has already
passed his great creative period. Life has caught up with him and
is in the process of submerging the artist in the vulgar supplicant
for a seat in the *Académie*. Elstir is at the height of his creative
powers and, in any case, is too great an artist to cadge for
awards and distinctions. He knows with a sure and modest
confidence that his work is good but, as Marcel sensitively notes,
when he pronounces the word 'gloire', a shadow flits over
Elstir's face. Fame will come only after his death. In these
conversations between the incipient artist and the great master,
as in Marcel's interpretation of Elstir's *Port de Carquetuit*, that
brilliantly sustained metaphor in paint where the sea is expressed
in terms of the land and the landscape gives one the illusion
that it is the sea, Proust reveals his own ideas on the creative
artist's way of perceiving life. In a reference to Bergotte, it
will be recalled, the words 'le pouvoir réfléchissant' were used
to define a faculty peculiar to the artist. Marcel's remarks on
Elstir throw further light on this expression:

L'effort qu'Elstir faisait pour se dépouiller en présence de la réalité
de toutes les notions de son intelligence était d'autant plus admirable
que cet homme qui, avant de peindre, se faisait ignorant, oubliait tout
par probité, car ce qu'on sait n'est pas à soi, avant justement une
intelligence exceptionnellement cultivée.[1]

In the course of this study we shall have many occasions for discussing Marcel's æsthetic concept, the gist of which surely is that, since art recomposes life, the duty of the artist is to communicate life as it is *immediately* presented to his consciousness and not indirectly, not as rationalized, and—as Proust would doubtless maintain—falsified by the intelligence. Like Elstir, the artist must drain his consciousness of all preconceived intellectual notions or cadres such as the non-artist is so prone to fit round the impressions made upon him by the impact of reality on his senses. In these Elstir pages are to be found other interesting ideas. One is cleverly woven into an incident which casts a sudden illumination on Elstir's past. Marcel, who is rummaging amongst the painter's early works, unearths a water-colour entitled *Miss Sacripant. 1872*, a provocative, equivocal portrait of a young woman in fancy dress, 'suggérant plutôt l'idée d'un jeune efféminé vicieux et songeur'. On interrogating Elstir who is clearly displeased and rather embarrassed, Marcel discovers that *Miss Sacripant* is Odette and that the painter is the disreputable 'M. Biche' of the early Verdurin *salon*. Now, this portrait, so beautifully executed, of a charming and seductive original suggests to Proust an idea which is later elaborated in Marcel's impressions of Mme Elstir. Perhaps, he thinks, there exist in nature certain objects so perfect in themselves that the artist need only copy them in order to produce a work of art. He need not interpret them or, if I may complete Proust's thought, extract from the impressions which have penetrated into the depths of the artist's consciousness their essential beauty, discover the intellectual equivalent of this beauty and reveal it to the world through the medium of his art. In the career of every artist, according to Proust, a time comes, after the decline of his creative power, when he will tend more and more to seek beauty, not within himself, but already realized externally, in a lovely woman, a Titian painting, a particular landscape or climate, in the frequentation of certain human types. That, Marcel now realizes, was the attitude of Swann to the beauty of life, the point beyond which Charles Swann could not advance, lacking creative talent.

Elstir is young Marcel's ideal of the creative artist or almost his ideal, for he makes one significant reserve. In a passage notable for its transparent and beautiful simplicity, he tells what happens when Elstir, after the admission that he was the young artist called 'M. Biche', notes an involuntary expression of disappointment on the face of his young admirer. Too great a master to take offence, he uses the occasion in order to teach Marcel a lesson about life. There is no man, he says, however wise and distinguished who has not in his youth spoken words or committed follies he would not like to forget. Yet this is the only way of acquiring wisdom.

'Les vies que vous admirez, les attitudes que vous trouvez nobles n'ont pas été disposées par le père de famille ou par le précepteur, elles ont été précédées de débuts bien différents, ayant été influencés par ce qui régnait autour d'elles de mal ou de banalité. Elles représentent un combat et une victoire. Je comprends que l'image de ce que nous avons été dans une période première ne soit plus reconnaissable et soit en tous cas déplaisante. Elle nē doit pas être reniée pourtant, car elle est un témoignage que nous avons vraiment vécu, que c'est selon les lois de la vie et de l'esprit que nous avons, des éléments communs de la vie, de la vie des ateliers, des coteries artistiques, s'il s'agit d'un peintre, extrait quelque chose qui les dépasse.'[1]

Marcel's conclusion is that these are the words of a great artist but he suggests that perhaps Elstir might have been a greater master had he remained silent, 'car un artiste pour être tout à fait dans la vérité de la vie spirituelle doit être seul, et ne pas prodiguer de son moi, même à ses disciples'.[2] I wonder how many of the world's masters have conformed to this austere criterion of genius.

[1] JF. ii, 149.   [2] JF. ii, 148.

Chapter III

LE CÔTÉ DE GUERMANTES

PROUST never acquired the Stendhalian habit of epigraphs; otherwise he might have found a most appropriate one for his Guermantes volumes in Constant's masterpiece, *Adolphe*. 'Il faut du temps', remarks Adolphe, 'pour s'accoutumer à l'espèce humaine, telle que l'intérêt, l'affectation, la vanité, la peur nous l'ont faite.' Marcel does not yet know what is meant by getting used to Society. Proust touches on this matter in the account of Marcel's conversation with Bergotte when the latter, having just uttered a malevolent remark about Swann, warns his young companion to keep it to himself. Marcel who has not learned the social clichés does not reply: 'Je ne répète jamais rien.' He simply inclines his head in silence. So far, to employ his own expression, he is not 'un personnage social'. His grand-aunt, in these circumstances, would have bluntly asked Bergotte why he ever made the remark in the first place since he does not want it repeated. But Combray society, as Marcel points out, bears no resemblance to 'le monde'. What of the society he met at Swann's? 'Celle des Swann était déjà un acheminement vers lui [le monde], vers ses flots versatiles. Ce n'était pas encore la grande mer, c'était la lagune.' Proust is now about to launch Marcel into deeper waters, into a milieu where he will enjoy a unique opportunity of observing and getting used to the human species in one of its most civilized forms.

Now, when we follow Marcel into the *salons* of the Faubourg Saint-Germain, it will become clear that Proust is a much more objective student of social manners and morals than any of the great nineteenth-century novelists. Chateaubriand, Balzac, Stendhal, Constant, Flaubert, Zola all express, in various ways, an attitude of revolt against Society, an attitude reflected in the Romantic ennui of René and Adolphe, in the demonic pride of Julien Sorel, in the spiritual frustration of Frédéric Moreau or

in the tragic defeatism of Lucien de Rubempré. By contrast, the
narrative of Marcel's social enlightenment appears undramatic
or, at any rate, unsensational. He is not a Romantic *incompris*
oppressed by a sense of spiritual isolation: his path is not
beset with the physical dangers or political intrigues which
surround Fabrice del Dongo or Julien Sorel and no shadow
of the prison or guillotine lies athwart his life. Nor, of course,
is Marcel's character ever subjected to the test of poverty,
that terrible proving-house in which so many of Balzac's
young men are stripped of their honour, their ideals and their
innocence.

Proust, although he appreciated keenly the effective use that
can be made of exciting situations and tensely woven plot, himself dispenses with such apparatus. This, as I have said, is not
because he lacks imagination. On the contrary, his imagination
is so active and powerful that it can find romance, strangeness,
beauty and mystery in the ordinary situations of life, in the
familiar objects of his usual surroundings, in the behaviour and
conversation of those whom one meets in everyday social commerce. But imagination, as Marcel's narrative has already
suggested, is not merely the faculty of creating, *ex nihilo* as it
were, an exciting world composed of beautiful unreal images.
There is another world, as Proust now reveals in the opening
pages of *Le côté de Guermantes* which is just as unreal and illusory,
also a creation of the imagination though we call it the real
world. It consists of our false perceptions of the social relationships, of the real attitude towards ourself of the other individuals
who compose the society we live in. Marcel tells us, for
example, of the shock he experienced on learning that Françoise had described him to her crony, Jupien, as a malevolent
person who was not worth the rope he should be hanged with.
Marcel is not very worried about Françoise whose opinions, he
knows, change with her moods. What appals him is the idea,
generated by Jupien's indiscreet disclosure, that the world he
had conceived as real, based on his intelligent perceptions, may
be just as illusory as the creations of his romantic imagination.
It is a tormenting and sobering thought, opening up an
infinite perspective. 'En était-il ainsi dans tous les rapports

sociaux. Et jusqu'à quel désespoir cela pourrait-il me mener un jour s'il en était de même dans l'amour? C'était le secret de l'avenir.'

In portraying Marcel's initiation into the ways of fashionable society, Proust develops his theme of the contrast between imagination and reality. As Marcel's direct contacts with society become more extensive and intimate, the tone of the narrative reflects increasingly the impressions of a mind which surveys the external world from the plane of its critical, analysing intelligence. Fortunately, the effect of Marcel's new experience of society is never such as to destroy his imaginative powers, his belief in the existence of a mysterious unknown. His imagination, yielding to the pressure of reality, continues to lose or modify its illusions but its activities are not suspended, merely transferred to other more promising objects. The history of his social education is not presented, therefore, as a romantic conflict between his ego and the massed resistance of an organism designed to subdue and discipline the individual. Always it reveals that fascinating spectacle to which I have alluded: the interplay of imagination and reality. Later, when Marcel deserts the Faubourg Saint-Germain for Albertine, the curtain will rise on another, more complicated and tragic version of this eternal theme.

Meanwhile, in order to prove that Marcel's faculty of imagination is still intact, Proust weaves into the pattern of his reflections on society the glittering thread of his romantic, hopeless infatuation for Oriane, the duchesse de Guermantes. Forgetting Gilberte, Andrée and Albertine, he falls in love with Oriane and, by a natural extension, with the smallest object in her enchanting ambience, beginning as far back as Marcel can remember, in his little room at Combray when the name Guermantes, associated with a child's magic-lantern pictures of medieval adventures, absorbed those rich and amaranth hues which, later, he saw reflected in the stained-glass windows of Combray church on that marvellous occasion when the duchess graced with her presence the marriage of Mlle Percepied. The reality, it will be remembered, shivered Marcel's bright image, but imagination quickly reassembled the glittering fragments, so that now the name of Guermantes conjures up a vision of a soft and brilliant mauve scarf and the sunny periwinkle blue of Oriane's smile. In such brief moments of reverie, Marcel breathes the hawthorn-scented air of Combray.

In these two volumes, wherever the name of Guermantes appears, Proust always discreetly reminds us of this alternation of imagination and experience, of reverie and reality which leads to a constant modification of Marcel's illusions. So it is with his images of the château de Guermantes with its aura of medieval chivalry and romance, of splendid feats woven into the blue and amaranth tapestries hanging on its ancient walls, a fairy setting indeed for the suzeraine Oriane. This insubstantial pageant fades, however, when Saint-Loup casually informs his friend that the château has only been called Guermantes since the seventeenth century and that the tapestries, by Boucher, were bought at a sale in the nineteenth century. Marcel's dream, ousted from its untenable position by the irresistible force of reality, is now transferred to the Paris residence of the Guermantes in one of the wings of which his parents, it so happens, have just rented an apartment. Since imagination can only operate on what is absent, surely now the name Guermantes will finally lose for Marcel the last vestiges of its magic and glamour. On the contrary, thanks to the gossip imported by Françoise from the servants across the courtyard, he now visualizes the existence of Oriane as something mysterious and altogether charming. The dances, dinners and receptions given at the hôtel de Guermantes must, he feels, be utterly different from the banal affairs to which he is invited. And when he hears that it is 'le premier salon du faubourg Saint-Germain', Marcel is convinced that the most exquisite but alas, the most inaccessible of pleasures would be to dine at the Guermantes', to meet the happy few who enjoy the friendship of the duchess and, above all, to listen to the conversation of this élite. The urban quality of these impressions does not, moreover, entirely dissipate the woodland fragrance of Marcel's boyish reveries. Françoise has only to mention that she saw a brace of pheasants hanging from the Guermantes' pantry-window remarking that no doubt the duke has been shooting on his estates for Marcel to forget Paris and think of 'la fraîcheur ombreuse et dorée des bois de Guermantes'.

Combray, Méséglise, Tansonville, Guermantes! Marcel hears these names almost every day on the lips of Françoise and the rustic tang of them impregnates the air of the Faubourg Saint-Germain. And this persistent charm of early associations influences Marcel's dawning admiration for the duchesse de Guermantes and her fashionable entourage. What transforms his admiration into a cult is undoubtedly the gala performance at the Opéra where the great La Berma is appearing in the declaration scene from Racine's *Phèdre*. Her acting is not, however, the spectacle which makes the deepest impression on his youthful imagination though Marcel appreciates now, for the first time, the unique gifts of the famous actress. But he is distracted by another vision which, to the marvelling gaze of the neophyte, acquires the splendour of an apotheosis. It is the presence, in the auditorium, of the élite of aristocratic France, the noblest descendants of the *ancien régime*, even of royalty to judge from the sweeping curtseys of the ladies to the anonymous fair-haired young man seated beside la princesse de Guermantes-Bavière. Here is Marcel's impression of this divinely beautiful creature on whom, until her cousin Oriane enters the box, all his attention is concentrated.

Comme une grande déesse qui préside de loin aux jeux des divinités inférieures, la princesse était restée volontairement un peu au fond sur un canapé latéral, rouge comme un rocher de corail, à côté d'une large réverbération vitreuse qui était probablement une glace et faisait penser à quelque section qu'un rayon aurait pratiquée, perpendiculaire, obscure et liquide, dans le cristal ébloui des eaux. A la fois plume et corolle, ainsi que certaines floraisons marines, une grande fleur blanche, duvetée comme une aile, descendait du front de la princesse le long d'une de ses joues dont elle suivait l'infléxion avec une souplesse coquette, amoureuse et vivante, et semblait l'enfermer à demi comme un œuf rose dans la douceur d'un nid d'alcyon. Sur la chevelure de la princesse, et s'abaissant jusqu'à ses sourcils, puis reprise plus bas à la hauteur de sa gorge, s'étendait une résille faite de ces coquillages blancs qu'on pêche dans certaines mers australes et qui étaient mêlés à des perles, mosaique marine à peine sortie des vagues qui par moments se trouvait plongée dans l'ombre au fond de laquelle, même

alors, une présence humaine était révélée par la motilité éclatante des
yeux de la princesse. La beauté qui mettait celle-ci bien au-dessus
des autres filles fabuleuses de la pénombre n'était pas tout entière
matériellement et inclusivement inscrite dans sa nuque, dans ses
épaules, dans ses bras, dans sa taille. Mais la ligne délicieuse et
inachevée de celle-ci était l'exact point de départ, l'amorce inévitable
des lignes invisibles en lesquelles l'œil ne pouvait s'empêcher de les
prolonger, merveilles engendrées autour de la femme comme le
spectre d'une figure idéale projetée sur les ténèbres.[1]

[Like a tall goddess presiding from afar over the frolics of the
lesser divinities, the princess had deliberately remained somewhat in
the background, on a sofa at the side of the box, red as a coral reef,
next to a vitreous glittering expanse which was probably a mirror and
suggested a vertical, dim and liquid section cut, as it were, by a sun-
beam in the dazzling crystal of the waters. At once feather and corolla,
like certain maritime plants, a great white flower, downy as a bird's
wing, hung down from the princess's forehead along one of her cheeks,
the contour of which it followed with coquettish, amorous and lively
suppleness as if half enclosing it like a pink egg in the softness of
a halcyon's nest. Thrown over the princess's hair, sinking as far as her
eyebrows, then caught up again lower down and level with her bosom,
was a net composed of those white shells that are fished up in certain
southern seas and which were intermingled with pearls, like a marine
mosaic but recently emerged from the waves and at times plunged
in the shadow in whose depths, even then, a human presence was
betrayed by the brilliant motility of the princess's eyes. The beauty
which raised her far above the other fabulous daughters of the
penumbra was not altogether materially and inclusively graven in the
nape of her neck, in her shoulders, her arms and waist. But the
delightful unfinished line of the latter was the exact starting-point,
the inevitable centre of attraction for those invisible lines into which
the eye could not help prolonging them—lines marvellously engendered
and surrounding the woman like the spectre of an ideal figure projected
against the darkness.]

This, as the reader has divined, is but a fragment of the
tableau viewed by Marcel from his place in the orchestra stalls.
Owing to the chiaroscuro produced in the auditorium by the
footlights, the boxes are transfigured into a series of submarine
grottos. In their shadowy pools one can just perceive the
movements of bearded Tritons, of one-eyed sea-monsters and

[1] *Guer.* I, 37.

of smiling alabaster nereids whose undulating fans of ostrich feathers and flashing eyes conspire, by their suggestion of softly waving marine flora and glittering gems, to lend a strange air of reality to this mythological fantasy.

In a miraculous atmosphere, miracles, of course, are to be expected. Yet Marcel, contentedly submerged in the throng of lowly creatures whose eyes are uplifted to Olympus, is staggered by the miracle now enacted when Oriane, suddenly recognizing him, leans forward, gaily waving her hand and smiles down, or rather, in his own charming words 'fit pleuvoir sur moi l'averse étincelante de son sourire'. The cynical Talleyrand used to advise his attachés to beware of yielding to first impulses because first impulses are always generous. For neglecting this harsh but wise maxim, the duchesse de Guermantes encounters in her path, every time she goes walking or shopping, a mooning and infatuated young man, pathetically hoping for a smile, a word of greeting or maybe, another miracle which will enable him to render this goddess some magnificent and indispensable service. Indifferent now to anything not directly or indirectly connected with the duchess, it is because of her that Marcel accepts Saint-Loup's long-standing invitation to Doncières where the latter is garrisoned. This is a notable sacrifice to Venus, for one of Marcel's greatest phobias is the dread of being alone in a strange hotel. On the other hand, he may contrive, through the unsuspecting Robert, to obtain an introduction to Oriane.

There are, in short, plenty of excellent reasons why Proust, at this juncture, should send Marcel out of Paris. Obviously he cannot keep his hero prowling eternally round the streets of the Faubourg Saint-Germain because, after all, though it is fascinating to read about Marcel's striking and varied impressions of the duchess who changes mysteriously, like Albertine, from day to day, Proust is too clever an artist not to know that the moment has come for a change of scene and of atmosphere. Was it Norpois, the diplomat, who said that when the political atmosphere becomes overcharged with tension often the best way to clear the air is to break the windows. The same is true of the atmosphere of certain types of novels but not of *A la recherche du temps perdu* where it is sufficient on occasion to open the windows: in other words, to transport the chief characters for a time away from their usual physical milieu. Therefore, Proust sends Marcel to Doncières, Saint-Loup's garrison-town. Though he is not yet aware of it, the crisis of his amorous fever has nearly passed. He needs a change of ideas and that is precisely what he will obtain in the company of Robert and the latter's intelligent brother officers.

His brief holiday at Doncières has a tonic effect upon Marcel, whose imagination is no longer exclusively preoccupied with Mme de Guermantes. Thanks to the society of Saint-Loup and the latter's friends the idea of never seeing Oriane again, even of forgetting her, although no doubt frightful, begins to present itself as a possibility. This, as we can perceive by reading between the lines of Marcel's narrative, is due to the influence of two factors. One is the force of Habit. The other is perhaps his growing consciousness that the inevitable trend of the imagination, unless it is checked, is towards hallucination. It so happens, and we shall see why, that Marcel becomes quickly and pleasantly accustomed to his new physical and intellectual milieu, so that in a few days, such is the force of Habit, it is Paris which now seems remote and strange. He realizes, too, and Saint-Loup's passion for the actress Rachel will drive the lesson home, the extraordinary magnifying force of imagination. This has always been for him a source of discouragement because in losing the illusions created by our imagination we also lose the self whom they rendered so happy and exalted. Now, however, listening to these young friends of Robert's discussing the latest theories of warfare, infected by their enthusiasm, Marcel feels that here, at last, is something of a permanent nature, with a solid core of intrinsic value, impervious to the distorting influence of imagination. These pages on the art of war are illuminating, but not just for the æsthetic pleasure to be derived from Proust's brilliant disquisition on war considered as an art in the *sens spirituel* of the term. Even more interesting is the implication that Marcel is changing his opinion of friendship, the pleasures of which he had thought incompatible with those of the intellect. One has the impression that, in the company of these young officers, passionately devoted to their vocation, observing their hero worship of Commandant Duroc, their brilliant professor of strategy, Marcel himself has unconsciously made one further step in his own progress towards a destined vocation. But he discovers other sources of durable happiness, for example, the rich contentment which men find in good fellowship, in friendly talk accompanied by excellent food and sound wine, in a snug restaurant on a bitter November night. Perhaps nowhere else in *A la recherche du temps perdu* does Proust so vividly display as in the Doncières episode, his genius for extracting interest and beauty from the homely things and the ordinary relationships of life. How well he interprets, for instance, the precious quality of comradeship in that scene where Marcel, utterly wretched and forlorn, awaits Saint-Loup on the wind-swept barrack square! Obsessed by the invalid's neurotic presentiments, he is dreading the thought of a night in a lonely hotel when, to his unspeakable relief, Robert suddenly announces that he has unexpectedly obtained permission from his captain, Prince Borodino, to put Marcel up in his quarters till next morning. It requires the peculiar talent of Proust to communicate the essential reality of this simple incident and to explain why a certain experience, apparently so trivial, encountering a certain state of soul, irradiates a zone of our existence, a zone immune to the influence of events which a biographer would infallibly chronicle in detail; regarding them as important, perhaps dramatic, or at any rate as determining factors in our life.

The whole of this Doncières episode is suffused with a kindliness and warmth which attains glowing intensity in the narrative of Marcel's visits to the restaurant used as a mess by Saint-Loup and his friends. I cannot at the moment recall any scene that illustrates in so few words, the meaning of comradeship. Picture Robert de Saint-Loup, his thin triangular face and green eyes alight with excitement and pleasure at Marcel's intellectual gymnastics, watching with breathless eagerness and pride the reaction of his brother officers, and, in order to show off his friend's talents as a raconteur, exhorting him to retail anecdotes which he, Saint-Loup, has certainly heard before though he swears they are new to him. Outside, a chill wind is blowing with a threat of snow, in ideal contrast to the light and colour and warmth of the interior depicted by Proust after the manner of the Flemish masters.

Et dans la grande salle à manger que je traversai le premier jour, avant d'atteindre la petite pièce où m'attendait mon ami, c'était aussi à un repas de l'évangile figuré avec la naïveté du vieux temps et l'exagération des Flandres que faisait penser le nombre des poissons, des poulardes, des coqs de bruyère, des bécasses, des pigeons, apportés tout décorés et fumants par des garçons hors d'haleine qui glissaient sur le parquet pour aller plus vite et les déposaient sur l'immense console où ils étaient découpés aussitôt, mais où — beaucoup de repas touchant à leur fin, quand j'arrivais — ils s'entassaient inutilisés, comme si leur profusion et la précipitation de ceux qui les apportaient, répondait beaucoup plutôt qu'aux demandes des dîneurs au respect du texte sacré scrupuleusement suivi dans la lettre mais naïvement illustré par des détails réels empruntés à la vie locale, et au souci esthétique et religieux de montrer aux yeux l'éclat de la fête par la profusion des victuailles et l'empressement des serviteurs.[1]

[And in the huge restaurant which I passed through on the first day, before entering the little room where my friend was waiting for me, one was also reminded of some Biblical repast delineated with the naïvety of olden times and Flemish exaggeration owing to the quantity of fish, chickens, grouse, snipe, pigeons carried in all garnished and smoking, by breathless waiters who slid along the polished floor for greater speed and placed them on the immense sideboard where they were immediately carved up, but where—as many diners were finishing as I came in—they piled up unused, as if their profusion and the haste of those who brought them, were inspired much less by a desire to meet the demands of the guests than by respect for the sacred text, the letter of which was being scrupulously followed though naïvely illustrated by realistic details borrowed from local life, and by an æsthetic and religious anxiety to display the splendour of the feast by the profusion of the viands and the alacrity of the servitors.]

And when Marcel returns to his own room it is to exchange one kind of happiness for another. His charming eighteenth-century hotel, belying his original fears, ridicules the notion of loneliness. On the contrary, all the rooms, the furniture, the twisting corridors, the surprising alcoves beckon to the guest with a gay and friendly air of welcome. I imagine that somewhere in France stands the original of Marcel's Hôtel de Flandres. If so,

[1] *Guer.* I, 88-9.

it should be glorified in the guide-books not with the classic three stars but with a constellation, if only for having induced Marcel Proust to offer us the first fruits of his meditations on Sleep, that mysterious palace which he will later describe in greater detail with singular charm and unique knowledge. Once again we are ravished and amazed by the touch of the magician who transmutes into beauty the ordinary experience of life and divests material things of their habitual, commonplace disguise, revealing them to us as they appear to the eyes of children or as they were seen long ago by those great, original and nameless artists who made the old fairy tales and illustrated the cathedrals of medieval Europe. In *Cinderella* the fairy princess turns a pumpkin into a gorgeous coach and that is admittedly very fine work. But look what Proust can do in the same direction with oysters, grapes and fish.

Je me sentais séparé (non seulement de la grande nuit glacée qui s'étendait au loin et dans laquelle nous entendions de temps en temps le sifflet d'un train qui ne faisait que rendre plus vif le plaisir d'être là, ou les tintements d'une heure qui heureusement était encore éloignée de celle où ces jeunes gens devraient reprendre leurs sabres et rentrer), mais aussi de toutes les préoccupations extérieures, presque du souvenir de Mme de Guermantes par la bonté de Saint-Loup à laquelle celle de ses amis qui s'y ajoutait donnait comme plus d'épaisseur: par la chaleur aussi de cette petite salle à manger par la saveur des plats raffinés qu'on nous servait. Ils donnaient autant de plaisir à mon imagination qu'à ma gourmandise; parfois le petit morceau de nature d'où ils avaient été extraits, bénitier rugueux de l'huître dans lequel restent encore quelques gouttes d'eau salée, ou sarment noueux, pampres jaunis d'une grappe de raisin, les entourait encore, incomestible, poétique et lointain comme un paysage et faisant se succéder au cours du dîner les évocations d'une sieste sous une vigne et d'une promenade en mer; d'autres soirs c'est par le cuisinier seulement qu'était mise en relief cette particularité originale des mets, qu'il présentait dans son cadre naturel comme une œuvre d'art; et un poisson cuit au court-bouillon était apporté dans un long plat en terre, où, comme il se détachait en relief sur des jonchées d'herbes bleuâtres, infrangible mais contourné encore d'avoir été jeté vivant dans l'eau bouillante, entouré d'un cercle de coquillages d'animalcules satellites, crabes, crevettes et moules, il avait l'air d'apparaître dans une céramique de Bernard Palissy.[1]

[1] *Guer.* 1, 105–6.

[I felt myself separated (not only from the great icy darkness that
stretched out into the distance and whence we could hear from time
to time the whistle of a train which but accentuated the keenness of our
pleasure in being there, or the chimes of an hour still happily distant
from that when these young men would have to pick up their sabres
and go home) but also from all external preoccupations, almost from
the memory of Mme de Guermantes, by the kindness of Saint-Loup to
which that of his friends added, so to speak, an extra layer of thickness;
by the warmth too, of that little dining-room, by the savour of the
exquisite dishes they brought us. These gave just as much pleasure to
my imagination as to my palate; sometimes the little bit of nature
from which they had been extracted, the ruguous holy-water font of
the oyster which still holds a few salty drops, or like a knotty sar-
mentum, the yellowed vine-twigs of a bunch of grapes, surrounding
them still, inedible, poetic and distant as a landscape evoking as we
dined, the successive images of a siesta under a vine and of sailing on
the sea; on other evenings this original peculiarity of the viands was
thrown into relief solely by the chef who presented them in their
natural cadre as a work of art, and a fish cooked in court-bouillon was
brought in a long earthenware platter, on which, since it stood out in
relief against masses of bluish herbs, unbreakable yet twisted from
having been thrown alive into the boiling water, surrounded by a ring
of shell-fish, of satellite animalcula, crabs, shrimps and mussels, it
looked like something out of a treatise on ceramics by Bernard Palissy.]

This alchemy of the imagination, however, is seldom entirely
gratuitous and only occasionally do these Proustian transpositions remind one of the marginal arabesques which beautify, yet
do not illustrate, the texts of medieval stories. Proust hardly
ever digresses from his tale, even when the loom seems to have
ceased to weave its inevitable pattern, and nothing apparently is
farther from the novelist's mind than the fate of his characters,
for example when his imagination is busy transforming an
ordinary long-distance telephone call into something legendary,
Greek and altogether wonderful. But look more attentively and
you will observe, running through this delightful fantasy, a
moving, sombre strand of the grand design. The imminent death
of Marcel's grandmother is foreshadowed in the young man's
frantic appeals to the *Vierges vigilantes* to reconnect him with the
old lady in Paris. 'Je continuais à répéter en vain "grand'mère!
grand'mère!" comme Orphée, resté seul, répète le nom de la
morte.'

The action quietly progresses in this Doncières episode. For the first time we catch echoes of the Dreyfus case, the social repercussions of which Marcel is shortly to observe in Guermantes circles; Robert, whose passion for Rachel is almost at its peak is a *dreyfusard*. Foreshadowed, also, in those conversations so fascinating to Marcel is the First World War, destined to complete the reversal of social values initiated by the *affaire*. Even the admirable impression of Saint-Loup's captain, Borodino, is not, as the architects say, *hors d'œuvre* but part of the edifice. Is it not because of Borodino's indulgence, regarded as criminal by Robert's mother, that he is able to go to Bruges with his mistress? Moreover, Borodino provides Marcel with a unique opportunity of observing the essential traits which differentiate the aristocracies of two regimes. For the prince, owing to his grandmother's intimacy with Buonaparte and his mother's weakness for Napoleon III, is doubly illegitimate and doubly imperial. Exploited by Proust, this unusual situation yields an interesting comparative study of manners and, besides, affords a remarkable illustration, in his impression of Borodino, of the survival and fusion in present time of what is loosely described as the historic past.

On his journey back to Paris, Marcel carries with him the memory of a puzzling incident. On his last morning at Doncières he had gone down to the barracks to say good-bye to Robert whom he met driving out of the gates in a dog-cart, accompanied by a friend. Out of deference to the latter, whom he knew only slightly, Marcel took off his hat without addressing Robert but fully expecting him to stop and offer a lift. To his stupefaction, however, Saint-Loup, monocled, expressionless and without a glance at his friend, raised his hand in a correct military salute and rattled off at full speed. Later, in Paris, still intrigued by this extraordinary incident, Marcel discreetly alludes to it. 'Ne m'en parle pas', replies Saint-Loup coolly. 'J'en ai été désolé; nous nous sommes recontrés tout près du quartier, mais je n'ai pu m'arrêter parce que j'étais très en retard. Je t'assure que j'étais navré.'

Now that, to the casual observer, is the sort of explanation which explains nothing. Not so to Marcel who is far from being a casual observer but an expert in deciphering psychological cryptograms. The explanation is that Saint-Loup, like all the Guermantes, and for that matter, like everyone who belongs to a closed and highly organized social or professional caste, is trained in a ritual the object of which is to simplify life for the members of the caste and thus conserve its integrity. Robert, as Marcel now realizes, is an experienced actor. In one of his parts he is a comrade, almost a brother. Yet, by a sort of reflex, in another setting, he assumes with admirable ease the role of the monocled, correct and aloof Saint-Loup who saluted Marcel as if he were a complete stranger. The latter, who is to have several opportunities of observing this curious aspect of social behaviour, does not allow the incident to interfere with his admiration for Robert. It is not one of those things which, as La Rochefoucauld would put it, 'nous dégoûtent de l'amitié'. On the contrary, he implies that it is something which must be accepted, with perhaps a certain regret. Otherwise, like Alceste, we shall be driven in despair to abandon society altogether. 'Il faut du temps pour s'accoutumer à l'espèce humaine.' Proust's attitude to such human defects, oddly enough, is that of the unimaginative Philinte in Molière's great play:

> Tous ces défauts humains nous donnent dans la vie
> Des moyens d'exercer notre philosophie.

One must hasten to add, however, that for him the exercise of philosophy is not, as Philinte says, 'le plus bel emploi de la vertu', but the disinterested pursuit of truth and knowledge.

On arriving at his parents' apartment, Marcel makes another discovery of a different and painful nature because it concerns his beloved grandmother. Remember that they have never before been separated for so long. Entering the room unnoticed, he glimpses her for a moment quite objectively, as a camera would have caught her, not as the grandmother of his early boyhood whose image, thanks to the conservative virtues of love and habit, has never altered but as a stranger, an old woman 'rouge, lourde et vulgaire, malade, rêvassant, promenant au-dessus d'un livre des yeux un peu fous, une vieille femme accablée que je ne connaissais pas'. As Marcel tells us, he sees his grandmother, for a fleeting instant, no longer in a fixed plane, in the past, submerged in the self who was Marcel the child but in a new world, that of Time. Who has not experienced such moments in which reality is tragically illuminated for us by the interruption of habit? Proust has many titles to greatness, not the least of which is this uncanny wisdom which enables him to recognize the truth that tragedy for the ordinary man and woman consists, not in the catastrophes portrayed by more dramatic novelists but in the recollection, so bitter and so futile, of moments such as that described by Marcel. Like him, we lack the courage to heed such warnings, impatiently dismissing them from our consciousness though surely they are mercifully intended to prepare us for the shock of a greater and more painful revelation, the termination of a friendship, the farewell to a lifelong dream, the end of love or, as in Marcel's case, the death of a dearly beloved.

But the pigeons are cooing down the chimney, spring is on the move, Robert has promised an invitation to the Guermantes. So Marcel hums merry tunes, selects his most attractive Charvet ties and resumes his sorties into the quiet streets of the faubourg, enriching his collection of dreams by several choice impressions of Mme de Guermantes, in various moods and costumes. Imperceptibly, the object of his romantic adoration has become more ethereal, the *princesse lointaine* of the artist's imagination. Marcel is now resigned to her inaccessibility, content, like the 'fin amant' of the medieval courtly romances, to love for the sake of loving, without hope of other reward. This spell, if we may anticipate events by a few weeks, is broken one day when his mother gently recalls her son to a sense of duty and of reality. Placing her hands over his eyes, as always she did when forced to speak of things that would hurt the boy, this wise and charming woman cures his 'mal imaginaire' by substituting for it a real and tangible sorrow. She points out to Marcel that his grandmother is seriously ill. It is time, therefore, to stop making himself the talk of the servants' hall and to give up his pursuit of a woman who must regard his behaviour as ridiculous and importunate. The great act of renunciation is accomplished with surprisingly little difficulty, perhaps because there is no longer very much left to renounce. A few hours of bitter tears, shed to the accompaniment of Schubert's *Adieu* and the whole business is over. One wonders whether it is because Rousseau and Chateaubriand had no mothers in their youth that we now possess *La nouvelle Héloïse* and *René*. Marcel, however, never had the genuine 'mal romantique', for the excellent reason that his temperament is the reverse of egotistic.

Meanwhile, Robert is back in Paris and eager to pay Marcel that compliment which is one of the penalties of friendship, an introduction to his mistress, Rachel. The lover, the sweetheart and the best friend! Here we have one of the oldest situations in civilized society and, of course, in literature. Curiously enough, however, Proust is the only important novelist I can think of at the moment who really has done justice to the best friend by appreciating the peculiarly difficult role of this unfortunate confidant, usually so scurvily and obliquely presented by writers of fiction. Here, for a change, we see the lovers through the eyes of the best friend. It is a pity that, for example, the abbé Prévost or Dickens did not imitate Proust's technique. It would have been fascinating to know what Tiberge really thought of Manon Lescaut or Traddles of Dora Copperfield. From Marcel we learn all about Rachel, including something which even a best friend dare not mention to Robert. But now we must briefly recount that first meeting with the lady whose perfections have so often been described by Saint-Loup.

Rachel with her birds, dogs and monkey has been obliged to vacate her Paris flat for a house in one of the outer suburbs. So far the situation has developed according to the general laws governing triangular situations of this kind. In the train Robert apologizes for not showing Marcel a photograph of Rachel. She is not, he says, particularly beautiful but possesses on the other hand, extraordinary intelligence and sensibility. Marcel, decoding correctly, guesses that Rachel is, at least in Robert's eyes, a raging beauty though this discovery is to be a delightful surprise. They arrive at one of those charming suburban villages peculiar, then, to the Paris of outside the fortifications. The lilacs and pear-trees are in full blossom and Marcel, dreaming of Combray, stands gazing in rapture whilst Robert hurries to fetch Rachel.

Un air frais y soufflait comme à Combray, mais au milieu de la terre grasse, humide et campagnarde qui eût pu être au bord de la Vivonne, n'en avait pas moins surgi, exact au rendezvous comme toute la bande de ses compagnons, un grand poirier blanc qui agitait en souriant et opposait au soleil, comme un rideau de lumière matérialisée et palpable, ses fleurs convulsées par la brise, mais lissées et glacées d'argent par les rayons.[1]

The surprise fatuously plotted by Robert is quite different from the one that hits Marcel between the eyes when he meets Rachel. Some years before he had seen in a house of call, but himself unobserved, a Jewess whom he nick-named humorously 'Rachel quand du seigneur', not an inmate but a free-lance always ready to barter her favours for twenty francs. This is Saint-Loup's Rachel, the woman for whom he has quarrelled with his family, on whom he has lavished a fortune and whose temperamental vagaries make his life a purgatory compared to which the worst marriage would be heaven itself.

The three return to Paris there to lunch in a restaurant and later to pay a visit behind the scenes of the boulevard theatre where Rachel has a rehearsal. Now Proust excels himself, for nothing could be more painfully and exactly true than his impression of an afternoon in the life of a confidant. Figuratively speaking, the best friend is always the teetotaller at a party where everyone else is hilariously or quarrelsomely intoxicated. For even if he is not a teetotaller, that is to say when he is familiar with the symptoms of this sort of intoxication, the fact remains that he is not at the moment 'under the influence'. Actually, to pass from the figurative to the literal, his only salvation on such occasions, is unlimited alcohol, the sole antidote to those sensations of hot embarrassment, shuddering boredom and painful bewilderment which assail a man condemned to watch and hear his best friend making ardent love to a woman who is intelligent enough to read the stranger's mind and from behind a gay screen of smiles and laughter, to examine him with scrupulous distrust. This rencontre, it happens, marks a crucial stage in Saint-Loup's passion and in Rachel's contempt for him and his class which, as far as she can

[1] *Guer.* I, 141.

see, is composed exclusively of wealthy loafers, snobs and philistines. That is because a performance she had recently given at
the Guermantes' of a symbolist play turned out to be a complete
and humiliating failure, a source of politely yet barely concealed merriment to a fashionable audience insufficiently versed
in the dramatic experiments of the *avant-garde* to appreciate the
genuine talent of an actress interpreting, in an original way,
a novel form of drama. Even Marcel, who discerns the intelligence underlying many of Rachel's intolerable mannerisms,
is shocked to hear her dismiss La Berma as a 'back number',
wrongly attributing to the envy of an inferior and third-rate
artist what is actually the sincere professional judgement of an
actress destined to enjoy a reputation as great as that of her
rival. Rachel in the role of mistress is, however, intolerably
vulgar and it pains Marcel to note the effect on Robert of her
calculated glances at other men, her amusement at Saint-Loup's
furious supplications and the inevitable, if very temporary, reconciliation in the private room to which her lover retires, in
a rage, to finish his lunch alone. Hostilities are renewed at the
theatre when Rachel throws Robert into another agony of
jealousy by pretending to make love to a dancer rehearsing his
ballet role. It is not on him but an unfortunate if boorish
journalist, however, that Saint-Loup vents his anger. The incident shows Marcel an aspect of Robert he has never suspected.
His friend, knowing that tobacco smoke is bad for Marcel's
asthma asks the journalist politely to throw away his cigar and
elicits the retort that people who are ill should stay at home.
'En tout cas, monsieur, vous n'êtes pas très aimable' says
Robert gently. Then, suddenly raising his hand vertically,
brings it across the journalist's face with a resounding smack.
Altogether, this is an afternoon of surprises, for Marcel's last
vision of his comrade before they part for the time being in the
Avenue Gabriel is of Robert administering a masterly thrashing
to a loathsome and seedy individual who has just accosted him
with an indecent proposition. Somewhat preoccupied by these confused events, Marcel proceeds to the *salon* of Mme de Villeparisis.

This visit might be said to mark his début as a man of fashion
though, strictly speaking, Mme de Villeparisis is not in Society.

A Guermantes and thus related to the noblest families in France she no longer, however, enjoys the social position normally occupied by a person of her birth. That she sacrificed when, as a young woman, she thought it amusing to scandalize her aristocratic relatives by her indiscreet liaisons and to shock the Faubourg Saint-Germain by her escapades in Bohemia. Yet who could now imagine that the sweet, white-haired old lady with the old-fashioned cap, seated at her easel and doing water-colours of flowers was once 'la gaie soupeuse' whose caprices reduced many a lover to bankruptcy? True, duchesses sometimes call and even an occasional royalty, but these are purely family and duty visits. The regular members of Mme de Villeparisis' *salon* belong to a very different class and are recruited largely by the ex-ambassador, Norpois, her faithful admirer and formerly her lover. Norpois, indeed, lives at her house, yet always, sometimes with amusing results, pretends to be a caller in order to preserve the conventions.

One of Marcel's favourite theories which delighted his Doncières companions is that our true formative milieu is not social but intellectual. 'On est l'homme de son idée.' Therefore, it is here that we must look for the fundamental cause of Mme de Villeparisis' loss of social prestige. In other words, what inspired her with contempt for the way of life of her set was a sense of intellectual superiority. Possessed of considerable talent and, as a girl, something of a blue-stocking, she indulged her merciless spirit of raillery at the expense of her less in-telligent friends who never forgot the sting of these barbed witticisms though they would have probably overlooked her immorality. And this habit of subtle mockery, as Marcel had already observed at Balbec, has limited and vitiated her artistic judgement so that this lady who once enjoyed the inestimable privilege of meeting at her father's dinner-table some of the greatest writers of France was never able to appreciate their true genius. So for her Musset is simply the young man who came late to dinner speechlessly drunk whilst Vigny struck her as rather absurd because he was so proud of his obscure nobility. Mme de Villeparisis possesses, in fact, the kind of literary talent which finds its most natural and highest expression in the writing of fashionable memoirs. This, as Proust justly points out, does not mean that she is wholly superficial: really superficial people cannot write memoirs, especially graceful and frivolous memoirs, the confection of which postulates a certain fund of seriousness and erudition.

Mme de Villeparisis has just written her memoirs which are now being revised by her secretary, a timid young archivist who watches the effect of her literary and historical reminiscences on the visitors. The latter, of course, except for Mme de Guermantes, here on one of her rare family calls, have no suspicion that they are being used for experimental purposes. On entering, Marcel observes in the little group round the marquise, his old comrade Bloch, now a rising dramatist. In spite of his frock-coat, pince-nez and imperial he strikes an exotic note. He is now, Proust infers, at an intermediate stage in the physical evolution of the Jew, that is to say, not yet so completely assimilated by French society as to resemble an English aristocrat but, on the other hand, no longer producing the impression, on entering a drawing-room, of a hyena loping in from the desert with head pushed forward and set at an oblique angle. Bloch, who is not yet trained in the idiom of the Faubourg Saint-Germain, naïvely accepts the most banal politeness as a tribute, a just recognition of his importance. He asks the most embarrassing questions, listens to the answers with a satanic leer of knowing disbelief, pontifically lays down the law on every subject and, as other Guermantes drift in to join Oriane, proceeds to interrogate them on their attitude to the Dreyfus affair, inviting, finally, the following crushing retort from the young duc de Chatellrault: 'Excusez-moi, Monsieur, de ne pas discuter de Dreyfus avec vous, mais c'est une affaire dont j'ai pour principe de ne parler qu'entre Japhétiques.' Mme de Villeparisis though she has no politics is under the influence of the archivist, a strong nationalist. Therefore, in order to intimate to Bloch that his further visits can be dispensed with, she discovers, as Proust expresses it, in her 'répertoire mondain' the classic scene for such occasions. Here it is:

Comme Bloch s'approchait d'elle pour lui dire au revoir, enfoncée dans son fauteuil, elle parut à demi tirée d'une vague somnolence. Ses regards noyés n'eurent que la lueur faible et charmante d'une perle.

Les adieux de Bloch, déplissant à peine dans la figure de la marquise un languissant sourire, ne lui arrachèrent pas une parole, et elle ne lui tendit pas la main. Cette scène mit Bloch au comble de l'étonnement, mais comme un cercle de personnes en était témoin alentour, il ne pensa pas qu'elle pût se prolonger sans inconvénient pour lui, et pour forcer la marquise, la main qu'on ne venait pas lui prendre, de lui-même il la lui tendit. Mme de Villeparisis fut choquée. Mais sans doute tout en tenant à donner une satisfaction immédiate à l'archiviste et au clan antidreyfusard voulait-elle ménager l'avenir, elle se contenta d'abaisser les paupières et de fermer à demi les yeux.

'Je crois qu'elle dort', dit Bloch à l'archiviste qui se sentant soutenu par la marquise, prit un air indigné. 'Adieu, madame', cria-t-il.

La marquise fit le léger mouvement de lèvres d'une mourante qui voudrait ouvrir la bouche, mais dont le regard ne reconnaît plus. Puis elle se tourna débordante d'une vie retrouvée vers le marquis d'Argencourt tandis que Bloch s'éloignait persuadé qu'elle était 'ramollie'. Plein de curiosité et du dessein d'éclairer un incident si étrange, il revint la voir quelques jours après. Elle le reçut très bien parce qu'elle était bonne femme, que l'archiviste n'était pas là, qu'elle tenait à la saynète que Bloch devait faire jouer chez elle, et qu'enfin elle avait fait le jeu de grande dame qu'elle désirait, lequel fut universellement admiré et commenté le soir même dans divers salons, mais d'après une version qui n'avait déjà plus aucun rapport avec la vérité.[1]

[As Bloch approached to say good-bye to her, buried in her deep armchair, she appeared to be only half-awakened from a dreamy somnolence. Her sleep-drowned eyes held only a faint, charming and pearly glimmer. Bloch's farewells, at which the Marquise's face relaxed into the shadow of a languid smile, evoked not a word from her and she did not hold out her hand. This scene completed the astonishment of Bloch, but as it was witnessed by a circle of bystanders, he did not think it could be prolonged without disadvantage to himself so, in order to force the Marquise, he himself thrust out the hand she had just refused to shake. Mme de Villeparisis was shocked. But no doubt, whilst still anxious to give immediate satisfaction to the archivist and the anti-Dreyfus clan, she did not, however, want to compromise the future. So she merely let her eyelids droop over her half-closed eyes.

'I do believe she's asleep', said Bloch to the archivist who put on an expression of indignation, feeling himself backed up by the Marquise. 'Goodbye, Madame', shouted Bloch.

The Marquise sketched the slight movement with her lips of a dying woman who would like to open her mouth but whose eyes reveal no

[1] *Guer.* I, 223.

sign of recognition. Then she turned, brimming over with resurrected animation, toward M. d'Argencourt whilst Bloch took himself off, persuaded that she was 'gaga'. Full of curiosity and with the intention of clearing up such a strange incident, he came back to see her a few days afterwards. She received him very affably because she was a kind woman, because the archivist was not there and she was keen on the little play which Bloch was to put on at her house and finally, because she had effectively staged her little *grande dame* act which was universally admired and commented upon that very evening in various drawing-rooms, but according to a version that no longer bore the slightest relation to the facts.]

It must not be assumed that this arresting incident reflects the general tone and composition of Proust's studies of fashionable life. Here, as in other similar episodes for example, Marcel's dinner at the Guermantes and the reception at the prince de Guermantes, the action takes the form of a gradual disclosure of character and *mœurs*. Of action, in the dramatic sense, there is very little indeed. What Proust does, superlatively, is to re-create, by an unobtrusive and natural process, the atmosphere of Mme de Villeparisis' *salon*, allowing us to judge for ourselves exactly how and why this milieu differs from that of the Guermantes. Here he is successful precisely because he refuses, unlike most of his predecessors, to imitate the methods of the dramatist who is obliged by the optics of the theatre, by the peculiar exigencies of his art—rapidity of the tempo, necessity for bold and immediate effects, imminence of the dénouement— to charge the atmosphere with tension so that a *salon* presented by Molière or Wilde or by Meilhac and Halévy is always, viewed in retrospect, an exceptional *salon* where a group of remarkably fluent and witty persons vie with each other in the brilliance of their epigrams or in the swiftness of their repartees. This is, of course, a retrospective impression, because during the performance the illusion of reality is maintained, not merely by the art of the dramatist, but also by the convincing fact that all these clever remarks and perfectly timed retorts are uttered by real people. That is why very often a play, read as one would read a novel, seems artificial or unreal. Proust seldom copies the technique of the playwright and that is one of many reasons why he is an original novelist of the first order.

Perhaps, therefore, I was wrong in using the word 'action' at all in order to express what takes place at this stage in the narrative. It is a gradual process of illumination or enlightenment, so gradual that Mme de Guermantes, even after Marcel is introduced to her by Robert, still retains an aura of mystery. Yet already he is astonished to find that somehow it is difficult, on closer quarters, to superimpose on this Parisienne in blue pekin the golden, autumnal, woodland tints, the rich, heraldic colours and the air of feudal romance which the name Guermantes persistently evokes in his memory. But since experience does not so easily conquer imagination, the presence of Oriane weaves a new spell, the charm of her eyes and her voice:

ses yeux, où était captif comme dans un tableau le ciel bleu d'une après-midi de France, largement découvert, baigné de lumière même quand elle ne brillait pas; et une voix qu'on eût cru aux premiers sons enroués, presque canaille, où traînait comme sur les marches de l'église de Combray ou la pâtisserie de la place, l'or paresseux et gras d'un soleil de province.

For the first time Marcel sees Oriane in her familiar milieu, surrounded by Guermantes, separated by the invisible wall of her indifference from himself, from the archivist, the historian of the Fronde and from everyone in this *salon* who does not belong to the world of the Guermantes. But at least Marcel can now begin to observe what Saint-Simon would have called the 'mécanique' of this world and discover for himself what its inhabitants mean when they speak admiringly of *l'esprit des Guermantes* or *l'esprit d'Oriane.*

Proust, who knew his Saint-Simon as well as Marcel's grandmother knew her Sévigné, used to regret, with some annoyance, that Saint-Simon whilst frequently alluding to *l'esprit des Mortemart* gives no illustrations which might help us to guess at its peculiar quality. In this, Saint-Simon, not being a novelist, was probably wise for I can imagine nothing more difficult to transfer to the printed page from the fragile and fleeting moment in which it was conceived than that intangible and almost indescribable entity known to the French as *esprit*. Like an Anjou wine it is apt to lose its sparkle after uncorking, though an expert and careful butler such as Proust can sometimes do wonders, especially if the temperature is right. Even so, though Oriane's *mots* do often possess the malicious impertinent sparkle of genuine *esprit*, her verbal felicities and audacities are more often humorous than witty, inspired as a rule by her amusement at the physical rather than the psychological oddities of her victims. Here she resembles Charlus, though of course he carries this game to the ultimate limits of decency and even beyond. No, Oriane is most spontaneously amusing when she cruelly seizes on a physical defect like Mme de Cambremer's *embonpoint*, and observing with a merry eye the delighted reception accorded to her first wicked metaphor, proceeds to embroider on it, skilfully abetted by her husband, Basin, who plays the role, more usually allotted to the wife on such occasions, of the stage accomplice whose feigned protests stimulate the verve of the chief performer.

'Je reconnais qu'elle n'a pas l'air d'une vache car elle a l'air de plusieurs', s'écria Mme de Guermantes. ' Je vous jure que j'étais bien embarrassée voyant ce troupeau de vaches qui entrait en chapeau dans mon salon et qui me demandait comment j'allais. D'un côté j'avais envie de lui répondre: "Mais, troupeau de vaches, tu confonds, tu ne peux pas être en relations avec moi puisque tu es un troupeau de vaches," et d'autre part ayant cherché dans ma mémoire j'ai fini par croire que votre Cambremer était l'infante Dorothée qui avait dit qu'elle viendrait une fois et qui est assez *bovine* aussi, de sorte que j'ai failli dire Votre Altesse royale et parler à la troisième personne à un troupeau de vaches. Elle a aussi le genre de gésier de la reine de Suède. Du reste cette attaque de vive force avait été préparé par un tir à distance, selon toutes les règles de l'art. Depuis je ne sais combien de temps j'étais bombardée de ses cartes, j'en trouvais partout, sur tous les meubles, comme des prospectus. J'ignorais le but de cette réclame. On ne voyait chez moi que "Marquis et Marquise de Cambremer" avec une addresse que je ne me rappelle pas et dont je suis d'ailleurs résolu à ne jamais me servir.'[1]

['I admit she doesn't look like a cow for she looks like several', exclaimed Mme de Guermantes. 'I swear I was quite taken aback on seeing that herd of cows with hats on, coming into my drawing-room and asking me how I was. On the one hand, I had a good mind to reply: "But, herd of cows, you're mistaken, you can't be on calling terms with me because you are a herd of cows." On the other hand,

[1] *Guer.* i, 208.

after racking my brains, I finally got the idea that your Cambremer was the infanta Dorothea who said she would come and see me one day and who is also rather bovine, so that I nearly called her "Your Royal Highness" and nearly spoke in the third person to a herd of cows. She's also got the Queen of Sweden's type of dewlap. By the way, this assault in force had been prepared by a long-range fire according to all the rules of warfare. For goodness knows how long I had been bombarded by her cards; I used to find them everywhere, on every article of furniture, like prospectuses. I had no idea what was the object of this advertising campaign. You could see nothing else in my house but "Marquis and Marquise de Cambremer" with an address I don't remember and which, moreover, I am determined never to utilize."]

It must not be imagined that Basin always thus plays second fiddle to Oriane though in company he loves to put her through her paces and is unmistakably proud of the sensation aroused by her performances in the *haute école* of fashionable society. He is not, however, a model husband. Proust in a lapidary phrase sums up his attitude to his wife: 'Le duc se parait de sa femme mais ne l'aimait pas.' Sometimes, indeed, this becomes suddenly and painfully evident as for example at Mme de Villeparisis' when in the middle of a discourse on the Dreyfus affair he is interrupted by a malicious, amused remark of Oriane's on the anti-semitism of his cousin Gilbert, the prince de Guermantes. Basin fixed his wife with one of those implacable looks that astonish and embarrass the observer as if, accidentally, he has intruded on a domestic altercation. The duc de Guermantes, debonair, of herculean build, fabulously rich, is a rare and complete example of egoism, brutality and pride; civilized but not entirely disciplined by the traditional respect for good form and the meaningless though charming urbanity inherited from several generations of courtiers. Intelligent enough to move with the times, he usually joins with Oriane in affecting to laugh at the prince de Guermantes and at his brother Charlus for their absurd and pedantic attention to questions of birth and precedence. But as Marcel later discovers, the most thoroughly Guermantes of all the family is Basin whose bonhomie and republicanism conceal an immense arrogance and a profound contempt for his social inferiors. A faithless husband, domineering and probably brutal in private, he exacts from his mistresses, who are always chosen from his own class and for their blonde, alabaster and statuesque beauty, the most absolute submission to his will and, with almost royal capriciousness, discards one favourite for another. Ironically, it is Oriane who has to listen to the complaints of the deposed paramour, a situation which, out of pride, she pretends to regard with ironical amusement or else, being a versatile actress, as the excuse for a disillusioned comment on the vanity of love illustrated by an apt quotation from Hugo or Musset and by a wistful, charming and dreamy smile. Whatever may be her reactions, in private, to Basin's tyrannical outbursts, she never forgets, in society, what is due to the duchesse de Guermantes, meeting her husband's intimidating silences and leonine stares with the unruffled composure of a practised tamer of wild animals. Certainly, too, the fear of his displeasure is never allowed to interfere with the free expression of her deliberately unorthodox opinions some of which indeed are designed to brave the anger of Basin and thus to assert Oriane's independence. But the fact is that although there is no longer any question of love between these two they are united by an unshakable belief in the grandeur and uniqueness of the house of Guermantes.

Proust has at least two good reasons for lingering over this description of Marcel's visit to Mme de Villeparisis. Where else could he assemble, so very naturally, such an assortment of characters? For although one would certainly expect to meet at any Guermantes function Robert's mother, Mme de Marsantes, her brother Charlus, the Belgian aristocrat D'Argencourt, or the duc de Chatellrault, one would be equally certain not to encounter there Bloch, Norpois, Odette Swann, the super-snob Legrandin, or the timid insomnia-ridden M. Pierre, the historian of the Fronde. Mme de Villeparisis' *salon* is also an excellent milieu for observing various repercussions of the Dreyfus case, which is already beginning to accentuate existing class schisms and to announce surprising regroupings. Charlus, in his usual exaggerated manner, proclaims indeed that it is destroying society 'par l'afflux de messieurs et de dames du Chameau, de la Chamellerie, de la Chamellière'. Odette, for instance, is an

active member of the Ligue de la Patrie Française, and as such
has entered into relations with Mme de Marsantes. Robert de
Saint-Loup, on the other hand, has been indoctrinated by Rachel
and is a confessed Dreyfusard though his convictions, as events
reveal, are not profound. The *affaire* is by no means, however,
the sole topic of conversation. Proust, who would have agreed
with Stendhal that politics in a novel are apt to resemble a
pistol-shot in a symphony, introduces the Dreyfus case at discreet intervals and always with good effect. We have already
referred to it in relation to Bloch's *congé*, an incident which
was preceded by a conversation between the young Jew and
Norpois. It is a little masterpiece of subtle irony and perception.
Marcel, listening to the ex-ambassador playing with the bewildered Bloch realizes that Norpois whom he had lightly
dismissed as a vain and garrulous old man, is an artist in
diplomacy.

This is one of the chapters in *A la recherche du temps perdu*
where, in order to convey an adequate idea of Proust's descriptive manner, a new tense of the verb would be desirable,
expressing the continuity of the past in the present, for that is
how the author sees life. Inseparable from the actuality of the
Dreyfus case, which is history in the process of conception, there
is History itself preserved yet alive, in all the Guermantes, as
in the annular rings of growing trees. And, like trees, every one
of them is set to grow in a certain direction, fixed generations
ago, and now unchangeable. Even the saintly Mme de Marsantes, whose sweetness and humility make it seem incredible
that she comes from the nursery which produced Basin and
Charlus, betrays the *grande dame* and the stock of Guermantes
in a dozen little unconscious insincerities of speech and manner.
Her perfect simplicity is, like that of a Paquin frock, an artistic
and expensive creation, though this is apparent only to the eye
of the connoisseur.

Yet it so happens that Marcel catches a glimpse of another
Mme de Marsantes when for a brief interval she is not being
a *grande dame* but just the adoring, anxious mother of Robert
de Saint-Loup, who is in Paris, after a long absence, on twenty-
four hours' unofficial leave. He has left Rachel in the circum-

stances we have already described and his one desire is to see
her again, that evening, in order to effect a reconciliation. Of
this, naturally, his mother knows nothing but Marcel, though
he can guess at his friend's unhappy state of mind, is pained by
the brutal petulance of Robert's response to Mme de Marsantes'
loving solicitude as she timidly begs him to dine with her at
home. More touching still is her bitter self-reproach when her
son, in a temper, rushes off to rejoin his mistress. Marcel, up
till then, has always sympathetically abetted Robert in his
amour but now he feels that there is nothing he would not do to
break it off and restore Saint-Loup to his mother. Yet, as he
whimsically observes: 'J'étais pourtant le même homme à quelques heures de distance.' Robert gone, Mme de Marsantes
turns to say good-bye and is immediately transformed into the
grande dame.

— J'ai été *intéressée, si heureuse* de causer un peu avec vous. Merci!
Merci!
Et d'un air humble elle attachait sur moi des regards reconnaissants,
enivrés, comme si ma conversation était un des plus grands plaisirs
qu'elle eût connus dans la vie. Ces regards charmants allaient fort
bien avec les fleurs noires sur la robe blanche à ramages: ils étaient
d'une grande dame qui sait son métier.[1]

Robert, before leaving, keeps his promise to introduce Marcel
to his aunt. Thus, at last, his greatest wish is realized, the event
he has schemed for and longed for so passionately. What happens is exactly what always happens when imagination outruns
reality. Apart from a polite remark that she has sometimes
noticed Marcel out walking in the morning, Mme de Guermantes offers him a tart and then, observing the arrival of
Odette whom she does not want to meet, rises and without
saying good-bye, leaves the *salon*.

Marcel is also about to go but is waiting to accompany the
baron de Charlus who, to his surprise, has expressed a desire
to speak to him. Flattered by such condescension on the part of
a man so much his senior and notorious for the absurd value he
places on the honour of being admitted to his acquaintance,
Marcel, in reply to a question from the marquise, announces with

[1] *Guer.* I, 254.

some pride that he is waiting for Charlus. Mme de Villeparisis, with a peculiar expression, earnestly advises him not to stay but to slip out before the baron turns round. Charlus, however, overtakes him on the staircase. They walk off arm in arm.

Now at this stage Marcel really knows very little about Charlus. At Balbec he had formed certain impressions which we have described, and from these a more experienced man would have guessed the reason for Mme de Villeparisis' odd anxiety. If Marcel himself had taken the trouble to reflect he would have remembered having noted, instinctively, in the baron's fixed, inscrutable gaze, something dangerous, possibly even sinister or slightly crazy. Yet since that time everything he has heard about Charlus from Robert is calculated to belie this impression. The baron is portrayed by his nephew as eccentric, no doubt, but harmless. A virile type with a passion for violent outdoor exercise, Charlus is inordinately fond of women and bitterly contemptuous of the effeminate younger generation. This is confirmed by the baron's behaviour in Mme de Villeparisis' *salon* for, to Robert's amusement, he makes straight for the most attractive and best dressed woman and engages her in conversation. Here is Marcel's vivid picture of Charlus seated beside Odette Swann:

Je regardais M. de Charlus. La houpette de ses cheveux gris, son œil dont le sourcil était relevé par le monocle et qui souriait, sa boutonnière en fleurs rouges, formaient comme les trois sommets d'un triangle convulsif et frappant. Je n'avais pas osé le saluer, car il ne m'avait fait aucun signe. Or, bien qu'il ne fût pas tourné de mon côté, j'étais persuadé qu'il m'avait vu; tandis qu'il débitait quelque histoire à Mme Swann dont flottait jusque sur un genou du baron le magnifique manteau couleur pensée, les yeux errants de M. de Charlus pareils à ceux d'un marchand en plein vent qui craint l'arrivée de la *Rousse*, avaient certainement exploré chaque partie du salon et découvert toutes les personnes qui s'y trouvaient.[1]

Inquisitive, eccentric, but not sinister. Marcel knows, however, that Charlus is incredibly susceptible and capable of astonishing vindictiveness. Yet, since he is at heart extremely kind, the baron is quick to regret his impulsiveness once he

[1] *Guer.* I, 242.

has taken his revenge for an imagined slight. Marcel remembers a typical example of this weather-cock mentality. At Balbec, Mme de Villeparisis, who was miserly in little things, found herself short of ready money and, in order to save the expense of wiring to her bank, borrowed 3000 francs from her nephew. Shortly afterwards, because of a fancied grievance, he telegraphed demanding the immediate return of the money which was sent to him less the cost of the postal order. Charlus, thinking the marquise had made a mistake, questioned her but learned that there was no error. Highly amused at this evidence of his aunt's stinginess, he laughed heartily. But some days later, convinced that she was attacking his interests in some family affair, Charlus wrote a terrible, threatening letter, announcing that he intended to expose her to the ridicule of the Faubourg Saint-Germain by relating in every *salon* the story of the money-order. Next day, full of remorse, he asked her pardon. This was quite sincere but, unfortunately, in the meantime, whilst on excellent terms with the marquise, he had already related the anecdote without the faintest desire to be malicious but simply as an amusing drawing-room tit-bit.

So far, therefore, there is nothing in what Marcel knows about the baron to announce the *éclaircissement* related in a subsequent chapter by Proust, the revelation, due entirely to chance, which retrospectively illuminates his ignorance of human nature. And, indeed, what is more usual in real life than this blindness followed by a sudden removal of the scales from our eyes? A man we have known for years as a colleague rings up late one evening. In his voice and in the tenor of his conversation there seems to lurk an undercurrent of strange mockery. It is only later, when we have dismissed the impression from our mind, that we learn quite accidentally that he has been removed to a home for dipsomaniacs and that his unfortunate weakness was known to many, even talked about, but not in our presence. Besides, there is a vast difference between the vice of drunkenness and that of the baron which is not—or, rather used not to be— a topic of drawing-room conversation. And when rumours begin to circulate, as they do when Charlus inadvertently betrays his perverted tastes, there are always well-meaning friends like

Swann, for instance, who are ready to dismiss them quite sincerely as stupid or ridiculous. Others, less sincere, also deny them, either in defence of their own caste or, from prudence, lest they be suspected of the same proclivities.

Perhaps the baron's conversation, as they leave Mme de Villeparisis' together, should have disillusioned Marcel. Instead, it arouses a suspicion which leads him farther from the truth. As Charlus expatiates on the grandeur of his own situation and the extent of his authority as a leader of society, Marcel confirms his early impression that this man is not only a monomaniac but, on certain topics, almost mentally unbalanced. Now, though everyone agrees that great literature reflects the truth about life, very few ever seriously compare the knowledge contained, for instance, in the world's great novels, with their own experience. If Marcel, who knew his Balzac better than he knew his own pocket, had really profited from his meditations on *La Comédie humaine*, the baron's first remarks would have rung a bell, and he would have seen ascending from the subterranean chamber of his consciousness the Balzacian counterpart of his interlocutor: Vautrin. In the hierophantic pronouncements of Charlus he would have detected the exultant, Mephistophelian pride of Vautrin describing his plans for the spiritual and moral domination of Lucien de Rubempré: 'Nous cultivons les bégonias, nous taillons les ifs, par pis aller, parce que les ifs et les bégonias se laissent faire. Mais nous aimerions donner notre temps à un arbuste humain, si nous étions sûrs qu'il en valait la peine.'[1]

Nevertheless, one may excuse Marcel for not attaching serious importance to the proposals of an elderly gentleman who calmly offers, in return for his friendship, that is to say, complete submission to his imperious decrees, the knowledge contained in a 'dossier secret et inestimable' of which, apparently, the baron is the sole possessor. There exists, according to Charlus, a freemasonry, including four European sovereigns, whose clandestine activities will furnish the explanation of many an enigma, a freemasonry with powers so great as to decide, sometimes, the fate of a nation. All this, admittedly, places a certain strain on

---

[1] *Guer.* 1, 256.

Marcel's credulity particularly when one recollects the strange
digressions which interrupt the stream of these revelations. For
example, the baron suddenly changes the subject to interrogate
Marcel about his comrade Bloch and stupefies Marcel with the
following suggestion:

Peut-être pourriez-vous demander à votre ami de me faire assister
à quelque belle fête au temple, à une circoncision, à des chants juifs.
Il pourrait peut-être louer une salle et me donner quelque divertisse-
ment biblique, comme les filles de Saint-Cyr jouèrent des scènes
tirées des *Psaumes* par Racine pour distraire Louis XIV. Vous pourriez
peut-être arranger même des parties pour faire rire. Par exemple une
lutte entre votre ami et son père où il le blesserait comme David et
Goliath. Cela composerait une farce assez plaisante. Il pourrait
même, pendant qu'il y est, frapper à coups redoublés sur sa charogne,
ou, comme dirait ma vieille bonne, sa carogne de mère. Voilà qui
serait fort bien fait et ne serait pas pour nous déplaire, hein! petit ami,
puisque nous aimons les spectacles exotiques et que frapper cette
créature extra-européenne, ce serait donner une correction méritée
à un vieux chameau.[1]

This peripatetic lecture ends as queerly as it began with
Charlus suddenly hailing a cab and driving off seated beside its
young, half-tipsy coachman though, to Marcel's puzzlement, the
baron had refused several other vehicles going in the same
direction. The explanation of this and other puzzling incidents
will be granted to him in due course. 'Il faut du temps pour
s'accoutumer à l'espèce humaine.' Especially, one might add,
when one is confronted by some of the rarer animals in this
human menagerie, although Charlus would deprecate our choice
of adjective. On the contrary, he tends always to overestimate
the population of his native city, Sodom. But we must allow, of
course, a certain margin for municipal pride and professional
bias.

What is now clear to the reader, if not to Marcel, is that
Charlus must no longer be regarded as a purely comic figure,
a twentieth-century version of *Le Glorieux*, an amusing monomaniac whose eccentricities, though often mischievous, produce
on the whole no serious harm. In the illumination furnished by the
above episode, unsuspected aspects of his nature are made visible.

[1] *Guer.* i, 258.

This man has undeniable virtues and talents but all are at the service of his terrible vice or, as Proust prefers to call it, his malady. Vice or malady, we need not for the moment quibble about that. The fact is that in Charlus lurk incalculable possibilities. Without a doubt, by virtue of his rank, wealth, his numerous and extensive political and diplomatic connections, he is a potential menace to society. It so happens that his interest in domestic and international public affairs is academic because he views them from the Everest of his indescribable pride and egotism. This applies even to the Dreyfus case. On the other hand, if goaded by unnatural jealousy, Charlus is capable of almost any crime, including murder. But the truth is that none can predict what Charlus will say or do in any given situation.

Chapter IV

LE COTÉ DE GUERMANTES
(continued)

T HERE are still, I suppose, certain experiences portrayed by
the novelist which must be taken, so to speak, on trust. However, with the progress of the applied sciences as demonstrated
in modern warfare, in the cinema and the radio, the extent
of the novel-reader's credulity is rapidly diminishing. As
a result, nowadays, very few novelists set out to *épater le
bourgeois*, as did the Zolaists, by exploiting his inexperience.
But when a novelist writes of domestic realities like illness and
its sequel, death, we meet him on even terms. He is no longer
in the privileged position of the explorer from far-off lands
addressing an audience of admiring, yet ignorant, laymen. On
the contrary, he has assumed the most difficult of all the artist's
tasks, which is to interpret these common experiences in such
a manner as to make every member of his public recognize that
his, the reader's, personal experience is no longer personal, that
it is one of the moments of existence when the individual enters
into communion with all humanity. No artist is great unless he
compels recognition of this simple truth. Therefore, although
hundreds of novelists have attempted to portray illness and
death, it is only in the creations of the masters that we are able
to discern beneath the intricate network of circumstances woven
around such experiences by the imagination of the novelist, that
unmistakable universal design repeated in the pattern of our
own life yet never hitherto apparent, that design we should have
lived and died without seeing but for the illumination furnished
by the artist.

Proust's account of the illness and death of Marcel's grandmother produces this effect of illumination. It is obtained, however, in a striking and original way, since he makes no attempt
to emulate the dramatic pathos of Balzac or the impassive

reportage affected by the Naturalists. Proust is original because whilst portraying the simple, ordinary circumstances which form the prelude and the accompaniment to illness and death, he succeeds in re-creating the pattern of an experience which all of us recognize. Its elements are self-delusion, false hopes, unspoken fears and, when the expected miracles of science have not materialized, the final, bitter acceptance of reality. Unlike Dickens or Balzac, he makes no attempt to harrow the sensibilities by morbid descriptions of suffering and grief. Yet, unerringly, Proust discovers a pathos so common in life that literature nearly always ignores it. I mean the pathos which springs from nobility of soul, the pathos of that gallant drama enacted in every home where mortal illness has elected to reside. Such is the theme of the admirable passage describing Marcel's outing with his grandmother when, in the little pavilion of the Avenue Gabriel, occurs the first serious attack paralysing one side of her face. After the interview with the specialist, Marcel knows that his grandmother is doomed. She also knows it and so does her daughter. Yet all three, until the end, play out that grim comedy of loving deception where every word and gesture is a saintly and pitiful lie, where every cry wrung from the patient by the agony of physical pain is stifled by the indomitable force of love or if, perchance, overheard by her dear ones, is attributed to some trivial cause.

To interpret the intensity of this silent despair and suffering the genius of Proust coins new expressions revealing the inexhaustible resources of the French language—'elle ne pouvait empêcher le gémissement de ses regards'; 'elle inclinait vers ma grand'mère toute sa vie dans son visage'; 'son visage pleurait sans larmes'; 'ma mère, au pied du lit, rivée à cette souffrance'. Proust, as we have remarked, has several styles. The style which predominates here is classic in its purity and tense restraint. It has the sculptural, achromatic quality of the language used by Marcel earlier to express the acting of La Berma in *Phèdre*. Nothing could more perfectly harmonize with his present theme, which is the dignity and beauty of unutterable and unuttered grief. 'Le soleil ni la mort', wrote La Rochefoucauld, 'ne peuvent se regarder fixement.' Proust is an exception. Now, as so often in *A la recherche du temps perdu*, the author gazes with reverent yet fascinated curiosity at the swift and mysterious operations of the unseen master sculptor and in at least two fine passages, one of which I quote, a great artist pays homage to the 'travail de statuaire' of that greater artist, Death. Here is Marcel's last impression of his grandmother as she lies on her death-bed:

Quelques heures plus tard, Françoise put une dernière fois et sans les faire souffrir peigner ces beaux cheveux qui grisonnaient seulement et jusqu'ici avaient semblé être moins âgés qu'elle. Mais maintenant, au contraire, ils étaient seuls à imposer la couronne de la vieillesse sur le visage redevenu jeune d'où avaient disparu les rides, les contractions, les empâtements, les tensions, les fléchissements que, depuis tant d'années, lui avait ajoutés la souffrance. Comme au temps lointain où ses parents lui avaient choisi un époux, elle avait les traits délicatement tracés par la pureté et la soumission, les joues brillantes d'une chaste espérance, d'un rêve de bonheur, même d'une innocente gaieté, que les années avaient peu à peu détruits. La vie en se retirant venait d'emporter les désillusions de la vie. Un sourire semblait posé sur les lèvres de ma grand'mère. Sur ce lit funèbre, la mort, comme le sculpteur du moyen âge, l'avait couchée sous l'apparence d'une jeune fille.[1]

There are, however, in this chapter, passages conceived in a very different style, reflecting the sensations produced in Marcel by experiences which belong to the domain of comedy. They are portrayed with great fidelity, though in language touched with satire and disillusionment. M. Albert Feuillerat, that eminent Proustian scholar, disapproves of these 'scènes de comédie moliéresque' on the ground that they 'détonnent dans l'ensemble du chapitre'.[2] And, in order to exculpate Proust, he points out that the offending scenes must have been written some years after the moving passages in which Marcel tells us of his mother's silent grief and his grandmother's stoical acceptance of pain. This is undoubtedly true yet the very fact that Proust deliberately included these *scènes de comédie* in the revised and greatly enlarged version of his novel shows that he regarded them as forming a necessary and integral part of this

[1] *Guer.* II, 35.
[2] Albert Feuillerat, *Comment Proust a composé son roman*, p. 187. Yale Univ. Press, 1934.

chapter. He would have been astonished to learn that by introducing comedy into a narrative relating to illness and death he was guilty of infringing an æsthetic law, for that is what is implied in M. Feuillerat's strictures. I cannot personally share the latter's misgivings, which appear to reflect a somewhat rigorous attitude to literature. As Balzac remarked: 'Il est dans la nature que le comique se trouve parfois mêlé aux choses les plus pathétiques.'

Perhaps it may be opportune to recall here what Proust conceived as the function of art: 'L'art recompose exactement la vie.' Later, I shall examine the implications of this statement. One of them is that the optics of the novel, to borrow Diderot's expression, are not the optics of drama, a fact which French novelists have been reluctant to accept. The comic passages in the episode under discussion are not to be compared, therefore, to 'moliéresque' scenes suddenly cropping up in a Racinian tragedy where indeed they would ruin the unity of tone. This chapter, with all deference to Proust's critic, is not an 'ensemble': the ensemble is *A la recherche du temps perdu*, which is a great and original novelist's attempt to recompose the history of the narrator's psychological life; of all the impressions made by life on his consciousness at its various changing levels or depths. Everyone who will honestly examine the sensations, emotions, sentiments and thoughts aroused in him by an experience such as that now interpreted by Proust must admit that they do not always conform to an ideal design; they do not always compose a uniformly coloured state of soul. Are there not sometimes involuntary impressions so terribly 'out of place' that he is obliged to dismiss them angrily from his consciousness. But they exist and Proust would maintain, I am certain, that they cannot be excluded from a truthful artist's recomposition of life.

It is useless then, to expect from Marcel a conventional transcription, in monotone, of his sensations or impressions at the time of his grandmother's illness and death. We must not expect a smoothly false translation which omits or glosses over the unconventional word, the phrase that seems at first discordant until we realize that there is only one unity, the unity

of truth, which the artist must respect if his work is to have the
durable quality of integrity. This Proust fully recognized when
he decided to portray not just the pathos of illness and death but
also the gleams of comedy that sharpen the edges of the shadows.

Marcel observes what all of us know to be true, that serious
illness, like birth and marriage and death, is a social act—
possessing its own special ceremonial or ritual, more or less
elaborate according to the theatre on which it is enacted. In
Marcel's house the ritual is punctiliously observed. His mother,
even in the midst of her sorrows, remembers the traditional
conventions, the language consecrated by usage: 'Vous n'irez
pas *là-bas*'; 'Vous, on ne vous dit pas merci.' These words are
addressed to the eupeptic, bearded cousin, irreverently nick-
named 'ni fleurs ni couronnes' who never misses a funeral,
whose presence in a house of illness is indeed equivalent to
a death-certificate. In those final days of waiting, Marcel has
every opportunity to observe the actors in this ancient morality,
the final scenes of which will be performed on another stage.
There is the famous specialist, Professor X, whose obsession is
that all disease has its origins in the nasal passages; the famous
Dr Dieulafoy, only called in when the patient is *in extremis*. His
rôle, which he has played superbly for forty years, is simply to
confirm the verdict of his colleagues.

Dans sa noble redingote noire, le professeur entrait, triste sans
affectation, ne donnait pas une seule condoléance qu'on eût pu croire
feinte et ne commettait pas non plus la plus légère infraction au tact.
Aux pieds d'un lit de mort, c'était lui et non le duc de Guermantes
qui était le grand seigneur. Après avoir regardé ma grand'mère sans
la fatiguer, et avec un excès de réserve qui était une politesse au
médecin traitant, il dit à voix basse quelques mots à mon père,
s'inclina respectueusement devant ma mère, à qui je sentis que mon
père se retenait pour ne pas dire: 'Le professeur Dieulafoy'. Mais
déjà celui-ci avait détourné la tête, ne voulant pas importuner et
sortit de la plus belle façon du monde, en prenant simplement le
cachet qu'on lui remit. Il n'avait pas eu l'air de le voir, et nous-
mêmes nous demandâmes un moment si nous le lui avions remis tant il
avait mis de la souplesse d'un prestigitateur à le faire disparaître, sans
pour cela perdre rien de sa gravité plutôt accrue de grand consultant
à la longue redingote à revers de soie, à belle tête plein d'une noble
commisération. Sa lenteur et sa vivacité montraient que si cent visites

l'attendaient encore, il ne voulait pas avoir l'air pressé. Car il était le tact, l'intelligence et la bonté même.[1]

[Attired in his noble black frock-coat, the Professor entered the room. Sad, yet without affectation, he uttered not one word of condolence which could have been construed as insincere, neither did he commit the slightest error in tact. At a death-bed it was he and not the duc de Guermantes who was the great gentleman. After having examined my grandmother without tiring her, with a scrupulous air of reserve which was a compliment to the physician in charge of the case, he whispered a few words to my father, bowed respectfully to my mother to whom my father, I feel, only prevented himself with an effort from saying: "Professor Dieulafoy". But already the latter had turned away so as not to seem intrusive, and made a perfect exit, merely accepting the sealed envelope handed to him. He did not appear to have seen it and we ourselves wondered for a moment whether we had given it to him, so remarkable was the dexterity with which, like a conjurer, he made it vanish, without on that account losing one iota of the gravity—which if anything was accentuated—of the distinguished consultant with his long frock-coat and silk lapels, and his fine countenance registering the most dignified commiseration. His deliberation and his vivacity combined to show that whilst he had still a hundred other patients to visit he did not want to give the impression of being in a hurry. For he was the incarnation of tact, intelligence and kindness.]

What a contrast with the duc de Guermantes who bungles his part in spite of a lifetime of training for occasions just like this! After the initial, obviously insincere phrases of condolence, Basin suddenly notices Marcel's mother and disregarding her son's violent protests, insists on being formally introduced. No other episode interprets so completely the fundamental insensibility, the sublime egotism of this *grand seigneur*, otherwise so perfectly styled in the ritual of politeness, as his inability to realize that no moment could have been worse chosen for the performance of that celebrated and complicated act known as a 'présentation à la Guermantes'. So the duke, whose antics are naturally ignored by Marcel's mother, is left standing, for once a completely ridiculous figure, deserted by his usual audience before he has really got into his stride. This has never happened before: no one has ever been known to reject the honour of knowing the duc de Guermantes. Therefore, the

[1] *Guer.* II, 33.

only explanation he can think of is that the poor lady is not quite right in her head. But as Marcel puts it: 'il avait encore dans les jambes tout le reste des saluts et réverences à reculons qu'on l'avait empêché de mener à leur fin.'

Nature, when she inflicts a deep wound, appears to provide her own anæsthetic, thus allowing her victims a respite before the inevitable onset of sharp and bitter pain. Marcel will not feel the real agony of loss until much later. In the meantime, he slips back into the old social routine, refusing to listen to the insistent pleadings of his artistic conscience. Robert, for the time being, has broken with Rachel whose lies, by poisoning her lover's mind against Marcel, had interrupted their friendship. This is, however, forgotten not because Saint-Loup disbelieves Rachel, but because he is now indifferent and has accepted a post in Morocco. Albertine pays Marcel a surprise visit and he divines from certain new tricks of speech that she is now a mature young woman although, as he is to discover to his eternal regret, she will always incarnate his nostalgic desire for Balbec. Albertine will always be 'comme une rose au bord de la mer'. But at the present he is not in love with her since his imagination is completely focused on another woman, an absolute stranger and a friend of Robert's. Yet on that autumnal misty Sunday afternoon, to Marcel's astonishment, the Albertine who had repelled his advances at Balbec not only returns his caresses but yields herself complacently to his desires.

Marcel is rather glad to see her go because, having arranged through Saint-Loup an assignation with a Breton lady called Mme de Stermaria—the Mlle de Stermaria of Balbec, now divorced and ready for adventure—he wants to make plans for their meeting. Mme de Stermaria is shortly to pass through Paris *en route* for her château in Brittany and Marcel can think of nothing but their rendezvous in a certain little restaurant in the Bois de Boulogne. The weather is grey and misty; the restaurant is situated on a small island on the lake, an ideal pastel-tinted atmosphere harmonizing perfectly with his vision of this mysterious Celtic princess. It was ever Proust's ambition 'to render Time visible'. Rarely has he done so with more success than in this description of Marcel's waiting for the realization of yet another dream, of the impatience that urges him to send a last minute note to ask if he may fetch Mme de Stermaria in his carriage only to receive the shattering reply that she regrets that, owing to an unfortunate change in her plans, she must postpone the pleasure to another time. Here we have the unchanging pattern of youthful despair, the design of that miniature, brief yet poignant desolation which will be repeated till the end of time whenever a Mme de Stermaria casually breaks an appointment with a romantic Marcel. Mercifully it is never a tragedy: tragi-comedy would be a better epithet. In this case Robert, on leave from Africa, is the jovial *deus ex machina* who whisks Marcel away from his misery to the friendly warmth of a crowded restaurant glowing bravely in the clinging fog of a November night.

Pause, however, for an instant, as Marcel descends the stairs of his apartment with Robert. Before leaving his room, he had suddenly been assailed by memories of Rivebelle. Now he relives in a flash the charming evenings at Doncières and, a moment later, one particular foggy evening at Combray. Yet, as he notes with a strange feeling of happiness, each of these resurrected states of soul has its individual quality. They are separated by differences which, he suggests, have nothing to do with conventional Time. The distances that lie between them are not measurable in terms of years. In reality, these three emotional experiences so unexpectedly imported into his consciousness by his involuntary memory are as remote from each other as totally different worlds. But for the presence of his friend, Marcel would try to find language to express the exaltation aroused by this realization, words adequate to interpret the substance of these memory-images, all so beautiful yet all so unlike. So another opportunity is lost. Otherwise, Marcel might have been spared that long journey he called afterwards *A la recherche du temps perdu*, the story of which he is now telling. 'J'éprouvais à les percevoir' he says of his memories, 'un enthousiasme qui aurait pu être fécond si j'étais resté seul et m'aurait évité ainsi le détour de bien des années inutiles par lesquelles j'allais encore passer avant que se déclarât la vocation invisible dont cet ouvrage est l'histoire.'[1]

---

[1] *Guer.* II, 82.

This statement by Proust of his intention, this conception of the narrator as the artist in the process of discovering his vocation must always be present in our mind if we are to understand this novel. Any other approach is bound to lead us astray. This is exemplified, I feel, in M. Feuillerat's remarkable study of Proust's method of composition, the thesis of which is that the novelist was guilty of æsthetic *lèse majesté* when he abandoned the first version of his work in favour of the very much larger book known to us as *A la recherche du temps perdu*. In so doing, according to this critic, the author sacrificed unity of plan, of characterization, of style, giving us, instead of a novel, a collection of memoirs. In building up his thesis, M. Feuillerat uses as part of his substructure, in addition to the page-proofs of the second volume of the novel in its original version, biographical material taken from the author's correspondence. Now the biographical approach, indispensable in the case of certain writers, is a risky method to employ with Proust. Let us take by way of illustration M. Feuillerat's interpretation of the scene to which I have recently alluded; the scene where Marcel dines with Saint-Loup in the café-restaurant on that foggy November evening when he so badly needed distraction. The clientèle is heterogeneous, composed of middle-class professional men, of amateur politicians discussing the Zola case and, forming a small exclusive group, arrogant young impecunious aristocrats some of whom, like the prince de Foix, are in Robert's set. Proust, however, in his acid commentary on their manners and conversation, sharply dissociates Saint-Loup from these fortune-hunting, degenerate snobs and, indeed, the whole episode is designed to illuminate even more vividly than in the Doncières scenes the attractive qualities of Robert. It also serves—and this is important—to elaborate Marcel's views on the nature of friendship. That point escapes M. Feuillerat, who plunges *in medias res*, concentrating on one aspect of this episode. On the strength of a remark in one of Proust's letters in which he mentions that in creating Saint-Loup he thought of his friend, Bertrand de Fénelon, a young aristocrat killed in 1915, M. Feuillerat interprets as follows the pages describing why Marcel admires Robert and the scruples that exercise his mind when he wonders whether Saint-Loup would regard this admiration as having the quality of true and disinterested friendship. Of these scruples, as the following quotation shows, M. Feuillerat says nothing. He writes:

> Se rappelant la douceur de cette soirée passée avec son ami, le narrateur dit la beauté, le charme, l'intelligence de Saint-Loup. Il s'incline devant cet être de pure noblesse qui réunissait en lui les meilleures qualités d'une race presque royale. Le ton de ce passage est si pathétique, si frémissant d'émotion révérencieuse qu'on sent naître en soi la conviction que Proust en écrivant ces lignes disait un dernier adieu à un ami disparu.

He concludes, in short, that this passage was written in 1916–17 as a tribute to Bertrand de Fénelon.[1]

Now, the passage in question is not 'pathétique'; neither can it be described as 'frémissant d'émotion révérencieuse'. Why should it be? Marcel is not bidding a last farewell to Robert de Saint-Loup whom he will see again on several occasions. It is only because M. Feuillerat, in defiance of Proust's repeated and categorical warnings, insists upon treating this novel as 'un roman à clef' that the description of the restaurant episode seems to him 'pathétique' and 'frémissant d'émotion révérencieuse'. But surely the proper way to interpret the passage is to see it as the reflection of Marcel's feelings towards Robert on a particular evening, or rather during part of that evening. For just before the two entered the café-restaurant, Saint-Loup had shocked and irritated Marcel by observing coolly:

> Tu sais, j'ai raconté à Bloch que tu ne l'aimais pas du tout tant que ça, que tu lui trouvais des vulgarités. Voilà comme je suis, j'aime les situations tranchées....

And Marcel, watching Robert's face observes:

> Du reste, sa figure était stigmatisée pendant qu'il me disait ces paroles vulgaires par une affreuse sinuosité que je ne lui ai vue qu'une ou deux fois dans la vie, et qui, suivant d'abord à peu près le milieu de la figure, une fois arrivée aux lèvres, les tordait, leur donnait

---

[1] The authentic tribute to Bertrand de Fénelon is to be found elsewhere in Proust's novel [*SG.* II (i) 198] where Proust in one of his extremely rare interruptions of Marcel's narrative, remarks à propos of the illustrious Fénelon: 'ayant pour ami le plus cher l'être le plus intelligent, bon et brave, inoubliable à tous ceux qui l'ont connu, Bertrand de Fénelon.'

une expression hideuse de bassesse, presque de bestialité toute passagère et sans doute ancestrale. Il devait y avoir dans ces moments-là qui sans doute ne revenaient qu'une fois tous les deux ans éclipse partielle de son propre moi, par le passage sur lui de la personnalité d'un aïeul qui s'y reflétait. Tout autant que l'air de satisfaction de Robert, ses paroles: 'J'aime les situations tranchées' prêtaient au même doute, et auraient dû encourir le même blâme. Je voulais lui dire que si l'on aime les situations tranchées, il faut avoir de ces accès de franchise en ce qui vous concerne et ne point faire de trop facile vertu aux dépens des autres.[1]

This disagreeable impression, however, is later dispelled by Saint-Loup's frank and charming generosity and by his anxiety when he notices that Marcel is shivering with cold in the draught of the constantly opening doors. Leaping impetuously to his feet, Robert nimbly tiptoes along the backs of the seats, borrows the prince de Foix's overcoat, repeats with the same graceful skill his balancing feat and with a little flourish, drops the coat shawlwise over his comrade's shoulders. The trivial incident, so typical of Robert, appears somehow for Marcel to epitomize the mood of their *tête-à-tête*: 'Pour lui, comme pour moi, ce fut le soir de l'amitié.' Yet, having pronounced the word, Marcel reflects once again, and with his former compunction, on the nature of friendship. After all, do these feelings of warm gratitude and admiration constitute friendship in the true sense of the word?

Now, to understand his scruples, we must compare them with certain reflections that occurred to Marcel earlier that evening, in fact, when Robert suddenly appeared at his flat, just after the arrival of Mme de Stermaria's desolating letter. Marcel was unfeignedly delighted to see Robert at that moment because, whatever his opinion of the value of friendship, and it is a very unorthodox opinion, Saint-Loup's gaiety, kindness and superabundant energy produce a tonic effect on his morale. But this does not alter his considered view that friendship is an overrated sentiment and that the pleasure derived from it does not compensate the artist for the time sacrificed to his friends. Therefore, basking in the warmth of Robert's conversation at dinner, admiring the elegance and perfection of his comrade's behaviour

[1] *Guer.* ii, 83–4.

as a host and of the inherited aristocratic qualities which find in him such natural and complete expression, Marcel is tormented by the following misgivings. Must not Robert sometimes perhaps think that Marcel likes and admires him for the wrong reasons; for the very accomplishments to which he, Saint-Loup, attaches no importance since they are not individual qualities but merely those common to his family or caste? In short, would not Robert be justified in thinking, with a certain disillusionment, that the pleasure derived by Marcel from their comradeship is an intellectual or artistic pleasure incompatible with real friendship? Marcel, in an attempt to 'voir clair dans son cœur', concludes that Robert would be wrong. The reason which he adduces is interesting precisely because it does not spring from the fullness of an *âme sensible*: it is the result of the artist's *acte intellectuel*, of that effort which, as he once told us, is essential if we are to grasp the reality of affective experience. If Robert had not cultivated something higher than the attainment of perfect grace of manner, if he had not constantly striven to rise above the prejudices of his class, his physical distinction would have been more self-conscious and therefore, less natural and perfect. So Marcel can honestly assert that he admires Robert not simply as a work of art, as the scion of a noble and historic family but for an intellectual quality that differentiates him from other young men of his caste, for the superior intelligence which impels Saint-Loup to make friends outside his own class. Observe, however, that whilst Marcel thus distinguishes Robert from the average young aristocrat, it does not follow that he has modified his estimate of the intellectual value of friendship or that he renounces the opinions to which I have referred. After all, one may share the views of a La Rochefoucauld on friendship and still be an excellent friend. An artist, says Marcel, may know that he carries within him a masterpiece and feel it his duty to spend all his time in work. Nevertheless, he will often give up his life for a perfectly useless cause.

In this perspective we must view the passage referred to by M. Feuillerat. To see it as a tribute to one of Proust's friends is to ignore the context, to present a misleading impression of the whole episode and, consequently, of Marcel's psychology.

We now come to the lengthy description of Marcel's first dinner at the Guermantes, the experience once regarded as unattainable, desirable above all others. But Marcel is no longer the moonstruck youth who shadowed Oriane in the quiet streets of the Faubourg Saint-Germain. The invitation so eagerly coveted, so patiently angled for, no longer excites his imagination. Indeed, as is the way of life, he is just as much interested in the prospect of seeing Elstir's paintings as of observing the behaviour of his host and hostess in their familiar milieu. Absorbed, therefore, in his examination of the pictures, Marcel suddenly realizes that for half an hour the duke and his guests have been hungrily awaiting his arrival in order to begin dinner. This absent-mindedness is significant, indicating an important readjustment of Marcel's scale of values, a change of perspective whereby even the most exclusive *salon* in Paris takes its proper place in relation to the genius of an Elstir. The incident explains also why the intelligent young bourgeois will be invited often by the Guermantes and eventually become one of their privileged intimates. For one of the characteristics of the 'esprit des Guermantes' is their admiration, which is half-genuine, for original talent, provided always that its possessor is otherwise socially acceptable. Dr Cottard, Elstir, or Brichot, the Sorbonne professor, though eminent in their particular speciality, would not qualify for admission to the Guermantes' *salon*. Their proper milieu, as we shall see, is that of the Verdurins. In the eyes of Basin and Oriane, talent and originality are not enough: one must be an amateur and preferably an amateur from choice, not from necessity. True, men of letters are sometimes invited by Oriane. But this is exceptional and if a poet comes for after-dinner coffee or to lunch it will be to play poker not to discuss poetry. That is also characteristic of the 'esprit des Guermantes'. Unconsciously, therefore, by keeping his host waiting for dinner, Marcel does more to establish himself in the esteem of the Guermantes than if he had written *Phèdre* or even discovered the theory of relativity. Besides, though the company happens to include a Royal Highness, the princesse de Parme, their hosts have seen these people too often to bother about their feelings whilst Marcel, on the other hand, is an interesting and unknown personality. Moreover, from the mere fact of having been invited at all, he must necessarily possess remarkable attributes. Certainly such is the opinion of the princesse de Parme, for whom a dinner at Oriane's always harbours the promise of rare and enchanting surprises. This pleasant expectancy is shared by all the guests who hope, nearly always with justification, that in the course of the evening, the duchess will launch another of her audacious *mots*, later to be repeated with variations, as 'la dernière d'Oriane'.

When Proust's critics assert that *A la recherche du temps perdu* too often resembles a collection of memoirs rather than a novel, they have in mind no doubt those sections where, as in this account of the dinner at the Guermantes, the author re-creates for us the atmosphere and what Saint-Simon would call *la mécanique* of a now vanished social group. Nothing could be farther from the mark. Such criticism reveals, in the first place, a basic misconception of Proust's art and in general of the art of the novel which, as so often happens, is confused by critics with the art of drama. This is not surprising, especially in France where a particular kind of drama, classical tragedy, has long exercised a strong influence on the novel. One observes it in the works even of the great nineteenth-century French novelists, notably in the dramatic form of their plots, in their predilection for *coups de théâtre*, for what Sarcey used to call *scènes obligatoires* and also in their method of presenting character. Now Proust, on the contrary, successfully attempts to break away from the influence of the theatre and exploits very fully the great possibilities of an art which, as Goethe pointed out, is fundamentally different from that of drama. With his accustomed genius for getting down to essentials, Goethe observes:

Im Roman sollen vorzüglich *Gesinnungen* und *Begebenheiten* vorgestellt werden; im Drama *Charaktere* und Taten. Der Roman muss langsam gehen, und die Gesinnungen der Hauptfigur müssen, es sei, auf welche Weise es wolle, das Vordringen des Ganzen zur Entwickelung aufhalten. Das Drama soll eilen, und der Charakter der Hauptfigur muss sich nach dem Ende drangen und nur aufgehalten werden. Der Romanheld muss leidend, wenigstens nicht im hohen Grade wirkend sein; von dem dramatischen verlangt man Wirkung und Tat.[1]

[1] *Wilhelm Meister's Lehrjahre*, pt. II, bk. v, ch. 7.

[But in the novel, it is chiefly *sentiments* and *events* that are ex-
hibited; in the drama, it is *characters* and *deeds*. The novel must go
slowly forward; and the sentiments of the hero, by some means or
another, must restrain the tendency of the whole to unfold itself and
to conclude. The drama, on the other hand, must hasten, and the
character of the hero must press forward to the end; it does not restrain but is restrained. The novel-hero must be suffering, at least he
must not in a high degree be active; in the dramatic one, we look for
activity and deeds. (*Carlyle's Trans.*)]

With the exception, perhaps, of Flaubert's *L'Education sentimentale* which is a study of frustration and of moral spinelessness,
A la recherche du temps perdu is probably the most complete
example in French literature of what a novelist can achieve with
the resources peculiar to his art and foreign to the art of drama.
No dramatist, except Shakespeare who was novelist, poet and
dramatist in one, could hope to emulate the manner in which
Proust, by the subtle employment of constantly shifting psychological and spiritual perspectives and sites, interprets the *Gesinnungen* as distinct from the *Charaktere* of his personages. To
dramatize Charlus, Marcel or Swann, that is to say, to present
them in opposition to a clear-cut dramatic situation, would be
to simplify and distort the picture unfolded by Proust. We should
have then a character in Goethe's sense of the term, in other
words, a vivid impression of their behaviour under the stress of
passion, at a time of crisis, a character in the manner of Prévost
(Des Grieux), of Balzac (Vautrin), or of Flaubert (Emma Bovary).
But we should not have what a novelist of Proust's originality
offers, that view of their real character, of their *Gesinnung*, that
view made possible by the Proustian continual change of approach
and of perspective which reveals not only the unexpected traits
concealed by habit and excavated or thrown into relief by drama,
but the modifying, equally surprising nuances which also form
part of the self, the ever-changing self known as Marcel, or
Charlus or Swann. To a critic afflicted with the tendency to
judge the novelist solely by the standards of classical drama,
A la recherche du temps perdu will of course seem to be formless
and the many pages devoted to the Guermantes and Verdurins
irrelevant though admittedly fascinating pictures of manners.

On the contrary, they represent a progressive illumination of character and a development of Proust's main theme.

Marcel is now observing Basin and Oriane in a milieu new to him, in their own house, surrounded by their intimate friends and familiar visitors. As a result, our earlier impressions, like Marcel's, have to be modified. For if certain ridiculous or displeasing traits are now confirmed these are sometimes mitigated, as in Basin's case, by this change of situation. We discover, for example, that the duke in the role of host is a charmer whose exquisite courtesy, good humour and eager attentiveness leaves his guest with the flattering illusion that the Guermantes have spent the afternoon wondering whether, after all, he might not let them down at the last moment; that, in short, all the pleasure is on their side, a pleasure tempered only by their concern lest Marcel may not find his evening rather dull. This note is never forced to the pitch of flattery. Every phrase and gesture has the naturalness of well-rehearsed acting; the duke lives the part, having played it and seen it played, since childhood. Thus when at last he observes Marcel emerge from the contemplation of Elstir's pictures, the famished master of the house makes no attempt to rush the presentations and his signal to the butler to serve dinner is almost surreptitiously discreet so as not to embarrass the late-comer. And from that moment until Guermantes helps him on with his overcoat and sees him to the door, the ritual of hospitality is observed to the minutest detail. All this is not entirely insincere. Marcel is obviously *persona grata*, whose qualities render him worthy of the honour of being received by the Guermantes. Besides, it is possible by the constant imitation of certain sentiments to acquire them, if only superficially, just as medical students often experience the symptoms of the diseases they study.

The picture of the duchess is also now presented in greater detail and no longer in the impressionistic manner of the earlier pages, a manner, be it noted, eminently natural during the period of Marcel's infatuation. Not that he sees her now with the objective eye of the camera or of the Naturalists, who prided themselves on their impassive realism. He looks at Oriane with the eyes of an artist whose sensitive appreciation of beauty is

for the moment unclouded by a lover's romantic dreams; of
a psychologist trained to observe and interpret much that his
predecessors had never noticed or else rejected as insignificant.
One might be tempted to compare Proust's uncanny acuteness
and range of perception to that of a delicate instrument which
can detect supersonics, or light vibrations invisible to the ordinary
eye. Yet such an analogy by its suggestion of a soulless, inhuman
observer would misrepresent completely Proust's attitude to
human behaviour which, although not sentimental, is one of
enlightened sympathy.[1] Indeed, many will think on observing
his reactions to abnormal vice, that it is almost reprehensibly
humane.

In these pages, we encounter two or three brief allusions to
Leibniz, a philosopher whom Robert and Marcel had obviously
studied and discussed, along with Bergson. Perhaps, therefore,
we may borrow the well-known Leibnizian metaphor and say
that Proust not only hears the roar of the sea but also the
beating of the individual waves. He apperceives, as Leibniz
would have expressed it, what most of us perceive but do not
apperceive. Proust agrees with Leibniz and Bergson on the
importance of what the former termed the *perceptions petites*,
the subconscious elements of our soul-life, which distinguish
our particular *moi* from that of others. What is Marcel's
vocation invisible if it is not the art of noting such *perceptions
petites*? To some extent, too, like every great artist he is a
Leibnizian in his acceptance of evil as a necessary component of
a perfect composition, ugly if viewed in itself, but when seen by
the artist and in relation to the whole, sometimes possessing
a strange beauty.

The description of the dinner-party at the Guermantes is
entitled 'L'esprit des Guermantes devant la princesse de Parme'.
From the outset, it is apparent that owing to the peculiar nature
of this new experience and, above all, to the altered state of
soul of the observer, the tone of this whole passage will reflect,
inevitably, an intellectual and critical rather than an intuitional
or a purely imaginative mode of approach to reality. Marcel, no

---

[1] I.e. in the original sense of the word, which does not necessarily exclude
antipathy.

longer in love with Oriane, has recovered from the shock of disappointment produced by the realization that the Guermantes of actuality stubbornly refuse to conform to the romantic images originally evoked by their name. But we need not fear that names have for ever lost their magic for Marcel, or that he will ever abandon the effort to establish by intuition that sympathetic communication with life which, in conjunction with the knowledge furnished by the analysing intelligence, results in a vision of reality that can never be achieved in any other way. On this very evening, he confesses, just before meeting the little dark woman called the princesse de Parme he had imagined her as a Sanseverina, perfumed with the scent of a thousand violets, a *princesse lointaine* dreaming in the breathless hush of an Italian summer evening, shut off from the rest of the world in her beautiful palace. Yet Marcel has progressed sufficiently in his *vocation invisible* to know that direct physical contact with external reality has a disconcerting habit of demolishing the magic of names. Proust, in a vivid if commercial simile, likens the first of these two operations, that of the pure act of 'fabulation' to the process which manufacturers of perfume call, I believe, *enfleurage*, whereby the block of grease absorbs the essential scents of certain flowers: the second operation, that of the disillusionment performed by reality, resembles the chemical action by which the essential oils or attars are brutally expelled.

In the case of the Guermantes and the magic of the name Guermantes, it will be remembered that this second operation led to a violent reaction which for a time disturbed the clarity of Marcel's vision. Unfairly, he dismissed them as merely aristocrats like a hundred others to be found in the Faubourg Saint-Germain. Common sense, however, regained the upper hand: 'Mais de même que Balbec ou Florence, les Guermantes après avoir déçu l'imagination parce qu'ils ressemblaient plus a leurs pareils qu'à leur nom, pouvaient ensuite, quoiqu'à un moindre degré, offrir à l'intelligence certaines particularités qui les distinguaient.' So Proust's chief objective in these hundred pages will be to portray distinctive qualities which are both physical and psychological. The former he dismisses summarily in a few lines. Marcel draws attention to the special Guermantes complexion, 'la couleur d'un rose spécial allant quelquefois jusqu'au violet'. He notes also the Guermantes fairness, 'une certain blondeur quasi éclairante des cheveux délicats, même chez les hommes, massés en touffes dorées et douces, moitié de lichens pariétaires et de pelage félin'. These traits, which might be called static physical features, do not interest Proust very much and indeed, we shall see that this is one of many differences which separate him from Balzac and the nineteenth-century realists. Marcel's intelligence is chiefly focused on the 'esprit' and on the 'génie de la famille' of the Guermantes although at the same time it discovers with uncanny divination the significant features expressing the normal psychological state, the disposition or the *Gesinnung* of their satellites, Mme d'Arpajon, the German 'prince Von', M. de Bréauté, the lady-in-waiting to the princess and many others, even of Poullein the wretched footman, whose rendezvous with his sweetheart is ruthlessly cancelled because the duchesse de Guermantes, in obedience to a passing malicious impulse, deliberately changes his day off.

Proust, as I remarked, asserts the novelist's right to exploit freely the possibilities of his special art without that almost servile deference to the prestige of drama which is so characteristic of his predecessors. Now, if there is one domain in which the novelist can really operate independently, unrivalled by the dramatist, it is that of descriptive narrative. On the other hand, since the exercise of every prerogative implies responsibility and incurs criticism, he is liable to expose himself to the reproach which has been levelled at Proust, that descriptive narrative, carried to excess, may transform a novel into a collection of memoirs. In his case, as we shall see, this reproach is quite unjustifiable and was probably inspired by the fact that Proust frequently alludes to Saint-Simon, whose *Mémoires* he knew by heart. But it is in the manner of a novelist, not of a memorialist, that he re-creates the mentality of the Guermantes, portrays the *mécanique* of life in their particular social 'monad' and throws into relief the hundred little details betraying 'le côté de Guermantes' of fashionable society.

Proust opens with a panoramic survey of two great families, the Guermantes and the Courvoisiers, a contrast that defines very clearly the original nature of the Guermantes *esprit*, an expression which must be interpreted here in the widest sense. He reveals also the family genius of the Guermantes which is not at all the same thing as their *esprit*. It is much deeper rooted so that, at certain moments, when the interest of the family is closely involved, a Guermantes will instinctively obey not the *esprit* but the genius, to use the word in its original Latin meaning, of the family. Thus Mme de Villeparisis, had she acted in a manner consistent with the *esprit des Guermantes* which affects to despise rank and ancient lineage, prizing only intellectual brilliance and independence, would have chosen for her niece, Oriane, a husband outside their own exclusive caste, perhaps an eminent writer, politician or professional man. Instead, to the surprise and chagrin of the Courvoisiers, she conformed automatically to the family genius and chose Basin, then prince des Laumes, colossally rich, intellectually mediocre, yet related to the greatest houses in Europe. The family genius discloses itself in other ways, always contrasting oddly with the Guermantes *esprit*. They may scandalize the Courvoisiers by their republican contempt of the nobility, by their refusal to admit to their *salon* anyone who is not 'intelligent' whatever their quarterings, in short by their apparent disregard of the traditional *bienséances* sacred to most ducal houses. Nevertheless, Oriane and Basin never fail to appear at the boring teas and dinners offered by dowagers who really matter; you will always find their names in the social columns of the *Gaulois* on the occasion of a fashionable burial: in the Guermantes residence you will never hear a flunkey address Oriane other than as 'Madame la duchesse'. A typical Guermantes characteristic, again at variance with the almost Voltairian persiflage of their normal conversational tone, is their trick of lapsing quite unexpectedly into an old-fashioned sententious vein of morality, usually discernible in their intonation, in their choice of vocabulary but also sometimes in the expression of their faces. One can hardly call it hypocrisy. It is rather a sort of reflex evoked by particular situations, for example by the marriage of Swann to Odette, or by Robert's passing access of Dreyfusism. The idea which the author implies rather than expresses directly is that the Guermantes tend to behave instinctively and naturally when they follow the channel grooved out by their family genius. The *esprit des Guermantes*, on the contrary, finds expression in more intelligent, deliberate and conscious action and speech. This is suggested in Marcel's account of his impressions as he observes and listens to Basin and Oriane. When the latter appear on the stage of society—and they are very seldom off it—every action, word and movement appears to have been carefully selected in order to surprise and delight an audience of admiring connoisseurs. Yet, as Proust subtly and gradually discloses, the very essence of this *esprit* is the Guermantes' pretence that they are always natural, that they despise the whole complicated artificial ceremonial which makes fashionable life resemble a theatre. Therefore, when all society is excited over a forthcoming event of the season, the Guermantes casually announce that they are off to the Norwegian fjords or on a tour of the French cathedrals. Or else, the duchess, if asked what costume she has decided on for a certain splendid masked ball, replies carelessly that she is going as—la duchesse de Guermantes. The same *esprit* is reflected in her judgements on people, on literature and on art. True, she does not share the duke's opinion that all Wagner is 'assommant' and much inferior to Auber and Boieldieu. No, Oriane magnanimously grants that Wagner despite his 'longueurs insupportables' displays genius in *Lohengrin* whilst here and there in *Tristan* there are curious passages. She finds the Victor Hugo of the *Légende des Siècles* detestable but admits that in his early manner he is sometimes a poet, even a great poet. But she is most typically Guermantes when, to the shocked delight of the princesse de Parme, she calmly pronounces, in the presence of the anti-Dreyfusard général de Beautreillis, the name of Zola, rejecting the current definition of him as a realist. Zola is not a realist but an epic poet—'il a le fumier épique. C'est l'Homère de la vidange. Il n'a pas assez de majuscules pour écrire le mot de Cambronne.' Equally unorthodox are Oriane's verdicts on her acquaintances, which are shaped according to the same pattern;

that is to say, of an intelligence formed in an unintellectual
social milieu at a period when Mérimée, Meilhac and Halévy
and Pailleron were the models of literary taste. 'Qui se fait
singulier pour avoir un caractère!' Sometimes it is hard to
resist the temptation to apply Voltaire's epithet to Oriane when
she is exercising her malicious wit, often with a serene disregard
of the truth, at the expense of her absent friends, zealously
abetted by the duke who plays the part of second murderer in
this amusing game of liquidating established reputations. But
Marcel shows us not only the duchesse de Guermantes who is
'stupidement Faubourg Saint-Germain' but also the Oriane who
unconsciously expresses in 'la perpétuelle et quiète après-midi
de ses yeux', in the Racinian purity of her vocabulary, something
quite remote from the *esprit de Guermantes*: the old-world charm,
the perfume of history which clings to the words 'la vieille
France'. The fusion of these two general impressions, the one
unconsciously and the other consciously produced by the duchesse
de Guermantes, constitutes the reality of her personality.
Proust's originality as a descriptive writer is largely due to his
talent for presenting such disparate, apparently inconsistent
aspects of character so that by a subtle adjustment of the
novelist's instrument of vision, these images finally merge into
one clear, true and unforgettable picture. Is it not one of the
functions of great art to discover unity where a less perceptive
intelligence sees only confusion?

Although none of the guests at this dinner-party is described
with that conventional and minute attention to physical detail
cultivated by the nineteenth-century novelists, all the characters
are individualized. The personal and memorable feature is unerringly located, brilliantly exposed. If it is a physical trait—
and that is rare—be sure that nearly always Proust has an
ulterior motive. If Marcel draws attention to the marmoreal
quality of Mme d'Arpajon's beauty, to the similar Victoire de
Samothrace physique of her successor Mme de Surgis-le-Duc, it
is to emphasize the fact that Basin's criterion never changes.
Even in his infidelities, he is instinctively faithful to the original
type of feminine pulchritude represented by his wife. He betrays
her only by choosing mistresses who lack Oriane's intelligence

and force of character. Note, incidentally, how effectively Proust employs the oblique method in his character illumination. The stupidity of Mme d'Arpajon emerges sufficiently, one would think, from her conversation as when she quotes Musset under the impression that he is Victor Hugo. But its ineffable quality becomes really evident when we listen in to Oriane's asides to the princesse de Parme or, better still, catch her merry and significant glance at Basin, the smile that reads: 'Est-elle assez idiote!'

On the subject of Proust's descriptive technique, it is instructive to compare him with Balzac or Flaubert, for instance, in the former's portrait of Ursule Mirouet or the latter's portrayal of Mme Dambreuse's *salon* in the *Education sentimentale*. These examples are chosen absolutely at random. In both, the care lavished on details of physique and on the reconstruction of the material setting appears to the modern reader excessive and perhaps often superfluous. The reason is probably that very few people, except professionals such as auctioneers, private detectives, women at fashion displays, and interior decorators ever remember persons or their material surroundings in this way. Proust, for whom life or reality is constant movement, retains preferably the expressive, animated traits which are usually combinations of features—the smile, the undertone, the gesture, the recurrent turn of phrase. As for the *décor*, it is significant that in this long description of dinner at the hôtel de Guermantes, there is scarcely a word about the furnishings except when Oriane, as a prelude to one of her audacities, refers to her Empire suite, identical with that owned by the Jena family who have usurped for their son the title of duc de Guestalla which rightly belongs to the heir of the princesse de Parme. Costume interests Proust more but here again, as in 'Un amour de Swann' not for its purely decorative value. In this episode, Marcel, who is surrounded by a bevy of lovely 'filles-fleurs', observes only that 'elles coulaient vers moi de longs regards caressants comme si la timidité seule les eût empêchées de m'embrasser'. Perhaps they were gowned by Paquin, Worth or Doucet: he does not seem to care. His motive is not, as when he introduces us to Odette, to show how clothes may reflect the *spiritualité d'une civilisation.* In the art of description the determining factor should be necessity, which implies intelligent selection. Proust selects only the traits necessary to his purpose. He wants to create the illusion that if tomorrow you met the princesse de Parme in a *salon* you would instantly recognize her not, indeed, in the sense of identifying her from a photograph. There might be other dark ladies with luminous jet-black eyes. But it would be impossible to mistake them for the princess who is seated next to the duchesse de Guermantes in a perpetual state of half-fearful expectancy, waiting for the latest *mot*, nodding violent assent when Oriane mentions an artist of whom Her Royal Highness has never heard before. When you are introduced to the princess, she will inquire anxiously after your health, insist upon holding your gloves and on drawing up a chair for you expressing, to your complete bewilderment, the regret that 'Albert' is not here to meet you. But she knows no more about you than she does about Marcel. Only, she has been trained by a royal mother to lavish charming meaningless attentions on those lesser mortals whom God recommends to the kindness of His elected daughters. It would be painfully simple, on the other hand, to identify the 'prince Von', as he is known to his intimates. He affects that bone-crushing handshake which is *de rigueur* in little Teutonic principalities. But he has other less striking but more disturbing characteristics which Marcel finds vaguely repellent and terrifying, refusing therefore the prince's invitation to accompany him as far as the Théâtre Français. Memorable, also, at the other extreme, is the imbecile lady-in-waiting to the princesse de Parme, the lady who insists maddeningly, despite Marcel's repeated disclaimers, that his uncle is a famous admiral. Her brightest remark, which even infuriates her indulgent mistress, is that it certainly will not snow because, she points out: 'On a fait le nécessaire pour cela: on a jeté du sel!'

These are but a few specimens, arbitrarily selected, from a group of sharply individualized people who combine nevertheless, to form a homogeneous and animated society. Proust, in re-creating this *salon* is not simply displaying his specialized knowledge of Parisian fashionable *mœurs*. He is not out to 'épater le bourgeois'. The whole episode has a necessary place in the novel, marking the end of Marcel's youthful illusions regarding the name Guermantes. He will no longer view Oriane, Basin, la princesse de Guermantes or their social milieu through the tinted screen of a romantic imagination. Only, however, the end of his youthful illusions, because now in the carriage, on the way to his rendezvous with Charlus, trying vainly to assemble the kaleidoscopic impressions of the last few hours, Marcel is possessed by a strange and almost physical sense of excitement. It is a special kind of exaltation which, although not to be under-valued, is not to be compared with the deep and satisfying joy he experienced during his drive in Dr Percepied's dog-cart at Combray, or in Mme de Villeparisis' carriage in the country roads round Balbec. On those two occasions, he realizes, the exaltation was of a different quality, a prelude to artistic creation, inspiring him to write that passage on the steeples of Martin-ville and the exquisite lines on the 'allée d'arbres', the trees that seemed to beg him desperately to stop and notice them, the trees he had never seen before yet which somehow he must have seen. The reader will remember the words: 'Je vis les arbres s'éloigner en agitant leurs bras désespérés, semblant me dire: "ce que tu n'apprends pas de nous aujourd'hui, tu ne le sauras jamais".' And Marcel's terrible sadness as the vision disappears and the carriage moves on: 'comme si je venais de perdre un ami, de mourir moi-même, de renier un mort ou de méconnaitre un Dieu'.[1] No, there is nothing of this quality in his present mood as he views through that 'stéréoscope intérieur' which magnifies their importance, the memories of the conversations at the Guermantes dinner: Oriane's judgements on literature, prince Von's stories of Botha and the Boer war, Bréauté's encyclopædic chit-chat, the duke's casual revelations of quaint customs still surviving in the aristocracy. All this, interesting as it may be to the writer of memoirs, is not, Marcel discovers, the raw stuff of which is composed the greatest art, precisely because it is known to the observer as an external experience, apprehended only by the surface of his intelligence, not, Proust implies, by his whole consciousness.

[1] *JF.* ii, 21.

Nous pouvons à notre choix nous livrer [thinks Marcel] à l'une ou l'autre de deux forces, l'une s'élève de nous-mêmes, émane de nos impressions profondes, l'autre nous vient de dehors. La première porte naturellement avec elle une joie, celle que dégage la vie des créateurs. L'autre courant, celui qui essaie d'introduire en nous le mouvement dont sont agitées des personnes extérieures, n'est pas accompagné de plaisir; mais nous pouvons lui en ajouter un, par choc en retour, en une ivresse si factice qu'elle tourne vite a l'ennui, à la tristesse, d'où le visage morne de tant de mondains, et chez eux tant d'états nerveux qui peuvent aller jusqu'au suicide.[1]

Once again we are reminded, by these reflections on art, of the basic theme of *A la recherche du temps perdu*, which seeks not merely to present through the medium of the narrator, a linear, a surface and cinematographical picture of life but the vision of life communicated by a man who is an artist in process of evolution, an artist sure that his approach to life is unique because it is never wholly objective or 'intellectual', who is constantly striving, on the contrary, to identify himself with the stream of which his own *moi* is a small but essential part. At certain moments of his existence Marcel did achieve an apparently complete and immediate consciousness of this identity with the reality which, as an artist, he must grasp and communicate through the work of art. What, then, of the misgivings now aroused in him as he writhes 'comme une pythonisse' in the cab on his way to the baron de Charlus? Here again Proust reminds us discreetly that Marcel is narrating the history of his 'vocation invisible'. He offers us a unique and absorbing interpretation of the artist's mental processes as he attempts to penetrate, intuitively and intellectually, into the reality, not of a single, individual experience such as a contact with natural beauty or the beauty of art, with an orchard in blossom or an Elstir painting, but with a complex restless flux of experience 'de nature sociale et non individuelle' like the memories of the conversations and events of the Guermantes dinner. Marcel feels rather despairingly how difficult it is to seize and communicate the true reality of such impressions. On one point, however, he has no doubts. They cannot be presented in the manner of the so-called realistic novelist who thinks naïvely that it is enough to transfer

[1] *Guer.* II, 209.

such material *en bloc* from life to the work of art, relying on the
old-world charm, the historic interest latent in these stories and
anecdotes to give the reader an illusion of reality. Marcel warns
us that such a novelist 'risque de croire que les choses du passé
ont un charme par elles-mêmes, de les transporter telles quelles
dans son œuvre, mort-née dans ce cas, dégageant un ennui dont
il se console en se disant: "C'est joli parce que c'est vrai."'
What Marcel means, surely, is that for the true artist there is no
such thing as the 'things of the past'; re-created by art, they
present themselves as part of the artist's consciousness. Their
charm is in the realization, procured for us by the artist that what
we wrongly call the past is alive precisely because we are still
conscious of it; it is real and actual just as what is loosely called
'the present' is alive and real.

The problem that torments Marcel has been well stated from
the rational point of view by Pope:

> Yet more; the diff'rence is as great between
> The optics seeing as the objects seen.
> All manners take a tincture from our own,
> Or come discolour'd thro' our passions shown;
> Or fancy's beam enlarges, multiplies,
> Contracts, inverts and gives ten thousand dyes.
>   Nor will life's stream for observation stay,
> It hurries all too fast to mark their way:
> In vain sedate reflections we would make,
> When half our knowledge we must snatch, not take.

Oddly enough, too, Voltaire glimpsed another aspect of the
same problem when in an article on the *Infinite*, he coined the
expression 'la fluence du temps' to distinguish between the
conventional nature of chronological time and what he calls,
anticipating Bergson, 'la durée' which cannot be separated
into past, present and future, 'puisque quelque chose a été
toujours, quelque chose est et sera toujours'.[1]

The force or creative urge emanating from Marcel's impressions of the 'Esprit des Guermantes devant la princesse de
Parme' is not, he admits, to be equated with that originating in
the profounder more concentrated impressions evoked by other

[1] *Dict. phil.* Art. *Infini.*

contacts with nature, especially external nature. This is clear from the absence of that unmistakable sense of joy which differentiates the exaltation of Combray with the febrile, confused excitement of his present mood when his mind seems 'vertigineusement emporté par une force centrifuge'. We should be naïve, however, to construe these reservations and misgivings as Proust's confession of defeat, as an apology or admission that in the long episode under discussion or in his other descriptions of life amongst the Guermantes or Verdurins, the author has abandoned his efforts to enter by the subconscious more deeply into the reality of experience. Indeed, he tacitly invites us, I feel sure, with the justifiable pride of the great artist who is aware of his originality, to judge the tree by its fruits; to compare these descriptions with those of other novelists and ask ourselves which are more real. One may agree with Pope and regard as hopeless Marcel's constant attempts to obtain direct knowledge of 'life's stream' by plunging into it and abandoning himself to the current instead of always resting content with the restricted, artificial views obtained by the self-styled objective and intellectual observer on the bank of the stream. One may deny that there is such a thing as an intuitive faculty which affords a more intimate knowledge of certain aspects of life than is possible by the analysing intelligence alone. Proust believed, however, in the superior 'pouvoir réfléchissant' of the novelist employing the intuitive approach to life: he saw life as movement, as duration, not as something to be cross-sectioned and stopped in its flow by an external, impassive, static and observing intelligence. And in spite of the doubts he attributes to Marcel, the re-creation of the dinner at the Guermantes has a vibrant, living quality. People and things lose that arrested, photographed character peculiar to the conventional 'tableaux de mœurs' of so-called realistic novelists and of writers of memoirs. Even the details concerning genealogy, heraldry, philology and ancient customs which delight Marcel as they fall from the lips of Oriane and Basin are merged into the flashing, vital stream of the narrative. They do not stand up like rocks indicating the finality, the inanimateness of a dead past. Presented by any other novelist, they might, as Marcel fears, render the work of

art 'mort-née'. Viewed, however, by Marcel they have the
vitality of the characters who narrate them, of whose lives they
are an essential element, of those selves into which Marcel tries
to enter by the force of intuition or imaginative sympathy, call it
what you will. They are not transported 'telles quelles' into the
work of art. They have first been assimilated by the consciousness of a great and sensitive artist.

The interview which now takes place between Marcel and
Charlus is extraordinary. Here Proust, that most undramatic
of novelists, presents us with what, in a play, would be called
a *coup de théâtre*, that is to say, an unexpected situation which
astonishes or disconcerts one or more of the personages although, as is subsequently revealed, it has a *necessary* liaison
with everything the spectator knows about the plot, the action
of the play, and with the psychology of the chief characters. The
situation exposed now by Proust is, of course, less surprising
to the reader than to Marcel, who does not yet possess the key
to the enigma of the baron's amazing behaviour. Some days are
to elapse before a chance encounter reveals to him the unnatural,
secret vice which distinguishes the psychology of a Charlus
from that of ordinary men.

Now, this scene of the interview is of capital interest. Proust
is about to embark on a difficult and perilous undertaking, the
nature of which is bluntly stated in the title of his next three
volumes: *Sodome et Gomorrhe*. One might say, indeed, over-
stated, since, as we shall see, these subjects do not, in fact,
constitute the main interest of this section. Proust knows,
however, that the success or failure of this venture will depend
on the first reactions of a public, the overwhelming majority of
whom, although ready to admit that unnatural vice is a social
fact, consider very strongly that it is not a subject to be treated,
save in the veiled manner of a Balzac or Maupassant, by the
novelist or playwright. Proust intends to extend the province
of the novelist by interpreting the psychology and behaviour of
Charlus and his fellow perverts, in short, to portray an aspect
of *mœurs* never hitherto studied in such detail by an imaginative
writer. Now, this scene describing Marcel's interview with
Charlus is, at least for the reader, the immediate prelude to

the *entrée en matière*, to the fortuitous incident which removes with the swiftness and dexterity of a surgical operation, the scales from the eyes of Marcel's intelligence. Proust realizes acutely, therefore, how vital it is at this juncture to discover the right tone, the correct mode of approach to a delicate and forbidden subject. How will Marcel react to this situation? That is very important because, even after his enlightenment, it is through the reflecting agency of his intelligence that we are going to view Charlus and to obtain an increasingly vivid impression of the baron's complex nature. In the scene of the interview it would be dangerously easy, by striking the wrong note, to inspire the reader with repulsion or loathing, with sentiments which Marcel himself, in the whole of his subsequent contacts with Charlus, never in fact experiences because always his attitude to the baron and his vice is that of an artist engaged in the disinterested search of truth, of an artist who believes that by enlarging and deepening his consciousness of life he can get closer to reality than by the purely external and rational approach of medical science.

How then does Proust present this extraordinary situation? First of all, by accentuating its unexpectedness. There is little in the way of preparation. The material setting is negligible for the excellent reason that Marcel, absorbed in his thoughts, only realizes with a start that for half an hour he has been kept waiting in the baron's *salon*, an immense apartment which, he vaguely notes, is predominantly greenish with a few portraits to relieve the austerity. The psychological *mise en scène* is also merely suggested by the attitude of the baron's flunkeys who, as Marcel already knows by hearsay, regard Charlus with the deference accorded to Louis XIV by his favourite courtiers. They are absurdly jealous of any of their companions whom the master has deigned to notice with benevolence.

Marcel, advancing cheerfully into the baron's presence finds him, arrayed in a Chinese dressing-gown, recumbent on a sofa. Lying on the floor is a superb, glittering top-hat. Charlus, ignoring the visitor's outstretched hand, fixes him with an implacable gaze. Completely taken aback, Marcel asks leave to sit down, is contemptuously waved to a Louis XIV *bergère* for

which he selects, instead, a Directoire *chauffeuse*, an error loudly
and derisively commented upon by his host. Marcel is now
treated to a bewildering harangue in the best Charlus manner,
rising swiftly from a studied note of melancholy reproach to
a pitch of ungovernable, almost insane vituperation, distinguished throughout, however, by the speaker's typical fluency
and originality in the choice of epithet. Marcel gathers con-
fusedly that by ignoring certain overtures, 'presqu'une déclara-
tion', symbolized by the gift of a volume ornamented by a
design of forget-me-nots, he has ignominiously failed in what
Charlus describes as the greatest and most terrible test to which
a person of his august position can subject an insignificant little
bourgeois to whom, nevertheless, by a royal caprice, he has
condescended to extend his friendship. This is 'l'épreuve de la
trop grande amabilité'. In medical symbols, Proust expresses
the maniacal rage of this strange and unpredictable creature.
'Je regardais M. de Charlus. Certes sa tête magnifique, et qui
répugnait, l'emportait pourtant sur celle de tous les siens; on
eût dit Apollon vieilli; mais un jus olivâtre, hépatique, semblait
prêt à sortir de sa bouche mauvaise.'[1] Listening, petrified by
the baron's accusations which now include perfidy and slander
as well as ingratitude, the young man senses the presence, in
this megalomaniac, of abnormal passions and irresistible
impulses. Whilst temporarily in the clutches of an *idée fixe*,
this man, he divines, might be capable of incredible hatred, of
sadism or even of murder. Proust, however, is too sure an
artist to linger on this theme.

Like all situations based on a misunderstanding, the situation
created by Marcel's bewildered ignorance of the real motive of
Charlus' fury is predominantly comic or, at most, ironical. I use
the word comic in its highest sense. Proust, therefore, decides
very wisely to treat the incident as comedy and for the reasons
already explained, Marcel's astonishment is swiftly transformed
by an outraged sense of justice by his conviction of innocence,
into an uncontrollable fit of temper. As he cannot strike an
older man, he seizes the baron's magnificent silk hat, jumps on
it, tears it to shreds and throws open the door, behind which he

[1] *Guer.* II, 216.

discovers two silent lackeys trying unsuccessfully to pretend that they are there by accident. Hence Marcel surmises that scenes of this kind are not infrequent. Charlus, whose rages apparently subside as quickly as they arise, follows his guest, protesting and conciliatory, though flaring up again when the latter insists on knowing the names of his accusers. In harmony with the strangeness of this whole episode is a final suggestion of the unreal. In the calm after the tempest, when Charlus has resumed the tone of arrogance mingled with Guermantes persiflage which characterizes his ordinary conversation, Marcel is arrested by the strains of an unseen orchestra playing the opening bars of the third movement of Beethoven's *Pastoral Symphony*.

The episode closes on this impression of unreality. Marcel is still bewildered since obviously he lacks the missing piece to this jig-saw puzzle. Without it he can only form a confused picture of the baron's recent behaviour which, rather vaguely, he describes as 'un état délirant de susceptibilité et d'orgueil'. Is the novelist placing here too great a strain on our credulity? After all, Marcel is a remarkably intelligent and well-read young man. Rumours of the baron's vice must surely have reached his ears if only through that cynic, Bloch. Again, we know that this is not his first private conversation with Charlus. Yet Proust asks us to believe that now, as well as on the occasion of his walk with the baron, Marcel's innocence prevents him from guessing the truth. I do not see why not. Swann, whom Marcel is shortly to meet again, Charles Swann who has known Charlus intimately for years, ridicules the suggestion that the latter is a pervert. And, Marcel, if he had not just then acquired positive proof to the contrary, would probably have believed him. One may quite reasonably conclude, therefore, that before his enlightenment, Marcel had no doubt frequently heard rumours about the morals of Charlus all of which, however, like Swann, he had dismissed as malicious, idle gossip.

Certainly now, listening to the baron's ecstatic praises of the princesse de Guermantes, whom Charlus sets on a plane far above the duchess, her cousin, amused by the Charlusian *boutades* on the social nullity of the Jéna family, the unvindictive Marcel, though anxious to get away without offending his host's susceptibilities, regards the latter with some compassion as an unbalanced egomaniac, fundamentally kind but rather lonely. And the baron's parting words convey just as little to Marcel as the previous crazy harangues:

'Mon rôle est terminé, monsieur; j'y ajoute simplement quelques paroles. Un autre vous offrira peut-être un jour sa sympathie comme j'ai fait. Que l'exemple actuel vous serve d'enseignement. Une sympathie est toujours précieuse. Ce qu'on ne peut pas faire seul dans la vie, parce qu'il y a des choses qu'on ne peut demander, ni faire, ni vouloir, ni apprendre par soi-même, on le peut à plusieurs et sans avoir besoin d'être 13 comme dans le roman de Balzac, ni 4 comme dans *les Trois Mousquetaires*. Adieu.'[1]

Marcel's imagination now plays round a new object, the princesse de Guermantes and her milieu into which no one, it seems, can hope to penetrate without the approval of Charlus. Out of the blue comes an invitation to a grand reception which is to be held in the famous gardens of the prince de Guermantes. Afraid of a mystification, Marcel decides to watch from his staircase for the return of Oriane and Basin who are expected back from Nice that afternoon. They will tell him whether he is the victim or not of a practical joke. But Marcel's curiosity has another, more scientific motive. At the Guermantes' dinner, the duchess had entertained her guests with an amusing account, borrowed from Darwin, of how certain flowers are fertilized, mentioning in particular a rare orchid which she has had placed in the courtyard to await the hazard of pollenation by a bee which must have previously visited a male plant of the same variety. This botanical phenomenon Marcel never witnesses. Instead, he observes an even more remarkable encounter between two members of the human species, Jupien and the baron de Charlus. Jupien is a very subordinate Civil Servant whose niece carries on his former tailoring business in a shop which abuts on the Guermantes property. But the story of this adventure is postponed. Meanwhile, let us follow Marcel to the Guermantes whom he finds on the point of leaving for a dinner at Mme de Saint-Euverte's, after which they are to come home so as to dress for a masked ball. Basin is eagerly looking forward to this event for he has a piquant rendezvous with a new mistress. Marcel finds Swann with the duke in the hall, where they are joined by Oriane, superb in red satin and rubies. Swann has brought the proofs of a study on the coins of the Knights Templar of Rhodes which Oriane, in spite of her husband's impatience, insists on examining.

Proust has two good reasons for reintroducing Oriane and Basin de Guermantes at this stage. One is to complete the fresco entitled *Le côté de Guermantes*; the other is to prepare us for the death of Charles Swann who now reappears after a long absence. Oriane and Basin we shall frequently meet again but no longer in a primary role. Charlus, Albertine, the Verdurins and the violinist, Morel, who is the baron's protégé, now move into the foreground of the novel. Marcel is a now privileged friend of the duke and duchess, the neighbour who drops in casually, the neophyte seeking enlightenment on the mysteries of social precedence.

For the first time we hear Oriane and Basin in conversation with Swann, whose marriage with Odette, naturally, had for a time suspended his former intimate relations with the Guermantes. The Dreyfus case, his increasing ill-health and marriage, have now combined to alter Swann's attitude to the Faubourg Saint-Germain, which he views with a sense of cynical disillusionment. Such is Proust's own prevailing mood as he puts the finishing touches to *Le côté de Guermantes*, accentuating the insensibility, the selfishness, the insincerity and shallowness of the Guermantes way of life. The La Rochefoucauld aspect of his satire emerges brutally in several incidents, notably in that where Swann, pressed by Oriane to say why he will not accompany her on an antiquarian visit to Italy, smilingly replies: 'Mais, ma chère amie, c'est que je serai mort depuis plusieurs mois. D'après les médecins que j'ai consultés, à la fin de l'année, le mal que j'ai et qui peut du reste m'emporter tout de suite, ne me laissera pas en tout cas plus de trois ou quatre mois à vivre, et encore c'est un grand maximum.' Oriane, about to enter the carriage, is for once disconcerted. There is nothing in the code of social etiquette to guide her in a situation of this nature. To be just, she is genuinely shocked by Swann's disclosure. Not so

her husband, who is alarmed lest they be late for dinner:
'Voyons, Oriane ne restez pas à bavarder comme cela et à
échanger vos jérémiades avec Swann, vous savez pourtant que
Mme de Saint-Euverte tient à ce qu'on se mette à table à huit
heures tapant.' Yet when Oriane is dejectedly stepping into the
carriage, Basin, noticing that she is wearing black slippers with
her red dress, sends her upstairs to change them. And, like the
perfect oaf which he can be with no effort whatever, the duke,
whilst waiting for his wife, hurries Marcel and Charles off,
bawling out the following parting words to his old friend: 'Et
puis vous, ne vous laissez pas frapper par ces bêtises des médecins,
que diable! Ce sont des ânes. Vous vous portez comme le Pont
Neuf. Vous nous enterrerez tous!'

This is the climax designed to modify the rather flattering
impressions offered in the description of the dinner-party. It
also affords us more than a glimpse into the conjugal relations
of the duke and duchess which, we learn, exist only in name.
As only Marcel and Charles are present, Basin makes no attempt
to hide his irritation at Oriane's flippant remarks on the stuf-
finess and pomposity of the prince and princesse de Guermantes
whose annoyance he shares at his wife's latest indiscretion
in calling on the President of the Republic. Oriane spiritedly
retorts that Basin never once refused an invitation to dine at
Chantilly when Napoleon III was in power. In these alterca-
tions the Guermantes' charm loses much of its attractive gloss
and Proust delicately suggests that the duchess, though still
beautiful and *spirituelle*, is about to lose her radiance. From
Marcel we learn that if no servants remain long with the Guermantes, it is because Oriane, using her *concierge* as a scapegoat,
maliciously foments their quarrels. Unhappy herself, she cannot
bear to see the naïve joy of Basin's footman when the duke gives
him the evening off. As on a former occasion she cancels the
permission on a frivolous pretext. 'Elle éprouva', notes Marcel,
'comme un serrement de cœur et une démangeaison de tous ses
membres à la vue de ce bonheur qu'on prenait à son insu, en se
cachant d'elle, duquel elle était irritée et jalouse.' And when, to
annoy the duke and entertain her two visitors, Oriane forces
her celebrated *esprit des Guermantes*, it rapidly degenerates into

something like preciosity. Thus, searching for an original reply to Swann's remark that King Théodose, whom they are soon to meet at the prince de Guermantes, is both agreeable and witty, the duchess, though delighted at the prospect, automatically camouflages her true sentiments by these words: 'Avez-vous remarqué parmi les princes que les plus gentils ne le sont pas tout à fait. Mais si, je vous assure! Il faut toujours qu'ils aient une opinion sur tout. Alors comme ils n'en ont aucune, ils passent une partie de leur vie à nous demander les nôtres, et la seconde à nous les resservir.' This is pure *marivaudage*; though Marivaux himself seldom descended to such a level of banality.

Chapter V

SODOME ET GOMORRHE

CERTAINLY Boileau never visualized the profound implications of the well-known lines which open the third canto of his *Art poétique*:

Il n'est point de serpent, ni de monstre odieux,
Qui, par l'art imité ne puisse plaire aux yeux....

We know from the context that he was thinking, immediately, of Racinian tragedy, probably of *Phèdre*. Nor did this orthodox Catholic and intransigent neo-classic ever mean us to interpret his couplet as a Magna Carta of the artist, or a challenge that fine art is above morals; that there is no subject, however repulsive, physically or morally, in real life, which cannot be alchemized by the great artist into a thing of beauty and thus, because it gives pleasure to the beholder, shorn of its habitual or traditional power to shock the latter's moral sensibility. Yet such is precisely the doctrine implicit in Boileau's lines and so it has since been interpreted, at least in theory if not always in practice, by generations of artists, whatever their other conceptions of art. Romantics, Realists, Naturalists, and more recently, Existentialists have all claimed that art, by virtue of its unique beauty, transcends morality. It is this attitude which has been most strikingly revealed, in literature, by the novelist and the playwright whose work brings them into direct touch with contemporary manners and morals. Indeed, viewed from this angle, the French novel is peculiarly interesting; Proust is only one of a series of novelists who have run counter to the accepted moral prejudices of their day by introducing 'forbidden' themes into their fictions. But Proust differs from his predecessors in two important respects. His subject, unnatural vice, is infinitely more revolting to the general public than any hitherto selected by a novelist for artistic treatment. He approaches it, moreover, in the spirit of a purely disinterested artist whose sole object is to present his vision of a certain aspect of life and by sheer art to

force us as did Racine in *Phèdre* to lose our moral revulsion in
our admiration for the genius of the artist. To paraphrase
Boileau's axiom, Proust's aim is to make us forget the odious-
ness of the 'monstre' in the pleasure we derive from its transformation into the work of art.

Marcel, whose intelligence is centred on the fascinating subject of botanical cross-pollination, is watching the orchid in the
courtyard of the Guermantes for the arrival of the problematical
humble-bee. At that moment, the baron de Charlus, who is
calling on Mme de Villeparisis, crosses the observer's field of
vision. Charlus, quite unaware of this, is off his guard. All the
severity and virility has vanished from his expression and his
demeanour. What the astonished Marcel observes is described
in the following words:

> Clignant des yeux contre le soleil, il semblait presque sourire, je
> trouvai à sa figure vue ainsi au repos et comme au naturel quelque
> chose de si affectueux, de si désarmé, que je ne pus m'empêcher de
> penser combien M. de Charlus eût été fâché s'il avait pu se savoir
> regardé; car ce à quoi me faisait penser cet homme qui était si épris,
> qui se piquait si fort de virilité, à qui tout le monde semblait odieuse-
> ment efféminé, ce à quoi il me faisait penser tout d'un coup, tant il en
> avait passagèrement les traits, l'expression, le sourire, c'était à une
> femme.[1]

This is swiftly followed by an even more stupefying revelation:
the meeting between the baron and Jupien whose grotesque
attitudes, gestures and expressions Proust, in a far-fetched simile,
compares to the poses that might have been adopted by the rare
orchid in the presence of the providential humble-bee. 'Cette
scène', pursues Marcel, 'n'était du reste pas positivement
comique, elle était empreinte d'une étrangeté ou si l'on veut
dire, d'un naturel dont la beauté allait croissant.' I doubt if any
reader will share this view. On the contrary, though Proust
employs every device of style—and that is saying a great deal—
to lend artistic beauty to his account of the sordid happenings
now enacted in Jupien's shop and overheard by Marcel through
the partition, the whole episode must be regarded as one of the
author's least successful transpositions or analogies. In vain, the

[1] *SG.* I, 257–8.

novelist tries to distract our attention from its essential and brutal ugliness by his allusions to oriental cities and by images borrowed from ornithological and botanical lore. The wealth of analogies which Proust seeks to establish between the fertilization processes of various species of plants and the abnormal *mœurs* of various subspecies of humanity form a most unconvincing and unpleasant prelude to a sombre exegesis of the origins, evolution and ramifications of paederasty. In connection with this particular section of *A la recherche du temps perdu* but with this section only, I am compelled to admit the justice of Alain's criticism, if not for quite the same reasons as those advanced by that brilliant and veteran critic:

Mais ce romancier, parmi d'idées vivantes en a gardé une à l'état de mort, qui est qu'il y a deux espèces d'hommes et aussi deux espèces de femmes; ce n'est que la folle idée de Lombroso, maintenant jugée. Et ce préjugé d'école fait tache et vilaine tache en cette œuvre magistrale comme un informe paquet de fil dans une toile bien tissée.

Proust, by accentuating the 'scientific' nature of his approach to the problem of unnatural vice, the exponents of which he regards as the predestined victims of a special racial heredity; by comparing their terrible 'goût spécial' to any other inherited disposition, exposes himself deservedly to the objections raised by Alain. How do we know, asks the latter, that a man is born a monster like Charlus or Jupien, that he *naturally* possesses their abnormal habits? I may be born with formidable hands but it does not follow that I am a born strangler. Alain echoes the common sense of Molière who echoed the common sense of the average Frenchman. Remember that passage in *Les Fourberies de Scapin* where Argante, enraged at the fatalist's cry that he has been 'poussé par sa destinée' retorts: 'Ah! ah! voici une raison la plus belle du monde. On n'a plus qu'à commettre tous les crimes imaginables, tromper, voler, assassiner, et dire pour excuse qu'on a été poussé par sa destinée.'

Now one may, like Alain, disagree with Proust's deterministic conception of homosexuality and prefer the more usual view that it is a vice which the law is right in punishing with great severity because its adepts are just as answerable for their behaviour as any other criminals. But this has nothing to do with the art of the novel. It is not a question of whether the reader considers perverts to be loathsome criminals or whether he regards them as the pitiable victims of fatality. In fairness to the artist, his work must be judged only from the æsthetic point of view. Charlus, Jupien and their kind are, as Proust is the first to admit, ugly people. The sensations and impressions they evoke are repellent. The question, however, is whether the novelist succeeds, by his art, in presenting them in such a light as to make the reader forget his moral objections, his involuntary revulsion. The murder of the good and venerable King Duncan is a horrible reality and so is the slaughter of Macduff's wife and children. Yet these events, woven into the beautiful pattern of *Macbeth*, acquire a new significance in the contemplation of which the spectator experiences not revulsion but a sense of wonder and of awe. At the close of *A la recherche du temps perdu* can it be said that Proust, in portraying his perverts and their perversity has achieved this miracle of art? That remains to be seen. Meanwhile, let us for a moment refrain from accepting Alain's sweeping verdict and consider the episode in which Proust claims to see a strange beauty and naturalness: the scene of Jupien's first meeting with Charlus. Here I think the author deludes himself. The actions and conversations he describes may have occurred in reality. But the method of their interpretation is unconvincing. The antics of the characters do not strike us as natural, beautiful or even comic but as unreal and revolting to our sense of human dignity. Moreover, Proust's exegesis of paederasty is a digression which, apart from anything else, suffices to break the unity of the artist's design. These twenty-seven pages of the first part of *Sodome et Gomorrhe* should have been entirely cut out or recast. It is these and not the many subsequent passages featuring Charlus and his satellites that constitute the 'vilaine tache' referred to by Alain. The trouble appears to have started with Proust's botanical symbol of the orchid and the humble-bee. This analogy is overworked until it dies an inevitable death. At no time does the author succeed in convincing us that what is natural, curious and beautiful in the world of plants is natural or beautiful in the human species. In other words, the 'monstre odieux' refuses to 'plaire aux yeux'.

That, however, is a vastly different thing from saying that Proust repeated this artistic blunder throughout the whole novel. We shall find, on the contrary, that Charlus emerges as one of the most interesting creations of the novelist's imagination. The incident we have just discussed and which Proust thought essential to the enlightenment of Marcel, does not really detract from the value of the author's complete study. The interpretation of the baron's relations with the violinist, Morel, like the terrible picture of Charlus in his last phase, which is on an entirely different plane, does much to abolish the unfortunate impression produced at the opening of *Sodome et Gomorrhe*. There are certain sense experiences which resist the efforts of the most talented artist to fuse them into the harmony and unity of the work of art. Proust was aware of this when, in portraying the Charlus-Jupien incident, he attributed the following words to Marcel: 'Quand je ne suivais que mon instinct la méduse me répugnait a Balbec; mais si je savais la regarder comme Michelet du point de vue de l'histoire naturelle et de l'esthétique, je voyais une délicieuse girandole d'azur.' He fails, nevertheless, to make us see Charlus and Jupien in this light. The jelly-fish remains a horrible jelly-fish. Not even Proust's art can transform it into an azure sea-flower. That is because we are not scientists looking at aquatic creatures but average human beings looking at creatures of our own species. It does not follow, either, that we are on this account what Baudelaire calls 'hypocrites lecteurs'.

Proust's habitual tact and sense of proportion are reasserted in the next volume. In all the scenes involving Charlus, the prevailing atmosphere is that of comedy. Witness the conversation between the baron and the fearful Vaugoubert, who are inspecting the guests, from their own peculiar viewpoint, as the latter queue up to be received by the prince de Guermantes! Comic, also, in the Le Sage sense, is the panic of the young duc de Chatellrault and the consternation of the stentorian flunkey who discovers the identity of the mysterious 'Anglais' of the Avenue Gabriel. In the same mood, transposing the sinister into the grotesque, Proust describes the baron's arrogant yet furtive approaches to Victurnien and Arnulphe, the marmoreal but half-witted twin sons of the regal Mme Surgis-le-Duc. Thus, whilst never abandoning the subject that is very much in Marcel's thoughts since his recent *éclaircissement*, Proust discreetly fits it into its proper perspective. His chief object, here, is to portray Charlus in society, the formidable arbiter in all matters affecting social precedence. Observe him, therefore, on the terrace commanding the gardens, a Whistler symphony in black and white, or as Marcel notes, in black, white and red for he is wearing the chevalier's cross of the Knights of Malta. Every guest, before descending the staircase leading to this modern Eden, must pass before the dark angel whose impertinent, ironical scrutiny is more intimidating than any flaming sword. If Marcel needed any confirmation of his previous impression of the 'lâcheté des gens du monde' here is ample demonstration. All save the Guermantes pay obsequious homage to this megalomaniac, cowed by the ever-present threat of the baron's implacable vindictiveness and by the inexhaustible verve of his malicious eloquence. Marcel is the embarrassed witness of an incident which reveals the astonishing quality of the Charlusian *libido dominandi* and the craven servility of these fashionable toadies. Mme de Saint-Euverte, whom Charlus detests, is giving a garden-party on the following day and is assiduously moving from group to group, making certain that her guests have not forgotten. As bad luck will have it, she is cornered in an alcove behind Charlus, Marcel and Mme de Surgis. The baron seizes the opportunity:

Une niaise question que je lui posai sans malice [says Marcel], lui fournit l'occasion d'un triomphal couplet dont la pauvre de Saint-Euverte, quasi immobilisée derrière nous, ne pouvait guère perdre un mot. 'Croyez-vous que cet impertinent jeune homme', dit-il en me désignant à Mme de Surgis, 'vient de me demander, sans le moindre souci qu'on doit avoir de cacher ces sortes de besoins, si j'allais chez Mme de Saint-Euverte, c'est-à-dire, je pense, si j'avais la colique. Je tâcherais en tout cas de m'en soulager dans un endroit plus confortable que chez une personne qui, si j'ai bonne mémoire, célébrait son centenaire quand je commençai à aller dans le monde, c'est-à-dire pas chez elle. Et pourtant, qui plus qu'elle serait intéressante à entendre. Que de souvenirs historiques, vus et vécus du temps du Premier Empire et de la Restauration, que d'histoires intimes aussi qui n'avaient certainement rien de "Saint" mais devaient être très "Vertes", si l'on en croit la cuisse restée légère de la vénérable gambadeuse. Ce qui m'empêcherait de l'interroger sur ces époques passionnantes, c'est la sensibilité de mon appareil olfactif. La proximité de la dame suffit.'[1]

[A silly question I asked him without any mischievous intention, furnished him with the opportunity for a triumphal tirade not one word of which could have been missed by the wretched Saint-Euverte who was, so to speak, immobilized behind us. 'Would you believe that this impertinent young man', he said, pointing me out to Mme de Surgis, 'has just asked me, without bothering in the least to observe the proper reticence in regard to needs of this sort, whether I was in the habit of calling upon Mme de Saint-Euverte, in other words, I imagine, whether I was afflicted with the gripes. I should endeavour in any case to relieve myself somewhere more comfortable than at the house of a person who, if my memory serves me right, was celebrating her centenary when I began to move in Society, that is to say, not in her house. And yet who would be more interesting to listen to than she? What a profusion of historic events seen and experienced under the First Empire and the Restoration, how many intimate revelations, too, which certainly did not merit the epithet "saint" but must have been extremely "vertes" if one may judge from the friskiness still left in those venerable hams. What would prevent me from questioning her about these exciting times is the sensitiveness of my olfactory organ. The proximity of the lady is enough.']

This is sufficiently outrageous and becomes more so. But what is really stupefying and what disgusts Marcel is the behaviour of Mme de Saint-Euverte when she finally manages to slip out of the alcove, inadvertently brushing against Charlus.

'Oh! pardon, monsieur de Charlus, j'espère que je ne vous ai pas fait mal', s'écria-t-elle comme si elle s'agenouillait devant son maître. Celui-ci ne daigna répondre autrement que par un large sourire ironique et concéda seulement un 'bonsoir' comme s'il apercevait seulement de la présence de la marquise une fois qu'elle l'avait salué la première, était une insulte de plus. Enfin, avec une platitude suprême dont je souffris pour elle, Mme de Saint-Euverte s'approcha de moi, et, m'ayant pris à l'écart me dit à l'oreille: 'Mais, qu'ai-je fait à M. de Charlus? On prétend qu'il ne me trouve pas assez chic pour lui', dit-elle, en riant à gorge déployée.[2]

'Ce sont les esclaves qui font les tyrans; ce ne sont pas les tyrans qui font les esclaves.' The profound truth of Duclos'

---

[1] *SG.* ii (1), 99–100.   [2] *SG.* ii (1), 101.

maxim is richly illustrated in this account of the reception at the prince de Guermantes'. The despotism of Charlus is explained by the snobbery and inane ambitions of the Faubourg Saint-Germain, which imagines itself still to be the apex of French society, refusing to admit, despite the Revolution, that it is now an anachronism, though often to be reckoned with by politicians because of its wealth and its military or international affiliations. What Marcel discovers is that the Faubourg Saint-Germain is not an assembly of peers but a society with various estates, a hierarchy in a perpetual flux, composed of subgroups with constantly altering contours. At the moment, the rhythm of this movement has been quickened by the Dreyfus case, which will shortly draw the *salons* of Odette and of Mme Verdurin into the sphere now dominated by the Guermantes, the Courvoisiers and other ancient houses. Inside the clan of the Guermantes a revolution is in progress, the story of which is narrated by Swann to Marcel.

Let us, however, follow the latter as he moves from group to group, vainly trying to find someone to introduce him to his host. He has already been received by the princess. Once again, Marcel encounters the 'lâcheté des gens du monde' of which Mme de Souvré furnishes a typical example. This lady, waiting till the prince is looking in another direction, takes the young man maternally by the shoulders and thrusts him forward, smiling at her host's averted profile. As a result, Marcel is exactly where he started. Charlus, to whom he appeals, is about to effect the introduction but when Marcel, in order to justify his request foolishly remarks that of course he knows the prince and princess quite well, the irascible baron turns his back: 'Hé bien, si vous les connaissez bien, en quoi avez-vous besoin de moi pour vous présenter?' At last, however, the obliging De Bréauté comes to his rescue. Now Marcel discovers, after a short conversation, that for all his grave formalism and aloofness, Gilbert de Guermantes is at heart simple and kindly; the really arrogant Guermantes is Basin, whose affected camaraderie and simplicity conceal an immense disdain for his social inferiors.

As Marcel unreels his ribbon of impressions one's mind turns unbidden to the great French classic observers, to La Rochefoucauld, Saint-Simon and La Bruyère. Proust does not imitate their style, yet the world he shows us here is still essentially the world they reflected with such forthrightness and perspicacity. Note, for example, the instinctive pleasure evinced by the prince's guests when Mme d'Arpajon is drenched by the spray from the fountain; their eager and absurd credulity when the rumour spreads that Gilbert de Guermantes, perceiving the entrance of Swann, had personally shown him the door; the fiction of the measles epidemic invented by the envious colonel de Froberville in order to dissuade Oriane from appearing at Mme de Saint-Euverte's garden party. Observe, too, the little comedy enacted by Basin and his duchess. The duke, in his typical more-in-sorrow-than-in-anger voice is stripping the last rag from the reputation of his old friend Charles Swann, now condemned as a Dreyfusard and, therefore, a bad Frenchman. Oriane, appealed to for corroboration, puts up a superb performance as a stage *ingénue*:

'Hé bien! je me rappelle quand elle a appris le mariage de Swann, elle s'est sentie froissée; elle a trouvé que c'était mal de quelqu'un à qui nous avions témoigné tant d'amitié. Elle aimait beaucoup Swann; elle a eu beaucoup de chagrin. N'est-ce pas, Oriane?' Mme de Guermantes crut devoir répondre à une interpellation aussi directe, sur un point de fait qui lui permettrait, sans en avoir l'air, de confirmer des louanges qu'elle sentait terminées. D'un ton timide et simple, et un air d'autant plus appris qu'il voulait paraître 'senti', elle dit avec une douceur réservée, 'C'est vrai, Basin ne se trompe pas.'[1]

I have always felt that great novels divide naturally into two categories. In one, the novelist selects a certain spiritual climate for the development of his theme, characters and of the action. *La Princesse de Clèves, Manon Lescaut* and *L'Education sentimentale* are novels of a single climate. In the second category I should place *A la recherche du temps perdu*. For it is a world of many climates and temperatures of the soul in each of which the author moves with the perfect ease that comes from long acclimatization, though that is, of course, the illusion produced by the genius of the artist whose powerful imagination and sensitive intuition would enable him to re-create an Amazonian

[1] *SG.* II (1), 69–70.

forest from the scent of an orchid in a Paris florist's shop. In the episode of the reception at the prince de Guermantes', the prevailing climate is that of intellectual comedy, the climate of Molière's 'philosophic' plays. From this atmosphere Proust now slips imperceptibly into that scene where Swann, who has not long to live, has a confidential talk with Marcel. The tone is now graver, in harmony with the circumstances. Their conversation, however, is continually and exasperatingly interrupted and this, in a very natural way, allows Proust to retain an undertone of comedy. Here is Marcel's impression of Swann; it needs no gloss.

Il y a certains Israelites, très fins pourtant et mondains délicats, chez lesquels restent en réserve et dans la coulisse, afin de faire leur entrée à une heure donnée de leur vie, comme dans une pièce, un mufle et un prophète. Swann était arrivé à l'âge du prophète. Certes, avec sa figure d'où, sous l'action de la maladie, des segments entiers avaient disparu comme dans un bloc de glace qui fond et dont des pans entiers sont tombés, il avait bien changé.[1]

Yet this is the same man whom Marcel, in the days of his infatuation for Gilberte, regarded as a sort of demi-god, shrouded in mystery, endowed with all the perfections.

Swann discloses a secret imparted to him by the prince de Guermantes. This confirmed anti-Dreyfusard confesses that for some time he has been tormented by doubts concerning the guilt of Alfred Dreyfus. After carefully examining the proceedings, he is now convinced that a terrible injustice has been committed, involving the honour of the French army. At the same time, unknown to her husband, his wife has undergone a similar change of heart. Both feel it their duty to inform Charles Swann of their conversion and to resume their former relations with him. Marcel observes the interesting effect of this revelation on Swann. As a Jew, of course, he is touched and pleased. But, as a volunteer of 1870 and a member of the Jockey Club he refuses, later on, to allow Bloch to send Gilbert de Guermantes a copy of the revisionist petition for signature. Moreover, he does not sign it himself. And, to the annoyance of Bloch and the Dreyfusards, when Charles Swann is buried

---

[1] *SG.* II (1), 86.

military honours are paid to the deceased, who is a chevalier of the Legion of Honour, in deference to the wish expressed in his will.

'A mesure qu'on a plus d'esprit, on trouve qu'il y a plus d'hommes originaux.' How often we are reminded of Pascal's words as we follow Marcel's efforts to discover the truth about his fellow-men. How often, also, as in the scene we are discussing, Proust illustrates his conviction that our relations even with our most intimate friends are largely based on misunderstanding and ignorance; that life, in short, is a play governed by no classic unities, where the action consists, no doubt, in a progressive enlightenment, but an enlightenment due to the effect of hasard rather than to the inductive powers of our intelligence. Marcel who now knows, or thinks he knows, the whole truth about Charlus listens with a certain irritation to Saint-Loup's furious outbursts against his uncle. Robert looks on Charlus as a *coureur de femmes*—witness his attentions to Mme de Molé and to Mme de Surgis. How dare this hypocrite set himself up as his nephew's mentor in the affair of Rachel which had led to the convocation of a family council in order to curb the young man's extravagance? Marcel is astonished, too, at Swann's blindness, forgetting that his own eyes have only recently been opened. However, these experiences sharpen his perceptiveness. In conversation with the princesse de Guermantes, he notes that when the baron's name crops up her attention is suddenly arrested. Soon afterwards, driving with her, Marcel insists, despite her embarrassment, in taking charge of a letter which she wants to post. Inadvertently he sees that it is addressed to Charlus. Now, when she alludes to the baron it is possible to decipher her language. He holds the key.

Whilst Marcel complacently notes the progress he has made in his researches into human nature, Proust sounds an ironical and ominous note. Swann, surveying that terrible period in his life which ended in his marriage to Odette, asks his young friend if he has ever been jealous. Marcel promptly replies that he has never experienced jealousy and does not even know what it is. Yet soon he is to know all its horrors though in a form unknown to Swann. No inkling of this clouds his mind, of course, as he gaily drives back with Basin and Oriane to keep his rendezvous with Albertine who is to visit him after the theatre. She has been to see *Phèdre*. It is only when he arrives at his flat and learns from Françoise that Albertine has not kept her promise, that Marcel has his first vague premonition of the sufferings which are to come from his association with this elusive and mysterious girl. As he waits anxiously for her telephone call, however, Marcel does not realize that the seeds of love and jealousy have already begun to germinate. His intelligence, which has taught him so much about the secret passions of others, does not illuminate his own soul. But the simple peasant, Françoise, who meets Albertine in the hall, knows instinctively from the girl's first words that she will bring sorrow to her master. And Marcel, who has already been irritated by Albertine's evasions on the telephone, is suddenly possessed by a sense of foreboding as he listens to Françoise:

> Celle-la, sans proférer aucune plainte, ayant même l'air d'étouffer de son mieux une toux irrésistible, et croisant seulement sur elle son châle comme si elle avait froid commença par me raconter tout ce qu'elle avait dit à Albertine, n'ayant pas manqué de lui demander des nouvelles de sa tante, — 'Justement j'y disais, monsieur devait avoir crainte que mademoiselle ne vienne plus, parce que ce n'est pas une heure pour venir, c'est bientôt le matin. Mais elle devait être dans des endroits qu'elle s'amusait bien car elle ne m'a pas seulement dit qu'elle était contrariée d'avoir fait attendre monsieur, elle m'a répondu d'un air de se fiche du monde: "Mieux vaut tard que jamais!"' Et Françoise ajouta ces mots qui me percèrent le cœur: ' — En parlant comme ça elle s'est vendue. Elle aurait peut-être bien voulu se cacher mais....'[1]

Albertine makes only a fleeting entrance: she will reappear at Balbec, which Marcel now revisits.

The narrative of this final sojourn at the Grand Hôtel opens a chapter called 'Les Intermittences du Cœur'. Proust very soon explains the meaning of this title. After a humorous impression of the manager of the hotel with his ineffable malapropisms, we are suddenly transported into those mysterious regions of the soul from which long imprisoned realities are liberated and presented to the intelligence by a process which one can only compare to the unexpected opening of a strong-room

[1] *SG.* II (1), 148.

door when someone accidentally stumbles on the essential missing letter of the combination. Marcel, who is suffering from cardiac fatigue, after his train journey, stoops painfully to take off his shoes.

Mais à peine eus-je touché le premier bouton de ma bottines, ma poitrine s'enfla, remplie d'une présence inconnue, divine, des sanglots me secouèrent, des larmes ruisselèrent de mes yeux. L'être qui venait a mon secours, qui me sauvait de la sécheresse de l'âme, c'était celui qui, plusieurs années auparavant, dans un moment de détresse et de solitude identiques, dans un moment où je n'avais plus rien de moi, était entré, et qui m'avait rendu à moi-même, car il était moi et plus que moi (le contenant qui est plus que le contenu et me l'apportait). Je venais d'apercevoir, dans ma mémoire, penché sur ma fatigue, le visage tendre, préoccupé et déçu de ma grand'mère, telle qu'elle avait été ce premier soir d'arrivée, le visage de ma grand'mère, non pas de celle que je m'étais étonné et reproché de si peu regretter et qui n'avait d'elle que le nom, mais de ma grand'mère véritable dont pour la première fois depuis les Champs-Elysées ou elle avait eu son attaque, je retrouvais dans un souvenir involontaire et complet la réalité vivante. Cette réalité n'existe pas pour nous tant qu'elle n'a pas été récrée par notre pensée.[1]

[But I had scarcely touched the topmost button of my boot when my bosom swelled, filled with an unknown, divine presence. I was shaken with sobs, tears streamed from my eyes. The being which came to my rescue, saving me from the aridity of my soul, was the one which, several years before, in a moment of identical distress and loneliness, at a moment when I no longer possessed anything of myself, had come in and had restored me to myself. For it was I and more than I (the container that is greater than the contained and was bringing it to me). I had just perceived, in my memory, bending over my fatigue, the tender, preoccupied, disappointed face of my grandmother, as she had been that first evening we arrived, my grandmother's face, not the face of her whom I had been astonished and remorseful at having so little missed, and who had nothing in common with her save her name, but of my real grandmother, of whom, for the first time since her stroke in the Champs-Elysées, I rediscovered the living reality in an involuntary and complete recollection. This reality does not exist for us so long as it has not been re-created by our thought.]

Once again we are reminded that *A la recherche du temps perdu* is not just the story of Marcel's (or Proust's) progressive efforts to understand and interpret the behaviour and the psychological states of the characters whose lives at every moment impinge upon and intermingle with his own life. It is not merely the narrative of his attempts to endow with the beauty or unity of art, to externalize for us, his sensations or impressions of the material world surrounding him. It is also the story of Marcel's gradual discovery that the self, the *moi* called Marcel which is always striving to penetrate by sympathy and at the same time to perceive by the intellect, the reality of external things and people—that this self is never static, never, as Proust says, 'une âme totale', in the sense that all its powers of imagination, sensation, perception and memory are completely and ever available. Sometimes this discovery, as in the present instance, is accompanied by the greatest anguish. Yet does not Proust tacitly imply that this suffering, for the artist, will eventually be tempered by the sense of spiritual satisfaction which comes from the possession of a truth, from the discovery of a reality?

In these pages, I think for the first time, a French novelist expresses in language of surprising lucidity, the reality of a spiritual experience which, although universal, has probably never been so arrestingly externalized by a novelist. Marcel, describes what happens when an everyday action—that of stooping to unbutton his shoes—releases from the subconscious the self, the spiritual state which was his on that evening of his first visit to Balbec. The psychological atmosphere surrounding the original action, like Marcel's image of his grandmother as she really was, had, in the meantime, remained in the Aladdin's cave of the subconscious waiting for the Open Sesame; the repetition of the original action in a milieu and in circumstances re-creating the cadre or ambience of his state of soul at Balbec, of the *moi* which was then Marcel. But why does he only now experience the living reality of his grandmother's death, so long after the fact? Proust explains what he calls this anachronism, this 'lack of synchronization between the calendar of facts and that of our feelings'. True, Marcel had often thought of his grandmother and in the year after her death, had often spoken of her. But other impressions, other memories, the habit of seeing her during her last illness had suppressed the memory of what she had *really* meant to him. 'Car aux troubles de la

mémoire sont liées les intermittences du cœur.' Probably, thinks
Marcel, it is because of the existence of our body that we are apt
to believe that all our past joys and griefs are perpetually in our
possession enclosed as in a vase. In point of fact, only a part,
often the part least important for our true or spiritual existence,
is present in our consciousness. The sensations and emotions
that are most truly and profoundly our *moi* are thrust down into
that *domaine inconnu*, the subconscious.

'Le moi [says Marcel] que j'étais alors et qui avait disparu si
longtemps, était de nouveau si près de moi qu'il me semblait encore
entendre les paroles qui avaient immédiatement précédé et qui
n'étaient pourtant plus qu'un songe, comme un homme mal éveillé
croit percevoir tout près de lui les bruits de son rêve qui s'enfuit.[1]

This theme, admirably described as 'l'incompréhensible contradiction du souvenir et du néant', has inspired some of the finest
pages in world literature. Explored anew by Proust, it acquires
a fresh density of meaning, chiefly, no doubt, because Marcel
exfoliates not only his conscious but his subconscious mind, even
his sleeping mind. For, as he tells us, the world of sleep reflects
and refracts 'la douleureuse synthèse de la survivance et du
néant'. This remarkable episode represents, therefore, the most
serious attempt ever made by a novelist to communicate, without
recourse to the language of mystic symbolism, all the sensations,
emotions, thoughts and even the hallucinations of a bereaved soul.

Marcel's involuntary memory of his grandmother produces
an immediate sense of infinite happiness, which swiftly disappears with the realization that she is lost to him for ever. Then
comes remorse, bitter and inexorable. With painful clarity,
tormented by futile self-reproach, he remembers his cruel and
thoughtless behaviour on that day when his grandmother had
asked Saint-Loup to photograph her. She wore, to Marcel's
annoyance, a wide-brimmed hat chosen deliberately, he now learns
from Françoise, so as to hide the ravages of her malady. To-day,
with almost masochistic tenacity, he broods on other recollections, equally painful, as if to atone thereby for the suffering he
inflicted on the beloved dead one. But Marcel suggests with
typical integrity that whilst he is trying to immobilize this mood,

[1] *SG.* II (1), 179.

to retain its terrible intactness; whilst he is striving to remain, as it were, naked and exposed to the excruciating frozen bleakness of this spiritual climate, he becomes aware of a subtle alteration. His intelligence, that vigilant and docile servant of the instinct for self-preservation, is already at work. Thus, even when Marcel clings remorsefully to these sad images they begin to fade. He experiences a certain sweetness and serenity and recalls happier moments spent in conversation with his grandmother.

Proust has a genius for penetrative observation, for revealing, as I said, the true density of his theme. To meditate on these observations of Marcel's is to realize the fallacy of La Bruyère's 'Tout est dit' and the wisdom of Bossuet who wrote: 'Après 6000 ans d'observation, l'esprit humain n'est pas encore épuisé; il cherche, et il trouve encore afin qu'il connaisse qu'il peut trouver jusqu'à l'infini.'[1] Certainly, to some extent, Proust's originality as a novelist is due to his courage and sincerity in exploring aspects of life and morals avoided by his predecessors. But he is most profoundly original when, as in the present instance, his great talent for psychological analysis is employed to investigate experience of a more universal nature. Note, for instance, the complexity and suggestiveness of his orchestration of a theme which, in the novels of the abbé Prévost, is expressed in six words: 'il était idolâtre de sa tristesse.' And yet, Proust retains the classic quality of restraint we admire so much in Prévost and Mme de La Fayette. His pages leave ample margins for our speculation: they are always richly suggestive. Do not let us be misled by Proust's lucidity of utterance into thinking, like one of his critics, that he has no philosophy. It is not difficult to prove the superficiality of that opinion. How is it possible, for example, not to discern the philosophic implications of Marcel's observations? Here, surely, we have in essence a 'philosophy of remorse', Proust's conception of remorse as a reassertion of the human spirit, or if one may so describe it— the operation of the law of spiritual gravity which can only function, however, intermittently because it is superseded by a much stronger law: the instinct for self-preservation, 'l'ingéniosité de l'intelligence de nous préserver de la douleur'.

---

[1] *Connaissance de Dieu et de soi-même*, v, 5.

In this way, Marcel finds relief from the intolerable memories, deliberately invoked by himself, of the thoughtless cruelties he inflicted on his grandmother. He notes, simply, that these painful recollections were gradually replaced by gentler ones when he recalled certain of her opinions. Undoubtedly he has in mind one particular conversation in which his grandmother, disturbed by Marcel's remark that he could not possibly live without her, gently said: 'Il faut nous faire un cœur plus dur que ça. Sans cela, que deviendrais-tu si je partais en voyage?' Does Marcel now grasp the wisdom, the eternal human sadness condensed in these words? It is the tragic truth uttered by Pascal: 'Il est injuste qu'on s'attache à moi, quoiqu'on le fasse avec plaisir et volontairement. Je tromperais ceux à qui j'en ferais naître le désir, car je ne suis la fin de personne et n'ai pas de quoi les satisfaire.'[1] Always Marcel's grandmother was haunted by this thought, for she knew her grandson's insatiable craving for affection, the desolating sense of loneliness when his sensibility met with no response. Yet, because she was not a religious woman, she could not honestly imitate the example of Pascal and warn the boy that, by concentrating his tenderness upon her instead of upon God, he was doomed to be tormented, after her death, by the incomprehensible contradiction between his surviving, vivid memories of what she had meant to him and the inexorable fact that she is dead.

But there is a domain where the subconscious is supreme. It is the mysterious world of sleep. Here the intelligence, the will, the instinct for self-preservation lose their powers. Here there is no escape from remorse.

Monde du sommeil où la connaissance interne, placée sous la dépendance des troubles de nos organes, accélère le rythme du cœur ou de la respiration, parce qu'une même dose d'effroi, de tristesse, de remords agit, avec une puissance centuplée si elle est ainsi injectée dans nos veines; dès que pour y parcourir les artères de la cité souterraine nous nous sommes embarqués sur les flots noirs de notre propre sang comme sur un Léthé intérieur aux sextuples replis, de grandes figures solennelles nous apparaissent, nous abordent et nous quittent, nous laissant en larmes.[2]

---

[1] *Pensées* (ed. L. Brunschvicg), p. 548, *Pensée* 471.   [2] *SG.* II (1), 183.

In his dreams, Marcel is transported into a country infinitely more desolate even than the region haunted by his waking remorse, into a country swept by bitter winds, the abode of darkness and death. Yet somehow, in his vain attempts to overcome the invisible obstacles that prevent him from reaching that solitary, weeping figure who is his grandmother, Marcel knows that she is not dead. His father, to whom he appeals for help, gently tries to persuade his son to abandon his search, returning evasive answers to Marcel's anxious questions. When the morning sunshine rescues him from this nightmare, he closes the shutters, unable to look upon the indifferent and superb beauty of the sea upon which his grandmother loved to gaze for hours on end. And when Marcel turns his face to the wall, it is to remember with keen, stabbing grief the first night in the Grand Hôtel when his grandmother, afraid lest the boy might have an attack in the night, told him to rap three times on the partition wall. So once again, very clearly, he can hear the answering knocks that seem to say: 'Ne t'agite pas, petite souris, je comprends que tu es impatient, mais je vais venir.'

In view of certain disconcerting observations which Marcel will shortly make on the subject of his bereavement, it might be well, at this stage, to form a clear idea of the experience he has just narrated. Briefly, the act of stooping painfully to unbutton his shoes, by its analogy with a similar act accomplished some years before, produced a sensation common to the past and the present, thus liberating from the cadre of Time the cluster of impressions, the state of soul, the fragment of reality or of truly lived experience overlooked by Marcel's voluntary memory but stored in the depths of his unconscious and now miraculously released by the modality of his involuntary memory. The Marcel of the present and the Marcel of the first visit to Balbec are momentarily identical. What is conventionally termed past and present have, in fact, no meaning. His being apprehends for a brief moment what Proust elsewhere calls 'un peu de temps à l'état pur'. Marcel experiences in this contact with the essence of reality what he had not felt during his grandmother's long illness. He experiences for the first time a poignant sense of bereavement. This realization, inevitably, arouses remorse. But almost immediately his intelligence, his voluntary memory, begin protectively to distort the newly apprehended reality and to superimpose on these real, subconsciously derived impressions of his grandmother other impressions which are less painful but also less accurate. Remorse, however, induces him to cling to the images revealed by involuntary memory in a desperate effort to retain them in their pristine intactness and purity. He feels, therefore, ennobled by his grief. And, as he awaits his mother's arrival at Balbec it seems to Marcel that his soul, like hers, is 'encircled with a crown of thorns'. He thinks that he will now be better able to understand her great sorrow. But suddenly Marcel tells us that this was a complete illusion.

Je le croyais; en réalité il y a bien loin des chagrins véritables comme était celui de maman, qui vous ôtent littéralement la vie pour bien longtemps, quelquefois pour toujours, dès qu'on a perdu l'être qu'on aime, — à ces autres chagrins passagers malgré tout comme devait être le mien, qui s'en vont vite comme ils sont venus tard, qu'on ne connaît que longtemps après l'événement parce qu'on a eu besoin pour les ressentir de les comprendre; chagrins comme tant de gens en éprouvent et dont celui qui était actuellement ma torture ne se différenciait que par cette modalité du souvenir involontaire.[1]

Does this mean that Proust has renounced his faith, to which he has so often testified, in the uniqueness of the involuntary memory as a reflector of reality? Are we to interpret Marcel's disparagement of his own grief, which is so ephemeral in contrast to his mother's immense and durable sorrow, as proof that Proust now attributes less value to the revelations of the subconscious? Has he abandoned his conviction that great art is essentially the re-creation by thought, not of the false and superficial notations made by the voluntary memory, but of the impressions rejected as unimportant by the intelligence, the impressions that have penetrated to the subconscious, and are restored by our involuntary memory, the vague sensations which alone contain the true reality of our experience?

Let us see how Marcel interprets the quality of his mother's sense of bereavement and how he tries to explain its genesis. There is no suggestion in her case of 'la modalité du souvenir involontaire'. This one may gather from the fact that, quite obviously, she misunderstands the cause of her son's present state of mind. Indeed, she thinks wrongly that Marcel, ever since his grandmother's death, has mourned his loss but that his grief has been revived by the sight of Balbec and of the places associated with his first visit. Wrongly, says Marcel because his is 'un chagrin tout nouveau' and not the reopening of an old wound. Nor, he insists humbly, is his grief to be compared with the profound and lasting sorrow that has transformed his mother spiritually and physically. When he sees her enter the hotel, it is to perceive something which had escaped him in Paris. His mother is now the living image of his grandmother, all of whose habits she has instinctively adopted, even the dead woman's infatuation for Mme de Sévigné. His grandmother, in her lifetime, had commanded her daughter's love and respect, but not this absolute veneration, this total surrender of individuality which distinguishes the latter's cult for her mother. Marcel implies that her grief, which coincided with his grandmother's death, has gradually achieved, though by a slower process, the same effect as that produced upon himself by a sudden operation of the involuntary memory. His mother has now obtained a complete and real image of his grandmother. Through brooding on the 'incompréhensible contradiction du souvenir et du néant', she has re-created a picture, fragments of which had been concealed by the habits of everyday intercourse, the fragments missed by the intelligence. When a daughter has lost a beloved mother, Proust thinks, death but accelerates that natural metamorphosis by which the survivor assumes not only the physical but also the psychological traits of the dead. She continues, so to speak, an interrupted life. Observe that Marcel's grief swiftly followed upon a moment of ineffable happiness when it seemed to him that his grandmother knelt by his side, uttering words of consolation and of reassurance. Such a moment his mother did not experience. She remembers only the terrible finality of the last words: 'Adieu, ma fille, adieu pour jamais.' Therefore, in order to re-create the living reality which was her mother, to understand everything they had meant to each other, she has had to go down into the very depths of her sorrow. 'Ce n'est pas assez', says Marcel, 'de dire qu'elle avait perdu toute gaieté; fondue, figée en une sorte d'image implorante, elle semblait avoir peur d'offenser d'un mouvement trop brusque, d'un son de voix trop haut, la présence douleureuse qui ne la quittait pas.'

How, then, are we to explain the ephemeral quality of Marcel's suffering which is, nevertheless, so poignant because of its almost miraculous provenance? Chiefly, I think, by the fact that Marcel is already, unconsciously, an artist and must subordinate his grief to the work of art he now carries within him. In the last volume of *A la recherche du temps perdu* occurs a passage which, in retrospect, illuminates our problem. The artist, says Proust, instinctively seeks to extract from his grief *la généralité*, the universal truth or psychological law which it contains. Thereby, no doubt, he achieves a certain appeasement, with the strength to continue his work. Nevertheless, Proust adds, there were times when Marcel, even though believing that the supreme truth of life is art, was profoundly distressed and revolted by his own inability to keep on mourning his grandmother. 'Ma grand'mère que j'avais, avec tant d'indifférence, vu agoniser et mourir près de moi. O puissé-je, en expiation, quand mon œuvre serait terminée, blessé sans remède, souffrir de longues heures abandonné de tous, avant de mourir.'[1]

Let us now return to the episode where Marcel, with the ruthless honesty of the artist, tries to communicate the truth about his state of soul. This truth is, he confesses, that the grief he feels is not, like his mother's 'un véritable chagrin'. This he will experience, later, through his love for Albertine. Meanwhile, he spends hours contemplating Saint-Loup's snapshot of his grandmother, thinking pitifully about the final stages of her illness. Imperceptibly, however, his intelligence pursues its work of alleviation, building, as he says, upon the smoking ruins. Perhaps, thinks Marcel, one's pity is inclined to exaggerate the reality of another's suffering. Or might it not be that death has actually and completely ended the beautiful relationship which existed between him and the dead woman? Perhaps it is wrong to think that they had been created 'uniquement l'un pour l'autre'.

[1] *TR.* ii, 58.

But two incidents interrupt his trend of thought. Marcel learns in detail from Françoise why his grandmother asked Saint-Loup to take her photograph. Moreover, Aimé, the *maître d'hôtel*, discloses casually that Mme Amédée had suffered more than one attack in her room and had begged him not to tell her grandson.

Marcel, in a fresh access of grief, walks out on to the dunes to brood over these revelations. He falls half asleep and dreams that he sees his grandmother who does not, however, respond to his loving advances. To his infinite distress she appears indifferent, even displeased. Yet Marcel is puzzled by the certainty that she is not really dead. Why then does she evince no interest in him? His father, who is present in this dream, replies carelessly: 'Que veux-tu, les morts sont les morts.' What Proust suggests is that sometimes, in certain states of soul, as in this day-dream which is part dream, part hallucination, the instinct for self-preservation, the *élan* of our inner life, is not interrupted. For Marcel's vision corroborates the idea that had just been whispered to him by his protective intelligence. Death has, it would seem, effectually severed the last link between the dead woman and himself.

And, some days afterwards, Marcel finds that despite what Françoise has told him about his grandmother's pathetic efforts to hide the ravages of her malady, he sees in her photograph only the likeness of an elegantly dressed old lady who seems much less unhappy than he had imagined. He does not see, as his mother does—and for that reason cannot bear to look upon the photograph—the image of a hunted creature, stalked down and finally brought to bay by disease.

This whole episode appears to mark an important phase in Marcel's evolution, that is to say, of Proust's own conception of art. It deserves, therefore, to be considered in relation to the final pattern of his ideas on the nature of art which will not, however, become clear until the last two volumes of *A la recherche du temps perdu*, that is to say, until he discloses the results of his search for vanished time. In *Du côté de chez Swann*,[1] alluding to this quest, Marcel roundly asserted that it is

[1] *Swann*, I, 69.

quite useless to try to evoke the true past by means of the intelligence:

> Il [le passé] est caché hors de son domaine et de sa portée, en quelque objet matériel (en la sensation que nous donnerait cet objet matériel) que nous ne soupçonnons pas. Cet objet, il dépend du hasard que nous le rencontrions avant de mourir, ou que nous ne le rencontrions pas.

Such was Proust's artistic doctrine in 1913. But in the last volume of his novel he expresses a different point of view:

> Je sentais pourtant que ces vérités que l'intelligence dégage directement de la réalité ne sont pas a dédaigner entièrement car elles pourraient enchâsser d'une matière moins pure mais encore pénétrer d'esprit ces impressions que nous apportent hors du temps l'essence commune aux sensations du passé et présent, mais qui, plus précieuses, sont aussi trop rares pour que l'œuvre d'art puisse être composée seulement avec elles....[1]

How are we to interpret his apparent change of front? On this question, the critics divide into two camps, reproducing, indeed, a situation which might be described as a twentieth-century version of the old quarrel of the ancients and the moderns. The traditionalists, such as Alain, M. J. Benda and M. Feuillerat extend to Proust the indulgence, mingled with reproof, which Voltaire used to reserve for the atheist: 'un honnête homme qui se trompe.' M. Feuillerat, as we shall see, goes farther. The general thesis of these twentieth-century ancients is that Proust, during the period 1905–12 became infected with the 'new-fangled' ideas on the role of the subconscious of which Bergson was the most notable exponent. He set out, therefore, to write a novel based entirely on material rescued from the unconscious by the involuntary memory. He did in fact write a very fine novel, but only because he employed with greater skill than his predecessors the traditional, intellectual approach to reality, the well-tried methods of the classic *roman d'analyse*. Proust, however, would never admit this. To quote M. Benda:

> l'œuvre de Proust est parfaitement bien une observation sur la vie, sur les mœurs, sur certains mécanismes psychologiques: elle est parfaitement bien critique; mais Proust ne veut pas qu'elle soit cela,

[1] *TR.* II, 53.

et toutes ses déclarations sur son œuvre protestent qu'il n'y a jamais voulu mettre que lui-même, qu'elle ne relève que de la méthode artistique en ce qu'elle est celle du poète et n'a rien a voir avec une méthode objective, soi-disant scientifique, pour laquelle il n'a que du mépris.[1]

M. Feuillerat's theory is that when the First World War interrupted the publication of the original three-volume *A la recherche du temps perdu*, its author perceived, as he began to write the greatly expanded novel we know by the same name, that his original conception of art was essentially untenable. In short, realizing that he could not dispense with the despised intelligence, Proust found it necessary to 'doctor' the new text. To quote M. Feuillerat: 'il insère donc, non sans audace, au milieu même des passages anciens où il avait affirmé que seule la mémoire involontaire mène à la réalité vraie, un certain nombre de phrases admettant que l'intelligence a son emploi dans le travail de reconstruction de la vie.'[2] These inserted phrases, according to this writer, are to be found only in the second volume of *Le temps retrouvé*, that is, in the last volume of the novel. The most damning of these, in his view, is that which I have quoted, and he regards it as a recantation of Proust's original conception of art. Thus M. Feuillerat interprets Marcel's admission that since the precious extra-temporal impressions released by the involuntary memory are too rare to compose in themselves a complete work of art, they must be supplemented by 'ces vérités que l'intelligence dégage directement de la réalité'. M. Feuillerat regrets that Proust was so slow to recognize his mistake since the effect of this extravagant aberration from the traditional methods of the classic psychological novelists (Stendhal, Fromentin and Bourget) was to ruin the unity of his original plan, to destroy the tonality of the novel and, unfortunately, to introduce confusion into his interpretation of the leading characters.

Now, in turn, I find it difficult to reconcile M. Feuillerat's own contradictory views on Proust. His book, in which he tells us how Marcel Proust must have composed his novel, is dedicated to Paul Bourget, 'au maître du roman d'analyse'.

---

[1] *Confluences*, No. 3 (April, 1945).　　[2] *Op. cit.* p. 265.

Naturally, therefore, all his admiration goes to the Proust who belatedly returned, he claims, to the tried and sound doctrine exemplified in Stendhal, Fromentin and Bourget. Yet, in the same breath, M. Feuillerat sadly regrets that Proust did not conserve in its pristine beauty and intactness the plan of his original *A la recherche du temps perdu* with its three dominant themes: *l'amour-désir*; the theme of Marcel's literary vocation and the Bergsonian theme of Time considered as duration. M. Feuillerat, who apparently does not believe that the subconscious contains any mysterious realities superior to those which are accessible to the analysing intelligence, applauds Proust for having eventually recognized the soundness of this view. And yet he reproaches him for not having adhered to the original plan of a novel based entirely on the unconscious.

Alain and M. Benda, on the other hand, view Proust quite simply as an intellectual who raised the art of psychological analysis to a remarkable degree of perfection. They dismiss good-humouredly the Proustian obsession with the unconscious. 'Ce peintre de l'âme n'avait nullement besoin de l'inconscient', says Alain, 'il n'en pouvait rien faire: aussi n'en fait-il rien, il le nomme pourtant.'[1] I like the deliciously casual 'il le nomme pourtant' so ingeniously slipped in as to give a totally wrong impression of Proust's attitude to the unconscious, of the conviction so often reiterated in his pages that the true reality of life, in its purest essence, is only to be found in the involuntary revelations of the unconscious.

We have, therefore, two views of Proust as he appears to the traditionalists: 'l'honnête homme qui se trompe' of Alain and M. Benda and the not so 'honnête homme' of M. Feuillerat whose Proust certainly 'se trompe' but only up to a point. Thereafter, although he discovered his error, Proust, if we believe M. Feuillerat, lacked the courage to admit his mistake and tried disingenuously to save his *amour-propre* by a system of last-minute attenuations and semi-concessions. Such is the harsh and bitter substance of M. Feuillerat's thesis despite the praise which he lavishly accords to Proust the redeemed psychologist and philosopher.

[1] *Propos de litt.* p. 255 (1934).

Now, having read *A la recherche du temps perdu* many times before acquainting myself with these criticisms, I find them, in the main, understandable but rather doctrinaire. Their authors seem to ignore the vital fact that Proust's work is, as he tells us, 'l'histoire d'une vocation invisible'. For them it is an axiom that the Proust of 1913 intended to base his novel entirely on the revelations of the unconscious. And indeed such is the impression which any reader of *Du côté de chez Swann* would glean from Marcel's forthright condemnation of the semi-truths presented by the memory of the intelligence. But these defenders of the classic methods of the traditional *roman d'analyse* go on to assume that nowhere, until the reluctant and belated concessions of *Le temps retrouvé*, does Marcel suggest that he has modified his original intransigent attitude to the intelligence. Are we to accept these assumptions without comment?

Let us first consider Proust's position in 1913. He had conceived and partially written the first version of *A la recherche du temps perdu*, then a relatively modest three-volume enterprise. For many years the trend of French philosophy and psychology had been anti-intellectual or anti-scientific. This movement, of which Henri Bergson was one exponent, denied that reality could be attained by the intelligence, by conscious thought. Reality, it was asserted, is so complex and so fluid as to defy the efforts made by conscious thought to grasp and dominate it. In the words of M. Parodi who has so clearly portrayed this revolutionary phase in the evolution of the European mind, 'the scientific intelligence, in attempting to impose on reality the abstract simplicity and homogeneity of its concepts and laws, only travesties and denatures it'. Proust, like hundreds of his intelligent contemporaries, was profoundly influenced by these views. For instance, this is what he writes in a letter which outlines the general plan of his original *A la recherche du temps perdu*:

C'est un livre extrêmement réel mais supporté en quelque sorte, pour imiter la mémoire involontaire (qui selon moi, bien que Bergson ne fasse pas cette distinction, est la seule vraie, la mémoire volontaire, la mémoire de l'intelligence et des yeux ne nous rendent du passé que des fac-similés inexacts qui ne lui ressemblent pas plus que les tableaux

des mauvais peintres ne ressemblent au printemps, etc.... De sorte
que nous ne croyons pas la vie réelle parce que nous ne nous la rappelons pas, mais que nous sentions une odeur ancienne, soudain nous
sommes enivrés; et de même nous croyons ne plus aimer les morts,
c'est parce que nous ne nous les rappelons pas, revoyons-nous tout
d'un coup un vieux gant, et nous fondons en larmes) par des réminiscences brusques une partie du livre est une partie de ma vie que
j'avais oubliée, et que tout d'un coup je retrouve en mangeant un peu
de madeleine que j'ai fait tremper dans du thé, qui me ravit avant que
je l'aie reconnue et identifiée pour en avoir pris jadis tous les matins,
aussitôt toute ma vie d'alors ressuscite, et comme je le dis dans le
livre, comme dans le jeu japonais, où des petits morceaux de papiers
trempés dans un bol d'eau deviennent des personnages, des fleurs,
etc...tous les gens et jardins de cette époque de ma vie sont sortis
d'une tasse de thé. Une autre partie du livre renaît des minutes du
reveil, quand on ne sait pas où on est et qu'on se croit deux ans avant
sans un autre pays. Mais tout cela n'est que le support du livre....[1]

[It is an extremely real book but underpinned [*supporté*] in a way, so
as to imitate the involuntary memory (which, according to me—though
Bergson does not make this distinction—is the only true one. The
voluntary memory, the memory of the intelligence and of the eyes
give us only inaccurate facsimiles of the past which do not resemble the
past any more than pictures by bad painters resemble the spring,
etc.... So that we do not believe life to be real because we do not
remember it. But if we smell an old perfume, we are intoxicated,
suddenly, and in the same way we think we no longer love the dead
because we no longer remember them. Yet, if we suddenly see an old
glove, we burst into tears) by sudden reminiscences. One part of the
book is a part of my life which I had forgotten, and which, suddenly,
I rediscover whilst eating a piece of 'madeleine' dipped in tea, which
delighted me before I had recognized and identified it as something
I used to eat every morning. Immediately, all my life belonging to
that period is resuscitated, and as I say in the book, just as in the
Japanese toy where little pieces of paper soaked in a bowl of water
become characters, flowers, etc., all the people and gardens of that
period in my life emerged from a cup of tea. Another part of my book
is resurrected from the waking moments when one does not know
where one is and imagines oneself to be in another country two years
previously. But all that is merely the underpinning of the book....]

As a rule, Proust's letters add nothing of substantial importance to the views on art expressed in his novel. This fragment,

[1] Quoted from Proust's correspondence by L.-P. Quint, *Marcel Proust*, p. 373.

however, is an exception. In addition to what we already know from *Du côté de chez Swann* and other volumes about Proust's enthusiasm for the new philosophy and psychology, it makes it quite clear that, even in 1913, he never believed it possible to construct his whole novel with material provided by the unconscious. 'Tout cela', he insists, 'n'est que le support du livre.' In other words, he was well aware that this method of approach was fortuitous and that the revelations of the unconscious though precious and unique as reflectors of true reality, were much too rare to provide the matter for a complete work of art. In fact we find him saying in 1913 substantially what he repeats in the final version of *Le temps retrouvé*.

And, if we follow in the novel itself the progress made by the narrator in his search for an ideal medium with which to interpret the reality of *le temps perdu*, it is equally evident that his early dogmatic views on the relation between art and reality underwent certain modifications. Marcel discovered that in practice, as opposed to theory, the artist who wants to be intelligible even to an élite of connoisseurs, must inevitably fall short of his ideal. It is clearly inaccurate to suggest that not until the close of *A la recherche du temps perdu* does Proust reveal this process of modification. Surely, for example, it is obvious at the end of the episode entitled 'L'esprit des Guermantes devant la princesse de Parme' that Marcel, writhing 'comme une pythonisse' on the seat of the cab that takes him to his rendezvous with Charlus is tormented by misgivings which contrast sharply with the serene confidence of the Marcel whose artistic credo is reflected in the lines I have just quoted from *Du côté de chez Swann*. Marcel, it is true, emerged unscathed from this brief and sharp trial of faith. His conclusion was, it will be remembered, that the creative artist always knows instinctively when he has obtained immediate contact with true reality, that is to say, with reality untouched by the contingencies of conventional Time. Therefore, impressions like those presented to him by the voluntary memory, by the memory of his intelligence as he drove away from the Guermantes' dinner were not to be compared in real value with the Combray impressions. The proof for Marcel is that the former, although they inspire him with a kind of exaltation do not fill his being with that deep and satisfying joy which is the prelude to the creation of the greatest art. Nevertheless this material, these external impressions collected by the intelligence, by the voluntary memory, although they contain a reality inferior to that secreted in the profounder impressions emanating from the subconscious, must also be employed in the creation of the work of art. This admission which is explicitly made only in the last volume of *A la recherche du temps perdu* and will be more thoroughly examined in this study, is already implicit in the section dealing with Marcel's visit to the Guermantes.

Now what of the experience that occurred during Marcel's second visit to Balbec? Here again, Proust anticipates the views which will be finally summed up in *Le temps retrouvé*. Surely it is clear from Marcel's deep impression of the extraordinary change wrought on his mother by her bereavement that he has divined a source of illumination which may be just as precious to the artist as the modality of the involuntary memory. Apparently, intense suffering may imitate to some degree the mysterious process by which the unconscious yields its truths. The intelligence, reinforced and sharpened by deep sensibility, may sometimes acquire a similar force of penetration, a similar faculty of divination. Marcel's mother, for example, is impelled by her incomparable sorrow to explore the depths of her conscious recollections in a pious, desperate resolve to seek and re-create by the *intelligence* reinforced by sympathy, the true image of her beloved dead one. And Marcel, witnessing the remarkable physical and spiritual transformation enacted in his mother, is convinced that in this particular case her search for the *temps perdu* has not been entirely vain. Thus, I venture to suggest, we must interpret the moving pages which describe the effect upon Marcel of this metamorphosis. He is aware at this stage that the precious but fortuitous revelations of the unconscious can be supplemented, given the proper emotional climate, by the truths abstracted from life by the formerly despised 'mémoire de l'intelligence'. The criterion of the reality of an impression is the depth to which it penetrates our consciousness. And when Marcel insists that his own grief, in spite of its provenance, the

unconscious, is not ' un véritable chagrin' this does not mean that
he doubts for one moment the unique reality of such involuntary
reminiscences. Proust implies, surely, that having grasped this
reality, Marcel's function as a creative artist is fulfilled. After
his belated and fleeting contact with the living reality, concealed
beneath the conventional words 'la mort de ma grand'mère',
Marcel the sorrowing grandson must give place to Marcel the
artist, the potential novelist who will pass on to other experiences in search of other fragments of *le temps perdu*. It is
quite different with his mother who is not an artist, and who has
not moreover been vouchsafed the brief yet authentic vision of
reality disclosed to her son by a chance analogy of sensations.
That is why all her intelligence, obedient to the command
of her immense sorrow, is now concentrated on the task of
reconstructing from the recollections laboriously assembled by
her voluntary memory, the true and living image of her beloved
mother. This is the process by which Marcel himself, in his
efforts to appease a very different and more terrible suffering,
lacking the illumination of involuntary reminiscences will strive
to extract the truth about Albertine's *mœurs* from a chaos of
conflicting impressions and memories; to decipher, under the
stimulus of his torturing and unavowable jealousy, the hidden
meaning of Albertine's most trivial actions, words, gestures
and intonations.

We need not at the moment enlarge upon the doubts, the
setbacks, the disillusionments experienced by Marcel in his
attempts to grasp reality by the objective and rational method,
to reconstruct, if possible, the existence of the Albertine who is
outside himself. For, as Marcel has learned: 'Les êtres ont un
développement en nous, mais un autre hors de nous.'[1] Which
is the real Albertine? Is it the Albertine who is reconstructed
and endowed with unity by Marcel's reasoning intelligence out
of the memories of their successive contacts? Or is it the Albertine of his inner vision, the creation of his desire for beauty,
love and happiness, the ever-changing image reflecting the extra-
temporal and varied climates of his subconscious, the Albertine
so real to Marcel because she is part of the substance of his soul

[1] *AD.* i, 134.

yet whose reality it is so difficult to communicate to others except, maybe, through the medium of art? Or again, is it not perhaps, as Marcel is inclined to believe, that the two visions are inseparable, for, after all, the moment he tries to retrace the the probable development of Albertine's existence outside himself, he is confronted by possibilities that cannot be measured, the possible effects of his own influence, of his fortune, of his jealousy in shaping the destiny and the character of Albertine.

Such, very roughly indicated, are the psychological problems that await Marcel the lover of Albertine. Although their full complexity is not revealed to him until he has known the true meaning of suffering, it is obvious, as I have tried to illustrate, that at no stage in his progress towards his vocation has Marcel ever really envisaged the art of interpreting experience simply as the notation and expression of unconscious revelations. And to corroborate this assertion I will quote from the first volume of *Albertine disparue* a passage which is illuminating not only for its content but because it is retrospective. Marcel, suddenly abandoned by his mistress, recalls the irrational fear that obsessed him on the eve of her flight:

Cette deuxième hypothèse n'était pas celle de l'intelligence et la peur panique que j'avais eue le soir où Albertine ne m'avait pas embrassé, la nuit où j'avais entendu le bruit de la fenêtre, cette peur [he remarks] n'était pas raisonnée. Mais — et la suite le montrera davantage, *comme bien des épisodes ont pu déjà l'indiquer*[1] — de ce que l'intelligence n'est pas l'instrument le plus subtil, le plus puissant, le plus approprié pour saisir le vrai, ce n'est qu'une raison de plus pour commencer par l'intelligence et non par un intuitivisme de l'inconscient, par une foi aux pressentiments toute faite. C'est la vie qui peu à peu, cas par cas, nous permet de remarquer que ce qui est le plus important pour notre cœur, pour notre esprit, ne nous est pas appris par le raisonnement mais par des puissances autres. Et alors, c'est l'intelligence elle-même qui se rendant compte de leur supériorité, abdique par raisonnement devant elles, et accepte de devenir leur collaboratrice et leur servante. C'est la foi expérimentale.[2]

[This second hypothesis was not that of the intelligence and the panic fear I had experienced on the evening Albertine did not kiss me, on the night I had heard the noise of the window opening—that

---

[1] My italics.   [2] *AD.* I, 13.

fear was not rational. But—and the sequel will show more clearly, what indeed many episodes may already have suggested—that just because the intelligence is not the most subtle, most powerful and most appropriate instrument for grasping the truth, this is but an additional argument for starting out from the intelligence and not from an intuitivism of the unconscious, a ready-made faith in presentiments. It is life which gradually, case by case, allows us to notice that what matters most to our hearts or to our minds is not taught us by reasoning but by other powers. And then it is the intelligence itself which, on realizing their superiority, abdicates, through reason, in their favour and consents to become their collaborator and servant. It is experimental faith.]

Here, sharply reflected, as in a crystal, is a view which, nevertheless, respects the integrity of Proust's original and essential belief in the unique powers of the unconscious. It is not a new attitude designed belatedly to 'save face' in view of an eventual apostasy. On the contrary, Proust simply expresses more clearly a viewpoint which, as we have noted, was adumbrated in the earlier volumes of his novel. Fundamentally, moreover, it is that conception of the artist's function and potentialities suggested in the letter of 1913 in which, after granting us an exciting glimpse of the enchanted realm of transcendent or unconscious reality, he let fall the curtain again with the regretful caveat: 'Mais tout cela n'est que le support du livre.' It is, in the last analysis, the attitude which Proust will adopt in *Le temps retrouvé* when, having discovered his vocation, he reaffirms his faith in the intuitivism of the unconscious yet confesses, with the sincerity of the great artist, that its precious truths will not in themselves suffice to compose his work of art. They must be supplemented by the less infallible verities discovered by the intelligence. In short, to borrow the jargon of the ultra-moderns, *A la recherche du temps perdu* does not claim to be *un roman pur* since no one can recover pure memory.

It is to be hoped that these comments will not be construed as a 'defence' of Proust, and least of all as an attempt to demonstrate by his example the superiority of that anti-intellectualist doctrine so fervently advocated in recent years by the *surréalistes* and at the moment illustrated in an extreme, somewhat repellent fashion by the neophytes of Existentialism. My remarks are framed, on the contrary, to serve as a warning against any such doctrinaire approach to the work of Proust. No doubt, as M. Benda says, *A la recherche du temps perdu* is 'une observation sur la vie' and thus a novel in the classic manner. But it is just as undoubtedly also the most successful attempt yet made by a French novelist to communicate the emotional states created in him by certain aspects of the outer world which, precisely because they have penetrated to the deepest recesses of his consciousness possess for him a more authentic reality than the more easily expressed yet more superficial notations of the critical intelligence. Both visions exist simultaneously and inseparably in Proust's novel so that any interpretation of *A la recherche du temps perdu* based on a dogmatic, exclusive conception of art such as that represented by the well-known though spurious antinomies: intellectualism or anti-intellectualism; realism and romanticism; objectivism and subjectivism, is necessarily misleading and valueless. With this in mind we can now rejoin Marcel at the Grand Hôtel de Balbec.

Chapter VI

SODOME ET GOMORRHE
(continued)

M a r c e l has completed half his journey of exploration. Moving along the route traced out by Marcel Proust with its shifting altitudes and hair-pin bends, our traveller has passed through a variety of climates. From various and unsuspected points of vantage he has acquired the components of a new and startling panorama reflecting not only what is conventionally termed the outer world but also the world that lies within himself. Even stranger discoveries await Marcel, whose narrative we must, however, interrupt for a moment to consider this *via Proustiana*, the unique advantages of which are so frequently noted in his log-book. Now, MM. Alain, Benda and other twentieth-century ancients would tell us that there is really nothing to consider since this *via Proustiana* has never existed save in Proust's imagination. It is simply, they would claim, the old *route rationnelle* used by his famous predecessors except that Proust, who happens to be a remarkably intelligent guide, has been able to give us a closer view of the true landscape. Perhaps MM. Alain and Benda are right but, in fairness to Proust, we might attempt a little essay in comparative geography.

From Mme de La Fayette to Flaubert, the great French novelists worked towards the same objective, which was to illustrate by their fictions the interaction of the external world and of the less visible inner world of the individual spirit. They viewed this process usually as a conflict, the intensity of which varied according to the energy displayed by the individual in his efforts to preserve the integrity of his ideal world or again, according to the degree of pressure exerted upon the individual by external human or material agencies. In the opinion of all these novelists this outer world is of such a nature as to be readily grasped by the reason and the senses. It has an objective,

real existence and is not, therefore, to be confused with the
irrational subjective world of the individual. It is very important
to note this attitude, which influenced in a most characteristic
fashion the art of these novelists and their followers. True, the
Romantics made intermittent attempts to identify the world of
external nature with their private spiritual universe but only to
discover, like René and Obermann, a fundamental dissimilarity
of climate. To none did it occur, however, to question as did
Proust the reality or the objectivity of this world so clearly
apparent to the eye of the reasoning intelligence.

Since the primary function of the novelist then was to stress
the incompatibility of these separate yet constantly interacting
worlds, the novel tended to imitate the structure of drama with
its classic exposition, peripeteia, dénouement and its penchant
for critical or exceptional situations, well designed to cast into
sharp relief the play of individual passions and sensibilities.
Moreover, the prevailing inclination was to view this interaction
of forces as tragic. Exceptions were Lesage, who portrayed it
ironically as farcical comedy, and Marivaux, to whom it appeared
both comic and touching. The individual was conceived by most
novelists as *une âme d'élite*, either on the defensive, striving to
guard the inner temple of the *moi* from violation or again, like
Vautrin, Troubert, Cousin Bette, Julien Sorel, Emma Bovary,
as a monomaniac determined to overcome the external force
called Society, to re-create the outer world after the image of
his individual and passionate ideal. A survey of the members of
this 'universal resistance' movement reveals few defeatists or
collaborators and the individual is nearly always presented
heroically, as an isolated figure, opposed to a world where everything and everybody conspires to prevent him achieving spiritual
harmony. The *simplisme* of such an outlook is reflected in the
novelist's characterization, in the tension of the atmosphere surrounding the characters and especially in the schematic progress
of the action. I suspect that M. Claudel had this conception
of the novel in mind recently when in a review of Aragon's
Aurélien, he observed: 'Le roman, c'est une confluence d'événements qui se poussent onde à onde et qui aboutissent finalement
à une série d'engendrements successifs, à une espèce de chronique,

à une histoire.'[1] M. Claudel's metaphors reflect precisely the method of interpreting life employed by the novelists I have just mentioned. The interaction of a certain individuality and of certain external circumstances produces a confluence of events which, in obedience to the law of causality, surge forward with irresistible and cumulative force towards an inevitable dénouement. It is doubtless an excellent method for interpreting the critical moments in the life of an individual but apt, surely, to produce an air of unreality when used by the novelist to portray the history of a whole existence unless, of course, he chooses as his subject a person governed by an *idée fixe*. But what of an individual like Marcel? The climates of his inner world show little respect for the reasons of the objective calendar year since at any moment the summer air of Combray is liable to invade the frosty December atmosphere of the Faubourg Saint-Germain. How is it possible to narrate in the chronological manner of Balzac or Flaubert the life-history of a man who is never quite convinced that the images of people and things re-created by his conscious memory reflect an essential reality, and is therefore discontented with the classic novelists and their historical, dramatic method of interpretation? And there is another complication. This Marcel who insists on narrating his own life is not simply the person who assures us that the people and events described in *A la recherche du temps perdu* are purely imaginary and composite creations. He is also identical with the mature artist who holds such unorthodox views on the functions of the novelist. Clearly, as we have already seen, Marcel has abandoned the *route rationnelle* of tradition for the more arduous but more exciting *via Proustiana*, stretches of which run parallel, yet never quite merge with the old route. You can follow his course if you look back, for it is traced in the spiralling narrative devised by Proust to portray the fluid swirling movement of life as expressed in terms of real and not conventional Time, a narrative reflecting also the perpetual *chassé-croisé* of Marcel's conscious and subconscious memories. Sometimes—and here, I think, is what has misled MM. Alain and Benda—this spiralling graph seems to adopt the familiar ascending curve of the dramatic

[1] *Les Etoiles* (15 May 1945).

roman d'analyse. But that is an illusion since Proust's co-ordinates are not those of Balzac, Stendhal or Flaubert. His geometry is not the space-time geometry of Descartes. Read Marcel's account of a country walk in Combray, of a matinée at the Comédie Française, a dinner at the Guermantes', a railway journey, a drive with Mme de Villeparisis, a night in a hotel at Doncières, a conversation with Charlus. Can anyone who knows his Balzac, Stendhal or Flaubert honestly maintain that their narrative method, admirable though it is, could ever produce the same kind of impressions as those obtained by Proust? I know there are moments in *L'Education sentimentale,* in *Lucien Leuwen* and *Armance* where Flaubert and Stendhal seem to have inadvertently found the Proustian way. But they are only moments. That the *via Proustiana* really does exist seems to me beyond doubt. Did Proust, I wonder, unconsciously symbolize it in that charming little incident which occurs in the first volume of his novel. On warm summer nights Marcel's father liked to take his wife and son for long complicated walks in the environs of Combray. They used to return in the moonlight, the boy drowsy with sleep and the perfume of lime-blossoms, dragging his tired legs and wondering if they would ever reach home.

Tout d'un coup [says Marcel] mon père nous arrêtait et demandait à ma mère: 'Où sommes-nous?' Epuisée par la marche, mais fière de lui, elle lui avouait tendrement qu'elle n'en savait absolument rien. Il haussait les épaules et riait. Alors, comme s'il l'avait sortie de la poche de son veston avec sa clef, il nous montrait debout devant nous la petite porte de derrière de notre jardin qui était venue avec le coin de la rue du Saint-Esprit nous attendre au bout de ces chemins inconnus. Ma mère lui disait avec admiration: 'Tu es extraordinaire.'

But it is time we returned to the Grand Hôtel de Balbec which Habit, that implacable enemy of Romance, has now transformed into a typical expensive Normandy *palace.* Marcel, on this second visit, no longer finds it intimidating, hostile or even mysterious, though in order to amuse Albertine he likes to imagine it as the theatre of a Racinian Biblical tragedy, a temple where the High Priest, the equivocal and furtive Nissim Bernard presides benignantly over the complicated and daily ritual expertly performed by a hurrying throng of ingenuous Levites agreeably represented by innumerable waiters, page-boys, chasseurs, lift-attendants and chambermaids. Marcel is no longer that timid youngster who suffered agonies of shame whilst his grandmother calmly bargained with the haughty reception clerk over the price of rooms. He is now the privileged client of standing, deferentially consulted by the ineffable *maître d'hôtel*, Aimé, and even by the once terrifying and aloof manager whose malapropisms are a continual source of joy. Accepted as a wealthy, rather eccentric semi-invalid whose odd desire for seclusion must be respected because his tips are absurdly lavish, Marcel is able to spend the early days of his holiday in the solitude of an aerial chamber, thinking sadly, behind drawn curtains, of his dead grandmother, refusing to see any visitors, not even Albertine, who is to pass the season at a neighbouring resort with her aunt Mme Bontemps.

On a glorious morning in early summer, when the sun is dancing on the waves and the air is clamorous with the mewing of gulls and the joyous shouting of children at play, Marcel chases away the black moths of sombre reverie. Seized by an urgent desire to live, to find perhaps durable happiness in the sensuous outer world of material beauty, he summons the docile, understanding Albertine, renews his contacts with *la petite bande*, with Andrée, Rosemonde, Gisèle and, through the Cambremers and Verdurins, drifts back into the social round. Once more, therefore, his narrative resumes its spiralling course, imitating not the forward march of calendar time but the evolution of that 'durée mobile' where past and present interchange and where, for instance, the Elstir or Charles Swann of the original Verdurin *salon* in the Quai Conti persistently invade the rusticity of Mme Verdurin's summer villa, La Raspelière, rented from the dowager marquise de Cambremer, mother-in-law to the snobbish sister of Legrandin, the same Legrandin whose casual mention of Balbec to Marcel's father at Combray is the primary cause of Marcel's presence at the Grand Hôtel. Into this society, too, comes Charlus for a reason that can be divined and will shortly be explained. And with Charlus early fragments of Swann-Odette history float into the Verdurin drawing-room in Normandy. Later, when Marcel begins to disclose the nature of his first 'véritable chagrin', it will seem at times as if we were listening to an old tune called *Un amour de Swann*. Yet soon it will be perceived that the original theme has been rearranged with new and disturbing variations when the Marcel who once naïvely replied to Swann that he did not know the meaning of jealousy discovers at the cost of painful researches, the profound or semantic value of this word.

We begin to understand, too, as this narrative uncoils, what Proust meant when he said that art recomposes life, because this is exactly the illusion presented by Marcel, the conviction that here we have the real story of his life and not a version arranged for dramatic effect or expurgated for reasons of *amour-propre*. Events are shown to us in the promiscuity of their natural occurrence and in their proper climate which is determined largely by the narrator's state of soul. For Marcel's narrative does not merely record the notations of his conscious intelligence but includes faithfully the other unobtrusive sensations that slipped unobserved through its outer screen or sentries and penetrated the regions of the unconscious. How rightly Proust insists on the originality of this aspect of Marcel's chronicle, on the importance of these sensations and impressions ignored by the reasoning intelligence until the mischief done by their delayed action is irreparable. Here again the illusion of reality is admirably sustained. Repeatedly Marcel receives yet fails to heed, the urgent signals of the intuitive unconscious. Remember that sudden image of his grandmother which confronts him on his return to his parents' flat from Doncières! Had Marcel paused to reflect upon its significance he might have spared himself the futile self-reproaches, the intolerable sufferings caused by his memories of the first visit to Balbec. Was he not also warned against Albertine by the same monitor? True, the sibylline utterances of Françoise might easily be explained away as the jealous backbitings of an old servant. But surely not his anxious curiosity as to Albertine's private existence, that terrible, inexplicably urgent need to see her, that feeling of hopelessness when he tries to break through the tangle of 'détails réels' and 'faits mensongers',[1] the inner conviction

---

[1] *SG.* II (1), 146.

that he will never know the truth about Albertine. Proust restores to the expression 'ignorance de la vie' its literal and profound significance. Marcel—and in this respect most of us resemble him—remains ignorant of many things in life because he does not want to know them, preferring the comforting meretricious interpretations of the reason to the more genuine though often distasteful intuitions of the unconscious. 'Le cœur a ses raisons que la raison ne connaît point.' There are many passages in *A la recherche du temps perdu* which send one back to Pascal's momentous saying.

Sodome et Gomorrhe, the challenging title selected by Proust for the fifth tome of *A la recherche du temps perdu* evokes an atmosphere of sulphurous gloom, malediction and damnation, which is rarely suggested in the novel itself. On the brief occasions when Marcel presents a synthetic vision of the Cities of the Plain there is no trace in his attitude of moral reprobation. The prevailing accent is rather one of scientific curiosity tinged with regret and pity. Proust's main concern as a student of *mœurs* is to reveal through Marcel's contacts with Charlus and Albertine the social repercussions and complexities generated by their special proclivities. He is extremely careful, here, in dealing with a subject which by its very nature is bound to act as a focal point, to avoid focusing the reader's attention exclusively or disproportionately on this particular aspect of Charlus or Albertine. In consequence, the character of the latter develops very slowly and indeed, this second 'monstre odieux', presented with every device of art that is consonant with veracity, never emerges with that sheer brutality of design which we noted in the case of the baron de Charlus. This is for the excellent reason that Marcel is never certain whether the Albertine whose existence develops outside himself corresponds in fact with the subjective Albertine whose image is the cause of his terrible suffering. As for Charlus, the nature of whose besetting vice was fully exposed in the Jupien incident, the novelist's task is henceforth to demonstrate by illustration the manifestations and effects of the baron's special *tare*, whilst at the same time revealing unsuspected and often apparently contradictory traits in the character of this strange creature. One must never forget that by the Proustian method of interpretation Marcel's own *moi* is also shown in a continual state of change because the habit of association constantly modifies his vision of Charlus, a factor never sufficiently emphasized by novelists before Proust. Familiarity, the proverb runs, breeds contempt. But it also breeds in certain milieus a tolerance of vices which in other spheres of life provoke revulsion and the harshest sanctions. This attitude to 'le charlisme', as Proust suggests in all the scenes which portray Charlus in society, is a by-product of snobbery, of apathy, of the half-fearful curiosity excited in normal people by the spectacle of aberration from the moral or physical norm. The Verdurins, for example, are well aware of the nature of the baron's relations with the musician, Charles Morel. These are indeed the subject of much private merriment amongst the members of the little 'clan'. But since Mme Verdurin's particular brand of snobbery is a precious cult of music and Morel is indispensable to her 'mercredis', she and Verdurin encourage this liaison. No French novelist has so completely and damningly exposed the blunting of the moral sense bred by snobbery as Proust, who is nevertheless frequently pilloried by inept critics as a dilettante and arch-snob. It is precisely because Charlus has all the prestige and *morgue* of a *grand seigneur*, because he is so contemptuous of public opinion, that Marcel is able to observe and interpret the characteristics of a vice extremely hard to detect in less exalted and more timorous members of the confraternity. Inevitably, the day will come when even the snobs will ostracize the baron, not, however, from an outraged sense of morality, but simply because he is no longer a social dictator in the Faubourg Saint-Germain. Pending that revolution the baron is free to gratify his strange pleasures. So potent and far-reaching is the influence of snobbery that his liaison with Morel is accepted and connived at not only by the Verdurins, the Cambremers and the Guermantes circle but, for instance, by that amiable professor from the Conservatoire, invited for Morel's sake to La Raspelière and who astounds even Marcel by inquiring casually in regard to the baron and his 'protégé': 'Est-ce qu'il y a longtemps qu'ils sont ensemble?'

Marcel's narrative, we have noted, reflects events in the promiscuous manner of their natural occurrence. As a result, the incidents and conversations evoking the Sodome-et-Gomorrhe aspect of life are presented in a flux of other co-existing elements which compose, in the mass, an equally arresting, yet saner panorama of human nature, an impression accentuated, moreover, by the material beauty of their setting. This is the charming stretch of Norman coast served by the *tacot*, the tiny local train which Albertine and Marcel so often take in order to visit the Verdurins or the Cambremers. During that long bright summer, this little shuttling train weaves its pattern of sensations into the fabric of Marcel's existence imitating, in miniature fashion, the eternal process by which sensations and their impressions gradually lose, under the influence of habit, the pristine, mysterious tints in which they are suffused by imagination, and eventually, in obedience to the ever-changing states of our soul, call up images that can never be completely or even adequately expressed because of the imperfections of our will to remember. Consider, for example, what happens to Marcel's impressions of the stations on this 'chemin de fer d'intérêt local': Saint-Pierre-des-Îfs, Saint-Mars-le-Vêtu, Hermenonville, Saint-Vaast, Arambouville, Egleville, Mainville, Parville and so many others. By the time the season draws to its close, they have lost the peculiar quality that intrigued Marcel's imagination on his first journey in company with Cottard, Brichot, Saniette, and the remaining members of the Verdurin 'clan'. The erudite Sorbonne professor, Brichot, was responsible for the first transformation when, in response to his young friend's eager questions, he substituted the etymologies of scientific research for the picturesque conjectures of that venerable amateur philologist the curé of Combray, formerly a parish priest in these parts. Yet Brichot only replaced one quality of mystery with another of equal charm. The larger and definitive transformation was due to a more gradual and subtle operation, namely the extension of Marcel's circle of relationships and the deepening of his intimacy with Albertine. Thus, before leaving Balbec for Paris he confesses that each one of these stations was now for him divested of its original mystery and had become 'un cadre de vie mondaine comme un autre'. Incarville is now the place where the marquis de Montpeyroux, returning from a shoot, comes forward to shake hands, or else the halt where Marcel has a word with that agreeable *pique-assiette* M. de Crécy, none other, as Marcel surprisingly discovers from a casual remark dropped by Charlus, than the Crécy who was once the husband of Odette and by her cleaned out of his last sou. And Doncières, so long associated with that memorable November visit to Saint-Loup, is now merely the station where Morel joins the 'clan' on his way to play Vinteuil's sonata at La Raspelière. Egleville is the stop where they look out for la princesse Sherbatoff, exiled from Guermantes society, and now the inseparable friend of Mme Verdurin. Mainville is linked only with Albertine who, on fine evenings, gets off here instead of at her own station, Parville, so as to have a little longer time in Marcel's arms.

During the first weeks of his stay at the Grand Hôtel, Marcel rarely sends for Albertine. But she has left him the addresses of her friends whom she is visiting in the region and with many of these delightful creatures he becomes more than intimate. In this Don Juan mood, reflecting, after all, that he can always see Albertine in Paris, after the holidays, Marcel begins to view their liaison with some complacency. He is not in love with her and indeed, but for a chance encounter with Dr Cottard at Incarville, their relationship might quite easily have drifted into a separation. All this, however, is changed by the hazard of a tram-breakdown. To pass the time, Marcel takes Albertine and Andrée into the casino where he is joined by Cottard who is on his way to La Raspelière. Invited by Marcel to admire the grace with which Andrée and Albertine are dancing together the doctor replies with typical oafishness: 'Oui, mais les parents sont bien imprudents qui laissent leurs filles prendre de pareilles habitudes.' He proceeds to adduce biological reasons for his outrageous statement and then, switching the conversation from this trivial topic, enlarges on his private feud with the local medical practitioner.

Cottard's lightly uttered words, acting like a slow poison are destined to corrupt Marcel's imagination, destroy his peace of mind and completely transform his sentiments for Albertine.

This incident forms, indeed, the prelude to a strange drama which no French writer had ever intensively explored. Its theme is touched upon by Balzac and Maupassant; the former in *La Fille aux Yeux d'or*, the latter in his short story, *La Femme de Paul*. It crops up, too, in several of Diderot's remarkable letters to Sophie Volland and in his disturbing *La Religieuse*. In applying the expression 'drama' to the story of Marcel's subsequent relations one must make certain reservations. To begin with, the Proustian narrative has not the traditional structure of drama, because, whilst revealing in slow motion the alternations of psychological states created by the development and conflict of Marcel's love and jealousy, it makes no pretence at imitating the continuity, the cumulative tension, the sense of inevitable catastrophe which we are accustomed to associate with dramatic action in the accepted sense of the term. On the contrary, there are great stretches where its stream apparently disappears underground, others where we are fascinated by the sinister darkness and depth of its waters, listening with a fearful expectation for the roar of the distant cataract. Instead, Marcel's tragedy meanders along with seeming aimlessness, ever diminishing, until finally it peters out in the desert sands of oblivion and indifference.

Marcel's reaction to Cottard's fateful words is not instantaneous. But soon he feels impelled to observe Albertine with close attention, suspecting every gesture, intonation and remark, consulting his memories, revising his opinion of her character. Was she, for instance, really the frivolous Albertine of his first visit to Balbec who could never be induced to give up for a *tête-à-tête* with Marcel her garden party, donkey ride or other trivial amusement? These excuses Marcel used to accept with amused indulgence. But now he wonders whether they do not perhaps camouflage more serious and disquieting pastimes. So he subjects Albertine to cunning and prolonged inquisitions, noting with a new and cruel sensation of pleasure her vain attempts to explain away obvious contradictions and lies. He dares not yet openly voice the reason for his jealous questions, though once, indeed, the forbidden epithet leaps out. This is when Albertine, driven into an impasse by his remorseless logic, escapes with the half-serious threat never to see him again. 'Je me noierai', she

exclaims in mock tragic accents, 'je me jetterai à l'eau.' And
Marcel with perfidious ambiguity interjects: 'Comme Sappho?'
Obviously something must happen to ease this intolerable
tension. Rosemonde, like the other members of the *petite bande*,
observes and comments on Marcel's harshness to Albertine who
finally asks him bluntly what she has done to deserve it. Before
coming to the point he invents a situation which, except for the
abnormal nature of the jealousy that motivates it, might have
easily inspired a scene in a Marivaux comedy, for instance, *Les
Fausses confidences*. With many elaborate explanations and apolo-
getic digressions Marcel pretends that although once on the
brink of falling in love with Albertine, he has conceived a violent
passion for Andrée. But he has just heard from someone who
must be anonymous of terrible rumours concerning the relations
between the two girls, rumours he would not have dared to
mention, of course, did they not affect his whole future happiness.
Albertine's response to his 'confession' of love for Andrée
reveals the golden qualities of her nature. There are no reproaches. With complete unselfishness and loyalty she tries to
hide her sadness and thanks Marcel for his frankness. The
second false confidence, however, arouses her anger. She flatly
denies the truth of the scandalous rumours and demands to be
confronted with the slanderer. Her attitude calms Marcel's
fears though his sense of reassurance is disturbed somewhat
by memories of Swann and Odette. Other circumstances increase his disquiet, in particular, the public scandal caused in
Balbec by the indecent behaviour of one of Bloch's sisters and
an actress friend of notorious morals. There is also the incident
of the young and beautiful woman with the remarkable star-like
eyes but vicious expression who pretends to her husband that
Bloch's cousin with whom she has just struck up an acquaintance,
is an old school comrade. Marcel's active imagination, inflamed
by unnatural jealousy, plays upon these incidents with such
intensity that it is difficult to judge when his narrative is re-
cording observed facts or hallucinations.

Souvent, quand dans la salle du casino [he says] deux jeunes filles
se désiraient, il se produisait comme un phénomène lumineux, une
sorte de traînée phosphorescente allant de l'une à l'autre. Disons en

passant que c'est à l'aide de telles matérialisations, fussent-elles
impondérables, par ces signes astraux enflammant toute une partie de
l'atmosphère, que Gomorrhe dispersée, tend, dans chaque ville, dans
chaque village, à rejoindre ses membres séparés, à reformer la cité
biblique tandis que partout, les mêmes efforts sont poursuivis, fût-ce en
vue d'une reconstruction intermittente par les nostalgiques, par les
hypocrites, quelquefois par les courageux exilés de Sodome.[1]

Proust, I have said, is not often swept into such exaggerations
and it is important to note the emotional atmosphere in which
they are generated. Quite evidently, Marcel has now begun to
view Balbec as a kind of summer rendezvous for the inhabitants of the accursed cities. In spite of his confidence in Albertine and the new frankness in their relations, he trembles for
her moral safety, hardly daring to leave her side. Fortunately,
Marcel stumbles upon a homeopathic remedy which, if it cannot
radically cure his malady, brings him at least temporary relief.
To distract Albertine, whose little friends have gone away for
a time, he takes her to meet Saint-Loup at Doncières station,
a junction for Paris, and recently linked up with the little local
railway. They travel happily, in a fond embrace, like any normal
engaged couple, ignoring the only other passenger in the compartment, a tall ugly over-dressed woman reading *La Revue des
Deux Mondes*, whom Marcel catalogues mentally as the pro-
prietrix of a high-class house of call, though vaguely surprised
to find that such ladies read the better reviews. She turns out, as
he discovers later, to be the princess Sherbatoff, Mme Verdurin's bosom friend. Saint-Loup, it transpires, can only stay
for an hour but, as events prove, this hour contains for Marcel
just sixty minutes too many, for Albertine, to his intense annoyance, turns the entire battery of her charms on his old
comrade. When the latter takes his leave Marcel, whose jealousy
is now switched to a more normal track, furiously reproaches
Albertine for having completely ignored his presence, so infatuated was she with Saint-Loup. He brushes aside her rather
lame excuse that since the latter had seen them embracing in
the train, she wanted, by her pretended indifference, to remove
any wrong impression from Robert's mind. This fails to convince

[1] *SG.* II (1), 85.

Marcel. On the other hand, his reason convinces him, at least for a time, that Albertine's behaviour with Saint-Loup is quite incompatible with the other more painful idea he had begun to form of her character.

Inevitably, our account of the early phases of Marcel's tragedy has simplified, and therefore distorted to some extent, the reality so admirably interpreted by Proust. In order to correct this error in perspective let us recall what has already been said about the intermittent, undramatic quality of Marcel's own narrative, where the psychological states just noted do not possess that air of fatality and of eventfulness which they immediately acquire when detached from the numerous other elements that combine with them to form the stream of the narrator's conscious experience. Marcel resembles a man stricken with a slow incurable malady so that, as Proust wisely and sadly remarks in another context, he has learned to live and compound with his detested invader. Like most incurables, he enjoys periods of complete freedom from suffering during which he even imagines himself definitely restored to health. It is this reality which Proust desires, above all, to reflect in Marcel's long story of his life with Albertine. We must not, therefore, imagine him in these summer months as a sort of René, conscious of naught but his terrible jealousy and suspicions. He is the identical Marcel whose description of his first meeting with the Cambremers is a masterpiece of satirical analysis; whose portrait of Mme de Cambremer-Legrandin is a brilliant and finished study of æsthetic snobbery. He is also the Marcel who extracts diabolic pleasure from the comic misadventures of Nissim Bernard with the tomato-faced twins; whose impressions of the 'liftier', of the manager and of the amazing *courrières*, Marie Gineste and Céleste Albaret yield pages brimming with gaiety and wisdom. He is, moreover, the Marcel whose excursions with Albertine in the lovely countryside round Balbec result in an exquisite array of sensations marked down for inclusion in the *livre intérieur* of his sweetest memories.

Very plausibly, therefore—and for the novelist, most opportunely—Proust grants Marcel an apparent reprieve at Doncières station. Opportunely, because Marcel is now about to resume his

Charlus saga, introduce us to the Verdurin coterie and, incidentally, tell us more about the Cambremers and the local
aristocracy of which they are the acknowledged leaders. Now
whilst it is true that social relations in a fashionable *plage*
are characterized by a *laissez-aller* unthinkable in the Faubourg
Saint-Germain, a much more powerful motive must be adduced
to explain why a Charlus mingles with the Verdurins and their
satellites: Brichot, the Sorbonne professor, Cottard, the eminent
clinician and member of the Academy of Medicine, the timid,
stammering archivist Saniette, the Polish sculptor, Ski, the
enigmatic Russian princess Sherbatoff, not to speak of the occasional guests who are invited to Mme Verdurin's Wednesday
dinner parties and 'musicales'. The baron's vice supplies the
motive. When Marcel has said goodbye to Robert at Doncières
station he catches sight of Charlus waiting for his train to
Paris, an exotic and curious figure to catch one's eye on a
railway platform under the merciless light of a summer day.

A Paris où je ne le recontrais qu'en soirée [Marcel observes],
immobile, sanglé dans un habit noir, maintenu dans le sens de la
verticale par son fier redressement, son élan pour plaire, la fusée de
sa conversation, je ne me rendais pas compte à quel point il avait
vieilli. Maintenant, dans un complet de voyage clair qui le faisait
paraître plus gros, en marche et se dandinant, balançant un ventre qui
bedonnait et un derrière symbolique, la cruauté du grand jour dé-
composait sur ses lèvres, en fard, en poudre de riz fixée par le cold-
cream, sur le bout du nez, en noir sur les moustaches teintes dont la
couleur d'ébène contrastait avec les cheveux grisonnants, tout ce qui
aux lumières eût semblé l'animation du teint chez un être encore jeune.[1]

[In Paris, where I saw him only in evening clothes, immobile, in
a close-fitting dress-coat, maintained in the vertical position by his
proud erectness, his eagerness to please, his verbal pyrotechnics, I did
not completely realize how much he had aged. Now in a light-
coloured travelling suit which made him appear stouter, waddling
along, with his swaying paunch and almost symbolic backside, the
cruel light of day disintegrated into paint, upon his lips, into rice-
powder fixed by cold cream, on the tip of his nose, into mascara on his
dyed moustache whose ebony hue stood out in contrast to his grizzled
hair, everything which in artificial light would have seemed like the
fresh complexion of a fairly young man.]

[1] *SG.* II (2), 97–8.

Another train, full of troops is standing on the opposite line, headed for Doncières. The baron suddenly asks Marcel to cross and bring over one of his relatives, a young bandsman of the regiment. Obligingly he carries out his mission, only to find that the soldier in question is Charles Morel, the son of his late uncle Adolphe's valet. Charlus interrupts their conversation, peremptorily informing Morel that he wants to hear some chamber music that evening and is willing to pay five hundred francs to the violinist. Marcel is blandly waved aside. Though used to the baron's insolence, he cannot understand the latter's inexcusable rudeness to anyone connected with the Guermantes, still less the sudden decision of Charlus to cancel his journey to Paris. Then the explanation dawns on him. The baron has never seen Morel before in his life. But the social gulf is now bridged since Morel, a brilliant student of the Conservatoire temporarily stationed for his military service at Doncières, has been invited to play at La Raspelière. And Marcel, at his first Verdurin *mercredi*, will hear from the Patronne herself of a young and talented musician who asks if he may bring with him a tiresome friend of his parents—a certain baron de Charlus.

The baron's situation, *mutatis mutandis*, exactly parallels that of Swann who, during his infatuation for Odette, practically deserted the Faubourg Saint-Germain for the Verdurin pseudo-bohemian *salon* in the rue de Montalivet. It will transpire also that Charlus, like Swann, basked for a spell in the Patronne's favour before incurring her suspicion and enmity. A similar analogy, we have observed, is established by Proust between Swann's passion for Odette and Marcel's unhappy love for Albertine, and, as later events reveal, he frequently accentuates this parallelism. It now becomes possible, indeed, to perceive the design which reflects in the author's challenging and unorthodox conception of the role played in the social scheme by sexual love. Viewed from this Proustian plane, Sodom and Gomorrha, hitherto excluded from the novelist's purview of human nature or at most only very dimly suggested on a distant horizon, now stand out boldly in the foreground of the canvas. To conform with this vision the inverted passion of Charlus and the Sapphism of Albertine—assuming, naturally, that the artist intends to retain a due sense of proportion—must be grouped along with *Un amour de Swann* as integral constituent elements of one complete design. Here Proust, I suggest, was influenced by that *esprit géométrique* which has led other searchers after truth to mistake trees for woods, hearsay for evidence, to generalize on exceptional cases in a laudable anxiety to establish those *lois générales* to which Marcel so frequently alludes. 'Tous les goûts' no doubt, as Voltaire said, 'sont dans la nature.' But this does alter the fact that certain tastes are fortunately rare, so rare as to strike the common sense of the ordinary man as the reverse of natural. Proust, who had plenty of common sense, recognized this and, as his novel developed, reduced the proportions of his infernal cities by a readjustment of perspective which we are now able to observe.

From now onwards the Verdurin clan and especially Mme Verdurin herself occupy an important place in *A la recherche du temps perdu*. This is a very natural arrangement since Marcel and Charlus are soon to become regular members of the coterie. It is excellent also for the novelist's dual objective which is to keep Charlus from stealing all the limelight and at the same time to create, as far as possible, a prevailing atmosphere of high comedy in the scenes which illuminate the baron's complex nature. Mme Verdurin or *la Patronne*, as she is affectionately referred to by her disciples, is a great comic figure vying indeed, from this point of view, with Charlus himself. She is surrounded, moreover, by characters whose several oddities combine to produce a tone of gaiety effectively distracting one's attention, in certain passages, from the grave and essentially sinister nature of the author's theme. Proust, for whom it was an axiom that characters appear static only when we are losing interest in them, always portrays them, physically as well as psychologically, in fluid movement so that at no stage in the stream of the narrative is it ever wise to form a dogmatic opinion on his creations. Usually, however, it will be found that Marcel seizes upon some recurring gesture, expression or trick of speech by which we may rapidly evoke the image of a particular person. Who does not recall, for instance, the shining hemispheres of Mme Verdurin's forehead inflamed by the concentrated ardour with which she has listened to a hundred sonatas, crouching with head buried in hands, in that typical Verdurin pose?—a convenient attitude for slumber, philistines are base enough to whisper. But this is almost certainly pure slander. Again, how can one forget that other attitude, a variant of the first, expressing the Patronne's high good humour. Observe her at one of the celebrated *mercredis* convulsed with silent mirth at one of Cottard's *pince sans rire* japes, her eyes again covered by her hands, or else with head burrowing girlishly in the princess Sherbatoff's shoulder. This particular *tic*, we learn from Marcel, originated in a very simple but rather painful contretemps when Mme Verdurin, in the midst of a peal of unrestrained laughter, once had the misfortune to dislocate her jaw.

The High Priestess of a temple devoted to the cult of Music— 'ce n'est pas de la musiquette qu'on fait ici'—Mme Verdurin also cultivates the other fine arts. It was she, in fact, who first discovered Elstir and, probably, as she claims, really did assist at the accouchement of his genius. All that remains, however, of their long friendship is a collection of the artist's exquisite flower paintings, the beauty of which owes a great deal to Mme Verdurin's sensitive and natural taste. For Elstir, resenting the Patronne's interference in his private life, deserted her circle on his marriage. With Brichot she was more successful because, on learning that the professor was about to marry his laundress, Mme Verdurin energetically intervened, stopped this nonsense and eventually pushed the romantic savant into the Institut, thus earning his undying gratitude. Her *libido dominandi*, her itch to organize the existence of her disciples springs naturally from Mme Verdurin's worship of Culture. This, in turn, originates partly in a genuine appreciation of artistic or intellectual talent, partly, however, in her snobbish ambition to be the queen of an exclusive *avant garde* society of painters, musicians, scientists and men of letters. Contemptuous of her own sex, the Patronne rarely invites women unless, like Mme Cottard and the princess Sherbatoff, they will accept the subordinate role of thurifers to the Priestess. A despot and therefore capricious of her favours, she is liable suddenly to turn on a member of the clan who seems to fall below her exacting standard, or excites the ill-humour of

M. Verdurin whom his wife maliciously encourages, for example, in his favourite sport of bullying the wretched Saniette. Yet so terrified are both the Verdurins at any sign of defection in the clan that even Saniette, after an evening in the course of which he has almost been reduced to tears of despair, is always, prior to his departure, mollified, flattered and reinvited. This is regularly the occasion of a little comedy where Verdurin is featured as the *faux grincheux* whose bark is worse than his bite, whose apparent exasperation conceals, indeed, a profound affection for his victim.

To Marcel every *salon* is a theatre, and the Patronne's is no exception. But Marcel is no longer the impressionable young critic whose infatuation for the leading actress and subsequent disenchantment we saw reflected in his review of the Guermantes comedy, though it would be inaccurate to say that he approaches La Raspelière in a completely objective mood. His companions, to begin with, are more than usually animated, for this is to be a very special *mercredi*, graced by the presence of the Cambremers. There are two other causes of excitement. Mme Verdurin's latest find, a young violinist who has been dining three times a week at La Raspelière, had unaccountably failed to appear on the previous Monday. The success of the *mercredi* is jeopardized by another event, the death of the musician Dechambre, an ancient discovery of the Patronne's, who has known him for twenty-five years. Now, there is one article in the Verdurin creed which every disciple knows by heart. It is that at all costs the Patronne must be protected against the baleful physical effects of her extraordinary sensibility. A martyr to her passion for Music, Mme Verdurin, before exposing her sensitive nervous system to the delicious but shattering ordeal of a symphony concert, is obliged to absorb large doses of aspirin. Without this prophylactic her temperature shoots up and she is prostrated by neuralgic headaches. On no account, therefore, must she learn of Dechambre's demise. But these are futile precautions. The princess Sherbatoff who has joined the train at Mainville, brings grave news.

'Oui, elle *sait tout* depuis ce matin', dit la princesse, 'on n'a *pas pu lui cacher*.' 'Ah! mille tonnerres de Zeus,' s'écria Brichot, 'ah! ça a du être un coup terrible, un ami de vingt-cinq ans. En voila un qui

était des nôtres.' 'Evidemment, evidemment, que voulez-vous,' dit
Cottard. 'Ce sont des circonstances toujours pénibles; mais Madame
Verdurin est une femme forte, c'est une cérébrale encore plus qu'une
émotive.' 'Je ne suis pas tout à fait de l'avis du docteur,' dit la princesse,
à qui décidément son parler rapide, son accent murmuré, donnait l'air
à la fois boudeur et mutin. 'Mme Verdurin, sous une apparence froide,
cache des trésors de sensibilité. M. Verdurin m'a dit qu'il avait eu
beaucoup de peine à l'empêcher d'aller à Paris pour la cérémonie; il
a été obligé de lui faire croire que tout se ferait à la campagne.' 'Ah!
diable, elle voulait aller à Paris. Mais je sais bien que c'est une femme
de cœur, peut-être de trop de cœur même....'[1]

By the time the carriages sent to fetch the guests at Féterne
are drawn up before La Raspelière, Marcel is enveloped in a
rosy cloud of happiness. The Doncières incident has dispelled
his terrible suspicions of Albertine so that the journey from
Balbec to Féterne is an experience fraught with ever mounting
delight, culminating in the marvellous drive along the cliff
road to La Raspelière. Intoxicated by the pure, soft, upland air,
by the grandeur of the quiet blue expanse below, and charmed
by the rose-smothered cottages gliding past the carriage windows, Marcel is invaded by a wave of tenderness. He could
have embraced the princess Sherbatoff, the Verdurins, the whole
world. Listening to his rapturous exclamations, the princess
thinks privately that this young man is an *exalté*, for, after all,
although the scenery is fine it does not strike her as surpassingly
beautiful. Nor does she understand Marcel's paroxysms of
gratitude to the Verdurins for having sent the carriages to meet
them.

Now the princess, who had slipped on to the train unobserved
by the other members of the clan and was eventually discovered
in an empty compartment reading *La Revue des Deux Mondes*, is
the very lady whose appearance had so amused Marcel and
Albertine on the way to Doncières. We now learn something
of her real history. Princess Sherbatoff, who for some years has
been ostracized by the Faubourg Saint-Germain, is like Mme
Verdurin, extremely wealthy. Having quarrelled with her
family, exiled moreover from her country, she has practically
no friends. Indeed, until her friendship with the Patronne she

[1] *SG.* II (2), 147–8.

knew only the Grand Duchess Eudoxie and the Baroness Putbus, and they only received her privately. Seeing no prospect of ever realizing her passionate desire to be taken back into society, the princess has not only made a virtue of necessity. She represents her position as the result of a deliberate and inflexible decision. 'Je ne vois *personne* d'autre', she tells the admiring clan, 'je ne fréquente que trois maisons.' Only Marcel, when he gets to know her better, discovers the pathos of her situation, the frustration and loneliness of this exile seated at the back of her box at the Opéra, longing to know the people whom the clan, out of deference for her imaginary desire for privacy, are careful never to present to the princess. That is why she adores Mme Verdurin, changing her *pension* when the Verdurins move house, following them on holiday, acting as *dame de compagnie* to the Patronne. Marcel does not find out her secret until one day he innocently offends her beyond hope of pardon precisely by respecting the illusory protocol. It is when, in the *tacot*, they chance to meet the marquise de Villeparisis whom he does not, of course, introduce to the princess. The latter, from that moment, never speaks to him.

Next to the princess Sherbatoff, the most assiduous devotee of Mme Verdurin is Brichot, the Sorbonne professor, whose very fidelity, however, is beginning to diminish his prestige with the High Priestess. A fine humanist, annoyed at the new Teutonic scientism that is creeping into the University of Paris, Brichot alternately charms Marcel by his erudition and irritates him by that tiresome affectation of frivolity so often found in distinguished scholars who feel impelled, perhaps because they are so familiar with their speciality, to 'debunk' history, to speak of the great figures of literature in the flippant idiom of contemporary slang. All the same, we need not allow ourselves to be deluded by Marcel's occasional exasperations, since Brichot's erudite *boutades*, as Proust knows very well, by their piquant contrast with the interesting matter of the professor's *ex cathedra* lectures, constitute a rich fund of entertainment. What is more important, if we recollect Boileau's dictum about art and the 'monstre odieux' is the subtle use made of Brichot, notably in *La Prisonnière*, in order to express Proust's unorthodox views on what Voltaire used to call *l'amour socra-tique*. As Marcel's narrative unfolds, we catch glimpses of another Brichot, surprised off-stage, when the stream of his eloquence is for a moment interrupted, the thoughtful rather sad Brichot, whose sight is rapidly disappearing along with his remaining illusions concerning friendship. 'Il n'ignorait pas que Mme Verdurin riait parfois publiquement de lui-même de ses infirmités, et sachant le peu qu'il faut attendre des affections humaines, s'y étant soumis, il ne considérait moins la Patronne comme sa meilleure amie.'[1] And who but Charlus could have divined, as he does to Marcel's stupefaction, that this elderly, myopic scholar is hopelessly in love with that elegant, hard, self-centred and incurable snob, the marquise de Cambremer?

For a character who appears so frequently in Marcel's nar-rative, Cottard reveals few surprising or contradictory traits. His author, possibly, was content to develop a fundamental contradiction which is sufficiently remarkable in itself. I mean the contrast between Cottard the distinguished specialist, the gimlet-eyed diagnostician and the Cottard whose abject puns and third-rate commercial traveller witticisms enchant the Verdurins, since the Patronne's great ambition is to collect great men and display them *en pantoufles* in her drawing-room. Marcel always keeps before our eyes the two images of Cottard.

Of modest, peasant stock, this brilliant professor of medicine has cultivated, during his long professional career, the inti-midating dogmatic manner which neurotic patients expect to find in their consultant physician. Moreover, in his capacity as *chef d'internat*, Cottard has long been accustomed to exercise unchallenged authority. Even at the Verdurins, should any guest dare to hazard an opinion on a medical subject, the doctor will abruptly stop his clowning in order to pulverize the unwary and profane individual who never fails, like the marquis de Cambremer or the princess Sherbatoff, to cower submissively beneath this traditional 'moliéresque' *veto* of the Faculty. On the other hand, Cottard has never quite managed to shake off the mannerisms of his village boyhood days. Watch him, for example,

[1] *SG.* II (2), 221.

at La Raspelière playing cards with Morel, the trump suspended in mid air, in approved *bistro* fashion, ready to smash down on his opponent's queen.

On entendait de temps à autre la voix de Morel et celle de Cottard. 'Vous avez de l'atout?' 'Yes.' 'Ah! vous en avez de bonnes, vous,' dit à Morel, en réponse à sa question, M. de Cambremer, car il avait vu que le jeu du docteur était plein d'atout. 'Voici la femme de carreau,' dit le docteur. 'Ça est de l'atout, savez-vous? Ié coupe, ié prends.' 'Mais il n'y a plus de Sorbonne,' dit le docteur à M. de Cambremer; 'il n'y a plus que l'Université de Paris.' M. de Cambremer confessa qu'il ignorait pourquoi le docteur lui faisait cette observation. 'Je croyais que vous parliez de la Sorbonne,' reprit le docteur. 'J'avais entendu que vous disiez: "tu nous la *sors bonne*,"' ajouta-t-il en clignant de l'œil, pour montrer que c'était un mot. 'Attendez', dit-il en montrant son adversaire, 'je lui prépare un coup de Trafalgar.' Et le coup devait être excellent pour le docteur, car dans sa joie il se mit en riant à remuer voluptueusement les deux épaules ce qui était dans sa famille, dans le 'genre' Cottard, un trait presque zoologique de la satisfaction. Dans la génération précédente le mouvement de se frotter les mains comme si on se savonnait, accompagnait le mouvement. Cottard lui-même avait d'abord usé simultanément de la double mimique, mais un beau jour sans qu'on sût à quelle intervention, conjugale, magistrale peut-être, cela était dû, le frottement des mains avait disparu. Le docteur, même aux dominos, quand il forçait son partenaire à 'piocher' et à prendre le double six, ce qui était pour lui le plus vif des plaisirs, se contenait du mouvement des épaules. Et quand — le plus rarement possible — il allait dans son pays natal pour quelques jours, en retrouvant son cousin-germain qui, lui, en était encore au frottement des mains, il disait au retour à Mme Cottard: 'J'ai trouvé ce pauvre René bien commun....'[1]

[From time to time one heard the voice of Morel and that of Cottard. 'Have you got trumps?' 'Yes.' 'Ah! *you've* got some good ones', said M. de Cambremer in reply to Morel's question, for he had noticed that the doctor's hand was full of trumps. 'Here's the queen of diamonds', said the doctor. 'That's trump, you know. I cut, I take my trick. But there isn't a Sorbonne any longer', said the doctor to M. de Cambremer. 'There is only the University of Paris.' M. de Cambremer confessed that he did not see the point of this remark. 'I thought you were talking about the Sorbonne', continued the doctor. 'I had heard you saying: "tu nous la *sors bonne*"' he added, with a wink to show that it was a pun. 'Wait', he said, pointing to

[1] *SG.* II (3), 23-4.

his opponent, 'I'm getting a Trafalgar ready for him.' And it must have been an excellent affair for the doctor because in his joy he began to laugh voluptuously, shrugging his shoulders, a movement which, in his family, in the 'genus' Cottard, was an almost zoological sign of satisfaction. In the preceding generation, this movement used to be accompanied by that of rubbing the hands as though soaping them. Cottard himself, originally, had employed both these forms of mimicry simultaneously but one fine day, it is not clear by whose intervention, his wife's or perhaps his professor's, the rubbing of the hands had disappeared. The doctor, even at dominoes, when he got his partner worried, forcing him to take the double six, which for him was the keenest of pleasures, contented himself with the shrugging movement. And when—which was as seldom as possible—he visited his native village for a few days, on meeting his first cousin who was still at the hand-rubbing stage, he used to say to Mme Cottard, on his return: 'I thought poor René very common.']

This particular Verdurin *mercredi*, although it is the occasion of the baron's first public appearance in the company of his 'protégé', furnishes Proust with comic material of the highest grade. If Marcel is surprised to learn that the missing violinist is Charles Morel and Charlus his tiresome old family friend, picture the astonishment and snobbish delight of the marquise de Cambremer, who regards this visit to her tenants as a species of obligatory slumming, when her hostess introduces to her the formidable baron, the Saint Peter of her earthly paradise, Guermantes society. To Charlus, for whom the Verdurins are socially non-existent, the experience of entering their drawing-room is rather like a visit to a *maison de passe*— amusing, strange and faintly improper. Mme Verdurin, on the other hand, has no idea of the baron's exalted rank, of his irascible *amour-propre* and his genius for studied insolence. In exploiting these promising situations, Proust surpasses even himself. The moment Charlus advances to greet his hostess is the prelude to a suite of misunderstandings, cross purposes and *gaffes*, the full and delicious import of which is grasped only by Marcel and superbly communicated in his narrative with a fascinating variety of comic nuances. His description of the baron's entrance is in itself a masterpiece to which no mere quotation can do justice. The following passage, however, reveals the philosophic quality which, on certain occasions, tinges the imagination and humour of Proust:

Quant à M. de Charlus, à qui la société où il avait vécu fournissait, à cette minute critique, des exemples différents, d'autres arabesques d'amabilité, et enfin la maxime qu'on doit savoir dans certains cas pour de simples petits bourgeois, mettre au jour et faire servir ses grâces les plus rares et habituellement gardées en réserve, c'est en se trémoussant avec mièvrerie et la même ampleur dont un enjuponnement eût élargi et gêné ses dandinements, qu'il se dirigea vers Mme Verdurin avec un air si flatté et si honoré qu'on eût dit qu'être présenté chez elle était pour lui une suprême faveur. Son visage à demi-incliné, où la satisfaction le disputait au comme il faut, se plissait de petites rides d'affabilité. On aurait cru voir s'avancer Mme de Marsantes, tant ressortait à ce moment la femme qu'une erreur de la nature avait mise dans le corps de M. de Charlus. Certes cette erreur le baron avait durement peiné pour la dissimuler et prendre une apparence masculine. Mais à peine y était-il parvenu que, ayant pendant le même temps gardé les mêmes goûts, cette habitude de sentir en femme lui donnait une nouvelle apparence féminine née celle-là non de l'hérédité, mais de la vie individuelle. Et comme il arrivait peu à peu à penser, même les choses sociales, au féminin, et cela sans s'en apercevoir, car ce n'est pas à force de mentir aux autres, mais aussi de se mentir à soi-même qu'on cesse de s'apercevoir qu'on ment, bien qu'il eût demandé à son corps de rendre manifeste (au moment où il entrait chez les Verdurin) toute la courtoisie d'un grand seigneur, ce corps qui avait bien compris ce que M. de Charlus avait cessé d'entendre, déploya, au point que le baron eût mérité l'épithète de ladylike, toutes les séductions d'une grande dame.[1]

[As for M. de Charlus, whom the society in which he had lived furnished, at this critical moment, with different examples, with various arabesques of affability, and especially with the maxim that in certain cases, for the benefit of ordinary lower-class sort of people, one must display and make use of one's rarest graces, usually held in reserve, it was with a fluttering mincing gait and the buxomness which, had he worn a skirt, would have enlarged and impeded his waddlings, that he bore down on Mme Verdurin with such a flattered and honoured air that one would have said it was for him a supreme favour to be presented to her. As he bent towards her, his face, on which satisfaction vied with good breeding, was creased with tiny wrinkles of affability. One might have thought it was Mme de Marsantes who was coming in, so vividly evident at this moment was the woman whom

[1] *SG.* ii (2), 162–3.

Nature by mistake had inserted in the body of M. de Charlus. That mistake, of course, the baron had struggled to conceal by adopting a masculine appearance. Yet scarcely had he achieved this than, having meanwhile retained the same tastes, this habit of feeling like a woman lent him a new feminine appearance, which derived not from heredity but from his individual way of living. And as he gradually came to consider even social matters from a woman's viewpoint, and quite unconsciously, for it is not merely by dint of lying to others but by lying to oneself that one ceases to notice that one is lying, although he had called upon his body to manifest (at the moment he entered the Verdurins' house) all the courtesy of a great nobleman, that body of his which had grasped so well what M. de Charlus had ceased to understand, displayed, to a degree which might have earned for the baron the epithet 'ladylike', all the charm of a great lady.]

More often, perhaps, Proust strikes a note midway between comedy and farce, as in the scenes where the baron grotesquely misinterprets, though only for a few moments, the ingratiating leer shot at him from above his eyeglasses by Cottard or again when Verdurin apologetically tries to explain to Charlus why, as a mere baron, he has been given a less important place at table than the marquis de Cambremer:

'Excusez-moi de vous parler de ces riens', commença-t-il, 'car je suppose bien le peu de cas que vous en faites. Les esprits bourgeois y font attention, mais les autres, les artistes, les gens qui en sont vraiment, s'en fichent. Or dès les premiers mots que nous avons échangés, j'ai compris que vous en étiez!' M. de Charlus qui donnait à cette locution un sens fort différent, eut un haut-le-corps. Après les œillades du docteur, l'injurieuse franchise du Patron le suffoquait, 'Ne protestez pas, cher Monsieur, vous en êtes, c'est clair comme le jour' reprit M. Verdurin! 'Remarquez que je ne sais pas si vous exercez un art quelconque, mais ce n'est pas nécessaire. Ce n'est pas toujours suffisant. Degrange qui vient de mourir jouait parfaitement avec le plus robuste mécanisme, mais n'en était pas, on sentait tout de suite qu'il n'en était pas. Brichot n'en est pas. Morel en est, ma femme en est, je sens que vous en êtes....' 'Qu'alliez-vous me dire?' interrompit M. de Charlus qui commençait à être rassuré sur ce que voulait signifier M. Verdurin, mais qui préférait qu'il criât moins haut ces mots à double sens. 'Nous vous avons mis seulement à gauche,' répondit M. Verdurin. M. de Charlus, avec un sourire compréhensif, bonhomme et insolent, répondit: 'Mais voyons! Cela n'a aucune importance *ici*!' Et il eut un petit rire qui lui était spécial — un rire qui lui venait probablement de quelque grand'mere bavaroise ou lorraine, qui le tenait elle-même, tout identique, d'une aïeule, de sorte qu'il sonnait ainsi, inchangé, depuis pas mal de siècles dans de vieilles petites cours de l'Europe, et qu'on goûtait sa qualité précieuse comme celle de certains instruments anciens devenus rarissimes. [1]

['Excuse my mentioning these trifles', he began, 'for I can well imagine how little they mean to you. Middle-class minds take them seriously but we artists, we who really belong, don't care a damn for them. Now, at the very first words we exchanged, I knew you were one of us.' M. de Charlus, who attached a very different meaning to this expression, gave a violent start. After the doctor's leering glances, the Boss's insulting frankness made him apoplectic with indignation. 'Don't protest, my dear Sir, you are one of us, it's as clear as daylight', M. Verdurin went on. 'Mind you, I don't know whether you practise any particular art but that isn't necessary. It isn't always sufficient. Degrange who has just died, played beautifully with the most vigorous execution but wasn't one of us; one felt at once that he wasn't. Brichot isn't one of us. Morel is, my wife is, I'm sure you are.' 'What were you going to say to me?' interrupted M. de Charlus, who was beginning to be reassured as to M. Verdurin's meaning, but preferred that he should utter the equivocal words less loudly. 'We only put you on the left,' replied M. Verdurin. M. de Charlus, with an understanding, genial, insolent smile replied: 'Come! come! That doesn't matter in the slightest, *here*!' And he gave a little special laugh of his—a laugh that came down to him probably from some Bavarian or Lorraine grandmother, who had herself inherited it, intact, from some ancestress so that it had gone on tinkling, unchanged, for a good many centuries in little, old-fashioned European courts, and one could appreciate its precious quality as one does that of certain instruments that have become excessively rare.]

In order to appreciate the originality and beauty of a great work of art, one must, of course, approach it experimentally and certainly not in the light of this or that literary doctrine. There are, on the other hand, certain æsthetic concepts which it may be profitable to bear in mind at this stage in our attempt to interpret the art of Proust. All art is a qualitative or emotional relationship between the self and the non-self. The greater the artist, the richer and more suggestive will be this relationship, the quality of which depends on the degree to which life penetrates his intimate consciousness. By way of illustration,

[1] *SG.* II (2), 207–8.

let me offer two extreme contrasts. Recall, for example, Marcel's impressions of the Gare St-Lazare; then imagine how a technician from the École Polytechnique would describe the same terminus. Which is the real Gare St-Lazare? Unhesitatingly, Proust would tell us that it is Marcel's, thus expressing a point of view which every artist understands. To return, however, to the question of the unique relationship to which I have just alluded, the greatest art, that is to say, art which extracts the essential reality of things, is only created when the artist *feels* this relationship and never when, in an effort to imitate the approach of the scientist or technician, he tries to *think* or judge it. The artist interprets the reality of life most completely, not when he is looking at life with his analysing intelligence alone, but in the moments when he is trying to enter into it sympathetically, to seize it through his deepest consciousness which is more extensive and receptive than that of his judging, reasoning self. To 'know' life, for the artist, is to experience it to the extreme limit of his sensibility. But he is a creative artist only in so far as he is able to communicate that experience. He must not only achieve a consciousness of spiritual identity with nature and life but also communicate the quality of this relationship in such a way that it can be felt or experienced by his reader, spectator or auditor. Now, as anyone knows who is familiar with the works of Bergson, there is a close affinity— a resemblance which is not an identity—between this conception of art and the philosophic intuition of Bergsonism. We are not surprised, therefore, to discern in the work of Proust, whose outlook on life is profoundly Bergsonian, a reflection of this affinity. Affinity, not identity: it is most important to remember this fact, since Proust is a novelist and not a metaphysician. As Marcel's narrative proceeds, we shall continue to observe what we have already noted: a rhythmic oscillation of two attitudes towards life. One is the judging, critical, analysing attitude of the self to the non-self; the other is the attitude which Bergson would call 'intuitive'. Here the self tries to merge with the non-self in the consciousness that both form part of that eternal stream of movement and change which is real existence. But obviously the quality of the experience interpreted by the

artist varies enormously in suggestiveness according to the
constant transformation which is taking place in his own observing self. This contraction and expansion of the narrator's
consciousness is very definitely reflected in the rhythm of Proust's
novel. But now it is time to return to Marcel's narrative and
observe at first hand this oscillation and rhythm.

Proust, having disarmingly charged the atmosphere with
comedy, proceeds tactfully and smoothly to expose the complex
character of the baron and in a few rapid traits, the fundamental
vileness of Morel. Here we have a typical example of that
gradual enrichment of quality, that intensification of suggestiveness which, we have observed, results from the ever deepening
interpenetration of the self and the non-self, from the artist's
effort to attain a profounder, more intimate relationship with
people and things, to discover the spirit hidden in matter, the
beauty, invisible to any other eye than his, concealed beneath
ugliness. Marcel's narrative presents at the outset two predominant and alternating images of Charlus. The first, intensely
comic, is that of the megalomaniac: the other, repulsive to our
moral sense, is that of Charlus the pervert. By an artistic
tour de force Proust contrives to hold these impressions in a
state of precarious equilibrium so that the spectator's dawning
sentiment of distaste is almost immediately dispelled by an
irresistible access of gaiety which sometimes gives way to
a sense of intellectual curiosity as when, for instance, Marcel,
adopting towards Charlus the attitude of the abstract positivist,
tries to discover the 'lois générales' exemplified in his behaviour.
This is the attitude which inspired the following lines:

Des rafraîchissements étaient servis sur un table. Mme Verdurin
invita les messieurs à aller eux-mêmes choisir la boisson qui leur
convenait. M. de Charlus alla boire son verre et vite revint s'asseoir
près de la table de jeu et ne bougea plus. Mme Verdurin lui demanda:
'Avez-vous pris de mon orangeade?' Alors M. de Charlus, avec
un sourire gracieux, sur un ton cristallin qu'il avait rarement et avec
mille moues de la bouche et déhanchements de la taille, répondit:
'Non, j'ai préféré la voisine, c'est de la fraisette, je crois, c'est
délicieux.'[1]

[1] *SG.* II (3), 12.

Why is it, Marcel reflects, that a certain order of secret acts are revealed thus by unmistakable modes of speech or gesture? We have only to hear Charlus say: 'Non, j'ai préféré la voisine, la fraisette', and to note his expression and intonation in order to be at once convinced that he is an invert. Yet how is it that by no analogous signs can we learn whether a man believes or not in the Immaculate Conception or in the innocence of Dreyfus? Observe now, however, the change in the quality of his language as he moves to a deeper, more intimate and larger consciousness of Charlus. To induce from the baron's speech and mannerisms the fact that he is a pervert does not require profound knowledge, remarks Marcel, perhaps even less than that required by a doctor who diagnoses general paralysis from certain peculiarities of speech. He continues:

Mais c'est qu'ici il y a rapport plus direct entre le signe révélateur et le secret. Sans se le dire précisément on sent que c'est une douce et souriante dame qui vous répond et qui paraît maniérée, parce qu'elle se donne pour un homme et qu'on n'est pas habitué a voir les hommes faire tant de manières. Et il est peut-être plus gracieux de penser que depuis longtemps un certain nombre de femmes angéliques ont été comprises par erreur dans le sexe masculin, où, exilées, tout en battant vainement des ailes vers les hommes à qui elles inspirent une répulsion physique, savent arranger un salon, composent des 'intérieurs'.[1]

Here we have Marcel the artist at work, engaged in the difficult task of beautifying 'le monstre odieux', trying to disengage the spiritual value implicit in every manifestation of human existence, however vicious, appealing through the sensibility of the artist to that of the reader, building up that vision of Charlus which, if it is to be real, must have all the complexity, the fluidity, the apparent contradictions, even the 'unreality' of a great artist's intuitive vision which, however, far from excluding the impressions gleaned by the analytic intelligence, fuses them with the impressions caught by the larger consciousness into that unique synthesis called a great work of art. Thus the integrity of the artist impels him to present for instance not only the admirably phrased description of Charlus accompanying Morel with the virtuosity of a great pianist but also that other un-

[1] *SG.* II (3), 13.

speakably revolting yet equally true impression of the baron's conduct at his wife's funeral service.[1]

It is the *côté Saint-Simon* of Charlus which Marcel now accentuates in portraying the genesis of the prolonged feline duel between Mme Verdurin and the baron. Its outcome will be to plunge the latter into a maelstrom of humiliation, grief and murderous rage. At present, however, we observe only the amusing preliminaries, the flexing and unflexing of the polished claws, the half-playful boxing feints, the still humorous green glint of the sleepy eyes. Picture the baron, insolently seated when his hostess remains standing, enjoying her growing irritated bewilderment as it begins to dawn upon her, from the baron's conversation with Cambremer and the *empressement* of the latter, that Morel's strange companion is not perhaps a modern baron von Münchausen, but really belongs to that world she affects as a true Bohemian to despise and probably does despise.

'Dites donc, Charlus,' dit Mme Verdurin qui commençait à se familiariser, 'vous n'auriez pas dans votre faubourg quelque vieux noble ruiné qui pourrait me servir de concierge?' 'Mais si..., mais si...,' répondit M. de Charlus en souriant d'un air bonhomme, 'mais je ne vous le conseille pas.' 'Pourquoi?' 'Je craindrais pour vous que les visiteurs élégants n'allassent pas plus loin que la loge.'[2]

Marcel only discovers little by little the extraordinary 'compositeness' of Morel's nature which he later compares to a medieval book 'plein d'erreurs, de traditions absurdes, d'obscénités'. That the dominant streak in the violinist's character is baseness emerges, however, very quickly in the following incident. Discarding his usual attitude of thinly veiled insolence and glacial aloofness which is only partly to be explained by the influence of Charlus, the musician approaches Marcel with the urgent plea, couched in the terms a flunkey might have used in asking a favour of his master, that 'Monsieur' be so kind as to seize a pretext for explaining to Mme Verdurin that Morel's father occupied the position not of valet but of estate agent, 'l'intendant de domaines si vastes que cela le faisait presque l'égal de vos parents'. Marcel, though he considers Morel's evident anxiety ridiculous, contrives, however, without exaggerating his grand-uncle Adolphe's situation, to magnify the situation of Morel *père*, in whom of course Mme Verdurin has not the slightest interest. Morel, having achieved his purpose, immediately drops the mask of obsequiousness. Alone with Marcel, he is friendly and increasingly cordial though for reasons which the former only discovers long afterwards when he finds out that the musician and Albertine, unknown to him, were very well known to each other. In company, Morel resumes his air of studied impertinence, pretending not to hear questions addressed to him by Marcel. The latter, who has, as he says, a good deal of his grandmother's tolerance and wisdom, accepts Morel as he is with all his vileness, his ruthless egoism, his absolute lack of gratitude and his occasional and charming moments of expansiveness. Yet, in Marcel's account of this first evening at the Verdurins it is easy to observe the rapid dissolution of the happiness that invaded his soul during the journey to Féterne and reached its climax in the drive along the cliff-road to La Raspelière. Once again, I think, he encounters a source of disillusionment which springs not from the despair of the moralist who finds humanity very different from what he had naïvely believed, but from the distress of the artist who cannot interpret the contents of his 'livre intérieur', the uniqueness of a vision achieved by intuition. He cannot escape the truth that what to him are realities of the first importance, charged with unlimited possibilities for happiness, are incomprehensible, trivial or absurd to most other human beings. This incommunicability, to judge from his conversations with Mme Verdurin and especially with the young marquise de Cambremer, appears to him to be the property of true reality.

Je ne touchai pas plus les Cambremer que Mme Verdurin par mon enthousiasme pour leur maison. Car j'étais froid devant les beautés qu'ils me signalaient et m'exaltais de réminiscences confuses; quelquefois même je leur avouais ma déception, ne trouvant pas quelque chose conforme à ce que son nom m'avait fait imaginer. J'indignai Mme de Cambremer en lui disant que j'avais cru que c'était plus campagne. En revanche je m'arrêtai avec extase à renifler l'odeur d'un vent coulis qui passait par la porte. 'Je vois que vous aimez les courants d'air,' me dirent-ils. Mon éloge du morceau de lustrine verte bouchant un carreau cassé n'eut pas plus de succès. 'Mais, quelle horreur!' s'écria la Marquise. Le comble fut quand je dis: 'Ma plus grande joie a été quand je suis arrivé. Quand j'ai entendu résonner mes pas dans la galérie je ne sais pas dans quel bureau de mairie de village, où il y a la carte du canton, je me crus entré.' Cette fois Mme de Cambremer me tourna résolument le dos.[1]

[My enthusiasm for their house had no more effect on the Cambremers than on Mme Verdurin. For the beauties they pointed out left me cold whilst I worked myself up into a state of excitement over confused memories; sometimes even, I confessed to them my disappointment because I found something inconsistent with what its name had made me imagine. I aroused Mme de Cambremer's indignation by telling her I had thought it was more rural. On the other hand, I halted to sniff ecstatically at a breeze that came through the door. 'I see you like draughts,' they said to me. I had no more success when I praised a bit of green lustre plugging up a broken window-pane. 'How frightful!' exclaimed the Marquise. The climax came when I said: 'My greatest joy was when I arrived. When I heard my footsteps echoing in the gallery, I thought I had walked into the office of some village *mairie* with a map of the canton on the wall.' Thereupon, Mme de Cambremer firmly turned her back on me.]

Do not let ourselves be misled by Marcel's tone of humorous, rather cynical resignation. We have heard it often already and we shall hear it often again. He will never give up this attempt to achieve a larger consciousness of existence, to find his most intimate *moi* and thus to penetrate beyond what Bergson calls 'le voile des concepts', the plausible transcriptions of the analytic intelligence, into the true reality of human nature and of things. So the history of Marcel's vocation will always reveal this continual shifting of the levels of his consciousness, this range and variety of attitudes to life.

A great artist, like a first-class artisan, is always dissatisfied with the instrument or method handed to him by his masters. But if he is always trying to evolve and exploit the potentialities of a better medium, he does not in a fit of petulance throw away the old one and abandon his job. On the contrary, he derives a kind of satisfaction from his ability to use the traditional method with even greater skill than his predecessors. The work

[1] *SG.* II (2), 211–12.

of art is therefore always an amalgam of old and new, of the traditional and the modern. So Marcel, for example, after his disappointing conversation with Mme Verdurin and Mme de Cambremer, turns with a kind of morose satisfaction to the business of analysing and judging their vices and follies, well aware that he can use this instrument, this method of approach, so as to obtain original and striking results.

He gives us, in fact, a fascinating comparative study in snobberies. Mme de Cambremer, the pushful little lady in *Un amour de Swann* whose 'forward' behaviour at Mme de Saint-Euverte's concert annoyed Oriane, is now a handsome young matron whose passion to be received by duchesses has cured her of what Marcel calls 'certains penchants à l'avarice et à l'adultère auxquels étant jeune elle était encline'. Mme Verdurin, whose dominating ambition is to preserve the integrity of her *salon* from the erosive influences of family and other ties, is transformed by snobbery into a sort of procuress who, although personally a chaste person, is so afraid of Marcel deserting the 'clan' for Albertine that she offers to put them both up at La Raspelière indefinitely, knowing perfectly well that they are not cousins. In both these women, the cult of modernistic art is ancillary to their main purpose, the establishment of a brilliant social position. Marcel, usually so indulgent and so broadminded where moral weaknesses are in question, is ruthless in his analysis of this sub-species of snobbery. Mme de Cambremer's brother, Legrandin, as he had already noted with sardonic amusement, is a good example of how easy it is to mistake the æsthetic Tartuffe for the genuine lover of art. Legrandin, who dwelt apparently in a purely spiritual world, used to impress and even shame Marcel by his contemptuous remarks on the frivolity of *la vie mondaine* until that illuminating encounter in the *salon* of Mme de Villeparisis which stripped off the mask and revealed the soul not of a poet, but of a flunkey and a snob. Yet as La Rochefoucauld observed: 'Il y a dans le cœur humain une génération perpétuelle de passions, en sorte que la ruine de l'une est presque toujours l'établissement d'une autre.' Legrandin must once have had a genuine passion for beauty before he sacrificed it to his cult of duchesses. At least,

so one may divine from the exquisite if somewhat baroque quality
of his conversations. This is probably in Marcel's mind when
he speaks of Mme de Cambremer's purity of language, which
undoubtedly reveals a seventeenth-century appreciation of formal
elegance. In her as in her brother, however, art has been
prostituted to snobbery. Thus, as Marcel observes, although
a disciple of the new philosophers who emphasize the unreality
of the external world, and an adept of the new literature which
interprets human nature through the medium of characters
drawn from the humblest ranks of society, Mme de Cambremer
redoubles her efforts to enter the charmed circle of the Faubourg
Saint-Germain. For, as Marcel observes, after Leibniz: 'Le trajet
est long de l'intelligence au cœur.' Wickedly probing the depths
of the lady's snobbery he discovers the perfect technique for
dealing with this type of humbug. Irritated by the insufferable
air of pity and contempt she assumes when he ventures to praise
'back numbers' like Poussin or Wagner—since, of course, anyone in the movement knows that Monet and Debussy are the only
artists who matter nowadays—Marcel gently insinuates that
M. Degas admires Poussin enormously and that the very latest
connoisseurs regard Debussy as a super-Wagner. Attack is
always the best defence. A few days later, Mme de Cambremer's
smile of pitying contempt will be reserved for the philistines
crazy enough not to appreciate the genius of Poussin and
Wagner! In this account of Marcel's second Balbec visit, as
indeed throughout the whole novel, there are lengthy passages
in this La Rochefoucauld vein when Proust, shedding his Bergsonian distrust of the analytic intelligence, appears to justify
critics like Benda and Alain who place him in the direct line of
the traditional *romanciers d'analyse*. There are also many others,
equally sustained, where by an unexpected introversion he is
carried down into a deeper region of the consciousness. That is
why Proust insists that his novel is *l'histoire d'une vocation*, in
other words, a narrative of trials and errors, of disillusions
and joys, of alternating doubts and intense convictions. Somewhere, referring to Dostoevski, who strikes him at that particular stage in his own evolution as superhuman, Marcel says
apologetically: 'Mais on ne se réalise que successivement.'

The phrase is significant and should be kept in mind as we follow his narrative.

Just as we must place ourselves in the perspective indicated by the artist in order to appreciate Monet's *Nymphea*, I think that in fairness to Proust we must adopt the viewpoint he tacitly recommends in defining his novel as the story of a vocation. For him, it would seem, as for the Impressionists of his time, the work of art is not an objective reproduction of nature executed according to the canons of a rational æsthetic and capable, therefore, of being grasped in its full significance by a spectator familiar with these canons. The purpose of the work of art is to serve as a means of linking the sensibility of the artist with our own. That is surely what Proust means when he says he has given us a new instrument by which to observe the world. In communicating to us the process by which Marcel realizes himself, by which his consciousness of existence is enlarged and enriched, he hopes that our own horizon will be enlarged, our ignorance of life diminished. But the reader must be willing to share in this experience. He must not, so to speak, retain the perspective from which one may best view a Poussin in order to appreciate the beauty of a Monet. It is this refusal to cooperate with the artist which has led some critics to view Proust's novel at one extreme simply as an exercise in critical observation, 'a judgement on life', or at the other as a 'novel of the unconscious', when, in fact, the work ranges over a wide field of consciousness. As we shall see, it is Proust's effort to break out of that restricted area in which most of us have to live, that 'champ clos' described by Bergson in the following memorable passage:

Ainsi, jusque dans notre propre individu, l'individualité nous échappe. Nous nous mouvons parmi des généralités et des symboles, comme en une champ clos où notre force se mesure utilement avec d'autres forces; et fascinés par l'action, attirés par elle, pour notre plus grand bien, sur le terrain qu'elle s'est choisi, nous vivons dans une zone mitoyenne entre les choses et nous, extérieurement aux choses, extérieurement aussi à nous-mêmes. Mais de loin en loin, par distraction, la nature suscite des âmes plus détachées de la vie. Je ne parle pas de ce détachement voulu, raisonné, systématique, qui est œuvre de réflexion et de philosophie. Je parle d'un détachement naturel, inné à la structure du sens ou de la conscience, et qui se manifeste tout de suite par une manière virginale, en quelque sorte, de voir, d'entendre ou de penser.[1]

[Thus, individuality escapes us even in our own individual self. We move amongst generalities and symbols, as in a tilt-yard where our strength effectively measures itself with other forces, and fascinated by action, drawn by it for our greater good, on to its chosen terrain, we live in a zone midway between things and ourselves, externally to things, externally also to ourselves. But from time to time, inadvertently, Nature raises up souls more detached from life. I am not speaking of that deliberate, reasoned, systematic detachment which is the work of reflection and philosophy. I mean a natural detachment, innate in the structure of the senses or consciousness and which manifests itself immediately in a virginal manner, as it were, of seeing, understanding and thinking.]

No one, as Bergson goes on to say, ever attained this detachment completely. 'Si le détachement était complet, si l'âme n'adhérait plus à l'action par aucune de ses perceptions, elle serait l'âme d'un artiste comme le monde n'en a point vu encore.' To what extent Proust succeeded in enlarging the confines of the 'champ clos' will emerge, it is to be hoped, from our study of his work. What we should keep in mind is that *A la recherche du temps perdu* represents the effort of a convinced Bergsonian and great artist to interpret nature according to the directive adumbrated in the above passage and explained, in all its implications, throughout Bergson's works. The view that Proust was saturated in the theories of Bergson has been expressed, of course, by many of his critics. As M. L-P. Quint has said: 'Proust semble avoir vécu, expérimenté personnellement toute la psychologie bergsonienne.' With this few will disagree, and if one knows Bergson well, it is a comparatively easy matter to extract the Bergsonisms that abound in Marcel's narrative, the maxims and reflections which paraphrase or condense the master's own pronouncements. It is less easy to show exactly to what extent and how Bergsonism, which shaped and profoundly influenced Proust's conception of art, was actually translated into practice; for philosophic theories, however

[1] *Le rire.*

suggestive and fascinating, cannot be strung together to make a novel. Of this, we know, Proust himself was well aware when he began to weave the precious yet scanty revelations of the involuntary memory into the tissue of a work of art. Here again, illumination can only be obtained gradually, from our impressions of Marcel's narrative. We must, therefore, rejoin him and the little 'clan' at La Raspelière and in particular note their attitude and his to Charlus and Morel.

The character of Charlus now begins to develop at a more rapid tempo and acquires increasing density. Proust is obviously trying to break with the traditional, deterministic method of characterization whereby the personality is represented as a succession of states of consciousness, of sentiments, sensations and ideas the strongest of which, often after a severe conflict, shapes a person's actions. Proust inclines to the opposite or Bergsonian view that this deterministic psychology is too simple. It is wrong to portray the *moi* as buffeted hither and thither between two conflicting sentiments, finally electing one rather than the other as its master and guide. We must not picture the ego as something always identical with itself, weighed down by conflicting sentiments which remain, moreover, identical during this process. This is what Marcel probably has in mind when he speaks of 'plane psychology'. Bergson refuses to accept such a psychology, based on the associationist theory, because it takes no account of the fact that the self is constantly changing and, therefore, continually modifying the feelings which agitate it. This theory is only applicable to the surface impressions made on the self, the impersonal sensations that do not penetrate our whole consciousness. Most of our daily actions, says Bergson, are no doubt shaped by sensations, feelings or impressions of this nature, so that the majority of our actions, although conscious, are really very like reflex acts. But any feeling, the moment it goes down deep enough, reflects the whole personality, the dynamic interfused series of states of consciousness which is the self. The acts, the 'free acts', as Bergson calls them, which emanate thus from the whole of our personality, from our *moi intérieur*, are naturally rare for the simple reason that, as a rule, the practical needs of everyday social existence make it advisable not to live at such a pitch of intensity. Thus, we have a second self whose existence, Bergson points out, is made up of distinct moments, whose states are separated from each other and easily expressed in words. But words fix only the impersonal, objective aspects of the multiplicity of emotions that stir the soul. Novelists, of course, know this and endeavour to reconstruct the history of the self, to reveal the inmost character of their creations. But, says Bergson, 'just as we can go on inserting points between two positions of a moving body without ever filling up the space traversed, in the same way, by the mere fact that we associate states with states and that these states are set side by side instead of permeating each other, we fail to translate completely what the soul experiences: there is no common measure between mind and language.'[1]

Now Proust constantly endeavours to avoid this error. He tries to distinguish between acts that express the *moi intérieur* and the everyday or empirical self. He shows us for instance, not in logical causal sequence but in lifelike dynamic interfusion his own ever modifying impressions of Charlus, the impressions made by the latter on Cottard, on the Verdurins, on Morel. He reveals, too, the contrast between the baron's illusory impressions of the 'petit clan', his images of Morel's character which are coloured by his profound sentiments for the violinist and on the other hand the realities observed by Marcel. Let me illustrate what I mean.

Cottard, influenced by Ski, and confusing our baron de Charlus with a homonym whose *mœurs* are known to the police, adopts an attitude resembling that of the average man who prides himself on his broadmindedness. Proust exploits this situation in a vein of wicked comedy sometimes bordering on farce. Take, for example, the scene where Cottard who has agreed out of vanity to act as second in a purely fictitious duel invented by Charlus, is accorded a private interview since the baron, having scared Morel into submission, now desires to thank the doctor for his kind but now unnecessary services. Alone with this formidable person, the Cottard whose

[1] *Essai sur les données immédiates de la conscience*: II. De l'organisation des états de conscience.

witticisms and *ex cathedra* pronouncements on the baron's vice
are an inexhaustible fund of amusement to his fellow-travellers
in the little train, is now transformed into a bundle of appre-
hensions. The baron in one of his most *vieille France* attitudes
takes the doctor's hand and with some repulsion strokes it
condescendingly in the true manner of a Guermantes taking
leave of a plebeian.

N'osant quitter sa chaise où la peur le tenait cloué, il roulait des
yeux d'épouvante, comme tombé aux mains d'un sauvage dont il
n'était pas bien assuré qu'il ne se nourrît pas de chair humaine. Enfin
M. de Charlus lui lâchant la main et voulant être aimable jusqu'au
bout. 'Vous allez prendre quelque chose avec nous, comme on dit, ce
qu'on appelait autrefois un mazagran ou un "gloria", boissons qu'on ne
trouve plus comme curiosités archéologiques, que dans les pièces de
Labiche et les cafés de Doncières. Un "gloria" serait assez convenable
au lieu, n'est-ce pas, et aux circonstances, qu'en dites-vous?'[1]

To the *fidèles*, these journeys, thrice weekly, in the little train
have all the excitement and romance of voyages to some exotic
country. Here, in their midst, is a strange and wonderful
specimen of the human species who can be induced by subtle
manœuvres to converse in the idiom of his tribe and even reveal,
perhaps, the secrets of its ritual and manners. This is all the
more probable since Charlus, naïvely convinced that he is thereby
camouflaging his vice, invariably affects to discuss it on the
lofty, impersonal plane of abstract speculation. And because he
is an artist as well as a monomaniac, prone also at certain
moments to view the whole world of reality and of art through
the eyes of a sexual invert, his impressions of literature, particularly of Balzac's novels, compose several of Proust's most
illuminating pages. It is this aspect of Charlus which impresses
the members of the clan, tickles their vanity, panders to their
love of sensation, lends them a flattering sense of intellectual
superiority and overcomes their natural feelings of repulsion.
Proust, in one of his most effective images, captures and interprets the quality of their sentiments.

Mais, au fond, si Charlus ne venait pas, on était presque déçu de
voyager seulement entre gens comme tout le monde et de l'avoir pas

auprès de soi ce personnage peinturluré, pansu et clos, semblable
à quelque boîte de provenance exotique et suspecte qui laisse échapper
la curieuse odeur de fruits auxquels l'idée de goûter seulement vous
soulèverait le cœur.[1]

Marcel himself, striving to obtain a more real vision of the
baron's personality, tries to place himself at the viewpoint from
which the latter must observe humanity and experience life. But
this is not easy. One cannot, for instance, simply assume that
Charlus, in his contacts with real people or with people in
literature, automatically transposes the sexes. No doubt such
inversion takes place, but since the baron is seldom unconscious
of his abnormality, most of his actions and speeches reflect a
complexity of motives not to be found in the exponents of other
types of anti-social vice. Fortunately, an invert, unlike the miser,
the snob or the hypocrite, can rarely express his total personality
in his behaviour. And even when the true character, the *moi
intérieur*, of Charlus is only partially exteriorized in his conduct,
the effect is often to shock the reader's prejudices and to impose
a momentary strain upon his credulity, thus rendering the
artist's task extremely difficult, for the artist's task is to bridge
the gap between his own consciousness and the sensibility of the
spectator. In Proust's case it is to communicate to the reader
a vision of reality such as can only be attained by the intuition
of a disinterested artist, by what Proust calls the novelist's
'pouvoir réfléchissant', though some might call it the artist's
power of self-hallucination. It is the power that enables him,
because he has the courage and sincerity to explore his own soul,
to experience vicariously through the artist's intuition, yet in
all their immediate tension and vitality, the seething emotions
and passions composing the individuality of a Charlus and which
will ultimately express themselves in behaviour when, in response to some irresistible and profound impression or situation,
the baron follows the dictates of his true nature. That is why,
as Marcel penetrates ever more deeply into the soul of Charlus,
the baron's personality slowly presents aspects which, if suddenly
revealed to us, would seem strange and unreal; as indeed they

---

[1] *SG.* ii (3), 116.

do when displayed in that nocturnal, war-time Paris of *Le temps perdu*, a Paris suspended in the blue, sublunary silences of a city out of the Arabian Nights.

The Charlus of the Verdurin period, the Charlus of the *tacot* and the La Raspelière Wednesdays is still presented, in the main, as a figure of *la haute comédie*. Sometimes, indeed, it would appear that Proust deliberately refrains at this stage from those deeper explorations which would immediately dispel the atmosphere of comedy and reveal the darker regions of the baron's inner life. Probably, he wants to emphasize, at the moment, the difficulties confronting the novelist who tries to see beneath that 'second nature', as Bergson calls it, which in the case of individuals like Charlus is so very hard to disentangle from their true and original self. Take, for example, the Charlusian glosses on Balzac to which I have alluded. He is talking about *Les illusions perdues*, about that scene where Vautrin, driving through Angoulême, asks his coachman the name of a château they are passing. On learning that it is called Rastignac, the home of the young man for whom he once entertained a platonic affection, Vautrin sinks into a profound reverie. This incident, says the baron, watching the effect of his words on the admiring 'petit clan', was christened by Swann 'la tristesse d'Olympio de la pédérastie'. But Marcel observes that though the baron sometimes derives an æsthetic pleasure from seeing himself as a Vautrin, the Balzacian character with whom he secretly compares himself is the romantic and tragically misunderstood princesse de Cadignan. And that to Marcel is more credible, for the baron in his relations with Morel, who is the male counterpart of Saint Loup's Rachel, experiences, just like his nephew, periods of deep humiliation, of impotent rage, examples of basest ingratitude, situations so complicated and obscured by the violinist's natural talent for prevarication as to drive Charlus to conduct bordering on the insane. Yet it should be noted that the baron is not primarily a man of reveries but of action and of inexhaustible verbosity. Moreover, as Marcel subtly implies, the majority of his acts and speeches should not be taken at their face value because, to a much greater degree than with men of normal *mœurs*, they are designed to camouflage the feelings of the inner self. However, Marcel learns to decode them, and sometimes, as in the scene where Morel is surprised by Charlus in the *maison de filles* at Maineville, we have what Bergson would recognize as the description of an *acte libre*. Stendhalians, too, will have no difficulty in identifying the original air for which Proust, in the following passage, has devised his own setting.

On ne peut comprendre à quel point cette inquiétude agitait et par là même avait momentanément enrichi l'esprit de M. de Charlus. L'amour cause ainsi de véritables soulèvements géologiques de la pensée. Dans celui de M. de Charlus qui, il y a quelques jours, ressemblait à une plaine si uniforme qu'au plus loin il n'aurait pu apercevoir une idée au ras du sol, s'étaient brusquement dressées, dures comme la pierre, un massif de montagnes, mais de montagnes aussi sculptées, que si quelque statuaire au lieu d'emporter le marbre, l'avait ciselé sur place et où se tordaient en groupes géants et titaniques, la Fureur, la Jalousie, la Curiosité, l'Envie, la Haine, la Souffrance, l'Orgueil, l'Epouvante et l'Amour.[1]

Yet it is typical of Proust to have created out of this situation one of the most farcical scenes in the whole novel, prolonged, moreover, in a second rocket-like explosion of gaiety, in the incident where the terrified Morel, on a nocturnal visit to the chalet of his admirer, the prince de Guermantes, observes, staring from a photograph, the implacable eyes of Charlus, whereupon, in an agony of fear, without stopping to greet his host the violinist darts like a hunted hare from the *guet-apens*. Reflecting on this incident and upon other equally crazy episodes, for instance, the bogus duel, one remembers Marcel's original impression of Charlus in Mme de Villeparisis' room in the Grand Hôtel de Balbec. He then felt, intuitively, that Charlus harboured a streak of madness, and since then it is clear from subsequent impressions that somewhere, amongst the many interacting and ever-changing selves composing the personality of this strange man, there lurks one that is really insane and virtually dangerous, a self which may at any time rush to the surface and express itself in violent, extraordinary and fatal actions. Meanwhile, however, it is interfused with and modified by less

[1] *SG.* II (3), 165–6.

harmful sentiments and finds expression chiefly in the baron's theatrical proclivities, in his childish fondness for romanesque charades and situations. Perhaps the most typical of such escapades, of which there are many, is that where the baron, in the role of a broken-down old family retainer, lunches with Morel in a restaurant farther up the coast. Here sparkling comedy is cleverly blended with darker and more expressive elements in order to accentuate the fundamental differences in the quality of two natures, that of the baron and of his protégé. The latter's innate vileness is reflected in the diabolic plan he confides to Charlus, of seducing and then deserting some innocent young girl just for the sheer fun of the thing. Morel's words suddenly release the mad sadistic impulses in the baron's nature, filling him with evil glee. But, learning that the intended victim is Jupien's hardworking little seamstress-niece, Charlus is overcome with horror and moves swiftly yet quite naturally into another order of sentiments which is instantly reflected in the tone of his conversation.

On remarquera [notes Marcel] qu'après une interpolation du langage vulgaire, celui de M. de Charlus était brusquement redevenu aussi précieux et hautain qu'il était d'habitude. C'est que l'idée que Morel 'plaquerait' sans remords une jeune fille violée lui avait fait brusquement goûter un plaisir complet. Dès lors ses sens était apaisés pour quelque temps et le sadique (lui, vraiment mediumnimique) qui s'était substitué pendant quelques instants à M. de Charlus avait fui et rendu la parole au vrai M. de Charlus, plein de raffinement artistique, de sensibilité, de bonté.[1]

As Marcel's narrative progresses, the affinity between the Proustian and the Bergsonian conception of life becomes more and more evident. Proust, in presenting the complex of psychological states which we call the individuality of a person, is clearly resolved to open up larger spiritual perspectives than any hitherto disclosed by the greatest even of his predecessors. Whilst the time has not yet arrived when it will be possible to define with assurance the place of Marcel Proust in the evolution of the French novel, it would seem, however, that his work marks an important phase in that evolution. Art, philosophy and

[1] *SG.* II (3), 72.

science are but various reflections of the consciousness of an era. Proust's great novel reflects, I think, with unusual clarity and directness the new trend of French consciousness in his era, the intellectual revolution which found in Henri Bergson its most brilliant and original protagonist. We must not, however, rush to the *simpliste* conclusion that Proust, because of his Bergsonian distrust of the analysing intelligence and its perceptions or because of his eagerness to break if possible with the Realists and their deterministic interpretation of life and nature, should be included in the category of what some of his critics describe as the 'anti-intellectuals'. But this is a question which can be more profitably examined in the concluding pages of our study.

Proust, who was certainly familiar with the *Essai sur les données immédiates de la conscience*, must have cordially agreed with most of the views expressed by Bergson on the question of the novelist's approach to the study of human nature. Bergson, it will be recalled, wages relentless war against the psychologists who try to recompose life by piecing together states of consciousness which have been cross-sectioned and, therefore, immobilized by the external, analysing intelligence. Here is what he says about such an approach by the artist.

Nous jugeons du talent d'un romancier à la puissance avec laquelle il tire du domaine public, où le langage les avait fait descendre, des sentiments et des idées auxquels il essaie de rendre, par une multiplicité de détails qui se juxtaposent, leur primitive et vivante individualité. Mais de même qu'on pourra intercaler indéfiniment des points entre deux positions d'un mobile sans jamais combler l'espace parcouru, ainsi, par cela seul que nous parlons, par cela seul que nous associons des idées les unes aux autres et que ces idées se juxtaposent au lieu de se pénétrer, nous échouons à traduire entièrement ce que notre âme ressent: la pensée demeure incommensurable avec le langage.

Beyond question, Proust had read and meditated on this passage, the substance of which you will find reproduced in the various sections of *A la recherche du temps perdu* where he criticizes the methods of the Realists. His own ambition probably was to surpass the type of novelist whose virtues and defects are described as follows by Bergson in his *Essai sur les données immédiates de la conscience*:

> Que si maintenant quelque romancier hardi, déchirant la toile habilement tissée entre notre moi conventionnel, nous montre sous cette juxtaposition d'états simples une pénétration infinie de mille impressions diverses qui ont déjà cessé d'être au moment même où on les nomme, nous le louons de nous avoir mieux connus que nous ne nous connaissons nous-mêmes. Il n'en est rien cependant, et par cela même qu'il déroule notre sentiment dans un temps homogène et en exprime les éléments par des mots, il ne nous en présente qu'une ombre à son tour: seulement il a disposé cette ombre de manière à nous faire soupçonner la nature extraordinaire et illogique de l'objet qui la projette; il nous a invités à la réflexion en mettant dans l'expression extérieure quelque chose de cette contradiction, de cette pénétration mutuelle, qui constitue l'essence même des éléments exprimés. Encouragés par lui, nous avons écarté pour un instant le voile que nous interposons entre notre conscience et nous. Il nous a remis en présence de nous-mêmes.

> [Now if some bold novelist, tearing aside the cleverly woven veil of our conventional self, shows us beneath that appearance of logic a fundamental absurdity, beneath that juxtaposition of simple states an infinite interpenetration of a thousand varied impressions which have already ceased to exist at the very moment they are named, we praise him for having known us better than we knew ourselves. This is, however, not so, and from the very fact that he unfolds our feeling in a homogeneous time and expresses its elements in words, he in turn is only presenting its shadow to us: but he has arranged this shadow in such a way as to make us suspect the extraordinary, illogical nature of the object which projects it; he has made us reflect by putting into the outward expression something of that contradiction, of that interpenetration, which constitutes the very essence of the elements expressed. Encouraged by him, we have thrust aside for a moment the veil which we interposed between our consciousness and us. He has brought us once more face to face with ourselves.]

Intermingled with his impressions of Charlus and of the other members of the Verdurin clan are the sensations and emotions evoked in Marcel by his numerous conversations with Albertine and by their excursions in the Balbec region. It is no mere chance that the narrator himself is in almost constant movement, either shuttling backwards and forwards in the diligent *tacot* or else weaving to and fro along freshly discovered roads, viewing well-known places from novel and astonishing sites in that latest invention of science—the motor-car. There is a fascinating page symbolizing the Proustian approach to reality, the continual effort of this modern artist to escape that fixation of the inner consciousness deplored by Bergson; to avoid the tendency, imposed on us by the imperative demands of everyday social existence, to solidify our ever-changing impressions, to let them crystallize round the external objects of our observation and thus, as Bergson would say, to confuse the feeling itself, which is in a perpetual state of becoming, with its permanent external object, and especially with the word which expresses this object. Here is the page in question.

Il peut sembler que mon amour pour les féeriques voyages en chemin de fer aurait dû m'empêcher de partager l'émerveillement d'Albertine devant l'automobile qui mène, même un malade, là où il veut, et empêche — comme je l'avais fait jusqu'ici de considérer l'emplacement comme la marque individuelle, l'essence sans succédané des beautés inamovibles. Et sans doute cet emplacement, l'automobile n'en faisait pas comme jadis le chemin de fer, quand j'étais venu de Paris à Balbec, un but soustrait aux contingences de la vie ordinaire, presque idéal au départ et qui le restant à l'arrivée, à l'arrivée dans cette grande demeure où n'habite personne et qui porte seulement le nom de la ville, la gare, à l'air d'en promettre enfin l'accessibilité comme elle en serait la matérialisation. Non, l'automobile ne nous menait pas ainsi féeriquement dans une ville que nous voyions d'abord dans l'ensemble que résume son nom, et avec les illusions du spectateur dans la salle. Il nous faisait entrer dans la coulisse des rues, s'arrêtait à demander un renseignement à un habitant. Mais comme compensation d'une progression si familière on a les tâtonnements mêmes du chauffeur incertain de sa route et revenant sur ses pas, les chassés-croisés de la perspective faisant jouer un château aux quatre coins avec une colline, une église et la mer, pendant qu'on se rapproche de lui, bien qu'il se blottisse vainement sous sa feuillée séculaire; ces cercles de plus en plus rapprochés que décrit l'automobile autour d'une ville fascinée qui fuyait dans tous les sens pour échapper et sur laquelle finalement il fonce tout droit, à pic, au fond de la vallée où elle reste gisante à terre; de sorte que cet emplacement, point unique, que l'automobile semble avoir dépouillé du mystère des trains express, il donne par contre l'impression de le découvrir, de le déterminer nous-mêmes comme avec un compas, de nous aider à sentir d'une main plus amoureusement exploratrice, avec une plus fine précision, la véritable géométrie, la belle mesure de la terre.[1]

[It might seem that my love of enchanted journeys by train ought to have kept me from sharing Albertine's wonder at the motor-car which takes even an invalid anywhere he chooses, and prevents one from thinking, as I had done up to now, that their actual site is the individual mark, the irreplaceable essence of static beauties. And of course the motor-car did not make this site, as the railway formerly did when I came from Paris to Balbec, a goal removed from the contingencies of everyday life, almost ideal at the moment of departure and remaining so at our arrival, at our arrival in that great dwelling where nobody dwells and which bears merely the name of the town, the station with its implied promise of accessibility to the city of which it is apparently the materialization. No, the motor did not convey us thus, magically, to a town which we first saw as the collectivity summed up in its name and with the illusions of a spectator at a theatre. It took us backstage into the streets, stopping to ask some inhabitant for information. To compensate one, however, for such a homely mode of progress, there are the fumblings of the chauffeur uncertain of his road and going back over his tracks, the *chassés-croisés* of the perspective making a castle play at puss-in-the-corner with a hill, a church and the sea, whilst one draws closer to it no matter how much it tries to cower beneath the shelter of its age-old foliage; those ever converging circles described by the motor-car round a spellbound town skeltering off in all directions to escape and down upon which it dives, head-on, perpendicularly, right into the bottom of the valley where it lies prone on the ground; so that this site, this unique point, which the motor seems to have shorn of the mystery of express trains, gives us on the contrary the impression of discovering it, of pin-pointing it for ourselves as if with a compass, of helping us to feel with a more lovingly exploring hand, with a more delicate precision, the true geometry, the beautiful contours of the earth.]

What Marcel does not guess is the threat to his future happiness latent in this wonderful machine. For if it can dispel certain mysteries and replace them by new realities, the motor-car also serves the purpose of those who, like Charlus or Morel or Albertine, have secret places in their lives. Unknown to Marcel, the intelligent young chauffeur, the *deus in machina*, in whom now and later, in Paris, he places absolute trust, is hand-in-glove with Morel. With the aid of the violinist he is busy juggling

[1] *SG.* II (3), 66–7.

with the kilometres to the considerable financial detriment of
the unsuspecting baron. Of all this, or of Morel's friendship
with Albertine, nothing reaches Marcel. So he traces eccentric
and carefree patterns on the Norman landscape, speeding along
roads that used to be lofty casements looking out on the sea—'la
plaintive aïeule de la terre, poursuivant, comme au temps qu'il
n'existait pas encore d'êtres vivants, sa démente et immémoriale
agitation'. Now they are just swift and convenient ways of
rejoining Albertine. Is Marcel in love with her? Looking into
his soul he finds it difficult to answer that question. The quality
of his feelings towards her varies from day to day, with the
fading or brightening of the halo of mystery generated by
Albertine's words, gestures, actions and absences. His jealousy,
though lulled, is only half asleep and he is still careful to invite
Saint-Loup only when she is away, even if this involves a certain
anxiety about her movements. There is so much that is purely
sensuous in their contacts: their drives on blazing summer days
to outlying farms and restaurants, their caresses on the moonlit
beach on warm summer nights. There is so much that may be
only partly Albertine and partly Marcel's returning *joie de vivre*,
his voluptuous and rhythmic sense of union with the mysterious
source of all vitality.

Quand la nuit était tout à fait venue et que, comme me disait le
directeur de l'hôtel, le ciel était tout parcheminé d'étoiles, si nous
n'allions pas nous promener en fôret avec une bouteille de champagne,
sans nous inquiéter des promeneurs déambulant encore sur la digue
faiblement éclairée, mais qui n'auraient rien distingué à deux pas sur
le sable noir, nous nous étendions en contrebas des dunes; ce même
corps dans la souplesse duquel vivait toute la grâce féminine, marine
et sportive, des jeunes filles que j'avais vu passer la première fois
devant l'horizon du flot, je le tenais serré contre le mien, sous une
même couverture, tout au bord de la mer immobile divisée par un
rayon tremblant; et nous l'écoutions sans nous lasser et avec le même
plaisir, soit quand elle retenait sa respiration, assez longtemps suspendue pour qu'on crut le reflux arrêté, soit quand elle exhalait enfin
à nos pieds le murmure attendu et retardé.[1]

On the morrow, Marcel's one anxiety is to prolong for ever
this halcyon existence, trembling always lest Albertine may not

[1] *SG.* II (3), 86.

be free or perhaps—intolerable thought—may have begun to weary of his company.

Je la regardais, [he says] je regardais ce corps charmant, cette tête rose d'Albertine, dressant en face de moi l'énigme de ses intentions, la décision inconnue qui devait faire le bonheur ou le malheur de mon après-midi. C'était tout un état d'âme, tout un avenir d'existence qui avait pris devant moi la forme allégorique et fatale d'une jeune fille.[1]

Here we have the answer to our question. Albertine is the lovely but impermanent materialization of a state of soul which itself is the unstable reflection of Marcel's dream of unbroken happiness. But this is not the love immortalized by Shakespeare, 'the marriage of true minds', the 'ever-fixéd mark, That looks on tempests and is never shaken'. On the contrary, Marcel's love diminishes as his sense of security, that is to say, of possession, increases: it alters with the alteration of his vision of happiness.

As the days slip past, Marcel begins to experience, once again, but now with greater urgency, the spiritual malaise of the artist who is letting his talents run to seed, wasting the precious and hurrying moments, failing in a duty to himself. The truth, although he is much too modest to visualize himself in such a splendid role, is that Marcel is a Pygmalion in search of a Galatea. But Albertine is not a Galatea. No doubt it is pleasant and amusing to watch the effect upon her tastes and ideas of his own views on art and life, but that is no substitute for the work of art now dimly shaping in the deep recesses of his consciousness. Hence Marcel's growing *désir d'évasion* to which he alludes in the remarkable passage describing his solitary ride on horseback along the cliff road to La Raspelière culminating in the shattering apocalyptic vision of his first aeroplane, incredibly moving and beautiful as must have been, says Marcel, the sight of a demi-god for an ancient Greek. Albertine, like Mme de Stermaria and Mme de Guermantes, is but the evanescent and illusory materialization of one of Marcel's familiar ghosts, 'des êtres dont la réalité était pour une bonne part dans mon imagination'. And so it will ever be with all the women with whom he thinks himself in love. Dimly and inter-

[1] *SG.* II (3), 87.

mittently the awareness comes to Marcel that no lasting happiness can derive from the pursuit of such phantoms. It can only
come from art. When he is alone in those quiet Balbec lanes,
reflecting that all this natural beauty will survive him, it seems
to Marcel as if the trees were trying to communicate to him
a message, a silent counsel to follow now his true vocation
before the coming of that eternal night when no man can work.
Swann, too, he reminds us, was an *amateur de fantômes*. Does
he remember, I wonder, that Swann, the irredeemable dilettante,
never finished his book on Vermeer? A Pygmalion *manqué*,
Swann took the easier way and, instead of Galatea, chose—
Odette. If we are to seize the inner rhythm of Marcel's existence
we must always keep before us this parallel with Swann if only
because it is always latent in Marcel's consciousness. Otherwise,
the episode called *Un amour de Swann* must seem to have no
necessary connection with the rest of *A la recherche du temps
perdu*, whereas of course it forms an integral part of the story
of Marcel's vocation.

The situation now exposed is not without irony. Who is the
greater victim of illusion, Marcel or the baron whose blindness
he considers with half-amused pity? In a little homily on the
salutory yet unrecognized properties of that hateful thing,
gossip, Marcel observes sagely that there is nothing like gossip
for jolting our mind out of its lazy and pleasant habit of seeing
the world, not as it is, but in the factitious image preferred by
our vanity. Rather smugly, he pictures the collapse of the baron's
'petit pavillon idéal' were he by some mischance to overhear
what the kind Verdurins, Brichot, Cottard, Ski or even his most
affectionate relations say about him behind his back. Marcel's
reflections on the situation of Charlus take the charming form of
a little parable which might have graced the vellum pages
of *Le Roman de la Rose*. Let us call it 'l'allégorie des deux
pavillons'. Marcel has just described the baron's 'pavillon idéal'
the atmosphere of which is so restful, cordial and sympathetic.

Mais, pour chacun de nous, ce genre de pavillon est double: en
face de celui que nous croyons être l'unique, il y en a un autre qui nous
est habituellement invisible, le vrai, symétrique avec celui que nous
connaissons, mais bien différent et dont l'ornementation, où nous ne

reconnaîtrions rien de ce que nous attendions à voir, nous épouvanterait comme faite avec les symboles odieux d'une hostilité insoupçonnée. Quelle stupeur pour M. de Charlus, s'il avait pénétré dans un de ces pavillons adverses, grâce à quelque potin comme par un de ces escaliers de service où des graffiti obscènes sont charbonnés à la porte des appartements par des fournisseurs mécontents ou des domestiques renvoyés.[1]

We know, of course, what people say about Charlus: Mme Verdurin's 'Nous n'attendons que ces demoiselles'; Cottard's medical student's japes; Ski's Quartier Latin witticisms and the rest. As for Charlus, although highly intelligent and suspicious, he deludes himself that whilst perhaps a few isolated individuals are, to use his own expression, 'fixés sur son compte', their opinion on his morals can only be founded on the vaguest of rumours and not on concrete, damning facts. But what about Albertine? Here we are obviously less well informed since it is Marcel who tells his own story. It does not seem, however, that the Verdurins or the other members of the clan entertain any suspicions whatever about his 'cousine', though he does seize one floating thread of gossip, one little 'potin'. Mme de Cambremer, he learns, had once remarked that Albertine had 'un drôle de genre'. But when confronted by Marcel, she said she was talking about one of Albertine's friends, the wife of a banker, called Lina, Linette, Lisette or Lia. None of these names flashes a warning signal: it is Albertine herself who blasts Marcel out of his 'petit pavillon idéal'.

This is how it happens. Weary of the pointless life he is leading, tired also of Albertine, Marcel resolves to break with her at the first convenient moment. He would in fact have done this already but for an inopportune reproach of his mother's about his extravagance. One evening, returning in the little train with Albertine to Balbec, he makes little effort to conceal his ill humour and when she casually assumes that they will go to the Verdurins as usual next day, Marcel replies that he is thoroughly sick of the whole stupid business. He will go once again, however, to La Raspelière because he wants to hear Morel play certain unpublished compositions of a musician of whom

[1] *SG.* II (3), 125.

Albertine has certainly never heard. He is called Vinteuil. Then the bomb crashes down.

'Vous ne savez pas comme vous m'amusez,' me répondit Albertine en se levant car le train allait s'arrêter. 'Non seulement cela me dit beaucoup plus que vous ne croyez, mais même sans Mme Verdurin je pourrai vous avoir tous les renseignements que vous voudriez. Vous vous rappelez que je vous ai parlé d'une amie plus âgée que moi qui m'a servi de mère, de sœur, avec qui j'ai passé à Trieste mes meilleures années et que d'ailleurs je dois dans quelques semaines retrouver à Cherbourg, d'où nous voyagerons ensemble (c'est un peu baroque, mais vous savez comme j'aime la mer), hé bien! cette amie (oh! pas du tout le genre de femmes que vous pourriez croire!) regardez comme c'est extraordinaire, est justement la meilleure amie de la fille de ce Vinteuil, et je connais presque autant la fille de Vinteuil. Je ne les appelle jamais que mes deux grandes sœurs.'[1]

In the blinding glare of a sudden and terrible recollection, Marcel re-lives that moment of his boyhood when, crouching behind a bush, he watched the unspeakable behaviour of Mlle Vinteuil and her actress friend, the notorious Lesbian. In the language of genius, that is to say, in words miraculously grouped so as to seem invented solely to express the spirit of one solemn unique and unforgettable experience, Proust renders visible for us the emotional upheaval produced in the depths of Marcel's soul by the suggestive power of Albertine's phrase, 'cette amie c'est Mlle Vinteuil'. Proust, with unerring intuition, discovers and isolates in the flux of sentiments which even now are shaping the contours of Marcel's new state of soul, that one sentiment dominating all others, stronger than remorse and horror and the dreadful certainty of suffering without an end. It is the queer sense of satisfaction he derives, in the midst of catastrophe, from this confirmation by reality of his former intuitive and unreasonable fears, of that pain with no apparent rational cause that invaded him in the casino at Incarville, the stabbing sensation of anxiety and jealousy provoked by Cottard's idle words. The reasonable intelligence, in short, now renders belated homage to the superior divinatory powers of the intuition.

We are now swept into the authentic climate of tragedy and the change is immediately reflected in the quality of Marcel's

---

[1] *SG.* ii (3), 214–15.

language and behaviour. For this of course we have been prepared although, as the writer intended, we had forgotten the
casino incident. Proust's object now is to transport us to a new
plane of observation viewed from which Marcel's actions will
seem not unreal, but natural and true. They are not to be analysed
and weighed by our intelligence: they are to be experienced by
our understanding sensibility. Tragedy, as Bergson profoundly
observes, offers nature her revenge on society, a truth now
confirmed and illustrated in the conduct of Marcel which is only
strange or improbable if we forget that, for the first time, his
acts and gestures express his total personality. A moment ago
he was ready to break with Albertine. Now, at all costs, she
must remain under his constant supervision. The mere thought
that she may leave him perhaps for a rendezvous with Bloch's
vicious cousins drives Marcel nearly mad. So he implores her
to put up for the night at his hotel in Balbec, inventing on the
spur of the moment a circumstantial and romantic account of
a purely imaginary love affair with a woman who is prepared to
give up everything in order to marry him though Marcel cannot
accept her sacrifice. Indeed, that very morning, she is leaving
France probably for ever.

   Albertine's quick and sincere sympathy takes the sharp edge
from Marcel's atrocious suffering, but only for a moment.
Looking out over the quiet sea now exquisitely tinted by the
rising sun, reflecting upon the absolute impossibility of an
existence without Albertine, he asks her to accompany him in
a few hours to Paris and, during the absence of his parents, to
stay for some days at their house until he has recovered from
the almost suicidal despair of his parting with the other woman.
Albertine, naturally with great reluctance, accepts the invitation.
Alone with his thoughts, Marcel abandons himself to his real
grief, which is spiritualized and transfigured by the genius of
Proust in the following 'Désolation au lever du jour':

La lumière du soleil qui allait se lever en modifiant les choses autour
de moi me fit prendre à nouveau, comme en me déplaçant un instant
par rapport à elle, conscience plus cruelle encore de ma souffrance. Je
n'avais jamais vu commencer une matinée si belle ni si douleureuse.
En pensant à tous les paysages indifférents qui allaient s'illuminer et

qui la veille encore ne m'eussent rempli que du désir de les visiter, je
ne pus retenir un sanglot quand, dans un geste d'offertoire mécanique-
ment accompli et qui me parut symboliser le sanglant sacrifice que
j'allais avoir à faire de toute joie, chaque matin, jusqu'à la fin de ma vie,
renouvellement solennellement célébré à chaque aurore de mon chagrin
quotidien et du sang de ma plaie, l'œuf d'or du soleil comme propulsé
par la rupture d'équilibre qu'amènerait au moment de la coagulation
un changement de densité, barbelé de flammes comme dans les tableaux, creva d'un bond le rideau derrière lequel on le sentait depuis un
moment frémissant et prêt à entrer en scène et à s'élancer, et dont il
effaça sous des flots de lumière la pourpre mystérieuse et figée. Je
m'entendis moi-même pleurer.[1]

[The light of approaching sunrise, by modifying the aspect of the
things around me, as if for a moment displacing my relationship to her
made me once again more sharply conscious of my suffering. I had
never seen the dawn of a morning so beautiful nor so full of sorrow.
Thinking of all the insignificant landscapes that were about to be
drenched with light and which, but only yester-eve it would have been
my one desire to visit, I could not stifle a sob when, with an oblatory
gesture mechanically performed and symbolizing, in my eyes, the
bloody sacrifice which I was about to make of all joy, every morning,
till the end of my life, a renewal, solemnly observed at every dawn, of
my daily grief and of the blood from my wound, the golden egg of the
sun, as if propelled by the interruption of stability caused at the moment
of coagulation by some change of density, barbed with flames as in the
paintings, shot through the curtain behind which one felt it had been
for a moment quivering, ready to enter upon the scene and to leap
forward, and whose mysterious clotted purple it annihilated with
floods of light. I heard myself weeping.]

The door opens softly and for an instant, Marcel thinks he is
gazing at an apparition. It is his mother whose striking resemblance to his grandmother he realizes as never before. More
than once in this narrative occur the words, 'la profanation des
mères'. He does not use them here because the scene itself is
eloquent enough. As Marcel is telling his mother about his
change of heart towards Albertine, whom he is now absolutely
resolved to marry, she draws her son gently towards the window,
remembering his grandmother's passionate love of natural
beauty. To Marcel, however, the dawn is like an unreal pageant,
a painted veil behind which he discerns other images, horrible

[1] *SG.* II (3), 233–4.

yet terribly real, of Albertine and Mlle Vinteuil at Montjouvain.
So Albertine goes to stay with Marcel and Françoise in Paris.
His mother, with one more sorrow engraved in her heart, goes
to Combray to nurse her aunt whilst her husband is absent on
a prolonged tour of inspection. During the ensuing winter
months Marcel rarely stirs from his room and seldom accompanies Albertine on her outings with Andrée and the intelligent
young chauffeur. This is only partly due to his recurrent attacks
of asthma. Satisfied that he knows exactly how Albertine has
spent her day, convinced therefore that she is safe from the evil
influence of bad companions, Marcel gradually recovers from
the shock caused by the revelation at Balbec. Indeed, he begins
to find Albertine's society rather tedious though Françoise,
like a good and vigilant servant, has trained the visitor to
respect her master's privacy. Docile, passive and good-tempered,
Albertine observes this unaccountable ritual with the obedience
of a well-trained domestic animal. Such is the unusual situation,
the slow evolution of which is now described minutely in *La
Prisonnière*.

Chapter VII

LA PRISONNIÈRE

IN *La Prisonnière* we are forcibly reminded of Marcel's remark that his narrative is, above all, 'l'histoire d'une vocation'. The fundamental and qualitative distinction, already so frequently illustrated, between his affective memories and those of his critical, analysing intelligence is now, I think, more pointedly emphasized than in any previous section of *A la recherche du temps perdu.* This is but another way of saying that Proust now brings into the foreground that aspect of Marcel's history which concerns his evolution as an artist. Consequently, it may be said that the affinity of the Proustian with the Bergsonian view of life becomes increasingly evident, though one must always bear in mind that Proust is a novelist, not a metaphysician or even, in the academic sense of the term, a philosopher. Because *La Prisonnière* reveals an important advance in Marcel's progress towards his true vocation, it betrays unmistakable affiliations with Bergsonianism. This will not surprise anyone familiar with Bergson's views on the primary function of the artist which is, as he states, in *La pensée et le mouvant,*[1] to see and to make us see what we do not ordinarily perceive. In fact, *La Prisonnière* shows us such an attempt by Marcel to give freer play to his faculty of intuition which, although so closely allied to intellection is more difficult to put into exercise and even then, as Bergson insists, can only be of short duration. That great philosopher thought it possible to achieve, by a conjoint effort of intelligence and intuition, a degree of consciousness which would result in a complete and immediate vision of life. He is speaking of the consciousness 'qui se prendrait enfin elle-même pour objet et qui, spectatrice et actrice spontanée et réfléchie, rapprocherait jusqu'à les faire coincider ensemble, l'attention qui se fixe et le temps qui fuit'.[2] Whilst it would be an obvious exaggeration to assert that Proust ever attains such consciousness,

---

[1] 1934.   [2] In *La pensée et le mouvant.* Lecture delivered in 1911.

it can be maintained that *La Prisonnière* reveals a serious and methodical effort by the novelist to move in the direction indicated by Bergson; to obtain, that is to say, a more direct knowledge of the impressions made upon him by life, to know more completely the reactions of his intelligence, of his sensibility and of his will to the external world of people and things.

Life, as Marcel has already divined, is essentially mobility, change, ceaseless re-creation—in short, what Bergson calls *le devenir*. He no longer confuses it, at any rate, with the easily intelligible and readily communicable suite of logically connected events and states of mind recorded, for instance, by the so-called Realists or even by the great masters of the traditional psychological novel. Of this Marcel has been made aware through certain involuntary memories, the quality of which struck him as incredibly richer and more genuine than anything ever recalled by his intellectual memory. The attentive observations of the analysing intelligence, he suspects, can only result in a false or very relative knowledge of life. The average intelligent man, situated always on the plane of imminent action, is never fully alive because his sole object is, necessarily, to live as comfortably as possible according to the rules governing social intercourse. He does not, therefore, *live* in the integral sense of the word: it is impossible for him to know his own real personality, much less to express it in behaviour. Nor does he ever really observe the characters of the individuals whose existence is daily touching his own.

Is this not now Marcel's own position? Relieved by his affluence from the necessity of earning a livelihood, blessed with unlimited leisure for meditation, he is guiltily and spasmodically aware of his shortcomings. Attracted by the pleasures of society, has he not confused this exciting process of getting accustomed to adapting himself to social intercourse with the real experience of living? Here, certainly, Marcel knows that he has grasped the shadow instead of the substance of life. On the other hand, there have been a few precious and joyous moments of profound introspection, revelations of the unconscious, brief glimpses of certain truths which, incidentally, resemble those so brilliantly demonstrated by Bergson. The inner life is a perpetual present, an indivisible and indestructible melody; it is only when we close our minds to this indivisibility that the 'past' seems separate from the present; the memory is not, therefore, a special faculty whose role is to retain the 'past' and decant it in doses into the present: our most distant 'past' adheres to our present and forms with it one uninterrupted process of change. Surely this is what Marcel so frequently discovers for himself the moment his attention is distracted from the business of living for immediate action; as, for example, in the reveries which illuminate the pages of his history.

What emerges from *La Prisonnière* is that Marcel is now advancing more rapidly towards his true vocation, art. But he is also at this stage a lover, an actor on the stage of life and not merely a disinterested spectator of the passions. Moreover, unlike the heroes of Shakespeare or Racine, he is not prepared to express his total personality in a series of volcanic *actes libres*. Nevertheless, in response to the stimulus of Albertine's revelation in the train at Incarville, he has already expressed a self that lay hidden in uncharted depths of his consciousness. Unable to endure the tortures of jealousy, he was impelled to persuade her to accompany him to his parents' flat in Paris. Now, under the pressure of the situation he has created, Marcel is driven to explore his own mind, to envisage life not as a concept but as a living reality, to obtain an enlarged vision of things. He can no longer view his inner existence as a succession of static, clear-cut states of soul which can be neatly analysed then recomposed by the cool and judging intellect. What confronts him now, on the contrary, is life, acutely felt and lived, a dynamic changing flux of emotions, of suffering, joy, anger, jealousy. Albertine's ingenuous allusion to her former relations with Mlle Vinteuil and her friend has generated sentiments which, like an electric current, traverse all the levels of his consciousness, thus discovering a new personality, a new Marcel. He is no longer the intellectually and æsthetically curious young man who once presided as a mere onlooker at the spectacle of Swann's jealous love for Odette, at the manifestations of the

baron's unholy passion for Morel. Now, as actor and spectator
—one might rather say, as patient and clinician—he contemplates and experiences in himself the nature, the rhythm, the
astonishing vitality of love, jealousy and suffering, that mysterious, indivisible trinity of the passions.

This tragic theme runs through *La Prisonnière* and is maintained to a large extent in *Albertine disparue*. Since it is also one
of the greatest themes in the grand symphony of man's inner
life, its subtle and secret undertones can only be perceived by an
artist like Marcel who possesses the courage, the patience and
the integrity to listen to the complete and terrible melody,
although, as a lover, he is tempted at every moment by the
reasonable, urgent pleadings of his reasoning intelligence to
subordinate what is called peace of mind to self-knowledge.
Such is the real tragedy on which the curtain is about to rise, this
conflict between Marcel's desire to know reality—his *recherche
du temps perdu*—and his natural, insistent craving for appeasement. How often we encounter in his narrative that word
appaiser and discern in Marcel's conversations, actions or reflections that narrowing of the field of perception which is produced
by a consciousness striving to ward off the thrusting spearhead
of memories, to elude the vision of reality and thus to purchase
an illusory and provisional sense of alleviation! Yet Marcel
ought to have learned from at least one experience of this kind
that, in the life of the individual as in the life of a nation,
appeasement is always bought at a terrible cost. I mean his
cowardice in running away from the memory of his grandmother.
But this he discovers only later when he admits: 'J'ai laissé
mourir ma grand'mere.' Nor does he yet know the reward that
crowns the search for self-knowledge, the difficult and apparently
hopeless effort to penetrate the reality of suffering and of evil.
It is, as every great artist knows, an incomparable sense of joy
and of fulfilment. Marcel has not yet, however, reached this
stage of his evolution as an artist. There will be times, indeed,
when art seems to him something outside and divorced from
reality, a beautiful illusion produced by a clever technician. But
these are not durable sentiments. They are inspired by the
inevitable flagging of a mind trying to enter into and to enlarge

its perception of things, to think, as Bergson would say, 'intuitively'. For if Marcel is to know the reality of his love, of his jealousy and suffering, he must disentangle himself from many acquired habits of thinking. He must see things not in their spurious space-time contours, as lifeless designs neatly cut out of the vast swirling ensemble of life by that expert *couturier*, the Intelligence—whose fashions are always changing—but in their right and proper reality, as integral, constituent elements of an ever streaming force that is life itself.

In this light we must read *La Prisonnière*, especially the first and third chapters which plainly reveal an intensification of Marcel's efforts to achieve something deeper than a merely intelligent vision of himself and the external world. They make it possible, also, to view the whole novel in better perspective. The criticisms levelled at Proust by the twentieth-century 'Ancients' cease to have any validity. These simply cannot be applied to this 'histoire d'une vocation' which, in harmony with the inner life to whose undulations the narrative constantly attempts to adhere, is itself a dynamic, evolutionary growth and not a static thing analysable into sections neatly labelled 'The Intelligence' and 'The Unconscious'. When we speak of the unity of design of Proust's masterpiece, the expression can have no meaning unless it is understood that Proust's design corresponds to Bergson's 'schéma dynamique', the contours of which are perpetually extending with the artist's extending consciousness. In short, the design of *A la recherche du temps perdu* resembles the grand design of life itself viewed as continuous movement and fresh creation. One can now guess, I think, what Proust would have replied to the traditionalists whose reproaches may be summarized as follows: 'You promised us a marvellous new instrument guaranteed to provide an entirely fresh vision of nature. No doubt your instrument shows things in better definition but it is the same as that used by your predecessors. Why not admit it?' To this Proust could retort: 'Since you concede that I give you a clearer view of life, then I have in fact presented you with a new instrument. It is, as you say, much the same as that employed by my predecessors, though, owing to the atmosphere in which they lived, an atmosphere heavily charged with intellectuality, their lenses were apt to be coated with a film which all but the greatest geniuses thought to be transparent. They suspected, whilst I *know*, that this film was opaque and, therefore, apt to distort the image of reality. Now, though this atmosphere of intellectuality still persists and always must, I have deliberately made the adjustments necessary to procure for you a closer vision of reality. This was not so easy as I originally imagined. But, as you admit, my efforts have been successful. It seems to me, therefore, you have little to cavil at and, for my part, I propose to keep on trying to rub off that film.'

To drop our little parable, Proust is using and endeavouring to perfect the method of approach to reality which every artist of genius has employed in his particular way and within the limitations of his art. For art cannot be equated with either philosophy or metaphysics, though no doubt in a loose, popular sense we can talk of philosophical novels or metaphysical poetry. Up to a point, great art involves what Bergson calls the intuitive approach to life, a method of perceiving the world which is typical of the great artists. The non-artist, he points out, automatically limits his field of perception, interested only in seeing what it is to his material advantage to see. Life demands that he wear blinkers so as to look neither to the right nor left, but straight ahead:

Notre connaissance, bien loin de se constituer par une association graduelle d'éléments simples, est l'effet d'une dissociation brusque: dans le champ immensément vaste de notre connaissance virtuelle nous avons cueilli, pour en faire une connaissance actuelle, tout ce qui intéresse notre action sur les choses; nous avons négligé le reste.

It is because the artist thinks less of *utilizing* his perceptions that he sees things more profoundly and more clearly, and perceives a larger number of things. In this respect, therefore, the great predecessors of Proust were all 'bergsoniens sans le savoir'. Proust, however, as a contemporary of Bergson, was intensely aware of this affinity between the uniqueness of the great artist's vision and the larger absolute vision which was the objective of Bergson's philosophy or rather of his metaphysics. Whilst his older and brilliant contemporary was unfolding his philosophy, Proust was creating his novel. I know, of course, that in the famous interview accorded to M. J-E. Bois in 1913, he deprecated the application of the epithet 'roman bergsonien' to his own novel. In a letter to Camille Vettard in 1922, however, he admitted certain affinities with Bergson though with the following reserve: 'il n'y a pas eu et pour autant que je peux me rendre compte de suggestion directe.' Nevertheless, without in the least impugning Proust's good faith or belittling his originality, it can be affirmed that Proust's history of Marcel's vocation reveals a progressive enrichment and deepening of Proust's own conception of the artist's function and object, in the course of which he expresses opinions that not only frequently coincide with those of Bergson but are sometimes illustrated by Bergsonian metaphors.

It is always unwise of a great artist, especially in mid-career, to explain to the public what he is trying to create. An excellent case in point is Proust's luckless interview with M. J-E. Bois in which, after pointing out that in certain characters he has revealed 'certaines impressions profondes, presque inconscientes' he goes on to say:

A ce point de vue, mon livre serait peut-être comme un essai d'une suite de romans de l'Inconscient, je n'aurais aucune honte à dire de 'romans bergsoniens' si je le croyais, car à toute époque il arrive que la littérature a tâché de se rattacher, après coup, à la philosophie régnante. Mais ce ne serait pas exact, car mon œuvre est dominée par la distinction entre la mémoire involontaire et la mémoire volontaire, distinction qui non seulement ne figure pas dans la philosophie de M. Bergson mais est même contredite par elle.

How misguided Proust was in releasing these views for publication, notwithstanding the reservations with which he tried to surround them, we have already observed in reference to the criticisms of M. Feuillerat, of Alain and M. Benda. The main thing, however, is to avoid their rigidity of outlook and to remember that, in 1913, Proust's knowledge of Bergsonism, like his great novel, was in process of evolution. What about the divergence which he believed to exist between his own conception of the role of the involuntary memory and that supposedly held by Bergson? My own opinion is that Proust's *mémoire involontaire* strongly

resembles Bergson's *mémoire pure*, that is to say, the memory as
it would be if it were divorced from any relationship with action
and with the external world, a state of reverie in which images
of past sensations reappear invested with the authentic, unique
quality of their original emotional climate. Bergson differentiates between *la mémoire pure* and *la mémoire-habitude* or our
voluntary memory which is primarily interested in the present
and in our immediate future action. But Bergson warns us that,
in fact, just as there is no such thing as pure perception, there is
no such thing as absolutely pure memory. After all, not being
disembodied spirits, we cannot live in a state of perpetual reverie,
so that our memory, in general, is always necessarily a compromise between purely intuitive memory and *la mémoire-
habitude*. Now, in the early years of this century the question of
'le souvenir involontaire' was being actively discussed in French
philosophic circles, notably by Pillon, Mauxion, F. Paulhan
and the Danish savant, Höffding. Paulhan, in a book on
the function of memory, particularly of affective memory, enlarges on a matter of great interest to Proust: Is the involuntary
character of a recollection sufficient assurance of its fidelity?
Paulhan thinks that, even without the inevitable intervention
of one's present personality which accompanies voluntary remembering, the memory may be falsified. But he goes on to
say that we have sometimes a more legitimate cause for believing
in the accuracy of an involuntary recollection. There are certain
things that happen to us, certain impressions which form in us
and then disappear for a long time. We forget them, and so
they are immune from the distorting influence of our sentiments
and ideas. Therefore, when they suddenly reappear, nothing has
occurred to change their original quality. Now we come to the
passage which must have interested Proust since it coincides
entirely with his views:

Ainsi se lèvent parfois des impressions de jadis que leur longue
disparition nous fait apparaître comme étrangères. Je crois que cette
apparence d'étrangeté, ce manque d'harmonie avec nos préoccupations,
nos idées, nos désirs actuels, cette brusque interruption de la vie
présente et ce retour obligé au passé dont nous avons l'impression sont
de bonnes garanties de la fidélité de la mémoire. Au contraire, lorsque

le souvenir s'adapte trop bien à notre état actuel, lorsque nous y
retrouvons trop complètement notre moi d'aujourd'hui, il est prudent
de nous en méfier. Il a probablement subi des retouches, il s'est tenu
au courant de notre propre évolution.[1]

These, obviously, are the very conditions described by Marcel
when he tells us of the involuntary and marvellous revelations
of his unconscious. Where Proust erred was in thinking that
Bergson would have discounted the value of the authenticity
of such 'souvenirs involontaires'. On the contrary, he would
regard them, like Marcel, as moments of intuition when the mind
directly seizes the 'past' in the lived 'present'. To Proust,
Bergson might have quoted the words of a lecture delivered in
1911 on 'L'Intuition philosophique':

...nous parlons du passé comme de l'aboli, nous voyons dans le
souvenir un fait étrange ou en tous cas, étranger, un secours prêté
à l'esprit par la matière. Resaisissons-nous au contraire, tels que nous
sommes, dans un présent épais et, de plus, élastique, que nous pouvons
dilater indéfiniment vers l'arrière en reculant de plus en plus l'écran
qui nous masque à nous-mêmes....[2]

We need not, however, dwell on a difference of opinion which,
even if it exists—and that is doubtful—cannot affect the fundamental similarity of the Proustian and Bergsonian attitudes to
reality. This philosopher, one must repeat, never claims that it
is easy to adopt the intuitive attitude to life and things. 'L'intuition est pénible et ne saurait durer.'[3] Whilst unflinching in
his conviction that it leads to a vision unobtainable, except in
the material sphere, by our habitual manner of thinking, he is
equally certain that we can never dispense with the intelligence
for the sufficient reason that man is destined always to live in
society. Here, as we have said, novelist and philosopher are
in complete agreement. Thus, in the scenes where Marcel is
shown in society, he automatically moves on the plane of action,
that is, of the surface intelligence. Only when alone does he
begin to move towards the disinterested, intuitive point of view
of the artist. *A la recherche du temps perdu* is the life-history of
a man whose normal milieu is fashionable society but who

[1] *La fonction de la mémoire*, 1904.   [2] *La pensée et le mouvant*, p. 162.
[3] *Ibid.* p. 39.

gradually deserts society in order to devote himself to art. It is totally wrong, therefore, to represent Proust as a kind of *intuitionniste manqué*, ignominiously obliged to fall back on the well-tried technique of the traditional novel of psychological analysis; to give up his ridiculous attempt at envisaging life as duration; to content himself with the scientific, analysing intelligence, that instrument which, after all, was good enough for Balzac, Stendhal or Flaubert. If this view of Proust's novel had any valid meaning it would be that its author was not a great artist: merely a fumbling amateur metaphysician posturing as a novelist. Besides, it ignores the fact that if Balzac, Flaubert and Stendhal had merely offered us what M. Benda calls a judgement on life, we should not rank them as masters. Genius, in any art, takes over at the point below which the analytic or judging part of our intellect cannot penetrate further. It is the intuitive effort which stimulates the imagination and produces that intensification of the senses and perceptions resulting in the vision of the great artist. Without such an effort at sympathetic insight the novelist remains in the category satirized by Proust in his vignette of the fashionable writer encountered in the Guermantes' *salon*. Asked by Marcel what he is doing he replies, screwing his monocle into his eye: 'J'observe.' But no amount of this kind of observation, of 'psychological analysis' however subtly practised, no arts of style will ever communicate that dynamic quality, that impression of fluid complexity, of fugitive emotional nuances, which confers on the creations of the great novelist their unmistakable cachet of individuality, of strangeness and yet, somehow, of reality. Intuition, says Bergson, 'représente l'attention que l'esprit se prête à lui-même, par surcroît, tandis qu'il se fixe sur la matière, son objet'.[1] Elsewhere in the same essay he makes a statement which, I think, helps us to follow the course of Marcel's evolution as an artist:

La pensée sociale ne peut pas ne pas conserver sa structure originelle. Est-elle intelligence ou intuition? Je veux bien que l'intuition y fasse filtrer sa lumière: il n'y a pas de pensée sans esprit de finesse, et l'esprit de finesse est le reflet de l'intuition dans l'intelligence.[2]

---

[1] *La pensée et le mouvant*, p. 98.   [2] *Ibid*. p. 100.

The miracle wrought by the Greeks, Bergson continues, was in expanding this very modest part of the intuition reflected in the intelligence. From this enlargement arose poetry and then prose, for the Greeks converted words, which were originally just signals, into an instrument of art. Yet this cannot alter the fact that thought and language are in their essence intellectual and that their intellectuality is necessarily vague—'adaptation très générale de l'esprit à la matière que la société doit utiliser'. At this point Bergson implies that the intuition of the literary artist is limited by the nature of his medium. Words, by their very nature, tend to acquire a definite meaning, a conventional fixed value, whereas intuition aims at reality, which is essentially mobility and change. Words are but symbols. On the other hand, the object of Bergson's metaphysics is to abstain from converting intuition into a symbol. It is not a generalization of experience but rather an attitude of mind towards life. Metaphysical intuition, although it cannot dispense with scientific knowledge, cannot result from scientific knowledge. Its relation to the latter, he says, is that of motive power to the road covered by the automobile, or the relation which the tension of the mainspring bears to the movement visible in the clock. Such absolute, intuitional knowledge, Bergson would say, lies far outside the scope of any artist, even of the musician. This is confirmed, indeed, by a specific allusion which he made, in 1934, to Proust's novel. Reviewing the progressive stages of his own advance towards a metaphysic of the intuition, Bergson recalls that his first step was to enlarge traditional logic, which is 'a logic of introspection', in order to render it more elastic, therefore more adaptable to 'une duration où la nouveauté jaillit sans cesse et où l'évolution est créatrice'. He then makes the following interesting remark:

Par là même nous nous replacerions dans le flux de la vie intérieure, dont la philosophie ne nous paraissait retenir, trop souvent, que la congélation superficielle. Le romancier et le moraliste ne s'étaient ils pas avancés, dans cette direction, plus loin que le philosophe? Peut-être; mais c'était par endroits seulement, sous la pression de la nécessité, qu'ils avaient brisé l'obstacle; aucun ne s'était encore avisé d'aller méthodiquement 'à la recherche du temps perdu'.[1]

[1] *Ibid*. pp. 27-8.

Now Proust, it seems, in *La Prisonnière* made a sustained effort to think intuitively, to replace himself in the flux of his inner life, to break through that film which, as Bergson suggests, the intelligence constantly tends to interpose between reality and our deepest consciousness. In the first place, he engineered a situation ideally favourable to this purpose, a situation which some, indeed, might consider far-fetched. Marcel, in order to obtain a more direct vision of his own mind, must have solitude. At the same time, if he is to penetrate the inner life of Albertine, assuming that to be possible, she must be constantly at his disposal. Now, these conditions have been realized. Marcel, although he has recovered from his asthmatic seizures, uses his illness as an excuse for seldom accompanying Albertine, Andrée and the intelligent young chauffeur on their excursions in Paris and its environs. He is now lulled into an uneasy sense of security by the thought that his docile prisoner is protected against evil influences. As a result, he begins to find Albertine's society rather irksome, grudging often the hours that interfere with his enjoyment of 'les vertus exaltantes de la solitude'. His senses, like those of most convalescents, are abnormally acute, and from his bedroom Marcel can perceive immediately from a hundred nuances of light and of atmosphere, the exact quality of the weather, the type of day that has just dawned. Lurking in the very depths of his being, he tells us, are two little 'bonshommes', two 'selves' who will be the last to survive when illness has destroyed all the other constituents of the individual called Marcel. One is a certain little philosopher, never happy until he has discovered what is common to two sensations or two works of art. The other little 'bonhomme' resembles the tiny weatherman of boyhood memory, in the optician's shop at Combray.

Je crois bien [says Marcel] qu'à mon agonie, quand tous mes autres 'moi' seront morts, s'il vient à briller un rayon de soleil, tandis que je pousserai mes derniers soupirs, le petit personage barométrique se sentira bien aise, et ôtera son capuchon pour chanter: 'Ah! enfin, il fait beau.'[1]

Solitude holds many other charms. Sensations unlock the floodgates erected against the inrush of the 'past' by the ordinary

---

[1] *P.* I, 14.

habits of social thought. Lying in his bath, watching the golden play of light on the artificially frosted windows, Marcel discovers within himself the youth who revelled long ago in the beauty of Combray. Or else, in bed, when Françoise lights his fire, the kindling twigs evoke by their woodland fragrance a similar miraculous enlargement of the consciousness, the substitution, for the constricted self of the immediate present, of a richer, more eager and vital personality.

L'odeur dans l'air glacé des brindilles de bois, c'était comme un morceau du passé, une banquise invisible détachée d'un hiver ancien qui s'avançait dans ma chambre, souvent striée, d'ailleurs, par tel parfum, telle lueur, comme par des années différentes, où je me retrouvais replongé, envahi, avant même que je les eusse identifiées, par l'allégresse d'espoirs abandonnés depuis longtemps. Le soleil venait jusqu'à mon lit et traversait la cloison transparente de mon corps aminci, me chauffait, me rendait brûlant comme du cristal. Alors, convalescent affamé qui se repaît déjà de tous les mets qu'on lui refuse encore, je me demandais si me marier avec Albertine ne gâcherait pas ma vie, tant en me faisant assumer la tâche trop lourde pour moi de me consacrer à un autre être, qu'en me forçant à vivre absent de moi-même à cause de sa présence continuelle et en me privant, à jamais, des joies de la solitude.[1]

[The perfume, in the frosty air, of the woodland twigs was like a fragment of the past, an invisible iceberg detached from some bygone winter moving forwards into my room, often, moreover, striated with this or that perfume or gleam of light, as with different annular markings, in which I felt myself once more submerged, overwhelmed, even before I had identified them, by the joyousness of hopes long since abandoned. The sun came up to my bed and passed through the transparent shell of my now frail body, warmed me, made me glow like crystal. Then, like the famished convalescent already feeding in imagination on all the dishes forbidden to him I wondered whether marriage and Albertine might not spoil my life, not only by making me assume the task, beyond my strength, of devoting myself to another creature, but just as much also by forcing me to live apart from myself because of her continual presence and by depriving me for ever of the joys of solitude.]

When Albertine is out, safely under Andrée's wing, Marcel can abandon himself to these and other pleasing reveries, gazing

[1] *P.* I, 34.

at the changing panorama of a unique and secret inner world, liberated spiritually by a temporary suspension of his usual preoccupations, of his worrying, jealous anxiety. Just because he knows that Albertine will infallibly return that evening, he can, by an almost physical act of the will, shut her off into a compartment of his brain where for the moment her possible behaviour is of no importance. He can then give himself up to dreams of an existence in which Albertine shall have no share. And when the day is bright and frosty, the happy recluse, thanks to the miraculous powers of imagination and memory, can experience with an immediate and original pleasure, not only the tonic sensation of that particular morning but the sensations of all the mornings, past or potential, of which it is the type or ideal.

Cette matinée idéale comblait mon esprit de réalité permanente, identique à toutes les matinées semblables, et me communiquait une allégresse que mon état de débilité ne diminuait pas: le bien-être résultant pour nous beaucoup moins de notre bonne santé que de l'excédent inemployé de nos forces, nous pouvons y atteindre, tout aussi bien qu'en augmentant celles-ci, en restreignant notre activité. Celle dont je débordais et que je maintenais en puissance dans mon lit, me faisait tressauter, intérieurement bondir, comme une machine qui, empêchée de changer de place, tourne sur elle-même.[1]

But these, after all, are largely material sensations, although no doubt interiorized, or transposed into psychological states. Temporarily released from the shackles of habitual thought, from the 'mouvements imaginatifs de l'intelligence' which are implied in the onerous task of trying to divine the possible actions and thoughts of Albertine, her captor is able to listen to the uninterrupted melody of his inner life, to live not in the fictitious universe of spatialized Time, but to some extent in real duration. Note how Proust and Bergson express, each in his particular manner, the same intuitional process:

Mais c'était surtout en moi que j'entendais, avec ivresse, un son nouveau rendu par le violon intérieur. Ses cordes sont serrées ou détendues par de simples différences de la température, de la lumière extérieures. En notre être, instrument que l'uniformité de l'habitude

[1] *P.* I, 33.

a rendu silencieux, le chant naît de ces écarts, de ces variations, source de toute musique: le temps qu'il fait certains jours nous fait aussitôt passer d'une note à une autre. Nous retrouvons l'air oublié dont nous aurions pu deviner la nécessité mathématique et que pendant les premiers instants nous chantons sans le connaître. Seules, ces modifications internes, bien que venues du dehors, renouvelaient pour moi le monde extérieur. Des portes de communication, depuis longtemps condamnées, se rouvraient dans mon cerveau. La vie de certaines villes, la gaîté de certaines promenades reprenaient en moi leur place. Frémissant tout entier autour de la corde vibrante, j'aurais sacrifié ma terne vie d'autrefois et ma vie à venir, passée à la gomme à effacer de l'habitude, pour cet état si particulier.[1]

[But it was above all in myself that I heard, with rapture, a new sound emitted by the violin within. Its strings are tautened or relaxed by mere differences in the temperature, in the light outside. In our being, that instrument which has been rendered mute by the uniformity of habit, song is born of these divergences, these variations, the source of all music: on certain days, according to the weather, we pass at once from one note to another. We recapture the forgotten tune, the mathematical necessity of which we might have divined and which for the first few moments we keep singing without recognizing it. These inner modifications alone, though they had come from without, gave me a fresh vision of the external world. Communicating doors, long since closed and disused, opened up again in my brain. The life of certain towns, the gaiety of certain excursions resumed their old place within me. With my whole being quivering around the vibrating string I would have sacrificed my former drab existence and my life to come, erasing them with the indiarubber of habit, for this so unique state of soul.]

Now here is the same process more completely envisaged by Bergson:

Je me bornerai donc à dire, pour répondre à ceux qui voient dans cette 'durée réelle' je ne sais quoi d'ineffable et de mystérieux, qu'elle est la chose la plus claire du monde: la *durée réelle* est ce que l'on a toujours appelé le *temps*, mais le temps perçu comme indivisible. Que le temps implique la succession, je n'en disconviens pas. Mais que la succession se présente d'abord à notre conscience comme la distinction d'un 'avant' et d'un 'après' juxtaposés, c'est ce que je ne saurais accorder. Quand nous écoutons une mélodie, nous avons la plus pure impression de succession que nous puissions avoir — une impression

[1] *P.* I, 32.

aussi éloignée que possible de celle de la simultanéité — et pourtant
c'est la continuité même de la mélodie et l'impossibilité de la décomposer
qui font sur nous cette impression. Si nous la découpons en notes
distinctes, en autant d'"avant' et d'"après' qu'il nous plaît, c'est que
nous y mêlons des images spatiales et que nous imprégnons la succession de simultanéité: dans l'espace, et dans l'espace seulement, il
y a distinction nette de parties extérieures les unes aux autres. Je
reconnais d'ailleurs que c'est dans le temps spatialisé que nous nous
plaçons d'ordinaire. Nous n'avons aucun intérêt à écouter le bourdonne-
ment ininterrompu de la vie profonde. Et pourtant la durée réelle
est là. C'est grâce à elle que prennent place dans un seul et même
temps les changements plus ou moins longs auxquels nous assistons
en nous et dans la monde extérieur.[1]

In Proust's novel there are other passages which seem to echo
the characteristic Bergsonian conception of life as perpetual
'becoming', as an uninterrupted inner melody, as real duration.
They reflect the effort to see existence not as an immobilized
segment called the 'present' but as a stream in which the
'present', when observed by the disinterested eye of the artist,
becomes fused with the 'past', since in reality the two compose
an indivisible oneness. That is why Marcel's history is so rarely
'history' in the conventional sense, but a moving panorama
rendered visible to us in its entirety by art, something resembling, in fact, the panorama seen in a flash, to quote one of
Bergson's illustrations, by a drowning man or by an Alpinist
slipping over a precipice. I need hardly recall the relevant
examples already furnished by Proust in the earlier volumes of
his novel. The point to emphasize now is that as Marcel's
artistic outlook develops, we can observe, especially in *La
Prisonnière*, that he no longer waits for the flashes of illumination
provided by involuntary memories. The artistic attitude which,
for Bergson, exemplifies the intuitive approach to life, is now
more deliberately cultivated. Marcel tells us, for instance, that
whilst he sees with the eyes of the body in the duchesse de
Guermantes only a middle-aged though still beautiful lady in
furs carrying an umbrella, the eyes of the mind, that is to say,
of the artist's mind, discern in her left hand châteaux, seigneurial forests, vast estates which Oriane carries with her, just

[1] *La perception du changement*, 1911. In *La pensée et le mouvant* (ed. cit.), pp. 188–9.

as the sculptured figures on the lintel of a porch hold in their hands the cathedral they have constructed. Similarly, in those moments of solitary reverie, Marcel's mind seems to gain a closer vision of itself even whilst remaining attentive to the sensations invading it from without: the keen, crisp air of the boulevards, the scent of approaching rainy weather, the charming Gregorian chant of the street-cries of Paris. Distinctions of space and time vanish when unconscious memories of other days, images of other experiences with their inseparable aura of sensations and emotions flood his consciousness, creating a joyous confusion of personalities, of dissolving states of soul. Impressions of the early Balbec Albertine enter into this vision, always silhouetted against their true and primitive background, the sea, which symbolizes their ever-changing quality. They form in the ensemble an Albertine vastly different from the girl now captive beneath his roof, so that Marcel, alone with his memories, reflects with growing chagrin that there is nothing new to be discovered in Albertine.

Chaque jour, elle me semblait moins jolie. Seul, le désir qu'elle excitait chez les autres quand l'apprenant je recommençais à souffrir et vouloir la leur disputer, la hissait à mes yeux sur un haut pavois. Elle était capable de me causer de la souffrance, nullement de la joie. Par la souffrance seule subsistait mon ennuyeux attachement. Dès qu'elle disparaissait, et avec elle le besoin de l'apaiser, requérant toute mon attention comme une distraction atroce, je sentais le néant qu'elle était pour moi, que je devais être pour elle. J'étais malheureux que cet état dûrat et par moments, je souhaitais d'apprendre quelque chose d'épouvantable qu'elle aurait fait et qui eût été capable, jusqu'à ce que je fusse guéri, de nous brouiller, ce qui nous permettrait de nous reconcilier, de refaire différente et plus souple la chaîne qui nous liait.[1]

[Every day she seemed to me less pretty. Alone, the desire she aroused in others when, upon learning of it, I began to suffer again and wanted to challenge their rights over her, raised her in my eyes to a lofty pinnacle. She was capable of causing me suffering, but no joy whatever. My wearisome attachment was kept alive through pain alone. No sooner had it vanished and consequently the need to appease it, requiring all my attention like some torturing distraction, than I felt

[1] *P.* i, 35.

how utterly meaningless she was for me as I must be for her. I was miserable at the thought that this state of affairs should persist and, at certain moments, I wished I could hear about something frightful she had done and which, until my recovery, might keep us on bad terms with each other and bring about a reconciliation, giving us a chance to alter the bonds that linked us and make them more flexible.]

Enclosed and condensed in these two sentences lies the dynamic pattern of Marcel's future relations with Albertine, the tragic design already emerging from the situation created by one spontaneous unreflecting action. His words suggest the presence, deep in Marcel's consciousness, of a motif whose dark undertones cannot forever be drowned in the ethereal flutings and arpeggios excited by sunshine and frosty weather. If he is to know the reality of his inner life and attain the longed-for state of self-harmony, he must listen to the whole symphony. But evening comes and with it 'la désolation du soir'. For when Albertine returns she will bring with her a cohort of other memories and sensations—all the memories deliberately thrust out of that delightful world created by the play of imagination upon pleasing and lovely reminiscences. These, however, do not compose the whole symphony, only its 'phrase de Vinteuil', to which all of us can listen with eager delight though we lack the patience and integrity to hear the rest. That is why our knowledge of ourselves, of others, of the material world around us is always fragmentary, superficial and fraught with disappointment. Is not this the position of Marcel, the lover of Albertine? Not quite, because a passionate jealousy often endows its victims with something akin to the artist's powers of divination and perception, inspiring in them an insatiable desire to see more deeply into their own hearts and at the same time to penetrate the mysterious veil, real or imaginary, concealing the true personality of the woman they love. Yet many jealous lovers, like Swann, remain only virtual artists. Unable to endure the strain inseparable from this revolution of their normal habits of thought and feeling, they yield to the persuasive counsels of reason which are so admirably suited to the requirements of ordinary social existence. Marcel, who is not only a lover craving appeasement but a born artist, is compelled instinctively to follow the direction of his vocation towards the plane from which the great artist envisages life, towards that disinterested attitude to one's personal emotions which art, sooner or later, exacts from her elected disciples. Such is the ultimate, the inevitable ordeal which confronts at some point in his experience every artist of genius. What distinguishes genius from talent is the possession of this supreme courage, this power to look steadfastly into the self and to reflect the perceived vision, truthfully, in the unique purity of a perfect image, the great work of art. Marcel's narrative portrays the tragic conflict implicit in such an ordeal which, although he cannot yet know it, will eventually bring him a joy far greater than the compromise, the false and temporary alleviation indicated in the closing words of the paragraph I have just quoted. Lifted to the plane of great art, he will acquire a sense of harmony, a higher knowledge of life's meaning, so that his passion for a Lesbian will appear, not as a tragedy on the dénouement of which must depend the fulfilment or annihilation of his spiritual existence, but an illuminating, rewarding phase in the ever changing process of living. In relation to his 'vaste amour' for Albertine, all his other loves, for Gilberte, for Oriane, for Mme de Stermaria had only been, as he later finds out, 'de minces et timides essais'. And it is profoundly significant that this revelation comes to Marcel when he is listening to the completed work of Vinteuil, the septet, to that thing of perfect beauty extracted by a genius who was also a loving father, out of the sufferings inspired by knowledge of his daughter's secret and terrible vice. Proust implies, surely, that here is a parallel and a lesson for Marcel who knows the story of Vinteuil's sorrowful love for his child. Listening to the triumphant septet, can he fail to perceive the joy that attends the creation of an immortal work of art, the spiritual harmony wherein are finally resolved all the discords, the ugliness, the contradictions of everyday life, of existence as it presents itself to the intelligence of the non-artist, of the ordinary man?

In the early stage of his cohabitation with Albertine, however, Marcel has not yet attained this degree of self-realization. On the contrary, he awaits her return with a sense of frustration and of anti-climax. Now that Albertine is virtually in his possession

—does he not control all her actions and possible contacts?—she begins to lose that perfume of mystery which in the Balbec summer days made her so excitingly attractive. Now Marcel has no difficulty in convincing himself that there is no longer any question of love between them. Why then does he not end a situation which his mother finds shocking and grossly unfair to the girl? In his moments of self-pity, Marcel reflects, like Constant's Adolphe, how pleasant and free would be an existence without an Albertine, how lovely it would be, for instance, to see Venice, the city of his dreams. As it is, though convalescent, he views the outer world almost exclusively from his bedroom. Sometimes, indeed, he slips downstairs to visit the duchesse de Guermantes, marvelling that this mysterious and beautiful creature, once his 'princesse lointaine' should now be just a charming lady whom he consults for Albertine's sake on the latest fashions. Very occasionally he encounters in Jupien's lodge Charlus and Morel; for the baron, whose notion of what is meant by possession is as imperfect as Marcel's, hopes that by marrying Jupien's niece to Morel, he will thus be able to tighten his hold on the musician. Morel is extravagant and, except when his vanity is touched, incurably lazy. 'Car la possession de ce qu'on aime' thinks Marcel, 'est une joie plus grande encore que l'amour.' This maxim, borrowed from La Rochefoucauld, he applies to Charlus though it completely describes his own state of illusion at this period of his relations with Albertine. Physical possession may be nine points of the law but, as Marcel is soon to discover, it does not constitute any real or necessary link between himself and his captive. This truth becomes daily more evident as the unusual situation imagined by Proust begins to produce its inevitable effects, generating strange thoughts, poisonous suspicions that flower vigorously in the 'atmosphère close' of Paris, so different in quality from the blue and spacious air of Normandy. Were it not, indeed, for the constant reminders that outside Marcel's windows is the familiar humming of the capital, the clatter and movement of her streets, the picture that forms irresistibly in our imagination is of some hushed and secret despot's palace. Proust, who is well aware that it is unusual for wealthy young bourgeois to live with their fiancées in the absence of parents or chaperones, makes an unconvincing attempt to justify the situation by explaining that Albertine is an orphan and has always been granted complete freedom of movement by her aunt, Mme Bontemps. He need scarcely have taken the trouble since his *mise en scène* is really in harmony with the abnormal character of the hero's jealousy and love. The fact is that no other situation would have suited Proust's purpose, short of presenting Marcel and Albertine as a married couple. On reflection, it is hard indeed to imagine how else the novelist could have arranged matters so as to explore with such incredible thoroughness and veracity the progressive enlargement of Marcel's consciousness resulting from his strange passion. In what other way could Proust have made it possible for Marcel to pursue simultaneously his effort to penetrate the real nature of his own emotions and decipher the true meaning of Albertine's conversations, silences and actions? Everything here, judged by conventional standards, seems abnormal and remote from the experience of ordinary social existence. No other novelist, it must be remembered, had ever embarked upon such an integral and concrete examination of jealousy, not even Stendhal in *La Chartreuse de Parme*. Moreover, for Proust, jealousy is not a clear-cut ascending passion which achieves its logical climax and full expression in violent action. Marcel is not a Moor of Venice. His jealousy—and there are, after all, nearly as many kinds of jealousy as there are jealous individuals—is an intermittent malady. The quality of its intensity varies not only with the shifting focus of the victim's perceptibility but with the changing personality of Albertine herself. For, as Bergson once remarked, it is only by an illusion comparable to that experienced by two travellers surveying each other from parallel moving trains that one individual sees the personality of another as something fixed and unchanging in space and time. *La Prisonnière* shows us Marcel's attempt to shake off that illusion, to break whenever feasible with the habit of logical, intellectual thought.

We must not, therefore, expect to walk now into a gallery hung with *Désolations* after the manner of that richly stylized *Désolation de l'Aube* in which Proust seized and immobilized the

sharp and sudden agony of Marcel on his last morning at Balbec.
No single metaphor or symbol can synthesize the multiplicity
of his present elusive and interfusing emotions, the torturing
images of Albertine in Mlle Vinteuil's room at Montjouvain,
the irrational anxieties which at twilight begin to gnaw into
his mind, the fear lest some evening Andrée may return without
her charge, the exhausting and hopeless attempts to reconstruct
from some half-remembered word or expression, the psychological state from which it sprang. So far, however, Albertine's
return never fails to dispel 'la désolation du soir'. In the long
hours spent in her arms, soothed by her caresses or listening
with the indulgence of a contented pasha to her laughter and
joyous chatter about frocks, books and music, reflecting with
a certain cruel satisfaction that no one else can enjoy these
pleasures, Marcel can almost persuade himself that, perhaps,
this is the durable happiness of his dreams. Love, after all, is
only the desire for complete possession and does he not possess
Albertine? Surely an intimate evening with his mistress is worth
all the other desires that beset him in her absence—to see Venice,
to write books, to be in the country in springtime when the
hawthorn blossom comes out? True, even in such hours of
ecstatic physical closeness, Albertine does not confer upon him
a positive sense of great joy. It is rather a sense of appeasement,
the satisfaction of that immoderate craving for affection which
his mother and grandmother both sadly observed to be a fundamental weakness of Marcel's character, that 'défaut de volonté'
against which they vainly tried to steel themselves. At last
we know what Proust meant by his dark allusion to 'la profanation des mères'. Now it is Albertine's good-night kiss that
brings the peace of mind without which, just as in his childhood
at Combray, Marcel cannot go to sleep. 'Je ne le redirai jamais
assez, c'était un appaisement plus que tout.'[1] And in a longer
passage, Marcel dwells with singular outspokenness on his
profane analogy.[2] It is interesting, here, to observe how Proust
exploits or orchestrates Bergson's idea that all our memories
are ever virtually present, always pressing forward like a cone
at the apex of which is the memory immediately necessary to

_____

[1] *P.* I, 103.   [2] *P.* I, 103–4.

our immediate need or imminent action. Thus Marcel, in the ardour of his carnal relations with his mistress, discovers himself automatically using the expressions of tenderness showered upon him long ago by his mother and grandmother. And when he is angry with Albertine the harsh and impatient words that rise unbidden to his lips are those employed by his father in moments of exasperation. Yet perhaps the most humiliating discovery is the presence within him of a self who resembles— of all people—Marcel's Tante Léonie, the half-crazy old *dévote* and hypochondriac whose antics were always a family joke at Combray. But he is forced to admit, on reflection, that it is the Tante Léonie part of his nature that keeps him lying in bed tormented by a hundred suspicions which, however, he is prevented from verifying by an invincible, hereditary lethargy.

Quand nous avons dépassé un certain âge, l'âme de l'enfant que nous fûmes et l'âme des morts dont nous sommes sortis viennent nous jeter à poignée leurs richesses et leurs mauvais sorts, demandant à coopérer aux nouveaux sentiments que nous éprouvons et dans lesquels, effaçant leur ancienne effigie, nous les refondons en une création originale. Tel, tout mon passé depuis mes années les plus anciennes, et par delà celles-ci le passé de mes parents, mêlait à mon impur amour pour Albertine la douceur d'une tendresse à la fois filiale et maternelle. Nous devons recevoir dès une certaine heure tous nos parents arrivés de si loin et assemblés autour de nous.[1]

When Marcel's attention is no longer fixed on the immediate present or future, his mind is free to wander over a constantly broadening zone where a swarm of reminiscences advance un-heralded and unbidden to greet him. On certain days this becomes an exquisite *promenade au soleil*. In the golden chime of a convent-bell he re-lives the early and charming sensations of Combray or Balbec, hearing again, from his shuttered room, the violins of the Grand Hôtel orchestra wafted upwards from the blue sea on the scented summer morning air. Suddenly, however, Marcel drifts into an odious bypath revealing a deso-late and infinite perspective. How did he first hear of Albertine? Ah! yes, it was through Aimé, the *maître d'hôtel*, who said she was a bad type. What exactly did he mean by that? Perhaps, by

[1] *P.* i, 105–6.

'mauvais genre', Aimé meant that Albertine frequented Lesbians. But what particular one? Was it perhaps Bloch's revolting cousin Esther, or again, might it not have been the two girls he caught Albertine looking at in the mirror of the Casino on the fateful afternoon of Cottard's disquieting remarks? He must write to Aimé; procure from Bloch a photograph of his cousin and show it offhandedly to Albertine, watching her reactions, scrutinizing her expression, deciphering her words, penetrating 'à travers son corps tout ce bloc-notes de ses souvenirs et de ses prochains et ardents rendezvous'. Marcel, who but a few hours ago had convinced himself that he was no longer in love with Albertine, rediscovers in the torments of reawakened jealousy the terrible resurrection of his love. And in the days to come he will know the unlimited possibilities for suffering and sadness implied in love and jealousy, the hopeless sense of having embarked in quest of a truth which must inevitably elude him. For Albertine, once she guesses at his jealousy, Albertine who is, moreover, by nature untruthful, will oppose to all his questions, however subtle, that impenetrable barrier of evasions, half-confessions and lies by which women, even when they are innocent and in love, defend the secret places of their soul against the assault of unreasoning and dominating jealousy. Love, as conceived by Marcel, is not a union comparable to Shakespeare's 'marriage of true minds', where although the fusion of two personalities is of a higher order than the individualities united, each lover respects the other's right to a certain spiritual privacy. Nor does Marcel resemble the passionate romantic lover who is willing to suffer for the woman he loves, nay to suffer almost gladly, deriving from suffering the sentiment that his love is thereby exalted, spiritualized and, therefore, fulfilled. *L'amour courtois* is very different from the conception of love defined in the following lines and illustrated in a hundred other passages:

Nous étions résignés à la souffrance, croyant aimer en dehors de nous, et nous nous apercevons que notre amour est fonction de notre tristesse, que notre amour c'est peut-être notre tristesse et que l'objet n'en est que pour une faible part la jeune fille à la noire chevelure. Mais enfin, ce sont surtout de tels êtres qui inspirent l'amour.[1]

[1] *P.* I, 124.

Love, in the Proustian sense, is the transformation into a kind of intellectual concupiscence of man's instinctive sexual desire, of that curiosity about women which is so frequently satisfied by carnal knowledge, but not in Marcel's case, although by making Albertine his virtual captive, he enjoys for a time an illusion of exclusive proprietorship. In fact, as he learns eventually, it is the jailer who is the virtual prisoner, the captive of his own nature, of an eternal desire that no woman can ever satisfy, since it is only one aspect of the artist's insatiable desire to know the reality of life and nature. Marcel's passion for Albertine, therefore, is but an intensified expression of a deep and urgent need for harmony, of what we often vaguely call 'dissatisfaction with life', because our mind, instead of turning inwards to view itself and thus to gain contact, however briefly, with life as it really is, seeks reality vainly outside, in the multifarious successive objects of its contemplation. Turn back the pages of Marcel's narrative and observe how often he tells us of such frustrated desires; they are all reflections of what he calls 'l'éternel désir, l'éternel regret de la vie'. Always their object is some girl fleetingly glimpsed, from Mme de Villeparisis' carriage, from the window of a train, from his car in the Bois, always inaccessible and because unknown, always desirable. These phantoms have always haunted Marcel and it will ever be so until in art he achieves a more direct approach to reality. In a passage expressing one of the most beautiful yet most double-edged compliments paid by an artist to the perennial and elusive charm of woman, Proust seeks the formula of what he calls the law of Marcel's 'curiosités amoureuses'. This formula, he thinks, is to be found in 'le maximum d'écart entre une femme aperçue et une femme approchée, caressée'.[1] For the curiosity excited by love resembles that evoked by names of countries—'toujours déçue, elle renaît et reste toujours insatiable'.[2]

There are times when the presence of an affectionate and almost domesticated Albertine shuts out of Marcel's vision the long perspective of Balbec images, his solitary contemplation of which renders her still desirable, mysterious and incomplete. If his love then turns to indifference it is because love is, above

---

[1] *P.* I, 193.   [2] *P.* I, 195.

all, as Proust diagnoses, 'l'exigence d'un tout'. On the other hand, how little is required to re-establish that 'maximum d'écart' which immediately revives his suspicious and intolerable curiosity. Jealousy needs hardly anything for the creation of its strange, nightmarish but terribly impressive tapestries. A chance word is enough, a silence, an involuntary gesture, a name trapped by the eye in the columns of a newspaper. Life as it presents itself to the jealous mind is no doubt often horrible and unreal. Yet is not jealousy also very often to some extent an intuitive attitude towards life? The language of ordinary social commerce, as we all know from reflection, is largely conventional, interposing a veil between us and the true personality of our fellows? By language, also, we conceal our true self from the world. The logic of ordinary conversation is a false logic: Bergson calls it the false logic of the intelligence. Underneath and parallel to it, at a deeper level, resides another more reliable logic which we adopt, however, only in moments of emotional crisis, when we are most profoundly individual. But outside art, outside great tragedy, how seldom does one dare to express his *moi profond* and obey the logic of real living. Coached by jealousy, Marcel quickly learns to ignore the apparent logic of Albertine's utterances, seeking beyond her words her real desires, her true intentions, the actual structure of her psychological life. Up to a point, this is often childishly easy since, as Marcel somewhere lightly remarks, the faculty of intuition is as widespread as the faculty of common sense. We need not stop to demonstrate the optimistic character of this opinion: Marcel's experience will provide the necessary commentary. It seems, however, not at all difficult at this stage to read Albertine's true thoughts because, although she is a charmingly natural and picturesque liar, she ceases to convince Marcel from the moment when, with painful surprise, he learns that she is naturally untruthful. No doubt he ought to have made the discovery long ago. Françoise, he remembers, had warned him at Balbec of this side of Albertine's character. But who believes a jealous servant? Now, however, Marcel, himself enlightened by jealousy, can automatically decode a remark such as: 'Il serait possible que j'aille demain chez les Verdurin, je ne sais pas du tout si j'irai mais je n'en ai guère envie.' This, of course, is an elementary anagram for: 'J'irai demain chez les Verdurin, c'est absolument certain car j'y attache une extrême importance.' As a result, Marcel instinctively assumes a similar air of casual indifference. Masking his anxiety and suspicions, he gently suggests alternative excursions which will make the Verdurin visit impossible.

Why should Albertine not go to the Verdurins? Marcel, if challenged, would be puzzled to find a rational explanation of his sudden resolve to prevent her visit. Nevertheless, the intuition of jealousy has its own peculiar logic which operates swiftly though, as events show, with varying accuracy. Meanwhile, it is enough for Marcel that Albertine is obviously determined to go to the Verdurins. For example, when he suggests that there is an interesting performance at the Trocadéro Theatre which she ought not to miss, watching Albertine's expression, Marcel discerns in her eyes a procession of fleeting images reflecting deep and mysterious emotions; such as suppressed anger, perhaps, or maybe the sadness and discouragement born of thwarted desires. What desires? His faculty of intuition disdains to answer that question. On the contrary, it tells him something he does not want to hear, namely, that he will never be able to enter into that guarded inner world, the real individuality of Albertine, into the self she will not and cannot disclose. For how can a woman conceivably satisfy the incredible demands of a jealous love which nothing less will satisfy than absolute possession, an impossible knowledge of every point in space and time that her consciousness has ever touched? Yet, no doubt, up to a point it is true, as Proust says, that the faculty of intuition is one of the most common of human attributes. But, like every other faculty, it can only be of real value to us if we have the courage and the will to exploit its full potentialities. For, whilst the intuitive approach to life will afford us a clearer and more immediate vision of reality than common sense or intelligence alone can obtain, how many of us possess the strength to face reality, even as mere spectators, when it is held up to our gaze, transmuted into the beauty of a work of art?

Albertine does not want to hurt Marcel. On the contrary, just
because she has now become aware of his jealousy, her lies are
mostly designed to save him from suffering. Is not the jealous
lover nearly always deceived in such a way, from motives of
kindness rather than of fear or malice? Gradually, of course,
Marcel learns this truth and the zone of his suspicions extends
to include even the trusted Andrée and, retrospectively, Gisèle
and all Albertine's Balbec companions. Progressively, therefore,
he is obliged to revise his former intelligent and logical versions
of certain experiences and impressions. After all, what does he
actually know about the 'jeunes filles en fleurs' of those luminous
summer days in Normandy? In what may be described as
a *pastiche* of Bergson's thought, Proust seizes and illuminates
most beautifully one of this philosopher's favourite ideas:

Et, en elles-mêmes, qu'étaient Albertine et Andrée? Pour le savoir,
il faudrait vous immobiliser, ne plus vivre dans cette attente perpétuelle
de vous où vous passez toujours autres, il faudrait ne plus vous aimer,
pour vous fixer, ne plus connaître votre interminable et toujours
déconcertante arrivée, ô jeunes filles, ô rayon successif dans le tourbillon
où nous palpitons de vous voir reparaître, en ne vous reconnaissant
qu'à peine, dans la vitesse vertigineuse de la lumière.... Je ne dis pas
qu'un jour ne viendra pas où, même à ces lumineuses jeunes filles,
nous n'assignerons pas des caractères très tranchés, mais c'est qu'elles
auront cessé de nous intéresser, que leur entrée ne sera plus pour notre
cœur l'apparition qu'il attendait autre et qui le laisse bouleversé chaque
fois d'incarnations nouvelles. Leur immobilité viendra de notre indifférence qui les livrera au jugement de l'esprit. Celui-ci ne concluera
pas, du reste, d'une façon beaucoup plus catégorique, car après avoir
jugé que tel défaut, prédominant chez l'une, était heureusement absent
de l'autre, il verra que le défaut avait pour contrepartie une qualité
précieuse. De sorte que du faux jugement de l'intelligence, laquelle
n'entre en jeu que quand on cesse de s'intéresser, sortiront définis des
caractères stables de jeunes filles, lesquels ne nous apprendront pas
plus que les surprenants visages apparus chaque jour quand, dans la
vitesse étourdissante de notre attente, nos amies se présentaient tous
les jours, toutes les semaines, trop différentes pour nous permettre, la
course ne s'arrêtant pas, de classer, de donner des rangs.[1]

[And, in themselves, what were Albertine and Andrée? To know
the answer to that, I should have to immobilize you, to stop living in

[1] *P.* I, 85 and 87.

that perpetual state of expectancy from which you emerge always transformed, I should have to give up loving you in order to fix your image, no longer conscious of your interminable and always disconcerting arrival, oh! girls, oh! flashing ray in the swirl of emotions with which we see you reappear whilst barely recognizing you, in the reeling velocity of light. . . . I do not say that a day will not come when, even to these luminous girls, we shall not assign very sharply defined characters, but that will be because they will have ceased to interest us, because their arrival will no longer be, for our heart, the apparition which it expected to be different and which, every time, leaves it overwhelmed with fresh incarnations. Their immobility will come from our indifference which will deliver them up to the judgement of our intelligence. The conclusions reached by the latter, moreover, will not be very much more categorical, for after judging that some defect, predominant in one, was luckily not present in the other, it will see that the defect was offset by some precious quality. As a result, out of the false judgement of the intelligence which only comes into play when we have lost interest, there will emerge well-defined, stable characters of girls, which will leave us none the wiser than did the surprising faces that confronted us every day when, in the bewildering velocity of our expectation, our friends presented themselves, daily, weekly, too different to allow us, for their progress was never arrested, to classify or to grade them.]

What of Andrée and her evening reports on Albertine's movements? Is she not perhaps secretly in league with the elusive captive? Marcel's intelligence, whetted by suspicion to the razor-keenness of an 'esprit de finesse' begins to probe the character of Andrée, discovering unobserved traits. He remembers now, for instance, her extreme susceptibility, the outrageous slanders she once invented at Balbec concerning the family of a young man, a certain Octave whom Andrée wanted to marry. A complex person, naïvely and greedily responsive to flattery, Andrée cannot bear, however, to witness the happiness of others. Thus when Marcel somewhat fatuously remarks that Albertine's uncle and aunt seem to like him, Andrée's displeasure is automatically registered in her expression.

Aussitôt je voyais son visage gluant se gâter; comme un sirop qui tourne, il semblait à jamais brouillé. Sa bouche devenait amère. Il ne

restait plus rien à Andrée de cette juvenile gaîté que, comme toute la
petite bande et malgré sa nature souffreteuse, elle déployait l'année de
mon premier séjour à Balbec....[1]

Marcel recalls, also, her curious trick, when she is giving
Albertine excellent advice, of appearing, by her expression and
tone of voice, to insinuate exactly the opposite. And when
Marcel has a quarrel with Albertine there is an extraordinary
contrast between Andrée's placatory affectionate intonation and
the obvious enjoyment irradiating her features. 'Pendant que
j'adressais à Albertine des reproches' observes Marcel, 'elle
[Andrée] avait l'air de sucer avec délices un sucre d'orge.'
Nevertheless, he telephones to her with instructions to prevent
Albertine at any cost from going to the Verdurins and, on
learning that the visit has been arranged for next day, mentions
casually that he will probably accompany the two girls. Is it
his imagination or does he catch in Andrée's exclamation a note
of irritation and alarm? One of the effects of jealousy, Proust
suggests, is to accentuate all the sense perceptions, so that
Marcel, for the first time, becomes conscious of the infinite
range of nuances distinguishing one woman's voice from another.
This is but one tiny aspect of the new external world which,
like the new world within him, is now beginning to unfold.
And in certain of his own gestures and intonations, Marcel
surprises, not for the first time, the existence of that disconcerting self, the one who resembles what his parents had been
to him. Once again exasperated by the ill-used air with which
Albertine listens to his suggestions about the Trocadéro Theatre,
her lover finds himself involuntarily mimicking the gestures and
reproaches, the wise admonitions used by his father, his mother
or his grandmother in a hundred similar family scenes. In the
heat of this quarrel a remark escapes Albertine which reveals
a deliberate lie she had told at Balbec. With the egoism of the
jealous lover, forgetting his own lies, the lie he invented, for
instance, to induce Albertine to come to Paris, Marcel is overcome with discouragement, with a certain deadly lassitude of
spirit. He will break with his mistress, renouncing this interminable, futile conflict. Knowing that the close of day will

[1] *P.* I, 82.

bring no reconciliation, invaded by the kind of anguish he used
to experience as a child yet, no longer a child, unable to say:
'Je suis triste', Marcel allows the precious minutes to slip
away. Albertine's door closes. He goes into his own room,
hoping she has left a handkerchief, some excuse for waking her.
But after fruitless pacings up and down the corridor—again so
reminiscent of Combray—listening for the word that transfigures mortal sadness into joy, Marcel goes to bed, shivering
with cold and spends half the night in weeping.

It must not, however, be thought that *La Prisonnière* is a *De
Profundis*, a dismal record of uninterrupted suffering. The intermittent character of jealous love is such as to procure for Marcel
frequent periods of blessed respite, almost of positive joy. If
I pause, once again, to draw attention to these sunny intervals,
it is because any interpretation of Proust, however sincere, is
apt to present a summary and therefore unfaithful impression
of his way of seeing life and of the style he created to express
his attitude. In short, it is very easy for the critic to adopt the
very mode of interpretation which Proust himself deplored and
condemned. The narrative of Marcel's tragic experience, we
have already noted, does not conform to the dramatic pattern
of the traditional French novel of psychological analysis. Proust
rejected that form because he thought it over-simplified and
thus distorted reality. His views on this question need not be
recapitulated. They appear to me, however, to have their tap-
root in a typically Bergsonian conception of the function of
language. I refer to his opinion that language is designed not
primarily for introspection but for the observation and analysis
leading to action, and on that account can never completely
embrace the sinuosities of our inner existence, of life's real
movement and change. Does not Proust's style reflect the
writer's effort to elude this obstacle which language by its
original nature interposes between the individual and his
intimate consciousness? Here probably we have the explanation
of what a scientific observer might very reasonably though
quite unjustly call Proust's digressions. Yet these apparent
breaks in the 'thread of the narrative'—to employ a cliché
much too linear to be applicable to the style of Proust—do not

really interrupt Marcel's story. On the contrary, they form an integral part of its substance.

The spiritual climate of *La Prisonnière* has, as Pascal might say, its fine and foggy days. Still, the atmosphere becomes progressively charged with tragedy as Marcel strives to penetrate more deeply into his own mind, and particularly when he tries to decipher the secrets of Albertine's inner life. Bergson, in *La pensée et le mouvant*, observes that between our consciousness and that of others the separation is less clearly marked than between our body and other bodies. He is convinced, indeed, that since experience shows many cases of 'psychological osmosis'—examples of the divinatory power of unreflecting sympathy or antipathy—it is possible for the individual to enter by intuition into immediate contact not only with his own inner life but with that of others. Bergson, indeed, goes very much farther. Why should not intuition introduce us into consciousness in general? 'Si tout être vivant naît, se développe et meurt; si la vie est une évolution et si la vie est ici une réalité, n'y a-t-il pas aussi une intuition du vital, et par conséquence une métaphysique de la vie, que prolongera la science du vital?'

Now, Proust reveals through Marcel's experience that, on this question, he is far from sharing Bergson's optimism. Indeed, viewed from this angle, the whole of *La Prisonnière* is the account of Marcel's failure to achieve what Bergson calls 'psychological osmosis', the record, in fact, of an experiment rendered nugatory by the sheer impossibility of seeing beyond the ever multiplying webs of lies spun by Albertine into her true nature. The narrative traces the process of this tragic and hopeless effort and in at least three notable passages confesses defeat. Yet, since no effort on the part of an individual to exploit the spiritual values latent in the mind is ever quite fruitless, one may say that Marcel suffered not defeat but only a temporary reverse. No doubt he was led to abandon his immediate purpose. But did this sense of failure not also lead to a reorientation of his intuitional powers and thus to the discovery that, in his case at least, it is only through art and not love that the individual can obtain contact with the spirit of another? Is not this what Proust means in the passage where Marcel, listening to Wagner's music, says:

La musique, bien différente en cela de la société d'Albertine, m'aidait a descendre en moi-même, à y découvrir du nouveau: la diversité que j'avais en vain cherchée dans la vie, dans le voyage, dont pourtant la nostalgie m'était donnée par ce flot sonore qui faisait mourir à côté de moi ses vagues ensoleillés. Diversité double. Comme le spectre extériorise pour nous la composition de la lumière, l'harmonie d'un Wagner, la couleur d'un Elstir nous permettent de connaître cette essence qualitative des sensations d'un autre où l'amour pour un autre ne nous fait pas pénétrer.[1]

Again, Marcel tells us that even in his moments of sweetest intimacy with Albertine he was always painfully sensible of an impassable barrier dividing them:

...je sentais que je touchais seulement l'enveloppe close d'un être qui par l'intérieur accédait à l'infini. Combien je souffrais de cette position où nous a réduits l'oubli de la nature qui, en instituant la division des corps n'a pas songé à rendre possible l'interpénétration des âmes (car si son corps était au pouvoir du mien, sa pensée échappait aux prises de ma pensée).[2]

Proust, clearly, does not believe it possible even for the intuition of a lover to achieve what Bergson calls 'psychological osmosis' and Marcel 'l'interpénétration des âmes'. Curiously enough, however, he seems to admit a degree of consciousness rather akin to Bergson's 'intuition du vital'. In half a dozen exquisite pages, Proust describes the impressions experienced by Marcel one afternoon when, on entering Albertine's room he discovers her fast asleep. For once, in her presence, Marcel is able to abandon himself to reverie and to recapture the charming pristine memories of Albertine at Balbec, during his first sojourn, an Albertine silhouetted against a background of sea and sky, the Albertine of the warm, moon-drenched nights on the beach, the Albertine composed of images ever-changing like the sea itself. Now, as he listens to the rise and fall of her breathing, she resembles some lovely and mysterious aquatic plant submerged in the rhythmic, eternal movement of the ocean, an integral element of the unconscious yet dynamic vital flux which pervades

[1] *P.* I, 217. [2] *P.* II, 250.

and animates the whole vast material universe. And, by some miracle, it seems to Marcel that never before has he been able to possess Albertine more completely, to obtain by an extension of love, such a coincidence of his whole being with that of Albertine. Asleep, reabsorbed into the unconscious life of plant and tree and flower, it is as if she has recalled to herself and interfused all the changing, varied selves which, by their dissociation, so torment him in her waking existence. It is as if all Albertine's life, her whole nature, were condensed now in this sleeping body.

En la tenant sous mes regards [thinks Marcel] dans mes mains, j'avais cette impression de la posséder tout entière que je n'avais pas quand elle était réveillée. Sa vie m'était soumise, exhalait vers moi son léger souffle.

J'écoutais cette murmurante émanation mystérieuse, douce comme un zéphyr marin, féerique comme ce clair de lune qu'était son sommeil. Tant qu'il persistait, je pouvais rêver à elle, et pourtant la regarder, et quand ce sommeil devenait plus profond, la toucher, l'embrasser. Ce que j'éprouvais alors, c'était un amour devant quelque chose d'aussi pur, d'aussi immatériel dans sa sensibilité, d'aussi mystérieux que si j'avais été devant les créatures inanimées que sont les beautés de la nature.[1]

The essentially tragic quality of Marcel's jealous love is communicated not directly, in the passages that narrate his painful attempts to decipher the truth concealed by Albertine's lies or evasions but, obliquely, when he tells us of his moments of unalloyed happiness, of respite from suffering. This breadth of vision which does not, by the way, impair the artist's powers of penetration and of reflection, marks, as I have suggested, a divergence from the French tradition in the novel. Stendhal, I think, is the only great novelist to make effective use of such 'moments de repos' which always seemed to him so typical of Shakespearian tragedy and so remote from the manner of the Greek or French neo-classic dramatists. Proust, by these rapid transfigurations of the emotional climate, subtly imitates the process by which in real life the true meaning and quality of human suffering and distress is most immediately communicated

[1] P. I, 93.

to our sensibility. To employ a trivial illustration drawn from everyday life, one is less moved by the appeals of a starving mendicant however sincere and eloquent they may be, than by the spectacle of the silent, avid enjoyment with which he devours the food given him by charity. In the same negative fashion, it is only by seeing the expression of ineffable happiness and blessed calm on his wife's face that a husband realizes the quality and intensity of the pain she has suffered to bring her child into the world. In *La Prisonnière* there are many exquisitely happy and profoundly moving interludes in the drama of Marcel's jealousy. One of Proust's beautiful pages describes the lover's sensations as he watches the sleeping Albertine and contemplates her grave, innocent, almost childlike expression. Then he is completely happy, no longer tortured by what those eyes seem to betray in her waking hours. Also, in the delicious moments of her first awakening, before her speech begins to trace the contours of Albertine's habitual conversation, Marcel tastes the perfect beauty of love undefiled by suspicion or anxiety. There are days when these happy awakenings are prolonged, infusing with their joyousness the world of external sensations that drifts into his room from the street below. To such a golden morning we owe a sparkling fountain of Proustian impressions of Parisian street-cries, that little masterpiece of imaginative transposition in which delicately nuanced perceptions of sound, colour and taste are caught and miraculously suspended in the invisible mesh of a marvellous style. There are long evenings, too, when behind drawn curtains Albertine, seated at the pianola, robed in her latest Fortuny creation, plays through for Marcel his favourite composers; or else listens to his exciting and unorthodox appreciations of the great novelists and musicians, often surprising and delighting him by her intelligent comments and questions. Yet these intermissions, as we have noted, serve only to accentuate the essential and tragic disharmony of their relations. They are fraught with the quality, perhaps, that evensong in a prison chapel might hold, in summer, for a convict sentenced to penal servitude.

The strain of this intolerable situation created by jealousy begins to tell upon Marcel. In one of his rare flashes of grim

humour, reflecting on all the subterfuges he has to adopt in order
to control the movements of his restless and agile captive, her
jailer compares his position to that of the unlucky Scheherazade
except that whereas the latter's ingenuity is directed towards
prolonging her life, the effect of his own eternal inventions is
more likely to produce the opposite results. Albertine has
agreed, however, to give up her Verdurin visit and to go instead
to the benefit performance at the Trocadéro. At this juncture,
Marcel discovers that the apostolic young chauffeur is not so
reliable as he had naïvely believed. However, Albertine sets off
for her matinée whilst Marcel, whose amorous curiosity has
been excited by a tall blonde shop-girl, gets Françoise to bring
this divinity from the *crémerie* to his flat on the pretext of an
imaginary errand. But jealousy, ever vigilant and treacherous,
intervenes and swiftly disposes of this incipient distraction.
Intimidated at close quarters by his visitor's flaring beauty,
Marcel hides his embarrassment behind a newspaper, pretending
to look for an address. Staring at him from the theatrical
columns of the *Figaro* is a short notice on the play that Albertine
has gone to see, the leading role in which is to be taken by an
actress called Léa. In a flash his memory connects her with
Albertine. This is the friend of the woman he caught Albertine
looking at furtively in the mirror of the Casino at Incarville.
Léa is the actress notorious for her Lesbian tastes and probably,
though he cannot prove exactly why, a source of potential
danger to his mistress. Anyhow, his jealous apprehension urges
instant prophylactic measures. The tall blonde is hustled out
and Françoise dispatched at once to the Trocadéro with
instructions to bring back Albertine at once. In a hurriedly
concocted note, Marcel, unable to think of any other excuse for
his irrational behaviour, revives the fictitious and romantic
affair of the heart that had served its purpose at Balbec, telling
Albertine he has just received a disturbing letter from the same
lady. This time Albertine does not hesitate. With unselfish and
reassuring alacrity she accompanies Françoise, thus allaying her
lover's suspicions and prolonging what he now ungratefully, in
such intervals of appeasement, regards as his slavery. Yet,
whilst regretting the charming possibilities for amorous ad-

venture of which he is deprived by Albertine's presence, Marcel
is honest enough to admit to himself that it is just because the
glittering and elusive star of Balbec *plage* is now boxed up in his
flat that all these mysterious dream-women retain in his imagination their infinitely romantic attraction. But for the presence of
his obedient captive, he would have visualized all these actresses
or midinettes as a continual and roving source of temptation to
his mistress, and thus as objects of fear and loathing. How
admirably and unobtrusively Proust illustrates once again the
psychological law which decrees that imagination shall always
tend towards hallucination! And Marcel, do not let us forget,
possesses the imagination of an artist and of a jealous lover. As
his memory begins to play on that Gomorrhe-sur-mer, Balbec,
his growing indifference towards Albertine is immediately
dispelled. His jealousy is also revived by her increasing
restlessness. A hundred tiny signs appear to indicate that she
is beginning to find her captivity intolerable. Marcel pursues
his subtle and persistent interrogations and is naïvely discouraged to observe her growing impatience. He finds her
out, triumphantly, though he is careful to hide his triumph, in
one flagrant untruth and elicits a confession that in the early
days of their relationship she had often lied to him. And when
with death in his soul he asks her with assumed and smiling
indifference for an example, Albertine tells him what is quite
obviously a harmless fib invented on the spur of the moment to
satisfy his curiosity and spare his feelings. Sometimes, but not
often, Marcel has the grace to remember that he himself is
a considerable liar although, like all jealous lovers, he places his
own fictions in a very different category from Albertine's. They
belong to the category of lies justified by their object, which is
to verify or refute his terrible suspicions and thus to protect this
girl against her own nature. Yet Albertine, on her side, could
plead with equal justification that by her evasions, Marcel is
spared incalculable distress. In every suspicious lover, as Proust
somewhere remarks, there lurks a pronounced streak of cruelty
and a suggestion of the *juge d'instruction*. There is also, I should
be inclined to add, a quality of rigidity or automatism which, in
less painful circumstances, might very easily excite, not pity,

but amusement. There are occasions, it must be confessed, when in spite of the prevailing air of oppressive and painful futility surrounding Marcel's interrogations, one is forcibly reminded of some Oriental tyrant in the pages of the *Arabian Nights* or perhaps even of the immortal Bartholo in *Le Barbier de Séville*. How often could Marcel, like Beaumarchais' jealous doctor, ask himself: 'Quelle rage n'a-t-on pas d'apprendre ce qu'on craint de savoir?' Indeed, the one contingency Marcel never faces in the midst of all his jealous imaginings is that whereby Albertine's guilt would be proved, beyond all possible doubt, by the evidence of his senses as in the case of Mlle Vinteuil and of Charlus. Yet, in many passages, Proust implies that even then, such is the implacable and fatal vitality of jealous love, Marcel would still not be cured of his malady. There are, as I have remarked, as many variants of jealousy as there are jealous lovers. Some, as Marcel observes, are aware beyond all doubt that they have been betrayed and yet are prepared to continue a liaison provided they know the identity of the successful rival. Others again there are, who are willing to submit to infidelities on condition that these are committed in some distant town and never brought to their notice. In a profound and subtle analysis which underlines the dynamic and vital quality of jealous passion, Marcel notes that Albertine is the type of woman whose very weaknesses often take the place of charm, and this applies not only to the faults such women have whilst we are in love with them but those they possessed before we knew them; that is to say, the faults inseparable from their nature.

Ce qui rend douleureuses de telles amours, en effet, c'est qu'il leur préexiste une espèce de péché originel de la femme, un péché qui nous les fait aimer, de sorte que, quand nous l'oublions, nous avons moins besoin d'elle et que pour recommencer à aimer il faut recommencer à souffrir.[1]

Now, if we link up this observation with our recollections of Marcel's first meeting with Albertine it will be remembered that what originally attracted him to the girl with the provocative eyes under the brim of her black polo hat, was an indescribable *air canaille* which indeed led him to classify her mentally as the

[1] *P.* i, 205.

mistress of some professional racing cyclist. At any rate, he never thought of her as of someone belonging to his own social milieu. Proust implies surely, once again, that there is a logic of the sentiment which is more reliable and more inexorable than the logic of the intelligence. Marcel's love originated in desire of a quality determined by those impressions of Albertine which so vividly illuminate the pages of *A l'ombre des jeunes filles en fleurs*. And, though Albertine is now his docile mistress, he is still chained to her by memories of the sensations she inspired during the first Balbec summer. Those memories have been immensely reinforced moreover by the terrible doubts he has since formed as to her sexual tastes. The latter, I think, constitute a second 'péché originel' which, retrospectively superimposed upon the first, produces an intolerable flux of shifting and conflicting images and emotions, reflecting a hundred Albertines. If he is ever to know happiness, appeasement of his torturing jealousy, Marcel must discover some kind of stability in this chaos: his mind must obtain a picture of the real, the fundamental *moi*, underlying all the changing and dissociated impressions of Albertine. Is there any certainty, however, that if, for instance, this picture revealed the unmistakable features of a Lesbian, Marcel's passion would automatically cease and with it all his sufferings? Might not his jealousy find, on the contrary, new avenues of exploration, new mysteries to solve, fresh and undreamt-of suspicions on which to batten? On the other hand, life has a way of forcing an exit out of situations that have no apparent issue because the essential reality of life is change and movement. No doubt there exist certain psychological impasses from which escape is only possible by a volcanic and total expression of the individual self which finds an outlet in some violent effort of the will culminating in explosive action. But Marcel, we have observed, is not a heroic character. The dénouement of his tragedy will be achieved by other, less spectacular means. Note, however, that it has not yet reached its crisis. Sensing Albertine's increasing restlessness which makes him all the more anxious to prolong her captivity, he now intends to play the comedy of the reasonable, grateful lover who feels that the time has come, in the interests of both parties, to end their liaison. Marcel's hope is that Albertine, thus realizing that she is not a prisoner but a free agent, will suggest a postponement of the rupture. Marcel reflects, how-ever, that there is no immediate necessity to put his scheme into operation. Albertine, by telephoning like an obedient little wife that she is hurrying back in response to Marcel's pathetic appeal, has restored to him a sense of calm, of security, even of in-difference. The time is not ripe for his hazardous bluff. Albertine arrives and Marcel's happiness is perfect. They drive along the boulevards on a cold, sunny February afternoon, leaving the car at Saint-Cloud to walk arm in arm towards the Bois. Watching their linked and clear-cut shadows cast on the banks of the tiny lake Marcel feels somehow that their destinies are for ever indissolubly joined. During the homeward drive through the avenues of the Bois de Boulogne with their leafless, ivy-clad and 'druidical' trees, Marcel experiences an almost pasha-like sensation of mastery and possession.

...c'était toujours ce même calme inerte et domestique que je goûtais à la voir ainsi lourde, empourprée, opulente et captive, rentrer tout naturellement avec moi, comme une femme que j'avais à moi, et, protégée par les murs, disparaître dans notre maison.[1]

The first chapter of *La Prisonnière* does not, however, close on this note of uxorious and possessive tranquillity. In one of those apparently irrelevant episodes which digress just sufficiently to reveal that Marcel's narrative contains very few actual digres-sions, we learn of the death of his former literary idol, Bergotte, whose novels, read in the golden hours of Sunday afternoons at Combray, had disclosed the vision of an unknown world. It was Bergotte who initiated Marcel into the secrets of art and philosophy, of that 'philosophie idéaliste' which reflected so exactly what the humble neophyte had perceived in his own thoughts and sometimes, to his unspeakable delight, had even contrived to express in his own apprentice, nocturnal scribblings. And now Marcel learns that Bergotte is dead, that Bergotte died as an artist should be happy to die—contemplating a frag-ment of perdurable beauty, a fragment of the material world

[1] *P.* I, 240.

alchemized by the genius of a brother artist into radiant
spirituality. Proust does not tell us, and it does not greatly
matter, whom he had in mind in creating Bergotte. Such
creations are usually a synthesis of the numerous impressions
left on a novelist's mind by a score of real individuals, a synthesis that is always greater and more true than any of its
component actualities. The narrative of the death of Bergotte is
Proust's beautiful tribute, not to any one person but to the Artist.

Bergotte has been for many years gravely ill, tormented by
insomnia and by ominous attacks of vertigo. Having read one
day that in Vermeer's *Vue de Delft*, lent by the Hague for an
exhibition of Dutch paintings in Paris, there is a little fragment
of yellow wall so exquisitely painted as to be in itself a little
masterpiece, Bergotte feels an irresistible desire to see it before
his death. I will quote the page where Proust describes the
last sensations of one whose life had been dedicated to the cult
and to the quest of beauty.

Bergotte mangea quelques pommes de terre, sortit et entra à l'exposition. Dès les premières marches qu'il eut à gravir, il fut pris
d'étourdissements. Il passa devant plusieurs tableaux et eut l'impression de la sécheresse et de l'inutilité d'un art si factice, et qui ne
valait pas les courants d'air et de soleil d'un palazzo de Venise, ou
d'une simple maison au bord de la mer. Enfin il fut devant le Vermeer qu'il se rappelait plus éclatant, plus différent de tout ce qu'il
connaissait, mais où, grâce à l'article du critique, il remarqua pour
la première fois des petits personnages en bleu, que le sable était rose,
et enfin la précieuse matière du tout petit pan de mur jaune. Ses
étourdissements augmentaient; il attachait son regard, comme un
enfant à un papillon jaune qu'il veut saisir, au précieux petit pan de
mur. 'C'est ainsi que j'aurais dû écrire,' disait-il. 'Mes derniers
livres sont trop secs, il aurait fallu passer plusieurs couches de couleur,
rendre ma phrase en elle-même précieuse, comme ce petit pan de
mur jaune.' Cependant la gravité de ses étourdissements ne lui
échappait pas. Dans une céleste balance lui apparaissait, chargeant
l'un des plateaux, sa propre vie, tandis que l'autre contenait le petit
pan de mur si bien peint en jaune. Il sentait qu'il avait imprudemment
donné le premier pour le second. 'Je ne voudrais pourtant pas,' se
disait-il, 'être pour les journaux du soir le fait divers de cette exposition.'
Il se répétait: 'Petit pan de mur jaune avec un auvent, petit pan de
mur jaune,' cependant il s'abattit sur un canapé circulaire; aussi

brusquement il cessa de penser que sa vie était en jeu et, revenant à l'optimisme, se dit: 'C'est une simple indigestion que m'ont donnée ces pommes de terre pas assez cuites, ce n'est rien.' Un nouveau coup l'abattit, il roula du canapé par terre où accoururent tous les visiteurs et gardiens. Il était mort.

On l'enterra, mais toute la nuit funèbre, aux vitrines éclairées, ses livres disposés trois par trois veillaient comme des anges aux ailes éployées et semblaient, pour celui qui n'était plus, le symbole de sa résurrection.[1]

[Bergotte ate some potatoes, went out and entered the exhibition. At the first few steps he had to climb, he suffered an attack of giddiness. He passed in front of several pictures and was struck by the aridity and pointlessness of such an artificial type of art which was greatly inferior to the sunshine of a wind-swept Venetian palazzo or of an ordinary sea-side cottage. At last he came to the Vermeer which he remembered as something more brilliant, more different from anything else he knew, but in which, thanks to the critic's article, he noticed for the first time some little figures in blue, that the sand was pink and, finally, the precious substance of the tiny bit of yellow wall. His giddiness increased; he fixed his gaze, as a child does on a yellow butterfly it wants to catch, on the precious little bit of yellow wall. 'That is how I ought to have written,' he said. 'My last books are too dry, I ought to have superimposed a few layers of colour, to have made my phrase valuable in itself, like that little bit of yellow wall.' However, the serious nature of his giddy spells did not escape him. There appeared to him as in a celestial balance, weighing down one of the scales, his own life, whilst the other contained the little bit of wall so beautifully painted in yellow. He felt that he had unwisely sacrificed the former for the latter. 'All the same,' he said to himself, 'I shouldn't like to be the headline news of the exhibition for the evening papers.'

He repeated: 'Little bit of yellow wall, with an overhanging roof, little bit of yellow wall.' Meanwhile he sank heavily on to a circular sofa; thereupon, he suddenly stopped thinking that his life hung in the balance and, with a return of his natural optimism, said to himself: 'It's merely indigestion from those potatoes; they were under-cooked; it's nothing.' A fresh attack struck him down, he rolled off the sofa on to the floor whilst visitors and attendants rushed forward. He was dead.

They buried him, but all through that funereal night, in the lighted shop-windows, his books, arranged in threes, kept vigil like angels with outspread wings and seemed, for him who was no more, the symbol of his resurrection.]

[1] *P.* I, 254–6.

Musing sadly on the death of his old friend and master, Marcel wonders casually at the inaccuracy of the journalists who record Bergotte's decease as of yesterday. Impossible, because yesterday Albertine, returning home late, told him of having met Bergotte and of their long and interesting talk. Not until much later does Marcel find out that Albertine never had any such conversation with the novelist for the excellent reason that the newspapers were right; Bergotte was already dead. But why did she invent this story? Here is one of the many enigmas concerning Albertine which no one will ever unravel, least of all Marcel. Was it to camouflage some other, very different and unavowable encounter? Or was it just because, arriving late and divining the cause of Marcel's eternal curiosity, she finds it simpler and kinder to imagine these convincingly natural and harmless adventures? At this stage, her lover does not guess how experienced is Albertine in what, retrospectively, he will describe as 'l'art charmant de mentir avec simplicité'. Albertine, far from desiring to arouse his jealousy, is only too anxious to dissipate Marcel's tormenting suspicions. He, on the other hand, is grateful for the caressing, the tender and adroit phrase which acts like a magic salve on the raw places of his soul. And if he now begins to realize that Albertine is naturally inclined to be untruthful, his knowledge is not so much derived from direct evidence of a specific contradiction between her words and known facts as from the intuition that Albertine's stories do not ring true, that she is too careful never to be alone when telephoning, or perhaps from a meeting with Gisèle who betrays in a chance turn of phrase like 'j'avais *justement* quelque chose à lui dire', that Gisèle and Albertine must have arranged a private interview.

But, for the moment, appeased and flattered by Albertine's obedient deference to his wishes, Marcel has only one unanswered question in his mind. Charlus has organized at the Verdurins' a very special recital, the object of which, of course, is to display the talents of Morel for whom the baron hopes to obtain the red ribbon of the *Légion d'honneur*. Marcel is curious to find out why Albertine was so oddly eager to go to this concert. To avoid exciting her suspicions, however, he conceals his real intention, which is to pay a personal visit of inspection, by remarking vaguely that perhaps he will call on the Guermantes or on the Cambremers. As he anticipated, his mistress has no desire to see these people, and says good night, standing up erect with shoulders thrown back and arm outstretched. In that instant, Marcel visualizes Albertine silhouetted against a background of sea and summer sky; for this is the attitude in which he first caught sight of her, at Balbec. So once again, as if mocking the futile attempts of the intelligence to make vertical sections in duration, in real time, the intrusive and disconcerting 'past' flaunts its perpetual survival in the 'present'.

In the second chapter of *La Prisonnière*, we are reintroduced to the society of the Verdurins and of the Guermantes. Moreover, Proust confronts us with a dramatic occurrence. It is nothing less than the public humiliation of Charlus, the revenge of Mme Verdurin for the slights, impertinences and petty tyrannies so long inflicted upon her by that irascible megalomaniac. Now, this change of milieu inevitably produces a corresponding alteration in the tone of Marcel's narrative, in the quality of his perceptions. Yet Proust, by devoting a lengthy section to the interpretation of Marcel's reflections and sensations during the rendering of Vinteuil's septet, contrives to pursue his *recherche du temps perdu*, to sustain and intensify the impression of a Marcel striving towards an intuitive, immediate perception of reality. As a result, this chapter presents a remarkable interfusion of mental states, illustrated by a fascinating variety of psychological observations ranging in density from Marcel's witty and ruthless *aperçus* of Faubourg Saint-Germain snobbery to the delicate and profound notations of his intimate consciousness. Here also, it seems to me, perhaps more than in any previous section of his novel, Proust reveals the extent of his indebtedness to Bergson, whose inspiration can be divined in many of the finest and most suggestive pages. And, if we accept the Bergsonian definition of evolution as 'a process, the continuous phases of which interpenetrate by a sort of inner growth', it is surely in the second and third chapters of *La Prisonnière* that the evolution interpreted in

Marcel's sinuous narrative attains a critical and dynamic stage. The humiliation and approaching disintegration of Charlus, together with the triumph of the former Zolaist, Mme Verdurin, signalize the irrevocable alteration that has occurred in the structure of French society. In Marcel himself one can observe the inception of a profound change with his discovery that the reality of existence is to be sought not in travel, in social intercourse or even in love, but in art. 'On ne se réalise que progressivement.' On various occasions in his life Marcel had been on the verge of realizing this affinity between art and philosophic intuition. After the Verdurin concert he knows that only by sympathy, by imitating the intuitive approach of the great artist is it possible for the individual to 'descend into himself'—his own phrase—and thus by a rejuvenation of his faculty of perception, to enter into the inner life of the external world. It was not until he listened to the inner melody of Vinteuil's tortured life, exteriorized and made real in the famous septet, that Marcel finally understood the power of art, the revelatory power of art. That is why, as we shall see, the death of Albertine and his subsequent discoveries about her habits, whilst causing him almost intolerable agony, do not shatter his existence, which is now oriented towards a greater objective, towards the creation of a work of art. One immediate result of this change of attitude, beautifully illustrated in *La Prisonnière*, is an intensification of Marcel's efforts to comprehend, rather than to judge and condemn, the unnatural and horrible vices exemplified in characters like Charlus, Morel, Mlle Vinteuil and her friend. Proust, in communicating the quality of the sensations and reflections evoked in Marcel by the septet, does not imply that the results of this catharsis produced by a work of art will be to transform immediately and utterly the relations linking his jealous lover to Albertine. This, as we shall observe, is not the case. Nevertheless, I think, Proust does mean that Marcel is now convinced in his inmost self, despite the contradictory suggestions of his intelligence, his jealousy, his craving for appeasement, that the aspect of experience seized by the artist is closer to the reality of life than the logical mosaic of plausible 'facts' grasped by the critical mind of the scientific observer, by a consciousness habitually turned outwards in its attempts to comprehend existence; as if the individual consciousness itself were something divorced from the life and matter composing the world and not part of their very essence.

The Charlus-Morel relationship, though subordinated in the first chapter of *La Prisonnière* to the author's immediate theme, is not entirely withdrawn from our attention. The baron himself looms in the background, a black and sinister guardian angel, directing the preparations for Morel's forthcoming marriage with Jupien's niece. Yet another page is turned in the cabbalistic manuscript of Morel's character, that queer jumble of hysterical viciousness and of sometimes delicate sensibility, a contradiction illustrated in two incidents narrated by Marcel. The first produces upon him an impression of unaccountable sadness. Passing by Jupien's lodge, he surprises the violinist in one of his ungovernable and almost primitive accesses of rage, directed this time at his trembling and bewildered fiancée. All that Marcel can distinguish is the phrase: 'Grand pied de grue, grand pied de grue!' reiterated with fearful automatism in accents that seem to emerge mysteriously from Morel's peasant childhood; accents and words containing no meaning for Marcel's intelligence, yet ringing long afterwards in his ears, quickening the beatings of his heart. The second incident, equally impressive yet also strangely unreal, occurs later as he is leaving for the Verdurins. It reminds one, somehow, of a scene from an eighteenth-century novel of love and adventure such as the Abbé Prévost used to compose, full of encounters that appear incredible if transferred to a twentieth-century setting. Just as he is about to hail a cab, Marcel hears a man sobbing bitterly. It is Morel, in evening dress, seated on a stone flanking the gateway, his head buried in his hands, genuinely overcome by remorse at his recent behaviour to his fiancée yet obviously worried about the effect on his playing of this shock to his nervous system. What strikes Marcel is the immense revolution that has occurred, during these few hours, in Morel's inner life; the transformation from the bestial rage of the afternoon to his present state of grief, shame and self-abasement. It does not alter his impression, however, that the violinist's nature is fundamentally vile; that Morel's general attitude to Jupien's niece corresponds, on the whole, to the sentiments implied in the abominable plan for seduction which he once outlined to Charlus. Morel, utterly self-centred and vicious, with his un-reasoning bouts of hysterical vindictiveness, is now ripe for Mme Verdurin's purpose. Even as Charlus, Brichot and Marcel are approaching her residence in the Quai Conti, the Patronne is preparing the interview between her husband and Morel which is to mark the first decisive step in the baron's fall from grandeur. Not that Mme Verdurin is influenced by any moral considerations. As she cynically admits, a liaison such as that between Charlus and Morel is much less of a threat to the homogeneity of the 'clan' than the normal sentimental entangle-ments of Swann or Elstir. What Mme Verdurin finds unendurable at this critical stage in her career as *salonnière* is the peremptory rejection by Charlus of one after another Faubourg Saint-Germain notability who had begun to attend her dinners. As a compromise the Patronne would have welcomed an opportunity of amalgamating the baron's guests with her own favourites. But Charlus, an expert in such affairs, contemptuously vetoes practically all Mme Verdurin's suggestions. This attitude, coupled with the atrocious manners of his duchesses, proves to be his undoing.

The baron, although the deterioration is so far perceptible only to Marcel, has reached the point where his vice is about to declare its presence beyond all possibility of error. He who once could find no language strong enough to express his virile contempt for the noisy bejewelled and powdered little perverts of the 'ma chère' brand; Charlus, who had always concealed his own inverted tastes behind a mask of almost military brusque-ness, has unconsciously shed his camouflage and now, involun-tarily, employs the gestures and utters the little cries of those 'petits messieurs' whom he used to imitate, hypocritically, but to perfection. To the observant Marcel, the baron's vice seems to ooze from every pore, from every movement, word and intonation. Even Brichot now feels vaguely uneasy in the presence of his old friend and, to dispel this malaise, the pro-fessor seeks reassurance in his memories of Classical literature forgetting, as Proust insistently reminds us, that there is no true analogy between the homosexuality of Charlus and of an era where an *amour* with an athlete was equivalent rather to the modern practice of keeping an actress. 'C'est l'homosexualité survivante malgré les obstacles, honteuse, flétrie qui est la seule vraie.' But Proust then proceeds to a generalization which is surprising in one so rarely guilty of inducing sweeping conclusions from uncertain data. The only genuine homosexuality, he continues, is that which usually corresponds to an intensification of the intellectual qualities.

On tremble [says Marcel], au rapport que le physique peut avoir avec celles-ci (les qualités morales) quand on songe au petit déplacement de goût purement physique, à la tare légère d'un sens qui expliquent que l'univers des poètes et des musiciens si fermé au duc de Guermantes, s'entre'ouvre pour M. de Charlus. Que ce dernier ait du goût dans son intérieur, qui est d'une ménagère bibeloteuse, cela ne surprend pas, mais l'étroite brèche qui donne jour sur Beethoven et sur Véronèse! [1]

Now, one might very pertinently ask, why should Marcel conclude that the æsthetic sensibility of the invert is a necessary result of his unnatural sexual proclivities? What of the swarms of 'louches individus' who, according to Marcel himself, are to be seen gliding in the baron's wake when the latter ventures on the boulevards or into the *salle des pas perdus* of the Gare Saint-Lazare? Quite certainly it would be absurd to claim that these creatures display the slightest appreciation of Beethoven or Veronese. Of course, when Marcel is on the subject of Lesbianism, his imagination blurs his sense of realities. But here, obviously, it is Proust himself to whom we are listening; Proust who always tends to assault our common sense when he begins to philosophize on the theme of 'le charlisme'. For instance, in his account of this *soirée musicale* at the Verdurins', Marcel records the curious and furtive remarks supposed to have been exchanged by six perverts who include two dukes, an eminent general, a great lawyer, a famous doctor and a celebrated author. Really, this is imposing too severe a strain on our credulity. When Marcel sees a potential Lesbian in every

[1] *P.* II, 8.

pretty woman who meets Albertine at Balbec we know that it is an insanely jealous man who is speaking, and we make the necessary allowances. Similarly, when an invert like Charlus, in order to impress the Sorbonne professor, assesses the proportion of homosexuals to normal males in fashionable society at three to ten, we can share the stupefaction and obvious disbelief of Brichot. Charlus is, after all, not a disinterested reporter. 'Vous êtes orfèvre, M. Josse', as Molière would say. But Marcel's mixed bag of dukes and brilliant professional men, and at one party, is a patent attempt to bolster up one exaggeration by another; to justify Proust's more than questionable theory on the relationship between sexual inversion and æsthetic sensibility. Here the most pertinent comment is surely to be found in Brichot's sensible remark to Charlus:

Or, aucun document ne venant authentiquer ce genre de phénomènes collectifs que les seuls renseignés sont trop intéressés à laisser dans l'ombre, on s'indignerait fort dans le camp des belles âmes et vous passeriez tout net pour un calomniateur ou pour un fol.[1]

I do not think, somehow, that Proust intends us to include him amongst these 'belles âmes'.

The truth is, I fancy, that Proust who inclines, on the whole, to present Charlus as a type and, therefore, as a figure of comedy in the highest sense of the term, finds himself in something of a quandary the moment he tries to penetrate deeply into the soul of this remarkable individual. In general, the traits most frequently accentuated by Proust are comic rather than tragic. They correspond, in fact, to those so admirably defined by Bergson in *Le rire* as peculiar to the comic type. Charlus is, *par excellence*, the character automatically following up his one idea, a Don Quixote living in an absurd world of his own imagining, governed by his own laws, unconscious of his monstrous egotism, rigidly following the track which it has marked out in his life. Here we have, in short, the type of the *Mégalomane*, admirably presented in all its nuances, a supremely comic creation, greater even than Homais, Flaubert's conception of *L'Imbécile*. But Proust, by trying to combine in Charlus two

[1] *P.* ii, 129.

types, *Le Mégalomane* and *L'Inverti*, began at once to encounter
difficulties. Society, up to a point, can laugh at avarice, hypocrisy and even other vices. But it is hardly disposed to laugh
very long or very heartily at sodomy. And it becomes very
evident, when Proust begins to observe the baron de Charlus
from this point of view, that there is no comic type one might
call *L'Inverti*. Here the artist at once enters perforce into a
deeper, more individual and tragic region of the human soul.
We are no longer in the atmosphere of comedy. Proust is no
longer concerned with a species, though by surrounding Charlus
with satellite perverts he attempts with very little success to
give this impression. No, the task he now confronts is one that
might tax the creative powers of a Shakespeare or Marlowe
and, as we know, it tempted the imagination of Balzac. Charlus,
from one point of view, represents Proust's effort to take over
where Balzac left off: in short, to improve on Vautrin. Inevitably, he encountered at once a fundamental obstacle. Most
men at some time in their lives have been at least vaguely tempted
by ambition, jealous love, by avarice, by the desire for revenge,
by many vices or passions which, if they had been allowed to
dominate their character would have completely disrupted their
social life. In other words, when we see in a tragedy or encounter in the pages of a novel, concrete examples imagined by
the artist of individuals who have utterly abandoned their soul
to the ravages of such vices, we are in a position to appreciate
the sincerity or truth of the vision communicated by the dramatist or novelist. Without being connoisseurs we can at least
say: 'There but for the grace of God goes John Bunyan—or
John Smith.' But *pace* Marcel Proust, by the grace of God, there
are very few who can apply this criterion to the novelist's
psychological study of a homosexual. Now, Proust was too
great and sensitive an artist not to be aware of this barrier. He
knows very well that Marcel's impression of the baron's inner
life, of Charlus considered not as a megalomaniac but as an
individual who is an invert, must frequently strike the reader
as strange and possibly as incredible. I think that is why he
felt it necessary to suggest, as he does in the following passage,
that there are occasions when in the absence of any link between

our own experience of life and the reality which the artist interprets, we must simply take him on trust. 'Ce serait une objection plus grave', says Proust apologizing to the readers who may be offended by certain strange descriptions,

si elle était fondée, de dire que tout cela nous est étranger et qu'il faut tirer la poésie de la vérité toute proche. L'art extrait du réel le plus familier existe en effet et son domaine est peut-être le plus grand. Mais il n'en est pas moins vrai qu'un grand intérêt, parfois de la beauté, peut naître d'actions découlant d'une forme d'esprit si éloignée de tout ce que nous sentons, de tout ce que nous croyons, que nous ne pouvons même arriver à les comprendre, qu'elles s'étalent devant nous comme un spectacle sans cause. Qu'y a-t-il de plus poétique que Xerxès, fils de Darius, faisant fouetter de verges la mer qui avait englouti ses vaisseaux.[1]

Proust's demands on our faith, as I have mentioned, will become increasingly great as Marcel's narrative enters on its closing phases. By then, too, Charlus will have shed most of the traits of the comic type, of *Le Mégalomane*. We shall see only the tragic individual, the homosexual called the baron de Charlus finally destroyed by his terrible vice. This fact will not of course deter superficially minded Proustians from using the epithet 'un Charlus' to designate an invert. But, as I have said, our final impression is one of uniqueness. The other impression which seems to me predominant, is of a type 'le grand seigneur quinteux', the despot of high society, the type worthy to rank with the greatest comic creations in fiction.

As it happens, this second chapter of *La Prisonnière* illustrates very well the difficulties experienced by Proust when he begins to move from the plane from which Charlus is observed and projected as a comic type to that deeper level of the consciousness where the artist is at once confronted by nuances of feeling, by forms of emotional reaction to external events which are peculiar to Charlus the individual and cannot be expressed in terms of averages. Proust multiplies his efforts to expose these secret places in the baron's personality, but it is not really until the dramatic situation which terminates this evening at the Verdurins' that he can be said to afford us a vision of the inner nature of

[1] *P.* I, 62.

Charlus. Until then, until the illumination suddenly produced by Morel's public act of apostasy, we see only the external traits of this 'grand inquisiteur peint par le Greco', the traits of a type already familiar to us though now greatly accentuated as Proust redoubles his attempts to individualize the baron's character. Despite his remarkable *flair* for the suggestive image and epithet, Proust does not essentially, at this stage, allow us to penetrate more deeply into the personality of Charlus. At times, indeed, the author quietly takes over the narrative from Marcel and proceeds to air his literary reminiscences or else to amuse us with a *pastiche* of Saint-Simon or perhaps of Anatole France. This is strikingly evident in the pages lavishly devoted to the dialogue between the baron and Brichot on the subject of *l'amour socratique*. Now, although Proust undoubtedly intended to show in these discussions that the baron's vice has now entered upon a phase in which apostolic zeal and vanity may readily outweigh considerations of secrecy and discretion, the reader is really much less interested in Charlus than in the obviously Proustian opinions expressed during this academic debate. But the moment that Proust, leaving these abstractions, effaces himself and resumes his interpretation of Charlus, 'le grand seigneur quinteux', the latter springs into life, monopolizing our interest just as he does when dominating the Verdurin *salon*. An expert and intimidating master of ceremonies, by a single commanding gesture Charlus imposes silence on this chattering throng of fashionable philistines. Here is Proust's admirable notation of a typically Charlusian attitude:

Morel était déjà monté sur l'estrade, les artistes se groupaient, que l'on entendait encore des conversations, voire des rires, des 'il paraît qu'il faut être initié pour comprendre'. Aussitôt M. de Charlus, re-dressant sa taille en arrière, comme entré dans un autre corps que celui que j'avais vu, tout à l'heure, arriver en traînaillant chez Mme Ver-durin, prit une expression de prophète et regarda l'assemblée avec un sérieux qui signifiait que ce n'était pas le moment de rire, et dont on vit rougir brusquement le visage de plus d'une invitée prise en faute, comme une élève par son professeur en pleine classe. Pour moi l'attitude, si noble d'ailleurs, de M. de Charlus avait quelque chose de comique; car tantôt il foudroyait ses invités de regards enflammés, tantôt, afin de leur indiquer comme un *vade mecum* le religieux silence qu'il convenait d'observer, le détachement de toute préoccupation mondaine, il présentait lui-même, élevant vers son beau front ses mains gantées de blanc, un modèle (auquel on devait se conformer) de gravité, presque déjà d'extase, sans répondre aux saluts de retardataires assez indécents pour ne pas comprendre que l'heure était maintenant au Grand Art. Tous furent hypnotisés; on n'osa plus proférer un son, bouger une chaise; le respect pour la musique — de par le prestige de Palamède — avait été subitement inculqué à une foule aussi mal élevée qu'élégante.[1]

[Morel had already mounted the platform, the musicians were taking up their positions and one could still hear conversations, laughter, such remarks as: 'Apparently, you have to be initiated in order to understand.' Immediately, M. de Charlus, throwing back his shoulders, as if he had entered a different body from the one I had seen, a short time before, dragging itself towards Mme Verdurin's, assumed a prophetic expression and looked at the assembly with a seriousness which indicated that this was no time for laughter, thus bringing a sudden blush to the cheeks of more than one lady, caught out like some schoolgirl by the master, in front of the whole class. To my mind, M. de Charlus' attitude, so noble in other respects, had a touch of the comic, for at one moment he paralysed the guests with his flashing eyes, at the next, so as to indicate by a kind of *vade mecum* the religious silence it was proper to observe, the detachment from any mundane preoccupation whatever, he himself presented, raising his white-gloved hands to his forehead, a model (to which they were expected to conform) of gravity, already almost of ecstasy, ignoring the greetings of late-comers who so forgot themselves as not to realize that it was the time for Great Art. All were hypnotized; no one dared to utter another sound, to move a chair; respect for music—by the sheer prestige of Palamède—had been suddenly inculcated in a crowd as ill-bred as it was elegant.]

Though the baron does not know it, this is the supreme act of his despotic regime, at least in the Verdurin *salon*. But the concert has begun and we can now observe the extraordinary change produced in Marcel's spiritual existence by Vinteuil's masterpiece. What is being played is the complete work, of which the well-known sonata is only a fragment. To this incident Proust devotes a score of magnificent pages, extracting from his memories and impressions, from his passionate and enduring love of great music a remarkable illusion of reality.

[1] *P.* II, 62.

There never was, of course, a *septuor de Vinteuil*. Yet no one, after reading Proust's marvellous critique, can possibly doubt the existence of a *septuor de Vinteuil*. Reversing the traditional functions of music and literature, by the magic of his incomparable style, Proust spins a gorgeous, iridescent web of sensations and moods into a unity which seems to require only a mechanical transposition of words into notes in order to be realized as a great musical composition.

Listening to Vinteuil's septet, Marcel is obliged to revise certain ideas on art which had crystallized in his mind that afternoon whilst he was comparing the scores of *Tristan* and of Vinteuil's sonata. Reflecting then upon the 'habileté vulcanienne' with which the great nineteenth-century artists, Wagner, Hugo, Balzac and Michelet lent to their essentially incomplete works an ulterior though by no means factitious unity, Marcel found himself assailed by doubts concerning the reality of art. In every great work of art there is something which appears to be the reflection of a superhuman reality. But might this not be, he wondered, merely the result of patient and clever technique? The effect of these meditations had been to convince Marcel almost that art was not, after all, something outside life, something divorced from the vanity and emptiness of our ordinary existence. On leaving his flat for the Verdurins' he was strongly tempted to believe that the uniqueness, the individuality of the work of art is simply an illusion due to the artist's cunning use of his medium. But the septet dispels these pessimistic views, restoring Marcel's faith in the reality of art, the function of which, he now feels, is precisely to discover reality and to render it visible. Nowhere does Marcel pronounce the name of Bergson. Yet the theme and substance of the reflections inspired in him by Vinteuil's music is essentially Bergsonian. Note how Marcel's conception of the object of great art tallies with that expressed by Bergson in the following words: 'l'art n'a d'autre objet que d'écarter les symboles pratiquement utiles, les généralités conventionnellement et socialement acceptées, enfin tout ce qui masque la réalité, pour nous mettre face à face avec la réalité même.'[1] The affinity between these sentiments and Marcel's is

[1] *Le rire.*

transparent in almost every page of this sumptuously imaged tribute to the genius of Vinteuil which reproduces, moreover, although in the form of an original and richly orchestrated commentary, the dominant notes of Bergson's own noble paean in honour of music and poetry:

D'autres creuseront plus profondément encore. Sous ces joies et ces tristesses qui peuvent à la rigueur se traduire en paroles, ils saisiront quelque chose qui n'a plus rien de commun avec la parole, certains rythmes de vie et de respiration qui sont plus intérieurs à l'homme que ses sentiments les plus intérieurs, étant la loi vivante, variable avec chaque personne, de sa dépression et de son exaltation, de ses regrets et de ses espérances. En dégageant, en accentuant cette musique, ils l'imposeront à notre attention; ils feront que nous nous y insérerons involontairement nous-mêmes, comme des passants qui entrent dans une danse. Et par là ils nous amèneront à ébranler aussi, tout au fond de nous, quelque chose qui attendait le moment de vibrer.[1]

Turn now to the following page from *La Prisonnière*. Could anything well be more reminiscent of Bergson's thought and yet so typically Proustian?

Ces phrases-là, les musicographes pourraient bien trouver leur apparentement, leur généalogie, dans les œuvres d'autres grands musiciens, mais seulement pour des raisons accessoires, des ressemblances extérieures, des analogies plutôt ingénieusement trouvées par le raisonnement que senties par l'impression directe. Celle que donnaient ces phrases de Vinteuil était différente de toute autre, comme si, en dépit des conclusions qui semblent se dégager de la science, l'individuel existait. Et c'était justement quand il cherchait puissamment à être nouveau, qu'on reconnaissait sous les différences apparentes, les similitudes profondes, et les ressemblances voulues qu'il y avait au sein d'une œuvre, quand Vinteuil reprenait à diverses reprises une même phrase, la diversifiait, s'amusait à changer son rythme, à la faire reparaître sous sa forme première, ces ressemblances-là voulues, œuvre de l'intelligence, forcément superficielles, n'arrivaient jamais à être aussi frappantes que ces ressemblances, dissimulées, involontaires, qui éclataient sous des couleurs différentes, entre les deux chefs-d'œuvre distincts; car alors Vinteuil, cherchant à être nouveau, s'interrogeait lui-même, de toute la puissance de son effort créateur, atteignait sa propre essence à ces profondeurs où, quelque question qu'on lui pose, c'est du même accent, le sien propre, qu'elle répond.

[1] *Le rire.*

Un tel accent, cet accent de Vinteuil, est séparé de l'accent des autres musiciens, par une différence bien plus grande que celle que nous percevons entre la voix de deux personnes, même entre le beuglement et le cri de deux espèces animales: par la différence même qu'il y a entre la pensée de ces autres musiciens et les éternelles investigations de Vinteuil, la question qu'il se posait sous tant de formes, son habituelle spéculation, mais aussi débarrassée de formes analytiques du raisonnement que si elle s'exerçait dans le monde des anges, de sorte que nous pouvons en mesurer la profondeur, mais sans plus la traduire en langage humain que ne le peuvent les esprits désincarnés quand, évoqués par un médium, celui-ci les interroge sur les secrets de la mort.[1]

[For those phrases, musicographers could no doubt find affinities and sources in the works of other great composers, but only for unessential reasons, external resemblances, analogies ingeniously discovered by the reason, rather than felt as the result of a direct impression. That conveyed by these Vinteuil phrases was different from any other, as if, in spite of the conclusions which seem indicated by science, the individual did exist. And it was precisely when he strove with might and main to be an original creator, that one discerned, beneath the apparent differences, the profound similarities; and the deliberate resemblances that lay at the core of a work, when Vinteuil went over a single phrase again and again, diversified it, amused himself by altering its rhythm, by reproducing it in its original form, those deliberate resemblances, the work of his intelligence, necessarily superficial, never succeeded in being so striking as those resemblances, disguised, involuntary, which flared up under different colours, between the two separate masterpieces; for then Vinteuil, trying to create something new, interrogated himself, with the full powers of his creative effort, made contact with his essential self at those depths where, no matter what be the question submitted, its reply will have the same accent, that is to say, its own. Such an accent, that accent of Vinteuil, is separated from the accent of other composers by a difference very much greater than that which we perceive between the voices of two people, even between the bellowings and the cries of two different animal species; by the difference, in fact, that exists between the thought of those other composers and the eternal investigations of Vinteuil, the question that he put to himself under so many forms, his habitual speculation, but as clear of analytic forms of reasoning as if it were operating in the world of the angels, so that we can gauge its depth although no more able to translate it into human language than can disembodied spirits when, evoked by a medium, they are questioned by him about the secrets of death.]

[1] *P.* ii, 72–3.

Under the spell of the septet, Marcel is now convinced that art is not just a continuation of life but that the paintings of an Elstir or the works of a genius like Vinteuil do undoubtedly possess the power to refract in their spectrum, to exteriorize the 'composition intime de ces mondes que nous appelons les individus'. Only through the medium of art can one communicate that ineffable something, that essential reality, that individual quality of one's sentiments which no conversation can ever transmit, not even, says Marcel, a conversation between friend and friend, master and disciple, lover and mistress. Does this mean that he himself, being neither a great painter nor a great musician, must despair of ever penetrating the veil interposed by language between consciousness and reality? No, because Marcel notes with inexpressible delight the affinity between the sensations evoked in him by a certain phrase of the septet and the quality of the impressions captured once in the pages he wrote on the steeples of Martinville. And, surrendering himself to the magic of the septet, Marcel begins to hear the melody of his own inner life and, in this mood, to survey the external world with a less analytic mind, with sympathetic insight. Viewed thus, from the serene and detached plane of art, life reveals unsuspected meaning and harmony.

The revelation that all Vinteuil's earlier works had been only incomplete and timid preludes to the triumphant perfection of the septet, alters Marcel's perspective. All the loves of his boyhood and manhood, like all the stages of his relations with Albertine were, he now realizes, merely fragments of a great design—his present and consuming love for Albertine. His mind, having attained at this moment an artist's purity of perception, grasps the eternal beauty and happiness which Vinteuil extracted from the terrible sadness and sordid ugliness of his existence. Before the concert, Marcel learns that but for the intelligence and devotion of Mlle Vinteuil's Lesbian friend, the septet would have remained for ever unknown. This fact, in conjunction with his new intuitive attitude to life, causes him to modify the harshness of his feelings towards the composer's daughter, a harshness, be it noted, which did not exist before Marcel fell in love with Albertine and began to suspect her of

unnatural tastes. The memory of the horrible profanation of
Vinteuil's photograph, of the sadistic incident witnessed at
Montjouvain cannot, of course, be effaced. But Marcel, who is
trying now to understand and not merely to sit in moral judgement on the evidence of that one action, feels that this sacrilege
was committed, surely, in one of those unaccountable moments
when an individual runs counter to her true inclinations. For
Mlle Vinteuil's sake he earnestly hopes that this is so, wishing
he could insert into her mind the idea that she can still pray for
her father and not despair of his forgiveness. Marcel reflects,
too, upon the strangely beautiful designs that can emerge from
the combination of our vices and virtues. Because of the terrible
attachment linking Mlle Vinteuil and her friend, linking Charlus
to Morel, a beautiful creation is now presented to the world.

How complete is the transformation produced in Marcel's
moral atmosphere by the septet may be gauged from the
following fact. On entering the Verdurin *salon*, he had learned
from the baron that Mlle Vinteuil and her friend, unctuously
described as 'deux personnes d'une terrible réputation' were
to have come to a rehearsal of the concert. This explains without
a shadow of doubt Albertine's peculiar eagerness to call on Mme
Verdurin. Obviously she had expected to meet these two women.
Marcel's jealousy is revived by this confirmation of his suspicions and he divines that the future will bring him fresh
suffering. On the other hand, he is now invaded by a new sense
of optimism induced by the conviction that in art it is possible
to realize a happiness, a self-harmony which he has failed to
discover in social intercourse or even in love. This mood is
fortified, moreover, by his diligent instinct for self-preservation
which persuades him, before the evening is out, that probably
Mme Verdurin, out of sheer boastfulness, had invented the
story of an expected visit from the composer's daughter.

Proust's increasing contempt for fashionable society, 'le
royaume du néant' is strikingly reflected in Marcel's account of
the quarrel between the Verdurins and Charlus. The immediate
cause of the baron's humiliation is the appalling manners of the
Faubourg Saint-Germain contingent, of the chattering, inquisitive and malicious duchesses who sail into the Verdurin

salon and, ignoring their hostess, make straight for Palamède whilst he accepts their homage with regal condescension, serenely oblivious of the Patronne's seething indignation. Only one guest, the Queen of Naples, enters into conversation with Mme Verdurin, thus subordinating the rules of etiquette to the impulses of her natural sensibility and tact. *Quos vult Jupiter perdere*...! The concert over, a second and more prolonged levee takes place. Charlus, delirious with the joy of the despot surrounded by his obsequious courtiers and of the talented impresario at the close of a triumphantly successful production, dispenses all the treasures of his eloquence and devastating wit for the benefit of the long queue of departing guests, not one of whom dreams of addressing a word of thanks to the hostess of the evening. The latter, enraged by this crowning insult, privately asks Brichot and Marcel to hold the baron in talk whilst M. Verdurin enlightens Morel as to the baron's true reputation, his evil designs on the violinist and the latter's situation as it appears to society. Marcel and the professor have no time to refuse the Patronne's request since the baron himself, in his sublime egoism and infatuation, joins their group and proceeds at once to inform Mme Verdurin how fortunate she is to have enjoyed the privilege of his unique and expert services as master of ceremonies, blandly driving home at every word another torturing spine into her raw and quivering *amour-propre*. But during this time, as Lady Macbeth observed on the occasion of another famous *guet-apens*, Mme Verdurin's husband 'is about it', closeted with Morel, killing one by one the violinist's sunny illusions concerning his immediate present and future. At the right moment, Verdurin is joined by his wife and the terrified Morel, for whom the only thing that really matters in life is the opinion of his colleagues, is informed brutally that he is 'la fable du Conservatoire', spoken of already as a society amateur and worse, because of his 'promiscuité honteuse' with Charlus. The Patronne, who has never complicated her life by absurd distinctions between truth and fiction, represents the baron as a social pariah, involved with apaches —which Morel knows to be true—a suspect to the police and, moreover, on the verge of complete and spectacular bankruptcy.

Expertly interweaving fact and invention, the Patronne dismisses with ridicule the baron's promise of a *Légion d'honneur* and cruelly repeating a remark made with no malice by the indiscreet and garrulous Charlus, pictures the latter as a false friend who jeers privately at the pretentions of Charlie Morel, the flunkey's son. This final stab penetrates the armour of Morel's conceit.

Mme Verdurin fut inondée de la joie d'une vieille maîtresse qui, sur le point d'être lâchée par son jeune amant, réussit à rompre son mariage. Et peut-être n'avait-elle pas calculé son mensonge ni même menti sciemment. Une sorte de logique sentimentale, peut-être, plus élémentaire encore, une sorte de réflexe nerveux, qui la poussait, pour égayer sa vie et préserver son bonheur, à 'brouiller les cartes' dans le petit clan, faisait-elle monter impulsivement à ses lèvres, sans qu'elle eût le temps d'en contrôler la vérité, ces assertions diaboliquement utiles sinon rigoureusement exactes.[1]

Since Morel's natural poltroonery is now submerged in an almost hysterical rage, he is ripe for Mme Verdurin's purpose. Charlus, in excellent humour, terminates his disquisition on pederasty and advances gaily towards his protégé, greeting him already as a chevalier of the Legion of Honour. But Morel, recoiling in horror, screams out: 'Laissez-moi, je vous défends de m'approcher. Vous ne devez pas être à votre coup d'essai, je ne suis pas le premier que vous essayez de pervertir.' The stupefied Marcel's one consolation in this painful instant is that Charlus will now proceed to pulverize the violinist and exhibit one of his most Charlusian and spectacular explosions of rage. Instead, the spectacle which now materializes before his amazed eyes is that of a Charlus, absolutely bewildered, turning his imploring gaze from Morel to the other witnesses of the violinist's astonishing outburst.

Toujours est-il [observes Marcel] que dans ce salon qu'il dédaignait, ce grand seigneur (à qui n'était pas plus essentiellement inhérente la supériorité sur les roturiers qu'elle ne le fut à tel de ses ancêtres angoissés devant le tribunal révolutionnaire) ne sut, dans une paralysie de tous les membres et de la langue, que jeter de tous côtés des regards épouvantés, indignés par la violence qu'on lui faisait, aussi suppliants qu'interrogateurs. Dans une circonstance si cruelle-

[1] *P*. II, 151.

ment imprévue, ce grand discoureur ne sut que balbutier: 'Qu'est-ce que cela veut dire, qu'est-ce qu'il y a?' On ne l'entendait même pas. Et la pantomime éternelle de la terreur panique a si peu changé, que ce vieux Monsieur, à qui il arrivait une aventure désagréable dans un salon parisien, répétait à son insu les quelques attitudes schématiques dans lesquelles la sculpture grecque des premiers âges stylisait l'épouvante des nymphes poursuivies par le Dieu Pan.[1]

How long Charlus might have stood there, mute and tearfully suppliant, it is impossible to say. A second *coup de théâtre*, fortunately, puts an end to this intolerable situation. The Queen of Naples who had forgotten her fan, a precious heirloom, returns personally to fetch it so that, quite unperceived, she has been a shocked spectator of the baron's profound humiliation. Advancing regally to her cousin's side, ignoring Mme Verdurin's sweeping curtsey and ill-timed attempts to introduce the expectant Morel, the Queen begins to chat quietly with the baron, desperately anxious to save at least a few remaining shreds of his tattered prestige:

'Vous n'avez pas l'air bien, mon cher cousin,' dit-elle à M. de Charlus. 'Appuyez-vous sur mon bras. Soyez sûr qu'il vous soutiendra toujours. Il est assez solide pour cela.' Puis levant fièrement les yeux devant elle (en face de qui, me raconta Ski, se trouvaient alors Mme Verdurin et Morel), 'vous savez qu'autrefois à Gaete il a déjà tenu en respect la canaille. Il saura vous servir de rempart.' Et c'est ainsi, emmenant à son bras le Baron et sans s'être laissé présenter Morel que sortit la glorieuse sœur de l'Impératrice Elisabeth.[2]

Proust disregards the patterns of behaviour which our objective and reasoning intelligence traces out in advance for the passions. Looking more deeply into the undercurrents of his own streaming psychological life, he can perceive for every state of feeling the rough outlines of many possible actions. If what is called our experience of life teaches us anything, it is surely the impossibility of foreseeing the exact shape of things to come, of predicting in what special way our individual personality will express itself in behaviour, the manner in which the individual consciousness will adapt or mould itself to the materiality of which it is largely composed. Most of us refuse

---

[1] *P.* ii, 154.   [2] *P.* ii, 160–1.

to accept this truth and that is often our tragedy. But the artist of genius whose genius consists precisely in his ability to observe life from a plane situated between the intelligence and the intuition, that is to say, closer to the true reality of life, is sometimes able to communicate to us something of the vision he has perceived and thus, in part, to diminish our ignorance of the human soul. Although, as Bergson has pointed out, pure perception or consciousness in absolute coincidence with life itself is impossible, there are, nevertheless, many possible states of conscious activity corresponding to all the imaginable degrees which lie between intelligence and intuition. There is, for example, that *esprit de finesse* whose operations we have just observed in Marcel's reflections upon a problem, insoluble by the processes of ordinary logic. I mean the problem presented by the apparent contradiction between the sadistic viciousness of Vinteuil's daughter and her undoubted cult of her father's memory. It is because Marcel has momentarily shifted from this plane of observation that the conduct of Charlus in the Verdurin *salon* now astonishes him, like the events which succeed this dramatic occurrence. For Charlus does not proceed to visit the lightning of his wrath upon the Verdurins. Not long afterwards, he contracts pneumonia and for months hovers between life and death, surprising all his friends by the saintly, almost mystic quality of his Christian sentiments. The effect, however, of this moral revolution gradually disappears with his return to health. Charlus then enters on the last, most rapid and decisive stage of his spiritual disintegration. Equally unpredictable by the logical processes of the intelligence is an action performed by the hateful Verdurins that very evening just after Charlus has left, though Marcel learns of it only many years afterwards from Cottard. But since this incident is indirectly concerned with the death of the princess Sherbatoff, we must go back to a moment preceding the concert when Brichot and Saniette enter the *salon* and break the news to Verdurin that his wife's old friend has just died.

A ce moment-là M. Verdurin vint à notre rencontre. M. Verdurin à qui nous fîmes nos condoléances pour la princesse Sherbatoff nous dit: 'Oui, je sais qu'elle est très mal.' 'Mais non, elle est morte à six heures,' s'écria Saniette. 'Vous exagérez toujours,' dit brutalement

M. Verdurin, qui, la soirée n'étant pas décommandée, préférait l'hypothèse de la maladie, imitant ainsi sans le savoir le duc de Guermantes.[1]

This insensibility shocks Marcel but not nearly so much as Mme Verdurin's callousness for, after all, she and the princess had been inseparable companions. Not only does the Patronne cynically admit that the death of her friend leaves her completely unmoved but appears, as Marcel observes, to derive therefrom 'une certaine satisfaction orgueilleuse de psychologue paradoxal et de dramaturge hardi'. Even more revolting is the epitaph she light-heartedly coins in the following conversation.

'Oui, c'est très drôle,' dit-elle, 'ça ne m'a presque rien fait. Mon Dieu, je ne peux pas dire que je n'aurais pas mieux aimé qu'elle vécût, ce n'était pas une mauvaise personne.' 'Si,' interrompit M. Verdurin. 'Ah! lui ne l'aime pas parce qu'il trouvait que cela me faisait tort de la recevoir, mais il est aveuglé par ça.' 'Rends-moi cette justice,' dit M. Verdurin, 'que je n'ai jamais approuvé cette fréquentation. Je t'ai toujours dit qu'elle avait mauvaise réputation.' 'Mais je ne l'ai jamais entendu dire,' protesta Saniette. 'Mais comment,' s'écria Mme Verdurin, 'c'était universellement connu, pas mauvaise, mais honteuse, déshonorante.'[2]

Yet this is the couple who, shortly after the success of their plot against the baron, secretly conspire to come to the financial rescue of Saniette, the long-suffering butt of M. Verdurin who is invariably driven into a frenzy of exasperation by Saniette's most innocent remarks. The latter has been speculating wildly and is now ruined. So the Verdurins arrange with Cottard to pay Saniette an annuity which is supposed to be a legacy from the princess Sherbatoff. Only at Saniette's funeral does Marcel discover this 'illogical' and unsuspected aspect of the Verdurins' character. And the discovery leads him to the following conclusion which is thoroughly Bergsonian.

...je conclus à la difficulté de présenter une image fixe aussi bien d'un caractère que des sociétés et des passions. Car il ne change pas moins qu'elles et si on veut clicher ce qu'il y a de relativement immuable, on le voit présenter successivement des aspects différents (impliquant qu'il ne sait pas garder l'immobilité mais bouge) à l'objectif déconcerté.[3]

[1] *P.* II, 35.   [2] *P.* II, 51.   [3] *P.* II, 167–8.

336 THE MIND OF PROUST

This phrase concludes the second chapter of *La Prisonnière*. But it is immediately preceded by a passage which I cannot resist quoting since it might have been transferred bodily from *La Vie de Marianne* by Marivaux, that remarkable exponent of *l'esprit de finesse*. 'C'était un homme', says Marcel of Verdurin, 'capable de désintéressement, de générosités sans ostentation, cela ne veut pas dire forcément un homme sensible, ni un homme sympathique, ni scrupuleux, ni véridique ni toujours bon.'[1] Proust, who used to delight in such literary reminiscences or resemblances, for instance when he discovered a phrase by Montesquieu cropping up in Flaubert, would have been the first, I feel sure, to smile at his own unconscious *pastiches* of Marivaux which occur quite frequently in *A la recherche du temps perdu*.

Marcel, having said good night to Brichot, stands for a while outside his flat, looking up at Albertine's lighted window. 'Il me sembla voir,' he muses, 'le lumineux grillage qui allait se refermer sur moi et dont j'avais forgé moi-même pour une servitude éternelle les inflexibles barreaux d'or.'[2] Enclosed in this brilliant image is the theme elaborated by Proust in the third chapter of *La Prisonnière* where Marcel narrates the last, most tragic phase of his hopeless attempt to know the real Albertine, to possess the secrets of her inmost life. But he is not now the artist who entered into sympathetic and immediate contact with the individuality of Vinteuil through the medium of the septet. Face to face with Albertine, striving to decipher the true meaning underlying her words, to divine her possible desires and future actions, he no longer possesses the humility, the spirituality and the disinterestedness of the artist. Marcel's perceptions, interfused with his memories and with the torturing images created by his jealous, possessive love, merely accentuate the opacity of the film interposed between his consciousness and the true nature of Albertine. Situated on a plane where the mind is oriented towards immediate action, his intelligence, instead of penetrating the object of its contemplation, strives to view it from as many angles as possible. How slight is the knowledge to be obtained by this approach Marcel knows only too well. Hence the reluctant admission wrung from him at the

[1] *P.* II, 166.   [2] *P.* II, 174–5.

conclusion of this long interview with Albertine. 'L'observation compte peu.' But this is the defeatist pronouncement of an irritated and tormented lover and not of the man who is to find his true vocation in art. Life, of course, does not reveal her secrets in response to the probings of the analytic intelligence alone: the intelligence must invoke the aid of the intuition which Bergson, who sees an excellent example of such an alliance in the æsthetic faculty of the artist, defines as 'l'instinct devenu désintéressé, conscient de lui-même, capable de refléchir sur son objet et de l'élargir indéfiniment'.[1] How clearly Proust now interprets Marcel's tragic conflict! Away from Albertine, not as at present listening to the stream of words beneath which he can so easily read the lies and evasions they pitifully try to camouflage, he is tortured by grief, rage and distrust. These emotions are inspired and magnified by the appalling picture constructed by his imagination on the evidence furnished by her silences, by the intonations of her voice, the changing expressions of her eyes and countenance. How, in such circumstances, can Marcel achieve that detachment of the artist, that power and depth of reflection, of sympathetic insight which enable the great artist to lower, as Bergson puts it: 'la barrière que l'espace interpose entre lui et le modèle'?[2] The prisoner of his own jealousy, Marcel strengthens and raises that barrier. As Proust implies, one of the inevitable and terrible results of jealousy is to impute to its object the jealous lover's own insatiable desires so that the latter's imagination becomes a kaleidoscope of horrible, unreal pictures. These are all the more torturing in Marcel's case, all the more obscure because of the unnatural quality which he imagines his own desires to have assumed in his mistress. Albertine, on her side, now intensely aware of her lover's jealousy and crafty surveillance, convinced as she says to Andrée that Marcel knows more about her life than she knows herself, tries, not from malice but rather out of compassion, to appease his devouring curiosity by lies, false confessions, by a docile obedience to his whims, and, most damning of all admissions, by the care she takes to avoid situations which might excite his suspicions. Albertine, as Marcel sadly notes, never

[1] *L'Evolution créatrice.*   [2] *Ibid.*

telephones except when he is within earshot and on returning
from an outing with Andrée invariably retires in order to allow
her friend to make her report privately. And whenever the
conversation veers round to girls of their mutual acquaintance,
Albertine, though never so adroitly as to deceive Marcel, contrives to change the subject. On the other hand, Marcel's
conscience is not altogether easy, particularly at the present
moment when he tells Albertine with affected casualness that
he has just come back from the Verdurins. The effect of this
remark surprises him. 'J'avais à peine eu le temps de prononcer
ces mots qu'Albertine, la figure bouleversée, m'avait répondu
par ceux-ci qui semblèrent exploser d'eux-mêmes avec une force
qu'elle ne put contenir. "Je m'en doutais."' Marcel replying
instinctively, not to her words but to the feeling betrayed in
their intonation, retorts: '"Je ne savais pas que cela vous en-
nuierait que j'aille chez les Verdurin.".…"M'ennuyer? qu'est-
ce que voulez que ça me fiche? Voilà qui m'est équilatéral. Est-ce
qu'ils ne devaient pas avoir Mademoiselle Vinteuil?"'[1]

If our psychological life were really the aggregate of logically
associated and distinct states of feeling imagined by the deter-
minists, how simple it would be for the novelist to interpret
the significance, the reality underlying the duel now engaged
between Marcel and Albertine. Proust, who has no illusions on
this score, knows that our emotional life is a living flux of
interpenetrating, changing sentiments and sensations, the nature
and direction of which it is almost impossible to refract in the
prism of language. This knowledge is reflected, as I have indicated, in the narrative of Marcel's despairing efforts to discover
the true links which exist between Albertine's disconnected
expressions. It is expressed also in his bewilderment when his
subtly phrased remark elicits, instead of the simple fact he
expected, a frightening array of sudden revelations which open
up a vista of new and hideous conjectures. Thus, when Marcel,
stung by Albertine's allusion to Mlle Vinteuil, involuntarily
pronounces the name of Léa, Albertine infers that someone must
have given away her relations with this notorious Lesbian,
blurts out that she knows the actress very well and, in fact,

[1] P. II, 177.

once visited her in her dressing-room at the theatre. Marcel whose jealousy in regard to Mlle Vinteuil had been appeased by the reflection that Albertine, after all, did not go to the Verdurin concert, is once again focused on the probable relations between his mistress and Léa. In his anger, he vaguely accuses Albertine of concealing other things and, purely at random, at a loss for an example, alludes to a three-day motor trip she had made to Balbec. To his stupefaction, Albertine confesses that she never went there but invented the journey out of kindness to the chauffeur who wanted three days off on urgent private business. So the post-cards Marcel received were posted in Normandy by one of the apostolic chauffeur's accomplices whilst Albertine was living with a friend at Auteuil, thoroughly bored and never out of doors, she says, except once, for fun, disguised as a man.

Horrified by these disclosures, by the annihilation of what he had believed to be realities, Marcel feels obliged, however, to hide the desolation of his soul. Smilingly he pursues his interrogation, the subject of which is now Mlle Vinteuil. Here, at least, is solid ground. What he saw through the window at Montjouvain is an indestructible fact. How can it be reconciled with Albertine's statement, on the eve of their departure from Balbec to Paris, that her relations with Mlle Vinteuil and her friend had been completely pure? Just as he is about to divulge his secret knowledge and thus triumphantly force Albertine into a confession of guilt, she suddenly admits that she had never been introduced to Mlle Vinteuil or her friend, that the story she invented at Balbec was inspired solely by the desire to make herself more interesting in her lover's eyes.

'Je sentais que je vous ennuyais, que vous me trouviez bécasse, j'ai pensé qu'en vous disant que ces gens-là m'avaient fréquentée, que je pourrais très bien vous donner des détails sur les œuvres de Vinteuil, que je prendrais un petit peu de prestige à vos yeux, que cela nous rapprocherait. Quand je vous mens, c'est toujours par amitié pour vous. Et il a fallu cette fatale soirée Verdurin pour que vous appreniez la verité, qu'on a peut-être exagérée du reste. Je parie que l'amie de Mlle Vinteuil vous aura dit qu'elle ne me connaissait pas. Mais naturellement, je ne suis pas assez chic pour des gens qui sont devenus si célèbres. Ils préfèrent dire qu'ils ne m'ont jamais vue.'[1]

---

[1] *P.* ii, 185–6.

The most horrible revelation comes, however, not from Albertine's conscious utterances but from one of those unguarded phrases which, in moments of distraction, express our unconscious thoughts. Marcel, touched by her admission that she lied from love of him and because she felt an outsider in the Verdurin *salon*, assures her tenderly that he would gladly have given her a few thousand francs to entertain the Verdurins in return for their hospitality. Then Albertine, in a retort most unflattering to the Verdurins, says that she would much rather he let her free once in order to—and here she utters only three words of a slang phrase which Marcel immediately racks his brains to complete. In spite of his gentle persistence Albertine hides her face in shame and refuses to finish her sentence. He therefore changes the conversation and Albertine, reverting to the Verdurin concert, accuses Marcel of having deliberately slighted her by going off alone, surreptitiously. During this time, Marcel's mind has been busily groping for the missing words. Suddenly the total, loathsome phrase rears itself up from his unconscious. To his unspeakable horror it is a slang expression so vile that not even the lowest prostitute would use it, assuming she consented to the infamous act which it translates. Incapable of hiding his despair, Marcel, as on a similar occasion at Balbec, invents on the spur of the moment a fictitious situation to account for his agitation. In this, he is merely continuing the policy of dissimulation which he has pursued throughout the whole painful interview where, we are reminded, none of his words reflects his true feelings. The effect of Albertine's involuntary disclosure is to make it more impossible than ever to break with her. They are linked, as he says, by 'l'étreinte d'une douleur', by Marcel's imperative need to know everything. Therefore, in asking Albertine, as he now does, to leave him that very night, he stakes his happiness on the outcome of a bluff. Seizing upon Albertine's complaint that she felt affronted when Françoise told her that her master had just gone out, Marcel, with a convincing display of contrition agrees that he was guilty of deceit. This, he pursues, is a trifle in itself but signifies the enormous change in his sentiments that has been steadily increasing for six months. The time has now come to part, for Albertine's sake, because quite obviously she is tired of the life she has been leading. So, for both, the best thing is an immediate separation. Gently ignoring Albertine's protest that she is perfectly happy and there is no alteration in her affections, Marcel pretends to regard the separation as a *fait accompli*. Occupied apparently now only with last-minute details of a material sort concerning Albertine's departure, he yet contrives to elicit a further admission, for instance, that she once spent a three weeks' holiday with Léa. Yet a short time ago, Albertine had sworn that she did not know the actress with the terrible reputation. Her lover's consternation is expressed in these words. 'Je regardais une flambée brûler d'un seul coup un roman que j'avais mis des millions de minutes à écrire. A quoi bon! A quoi bon!' His questions press her more closely:

'Mais Léa a été tout le temps de ce voyage parfaitement convenable avec moi', me dit Albertine. 'Elle était même plus réservée que bien des femmes du monde.' 'Est-ce qu'il y a des femmes du monde qui ont manqué de réserve avec vous, Albertine?' 'Jamais.' 'Alors qu'est-ce que vous voulez dire?' 'Eh bien! elle était moins libre dans ses expressions.' 'Exemple.' 'Elle n'aurait pas, comme bien des femmes du monde qu'on reçoit, employé le mot: embêtant ou le mot: se ficher du monde.' Il me semblait qu'une partie du roman qui n'avait pas brûlé encore, tombait enfin en cendres.[1]

There is a passage from Bergson's *Le rire* which holds a challenge for every artist. 'Quand nous éprouvons de l'amour ou de la haine, quand nous nous sentons joyeux ou tristes, est-ce bien notre sentiment qui arrive à notre conscience avec les mille nuances fugitives qui en font quelque chose d'absolument individuel? Nous serions alors tous romanciers, tous poètes, tous musiciens.' I expect this challenge was often in the forefront of Proust's mind, especially when he composed those pages of Marcel's narrative where the latter, as at present, in a crucial stage of his jealous passion, tries to communicate an accurate picture of his inmost feelings. Why does he play out the bitter comedy of a separation when his sole desire is to hold Albertine? One result of his bluff, of what he calls the great battle where he must conquer or succumb, is the positive assurance that his

[1] P. II, 204–5.

mistress does not want her freedom. He has, therefore, gained his objective. Why then does Marcel postpone the inevitable reconciliation? Proust, with his amazing talent for discovering the varied and fleeting nuances of emotion which compose an individual state of soul, contrives to reflect in Marcel's narrative this very complexity. The latter, comparing himself to a general who has just put on a feint attack to deceive the enemy, tells us significantly, however, that in doing so he engaged almost the full strength of his sensibilities. In consequence, as the play evolves, he is invaded gradually by feelings of sadness and of desolation just as intense as those which would have been evoked by a genuine separation. Marcel's little comedy is fraught with dangers, the least of which is the chance that it may end in a real parting. Consciously, Marcel is being insincere when he talks of separation. Yet it is his unconscious which really dictates his words, gestures and intonations.

Ces conversations que l'on tient ainsi, on croit le faire non seulement sans sincérité, ce qui est en effet, mais librement. Or, elles sont généralement à notre insu, chuchotées malgré nous, le premier murmure d'une tempête que nous ne soupçonnons pas. En réalité, ce que nous exprimons alors c'est le contraire de notre désir (lequel est de vivre toujours avec celle que nous aimons) c'est aussi cette impossibilité de vivre ensemble qui fait notre souffrance quotidienne, souffrance préférée par nous à celle de la séparation, et qui finira malgré nous par nous séparer.[1]

Other factors come into play when Marcel's instinctive urge to conceal the true cause of his agitation suggests the fiction of a love now practically dead and merely awaiting decent burial. Life has taught him the fallacy of his original naïve conceptions of love and of friendship. 'Tout ce que j'avais, enfant, rêvé de plus doux dans l'amour et qui me semblait de son essence même, c'était, devant celle que j'aimais, d'épancher librement ma tendresse, ma reconnaissance pour sa bonté, mon désir d'une perpétuelle vie commune.' Bitter experience has shown him the folly of surrendering to such natural impulses. He remembers, for instance, his adolescent passion for Gilberte, whose cruel reactions to Marcel's adoration proved how fatal it is to reveal the intensity of one's sentiments. From this and the other

[1] P. II, 213.

rebuffs encountered in his sentimental life, Marcel has derived a desolating philosophy in which, by the way, one can detect the peculiar twist given by Proust to Bergson's views on the impotence of ordinary language to reproduce the individuality of the sentiment it claims to express. Marcel, reflecting upon his conversation with Albertine, observes:

Et sans doute il en est toujours ainsi quand deux êtres sont face à face, puisque chacun d'eux ignore une partie de ce qui est dans l'autre (même ce qu'il sait, il ne peut en partie le comprendre) et que tous deux manifestent ce qui leur est le moins personnel, soit qu'ils n'aient pas démêlé eux-mêmes et jugent négligeable ce qui l'est le plus, soit que des avantages insignifiants et qui ne tiennent pas à eux leur semblent plus importants et plus flatteurs. Mais dans l'amour ce malentendu est porté au degré suprême parce que, sauf peut-être quand on est enfant, on tâche que l'apparence qu'on prend, plutôt que de refléter exactement notre pensée, soit ce que cette pensée juge le plus propre à nous faire obtenir ce que nous désirons, et qui pour moi, depuis que j'étais rentré, était de pouvoir garder Albertine aussi docile que par le passé, qu'elle ne me demandât pas dans son irritation une liberté plus grande, que je souhaitais lui donner un jour, mais qui en ce moment où j'avais peur de ses velléités d'indépendance, m'eût rendu trop jaloux. A partir d'un certain âge, par amour-propre et par sagacité, ce sont les choses qu'on désire le plus auxquelles on a l'air de ne pas tenir. Mais en amour, la simple sagacité — qui d'ailleurs n'est probablement pas la vraie sagesse — nous force assez vite à ce génie de duplicité.[1]

[And no doubt it is always so when two creatures are face to face, since each of them is ignorant of a part of what is in the other (even what he does know, he can only partly understand) and when both reveal what is least personal to them, either because they have not deciphered themselves and regard as negligible what is most individual or because certain insignificant advantages which do not belong to them particularly appear more important and more flattering to themselves. But in love this misunderstanding is carried to its supreme limit because, save perhaps in childhood, we strive to make the appearance we assume, rather than let it exactly reflect our thought, be what that thought considers best calculated to gain for us our desire, and this, in my case, since I had come in, was to be able to keep Albertine as docile as in the past, to take care she did not, in her irritation, ask me for a greater freedom, which I wanted to grant her some day, but which, at this moment when I was afraid of her

[1] *P.* II, 195–6.

THE MIND OF PROUST

hankerings after independence, would have made me too jealous. After a certain age, from *amour-propre* and sagacity, it is the things we most desire that we pretend not to care about. But in love, mere sagacity — which in any case is probably not true wisdom — drives us rather quickly to this genius for duplicity.]

Our character, as Bergson somewhere remarks, is a synthesis of our memories, a truth admirably illustrated by Proust in his account of Marcel's behaviour towards Albertine. The memories of other loves conspired, without doubt, to suggest the comedy of a separation. Possibly too, as Marcel remarks, he may have been influenced by unconscious reminiscences of Charlus, that adept in 'scènes menteuses'. Perhaps, also, in his ruthless interrogation of Albertine, Marcel is unwittingly imitating his father, who sometimes takes a similar cruel pleasure in disturbing people's sense of security. There is also something of Aunt Léonie in Marcel's character as he discovers later from an anecdote related by his mother. When Léonie found out that Françoise had secretly arranged a little outing, certain that her mistress would be asleep, that formidable old lady used to announce calmly that she proposed going for a drive. Slyly watching Françoise, she would arrange all the details of her day until her servant, convinced that the old invalid really intended to go out, was forced to confess that she herself had made other plans. The same malicious policy is now adopted by Marcel in order to bluff Albertine. Only when she begins to express her sorrow at leaving him and her familiar surroundings does Marcel, with a fine air of reluctance, propose what he calls a renewal of their lease, but on a weekly basis. The hour is late, and Albertine, completely exhausted, retires to her room. 'Je suis comme une morte,' she tells her lover. And indeed, a few minutes afterwards, watching his sleeping mistress, it seems to him as if she were, in fact, dead.

Elle s'était endormie, aussitôt couchée, ses draps roulés comme un suaire autour de son corps avaient pris, avec leurs beaux plis, une rigidité de pierre. On eût dit, comme dans certains Jugements Derniers du Moyen-Age, que la tête seule surgissait hors de la tombe, attendant dans son sommeil la trompette de l'archange. Cette tête avait été surprise par le sommeil presque renversée, les cheveux hirsutes.[1]

[1] *P.* II, 214.

Next morning, whilst Albertine is still asleep, Marcel tries to fathom her state of mind at this juncture. Is she really happy, as she protests, under his roof? Can he place any credence on her words? What about the suppressed flashes of impatience, of anger which he intuitively perceives beneath the camouflage of her language? What of that involuntary exlamation: 'J'en étais sûre!'[1] when he informed her of his visit to the Verdurins? His instinct tells him that without doubt, Albertine is possessed by frequent and sudden desires for freedom, for independence. Yet, instead of following the direction of his intuition, he tries to go counter to it, to follow, that is to say, the smoother, inverse stream of his reason. This of course makes everything quite simple. Albertine considers herself engaged to him. But since Marcel talks of a separation, he has obviously no intention of getting married. Logically, therefore, Albertine must often say to herself that all her original conjectures were right: there will be no marriage. Why not, therefore, end a situation which can lead nowhere? Marcel is confirmed in his optimistic hypothesis by a letter from his mother who expresses her shocked surprise not only at the length of Albertine's visit but at her son's continuing to monopolize the society of a girl whom he does not apparently intend to marry, thus preventing her from accepting another proposal. How very reasonable! There is no need to look for mysteries: there is nothing peculiar in Albertine's fits of suppressed irritation. But Proust, with a Bergsonian distrust of the plausible explanations furnished by the intelligence, does not leave Marcel long with his illusion. What his reasonable hypothesis fails to reflect is the essential reality of his liaison with Albertine: and this reality is not really covered by the cliché of the hesitating fiancé and the broken engagement. Marcel who is living his life with Albertine 'par le dedans' and not superficially, knows intuitively by his torturing anxieties, by what he reads in Albertine's eyes that she harbours secret, impenetrable desires. But, argues Marcel's reason, he may be completely mistaken in all his suspicions. These intuitions may be unreliable, distorted by jealousy.

[1] She said: 'Je m'en doutais!' But Marcel, naturally, reproduces the reality of her emotions rather than her actual words.

Perhaps. Yet why, at the sudden opening of a door, that sudden flash of warning from his unconscious, leaving him trembling with a nameless fear? And Marcel remembers how his grandmother, in her final agony, although in a coma, used to start every time her grandson rang for Françoise.

Jealousy, as interpreted by Proust in the last chapter of *La Prisonnière*, is an inner dialogue between the intuition—or as he nearly always calls it, the instinct—and the reason. It is a tragic dialogue, which may sometimes terminate in acts of violence. More often however, it slowly languishes into the silence of indifference, leaving a trail of frustrated hopes, of wasted happiness, a scorched zone of the spirit which may never recover its pristine vitality and beauty. Such, I think, is for Proust the real tragedy of jealous love, of the love that seeks only to possess and, therefore, is foredoomed to disappointment since great love is the spiritual fusion of two individuals and not the spiritual domination envisaged by Marcel. Great love, like religion, aspires to an absolute and superhuman union. That has never been Marcel's aspiration. Desire, even when it extends beyond physical concupiscence, will not lead to such a union if, as in his case, it assumes the form of insatiable intellectual curiosity. Marcel's love brings him intense suffering. Only, unlike the romantic, passionate lover, he is not prepared to cherish his sufferings nor even to derive from them a sense of exaltation and of completion. His passion for Albertine is really an expression of his consuming desire to know reality, to obtain a direct vision of himself, of the external world of individuals and things. The unity he seeks is inaccessible because it implies the total coincidence of two ever-changing selves, one of which is called Marcel and the other Albertine. It implies the knowledge of her inner life at every point of its evolution, knowledge of all the contacts she has ever made with other people, knowledge of all her secret desires and sensations. On the other hand, the very existence of what he calls love depends on the absence of such a total coincidence, on the impossibility of such a spiritual osmosis. Therefore, for Marcel, love is always equated with suffering and frustration. Observe however that Albertine, with every temporary appeasement of her lover's jealous curiosity, loses her beauty, mystery and attraction. This is what happens now when Marcel, reassured by her eager acceptance of his 'renewal of the lease' begins to chafe at his own slavery. Changing its object, his curiosity is once again focused upon art. Whilst Albertine, at the pianola, plays Vinteuil's septet, Marcel feels convinced that music could not give this impression of profundity and of truth unless it symbolized a 'certain spiritual reality'. And the genius of a Vinteuil, of every great artist, is to be found, he thinks, not so much in the content of the work of art itself, as in the individual, original quality of the artist's vision of the world, 'cette qualité inconnue d'un monde unique'. This unique mode of perception it is, surely, that constitutes the special beauty lent to the world by the musician, the sculptor, the painter or novelist. It is refracted in all their works in what Marcel calls *phrases-types*, a Proustian variant, by the way, of Bergson's remark that 'les grands philosophes n'ont jamais dit qu'une chose'. And Marcel borrows examples from Barbey d'Aurevilly, Hardy, Stendhal and Dostoevski to illustrate his theory. Yet, on reflection, he is assailed by certain misgivings. No doubt these *phrases-types* seem to express states of soul containing an indefinable quality of happiness, resembling states of his own consciousness. But is this ineffable quality of joy a sign of their profound reality? Or is it simply because they are unanalysable by the intelligence? 'La beauté d'une phrase de musique pure', whispers the spirit of doubt, 'paraît facilement l'image ou du moins la parente d'une impression purement intellectuelle que nous avons eue, mais simplement parce qu'elle est inintellectuelle. Et pourquoi alors croyons-nous particulièrement profondes ces phrases mystérieuses qui hantent certains ouvrages et ce septuor de Vinteuil?'[1]

Bergson, I fancy, shows us how needless are Marcel's misgivings. In his essay, *La perception du changement*,[2] he tells us that the object of art is to show us in nature and in the mind, outside us and inside us, things which do not explicitly strike our senses and our consciousness. The artist, when he expresses

[1] *P.* II, 243–4.
[2] 1911. In the volume: *La pensée et le mouvant*.

a state of soul, discloses nuances of emotion and of thought, which, without him, would never have been revealed to us and might have remained for ever, as Bergson puts it, in the form of an undeveloped negative. The great artist obtains and communicates a unique vision of things. Moreover, it is only half true to say that, after the revelation of a great artist, we see nature henceforth only through the image he has traced. His image does not only give us pleasure: it has the stamp of truth. That is because the vision we usually have is a limited one, cut out of reality by our intelligence in order to conform to the needs of our practical existence. It is just because the artist thinks less of *utilizing* his perceptions, Bergson insists, that he perceives a larger number of things. And, elsewhere in the same volume, he warns us that whereas the concept of intellectual origin is immediately clear, the idea that issues from an intuition is at first obscure, whatever our force of thought. 'C'est qu'il y a deux espèces de clarté.'

As the days lengthen and the pigeons resume their early morning cooings, it seems to Marcel that Albertine's thoughts are turned towards the pleasures of the open air and fine weather. Convalescent, he himself is invaded by a restless desire to escape from his captivity in Paris. In the new leafy world now awakening, there are so many delightful things he would like to do, so many places he would love to see. But always, with a sense of irritation, he finds Albertine interposed between these desires and their realization. What Proust implies is that now early memories of Albertine are revived, counselling increased vigilance, memories of the unstable, pleasure-loving Albertine of Balbec which are coloured and modified by jealousy. Reviewing all these past sensations and impressions with their synthetic picture of loveliness, Marcel strives incessantly, in his conversations with Albertine, to get her to complete the intolerable gaps in this fresco of vanished time. But what avails it now that she is in his room, that he holds her in his arms? It is, he says, like handling a stone that contains the salt of immemorial oceans or the ray from an infinitely remote star. Therefore day after day, until Albertine

begins to assume the enigmatic appearance of some fabled
Goddess of Time, her lover muses upon the past, sometimes
with pleasure, often with painful anxiety. The memory of some
of those hours they spent together torments him because of
a revelation which now presents them in a new and disturbing
aspect. It has just transpired in a talk with Mme Bontemps
that her niece, just before she suddenly changed her mind and
accompanied Marcel to Paris on the fifteenth of September, had
received a telegram informing her that Andrée was not coming
to Balbec but staying in Paris. His jealous imagination, playing
upon this fact, creates a vivid and terrible picture. The charming,
innocent friendship of the two girls is transformed into something evil which, nevertheless, fascinates Marcel by its horrible
beauty. Reason kindly intervenes, reminding him of Albertine's
habit of using one and the same action so as to give pleasure to
a number of people, each of whom imagines himself or herself
to be its exclusive object. With the malicious cunning of
jealousy, Marcel guards his information for the moment, partly
because if divulged now it may give Albertine a clue to the
identity of his informant, partly because, in a fit of rage, she
might leave him. His own ill-temper, however, precipitates
events. Marcel, on learning from Françoise that his mistress is
never pleased with anything and receives his messages with
scarcely disguised petulance, taxes her with ingratitude. But
like Des Grieux with Manon Lescaut, he relents immediately,
remembering how his anger frightens Albertine. To justify this
outburst, he pretends to have received anonymous letters concerning her relations with Andrée, in this way revealing what
he heard about Andrée's change of plans. Naturally, Albertine
flies into a rage which includes her friend who, she says, has
always exasperated her. She admits the telegram, claiming,
however, that it arrived after the fifteenth of September and had
nothing to do with her own change of mind, with her sudden
resolve to accompany Marcel to Paris. To Marcel, who eagerly
begs forgiveness, she replies gently that there is nothing to
forgive. But her lover, anxiously watching her features, seems
to detect beneath her sadness the crystallization of a secret
resolve. That night, she turns away from his kisses and Marcel

is seized with an indefinable presentiment, inspired by her gesture. 'Mais une seconde fois, elle s'écarta et au lieu de me rendre mon baiser, s'écarta avec l'espèce d'entêtement instinctif et fatidique des animaux qui sentent la mort.' In the days that follow, he tries vainly to resume their former intimacy. But Albertine, though sweet and kind, is now just a comrade. Somehow, in her heavily brocaded Fortuny dress with its design of symbolic oriental birds that signify either death or life, she is invested with a strange beauty, dignity and aloofness.

Caught once more in the rhythmic alternation of reason and instinct, Marcel suffers agonies of apprehension. In the night, he is awakened by the sound of Albertine's window being violently thrown open and is seized with an agitation such as he had never experienced since that evening long ago in Combray when, as a little boy, he waited in vain for his mother's good-night embrace. Why this unreasonable panic over an opened window? It is because Albertine knows that, because of Marcel's asthmatic attacks, no windows are ever opened at night. Obviously, now, having already resolved to leave, she no longer cares. With unspeakable relief, Marcel learns next day that she is still in her room. But as she persists in her aloofness, Marcel's restlessness and irritation increase. Albertine's Fortuny dress reminds him of Venice, of his long cherished desire to see this dream city.

Venise, un printemps décanté, qui est réduit à son essence, et traduit l'allongement, l'échauffement, l'épanouissement graduel de ses jours par la fermentation progressive, non plus d'une terre impure, mais d'une eau vierge et bleue, printanière sans porter de corolles, et qui ne pourrait répondre au mois de mai que par des reflets, travaillée par lui, s'accordant exactement à lui dans la nudité rayonnante et fixe de son sombre saphir. Aussi bien pas plus que les saisons à ses bras de mer infleurissables, les modernes années n'apportent de changement à la cité gothique; je le savais, je ne pouvais l'imaginer, mais, voilà ce que je voulais contempler de ce même désir qui jadis, quand j'étais enfant, dans l'ardeur même du départ, avait brisé en moi la force de partir; je voulais me trouver face à face avec mes imaginations vénitiennes, voir comment cette mer divisée enserrait de ses méandres, comme les replis du fleuve Océan, une civilisation urbaine et raffinée, mais qui, isolée par leur ceinture azurée, s'était développée à part, avait eu à part ses écoles de peinture et d'architecture, admirer ce jardin fabuleux de fruits et d'oiseaux de pierre de couleur, fleuri au milieu de la mer qui venait le refraîchir, frappait de son flux le fût des colonnes et, sur le puissant relief des chapiteaux, comme un regard de sombre azur qui veille dans l'ombre, posait par taches et faisait remuer perpétuellement la lumière.[1]

['Venice', a decanted springtime which is reduced to its essence, and reflects the lengthening, the warming, the gradual unfolding of its days in the progressive fermentation, no longer, now, of an impure soil, but of a virginal and blue water, springlike though it bears no flowers and which could have no affinity with the month of May were it not for the gleaming facets lovingly sculptured by May, exactly in her own image, in the radiant and immobile nudity of its dark sapphire. Likewise, too, no more than the seasons to its flowerless arms stretching into the sea, do modern times bring any change to the Gothic city; I knew it, I could not imagine it, but that is what I wanted to gaze upon with the same desire which long ago, when I was a boy, in the very ardour of departure, had broken and robbed me of the strength to make the journey; I longed to find myself face to face with my Venetian imaginings, to observe how that divided sea held in the clutches of its meanderings, like the sinuosities of the ocean stream, an urban and sophisticated civilization, yet which, isolated by their azure girdle, had evolved independently, had possessed its own schools of painting and architecture; to admire that fabulous garden of fruits and birds in coloured stone, blossoming in the midst of the sea which gave it freshness, lapping with its tide the base of the columns and, upon the bold relief of the capitals, like a sombre azure gaze lurking in the shadows, laid spots of light which it kept in a perpetual state of movement.]

Marcel now decides to break with Albertine, though not immediately. He will choose a fine sunny day in spring when he can no longer resist the desires that beckon him away from Paris to other, more romantic climes. Then, having made all his preparations for the journey, he will leave a farewell note for Albertine. Such are his thoughts one morning when he asks Françoise to get him the railway time-table with the trains for Venice. But his old servant has incredible news. Albertine has packed all her trunks and gone, leaving a note for Marcel:

Alors — tant on peut ignorer ce qu'on a en soi, puisque j'étais persuadé de mon indifférence pour Albertine — mon souffle fut coupé,

---

[1] *P.* ii, 283–4.

je tins mon cœur de mes deux mains brusquemment mouillées par une certaine sueur que je n'avais jamais connue depuis la révélation que mon amie m'avait faite dans le petit tram relativement à l'amie de Mademoiselle Vinteuil, sans que je pusse dire autre chose que: 'Ah! très bien, vous avez bien fait naturellement de ne pas m'éveiller, laissez-moi un instant, je vais vous sonner tout à l'heure.'[1]

[1] *P.* ii, 287.

Chapter VIII

ALBERTINE DISPARUE

THE flight of Albertine marks the climax of the tragic conflict so minutely interpreted in *La Prisonnière*. Marcel's desperate attempts to satisfy his jealous curiosity—his *désir moral*, as Proust calls it—have been defeated by Albertine's inflexible resistance. Obediently responsive to all her lover's other desires, she refuses, very naturally, to surrender to him the freedom of her soul, obstinately guarding the secrets of her private life. The two volumes entitled *Albertine disparue* show us the way out of this labyrinth, the complicated and fascinating process by which Marcel's love, his passionate obsession for spiritual domination peters out into indifference and is finally dissolved in oblivion. Here Proust makes a supreme intellectual effort and by mustering the combined forces of his intelligence and intuition, achieves a remarkable penetration of the mind by itself, resulting in a unique, illuminating and realistic vision of human nature. Beyond question, *Albertine disparue* represents the most brilliant experiment ever made by a French novelist in subjective psychology. It is, to some extent, an original and superbly illustrated essay in the psychology of Bergson. Drama, perhaps, would be a better epithet, for nothing could well be more dramatic than this interplay of memory, imagination, intelligence and intuition, those diligent yet rival vice-regents of a mind eager to know its own reality and in the light of that knowledge, to discover the reality hidden in other minds. Clearly, a very special idiom was necessary in order to reflect the fluid, ever-changing and interfusing psychological movements involved in such a spectacle. For this task, however, Proust is perfectly equipped and in *Albertine disparue*, he reveals the full potentialities of his narrative method, the profound originality of which is now triumphantly demonstrated. This sinuous and spiralling narrative, with its constantly shifting sites of observation, reproduces in admirable fashion the mobility and creative *élan* which, for Proust as for Bergson, constitute the very essence of life's reality. Marcel, launched on the steeply inclined plane of introspection, is revealed to us, as it were, in the act of reascending the stream of his memories, knowing them to be deceptive because they have changed; determined, nevertheless, to perform this journey in reverse in order to obtain a real vision of 'le temps perdu'.

Proust has now thrown down a challenge to himself. He must now adapt his style so as to reflect the processes of a mind turned inwards, striving to grasp its own restless complexity. That he was by no means unprepared for this self-imposed task we know from his achievements in *Du côté de chez Swann* and *La Prisonnière*. But here is an occasion demanding still greater feats of penetration and reflection. With the disappearance of Albertine, the solitude of Marcel is practically unbroken except for brief intrusions by Saint-Loup and Andrée. Proust has undertaken, in fact, something never attempted by a novelist: to interpret, in some three hundred pages, the 'monologue intérieur' of a bereaved and desolate lover whose jealous love, however, because of its essentially subjective nature, long survives the death of his mistress. Now, as everyone is well aware who is familiar with the fifteen volumes of his novel, Proust has various styles. It would be very easy, indeed, to select from this ample repertoire, scores of passages, even whole pages, which if presented anonymously in an anthology of contemporary French prose would be hard to identify as unmistakably Proustian. However, every page in *Albertine disparue* is stamped with the individual cachet of Proust. Here, perfected and adapted to fulfil the author's immediate plan, we encounter once again that remarkable creation, the Proustian period, with its profusion and exfoliation of subordinate clauses, its purposeful and relentless parentheses, its surprising inversions that arrive so often, in the nick of time, to preserve the life and integrity of an organism apparently on the verge of collapse. One observes, on the other hand, in the periods of this later Proustian phase the expression of a new quality, a greater urgency of rhythm, a suppressed anguish in the undertones. Moreover, it is always a period, a unity and never, as so often in the earlier volumes,

ALBERTINE DISPARUE   355

notably in *Du côté de chez Swann*, a paragraph masquerading as
a period in order to enframe an impressionistic and charming
word-painting. The Proustian period, in *Albertine disparue*, is
a dynamic and organic entity like the cell of a living tissue.
What is truly remarkable is that Proust, in adjusting his style so
as to reflect the inner melody of life, respects the armature or
discipline of syntactical usage whilst achieving, inside the
traditional cadre of the French language, a reorganization that
has an original air of revolution if not of anarchy. Yet there is
nothing, for example, in the structure of his prose, to suggest
comparison with the linguistic audacities committed, in poetry,
by Mallarmé or Valéry. Where the peculiar genius of Proust's
style is perhaps most strikingly displayed is in the art with which
he seizes upon and refracts in the prism of a metaphor or other
image the most delicate and fugitive vibrations of Marcel's
sensibility. Writing on the subject of Flaubert's prose, which he
did not wholly admire, Proust remarked that only the metaphor
can lend eternity to a writer's style. Many, no doubt, will not
agree with this view, but few will deny that Proust's superb use
of metaphor or simile is largely responsible for the unique
quality of his own writing. It is rare to encounter a page un-
illuminated by an image. In such a case, the reader is at once
sensible not so much of a slackening of his interest as of being
transported to a more superficial plane of consciousness.

Let us now rejoin Marcel at the point where Françoise informs
him that Albertine has packed her belongings and suddenly
disappeared. In a poignant sentence, Proust suggests the
terrific force and depth of penetration achieved by this simple,
external fact. Simultaneously, he formulates the psychological
law governing every situation of this nature. 'Comme la
souffrance va plus loin en psychologie que la psychologie!' The
evening before, Marcel, in analysing his sentiments, had at last
clearly perceived—or so he was convinced—their final and
authentic contours. Without doubt, the only possible solution
to his problem lay in a separation with Albertine, preferably
initiated by her, uncomplicated by prolonged farewells or hopes of
subsequent meetings. What he envisaged was, in every respect,
exactly the situation enclosed in the words: 'Mademoiselle

Albertine est partie.' The shape of events coincides absolutely, for once, with that of his desires. By all the rules of logic, Marcel ought to feel perfectly happy, in a state of complete self-harmony. In reality, he experiences the most atrocious suffering, whilst all the forces of his will are instantly directed to one exclusive act. He must get Albertine back immediately to the flat. His sense of desolation has the concrete reality of an intolerable physical agony. Automatically he finds himself uttering the words of consolation and pity used by his grandmother on that first evening in the hotel at Balbec when Marcel was overtaken by one of his painful asthmatic seizures. 'Aie une seconde de patience, on va te trouver un remède, sois tranquille, on ne va pas te laisser souffrir comme cela.'

'Comme la souffrance va plus loin en psychologie que la psychologie!' Spiritual pain can teach us more about the true nature of the self than any psychology based on an associationist conception of the human mind. That is surely what Proust implies. Once again, we find him in complete agreement with Bergson. Note, for example, the Bergsonian ideas expressed in Marcel's reflections:

Oui, tout à l'heure, avant l'arrivée de Françoise, j'avais cru que je n'aimais plus Albertine, j'avais cru ne rien laisser de côté; en exact analyste, j'avais cru bien connaître le fond de mon cœur. Mais notre intelligence, si grande soit-elle, ne peut apercevoir les éléments qui le composent et qui restent insoupçonnés tant que, de l'état volatil où ils subsistent la plupart du temps, un phénomène capable de les isoler ne leur a pas fait subir un commencement de solidification. Je m'étais trompé en croyant voir clair dans mon cœur. Mais cette connaissance que ne m'avaient pas donnée les plus fines perceptions de l'esprit, venait de m'être apportée, dure, éclatante, étrange, comme un sel cristallisé, par la brusque réaction de la douleur.[1]

This whole scene might have been designed to illustrate the views enunciated by Bergson in the second chapter on his *Essai sur les données immédiates de la conscience* where he points out that the error of the associationist school of psychology is in regarding the self as an aggregate of juxtaposed facts of the consciousness; of sensations, ideas and sentiments which have

[1] *AD.* i, 8–9.

only to be reconstructed in the proper order of their association in order to present a clear picture of the self. But, says Bergson, we do not obtain in this way a picture of the real, of the individual self, merely a picture of that superficial part of the self which touches the external world and retains its imprint. However, the moment the individual is really an individual, that is to say, when the states of his consciousness begin to interfuse and blend their emotional colours, this rough-and-ready psychology of the associationists proves its limitations. All it can do, in fact, is to reveal liaisons of simple, impersonal sensations. To borrow a phrase which crops up later in Marcel's narrative, it is really 'une psychologie plane'. It is wrong, continues Bergson, to think that we have only to associate several facts of consciousness so as to recompose, for instance, the personality, the soul of a man passionately in love or obsessed by hatred. The whole personality will be found refracted in any one intense feeling if only we know how to select it. The true history of the self is reflected in a sudden passion, such as violent anger, or to take Marcel's case, in an access of intolerable suffering. Bergson would have compared the effect of the shock produced by Françoise's announcement to that of a hypnotic suggestion. And, in fact, the violent anguish evoked by the news of Albertine's sudden departure does act upon Marcel like a hypnotic suggestion. His grief reflects his total personality, his fundamental self. It is quite different from the spurious self constructed by his analysing intelligence, from the Marcel whose sole desire was to break with Albertine. Proust likens this new self to a 'crystallization'; Bergson speaks of the 'masse compacte' of this fundamental, real self.

Why did Albertine go away? In her letter she says it is because life with Marcel had become impossible. His outburst of anger, though followed by a reconciliation, convinced her that they had better separate whilst still good friends rather than wait for the inevitable transformation of Marcel's love into indifference or even hatred. Decoded by reason, that obedient servant of our instinct for self-preservation, Albertine's letter seems at first to her lover a clear indication that his fiancée, exasperated by her virtual imprisonment and tired of her

equivocal position, had staged this flight merely to force Marcel
into marriage. Does not this common-sense hypothesis explain
everything? Still, Marcel is bound to admit to himself that
there is another one, suggested by his intuition at Incarville and
subsequently justified by events, by certain intermittent sensations of dreadful apprehension, on that night for example when
he heard Albertine throw open her window as if to let in the
fresh air of liberty or again, on that other evening when she
allowed him to leave without their good-night kiss. Life, in
short, has confirmed, experimentally, what Bergson would call
'les données immédiates de la conscience' and established the
superior reliability of the intuition as a reflector of reality.
Strange, therefore, that this reality which Marcel had always
known intuitively should now strike him as new and unpredictable: the grief it causes him is more intense than anything
he could possibly have imagined. As Marcel observes, the
imagination cannot picture to itself an unknown situation
because it can only work upon known elements. The same
truth is more profoundly expressed by Bergson in *L'Évolution
créatrice*. The imagination can only foresee the external con-
figuration of a situation and any attempt to fill up the internal
content of this cadre would occupy a duration which would
take us up to the moment when the event or state of soul
in question is already accomplished. How can we know what
we are going to think or experience even twenty-four hours
ahead since our then state of soul will comprise all the life we
have lived in the meantime, plus what will be added by the
particular moment we are trying to imagine? 'On ne prévoit de
l'avenir que ce qui ressemble au passé ou ce qui est recomposable
avec des éléments semblables à ceux du passé.'

How different for Marcel is the reality he now feels from
anything he had imagined! In a powerful metaphor, Proust
reaffirms his conviction that the essential reality of life can only
be known through feeling and not by concepts. Our sensibility, to
quote Marcel, even when it is purely physical sensibility, receives
the authentic, original and almost indelible imprint of a new event
as a material object receives the furrow made by the flash of
lightning. Therefore, his grief is not 'une conclusion pessimiste

librement tirée d'un ensemble de circonstances funestes'.[1] He means that it is not something which could have been logically foreseen and for which, consequently, his sensibility could have been prepared. Marcel's suffering is the 'reviviscence intermittente et involontaire d'une impression spécifique venue de dehors, et que nous n'avions pas choisie'.[2]

As always, in order to grasp what is new or original in any novelty, one must relate it with the past. The history of the French novel reveals several attempts to interpret the emotions and sensations of a man deserted by the woman he loves. The most striking example that occurs to my mind is that of Des Grieux in Prévost's *Manon Lescaut* although, no doubt, there is an immense qualitative difference between the chevalier's passion for the unstable, frivolous Manon and Marcel's jealous, possessive love for the enigmatic Albertine. Nevertheless, if we consider Des Grieux at the stage where he knows that his mistress has wilfully deserted him, the situation is fundamentally the same as that now depicted by Proust. The great eighteenth-century novelist condenses, however, in a few pages a theme, the transition from grief to forgetfulness, from 'le chagrin' to 'l'oubli' to which Proust devotes the greater part of *Albertine disparue*. In letters of fire, Prévost swiftly traces the evolution of Des Grieux's state of soul. The irrefutable fact that Manon connived at his removal from Paris literally stuns him. 'Je n'eus pas la force de soutenir plus longtemps un discours dont chaque mot m'avait percé le cœur. Je me levai de table et je n'avais pas fait quatre pas pour sortir de la salle, que je tombai sur le plancher sans sentiment et sans connaissance.' On recovering consciousness, Des Grieux instinctively seeks refuge from his intolerable suffering and, like Marcel, turns for help to reason and imagination. Manon had no logical motive for betraying him. Therefore, she must have been seduced by some charm or potion or else forced at the point of the dagger to obey his foul rival. Des Grieux would give a thousand livres for one quarter of an hour in Paris but it is impossible to escape from his father's house. In despair, he refuses food and resolves to die. '"Je puis mourir!" disais-je, "je le devrais même, après

---

[1] *AD.* I, 25.   [2] *AD.* I, 25–6.

tant de douleur et de honte; mais je souffrirais mille morts sans pouvoir oublier l'ingrate Manon.''' The father succeeds finally in convincing his son of Manon's perfidy and the chevalier is seized with an insane lust for revenge, a mad obsession to set fire to the house that shelters his rival and mistress. Six months pass during which, says Des Grieux: '''Tous mes sentiments n'étaient qu'une alternative perpétuelle de haine et d'amour, d'espérance ou de désespoir selon l'idée sous laquelle Manon s'offrait à mon esprit. Tantôt je ne considérais en elle que la plus aimable de toutes les filles et je languissais du désir de la revoir; tantôt je n'y apercevais qu'une lâche et perfide maîtresse et je faisais mille serments de ne la chercher que pour la punir.''' From books, from art, the chevalier derives a certain appease- ment of his sufferings and his former studious inclinations begin to return. Under the influence of his friend, Tiberge, he gradually moves back to the plane of his pre-Manon existence. Piety, ambition and pride combine to make him forget her and the aspect of life which Manon represents. '''Je mépriserai ce que le commun des hommes admire; et comme je sens assez que mon cœur ne désirera que ce qu'il estime, j'aurai aussi peu d'in- quiétudes que de désirs.''' Imagination paints a charming picture of the future: a little house in the country with a copse and a stream flowing through the garden; a few chosen friends, a good library, a modest but well-appointed table; a correspondence with comrades in Paris so that, by contrast, he may the better appreciate the happiness of the secluded life. But Des Grieux knows in his heart that, without Manon, his dream of happiness is only a dream. Sensibility knows more about reality than reason. Need I tell what happens next? Des Grieux returns to Paris, to the seminary of Saint-Sulpice. Now the abbé des Grieux, immersed in study, living on the plane of action, entering upon a brilliant career, he has forgotten his passion for Manon. The transition from 'le chagrin' to 'l'oubli' is now effected. But one glimpse of his mistress in the parlour of Saint-Sulpice destroys in a moment this apparently solid edifice of virtue and resolution.

No two situations, either in life or in fiction, are ever identical. History never repeats itself. Yet, if we allow for the basic difference between Prévost's conception of love, by which Des Grieux lives in Manon, and Proust's, which always presents Albertine as living in Marcel, the two situations are analogous. It is, therefore, interesting to observe, in this connection, by comparing the respective methods of these two masters, the revolution achieved by Proust in the art of the novel. Prévost, with all his genius offers us, in this particular episode, a very summary chart of feelings and sensations which in Proust's narrative are projected in their original relief, depth and inter-penetration. Prévost's schematic exposé is remarkably suggestive considering the prevailing rationalism of the intellectual climate in which he lived and the almost geometric symbolism of the French language during the Regency. Indeed, one of the great services rendered to literature by the author of *Manon Lescaut* was to react strongly against this *esprit géométrique* and this reaction is very marked in the general tone of his novel especially in the scenes where Des Grieux, after his second lapse, broods on the consequences of this final *acte libre*, this total expression of his inmost self. Proust, however, shows us deeper regions of the consciousness. He expresses, with much greater force and clarity than Prévost the essential mobility and inter-fusion, the extraordinary and illogical nature of the elements that compose our psychological life. It is often maintained and no doubt, in certain arts, with truth, that genius ignores contemporary artistic conventions and fashions its own laws. Yet I find it hard to imagine how Proust, if he had lived in the eighteenth century, would have surmounted the obstacles confronting Prévost and other novelists of this era which, at least until the influence of Rousseau began to make itself felt, was *par excellence* the classic age. For when Prévost practised his art, the classic or rational æsthetic was very stringently observed despite the increasing protests of those writers, mostly theorists, who wanted literature to reflect a larger and deeper consciousness of life and nature. Proust, on the other hand, arrived upon the scene at a time when French literature and philosophy reflected a powerful reaction against classic finalism and all its implications, the chief of which was that the real process of life is equivalent to that of the intelligence, that the movement and integrality of life can be perfectly grasped and communicated by a scientific or analysing intelligence.

Marcel's agony of grief is such that, unlike Des Grieux, he is unable to form in his mind a physical image of his vanished mistress. This is well observed. For one of the most poignant effects of a spiritual upheaval, as Marcel inferred in alluding to his mother's bereavement, is precisely the inability to visualize the traits of the absent and beloved one. In this phenomenon, Proust notes what he calls a symbol and a truth. Though by chance and by habit, Marcel's anxiety is riveted to the person of Albertine, she counts, as a person, for very little in the flux of his emotions. Whilst she was with him, Albertine's lover had always thought that his happiness depended upon her physical presence. But, in reality, it depended on the cessation of his anxiety. The unconscious, more clairvoyant than the intelligence, knows this and therefore automatically diminishes the image of Albertine, thereby placing it in proper perspective. 'Proportions minuscules de la figure de la femme, effet logique et nécessaire de la façon dont l'amour se développe, claire allégorie,' concludes Marcel, 'de la nature subjective de cet amour.'[1] Few of us have the courage to face this bitter truth, to meditate on its painful implications. Who does not, like Marcel's mother in her bereavement, experience a sense of betrayal and shame as the image of the dead becomes ever fainter in the memory? Now and later, when Albertine is killed, Marcel confronts this truth but it does not abolish the intolerable longing for her presence. At the moment, though unable to visualize her physically, he is obsessed by the idea linked to his suffering. This idea, he tells us, is composed alternately of his doubts as to the motives for Albertine's flight and of the methods which he must adopt to bring her back, to keep her under supervision and away from evil. Such, indeed, he reminds us, was the genesis of his love for Albertine: the desire to be continually in her society played only a secondary part.

Marcel's plan is to send his friend Saint-Loup secretly to Mme Bontemps, who is in Touraine, and to offer her if necessary thirty thousand francs for her husband's electoral committee if

[1] *AD.* i, 30.

she will procure her niece's return to Paris. His story will be that this sum was given to him by a relative as a present to his fiancée on the occasion of their betrothal. Saint-Loup does not sound very convinced but, like a faithful comrade, he accepts the commission. The second part of Marcel's plan is to write, meanwhile, a casual letter to his mistress, feigning indifference although, as he remembers from his experience with Gilberte, such letters are apt to be taken at their face value. Their effect is often, therefore, to kill an expiring love rather than to revive it. However, as Proust remarks, the commonest plagiarism in the world is our plagiarism of ourselves. Certainly this is true of Marcel who, it will be recalled, began the habit of writing mendacious letters as a small boy at Combray when, in a desperate bid to lure his mother away from a dinner-party, and thus to obtain her good-night kiss, he made Françoise carry a note to the dining-room, pretending it contained a message expected by her mistress. His present behaviour is determined by motives of prudence and *amour-propre*. Convinced that Saint-Loup's mission will succeed, Marcel does not want to appear as a suppliant, for that would greatly lessen his authority on Albertine's return.

Stendhal used to say that the best way to escape the clutches of despair is to do something, even if only to break an arm. Probably this was in Marcel's mind when he explains the extraordinary cheerfulness that follows on his decision to send Robert to Touraine. 'Le spécifique pour guérir un événement malheureux (les trois quarts des événements le sont) c'est une décision.' The effect, he claims, of this sudden reversal of our thoughts, is to oppose to the inflow of the thoughts which come from the past event, the counter-current of those which arrive from outside, that is to say, from the new incident. However, the true cause of his relief lies in the hopes built upon Saint-Loup's journey. But, as the hours pass, bringing no news, Marcel's anxieties return. Like Des Grieux, he experiences an oscillation in his feelings towards his mistress, between the extremes of profound aversion and of the passionate longing to get her back on any terms. Yet he knows perfectly well that if she does return, after the initial joy of reunion all the old

difficulties will close in upon their happiness. For, as Marcel
puts it: 'La recherche du bonheur dans la satisfaction du désir
moral était quelque chose d'aussi naïf que l'entreprise d'atteindre
l'horizon en marchant devant soi.' Observe that Proust is using
the adjective 'moral' in the sense of intellectual or pertaining to
the mind, for indeed, Marcel's 'désir moral' is very far from
moral. It is a *libido dominandi*, a monstrous concupiscence of
the spirit. His salvation, therefore, will come, not from the
satisfaction of this extraordinary desire, but from its gradual
obliteration by indifference and forgetfulness. At the moment,
however, this stage seems very remote for he lacks the strength
of will to leave matters as they are. How then will he achieve
forgetfulness and peace of mind?

From Marcel's reflections there emerges a thoroughly
Proustian view of the sentimental relations between man and
woman. Love, and for that matter, friendship, is a completely
subjective emotion. We are linked to others only by our own
thoughts so that memory, as it begins to fade, severs the bond.
Most of us, however, refuse to face this cruel fact and try to
disguise it for various wrong though laudable reasons. Yet, as
Proust insists: *nous existons seuls*, and it is sheer illusion to
pretend that we can ever know others except in ourselves.
Albertine, as he repeatedly observes, lives only in Marcel. She
might easily have been Gilberte or Mlle de Stermaria. But a
series of hazards ordained that Albertine should inspire his
'désir moral' and become its living symbol. By a mere chance,
Marcel's imagination extracted from the girl called Albertine
Simonet the notion that she was the individual predestined for
him and essential to his happiness. The woman a man loves is,
therefore, his creation. It is his imagination that endows her with
the unique personality whose influence welds all the fragmentary
elements of his tenderness into that compact sentiment known
as love.

When Saint-Loup arrives to receive Marcel's instructions,
Proust offers us in reverse the scene where Robert first introduced his comrade to Rachel. Saint-Loup is obviously amazed
when he sees Albertine's photograph and Marcel can read the
unspoken exclamation: 'Comment, c'est pour ça qu'il a pu se

faire tant de bile, tant de chagrin, faire tant de folies!' But that is because Robert perceives only the 'résidu' of the sensations inspired in Marcel by Albertine. Bergson calls it 'le résidu impersonnel', that mere shadow of our real self which is transmissible in our conversations, our ordinary relations with others.

The mission fails because Albertine catches sight of Robert and sends a brief note to her lover begging him ironically not to repeat these theatrical manœuvres. To see her, all Marcel had to do was to write. 'J'aurais été trop heureuse de revenir.' Reassured by her words, certain that Albertine is simply waiting for an excuse to come back, Marcel feels that he is about to live once again with the Albertine of Balbec days whose primitive and individual setting is the blue and sunlit ocean. Just because this is certain, however, there is no need for haste. Moreover, the unfortunate impression produced by Saint-Loup's clumsiness must be removed. Therefore, he sits down to compose one of those letters which, like so many of his conversations with Albertine, says the opposite of what he means, a letter couched in a tone of indifference, suggesting that it is always imprudent to go back on a decision already made, Albertine's own wise decision. True, at the moment, her departure caused him great distress but, after all, he is a creature of routine. Incidentally, says Marcel, his mother had just written consenting to their engagement on the very morning Albertine left so suddenly. Perhaps, therefore, that was just as well since this news might have made her feel obliged to remain out of a mistaken sense of gratitude. Meanwhile, as Marcel had always taken his mother's consent for granted, he ordered a Rolls Royce and a yacht, in Albertine's name, which is rather a nuisance because it involves their meeting again to discuss these and other material details. And, as Marcel points out, this might lead to his falling in love with her again. In a postscript, he touches amusedly on the Saint-Loup affair. Albertine must be completely mistaken: 'C'est du Sherlock Holmes. Quelle idée vous faites-vous de moi?' Françoise takes this letter off to the post.

In concocting this epistle, Marcel is plagiarizing himself, repeating the comedy of separation I have already described.

Every sentiment and wish expressed in his letter is the exact opposite of what he really feels and desires. Yet, oddly enough, Marcel is convinced that its result will be to bring Albertine back and, in fact, begins to regret having written because her return will mean the loss of his liberty. At this moment, Françoise comes in to ask for stamps and Marcel has an unexpected chance of revising his decision. Yet he gives the letter to his servant to post. Why?

This twentieth-century *cas de conscience* is seized upon by Proust as an excuse for a display of mental gymnastics which seems to me a little overdone, though amusingly reminiscent of the seventeenth-century manner. We are told in great detail by Marcel what he should have foreseen, namely that the effect of such a letter, whether Albertine took it literally or not, would be to invite a negative reply. Yet, at the time, such a possibility never occurred to him. He wrote the letter unhesitatingly because, as Proust explains, owing to the disastrous way in which our psycho-pathological universe is constructed, it is just this sort of clumsy and impetuous action which invariably restores our peace of mind, at least for a time, by holding out new perspectives of hope. Besides, whilst acting this pretence of a final rupture Marcel derives from it, one gathers, a rather pleasant sensation of melancholy, since of course he does not believe for one instant that Albertine will not return. Indeed, he observes the situation with all the detachment of an artist. Reviewing his love experience, he notes a rhythmic oscillation in his sentiments between the two extremes of indifference and anxiety. When assured of the possession of Albertine her presence invariably seemed a burden. On the other hand, the moment that sense of security was threatened as, for instance, after her recent departure, life without Albertine became unthinkable. Glancing idly at his newspaper, he sees that La Berma is to reappear in *Phèdre* and the famous *scène de l'aveu* of Racine's masterpiece strikes Marcel in a new light, presenting indeed a remarkable analogy with his own emotional experience. Phèdre, he argues, on realizing that Hippolyte did not love her, did everything possible to excite his enmity, because she no longer cared. But, on learning of Hippolyte's imminent departure, her passion revives and we have the immortal confession scene. Probably, thinks Marcel, if Hippolyte had evinced no indignation, if Phèdre, that is to say, had been assured of her happiness, she would have regarded its attainment with indifference. The moment it eludes her grasp, however, the queen gambles everything on one throw of the dice, resolved that the refusal shall come from Hippolyte just as Marcel, now, for the second time, hands back to Françoise the letter for Albertine. The question of Phèdre's pride, 'le soin de sa gloire', is not, says Marcel, of paramount importance. Indeed, had she not learned that Aricie was her successful rival, the queen would have rejected Oenone's advice and forgiven Hippolyte. Jealousy, which is equivalent to the total loss of happiness, is more powerful than mere loss of reputation. That is why Phèdre sends Hippolyte to his fate, although this act brings her no consolation and indeed drives her to suicide.

I confess to a certain difficulty in following Proust's argument. As Marcel once apologetically remarked when he compared Mme de Sévigné with Dostoevski: 'C'est très tiré par les cheveux.' The Racinian analogy is not only far-fetched: it is based on a distortion of the text, of the facts. For instance, at no point can one reasonably maintain that Phèdre 'devant le bonheur atteint', lapses into that state of indifference which invades Marcel whenever Albertine loses for him her mystery, that 'inconnu' which admittedly is the very essence of his love for her. And what of the 'analogy' between Phèdre's confession and Marcel's letter which could be interpreted as a confession of love only by a woman of a very subtle, italianate cast of mind, that is to say, certainly not by Albertine. The fact is that no valid parallel can be established between Racine's conception of love as 'Vénus toute entière à sa proie attachée' and Marcel's fluctuating 'désir moral' which is predominantly the intellectual curiosity of an imaginative artist blended with the supersensitive invalid's craving for tenderness and consolation. Therefore, to describe Racine's *scène de l'aveu* as a statement of the laws which Marcel had obeyed in the course of his sentimental life is completely inaccurate. Phèdre is constantly tormented by the consciousness that in loving her stepson she is sinning against an immutable and eternal moral law. Because of this, the rhythmic and terrible current that traverses her being alternates between guilty remorse and passionate desire. In the scene where she declares her passion, her dignity, remorse, self-esteem are swept away temporarily by the sudden explosion of desire, by the irresistible urge to know her fate. What possible analogy can there be here with the rhythm of Marcel's love for Albertine 'tour à tour livré' he says, 'à la confiance et au soupçon jaloux'?

Waiting for Albertine's reply, Marcel feels that perhaps as the days pass, the habit of being separated from her will gradually allow forgetfulness, 'l'oubli', to begin its slow destructive work. But Françoise enters with two rings left behind by his mistress. One has a ruby, the other is plain; but curiously engraved inside each, as his old servant ruthlessly insists, are the same initials. Obviously they are gifts from the same person though Albertine had said that one was a gift from Mme Bontemps and the other purchased by herself. Yet another lie! Marcel's jealous suspicions are revived and once again he is confronted by a train of painful conjectures and imaginings. At last he hears from Albertine but it is only for the name of the agent to whom she must write in order to countermand the Rolls and the yacht. To break this deadlock, Marcel has recourse to a stratagem which is not very original. He invites Andrée for a few days, asking her to inform Albertine, who is in Touraine. Simultaneously, he writes to the fugitive, explaining that since, owing to the fatality of their different characters Albertine can never be his wife, he has almost decided to marry Andrée, the next most charming of the little Balbec group. What will be the effect of this letter? From Saint-Loup, Marcel had gathered that Mme Bontemps' house in Touraine was full of guests, all young girls. Torturing images present themselves, pictures of an Albertine free to abandon herself to her terrible vice, only too pleased at the prospect of Marcel's marriage with Andrée which would give her absolute liberty. On the other hand, a conversation overheard between Saint-Loup and one of Mme de Guermantes' footmen on the day Robert left for Touraine leads Marcel to wonder whether his old friend is absolutely trustworthy. It will be observed that by no means for the first time, a pure hazard reveals to Marcel something which he would have never learned in any other way. To this Proust could retort, I suppose, that in real life such chance revelations are more common than we are ordinarily disposed to believe. In this case Marcel, who was impatiently waiting for Robert to come upstairs, stepped out to the landing and overheard Saint-Loup imparting the most diabolic advice to one of his aunt's flunkeys who wants to procure the dismissal of a detested fellow-servant. Nothing, remarks Saint-Loup, could be simpler. And he proceeds to enumerate a list of abominable tricks, the effect of which will be to exasperate the duchess against the wretched victim of this satanic conspiracy and to have him dismissed without character.

'Mais il faut bien que chacun gagne sa vie,' dit son interlocuteur, 'que j'aperçus alors et qui était un des valets de pied de la duchesse de Guermantes.' 'Qu'est-ce que ça vous fiche du moment que vous serez bien?' répondit méchamment Saint-Loup. 'Vous aurez en plus le plaisir d'avoir un souffre-douleurs. Vous pouvez très bien renverser des encriers sur sa livrée au moment où il viendra servir un grand dîner, enfin ne pas lui laisser une minute de repos jusqu'à ce qu'il finisse par préférer s'en aller. Du reste, moi je pousserai à la roue, je dirai à ma tante que j'admire votre patience de servir avec un lourdaud pareil et aussi mal tenu.'[1]

Marcel's faith in Robert is badly shaken but he listens with avidity to every detail of his report, reconstructing a vision of the house in Touraine which now seems to him accursed, no longer a possibility but a reality. Robert unwittingly increases his despair when he casually remarks that on his arrival Albertine was singing joyously in her room. Furiously Marcel rounds on his friend, accusing him of unpardonable clumsiness, suggesting ungratefully that he might have displayed more zeal. The upshot of their talk is to convince Marcel that he ought to have gone to Touraine himself, that he must get his mistress back immediately. At any cost she must be removed from the temptations now surrounding her in that infernal place. His imagination, intensified to the point of hallucination, does not exclude the possibility of a conspiracy involving perhaps Saint-Loup, to

---

[1] *AD.* I, 89.

separate him from Albertine. Swann, in the throes of his
jealousy, used to hope that Odette might be the victim of some
accident. Marcel has not the courage to form such a terrible
wish but now, taught by his own suffering, he understands what
Swann endured and what he meant by 'la liberté de vivre'.
Casting prudence to the winds, he sends a despairing telegram
to Albertine begging her to come back, promising her anything
she wants. But Albertine never comes back. Immediately after
sending his own telegram, Marcel receives one from her aunt
telling of Albertine's sudden death in a riding accident.

Death simplifies many things for those who survive, but not
everything. The death of Albertine does not terminate Marcel's
sufferings. For that, he says, she would have had to die not
merely in Touraine, but in him. And so his narrative enters
upon a new phase. Now Marcel has all the freedom in the world
to reorganize his life. There is nothing any more to interfere
with his 'liberté de vivre', nothing to prevent him enjoying
those 'vertus exaltantes de la solitude' for which so often he
longed when Albertine was alive. This is the profound and
moving subject of his present narrative which interprets the
crucial phase of Marcel's search for vanished time, his effort to
grasp and to exteriorize the true movement and direction of his
inner life, his life as it was lived in what Bergson calls *la durée* as
opposed to the conventional space-time of analytic science. What
Proust now illustrates, therefore, in *Albertine disparue* is the
beginning of Marcel's evolution, of his self-realization, of his
transition from the plane of action to that of art. Speculation,
as Bergson insists, is a luxury: action is a necessity for mankind.
So long as Marcel is tortured by jealousy his imagination which,
as he rightly notes, is always concerned with actuality, obscures
the reality of the emotional experience contained in memory.
The picture now unfolded by Proust shows us how Marcel, by
a supreme combined effort of his intelligence and intuition,
endeavours to seize a true vision of his mind's history, of his
spiritual life. Thanks to Proust's unique style we are able to
perceive this vision, and thus to glimpse the real meaning and
quality of living, the continuous, dynamic mobility which is normally hidden from the eyes of the intelligence. But first, before

he can attain such a vision, Marcel must face the terrible ordeal of re-living, in memory, the years he spent with Albertine, his love for Albertine. In seeking the truth about the past, he must confront all his memories, not only the happy reminiscences which it is so tempting to fit into the cadre of his actual tormented and be-reaved self, the self that is only too eager to accept such facsimiles of reality and is busy even now trying to amass new perceptions in order to refute the intolerable doubts inspired by jealousy.

This, it seems to me, is the complicated process which Proust means to illustrate in the narrative of Marcel's futile investiga-tions into Albertine's past life. They are futile, he suggests, because Marcel is trying to reconstruct a real picture of Alber-tine's secret existence from unreliable data, from 'facts' clumsily assembled by the memory of the intelligence, 'facts' which, moreover, cancel each other out, leaving the unhappy lover with a despairing sense of frustration. On the other hand, must we not regard this sustained effort by Marcel to form a synthesis of his memories and of his perceptions of new external incidents as a necessary preliminary to that deeper exploration of the self, that more intense search for 'le temps perdu' which alone can bring him close to reality? Proust shows how Marcel, having broken away from mechanical causality, is now launched on the steeply inclined plane of introspection. In other words, he is really fulfilling his vocation of artist and thus will gradually obtain relief from suffering. His jealous, selfish and possessive 'désir moral' will never, of course, be satisfied. Instead, it disintegrates under the influence of 'l'oubli'. That, he suggests, was inevitable since the essential movement and intention of life is re-creation. Our desires do not change but we change, so that our desires cease to exist as problems. Only when Marcel grasps this truth, only when he envisages life from the plane of art can he achieve the inner harmony, the appeasement he has always craved. For, as Bergson remarks profoundly: 'L'art vit de création et implique une croyance latente à la spontanéité de la nature.' In such a perspective, I think, we must situate the central theme of *Albertine disparue*, the first chapter of which is entitled 'Le chagrin et l'oubli'. Let us now examine, however, the genesis of the process, so delicately

interpreted by Proust, by which Marcel's suffering, his love for
Albertine gradually dissolves in oblivion.

Two letters from Albertine arrive just after the telegram
announcing her death. In the first, she thanks Marcel for his
confidence, warmly agreeing that Andrée will make an ideal
wife. But the second is a brief, urgent appeal to be taken back
if it is not too late. Never had Albertine been so completely
alive in her lover's consciousness: yet Albertine is dead. Where
then, is the reality? Marcel, in an agony of grief, tries to penetrate the enigma thus presented, the commonest yet the most
profound and solemn of all the contradictions that make up the
tissue of human experience. Albertine lives on in Marcel, but
not in the form of a static, material and complete image which
may be quickly forgotten. In Proust's beautiful metaphor,
Albertine had to assume the shape, adapt herself to the cadre of
Time in order to enter into Marcel's consciousness. In a passage
which might have been expressly designed to illustrate
Bergson's views on perception and memory,[1] Proust describes
the process by which Albertine had gradually appeared to
Marcel's consciousness, in the form of a succession of impressions, of moments, each of which, however, photographed only
one tiny aspect of her personality.

Grande faiblesse sans doute pour un être de consister en une simple
collection de moments; grande force aussi; il relève de la mémoire, et
la mémoire d'un moment n'est pas instruite de tout ce qui s'est passé
depuis; ce moment qu'elle a enregistré dure encore, vit encore et avec
lui l'être qui s'y profilait. Et puis cet émiettement ne fait pas seulement
vivre la morte, il la multiplie. Pour me consoler ce n'est pas une, ce
sont d'innombrables Albertine que j'aurais dû oublier. Quand j'étais
arrivé à supporter le chagrin d'avoir perdu celle-ci, c'était à recommencer
avec une autre, avec cent autres.[2]

Proust now devotes some of the most profoundly moving pages
he ever wrote to his favourite subject: the role played in our
psychological life by the involuntary memory, by the recollections suddenly evoked by the influence of what he calls 'moments
identiques'. By this expression he means sensations analogous
to those which presided at the birth of past impressions,

---

[1] *Matière et mémoire.*   [2] *AD.* I, 100.

of states of soul we have forgotten. These, says Marcel, had composed, in their ensemble, the sweetness of his life yet quite apart from his existence with Albertine. The perfume of the lilacs at Combray, for instance, was always recalled by the sound of pattering raindrops; the pigeons of the Champs Elysées by the restless sunbeams on his balcony; the cool, sweet taste of ripe cherries by the muffled street noises in Paris on a hot summer's morning; the longing for Venice or Brittany by the fresh winds of returning Easter days. Now, however, all these lovely memories are retrospectively impregnated with sadness, by the memory of Albertine. Sitting in his darkened room, just before sunset on a glorious evening, when Françoise moves the curtains, letting in a brilliant ray of sunshine, Marcel feels as if something has ripped his soul apart. For, in the memory swiftly evoked by that flashing shaft of light, he can see little Albertine standing outside the church at Bricqueville, looking up at its facade and, proud of her recently acquired architectural lore, saying: 'Elle est restaurée.' And since, in these moments, our words never interpret our state of soul, all Marcel can find to say to Françoise is 'J'ai soif.' But, when his old servant brings him cider and fresh cherries, another image fraught with a different quality of anguish, flits across his mind. It is the image of a farm, Des Ecorres, where, he now thinks, Albertine probably used to keep secret rendezvous whilst her lover fondly awaited her at the other farm, Marie Antoinette, where so often they halted, on torrid days like this, for cider and cherries. Marcel draws the curtains but he cannot shut out these memories: he cannot silence memory itself or arrest the inexorable working of imagination. There is no art to escape the murderous barrage of his involuntary recollections, this relentless pressing of the past laden with the totality of its memories—to borrow Bergson's striking metaphor—against the door which the brain reluctantly half opens into present consciousness. For although the imagination, as Marcel complains, is singularly uninventive when called upon to predict a future reality, who knows better than he that the imagination can display a terrible and sadistic inventiveness when it sets to work upon our recollections?

In words of poignant beauty, Proust now reveals the rapid saturation of Marcel's actual perceptions and sensations by invading memories. This is a mode of transfiguration which, so often when Albertine was alive, granted to her lover a blessed respite from suffering. But now that she is dead, every object, in striking his senses, evokes a memory now tinged retrospectively with his present sorrow. Albertine, transformed by the idea of her death, has become a symbol of desolation. I will simply quote here the following passage, for it requires no comment:

Que le jour est lent à mourir par ces soirs démesurés de l'été. Un pâle fantôme de la maison d'en face continuait indéfiniment à aquareller sur le ciel sa blancheur persistante. Enfin il faisait nuit dans l'appartement, je me cognais aux meubles de l'antichambre, mais dans la porte de l'escalier, au milieu du noir que je croyais total, la partie vitrée était translucide et bleue, d'un bleu de fleur, d'un bleu d'aile, d'insecte, d'un bleu qui m'eût semblé beau si je n'avais senti qu'il était un dernier reflet, coupant comme un acier, un coup suprême que dans sa cruauté infatigable me portait encore le jour. L'obscurité complète finissait pourtant par venir, mais alors il suffisait d'une étoile vue à côté de l'arbre de la cour pour me rappeler nos départs en voitures, après le dîner, pour les bois de Chantepie, tapissés par le clair de lune. Et même dans les rues, il m'arrivait d'isoler sur le dos d'un banc, de recueillir la pureté naturelle d'un rayon de lune au milieu des lumières artificielles de Paris, — de Paris sur lequel il faisait régner, en faisant rentrer un instant, pour mon imagination, la ville dans la nature, avec le silence infini des champs évoqués, le souvenir douloureux des promenades que j'y avais faites avec Albertine. Ah! quand la nuit finirait-elle? Mais à la première fraîcheur de l'aube je frissonnais, car celle-ci avait ramené en moi la douceur de cet été, où, de Balbec à Incarville, d'Incarville à Balbec, nous nous étions tant de fois reconduits l'un l'autre jusqu'au petit jour. Je n'avais plus qu'un espoir pour l'avenir — espoir bien plus déchirant qu'une crainte, — c'était d'oublier Albertine.[1]

[How slow the day is in dying on these interminable summer evenings! A pale ghost of the house opposite continued indefinitely to paint upon the sky its lingering whiteness. At last it grew dark in the apartment, I stumbled against the furniture in the hall, but in the door leading to the staircase, in the midst of the blackness I had thought to be complete, the glass panel was translucent and blue, with the

[1] *AD*. I, 105–6.

blueness of a flower, the blueness of an insect's wing, a blueness that would have seemed beautiful had I not felt it was a final glint, sharp as a steel blade, a supreme blow that was being dealt me, in its indefatigable cruelty, by the day. Finally, however, came utter darkness, but then I had only to see a star beside the tree in the courtyard to remember the times we had set out for a drive, after dinner, for the woods of Chantepie tapestried by the moonlight. And even in the streets I would chance to isolate upon the back of some bench, to cull the natural purity of a moonbeam amidst the artificial lights of Paris— of Paris over which, by relegating, in my imagination, the city to a state of nature, with the infinite silence of the fields thus magically evoked, it enthroned the painful memory of the walks I had taken there with Albertine. Ah! when would the night end? But at the first coolness of dawn I shivered, for it had brought back to me the sweetness of the summer, when, from Balbec to Incarville, from Incarville to Balbec, we had so many times seen each other home until daybreak. I had now but one hope left for the future—a hope much more poignant than a fear —it was that I might forget Albertine.]

No sooner has Marcel conceived this hope than he is assailed by tormenting thoughts. Experience reminds him that he will assuredly forget Albertine just as he has forgotten Gilberte, Mme de Guermantes, even his beloved grandmother. This knowledge is like a stab in the heart. The price we pay for the oblivion that shuts out the memory of our dead is the awareness in the throes of our bereavement that a day will come when we shall be able to forget them, or that if we think of them, it will be without sorrow, nay with indifference. And what of the intervening years of this transition from grief to oblivion? As Marcel, in the silence of his room, dwells on his tender memories of Albertine, he can scarcely bear to contemplate a future in which they will have no existence. To forget his love for her and all its torments, he must first strip his soul for ever of a 'tégument de caresses, de baisers, de sommeils amis'. At the moment, this seems unthinkable. It is, Marcel implies, like a betrayal of the dead to purchase eventual appeasement in such a way. Nothing, however, can alter the fundamental law of our psychological life, in obedience to which our consciousness is normally oriented towards action, towards the future. So Marcel will soon be compelled to admit, though with a sense of guilt, that the great sorrow of his life may prove perhaps to have been a necessary phase in his evolution towards a vocation. Is not this implied in the passage where he reflects that precisely because Albertine, in dying, became an instrument of grief she proved, therefore, of greater utility to his life than if she had been a source of unalloyed happiness? He means that Marcel the artist will eventually recognize the value of these truths revealed to him in the agonies of his bereavement, the truths infinitely more precious than would have been the possession of Albertine. In the meantime, however, brooding upon the past which he tries to project into the future, what appals Marcel is the thought that her memory is linked with all the seasons, with everything in the universe. Every day will be an anniversary, recalling some fragment of existence as it used to be when Albertine was alive. Soon it will be exactly a year since jealousy transformed his love into a complex of selfish, unattainable desires, all of which, however, seemed to Marcel attainable if only he could penetrate that secret, locked in an inner chamber, the soul of his mistress. Now she is dead. Why then should these desires persist and instead of vanishing, thrust themselves into the forefront of his consciousness, endowed with fresh vitality? Albertine, whose body was broken and destroyed in Touraine, was never more alive in Marcel's being, resurrected by her very death, by her now eternal absence. The tragedy enacted during her lifetime, with its rhythmic alternation of loving confidence and torturing suspicion, is now about to be replayed. But this time it will take the form of a monologue reflecting, surely, the most original spectacle ever recorded by a novelist.

It is the spectacle of a mind tortured by jealousy and grief, a mind turned inwards upon its inmost, ever changing self in a supreme effort to know its own nature and history. One might call it a reverie except that it is essentially different from any reverie we have met with in literature because the narrator, quite clearly, is obsessed by an inveterate distrust of the voluntary memory, of that plausible, spurious guide whose comforting reports are so eagerly accepted by the intelligence as genuine. The narrator is also very keenly aware, I suspect, of that gulf, first revealed by Bergson, which separates pure memory from our habitual way of remembering. Nowhere does Proust mention Bergson in this illuminating re-creation of the processes by which Marcel strives to visualize his own consciousness, to enter into the processional dance of his own memories and perceptions. Yet one cannot ignore the striking affinities between the revolutionary discoveries recorded in *Matière et Mémoire* and the Proustian views on memory and perception so brilliantly exemplified here in the subjective character of Marcel's narrative. Certainly, if we are to grasp the tragic nature of his ordeal we must recall what Bergson says about pure memory as opposed to habitual memory and note especially his remarks on the relation between remembering and perceiving.

According to Bergson, our mind or consciousness signifies, above all, memory. Our whole past is retained in memory though, in great part, subconsciously. If we possessed pure memory, all our past life exactly as we lived, felt and perceived it, would be present in our consciousness. In fact, however, we only remember that small part of our past which is of use to our present action, to the purposes of our actual existence as social beings. The function of the brain, indeed, is to select from the swarm of memories pressing forwards for admission into our immediate consciousness only those that interest our present situation. Yet, as Bergson insists, all our past life in the minutest details is preserved indefinitely: everything we have ever perceived, willed or thought. But the mass of such memories remain for ever invisible to us, shut down in the darkness of the unconscious. Sometimes, when the tension of our mind, which is normally oriented towards the immediate future, is relaxed, the door is opened to admit a larger inrush of memories. This happens often in sleep, or in exceptional cases where an individual is on the brink of what appears sudden death. But great artists, too, experience something of this 'disinterestedness in life', this attitude of detachment from the utilitarian demands of everyday social existence. That is precisely why, situated on this plane, they are able to procure a truer vision of life's direction and nature, a truer vision of the past. Less concerned than the ordinary individual in choosing memories that fit usefully into the moving framework of his present consciousness, the artist abandons this 'habit-memory' for something approaching pure memory. The sensations of the past are thus revealed to him in their true quality, surrounded by their original emotional atmosphere. He attains in these creative hours a clarity of memory, an acuity and depth of perception denied to other men. He also experiences a sense of joy, of inner completeness which others could never divine were it not communicated in the work of art.

What is Marcel's situation? Is his mind equipped to grasp even that fragment of its own past enclosed in the few years of his intimacy with Albertine? The idea of her death casts a backward shadow over all the sensations and emotions of the days they spent together, over the places they inhabited, over his many and varied images of Albertine. Besides, his jealousy still survives; liable at any moment to bring into play the distorting influence of imagination upon the memories of incidents long forgotten, endowing them suddenly with painful actuality. How difficult it is to remember, to replace oneself in the authentic spiritual climate of the past whilst new sensations stream into the consciousness! For Marcel, even whilst he strives to look backwards in an effort to seize the reality of 'le temps perdu' is continually distracted by the emotions born of fresh knowledge, of new 'facts' resulting from his jealous investigations into Albertine's mysterious other life. And what of the future, the shape and nature of things to come? For although a man may force his mind to dwell upon its past he cannot alter its inevitable orientation, which is in the direction of future action. Marcel, says Proust, wears the double harness of the past and the present, a metaphor which seems to me to illuminate admirably the nature of the ordeal exteriorized in *Albertine disparue* with such rare integrity, with such consummate art. Suffering craves appeasement which can only come with forgetting: jealousy demands more and still more knowledge of Albertine's past. Marcel's sorrowful love recoils from the desolate prospect of a future without Albertine and seeks relief in the contemplation of happy memories. Yet the intellectual whose vocation is art demands the truth, the real 'temps perdu'. But what is meant by 'remembering'? For instance, does he honestly remember that day when Albertine's obedient, submissive telephone call from the Trocadéro stilled her lover's horrible and torturing suspicions; inspiring him, as he then thought, with a victorious sense of pride and possession? Now, however, he knows that the cause of his elation was not pride: it was love, the real love of which Marcel had always dreamed. Yet this, Proust tells us, is also an illusion. The fact is that Marcel, in his present state of emotional chaos, does not actually remember the unique and exquisite quality of that particular day. It will only be disclosed to him very much later when he is able to think of Albertine's death without suffering, to think of his love with indifference. Proust's implication is that Marcel will never be able to grasp the reality of 'le temps perdu' until he attains the plane from which the great artist surveys life. Meanwhile, how can he look upon the last few years in this spirit of serene detachment, obscured as they are by a grey film of sadness, by the memory of her death upon which, in turn, those years have left their imprint, 'la couleur successive, les modalités différentes de leurs saisons ou de leurs heures'?[1]

In words so transparent that nothing seems to intervene between our perception and the artist's creation, Proust shows us a fascinating spectacle which I can only liken to a ballet of the memories. On the brightly lit stage of Marcel's consciousness are two groups of dancing, interweaving memories. In one can be discerned the reminiscences of all the lovely sensations evoked by June afternoons in Balbec, by moonlight on the ocean, by frosty winter evenings in Paris, by the scent of autumnal leaves at Saint-Cloud. These are memories of the seasons, capturing the perfume and luminosity of happy, vanished days. The other group embraces Marcel's memory-images of Albertine herself, of her physical attitudes, of his anxieties when she was late for a rendezvous, of his desires, hopes, disappointments. Now, gliding into the mazes of this ballet comes the moth-grey, diaphanous memory of a dead Albertine, weaving athwart the brilliant throng a pattern of shadows, losing thereby a little of its own sadness, yet robbing the other memories of their bright gaiety. The perspective swiftly lengthens until one can no longer

[1] *AD.* I, 114.

discern the individual features of the dancers who are instantly replaced by others. These are memories of the solar years, each linked with its spiritual associate, its sentimental counterpart, with Marcel's memory of his love for Albertine. For in his vision of the past, inseparable now from the sensations evoked by the pageant of the seasons, are the temperatures and climates of vanished time, the ever-changing states of soul inspired by Albertine. Time, viewed thus, assumes a double aspect because, in addition to every solar year, there was another year whose days and hours are to be read only in a unique, subjective calendar, where, to quote Proust's charming words:

les heures n'étaient pas définies par la position du soleil, mais par l'attente d'un rendezvous, où la longueur des jours, où les progrès de la température, étaient mesurés par l'essor de mes espérances, le progrès de notre amitié, la transformation progressive de son visage, les voyages qu'elle avait faits, la fréquence et le style de ses lettres qu'elle m'avaient adressées pendant une absence, sa précipitation plus ou moins grande à me voir au retour.[1]

But, Marcel observes, although memory holds a procession of different Albertines, this is not just because the recurrence of a spring or summer day evokes by analogy a certain image of his mistress as she then impressed herself on his consciousness. Before he fell in love, there awoke to greet the new day a Marcel quite different from the self of the preceding evening, a Marcel whose desires, hopes and beliefs had undergone a sea-change in the interval between sleep and awaking, thus altering the 'visibilité' of his love which sometimes filled the whole area of his mind, at others receded towards the horizon, thrust out by other emotions. 'On n'est que par ce qu'on possède', he reflects, 'on ne possède que ce qui vous est réellement présent.' And now, in a striking image, Proust illustrates a theory of memory and its role in consciousness which is quite Bergsonian. Many of our memories sail away on a voyage of their own, far out of sight. But one morning, on awaking, we find a whole fleet of them in the harbour of our consciousness. So Marcel, whose search for the past brings him one evening nothing but happy recollections, arises, nevertheless, at dawn to confront a serried mass of

[1] *AD.* i, 115.

different memories, the memories of Albertine's lies and betrayals. Two different Albertines: two different Marcels. He does not try to explain this transformation except to say that memories have secret roads by which they return to our consciousness. But we have only to recall what he has told us of his dreams to understand what is implied in his metaphor. In sleep, his repressed memories have been thrusting eagerly upwards towards what Bergson calls the trapdoor of the consciousness, so that when he awakes it is to discover to his dismay that some have contrived to force an entrance. Such are the painful recollections that now confront the Marcel who emerges from slumber.

Let us now examine the state of soul of the Marcel 'portant le double harnais du présent et du passé'. Whilst seeking to recover from memory a true vision of Albertine he is intensely preoccupied by the idea of her death. Retrospectively, as is clearly evinced in the tone of the narrative, this idea of a dead Albertine predominates for a time over the other idea of a guilty Albertine, suffusing his thoughts with sorrow and pity. Automatically, therefore, the recollections admitted into his consciousness are chiefly those which harmonize with his actual emotional state. Physical images crowd into his mind: Albertine, the swift and agile cyclist, bent over her 'roue mythologique', her tresses streaming in the wind; provocative images that fill Marcel with the regret of unsatisfied carnal desires. Vividly he remembers the Albertine of the Chantepie woods and the moonlit beach, flushed, exciting, alluring. Or again, he sees her silhouetted against the sea, an honest, sturdy little figure like a statuette; or else, motionless, smiling, diaphanous, in her Fortuny gown, seated at the pianola, in his flat, like a Saint Cecilia, an angel of music. How is it possible to reconcile all these memories all so vital, with the fact of Albertine's death? Is not this Albertine, the Albertine recomposed from his memories, not also a fact, a reality? Brooding on this contradiction, Marcel feels as if he must make a choice, decide which of these facts is true, which an illusion. Whilst his mind is crowded with sentiments exclusively implying a living woman, how can he believe that she died in Touraine, a place unknown to him? Simultaneously, however, arise Marcel's memories of himself. He, too, is a succession of moments, of emotional phases reflected in the complexity of his love: intellectual curiosity about the unknown: sensual desire mixed up with feelings of almost uxorious tenderness; jealousy; indifference; regret. Memory, therefore, resurrects the march past, as it were, hour by hour of a 'compact army' of dissimilar Marcels, of passionate or indifferent or jealous Marcels. And no doubt, he argues, this will be his eventual salvation: in this very multiplicity lies the certainty of his release from suffering. Proust's arguments are ingenious but I do not think they interpret the true nature of our psychological life. There are, he maintains, in this serried moving army of different selves composing Marcel's total self or personality, certain elements which imperceptibly drop out and are replaced by others until, finally, a complete change has taken place which could never have been accomplished if Marcel had been one uniform self and not a multiple self. I wonder, however, whether the phenomenon called forgetting can be so easily explained. Proust himself has shown a hundred times in Marcel's narrative that these memory-images of past states of soul certainly do slip out of the ranks of that 'armée compacte', in other words out of our mind or soul or consciousness. Yet they also have a singular trick—since conventional time means nothing to them—of slipping back into the ranks again and, moreover, of working their way to the head of the marching column. Perhaps Marcel is unlucky in his choice of metaphor which leads him to emphasize the differences separating the constituent elements of his 'armée compacte', and thus to obscure their essential quality of dynamic interpenetration or interfusion. Marcel's error consists here in seeing his inner life, not as duration, but in space-time, as a chain of states of consciousness, individual links of which may disappear or be replaced by others, without the continuity being broken. To this view he is inevitably committed by his image of the 'armée compacte'. Situated on another plane, that of the artist, he would have obtained a more intuitive vision. He would have seen, as Bergson says, that the past and present states of the consciousness, whilst resembling the distinct notes of a musical composition, nevertheless melt into each other to form that unbroken melody which alone can interpret the meaning and quality of the inner life, of real existence. Yet, in justice to Proust, do not let us forget that Marcel's narrative is 'l'histoire d'une vocation', projecting therefore the various phases of his search for reality, of his self-realization.

Ironically, as if to refute Marcel's logical theorizings, a battalion of stragglers composed of his forgotten jealous 'selves' unexpectedly rejoins the 'armée compacte'. But how can he be jealous of a dead woman, of an Albertine no longer able to commit the terrible acts, to enjoy the loathsome pleasures created by his imagination and retained by his memory? Reasonably, it is impossible to be jealous of the dead. Yet Albertine's betrayals and lies, Marcel's horrible suspicions are vividly actual: he has only to think of her in order to resuscitate them. Looking back along the avenue of time, he can see hundreds of guilty Albertines each linked inevitably with a jealous Marcel. Perhaps, if only she were still alive, if only he could shower upon her the treasures of his love, all those images would prove to be hallucinations, dispelled by one word from Albertine. As it is, even though she is dead, his imagination pictures his mistress, somewhere, away from his jealous surveillance, prostituting her liberty. During her lifetime, it was the uncertainty of the future that most tormented Marcel: now it is the past. 'Son Passé? C'est mal dire, puisque pour la jalousie il n'est ni passé ni avenir et ce qu'elle imagine est toujours le présent.'[1] Twenty years ago, when I first read *Albertine disparue*, this theme of Marcel's jealousy for his dead mistress seemed to me, if not exactly far-fetched, at least rather exceptional. That was because my ignorance of life was more profound then than perhaps it is now. Jealousy of the dead, though it does not always take the form of sexual jealousy, is surely one of the most commonly observed traits in human nature. *De mortuis nil nisi bonum.* Who has not frequently heard, with a pang of distress, the old Latin tag, uttered as a placatory offering to invisible gods but also as the prelude to a derogatory comment revealing the survival of

[1] *AD.* I, 120.

an inveterate and reinvigorated jealousy? It may be reasonably objected, however, that this is very different from the situation described by Proust because, to take the hypothetical case of an author who is still jealous of a deceased rival, the latter's works and reputation are still very much alive. Marcel's mistress, on the other hand, is dead so that he need no longer torture himself with endless conjectures as to her possible sexual relations with others. That would be true except for the peculiar quality of his love in which, as we have so frequently noted, the predominant element is his 'désir moral' and not physical desire. Albertine's death, instead of simplifying Marcel's existence, complicates it, for she is now beyond the reach of his jealous interrogations although his insatiable curiosity later discovers other less direct sources of information. No, the dead are never immune from the passions of the living, from the jealousy, envy, hatred or contempt that pursued them in life, so often without their knowledge. We know from everyday observation that envy, hatred or contempt of the dead are not uncommon: it is obviously not so easy to discover whether this is equally true of sexual jealousy. Proust does not go into this matter nor, until the close of his remarkable analysis of Marcel's thoughts and feelings does he try to account for this persistence of jealousy after the death of its object. Might not one regard it as the survival of a habit, analogous for instance to our persistence in trying to use a certain exit long after we have been told it is permanently closed? Only, strangely enough, that is a finality to which we get more quickly accustomed than to the idea of death.

The return of summer days laden with threats of thunderstorms bring memories of Balbec, and of Albertine, wrapped in her close-fitting waterproof, setting out for long cycle rides. Where she went Marcel never knew. Jealously and idly drifting on the 'fluide et invisible étendue de la mémoire', he encounters the recollection of a tiny incident that occurred before he fell in love with Albertine. The passage is worth quoting since it illustrates what I have just noted regarding the peculiarly intellectual quality of Marcel's jealousy.

Ainsi il y avait plusieurs années, comme on parlait de son peignoir de douche, Albertine avait rougi. A cette époque-là je n'étais pas

jaloux d'elle. Mais depuis, j'avais voulu lui demander si elle pouvait
se rappeler cette conversation et me dire pourquoi elle avait rougi.
Cela m'avait d'autant plus préoccupé qu'on m'avait dit que les deux
jeunes filles amies de Léa allaient dans cet établissement balnéaire de
l'hotel et, disait-on, pas seulement pour prendre des douches. Mais
par peur de fâcher Albertine ou attendant une époque meilleure, j'avais
toujours remis de lui en parler, puis je n'y avais plus pensé. Et tout
d'un coup, quelque temps après la mort d'Albertine j'aperçus ce
souvenir, empreint de ce caractère à la fois irritant et solennel qu'ont
les énigmes laissées à jamais insolubles par la mort du seul être qui
eût pu les éclaircir. Ne pourrais-je pas du moins tâcher de savoir si
Albertine n'avait jamais rien fait de mal dans cet établissement de
douches? En envoyant quelqu'un à Balbec j'y arriverais peut-être. Elle
vivante, je n'eusse sans doute pu rien apprendre. Mais les langues se
délient étrangement et racontent facilement une faute quand on n'a
plus à craindre la rancune de la coupable.[1]

[Thus, many years ago, when someone mentioned her bathing-
wrap, Albertine had blushed. At that period I was not jealous of her.
But since then I had intended asking her whether she could remember
that conversation and to tell me why she had blushed. This had occupied
my mind all the more because I had been told that Léa's two girl-friends
used to frequent that bathing establishment belonging to the hotel
and, it was said, not merely to take baths. But, for fear of annoying
Albertine or else pending a more favourable opportunity, I had always
put off mentioning it to her, then it had gone out of my head. And
suddenly, shortly after Albertine's death, I perceived this recollection,
stamped with that character, at once irritating and solemn, peculiar to
enigmas that are left for ever insoluble by the death of the one creature
who could have explained them. Might I not at least try to find out
whether Albertine had ever done anything wicked in that bathing
establishment? By sending someone to Balbec I might perhaps succeed.
Had she been alive I should not of course have been able to learn anything. But tongues become strangely loosened and readily talk about
a misdeed when the culprit's resentment need no longer be feared.]

In Albertine's lifetime, although he was often tormented by
such enigmas, Marcel had never summoned up the energy to
track them down to their source. Like Dr Bartholo, it will be
recalled, he preferred to employ the methods of the *juge d'instruction*. Now, however, he calls in a detective. Aimé, the former
maître d'hôtel, is sent for and dispatched to Balbec with instructions to make inquiries on the spot. No sooner has Aimé gone

[1] *AD.* I, 121–2.

than Marcel finds himself thinking involuntarily that, of course, he ought to have interrogated Albertine herself. In imagination, for a few brief moments, she is at his side answering his questions whilst almost simultaneously comes the realization that she is dead and will never speak to him again. All hateful suspicions vanish in a surge of pity and sadness. The memories that now flood his mind picture an innocent, loving Albertine with whom he passed only happy hours. In retrospect, his life with her, the life he so often thought intolerable either because of his in-difference or because of his jealousy, now seems to have been wholly delightful. The tragedy is that Albertine had to die so that her lover might know what he has lost. In the pages describing Marcel's inconsolable grief, Proust subtly and beauti-fully exteriorizes the process by which memory can distort the reality of past experience in deference to the exigencies of our present state of mind, offering us only those recollections which interest our immediate preoccupation. That is not the fault of memory. It is because we refuse to see our inner life as it really is, as indivisible continuity and change in which our 'past' and 'present' are one; only when an incident ceases to interest us does it really belong to our past. For Marcel now, the only events that count are those which harmonize with his present attitude of mind, which fit into this actual spiritual phase and complete the picture of a love unsullied, of an Albertine without a blemish. Approached from this direction, other memories are instantly revised. An invitation from Mme Verdurin, angrily thrown aside, recalls Brichot and Marcel's return to his apartment on the night of the concert. How could he then, looking up at Albertine's window, have possibly compared those vertical stripes of light to the bars of his prison?

Je compris combien cette lumière qui me semblait venir d'une prison contenait pour moi de plénitude, de vie et de douceur, et qui n'était que la réalisation de ce qui m'avait un instant enivré, puis paru à jamais impossible: je comprenais que cette vie que j'avais menée à Paris dans un chez moi qui était son chez elle, c'était justement la réalisation de cette paix profonde que j'avais rêvée le soir où Albertine avait couché sous le même toit que moi, à Balbec.[1]

[1] *AD.* I, 127.

He remembers the evening preceding the Vinteuil septet, his charming talk with Albertine about literature and music. Yet once at the Verdurins, Mme de Cambremer had reproached him with neglecting Elstir because of Albertine. She was wrong, of course, yet, until now, Marcel had never thought of Albertine's intelligence; never indeed, tried to think of her objectively, to understand her character as he would have done had she not been his mistress. His purely subjective attitude to her he now feels, was perhaps a mistake. He should have made an attempt to know her better, in herself, not just as the vessel containing his love, his fears and hopes. Thus, for the first time, the selfishness of his love begins to dawn upon Marcel. Jealous and possessive, he had never admired Albertine's qualities for their intrinsic value but merely because they enhanced his sense of ownership. But how difficult it is for a lover to see his mistress objectively, especially when she is so lodged in his own body that one little suspicion concerning her movements produces an almost physical pain. The great injustice implanted in us by love, thinks Marcel, is that it conditions, so to speak, our morality. Why should we need to be in love before lies have the power to excite our indignation or kindness our gratitude? Few of Proust's readers, I imagine, will accept this La Rochefoucauld sentiment, particularly from Marcel who, on his own admission, does not possess a very active or highly developed moral sense. He appears, for instance, to observe nothing unusual in his maxim: 'Le désir physique a ce merveilleux pouvoir de rendre son prix à l'intelligence et des bases solides à la vie morale.' Significantly it never occurs to him that in the moral life of millions of people religion, in some form, constitutes a very solid foundation, more permanent, certainly, than carnal desire.

Actively reconstructing, out of these selected memories, a completely one-sided picture of his sentimental life with Albertine, her lover now sees her as the only human being in whom he could absolutely confide, to whom he could talk about anything. He remembers, too, her caresses and with passionate regret though not, he insists, with despair. To feel despair, one must still cling to life, and the Marcel now surveying his past is no longer the self who possessed a treasure. Or did he really possess Albertine's love? Was this not simply imagination? Because she lived in his heart, because of their semi-domestic intimacy and her obedient responses to his tenderness, he had persuaded himself to believe in her love. Illusion or not, at any rate, during the period of his intense jealousy he was more fortunate than Swann, who rarely saw Odette at that stage of their relations. Yet Swann did not lose Odette and Marcel has lost Albertine. Indifferent now as to what life holds in store, he dwells on the happy memories of their short life together and from this contemplation derives a sense of spiritual well-being.

Situated on the steeply inclined plane of introspection, Marcel, to judge from his subsequent reflections, moves towards a profounder and more disinterested perception of his own character. Grief, as he truly observes, can distort reality just as powerfully as intoxication. Yet it is clear from the tenor of Marcel's thoughts that it can also be a precious source of self-knowledge. Thus, for the first time, he sees his possessive and selfish love not just as a series of states of consciousness reflected in his memory-images of Albertine, not merely as a purely subjective experience fraught with melancholy beauty. These memories on which it is so pleasant to dwell were not, from Albertine's point of view, mere pictures: they were the active substance of her brief, tragic existence. Whilst he was obsessed with his selfish, futile desire to know the inner life of Albertine, to superimpose his subjective vision of Albertine on her real personality, it never once occurred to him to consider the possible effects of this experiment. Viewing his life in this new light, in relation to the evolution of Albertine's existence as an individual and not as the mere symbol of his own desires, Marcel is forced to confront the banal, the solemn, appalling truth that every human being, by the simple fact of existing, influences at every moment the destiny of some other living creature. Such is the truth expressed in the following passage:

Si bien que cette longue plainte de l'âme qui croit vivre enfermée en elle-même n'est un monologue qu'en apparence, puisque les échos de la réalité la font dévier et que telle vie est comme un essai de psychologie subjective spontanément poursuivi, mais qui fournit à quelque distance son 'action' au roman purement réaliste d'une autre réalité, d'une autre existence, dont à leur tour les péripéties viennent infléchir la courbe et changer la direction de l'essai psychologique.[1]

One day, for instance, Marcel read a description of Balbec church which, according to Swann, was of Byzantine origin. And so, although he never found this church, he met Albertine and fell in love. Because of his wealth, perhaps, he was able to persuade her to remain in his Paris flat as a virtual captive. His monstrous jealousy, therefore, set in train a complex interaction of problems and events culminating in the death of Albertine, killed by a horse which, but for him, she would never have possessed. Yet, even having met Albertine, it was not predestined or necessary that he should have fallen in love with her. If Mme de Stermaria, for example, had kept that rendezvous in the Bois de Boulogne, she might have been the unique, the apparently irreplaceable woman of his desires. No doubt, a man falls in love with a certain type of woman though not a physical type. This reservation is prompted by Marcel's recollection of Gilberte, whose blonde slenderness is so different from Albertine's beauty. The resemblance, however, is there but it lies deeper.

Je pouvais presque croire que l'obscure personnalité, la sensualité, la nature volontaire et rusée de Gilberte étaient revenues me tenter, incarnées cette fois dans le corps d'Albertine, tout autre et non pourtant sans analogies. Pour Albertine, grâce à une vie toute différente ensemble et où n'avait pu se glisser, dans un bloc de pensées où une douleureuse préoccupation maintenait une cohésion permanente, aucune fissure de distraction et d'oubli, son corps vivant n'avait point comme celui de Gilberte cessé un jour d'être celui où je trouvais ce que je reconnaissais après coup être pour moi (et qui n'eût pas été pour d'autres) les attraits feminins. Mais elle était morte. Je l'oublierais.[2]

His love for Gilberte, then, had been like the 'phrase de Vinteuil' in relation to the septet, a fragment of his greater love, his passion for Albertine. And probably this, in turn, is but a phase in a vaster love, a movement in the continuous, inner melody of his emotional life. Habit, says Marcel, according to a certain school of philosophy, lends to the mere association of ideas between two phenomena the illusory necessity and authority

---

[1] *AD.* I, 135.   [2] *AD.* I, 138–9.

of a causal law. Was it not, therefore, just because he lived with Albertine that he came to associate her indissolubly with his love, with a sentiment she had not inspired yet of which he believed her to be, wrongly, the special and necessary cause? On the other hand, Marcel suggests, the original act of falling in love is surely a choice, an act of the free will though later, once a man is passionately in love, he acquires the illusion of fatality or necessity. Marcel, remembering the Balbec days, sees that, in turn, first Albertine then Andrée seemed to be the chosen one. What tilted the scales definitely in favour of Albertine was the knowledge that she had once been a friend of Mlle Vinteuil. Up till then, if Andrée had kept him waiting, or had missed a rendezvous, would it not have been her absence that had inspired him with sentiments of anxiety, of desire and, therefore, of love? How strange, he reflects, that an absent creature, a woman whose features we cannot exactly visualize, whose inner life is unknown to us, should be capable of generating emotions we should perhaps never have experienced but for this separation! A woman fails to keep an appointment and at once the imagination fastens on a shapeless complex of perceptions and sentiments, rapidly weaving them into the design of a passionate love, astonishing, says Marcel, the bewildered, laggard intelligence which protests in vain at the crazy unreality of such behaviour. 'L'intelligence qui n'a pas rattrappé le cœur, s'étonne, s'écrie: "Mais tu es fou, dans quelles pensées nouvelles vis-tu si douleureusement? Tout cela n'est pas la vie réelle."' So Marcel now looks on Albertine's departure as an allegory, the allegory of many other separations, of other absences, of other frustrated expectations.

Proust does not unfortunately probe more deeply into this interesting question of 'l'attente vaine' and its relation to the genesis of the passions and emotions. Why should this fact of having to wait, apparently in vain, for someone or something play such an important role in the evolution of our inner life? Obviously, its action is by no means confined to love. Many vague human desires there are which had never crystallized into passionate, urgent needs of the spirit but for the stimulating and directive influence of this obligation to wait. Is there any more common psychological fact than this rapid modification of our feelings and sensations, the spiritual disequilibrium, the anxiety varying in its degree of intensity which is produced in us by having to wait for a woman to keep a rendezvous, for an answer to an important letter or merely for summer to come back? In this state of tension we measure time by a clock within ourselves, by real duration which for us is always standard time although, unfortunately, no one else accepts it as such. Meanwhile, our imagination, summoned by our intelligence to end an intolerable situation, constructs a hundred possibilities in a vain attempt to close the gap between the present and the future, playing backwards also upon memories of past experience, or rather upon such memories as seem likely to restore our inner harmony, our peace of mind. The woman arrives two hours late, by that abstract mathematical time which for us has no connection with real time, our reckoning. Our correspondent, who has completely forgotten our existence until reminded by his secretary, finally dictates his reply. Summer, which evolves according to as many clocks as there are individuals in the world, emerges from the clutch of spring. All, however, acquire in the eyes of our spirit a special and precious quality because they have released us from an unbearable state of tension. So they will always retain in our memory that air of uniqueness until the lady begins to keep her appointments punctually, until our correspondent ceases to interest us, and until, with the disappearance of summer, we begin to wait for the desirable and frosty winter season.

Now, the root cause of Marcel's anxiety is the illusion that his inner life is a succession of states of soul whose future direction and quality he can divine by stopping to examine certain particular 'past' states. He is, therefore, naïvely astonished at the totally unexpected revolution which occurs in his emotions when the disappearance of Albertine completely falsifies the image, so logically constructed by his intelligence, of what he would think and feel and want in such an eventuality. The rough frame-work formed of incident and actions is certainly there. But how woefully different is its spiritual content from what he had foreseen! No one can anticipate a state of soul, not even his own, least of all that of another. It never exists as a possibility, only as an accomplished fact, except to our deluded intelligence which persists in mistaking the backward shadow cast by an event for a reality from which it ought to have been possible to foresee the event itself. In fact, all of us tend subconsciously to think that our 'past' is separate from our future, supposing that the memories of past experience, if scientifically examined, will reveal the future shape and direction of our life in a given situation. We forget, as did Marcel, that our inner life is continuous change and that the history of our consciousness never repeats itself: that the state of our soul cannot be measured like the phenomena of a natural system. There is no such thing as psychological astronomy.

This is the truth which, I think, Marcel vaguely discerns as his consciousness alternately dilates and contracts in its efforts to view its own history or rather that phase of its history which concerns Albertine. Such appears to be the process so minutely and subtly illustrated in Marcel's narrative. We observe, in fact, two aspects of him, the lover and the incipient artist. The lover's urgent need, of course, is to reconstruct, if possible with the help of new evidence as well as of his unconsciously selected, happy memories, the image of an innocent Albertine. It is necessary to his future tranquillity, which must hold only the idea of an Albertine who never possessed abnormal and evil tastes. Here, as we have seen, Marcel is the victim of a common illusion. Bergson would have warned him that the function of the brain is precisely to admit into our consciousness only such recollections as will fit easily into our immediate plan. On the other hand Marcel, the artist, as his mind looks backward and inwards upon itself, discovers a more real vision of its own life and nature. Just as when he was listening to the Vinteuil septet, he moves once more to a plane, viewed from which the matter of Albertine's guilt or innocence appears less important than the larger question of his own responsibilities towards this girl, the object of his monstrous 'désir moral'. Then pity, remorse, dispelling jealousy, conjure up only memories of her frankness, her unselfishness and adorable charm. It seems that the perfect love he had always dreamed of had in fact been attained. 'Je comprenais que cette vie que j'avais menée à Paris dans un chez moi qui était son chez elle, c'était justement la réalisation de cette paix profonde que j'avais rêvée le soir où Albertine avait couché sous le même toit que moi, à Balbec.'[1] Suddenly, however, that involuntary recollection of the 'peignoir de douche' produces a narrowing of Marcel's zone of conscious-ness. The mind of the jealous lover is now focused again on something of imperative interest to his immediate present and future state of soul, the question of Albertine's innocence or guilt. Whilst awaiting Aimé's report he tries, by purchasing the favours of women who might have known Albertine, to probe the secrets of her private life.

These researches, needless to say, lead to nothing and are soon abandoned. In the solitude of his room, Marcel continues his 'recherche du temps perdu' on another plane, that of introspec-tion. His thoughts dwell on certain conversations that took place just before Albertine's death, at the time when both were acting a comedy of separation which, had they but known, prefigured a reality. He recalls now many phrases, insincere at the moment of their utterance yet retrospectively fraught with truth. 'Plus je vous verrai, plus je vous aimerai'; 'Tâchez d'être prudente. Pensez s'il vous arrivait un accident je ne m'en consolerais pas.' The same prophetic quality was contained in many of Albertine's pronouncements, though certainly at the time she did not believe her own words. 'Laissez-moi vous regarder encore puisque bientôt je ne vous verrai plus et que ce sera pour jamais'; 'Dire que je ne verrai plus cette chambre, ces livres, ce pianola, toute cette maison, je ne peux pas le croire et pourtant c'est vrai.' And that last phrase in the letter written on the eve of her death: 'Croyez que de mon côté je n'oublierai pas cette promenade deux foix crépusculaire et qu'elle ne s'effacera pas de mon esprit qu'avec la nuit complète.' In that supreme moment, riding madly through the gates of eternal night, did Albertine, he wonders, call out to him for help? Was her last thought of Marcel, as he is cruel enough now to hope? Did she at last, like him, discover her true self? Did she finally confess herself to her lover, die in him? Even so, how would that avail either of them since, during

[1] *AD.* I, 127.

THE MIND OF PROUST

her lifetime neither knew where happiness lay? Only when it was no longer possible did they know what should have been done to realize it.

I would ask the reader to observe the trend of Marcel's reflections which are leading him gradually towards the idea expressed by Bergson in his luminous phrase, 'le mirage du présent dans le passé'. So long as things are only possible, says Marcel, we put them off because they are never attractive or desirable: only in retrospect, by an illusion, do they seem easy to realize. At least, this is probably what he means to convey in his grandiloquent sentence:

Tant que les choses sont possibles on les diffère, et elles ne peuvent prendre cette puissance d'attraits et cette apparente aisance de réalisation que quand, projetées dans le vide idéal de l'imagination, elles sont soustraites à la submersion alourdissante, enlaidissante du milieu vital.[1]

Marcel's illusion is that a happy life with Albertine might have been possible if only they had foreseen the possibility. This, however, as Bergson would have pointed out is a retroactive effect of his judgement. The happiness and the idea of that happiness, its reality and its possibility were simultaneously created.

Le jugement qui constate l'apparition de la chose ou de l'événement ne peut venir qu'après eux; il a donc sa date. Mais cette date s'efface aussitôt, en vertu du principe, ancré dans notre intelligence, que toute vérité est éternelle.[2]

Marcel does not at once grasp this truth because at first he feels that Albertine's action in sending the telegram expressing her wish to return lends to their tragedy an air of completeness, of æsthetic and indispensable finality. On reflection, however, he concludes that every event, retrospectively, bears a spurious cachet of finality.

En réalité il l'eût eu tout autant s'il eût été autre; car tout événement est comme un moule d'une forme particulière, et, quel qu'il soit, il impose, à la série des faits qu'il est venu interrompre et semble en conclure, un dessin que nous croyons le seul possible parce que nous ne connaissons pas celui qui eût pu lui être substitué.[3]

[1] *AD.* i, 148.   [2] *La pensée et le mouvant*, p. 21.   [3] *AD.* i, 149.

This is a virtual paraphase of Bergson's words:

Par le seul fait de s'accomplir, la réalité projette derrière elle son ombre dans le passé indéfiniment lointain; elle paraît avoir préexisté, sous forme de possible, à sa propre realisation. De là une erreur qui vicie notre conception du passé; de la notre prétention d'anticiper en toute occasion l'avenir. Nous nous demandons, par exemple, ce que seront l'art, la littérature, la civilisation de demain; nous nous figurons en gros la courbe d'évolution des sociétés; nous allons jusqu'à prédire le détail des événements. Certes, nous pourrons toujours rattacher la réalité, une fois accomplie, aux événements qui l'ont précédée et aux circonstances où elle s'est produite; mais une réalité toute différente (non pas *quelconque*, il est vrai) se fût aussi bien rattachée aux mêmes circonstances et aux mêmes événements, pris par un autre côté.[1]

[By the mere fact of happening, reality projects its shadow behind itself in the indefinitely distant past; thus it appears to have existed, in the form of a possibility, before its own realization. Hence an error which vitiates our conception of the past; hence our claim to be able to anticipate the future on every occasion. We wonder, for instance, what will be the art, the literature, the civilization of tomorrow; we imagine roughly the evolutionary curve of societies; we go so far as to predict the details of events. No doubt we can always link up the reality, once it has happened, with the events that have preceded it and the circumstances in which it occurred; but a very different reality (not, it is true, just any reality whatever) might as well have been linked up with the same circumstances and the same events, taken from another angle.]

Yet who does not share this illusion, this subconscious belief in what Bergson calls 'la valeur rétrospective du jugement vrai' which, at the moment, appears to saturate Marcel's thoughts? For example, brooding on Albertine's lies, redeemed no doubt by flashes of sincerity as when she refused to swear that the pleasure of seeing Mlle Vinteuil had nothing to do with her desire to go to the Verdurins, Marcel ardently wishes now that she had been consistently and utterly frank. If only she had come to him and said: 'J'ai ces goûts.' Here is a classic example of 'le mirage du présent dans le passé'. For Marcel is projecting his present state of soul on the past, deluding himself that if Albertine had only confessed her guilt, his reaction would have been one of pity and gratitude, forgetting the inevitable

[1] *La pensée et le mouvant*, 15.

alteration since produced in his love by the encroachments of 'l'oubli'.

Perhaps, he thinks, it was his fault that Albertine did not confess. Vaguely he seems to remember her blushing when in the early days of their intimacy he once expressed his horror of Lesbianism. Very probably, Albertine was thus deterred from confessing her own guilty inclinations. Observe, by the way, that it never occurs to him that an outrageous remark of this sort would be liable to embarrass—and that is a mild way of putting it—any *jeune fille*, whether innocent or guilty of the vice in question. However, Albertine is dead and for everyone else, merely a name. Her being, except in her lover's mind, has been submerged by the reality we call death although for him she is so alive that he cannot conceive her death as a reality. To judge from the persistence of his jealous curiosity she might be still in France, in Touraine. Reason, of course, harks back to the case of Gilberte and tells him that jealousy will drift into nothingness. Yet reason is powerless to blunt the sharpness of grief, to quiet his desire for her presence. And desire, he finds, can engender belief, even faith in the immortality of the soul, in spiritualism, in miracles. For Marcel wants an Albertine exactly as she was in life, as he remembered her, though more completely his, explaining away all the enigmas that had tortured him. Since her death appears to his imagination like a sort of dream, he is visited by the hallucinations we have in dreams. Perhaps a letter will come informing him that Albertine was not really killed but only injured; that she had preferred to wait for her complete recovery before asking Marcel to take her back, loving and repentant. Proust reveals in this passage how memory and imagination, intensified until they touch the fringe of madness, combine to subserve the immediate needs of Marcel's emotional state, ransacking the distant past, nay, the Infinite, for anything that will attenuate his spiritual distress.

Thoughts of Aimé, however, produce an inevitable refocusing of Marcel's attention. It is now directed towards what are called 'facts'. The logic of the intelligence is summoned to perform its normal functions, in this case, to pass judgement on an individual by the name of Albertine, a synthetic personality reconstituted from various notations made by her lover at various stages of his sentimental life with this woman. A single little fact, he argues, provided it is properly selected, often helps the experimental scientist to discover a general law and thus to know the truth about thousands of analogous facts. Perhaps Aimé, who has been sent to question the woman in charge of the bathing establishment frequented by Albertine at Balbec, may bring back that illuminating fact which will settle, once for all, Marcel's doubts. Quite so. But one might remind Marcel that the significant fact must not only be carefully selected: it must be really perceived.[1] That is the crux of the matter. Moreover, the experimental psychologist must be absolutely unprejudiced, ready at any moment, in the course of his researches, to abandon his original hypothesis and to remodel it on the evidence of other facts. Marcel thinks he is a dispassionate seeker after the truth. But, as he discovers on receiving Aimé's report, this is an illusion produced by the fact that, deeply rooted in his mind is the idea of an innocent Albertine. Aimé's letter, however, contains an objective fact. Is this the 'petit fait bien choisi'? The bathing attendant asserts that Albertine had many guilty rendezvous with a lady in grey, notorious for her abnormal habits. On the details furnished by Aimé, Marcel's imagination constructs a picture of Balbec which is like a vision of Hell. In retrospect, everything connected with that accursed Gomorrha becomes invested with a new, lurid quality of horror. Even the familiar, peaceful names of little stations on the 'chemin de fer d'intérêt local', Toutainville, Evreville, Incarville are now impregnated with the loathsomeness generated by one little 'fact'. If only Marcel could now send for Albertine and hear from her own lips, read in her frank, kind eyes, the truth grotesquely distorted and transformed into this monstrous lie! But Albertine is dead and he will never learn that truth.

Stored away in memory, however, is an unlimited repertory of recollections which are situated in the wings of the stage

[1] Bergson, *La perception du changement* (1911). 'Les conceptions le plus ingénieusement assemblées et les raisonnements le plus savamment échafaudés, s'écroulent comme des châteaux de cartes le jour où un fait — un seul fait réellement perçu — vient heurter ces conceptions et ces raisonnements.'

known as our consciousness, all eagerly demanding the right to play a part in the drama actually in progress. This, obviously, is what Proust now illustrates when he depicts Marcel suddenly remembering a remark made to his grandmother by Mme de Villeparisis concerning this identical bathing attendant. 'C'est une femme qui doit avoir la maladie du mensonge.' Here, then, is a new fact, an objective fact, clearly better chosen, more reliable than the one reported by Aimé. After all, the woman had seen nothing. Because two friends use the same bathing hut, even if one of them does tip with excessive generosity, why assume that they have had guilty relations? Partly reassured yet still obsessed by a desolating, futile longing for Albertine that makes his heart leap, foolishly, whenever the lift stops outside his door, Marcel decides to send Aimé to Châtellrault, near the villa inhabited by Albertine's aunt, Mme Bontemps. Very swiftly, as if to punish him for his jealous curiosity about the past of a woman now dead, comes positive proof of her guilty relations with a young laundress. The details are too exact to be false: Albertine's very words are remembered and quoted.

Televised by imagination and projected on the screen of Marcel's immediate consciousness is a brilliant fragment of Albertine's mysterious past. The scene is a meadow at sunrise in high summer, on the banks of the Loire, and it reveals a group of beautiful naked girls; some disport themselves, like nymphs, in the river, others recline in graceful attitudes on the sward beneath great, shady trees. To an objective spectator, they represent, of course, the stylization of Marcel's memories of Elstir's paintings and of the classic Leda myth: to him they are the girls described in Aimé's letter. In the centre of the group is Albertine.

All reality is subjective: we only really know through our sensibility. The familiar Proustian conviction assumes, in the pages now before our eyes, a fresh intensity of expression. Marcel's idea of an innocent Albertine is replaced by a new idea, that of a guilty Albertine, of a Lesbian. What is now visible in his memory is this stranger, this woman of an alien race, different from, yet intermingled with the feminine human species. But she is not only different in the ordinary sense of the term, in the sense we give to the word when we say that someone is different from what we thought. And Proust with his genius for interpretation, seizes the opportunity, at this point in Marcel's narrative, to illustrate certain views on the nature of thought and perception which, once again, irresistibly suggest comparison with Bergson. The intuitive approach to life affords a dynamic, integral vision of reality; whilst the scientific attitude of the rationalist confuses fragmentary notations of psychological states with the truly constituent parts of a personality. However, before commenting on this particular analogy I should like to repeat that the existence of such affinities must not be interpreted to the disadvantage of Proust, so as to present him, for example, as a writer whose main achievement was to reproduce the philosophy of Bergson in terms of his particular art, the novel. This would be to ignore the fact that Proust is a great and original artist and that every great artist, as Bergson always insisted, employs the intuitive approach to reality. He also insisted that there is a frontier between art and philosophy. The former no doubt enlarges our perceptions but on the surface rather than in depth. Art certainly enriches our present; yet it is only by cultivating the philosophy of intuition that we shall learn never to isolate the present from its inseparable companion, the past. Personally I am sure that Proust knew and sympathized with the views expressed in Bergson's works. At the same time, because he was a great artist whose novel narrates the vocation of one who finally discovered that his vocation was art, Proust was bound to reveal certain affinities between his own vision of life and the immensely greater vision so brilliantly disclosed by Henri Bergson. It is not surprising, therefore, to discover in the pages of *A la recherche du temps perdu* concrete illustrations of psychological truths enunciated by Bergson. Sometimes, perhaps, they are deliberately introduced, or so it would seem. On the other hand, if one may modernize Boileau's well-known maxim and ruin his alexandrine: 'L'intuition pour marcher n'a souvent qu'une voie.'

We may now return to Marcel and observe the effects of the emotional upheaval produced by Aimé's letter. Here certain phrases, echoing the language of Bergson, suggest that this particular incident might have been designed to illustrate what the latter would have called an intuitive act, an effort of the mind to enter by sympathy into the essence of its object. Of course, I use the word sympathy in its Bergsonian connotation, which includes both what we ordinarily call sympathy and, also, antipathy. Marcel, however, forgets that true intuition is 'l'instinct devenu désintéressé, conscient de lui-même, capable de réfléchir sur son objet et de l'élargir indéfiniment'. In other words, one cannot obtain an intuition of a reality without a preliminary and searching examination of its external aspects. And Marcel can scarcely be called disinterested. He accepts, without question, Aimé's report. For him it contains 'la réalité du vice d'Albertine'. That is why he says she is now different though not just in the way that ordinary people turn out to be different from what we had thought. That kind of difference, says her lover, does not penetrate deeply into one's conscious-ness, 'le pendule de l'intuition ne pouvant projeter hors de lui qu'une oscillation égale à celle qu'il a exécutée dans le sens intérieur, ce n'est que dans les régions superficielles d'eux-mêmes que nous situons ces différences'. Here we have an obvious variant of Bergson's remark: 'Descendons alors à l'intérieur: plus profond sera le point que nous aurons touché, plus forte sera la poussée qui nous renverra à la surface. L'in-tuition philosophique est ce contact, la philosophie est cet élan.'[1] In Marcel's case, as we have seen, there can be no question of true or philosophic intuition: the instinct of a jealous lover can never be 'disinterested, capable of reflecting on its object and of enlarging it indefinitely'. He tells us that, formerly, when he learned that a woman had unnatural sexual proclivities it never occurred to him to think of her as being, on that account, *essentially* different from others of her sex. Now, however, impelled by his torturing jealousy, he is convinced of Albertine's terrible uniqueness.

Je souffrais jusqu'au fond de moi-même, jusque dans mon corps, dans mon cœur — bien plus que ne m'eût fait la peur de perdre la vie — de cette curiosité à laquelle collaboraient toutes les forces de

---

[1] *L'intuition philosophique* (1911), p. 2.

mon intelligence et de mon inconscient: et ainsi c'est dans les profondeurs mêmes d'Albertine que je projetais maintenant tout ce que
j'apprenais d'elle.[1]

Aimé's revelation, especially a certain phrase of Albertine's
remembered by the little laundress strikes down into the regions
of Marcel's fundamental self, resulting in a swift tension and
upheaval of his sentiments and ideas. It is followed by the
outward, indivisible *élan* he has just described, the effort to
penetrate the secret thoughts, sensations and desires, 'l'essence
particulière' of Albertine's nature. No wonder, therefore, if she
now appears totally different, the inhabitant of a strange, remote
and sinister country.

But intuition, false or true, is of brief duration. Very quickly
the mind resumes its habitual attitude to things and if intuition
has laid bare a painful reality, the instinct for self-preservation,
which is the reverse of the 'instinct devenu désintéressé', mentioned by Bergson, performs its usual function. Perhaps this is
what Proust intends to illustrate in portraying the reorientation
of Marcel's attention towards exclusively pleasant memories of
his dead mistress. He thinks now only of the moments when
she was kind or serious, interested in his conversations about
art and literature, schoolgirlishly keen on every kind of sport.
It is this 'fractionnement d'Albertine en de nombreux fragments',
observes Proust, which restored calm to Marcel's agitated soul,
melting his cruel and pitiless rage. Whilst admitting that this
fragmentation does not reflect a reality, it helped to counteract
the appallingly simple idea of a continuously vicious Albertine
by presenting a multiple vision of her character. That the human
mind should normally operate in this way, Proust implies, is
a blessed thing for humanity. By a wise dispensation of nature,
it nearly always happens that, before discovering the ugly truth
about another person we had already formed an earlier, favourable impression. It was false, yet the memory of it frequently
persists, impinging on the new and real perception, especially
if the person concerned is someone we dearly loved. So Marcel
treasures all the little recollections of that different, innocent
Albertine who once lived within him. He begins to visualize also

[1] *AD.* I, 176.

the process by which his suffering will fade into oblivion. Continuity is the principle of all life. If he can break that continuity by enlarging the intervals between his thoughts of Albertine, will not these thoughts eventually die of inanition? Albertine is dead, and his memory, after all, reflects but the afterglow of his love. Whilst it is true that memory has a trick of suddenly reviving after a certain lapse of time, surely, however, it is governed by the principle of all life, by the laws of continuity, of eternal change. Was it not thus that Marcel grew to forget even his beloved grandmother and to think of her with indifference, though hating himself for his betrayal?

As Proust traces with admirable subtlety the process by which Marcel's grief slowly passes into a state of indifference, we are immediately reminded of his image of the 'armée compacte' and, naturally, of Bergson. The painful memories composing his grief slip back into the unconscious, permitting the happy ones to move to the head of that thrusting queue, milling their way forward into Marcel's immediate consciousness. Proust, it will be observed, felt that forgetting, 'l'oubli', would come from repeated breaks in the 'armée compacte' in the continuity of his memory. This view would not be disputed by Bergson though he would make the important reservation that we can only really see life as it is by seeing it as continuity, as indivisible change in which past and present are always interfused. On the other hand, he agrees that it is natural and indeed necessary for humanity to obtain the other fragmented vision mentioned by Proust. 'Rien de plus naturel, je le répète:' we read in *La perception du changement*, 'le morcelage du changement en états nous met à même d'agir sur les choses, et il est pratiquement utile de s'intéresser aux états plutôt qu'au changement lui-même. Mais ce qui favorise ici l'action serait mortel à la spéculation.' In other words, the average man has to live in society. His consciousness, therefore, is normally directed towards the immediate future, so that the part of our consciousness we call our 'present' tends as we grow older to change its quality and to let slip back into the unconscious all but the memories of immediate interest. In dreams, however, and also sometimes in the waking state, these repressed memories are always liable to house themselves in our actual sense-impressions. The difference is that in dreams the memory never completely fits the sensation whilst in consciousness there must be an absolute coincidence of memory and sensation.

Let us now observe in Marcel's narrative how ingeniously Proust illustrates this mechanism of memory and perception. Occasionally, says Marcel, his grief assumes unrecognizable forms. For example, when he longs for a great love, for marriage, or wishes he had a sister, he thinks that he no longer misses Albertine, whereas these are merely camouflaged unconscious forms of his grief. Similarly, when he imagines himself to be jealous of Andrée, the latter is simply a disguise for Albertine. In dreams, as he points out, after Bergson, we frequently give another face or name to a person whose individuality, however, we know perfectly well. In short, unconscious memories of Albertine constantly interfuse with his actual perceptions and ideas. This is simply another way of expressing Bergson's view that if we want to form an idea of the interpenetration of our concepts in the waking state we have only to note how, in dreams, two images will superimpose themselves on each other, presenting simultaneously one and two different persons. In this context Bergson, enunciating his well-known theory, employs a simile which probably inspired the passage in *Albertine disparue* where Marcel speaks of his 'bipartite self' the upper part of which is already hard and chilled though the base is intermittently traversed by a live current of sensibility. Bergson, it will be recalled, says that in our conscious state all our memories form at a given moment a solid unity, a pyramid as it were, whose apex coincides with our present which is ceaselessly plunging forward into the future. Although only the memories which interest our actual preoccupations are admitted by the brain there are images retained by the subconscious memory, not dormant but very alert, waiting for the first opportunity to insert themselves into the apex of the pyramid. Such is surely the process that Proust is trying to interpret. The present cadre of Marcel's consciousness no longer holds the hallucinatory idea of a still living Albertine but of a woman who is really dead. Tremors of emotion,

THE MIND OF PROUST

however, persist in the deeply situated mass of his unconscious. That appears to be the significance of the beautiful passage where Marcel confesses that long after Albertine's image has faded from his mind, a chance sensation, a cold breeze, for instance, like the wind that ruffled the apple-blossom at Balbec is enough to make his heart beat faster and flood his soul with desolation.

Proust, in common with Bergson, has the gift of being able to see the movements of his own mind in almost physical concreteness. Moreover, as a novelist, he has the benefit of a privilege denied to the philosopher. A confirmed invalid, he took a rather pathetic interest in medicine and was familiar with the symptoms of most diseases. His novel, therefore, reveals him constantly on the watch for analogies between the behaviour of the mind and of the body. Marcel, for example, now compares the suffering caused by Aimé's revelation to one of those 'secondary accidents' which a patient is apt to confuse with the malady itself. 'Mais, un médecin de l'âme', he observes with a touch of *marivaudage*, 'eût trouvé que pour le reste, mon chagrin lui-même allait mieux.' Such analogies though ingenious, are dangerous. They are based on the assumption, which may not be valid, that the operations of a sane mind can be legitimately compared to those of a diseased body. What Marcel wants to say is that despite the temporary shock produced by Aimé's letter, he was already far advanced towards a state of indifference as to Albertine's past guilt or innocence. To compare the effect of this emotional upheaval to a 'secondary accident' is to explain nothing, but merely to note a fact. It throws no light on the problem of 'l'oubli', of how such painful memories are gradually thrust out of our minds into the subconscious, without, however, being thereby definitively abolished, or forgotten. They are liable to return to us in sleep or in what Marcel calls his 'inconscientes songeries'. But now, dominated by the idea that Albertine is really dead, he is able to think of her with an increasing detachment. What now surprises him is not, as formerly, that being such a living creature for him she could possibly be dead, but that being dead, she can still be alive in him. In a striking metaphor,

Proust communicates this new quality in Marcel's sentiments, this dawning hope of imminent spiritual harmony.

Maçonné par la contiguité des souvenirs qui se suivent l'un l'autre, le noir tunnel, sous lequel ma pensée revâssait depuis trop longtemps pour qu'elle prît même plus garde à lui, s'interrompait brusquement d'un intervalle de soleil, laissant voir au loin un univers souriant et bleu où Albertine n'était plus qu'un souvenir indifférent et plein de charme. Est-ce celle-là, me disais-je, qui est la vraie, ou bien l'être qui, dans l'obscurité où je roulais depuis si longtemps, me semblait la seule réalité? Le personnage que j'avais été il y a si peu de temps encore et qui ni vivait que dans la perpétuelle attente du moment où Albertine viendrait me dire bonsoir et m'embrasser, une sorte de multiplication de moi-même me faisait paraître ce personnage comme n'étant plus qu'une faible partie, à demi dépouillée de moi, j'éprouvais la fraîcheur rajeunissante d'une exfoliation.[1]

[Solidly held together by the contiguity of the memories that followed one another, the black tunnel beneath which my thought had lain too long a-dreaming to be any longer conscious of it, was abruptly broken by an interval of sunlight, revealing in the distance a blue and smiling universe where Albertine was now merely an insignificant and wholly charming memory. Is that, I asked myself, the true one or is it the creature who, in the darkness through which I had so long been travelling, used to seem to me the one reality? The person I had been so short a time ago, who was kept alive only by the expectation of the moment when Albertine would come in to say good night and kiss him, a sort of multiplication of myself presented this person to me as no longer anything more than a feeble part, already half-detached from myself and, like a flower unfolding its petals, I experienced the rejuvenating freshness of an exfoliation.]

True, such 'brief illuminations', Proust is careful to note, perhaps serve to preserve the memory of Marcel's love, a view he illustrates by an interesting analogy. Frenchmen who went through the 1870 war often said that the idea of war had become so natural because it was always in their consciousness, that only when wrenched out of this habitual obsession by something which made them forget the war did they realize in its full horror the experience in which they were actually plunged. The passage from suffering to forgetting reveals how memories ebb out of the conscious into the unconscious, that

[1] *AD.* I, 189.

is to say not simultaneously but in a spasmodic irregular fashion so that as Proust acutely observes, Marcel was often stung by remembrances of Albertine's betrayals when the image of the other innocent Albertine was already too remote to be recalled in time to bring him consolation. He learns in such moments to accept the idea of Albertine's guilt, however intensely it hurts, because, as he finally realizes, in order to be cured of suffering one must experience it fully and completely. All he had done by cherishing the illusion of her innocence was to postpone the hour of his deliverance from grief. Habit will perform its magic work of transformation. Meanwhile, unused to this new idea of Albertine's certain guilt, Marcel is at the mercy of his ebbing memories, which often capriciously reverse their course, in response to a chance sensation, bringing with them a temporary revival of jealous love. A name accidentally encountered, even a syllable common to two different names, is enough sometimes to establish contact between his heart and Albertine, thus, says Marcel, half reopening the door of a past which literally he no longer possessed since he had ceased to give it his attention.

Those who know Bergson's famous lecture on Dreams given at the Institut psychologique in 1901 will appreciate in this part of Marcel's narrative how brilliantly Proust has embroidered upon that philosopher's illuminating remarks on the mechanism of true perception. Marcel's experience with names is a typical example. Bergson, it will be remembered, describes what happens in the case of a man whose mind is preoccupied at the moment he glances at a newspaper. Suddenly his attention is arrested by a word that responds exactly to his preoccupation. But, on closer scrutiny, the whole sentence turns out to have no special meaning: the word he read is not the word printed in the paper. It had merely a vague resemblance, some features in common. What has occurred, explains Bergson, is that the idea preoccupying the reader aroused, in his unconscious, all the recollections of corresponding words, all the images of the same family, giving them a hope of returning to consciousness. These are memories trying to encase themselves in an impression or sensation, seeking integral realization. Marcel expresses the same idea when he tells us how certain words or names ' suffisaient

pour incarner une jalousie virtuelle, inexistante, à la recherche
d'un corps, d'une demeure, de quelque fixation matérielle, de
quelque réalisation particulière'.[1] In the second volume of
Albertine disparue Proust returns to this subject and out of Marcel's
incomplete perceptions creates a most interesting episode.

Proust, who had certainly read Bergson's profoundly suggestive remarks on the mechanism and nature of dreaming, had,
moreover, undoubtedly studied the functioning of his own mind
in sleep and on emerging from slumber. Quite naturally, therefore, he devotes some attention to the narrative of Marcel's
dreams. His object, probably, is to accentuate the role played
by the unconscious in the latter's transition from 'le chagrin'
towards 'l'oubli'. Dreams, as a rule, says Bergson, create
nothing. Such is Marcel's experience in his dream conversations
with Albertine who, somehow, always just fails to supply the
vital information which would explain away the incidents mentioned in Aimé's letters. Or perhaps, because of that sleep-
disinterestedness which according to Bergson is the essential
difference between the dream and the waking self, Marcel keeps
on postponing his interrogation, especially since Albertine has
assured him that she was not doing anything wrong in kissing
Mlle Vinteuil. Meanwhile, with the same astonishing detachment, Marcel observes his grandmother silently moving to and
fro at the back of the room, noting with vague interest that the
lower part of her face is crumbling into fragments. Bergson
and Proust are interested in dreams for the same reason; the
analogy between the operations accomplished by the mind in
waking and in sleep, except that the conscious mind is in a state
of tension. Proust, however, seems to go farther than Bergson
when he writes:

D'ailleurs, dans l'histoire d'un amour et de ses luttes contre l'oubli,
le rêve ne tient-il pas une place plus grande même que la veille, lui qui
ne tient pas compte des divisions infinitésimales du temps, supprime
les transitions, oppose les grands contrastes, défait en un instant le
travail de consolation si lentement tissé pendant le jour et nous ménage,
la nuit, une rencontre avec celle que nous aurions fini par oublier à
condition toutefois de ne pas la revoir?[2]

[1] *AD.* i, 195.   [2] *AD.* i, 196.

It is of course impossible to reject a conclusion which emerges logically from the evidence just supplied by Marcel concerning his own dreams. But Proust obviously expects us to accept his theory as a general law and that is something quite different, because a novelist is always in the happy situation of being able to invent the premises from which his conclusions are induced. All one can say, therefore, is that Marcel's narrative illustrates vividly and plausibly the immense dilatation of the memory which is peculiar to the dream-state with its characteristic panorama of kaleidoscopic images, of sensations normally excluded from the consciousness in its waking condition. It is for the professional psychologist to judge of the accuracy of the novelist's interpretation.

These dreams, however, lend a hallucinatory quality to Marcel's waking state so that in the daytime he sometimes finds himself involved in long, silent conversations with Albertine only to discover with a start that his anxious questions are addressed to a non-existent being. Turning for relief to one of Bergotte's novels, he experiences in regard to these creatures of fiction sentiments just as profound as those aroused by his communion with his dead mistress. It appears, therefore, that the intensity of his emotions is absolutely no guarantee that the personality of Albertine is real or eternal. The novel he has just thrown aside pictures a man, who after a lapse of years sees once again the woman he had passionately loved yet now fails to recognize. And Marcel is overwhelmed by the idea that some day, he will have completely forgotten Albertine. But this seems quite incredible when, merely by looking at a map of France, at certain names such as Tours or Balbec or Doncières, he can experience, in turn, profound happiness and intolerable sorrow. Our memories, he says, become, after a certain age, so inextricably entangled and there is so much of ourselves in the objects of our external world that almost anything with which we come into contact may be a fertile source of danger to our peace of soul. On the other hand, such chance encounters, Marcel implies, may be of inestimable value to our self-knowledge. So at least one may interpret the following passage: 'on peut faire d'aussi précieuses découvertes que dans les

Pensées de Pascal dans une réclame pour le savon.' The inference which I draw from these words and from the paragraph that follows is that a chance perception, in this case of a book or an advertisement, may release an involuntary recollection and thus launch the mind on a voyage of introspection which may carry it down below the superficial film composed of impressions made by the objects of an external world towards a vision of its own inner life, towards an intuition of itself as seen in real time—or to borrow a Bergsonian expression, *sub specie durationis*.

As it happens, we now encounter, once again, Proust's favourite obsession—the importance and peculiar validity of the involuntary memory as a guide to the reality of our past. Marcel, led by a chain of apparently unconnected images stumbles on the name Buttes-Chaumont, which causes him an unaccountable stab of pain until he connects it with one of Albertine's many lies. Even then, why should this fact penetrate more deeply into his sensibility than for instance the much graver facts mentioned in Aimé's letter? Proust argues that an involuntary memory carries this greater power of conviction precisely because it is involuntary, thus, so to speak, catching our imagination off its guard with all its powers intact. It produces, in consequence, more intense suffering. On the contrary, when we set out deliberately to seek a certain memory our power of imagining is partly used up before the particular recollection is encountered. Besides, the memories evoked by Aimé's letter have now been long exposed to the devitalizing influence of Habit, whereas it is years since Marcel thought of Buttes-Chaumont. But observe the miracle wrought by involuntary memory.

Soulevant un coin du voile lourd de l'habitude (l'habitude abêtissante qui pendant tout le cours de notre vie nous cache à peu près tout l'univers, et dans une nuit profonde, sous leur étiquette inchangée, substitue aux poisons les plus dangereux ou les plus enivrants de la vie, quelque chose d'anodin qui ne procure pas de délices), un tel souvenir me revenait comme au premier jour avec cette fraîche et perçante nouveauté d'une saison reparaissante, d'un changement dans la routine de nos heures, qui, dans le domaine des plaisirs aussi, si nous montons en voiture par un premier beau jour de printemps, ou sortons de chez nous au lever du soleil, nous font remarquer nos actions insignifiantes avec une exaltation lucide qui fait prévaloir cette intense minute sur le total des jours antérieurs.[1]

Something in this exquisite passage sets a tiny bell chiming in the memory. It is of course a Proustian rearrangement, but with variations, of Bergson's charming passage in *Le rire*: 'entre nous et notre propre conscience un voile s'interpose, voile épais pour le commun des hommes, voile léger, presque transparent, pour l'artiste et le poète. Quelle fée a tissé ce voile?' For Proust and Bergson both it is the veil woven by Habit: in the eyes of the former, however, not a fairy but a stupid old crone. Proust's fairy is the involuntary memory, at one wave of whose wand the ugly, heavy veil disappears. Bergson, on the other hand, attributes this miracle to the genius of art, to the superior perceptiveness of the artistic mind. We need not take Proust too literally. It is clear from the subsequent pages where Marcel reveals what lies behind the veil, that whilst the immediate cause of this splendid revelation may be an involuntary memory, its adequate cause, to employ a term borrowed from metaphysics, is the genius of the artist.

The reappearance of Andrée marks the closing phase of the psychological process interpreted by Proust in the chapter entitled 'Le chagrin et l'oubli'. Andrée's chief interest for Marcel is that she now seems to incarnate Albertine's mysterious and unholy desires. His interrogations, therefore, display the technique he used to employ with Albertine, the same air of casual indifference suggesting the manner of the *juge d'instruction* who feigns a knowledge he does not possess in order to trap the unwary and elicit the decisive and damning admission. But the significant fact still remains unaltered. Marcel is not a disinterested, professional investigator and so, for all his carefulness, betrays something of his eager anxiety. Andrée makes no attempt to conceal her own abnormal tastes yet firmly denies that they were ever shared by her dead friend who, she maintains, detested such practices. Is Andrée, however, telling the truth? Marcel, knowing she is on her guard, thinks she is probably lying, though her assurances calm his troubled heart,

[1] *AD.* I, 204–5.

against his better judgement. Through other women he tries to establish some contact with the milieus probably frequented by Albertine before he met her at Balbec. From none does he derive any real pleasure, yet somehow, just as in Combray his walks out Méséglise way or in the direction of Guermantes had formed his preferences for a special type of scenery with old churches and fields gay with cornflowers and buttercups, he realizes that, if he now prefers the society of a certain type of woman, it is because there is a 'côté d'Albertine' in his senti-mental life. But she herself is irreplaceable: experience confirms his original intuition of her uniqueness.

In these closing pages where Marcel gives us his final reflections on the theme of the transition from 'le chagrin' to 'l'oubli' the narrative acquires an elliptical character which, I believe, is due to the fact that Proust, at this point, is very largely engaged in echoing Bergson's now familiar views on the psychology of memory and on duration. Not altogether, how-ever, since as we shall see, he diverges from Bergsonism in regard to the role of *l'oubli* or forgetting in our spiritual life. Let us, therefore, try to sum up very briefly the results of Marcel's final survey of his recent ordeal, his transition from 'le chagrin' to 'l'oubli'. In seeking the company of women who recall 'le côté d'Albertine' he finds only disillusionment, for each new fleeting desire is but the revival of his memory of Albertine. He is trying, unconsciously, to re-live, in the sensa-tions experienced with these newcomers, the time, the past which belonged to his life with Albertine. But this past exists only in what Marcel calls 'l'imbrication contingente et indis-soluble de mes souvenirs'. His love for Albertine is composed of a tissue of such memories, memories of intimate contacts peculiar to him and to his dead mistress in which, of course, other women can have no place. So the latter merely accentuate his longing for Albertine because memory, he concludes, is not inventive and cannot desire anything different from what we have possessed. Moreover, it is spiritual, of the mind, and cannot, therefore, find in reality—he means in the immediate zone of his consciousness—the state in which it would like to house itself.

Proust's meaning becomes less obscure if we replace these thoughts in their original Bergsonian context. In *Ame et Matière*, but more precisely in an article dealing with the theme of false recognition[1] or memory of the present, Bergson describes the causes of an illusion which strongly resembles that now discovered by Marcel. Defining 'perception' as the consciousness of anything that is present whether it be an external or internal object, he shows that the formation of a memory never comes after the formation of a perception; it is contemporaneous with it. But as we are not normally conscious of this simultaneous process by which our existence is continuously splitting up into perception and memory, into the actual and virtual, we wrongly suppose that the memory succeeds the perception, that the memory of a perception is identical in nature if not in intensity with the perception itself. The reason for this, Bergson explains, is that the reanimated or conscious memory has the curious, almost hypnotic power of producing what appears to be a resurrection of the original perception or sensation. We think, therefore, that the recollection is only the sensation itself in a weaker degree; that it grows stronger, however, the more we fix our attention upon it. This, Bergson insists, is an illusion, for the recollection is distinct from the sensation which it suggests. It is because we feel the suggestive power of memory that we localize the cause of the suggested sensation in the past. In fact, however, perception or sensation is always actual or present, though memory, as Proust has noted also, is always looking for a present or actual state in which to house or actualize itself. A memory possesses, says Bergson, that power *sui generis* of things that no longer exist but would like to exist again. Is not this what Proust has been trying to picture in Marcel's efforts to fit into the sensations aroused by these women who resemble Albertine, the memories of emotions once aroused by his innumerable perceptions of his dead mistress? His memories of Albertine, as is the way of all recollections, want to realize themselves in sensations: his actual sensations, on the other hand, seek to achieve the form of a memory. This process, Bergson tells us, operates without hindrance only in

[1] *Revue philosophique* (December 1908).

sleep. It is checked in our waking state by the fact that our normal attitude to life is one of attention, of tension, of a continual exact adjustment of memory to sensation. Such is precisely the function of the brain, which sees to it that memories are fitted only into the appropriate sensations; choosing only those which practically interest our immediate or future situation and will illuminate it. In ordinary remembering, then, the mass of memories composing the totality of our past is, most unfortunately for us, contracted into a very small zone of our consciousness. As a result, our mind tends, naturally, to represent our whole inner life as modelled on this very small part of our self which is inserted into present reality: the part of our self that perceives this reality and acts upon it. Now, if we survey Marcel's narrative it will be found to reflect not only this narrowing of the consciousness, but the picture of a mind in varying stages of tension and relaxation or distraction, for example, in dreams or in the 'inconscientes songeries' of Marcel's waking state.

I likened the spectacle presented in this section of *Albertine disparue* to a ballet of memory-images: it is also a ballet with music. The various figures or patterns increase in complexity with the altering rhythms of the interpretative memory. For Marcel, as we have seen, surveys his past from many changing sites of the self, from different states of soul. Sometimes he is obsessed by the idea of a guilty, sometimes of an innocent Albertine. Or again, having finally accepted the idea of her death, indifferent to her guilt or innocence, he simply longs for her presence. But whatever his actual psychological state, the past, he discovers, will always obligingly produce from its inexhaustible store, the recollections capable of fitting into the moving frame of his changing consciousness. The past itself, however, even that fragment representing his life with Albertine, will always elude the grasp of his inquisitive and eager intelligence. For the unaided intelligence cannot seize the reality of a past continuously flowing into and forming one with an advancing present. Marcel recognizes this truth when he tries to explain the extraordinary persistence of his grief and jealousy which, of course, must always seem permanent so long

as they are viewed as 'états immobiles' in an existence divided
into fractions called 'past', 'present' and 'future', that is to
say, in an existence where time is identified with space. This
'psychologie plane', Marcel admits, cannot interpret the reality
of life which is indivisible change, Bergsonian *durée*. Marcel
calls it 'un système plus vaste où les âmes se meuvent dans le
temps comme les corps dans l'espace'. His words have a
familiar ring. Turn to *Ame et matière* and you will find this
passage: 'elle [l'intelligence] est découpée dans quelque chose
de plus vaste ou plutôt elle n'est que la projection plane d'une
realité qui a relief et profondeur'. The intelligence, therefore,
can never give us more than a fragmentary view of the evolution
of life because the intelligence itself, in its career, is fashioned
by that evolution. The intelligence, says Bergson, always places
itself outside Time and is itself merely the flat projection of
a reality which has depth and relief. It employs what Proust
calls a 'plane psychology' and cannot, obviously, explain the
true life of the human soul. Aided, however, by intuition the
intelligence can sometimes catch a fugitive vision of the intrinsic spontaneity and change, the vital rhythm of our thoughts
and emotions before they are immobilized in words or in action.
Of this, it seems, Marcel now has some inkling: he has a brief
vision of existence in duration, as part of an evolution where
everything is indivisible change, where every living creature is,
to quote Bergson, 'surtout un lieu de passage'. But Proust, at
this point, parts company with Bergsonism. For Marcel tells us
that forgetting, 'l'oubli', destroys the surviving past, 'l'oubli
dont je commençais à sentir la force et qui est un si puissant
instrument d'adaptation à la réalité parce qu'il détruit peu a peu
en nous le passé survivant qui est en constante contradiction
avec elle'.[1] Now Bergson maintains, on the contrary, that
reality is change; change is indivisible and in indivisible change
the past is incorporated in the present.[2] For him this is axio-
matic. The past only seems to be abolished; it always exists
subconsciously. To have the revelation of it, however, our
consciousness must remove a veil, an obstacle which is the
habitual forward orientation of our mind whose life is essentially

[1] *AD.* i, 224.   [2] *La perception du changement*, p. 196.

concentration on action. It is interesting that Proust should close this narrative of Marcel's search for his past with Albertine on a very orthodox and un-Bergsonian sentiment.

The volume ends, however, on this note. Marcel is convinced that since his love was largely subjective, a state of mind having no real link with Albertine, no support outside itself, it is bound to be replaced like every 'état mental' and to become extinct. The day is, therefore, at hand when he will hand over Albertine's room to the first newcomer just as once, without the slightest pangs, he gave Albertine the precious agate marble, Gilberte's present, which formerly seemed to materialize his now vanished adolescent love. But is it really so easy, I wonder, to destroy the past?

Marcel's theory rests on a fallacious conception of what he calls 'un état mental'. Quite rightly he recognizes that every state of soul, however simple, is continuously changing, yet supposes wrongly that in the process certain of its constitutive elements or memories pass into nothingness. His error lies in viewing his inner life merely through the intelligence, that convenient but unreliable instrument which sees existence, in space-time, as a succession of individual and separate states of consciousness. If that were reality, then of course Marcel would be right in saying that every 'état mental' is replaced and obliterated by a new one. Life, however, does not evolve in this way, as experience ought to have taught Marcel. If a state of soul is a process of continuous change it is precisely because there is no consciousness without memory and the continuity of a state of soul necessarily implies the addition to an actual sentiment of the memory of past moments. That, as Bergson tells us, is *la durée intérieure* which he further defines as the continuous life of a Memory which prolongs the past in the present. And, he observes, as we grow older, our present consciousness bears witness by its continual change of quality to the ever increasing load which it drags behind it. The past, however, always survives in the present though, happily for us, our mind possesses an excellent mechanism for regulating the inflow of memories into the present zone of its consciousness.

Chapter IX

ALBERTINE DISPARUE (continued)

THE second chapter of *Albertine disparue* is entitled ' Mademoi-selle de Forcheville' because it reintroduces Marcel's first love, Gilberte Swann, who has now adopted her stepfather's name. However, before narrating the curious and amusing incident that brings Gilberte once again into Marcel's life, Proust traces, in a few pages of delicately spun prose, the ultimate phase of Marcel's love for Albertine.

Unconsciously inspired no doubt by recollections of Balbec, Marcel compares his intermittent excursions into the past, to a journey in reverse along a once familiar railway line where, lingering at certain stations, he experiences the odd sensation of setting out for the first time for a destination which, however, lies now in the past and not in the future. Thus, rereading one of Albertine's letters arranging a rendezvous for the evening, Marcel is transported with all the force of an hallucination into the state of soul of joyous expectation and impatience of that vanished summer's day. Such, he remarks, is the cruelty of memory. But, in general, his memories of Albertine are no longer painful: all are now tinged with a pleasant, wistful melancholy. Alchemized by indifference, his reminiscences, far from evoking sadness, have acquired a kind of historical value. For instance, as Marcel walks on a fine October morning through the Bois, he recalls, indeed, the sadness of that afternoon when Albertine went to the matinée at the Trocadéro. But it is a sadness blended with pleasure for, as he explains, the fact that what he remembers has now no reality, although it communicates a quality of melancholy to the present afternoon yet invests it with a certain beauty and individuality. In the same way, when he finds himself humming the little phrase from Vinteuil's sonata and recalls one of the reflections Albertine used to make as she played this passage, there is no real emotion in the words: 'Pauvre petite!' that rise to his lips. What interests him is the recurrent emergence of the little phrase in the sonata—or its 'devenir' to quote the Bergsonian epithet borrowed by Marcel who sees in the evolution of the 'phrase de Vinteuil', the pattern traced by his own love for Albertine.

Et maintenant sachant combien chaque jour un élément de plus de mon amour s'en allait, le côté jalousie, puis tel autre, revenant en somme peu à peu dans un vague souvenir à la faible amorce du début, c'était mon amour qu'il me semblait, en la petite phrase éparpillée, voir se désagréger devant moi.[1]

However, the most tangible proof that Marcel's love for Albertine is now dead comes from his reawakened interest in other women. One day, entering his own apartment he sees three girls leaving the residence of Mme de Guermantes. One of them, a slender blonde, glances at him, passes on and then looks back. Marcel, inflamed with the ardent desire to see her again, discovers from the concierge that she is called d'Eporcheville. In a flash he remembers what Saint-Loup once told him about a girl of his own set, belonging to an excellent Faubourg Saint-Germain family who frequented, however, a certain *maison de passe*. This, of course, explains the provocative backward glance. Marcel at once dispatches a telegram to Robert who is in Tunisia, in order to confirm the name and obtain an exact description of this exciting young woman. And on learning from the concierge that she is to call again shortly on Mme de Guermantes, he resolves to be there arrayed in resplendent garments. At home, there is a violent scene when his father proposes that Marcel should accompany him on a trip which would entail a two days' absence from Paris and wreck his romance. Finally, after a night of pleasurable insomnia, Marcel receives Saint-Loup's telegram. The anti-climax is complete. The name of the adventurous young society woman is De l'Orgeville and she is in Switzerland. Proust, as we have already noted, has a malicious penchant for situations based on hasty and inaccurate perceptions because they illustrate the unreliability of our normal mode of observation, of our habitual impressions of life. Of this, he will shortly offer us an even more striking example.

[1] *AD.* II, 10.

Yet life has a kindly way of compensating us for the loss of expected pleasures by the sudden largesse of totally unexpected joys. Glancing at the morning's *Figaro*, Marcel catches sight of an article with the very title of one he had submitted months before. What is doubly tiresome is that some of the phrases are identical with his own. It is, in fact, Marcel's article, long and vainly awaited until all hope of its acceptance was finally renounced. I know of nothing more charmingly natural than the impressions which Proust now gives us of a young author who sees himself for the first time in print and, with alternating emotions of reassurance and despair, surveys his own work now from the multiple viewpoints of his invisible readers, now from the solitary and bleaker site of his private judgement. Here Proust, the brilliant and fêted creator of *A la recherche du temps perdu* resuscitates the unknown and diffident author of *Les Plaisirs et les Jours* smiling ruefully at the naïve optimism of the Marcel who believes that his own thought is transmitted intact and directly through the medium of the printed word to the mind of his reader. In reality, however, the value of beauty of a literary essay lies in the ensemble of all the different impressions which it leaves on its various readers not one of whom will bring to his reading a mind undistracted by other preoccupations, tastes and prejudices.

'Et c'est la tare originelle de ce genre de litterature', concludes the older and wiser Proust,

dont ne sont pas exceptés les célèbres *Lundis* que leur valeur réside dans l'impression qu'elle produit sur ses lecteurs. C'est une Vénus collective, dont on n'a qu'un membre mutilé si l'on s'en tient à la pensée de l'auteur, car elle ne se réalise complète que dans l'esprit de ses lecteurs. En eux, elle s'achève. Et comme une foule, fût-elle une élite, n'est pas artiste, ce cachet dernier qu'elle lui donne garde toujours quelque chose d'un peu common.[1]

However, young Marcel has not yet attained this mood of critical and gloomy sagacity. True, when he regards his article with the severe and disillusioned eye of the author, its shortcomings are painfully visible. No one better knows the gulf that separates the ideal visions which haunted his mind and their

[1] *AD.* ii, 26.

woefully inadequate expression in these repellent printed sentences. But when Marcel resolutely places himself at the viewpoint of his potential readers he discovers excellent reasons for
confidence and hope. After all, there is something here for every
palate. The image whose charm is unperceived by Bloch will
delight M. de Guermantes, whilst Legrandin will certainly
appreciate the profundity of a phrase that will have no meaning
for the duke. Reviewing the list of his many friends, anxious to
learn their impressions, to hear their praises, Marcel convinces
himself that nothing could be more delightful than to reappear
in society in his new role, a contributor to *Le Figaro*. Marcel the
artist, on the other hand, knows very well that the admiration
of society is of little or no importance. What really matters is
the pleasure derived from the practice of art, above all, from the
dawning confidence in his own talent.

When Marcel, after a long absence, now revisits the Guermantes, it is really to find out what the duchess thinks of his
Figaro article, and not to make the acquaintance of Mlle
d'Eporcheville who turns out, indeed, to be Gilberte Swann or,
as she is now known, Mlle de Forcheville. Here, notes Marcel,
is but one more example of how difficult it is for the average
individual to perceive the reality of life. Embroidering on one
of Bergson's favourite themes he remarks: 'Nous n'avons de
l'univers que des visions informes, fragmentées et que nous
complétons par des associations d'idées arbitraires, créatrices
de dangereuses suggestions.'[1] We think wrongly that things
present themselves as they really are but our ordinary perceptibility is so inaccurate that we rarely see names as they are
actually written or people as they really are. So the tall blonde
whom Marcel nearly accosted outside the Guermantes is the
Mlle de Forcheville who now has to remind him of their childhood
romance in the Champs Elysées.

Marcel's impressions of the Faubourg Saint-Germain, after
his long eclipse, are strongly tinctured with cynicism and contempt. The spirit of La Rochefoucauld hovers over the pages
describing Gilberte's final and successful efforts to break into
Guermantes' society, which she owes in the last resort to Oriane's

[1] *AD.* ii, 33.

curiosity. Marcel, listening to the conversations between Gilberte, now an arrant snob, and her father's lifelong friends, experiences mingled sentiments of disgust and sardonic amusement. For if Gilberte is obviously ashamed of her bourgeois and Jewish origins, the Guermantes maintain the insufferable pretence that Swann, who for twenty-five years had been a daily visitor, was just a casual acquaintance but a good fellow whom they remember very well indeed. Listen to the duchess replying to Gilberte's timid allusion to Swann's relations with the Guermantes:

'Je sais très bien qui c'était, je vais vous dire,' ajouta-t-elle, comme si elle avait voulu expliquer à la fille qui elle avait eu pour père et donner à cette jeune fille des renseignements sur lui, 'c'était un grand ami à ma belle-mère et aussi il était très lié avec mon beau-frère Palamède.' 'Il venait aussi ici, il déjeunait même ici,' ajouta M. de Guermantes par ostentation de modestie et scrupule d'exactitude. 'Vous vous rappelez, Oriane. Quel brave homme que votre père. Comme on sentait qu'il devait être d'une famille honnête, du reste j'ai aperçu autrefois son père et sa mère. Eux et lui, quelles bonnes gens!'[1]

As Marcel acidly comments, one feels that if Swann and his parents had been alive, the duke would not have hesitated to recommend them for jobs as gardeners on a friend's estate. With some bitterness he remembers Charles Swann's dearest wish, never granted in his lifetime, that his daughter might be received by Oriane and Basin. And now Gilberte blushes with mortification if anyone asks her father's name, deliberately mispronouncing it even, so as to deceive the curious and tiresome inquirer. Into Marcel's mind there comes the distressing image of Swann drawing his little daughter close to him and saying: 'C'est bon, ma chérie, d'avoir une fille comme toi, un jour que je ne serai plus là, si on parle encore de ton pauvre papa, ce sera seulement avec toi et à cause de toi.' Now, on the contrary, it is precisely because Gilberte is Swann's daughter that his name is seldom mentioned in the Guermantes' *salon*. Death and forgetfulness have almost completed their inevitable task.

[1] *AD.* ii, 43–4.

Not only in the case of Swann, however, for Albertine has also begun to fade from Marcel's sentimental life and with her memory his suffering also begins to disappear. What is now being created in him is a new self, one of those 'spare selves' as Proust puts it, which destiny mercifully holds in reserve for us when life has dealt one of its shattering blows. No doubt this new self occasionally remembers the old one and respects its tears. But nothing can arrest the forward movement and re-creation which are of life's very essence. So gradually, Marcel discovers himself talking in the language of conventional grief about the loss of Albertine, sure sign that the memory of her death is but the shadow of a reality because he no longer feels the pangs of suffering. This is Marcel's state of soul when Andrée suddenly, one afternoon, reveals an aspect of Albertine totally at variance with the impressions she had communicated only six months before. We need not dwell upon the details of this startling picture except to note that it is even more horrible than anything ever imagined by Marcel and discloses, moreover, a long and vicious complicity between Albertine and Morel. From Andrée's story, Marcel gathers that his mistress was not only addicted to unnatural and criminal sexual practices but that her malady had assumed a pathological form so that most probably her death was due not to an accident but to suicide. Albertine, says her friend, lived in daily terror that Marcel would discover her vice which she was powerless to resist although every fresh lapse cost her the most terrible remorse.

Andrée's revelations leave Marcel strangely unmoved. Time and oblivion, he says, have robbed her words of their toxic effect. At most he feels a certain surprise that the truth he had so long dreaded and so long pursued should now emerge, casually, in the flow of an ordinary conversation. Somehow it ought to have been manifested in a special way, not just in the words of everyday social commerce. After all, what proof has Marcel that Andrée is not lying? And he remembers her absurd, slanderous attack on Octave, the wealthy young idler at Balbec whom she would have liked to marry. Certainly, thinks Marcel, one cannot ignore this hysterical streak in Andrée's character, as indeed is proved by subsequent events since in fact she eventually does marry Octave who becomes, incidentally, one of the most brilliant and original scenic artists of his generation.

Other surprises await Marcel. He learns that the chief reason for Albertine's departure was her respect for convention, for the opinion of her girl friends who thought it shocking that she should live under the same roof as a young bachelor even if they were engaged. In a second interview with Andrée, Marcel discovers another motive for Albertine's sudden disappearance and for the strange behaviour on the evening of the Verdurin's concert. Her aunt, Mme Bontemps, seeing that there was little prospect of her niece marrying Marcel, had recalled her to Touraine, principally to discuss a proposal made on behalf of their son by the parents of Octave who had fallen in love with Albertine. One by one, the elements of Marcel's carefully reconstructed edifice begin to crumble. So that was really why Albertine wanted so desperately to call on the Verdurins. It was not to see Mlle Vinteuil but to meet Octave, her former golfing partner of Balbec, the young man whom everybody regarded as a complete idiot, interested only in the latest fashions in sport and attire, whose chief preoccupations were cocktail mixing and the cut of his dinner-jacket.

I know how easy yet how futile it is to prophesy on past events. Yet it has always seemed to me at each re-reading of *Albertine disparue* as if Proust, intuitively aware that time was pressing, felt impelled in this third chapter, to accelerate the rhythm of Marcel's narrative and to condense in the few pages devoted to Andrée's revelations, final and conclusive evidence in support of the Proustian (and Bergsonian) thesis that the truth of life can never be grasped by the intelligence alone. In order to seize the reality of existence, our intelligence must always enlist the co-operation of our 'instinct', of our intuition. Proust, in the scene where Andrée by her disclosures completely shatters Marcel's carefully reconstructed conception of Albertine's life and personality, makes his object very clear. Some may think, indeed, that he is guilty of over-simplification; for the novelist, unlike the professional psychologist, can always manufacture his data. Marcel's logical, intelligent diagnosis of Albertine's motives is all wrong and viewed in the light of Andrée's revelations—if they are true—represents no reality at all. On the contrary, his original intuitive impressions were correct. This is how Marcel sums up the position:

J'avais d'abord cru Albertine coupable, et seul mon désir employant à une œuvre de doute les forces de mon intelligence m'avait fait faire fausse route. Peut-être vivons-nous entourés d'indications électriques, séismiques, qu'il nous faut interpréter de bonne foi pour connaître la vérité des caractères. S'il faut le dire, si triste malgré tout que je fusse des paroles d'Andrée, je trouvais plus beau que la réalité se trouvât enfin concorder avec ce que mon instinct avait d'abord pressenti, plutôt qu'avec le misérable optimisme auquel j'avais lâchement cédé par la suite. J'aimais mieux que la vie fût à la hauteur de mes intuitions. Celles-ci du reste que j'avais eues le premier jour sur la plage, quand j'avais cru que ces jeunes filles incarnaient la frénésie du plaisir, le vice, et aussi le soir où j'avais vu l'institutrice d'Albertine faire rentrer cette fille passionnée dans la petite villa, comme on pousse dans sa cage un fauve que rien plus tard, malgré les apparences, ne pourra domestiquer, ne s'accordaient-elles pas à ce que m'avait dit Bloch quand il m'avait rendu la terre si belle en m'y montrant, me faisant frissonner dans toutes mes promenades, à chaque rencontre, l'universalité du désir? Peut-être malgré tout, ces intuitions premières, valait-il mieux que je ne les rencontrasse à nouveau vérifiées que maintenant.[1]

[I had at first believed Albertine to be guilty and it was solely my desire, by utilizing the powers of my intelligence to construct an edifice of doubt, that had put me on the wrong track. Perhaps we live surrounded by electric, seismic indications which we must honestly interpret in order to know the truth about characters. If I must be outspoken, saddened as I was in spite of everything by Andrée's words, I thought it far finer that the reality should happen finally to accord with what my instinct had originally foreseen rather than with the wretched optimism to which I had eventually so weakly surrendered. I preferred that life should be situated on the same plane as my intuitions. Those, moreover, which I had had the first day on the beach when I had believed that these girls were the incarnation of frenzied pleasure, of vice, and on the evening, too, when I had seen Albertine's governess leading that passionate girl home to the little villa, as one drives into its cage a wild animal which nothing, afterwards, despite appearances, will ever succeed in taming, did not those intuitions agree with what Bloch had told me when he had made the world so fair to my eyes by showing me, making me quiver with excitement

[1] *AD.* ii, 88–9.

on all my walks, at every turn, the universality of desire? Perhaps, in spite of all, it was better that I should only now have encountered those first intuitions verified anew.]

The novelist, we remarked, has this advantage over the professional psychologist, that he can at any moment invent convincing data in support of his individual conception of life and human nature. But it would be quite wrong to interpret this, especially in the case of a genius like Proust, as serious criticism, impugning his intellectual integrity. Aesthetically, I think, the sudden introduction of the scene between Andrée and Marcel was a mistake. Proust, it seems to me, was in too great a hurry to tie up the loose ends of his design. This, however, does not in the least detract from the value and truth of his conception of life. As Proust, in this chapter, reveals by numerous examples drawn from his vast knowledge of the world, Marcel's particular experience, although expressed in an unusual and striking fashion, illustrates a truth which all of us may discover if we will only take the trouble to examine our own attitude to life. It is the truth, never perhaps more finely expressed than by Bergson in the following words: 'Car le monde où nos sens et notre conscience nous introduisent habituellement n'est plus l'ombre de lui-même, et il est froid comme la mort.'[1] Marcel compares this deceptive view of the universe to a tapestry the true pattern of which is only visible if we look at its other side: 'Car l'envers de la tapisserie, l'envers réel de l'action, de l'intrigue — aussi bien que celui de l'intelligence, du cœur — se dérobe et nous ne voyons passer que des silhouettes plates dont nous disons: c'est ceci, c'est cela.'[2]

From Marcel's reaction to Andrée's revelations, but above all from the tone of the reflections which they provoke, he is practically cured of his strange and jealous passion for Albertine. The 'intellectuel sensible' is now, in fact, an artist who can, therefore, survey his own past and that of Albertine from the detached plane of art. Thus, although believing in her guilt, Marcel's thoughts of Albertine are devoid of harshness or repulsion. He feels nothing but pity and sadness for this victim

---

[1] *Intuition philosophique* (1911).   [2] *AD.* ii, 105.

of his insatiable 'désir moral', this woman whose true nature, because of his hideous suspicions, Marcel never really knew. As he now realizes, Albertine's terrible vice did not prevent her from possessing all the innocent desires of normal girls of her age, not excluding the desire for marriage. Marcel can think of her now as he thought of Mlle de Vinteuil whilst listening to the immortal septet, with that profound mansuetude and understanding which characterizes the great artist or the saint. The sufferings inflicted on him by love were greater than anything he could have imagined. Yet he does not regret that experience if only because it has shown him that love, which Marcel once naïvely regarded as a direct mode of access to reality, serves only to render even more impenetrable the veil interposed between our consciousness and the soul of women we love. On this note Proust concludes the third chapter of *Albertine disparue*.

The fourth chapter, 'Séjour à Venise', culminates in an incident designed not only to reinforce Proust's views on the perceptions of the intelligence but also to mark the final stage of Marcel's transition from 'le chagrin' to 'l'oubli'. We are reintroduced, moreover, to Norpois and Mme de Villeparisis by one of those typically Proustian backward sweeping movements which telescope 'past' and 'present' into something resembling Bergson's pure duration, whereby conventional Time is shown to have no valid reality. Need I add, in view of the title of this chapter, that its text is richly illuminated by marginal arabesques which subtly blend Marcel's memories of Combray with his impressions of Venice, the city of his dreams? As Elstir, painting a little Norman seaside town, amused himself by transposing the urban and marine, so Proust in the following passage, superimposes Combray on Venice with charming effects:

Mais dès le second jour, ce que je vis, en m'éveillant, ce pourquoi je me levai (parce que cela s'était substitué dans ma mémoire et dans mon désir aux souvenirs de Combray), ce furent les impressions de ma première sortie du matin à Venise, à Venise où la vie quotidienne n'était pas moins réelle qu'à Combray, où comme à Combray le dimanche matin on avait bien le plaisir de descendre dans une rue en fête, mais où cette rue était toute en une eau de saphir, rafraîchie de souffles tièdes, et d'une couleur si résistante, que mes yeux fatigués pouvaient pour se détendre et sans craindre qu'elle fléchît, y appuyer leurs regards. Comme à Combray les bonnes gens de la rue de l'Oiseau, dans cette nouvelle ville aussi, les habitants sortaient bien des maisons alignées l'une à côté de l'autre dans la grande rue, mais ce rôle de maisons projetant un peu d'ombre à leurs pieds était à Venise confié à des palais de porphyre et de jaspe, au-dessus de la porte cintrée desquels la tête d'un Dieu barbu (en dépassant l'alignement, comme le marteau d'une porte à Combray) avait pour résultat de rendre plus foncé par son reflet, non le brun du sol, mais le bleu splendide de l'eau. Sur la piazza l'ombre qu'eussent développée à Combray la toile du magasin de nouveautés et l'enseigne du coiffeur, c'étaient les petites fleurs bleues que sème à ses pieds sur le désert du dallage ensoleillé le relief d'une façade Renaissance, non pas que quand le soleil tapait fort, on ne fût obligé, à Venise comme à Combray, de baisser au bord du canal, des stores, mais ils étaient tendus entre les quadrilobes et les rinceaux de fenêtres gothiques.[1]

[But no later than the second morning, what I saw on awakening, what made me get up (because they had taken the place in my memory and in my desire of the recollections of Combray) were the impressions of my first morning outing in Venice, in Venice where everyday life was no less real than in Combray, where, as in Combray on Sunday mornings one had the delight of stepping down into a gay street, but where that street was entirely paved with sapphire-blue water, cooled by warm zephyrs and of a colour so durable that my tired eyes might, in order to relieve their strain and with no fear of it giving way, rest their gaze upon it. Like the good folks of the rue de l'Oiseau at Combray, so also in this other town, the inhabitants actually emerged from houses lined up side by side in the main street, but the role played there by houses of casting a little patch of shade at their feet was entrusted in Venice to palaces of porphyry and jasper, above the Gothic doorway of which the head of a bearded god (jutting out from the façade like the knocker on a door at Combray) had the effect of lending, because of its shadow, a deeper hue not to the brownness of the soil but to the splendid blueness of the water. On the piazza, the shadow which would have been produced in Combray by the awning over the haberdasher's shop and the barber's pole, was here replaced by the little blue flowers strewn at its feet upon the desert of sun-baked flagstones by the relief of a Renaissance façade, which does not mean that when the sun was hot we were not obliged, in Venice as at Combray, to lower our blinds on the bank of the Canal, but they hung between the quatrefoils and foliage ornaments of Gothic windows.]

[1] *AD.* ii, 111–12.

Marcel is in Venice with his mother and her old friend, Mme
Sazerat, whom they have invited to dine at a hotel some distance
from their own. Whilst waiting for the ladies, Marcel notices
at an adjoining table an old woman whom he recognizes in spite
of the eczematic blemishes that disfigure her, as the marquise
de Villeparisis. She is dining with her octogenarian lover, the
ex-ambassador Norpois, who has not, however, as Marcel
gathers from their conversation, renounced his ambitions or
lost his remarkable *flair* for impending diplomatic events. At
this moment Mme Sazerat enters and to her Marcel casually
mentions that he has just seen Mme de Villeparisis. To his
amazement Mme Sazerat, pale with emotion, almost on the
point of fainting, asks him if he means Mme de Villeparisis,
née Mlle de Bouillon, for this is the woman she has wanted all
her life to see. Mme Sazerat's father, we learn, fell madly in
love with Mme de Villeparisis, then by her first marriage the
duchesse d'Havré, who stripped him of his last sou and deserted
him. As a result, Mme Sazerat was brought up in semi-poverty
yet with the one consolation that her father had loved the most
beautiful if the most wicked woman of his epoch. Marcel takes
Mme Sazerat into the restaurant, indicating Mme de Villeparisis'
table.

'Mais elle doit être partie, je ne la vois pas où vous me dites.'
Et elle cherchait toujours, poursuivant la vision détestée, adorée,
qui habitait son imagination depuis si longtemps.
'Mais si, à la seconde table.'
'C'est que nous ne comptons pas à partir du même point. Moi,
comme je compte, la seconde table, c'est une table où il y a seulement,
à côté d'un vieux monsieur, une petite bossue, rougeaude, affreuse.'
'C'est elle!' [1]

The memory of Albertine is now buried deep in Marcel's
unconscious though an occasional incident, by a complicated
association of ideas, allows some little recollection to slip into
his conscious mind. A stockbroker's letter, for instance, recalls
certain disastrous speculations the object of which was to get
more money to spend on Albertine. Once Marcel, examining an
eagle carved in the porch of San Giorgio dei Schiavoni feels

[1] *AD.* II, 125.

a momentary twinge of pain. He remembers the eagles engraved on Albertine's two rings. But one evening something
occurs which seems to indicate the resurrection not only of
Marcel's memories of Albertine but of Albertine herself. A
telegram is handed to him which reads: 'Mon ami, vous me
croyez morte, pardonnez-moi, je suis très vivante, je voudrais
vous voir, vous parler mariage, quand revenez-vous? Tendrement. Albertine.'

Proust invented this episode for two reasons, one of which, if
we may anticipate its conclusion, was to emphasize once again
the unreliability of our habitual perceptions. The telegram is, of
course, from Gilberte whose handwriting, with its pretentious
flourishes, had misled the post-office clerk, who transcribed her
name as Albertine. The rest was due to Marcel's hasty and
inaccurate perception reinforced by imagination. For a more
detailed and authoritative explanation of this process the reader
should consult Bergson's *Energie spirituelle*, which most probably
suggested the incident.

Proust, however, is chiefly interested in the reactions which
it produced in Marcel, who believes for a few hours that
Albertine was not killed and has recovered from her accident.
When Marcel learned of his grandmother's death he experienced,
at first, no grief: that came afterwards when she was reanimated
for him through the modality of certain involuntary memories.
Now exactly the opposite takes place. The news that Albertine
is alive brings him no joy because in his thoughts she is now
dead. The psychological fact emphasized by Proust is that life is
essentially change. A new self has supplanted in Marcel the
self who loved Albertine and suffered because of his love. In
this, Proust argues, there is nothing remarkable. In the course
of a day, we can observe the same process in our own character.
An individual can be, in turn, malicious, sensitive, caddish, disinterested, ambitious, in the space of twenty-four hours. These,
however, are brief or temporary 'selves'. On the contrary, if
our passions are involved the eclipse of the former self, in
Marcel's case the self who loved Albertine, is permanent and
irrevocable. Life, which is imperceptibly changing the face of
the world, has gradually transformed the Marcel who loved

Albertine into someone who has forgotten his love for her and now, since his desire is in fact directed towards a beautiful Italian shopgirl, regards the resurrection of his former mistress as a tiresome obstacle to his plans.

Here Proust grazes the surface of a question explored by Bergson in *L'Evolution créatrice*. At a given moment in my personality, is my 'self' multiple or unique? For lack of a better image we must, no doubt, compare life to an *élan*, a continuous rushing forwards. But this is only a convenient image which should not blind us to the fact that life is really of a psychological nature, involving, that is to say, a constant interpenetration of states of soul. Only if viewed abstractly in terms of space-time can we say that one is distinct from the other. Now, this is really the point of view adopted by Proust when he describes the personality as a multiplicity of juxtaposed psychological states each of which, temporarily or permanently, according to its degree of intensity, eclipses the other.

Bergson, who is a philosopher and not a novelist, does not regard this problem as quite so simple. If I declare, he says, that the personality is a unity, the inner voices of my sensations and sentiments are at once raised in protest. On the other hand, if I assert the multiplicity of the personality my consciousness affirms that my sensations, feelings and thoughts are abstractions which I operate on myself, that each of my psychological states implies all the others. The truth is, then, that if we adopt the language of the understanding, the self is at once a multiple unity and a unique multiplicity. But, concludes Bergson, that is because unity and multiplicity are merely aspects of my personality seized by the understanding which projects its categories on the self. The reality is different. I enter into neither category, nor simultaneously into both, though, together, multiplicity and unity give us a rough imitation of that reciprocal interpenetration and continuity which constitute the true nature of the self, of my inner life. Everything depends on whether we consider life in itself or in its contact with matter. In the former case one may compare life to an impulse or *élan*: in the latter, however, it appears as what Bergson calls 'une immensité de virtualité', a mutual interflux of thousands of

tendencies which only become dissociated when they are exteriorized in relation to each other, or in other words, spatialized.
It is, says Bergson, contact with matter which decides this dissociation or individuation. This process, which is partly the
work of matter, partly due to the nature of life itself, Bergson
illustrates by the following example. When a poetic feeling is
rendered explicit in distinct stanzas, lines or words, it may be
said to have contained this multiplicity of individuated elements
and yet that this multiplicity was created by the materiality of
language. Nevertheless, there runs through these words, stanzas
and lines the unique inspiration which is the essence of the poem,
which *is*, indeed, the whole poem.

The object of my parenthesis is to show that Proust, although
he has many affinities with Bergsonism, was deterred by the
limitations of his medium, the novel, from interpreting life in
absolute Bergsonian terms, even assuming that such was ever
his intention. Art is not identical with metaphysics and the
example I have chosen is a fairly typical indication of the difference separating Proust from Bergson which, as the latter
always rightly suggested in his allusions to novelists, is a
difference of depth: to appreciate this, one has only to read, for
instance, everything that Bergson has written on the subject of
Time and then to note, in *A la recherche du temps perdu*, Proust's
original attempts to show, by concrete illustrations, how *la durée*
or real time differs from conventional or space-time. Certainly,
he goes much further than any previous novelist; yet not even
his most fanatical admirers would claim that the light thrown
on this subject by Proust is comparable to the illumination
provided by Bergson. This is not a reproach, merely a restate-
ment of the fact that the function of the novelist is not that of the
metaphysician.

Marcel, analysing his own feelings, notes that his love is now
completely engulfed in oblivion. Viewed retrospectively, its
persistence after the news of Albertine's death seems now to
have been due to the very fact that she was reported killed,
coupled with that of her disappearance and their previous resolve
to break off relations. He tries to remember Albertine but the
image presenting itself to his mind is that of a rather stout

masculine woman whose features reveal already the profile of Mme Bontemps. It is, at any rate, the image of a woman whose relations with Andrée or anyone else leave Marcel completely indifferent. Proust gives us two explanations of this phenomenon, the first of which appears to me unconvincing. Comparing Marcel's former longing for Albertine, like the survival of his jealousy, to physical maladies such as tuberculosis or cancer, he differentiates between those which have a purely physical cause and those which act upon the body only through the medium of the intelligence. Now, the part of the intelligence that serves as a communicating link is the memory, which gradually fades or is destroyed. Therefore, whilst the victim of a cancer will surely die, not so the victim of jealous love, since our thoughts, unlike our tissues, are powerless to retain our memories. Here Proust's psychology is, I feel, very questionable. Our mind has a remarkable faculty for preserving our memories even if, as in Marcel's case, our thoughts are turned towards immediate or future action. I prefer, therefore, his second explanation, which is that Marcel is already thinking of another woman on whom all his desires are focused, the woman who is what Albertine once was. And if Marcel's image of his former mistress is so repulsive it is, as Proust should have explained, because our brain has a convenient habit of fitting into the cadre of a present state of soul only those memories that adapt themselves to this environment. The image of the little Albertine of Balbec days, arising at this moment, would have conflicted awkwardly with that of the 'éclatante fille' of Marcel's recent memory. No, as Bergson once suggested, one of the most difficult problems to explain is that of why we forget, and it is never really explored by Proust.

One interesting reflection, however, emerges from Marcel's introspections. It concerns a problem, that of our life after death, which occasionally crops up in this narrative. One can hardly say that Proust ever approached the question with any deep sense of anxiety: the curiosity which it aroused in him was mainly academic. Marcel tells us that once he loved Albertine more than himself, a singular assertion on the part of a man who always insisted that she had no real existence outside himself, that 'elle

vivait en moi'. Such, however, is his present illusion. Marcel
observes now that this desire never to be separated from his
mistress did not long survive their physical separation. What
about his desire for immortality, the desire never to be separated
from himself after death, which still persists? Is that because
Marcel thinks himself more precious than Albertine or his
love for himself more important than his love for her? His
conclusion is that, just as in the case of Albertine, so, when the
links attaching his spirit to his body are severed by death, his
desire for eternal life, for immortality will automatically disappear. 'Notre amour de la vie n'est qu'une vieille liaison dont
nous ne savons pas nous débarrasser. Sa force est dans sa
permanence. Mais la mort qui la rompt nous guérira du désir
de l'immortalité.'[1]

All this has a rank flavour of sophistry. Proust's argument is
based on the fallacy that his love for Albertine can be equated
with his desire for eternal life. But he has just admitted that
his love for Albertine had been only one fleeting aspect of his
love of women; that, in fact, his desire is already fastened on
a young Italian beauty. His parallel, therefore, has no validity.
For, even granting that one's sexual love can be regarded as
identical in quality with the desire for everlasting spiritual life,
it is absurd to conclude, from the impermanence of Marcel's
love for one woman, Albertine, whilst at the same time admitting
the permanence of his love for women in general, that, therefore,
death will remove his desire for immortality. How does Marcel
know whether his next liaison, for example with the brilliantly
tinted young Italian girl, may not, perhaps, be the lasting love of
his existence? Proust does not, as a rule, venture far into the
realm of metaphysics and to judge from the result of this ex-
cursion, possessed no special talents in that direction. Nevertheless, to revert to the passage under discussion, it is surprising
that one who tried always to envisage life as duration, that is to
say, to perceive Time as indivisible, could produce these superficial arguments in defence of materialism.

Dismissing Albertine and the telegram from his thoughts,
Marcel sets out to explore Venice by moonlight. There are few

[1] *AD.* II, 142.

nocturnes in *A la recherche du temps perdu*; I fancy, indeed, that in an exhibition of Proustian word-paintings the main effect would be one of lights and colours ranging through the entire spectrum of Nature from dawn to sunset in all her seasons. At the moment I can recall, of genuine nocturnes, only three examples though, no doubt, there are others. The first is that charming Hubert Robert impression of Marcel's walk with his father and mother at Combray; the second, in *Le temps retrouvé*, is an immense, apocalyptic and sublunary interpretation of wartime Paris by night. The third, which I now present, is a little Venetian study inspired by dreams of the *Arabian Nights*.

Je m'étais engagé dans un réseau de petites ruelles, de calli divisant en tous sens, de leurs rainures, le morceau de Venise découpé entre un canal et la lagune, comme s'il avait cristallisé suivant ces formes innombrables, ténues et minutieuses. Tout à coup, au bout d'une de ces petites rues, il semblait que dans la matière cristallisée se fût produite une distension. Un vaste et somptueux campo à qui je n'eusse assurément pas, dans ce réseau de petites rues, pu deviner cette importance, ni même trouver une place, s'étendait devant moi entouré de charmants palais pâles de clair de lune. C'était un de ces ensembles architecturaux vers lesquels, dans une autre ville, les rues se dirigent, vous conduisent et le désignent. Ici, il semblait exprès caché dans un entrecroisement de ruelles, comme ces palais de contes orientaux où on mène la nuit un personnage qui, ramené chez lui avant le jour, ne doit pas pouvoir retrouver la demeure magique où il finit par croire qu'il n'est allé qu'en rêve.[1]

[I had got myself entangled in a network of little alleys, *calli* splintering in all directions, by their groovings, the chunk of Venice hacked out between a canal and the lagoon as if it had crystallized in obedience to these innumerable, tenuous and minute patterns. Suddenly, at the end of one of these little alleys, it seemed as if in the crystallized substance a dilatation had occurred. A vast and sumptuous campo which, in the network of little streets I should certainly never have guessed to be so considerable, or even found room for it, stretched out before me surrounded by charming palaces pale with moonlight. It was one of those architectural *ensembles* towards which, in any other town, the streets converge, lead you and point it out. Here it seemed to be deliberately concealed in a tangle of alleys, as in those oriental fairy-tale palaces whither, by night, one of the characters is taken, who, having

[1] *AD.* ii, 143–4.

been brought back home before daybreak, is not supposed to be able to rediscover the magic dwelling, to which, as he ends up by believing, he had only gone in a dream.]

The close of this sojourn in Venice is marked by a curious incident. Long ago, Marcel heard from Saint-Loup that a certain Baronne de Putbus possessed a superbly desirable ladies' maid. Yet, owing to a variety of unexpected happenings, all his efforts to make the acquaintance of this elusive person had been frustrated. Now, however, learning that Mme de Putbus has just arrived in Venice, he asks his mother, on the day of their departure for Paris, to prolong their visit. Accustomed to her son's disconcerting whims, she does not even pretend to take him seriously, whilst Marcel, who has never outgrown his juvenile rebellious fits of obstinacy, lets his mother go off to the station without him, announcing his determination to stay in Venice. He has, of course, forgotten all about Mme de Putbus and the elusive *femme de chambre*. The latter was merely Proust's excuse for a remarkable fragment which might very well be entitled: 'Sur la psychologie de l'attente'. So much of our life is spent in waiting for something to happen that it has always seemed to me astonishing that novelists, who often lavish their powers of analysis on quite unimportant aspects of the soul, neglect this most significant psychological fact. The reason is, probably, that this fascinating subject is really one for the social philosopher rather than for the novelist, since modern civilization, viewed from this angle, is an organized attempt to relieve the individual of the necessity for waiting, and thus of a psychological experience which may vary in degree from mere boredom to almost intolerable anxiety. To take one example, think of the vast sums squandered every year in the world by travellers waiting in railway stations for trains to start or to reach their destination; the thousands of pounds gladly expended on penny-in-the-slot machines, cheap literature, news-cinemas, revolting buffet-car meals, by the millions of individuals whose instinctive urgent desire is to escape the ordeal of waiting, to escape, in other words, the consciousness of their real, their inner life. This, however, is taking us very far from Proust, who is concerned only with Marcel's state of soul as he sits alone outside the hotel listening to a gondolier bawling 'O sole mio' and visualizing his mother at the station on the point of leaving for Paris.

As his sense of isolation deepens, all the surrounding objects acquire an air of strangeness and of vulgarity. The beauty which constituted for Marcel the individuality of Venice crumbles away. Her palaces become ordinary aggregations of stone and mortar; the Rialto a rather inferior bridge, the canals mere receptacles for a mixture of hydrogen and oxygen. There is no longer the remotest suggestion of Turner's 'Venice', of the ancient city of the Doges. His environment assumes a foreign, unfriendly and rather frightening look. Meanwhile, although repelled by the singer and his interminable song, Marcel, hypnotized somehow into a state of complete irresolution, finds himself mechanically following the phrases of 'O sole mio' which seems now to echo the anguish of his loneliness. It is as if, he tells us, the edifice of his spiritual distress was being slowly and artistically constructed before his very eyes, with each successive note of that dreadful, hackneyed composition. His will, on the contrary, is rapidly crumbling into fragments. Suddenly from the caves of his innermost being, swiftly mobilized by Habit, arise the forces of self-preservation and the elements of action. Hurling himself from his seat, tearing in the direction of the station like a hare, Marcel reaches the station in the nick of time, to find his mother almost in tears and his train about to start for Paris.

The return of Gilberte together with Marcel's glimpse of Norpois and Mme de Villeparisis in Venice, suggest how Proust intends to complete the design of *A la recherche du temps perdu*. Eventually, we shall observe the re-entry into Marcel's existence of all the men and women whose lives were once linked with his own, whose personalities in varying degree once influenced the quality of his own feelings or sensations, the trend of his desires or actions. Encountered thus, after a long period of absence, materializing the interfusion of 'past' and 'present' they will exteriorize for Marcel the indivisibility of real Time or duration, the change, mobility and eternal 'devenir' of life as it really is, as it never appears, however, so long as we view it only through the distorting lens of our analysing intelligence. This, it seems to me, is already foreshadowed in the final chapters of *Albertine disparue*, in the last of which, indeed, Proust's shuttles work at an accelerated rhythm as if eager to complete their task.

In the journey to Paris, Marcel and his mother open their letters from home which contain startling news. Gilberte writes of her forthcoming marriage with Saint-Loup, incidentally revealing herself as the 'Albertine' of Marcel's telegram. More astonishing, however, is the announcement of another marriage, that of the young marquis de Cambremer to Jupien's niece, the little seamstress who once loved Morel and now, adopted by Charlus, is known as Mlle d'Oloron, an old title belonging to the Guermantes family. Just like the ending of a novel by George Sand and the reward of virtue, says Marcel's mother. Less innocent, because he is better informed, her son, reflecting on this strange alliance, sees in it the ending of a novel by Balzac—the wages of vice. After this domestic commentary, which exposes in Proust's astringent Saint-Simon manner the Faubourg Saint-Germain technique in the arrangement of profitable *mésalliances*, we are suddenly presented with a totally new aspect of Saint-Loup. To his profound distress Marcel hears from various sources, including Jupien, that his friend has now adopted his uncle's vice. Moreover, as Marcel is able to observe for himself, Robert is extremely intimate with Morel though, in order to camouflage his perverted tastes, he publicly advertises his liaisons with brilliant society *cocottes*. Here Saint-Loup is almost too successful and only the intervention of his mother prevents Gilberte from suing for a divorce.

Why does Proust introduce this hideous and unexpected transformation? Probably, if called upon to justify it, he could reply with truth that life affords many examples of similar psychological revolutions, that it is no uncommon experience to discover that friends, encountered after a period of absence, have acquired in the interval a new character, often diametrically opposed to that which we once knew and admired. The young man whose generosity was a byword at college is transfigured at fifty into a hard-fisted business-man. The painfully shy young girl of twenty develops into the loud-voiced, assertive President of some Woman's organization. All this is unquestionably true

and to deny it would be to reveal a great ignorance of life. Yet
the novelist, whose function is to enlighten our ignorance of life,
must at the same time attempt to explain the reasons for such
transformations, especially when as in the case of Saint-Loup,
they assume the form of a profound and volcanic upheaval of the
individual self. Now that is precisely what Proust fails to do. It
seems, at first, from certain revelations made by Aimé that
Marcel's original perceptions were at fault, that even at Balbec
Saint-Loup secretly possessed these unnatural tastes. But
Marcel, who remembers his friend's undoubted passion for
Rachel and the incident in the rue de l'Elysée, quite naturally
rejects this explanation. Jupien, on the other hand, blames the
evil influence of Morel and Proust, rather feebly, leaves Marcel
and his readers in a state of complete uncertainty as to the
motives determining the appalling inversion of Robert's original
habits and desires. The weakest of his conjectures is that homosexuality is a hereditary Guermantes vice from which only the
duke enjoys an exceptional immunity. My personal impression
is that Proust, whenever this distasteful subject crops up, is
prone to abdicate his customary good sense and to lose his
sense of proportion. We learn, for example, that Legrandin the
snob and dilettante, Mme de Cambremer's brother, is also
a member of the *confrérie*. This, indeed, is one of the reasons
why Charlus, who shares Proust's belief in the hereditary nature
of unnatural vice, particularly through avuncular channels,
regards Legrandin's nephew as an excellent husband for his
adoptive niece. Every great novelist has his favourite and
peculiar mania, just as every painter of genius has his predilection for a particular colour. It is regrettable that Proust's
should have assumed this special form though, fortunately, so
vast is the canvas of *A la recherche du temps perdu* that the
integrity of this unique work of art is unimpaired by Marcel's
occasional exaggerations and optical errors.

These final pages of *Albertine disparue* are fraught with a
spirit of lassitude and of profound sadness. Marcel, who is the
guest at Tansonville of Gilberte and Robert, can hardly bear to
think of the contrast between his memories of the Saint-Loup of
Balbec, Doncières or of that foggy evening in the restaurant on

the Boulevards, and the husband of Gilberte, this total stranger
whose behaviour towards his wife is a distasteful comedy.
Remembering the old days of his friend's mad infatuation for
Rachel, knowing his secret, loathsome relations with Morel, it is
painful for Marcel to dine out with the Saint-Loups, to observe
the quick, furtive inquisitional glance which reveals the mockery
of Robert's elaborate, protective and uxorious attentiveness to
his young wife.

This evil, almost unrecognizable Saint-Loup was designed by
Proust, I think, to express an idea which pervades and dominates
this section of his novel. In the new Robert, who comes back
into his life after a long period of separation, Marcel sees the
death and corruption of impressions which were once closely
woven into the tissue of his inmost self. Such is the theme pursued in the closing pages of *Albertine disparue*. Its essential and
desolating quality, however, can only be appreciated by the
reader who will lay down this volume and return in memory to
Du côté de chez Swann, where Marcel in words and images
pulsating with the virginal freshness of a perfect morning in
June, resurrects the glorious emotions and sensations created
by that unique, momentous experience in life—a child's first
consciousness of natural beauty. Now it seems to Marcel, as he
rambles with Gilberte through the countryside they knew so well
as children, that all these are lovely illusions, unreal as dreams
which, on our awakening, dissolve in fragments. This at least is
suggested by his discouragement, by the admission 'j'étais
désolé de voir combien peu je revivais les années d'autrefois',[1]
and again, 'Mais ce qui me frappa le plus, ce fut combien peu,
pendant ce séjour, je revécus mes années d'autrefois....'[1]

Here Proust, as I said, merely re-enunciates a theme anticipated and more fully orchestrated in *Du côté de chez Swann*
where the gorgeous pageant of Marcel's boyhood impressions
is projected on the horizon of the future as a cortège moving
towards oblivion. Is not this what Proust intended to suggest
when he wrote: 'On cherche à retrouver dans les choses,
devenues par là précieuses, le reflet que notre âme a projeté
sur elles, on est déçu en constatant qu'elles semblent dépourvues

---

[1] *AD.* II, 204 and 206.

dans la Nature, du charme qu'elles devaient, dans notre pensée, au voisinage de certaines idées....'[1] And now Marcel, re-visiting the scenes of his boyhood, tries in vain to recapture the lovely impressions of long ago. But the Vivonne is no longer the enchanted, crystalline, aquatic garden of *Du côté de chez Swann*, the river of which the source was the entrance to a dark and mysterious underworld. All Marcel can see is a rather ugly little stream which springs from a square hole not unlike a public wash-pit. So, also, with 'le côté de Guermantes' and 'le côté de Méséglise' which used to symbolize two different ideals of natural beauty, each leading to an inaccessible, miraculous country, both, however, always separated in Marcel's imagina-tion by a zone, measurable no doubt in kilometres, yet of such a quality as to situate those two roads on completely dissimilar planes of reality. Now, however, Gilberte lightly proposes a walk which, if they set out from Tansonville, will take them striding through Méséglise and Guermantes, and thus annihilate one more illusion of adolescence. Even the steep little field-path bordering Swann's estate, where Marcel first really perceived the miracle which, owing to the poverty of words, men are obliged to describe as a hawthorn hedge in blossom, even 'le raidillon' where first he met and fell in love with Gilberte has lost the power to arouse his sensibility and imagination. Perhaps, Marcel wrongly assumes, that is because these faculties have lost their former virtue, forgetting that, in the intervening years, they have been oriented with unimpaired intensity towards other objects. The Vivonne, Guermantes, Méséglise, the 'raidillon' have not appreciably changed, but the Marcel who now perceives them no longer brings to their contemplation the state of soul of the boy who once passionately believed in their unique and wonderful beauty, nay, who created, perhaps, that beauty in the form of a hundred changing sensations, which ever since have been merged in the advancing stream of his consciousness along with the hundreds of other sensations, feelings and ideas composing that continuous indivisible process of re-creation we call life.

Proust does not really explore the causes of Marcel's present

---

[1] *Swann*, I, 128.

disillusionment. True, the latter says rather vaguely: 'Mais, séparé des lieux qu'il m'arrivait de retraverser par toute une vie différente, il n'y avait pas entre eux et moi cette contiguité d'où naît avant même qu'on s'en soit aperçu, l'immédiate, délicieuse et totale déflagration du souvenir.'[1] This dazzling metaphor, however, can scarcely be said to illuminate the psychological experience to which Proust alludes in these pages. It simply restates the fact that Marcel is discouraged because, somehow, he cannot now re-live the years of his boyhood. But why? Is it not because, although no doubt pure memory exists in theory rather than in fact, it is possible sometimes to re-discover the images of past impressions surrounded by their original individual and unique emotional atmosphere? But in order to remember the past in this way, to achieve this intuition of a personal intimate experience we must situate ourselves on the disinterested plane of art. That is probably what Proust means when he speaks of Marcel's failure to establish between himself and the places now revisited, that contiguity without which there can be no 'déflagration du souvenir'. Marcel's illusion is to suppose that his memories are somehow locked up in the sites of his contemplation and must infallibly be evoked merely by the sight of these objects. But 'le temps perdu' is not so easily recaptured. Our consciousness, normally oriented towards immediate action, tends to utilize only such of its memories as are of most use to the purposes of social life. To remember our true past we must imitate the state of mind of the artist who, precisely because he can detach himself from the present, is able thus to achieve something approaching pure memory, to grasp and communicate the reality of past sensations.

From his conversations with Gilberte, however, Marcel derives some happiness, albeit tinged with regret. In an access of expansiveness, referring to their first meeting beside the 'raidillon', he confesses to his boyish infatuation for the little girl with the golden hair whose rude gesture, however, seemed to express the utmost contempt for his person. To his surprise, Gilberte explains that this was her crude and unmaidenly way of expressing her love, of throwing herself at his head. Moreover,

[1] *AD.* ii, 204.

years later outside the Guermantes residence, she made a second equally fruitless effort to indicate her sentiments. Marcel naturally reminds her that he was madly and hopelessly in love at the time they used to play in the Champs Elysées. But then, as Gilberte remarks significantly: 'Oui, mais là vous m'aimiez trop, je sentais une inquisition sur tout ce que je faisais.'

Marcel, looking back on his sentimental life, sees that with two women, Albertine and Gilberte, he was within an ace of realizing his dream. Both opportunities he missed for the same reasons. Only now does it dawn upon him that the real Gilberte and the real Albertine were the girls who spontaneously displayed their love for him, in a glance which he was too obtuse to read, one beside the hawthorn at Combray, the other on the beach at Balbec. Afterwards it was too late, for then, as Gilberte implies, his ardour defeated its own object. Both, sensing the possessive, inquisitional quality of his 'désir moral' abandoned their original frankness and erected a barrier of reserve against his threat to their spiritual independence. Yet there was a time during Marcel's infatuation for Gilberte when he might have swallowed his pride and attempted a reconciliation. His intention, however, was never carried out because, one evening in the twilight, he surprised Gilberte out walking with another young man. The latter as he discovers long after these Tansonville confidences was the actress, Léa, disguised in male attire. From these revelations Marcel derives at least one consolation. The happiness that now lies beyond his grasp might, after all, have been achieved. It was not, he now knows, a creation of imagination stimulated by desire. It existed, in reality, very close to him, 'Plus complètement encore que je n'avais cru, Gilberte était à cette epoque-là vraiment du côté de Méséglise.'[1]

[1] *AD.* ii, 212.

Chapter X

LE TEMPS RETROUVÉ

In Proust's chronicle there are no unnecessary journeys. It is only the mediocre novelist who is compelled to distract our attention from the shallowness of his characters by sudden changes of scene and to refocus it upon their exciting physical adventures or else upon the attractive picture of their new material environment. One may be quite sure, therefore, that in now transferring Marcel and Gilberte to Tansonville the author has a motive which directly concerns the general design of *A la recherche du temps perdu*. Let us pause for a moment to consider the progress achieved by Marcel in this search for his lost past, that is to say, the past as it was really lived by him in the deepest regions of his being. The other past is that perceived by his intelligence and preserved in his conscious or voluntary memory. This, Proust always infers, can be easily recovered.[1] But the real past can be evoked only when the intelligence is reinforced by the 'intuitivism of the unconscious'.[2] Yet, as Marcel has learned, such intuition is of brief duration: the unconscious memory operates capriciously. The implication is that one cannot spend a lifetime waiting for that chance sensation which will miraculously release from the unconscious a fragment of existence *sub specie durationis*, a moment complete with its primitive aura, sensations and emotions. So, even if the intelligence yields only a distorted or imperfect view of reality, the route of the intelligence is the one we must perforce adopt at the outset of our journey of exploration. Experience will later confirm the superiority of the other, of the intuitive approach which is for most of us, however, a strange, lonely and arduous way. It is not so for the happy few—the artists and philosophers of genius. They are undaunted by the difficulties and labours of the ascent, believing as they do that it will lead to a 'vision splendid'.

[1] *Swann*, I, 68.　　　　　　　　　[2] *AD.* I, 14.

With philosophy Marcel is not immediately concerned and he seems, at this phase, more than ever remote from his destined vocation, art. The long and painful experiment narrated in *La Prisonnière* and in *Albertine disparue*, though not entirely profitless, has failed in its object, which was to reveal the real Albertine, the essential quality of his relationship with Albertine. Proust suggests that no other result was to have been expected since the intuitions of Marcel, the jealous lover, were constantly interfused and at variance with those of the other self whose ultimate vocation is art, whose attitude to life, though Marcel only realized this intermittently, is that of the artist. From such a continual shifting of Marcel's sites of observation there could only emerge a bewildering vision of the past, a confusion of sweet memories traversed by dark hallucinations, a vision reflecting the expansion and contraction of his consciousness, the alternating rhythm of his love.

Now, in every spiritual ordeal there comes a time when, to borrow a popular expression, 'il faut se faire une raison'. Our mind, exhausted by the introspective effort to seize its own, inner history, yet simultaneously conscious of being swept forward in the irresistible *élan* of a soul of which it is an indivisible element, turns outward in an attempt to reach permanence or finality. Is not this Marcel's situation when, having failed to grasp the reality of his past as he lived it during his love for Albertine, he listens with relief to the reassuring voice of reason which tells him, in effect, that it is futile to pursue his search for 'le temps perdu' since the past is in continual process of disintegration? Our ancient memories, whispers reason, especially those which tend to upset the harmony of our inner self, do not survive. After all, is not this Marcel's own experience? A merciful oblivion is even now rapidly liquidating his recollections of Albertine and, with them, the last vestiges of the greatest sorrow of his life. And is it not reasonable to conjecture that such is the essential nature and tendency of life? So, I think, we must interpret the section of Marcel's narrative which deals with the theme of 'Le chagrin et l'oubli'.

The terrible force of every doctrine of defeatism lies in its reasonableness. It coincides at all points with the facts of our experience or of what we call our experience. Now, it may be objected, Marcel ought to be the last to accept a philosophy which, although corresponding no doubt to his present desires, is belied by his experience of the unconscious memory and its miraculous powers of resurrection. One thinks of the revelations so beautifully recorded in *Du côté de chez Swann*, of those impressions which might have been properly written off as long ago extinct yet were later magically restored to existence by the involuntary memory thanks to the evocative virtue of a chance sensation, by the taste of a *madeleine*, the bubblings of a radiator in Paris, the clink of a teaspoon at a garden-party in the Faubourg Saint-Germain. And Marcel is now back in Combray, in the tangible, material surroundings of his childhood. The steeple of Combray church thrusts upwards out of its mass of verdure cleaving the soft blueness of a summer sky. He can see it, neatly engraved in miniature, on the central pane of his bedroom window at Tansonville. In the evenings he wanders with Gilberte along the once enchanted roads that lead to Guermantes and to Méséglise. He lingers on the little bridge over the Vivonne where long ago the swift beauty of water alive with light could pierce his inmost being, so that his soul was flooded with exultancy and he shouted and danced for joy. Everything is here that ought to resurrect the springtime of Marcel's life. Yet 'le temps perdu', the real past, has apparently vanished beyond recall, like his boyhood love for Gilberte, his foolish adolescent cult of the feudal princess, Oriane, the deep tenderness that made existence without his beloved grandmother seem unthinkable, and finally, his torturing jealous passion for Albertine.

Marcel does not speak of these things. He confines himself to the bare statement that Combray revisited was a source of profound disappointment. It is as if he has accepted the defeatist conclusion that life, because of its essential properties of change and new creation, involves, necessarily, the death of a part of ourselves, of our past; that the survival of the past is not a reality but an illusion spun by the imagination out of nothing. That marvellous tissue of sensations and emotions which we fondly believe to have been extracted from life by our childhood-self and lovingly kept intact by memory was something, then, that never really existed; merely a complex of images we have been engaged in fabricating out of nothing. Is this the mirage which Marcel is now vainly trying to project against the material setting of his childhood?

Proust, it would seem, is now interpreting a crucial phase in Marcel's psychological life, in that history of his vocation which is an inseparable part of the account of his 'recherche du temps perdu'. One must not forget that the Marcel who has just emerged from the ordeal of loving and losing Albertine, who fails now to rediscover the Combray of his childhood or the comrade of his youth is not the Marcel who recorded the exquisite impressions contained in *Du côté de chez Swann*. These were narrated, as Proust clearly indicated in the opening pages of his novel, by a Marcel who had surmounted the spiritual defeatism of the Tansonville period, by one whose sudden reconversion to a lasting faith in the revelatory powers of art we shall find described in the prelude to the second volume of *Le temps retrouvé*. Only, therefore, in this oblique fashion, by collating the impressions contained in these first and last volumes, may we gauge the true quality of Marcel's feelings at Tansonville and realize how close he is to surrender. For if there is one fragment of our past which all of us believe indestructible, preserved as long as our breathing, it is our childhood. The sentiments one experienced in the ecstasy of a first love may sometimes elude all our efforts at recall but not, surely, the bright and marvellous impressions of childhood, the unique, incommunicable sensations and emotions aroused in us by certain objects of our perception, by things of trivial importance to the analysing intelligence of the grown-up, yet to us more real, more individual than any others of their species. Why is it then, like Marcel now in Combray revisited, we sometimes fail to recapture that vanished time which intuition tells us was an eternal springtime, towards which so often our mind looks back as a relief from the other impressions housed in its consciousness? To revisit the scenes of childhood is sometimes to court the bitter disappointment of Marcel at Tansonville, but not always. If the reader will forgive the intrusion of a personal experience, the writer of this study, on revisiting, after a lapse of forty years, the scenes of his early childhood did, in fact, recapture the original emotional climate with which they had always been linked in his memory. Or rather, it would be more accurate to say that the distant past as conserved in memory was not dissolved by the impressions aroused by the objects contemplated once again, after so many years. Perhaps that was because unlike Marcel, the present writer had not returned to his native place in deliberate search of 'le temps perdu' but on the more earthy business of university examining, expecting if anything to discover that, as the saying goes, 'the old place had changed out of all recognition', which is nearly always another way of saying that the self who first observed that place has altered but does not know it.

If Marcel fails to recapture, after many years, the state of soul in which he first perceived Combray, it is because his mind is still preoccupied with the task of burying unpleasant memories of Albertine and is incapable of that expansion and relaxation, of that slackening of its attention to the immediate business of living which distinguishes the attitude of the child or of the artist, who are in this respect alike. Instead, Marcel has the illusion which all of us share, that the impressions of childhood, of our past, are mental snapshots neatly filed away for future reference and for comparison *in situ* with their originals. But the objects perceived in childhood only possessed their unique, original quality because we believed in them and looked upon them with a mind detached from any thought of their utility to our lives, in short, with the detachment of the child or the artist. The things that arrested our attention were marvellous because we saw them in their complete reality, not superficially, with our appraising intelligence. In a moment of total perceptiveness, we entered through sympathy into their very essence, into the very rhythm, as it were, of the life of which they and we form part.

As the child grows into the man, he tends to lose this intuitive approach to life, and in view of the structure of our social existence that is almost inevitable and certainly necessary. It is retained intact, however, by a very few individuals, by the great artists whose poetry, music, paintings or novels serve to remind us of a faculty which most of us have almost lost. That is why Marcel's search for 'le temps perdu' will only be crowned with success when he discovers his vocation and learns that his search, apparently so fruitless, was really the artist's eternal quest for truth. For no one may hope to succeed in this quest unless he believes that through art it is possible to obtain a direct vision of the essential reality and meaning of life. One may compare it without irreverence to the quest for a Holy Grail; demanding, therefore, the immolation of all selfish, utilitarian desires to a single purpose. Viewed from the plane of art, there can be no such concept as an irrecoverable past because there is no real line of separation possible in an evolution which is life incessantly creating itself and, simultaneously, reflecting its own image on the indefinite past. Marcel at Tansonville, however, has not yet attained such illumination. At no time, moreover, has he possessed so little faith in the power of art to recompose the reality of existence. That is why his present disappointment at Tansonville seems to him merely another facet of the disillusionment caused by his failure to recover the true impressions of his life with Albertine. What he does not see is that he has never honestly attempted to re-live, to re-create those impressions. In surveying that part of his existence Marcel did not seek reality but, as he often confesses, an appeasement of his intolerable suffering. His intelligence, reinforced by imagination, was too often called in to offer a comforting facsimile of reality though the instinct or, if you prefer, the intuition of the incipient artist within him knew it to be a facsimile. The same instinct warned him that there is no true knowledge without an apprenticeship involving suffering as well as happiness. If the artist is to interpret what is written in the 'livre intérieur', in the record of his whole past, he must learn to read every page faithfully. The great work of art is not an anthology of passages selected and paraphrased in deference to a current mode of taste or morality. It is the reflection, through a medium chosen for its transparency, of an original lovingly studied by one who has tried to enter by sympathy into its very spirit. This is the attitude from which Marcel, as I see him at Tansonville, is so very remote. The history of every vocation reveals a similar phase of doubt and hopeless resignation. Yet it is nearly always the prelude to an illumination followed by an enduring conversion because this spiritual defeatism is rooted not in obstinate pride but in humility. In Marcel's case, however, many years are to elapse before that hour strikes. It will strike in a world still quivering from the shock of war, in a France gazing sombrely on a hail-swept garden strewn with the bravest of her lilies. But we must go back to the years preceding this tragic season, to the Tansonville which is not yet 'Hill 307' but the Saint-Loup's estate inherited from Swann, who in his lifetime had often dreamed that Gilberte might some day be received by the Guermantes. Never, in his wildest dreams, had he imagined her married to Oriane's nephew.

Marcel, living under the same roof as Gilberte and Robert de Saint-Loup, can see from his window the steeple of Combray church. Observing him thus, once again in the setting so marvellously described in *Du côté de chez Swann* one feels tempted to quote that famous phrase from *Lear*: 'the wheel has come full circle.' But it would have no real application to Marcel's position. For that to happen, Combray, Gilberte and Robert de Saint-Loup would have to resurrect the state of soul in which he first contemplated them, long ago. They cannot do so because Marcel himself does not believe that 'le temps perdu', the authentic emotional climate of his boyhood, can be resurrected. And such, on the whole, will be his attitude until he recognizes the potentialities of art and discovers his vocation. We must not, then, expect to hear in this first chapter of *Le temps retrouvé* the echoes of that 'mélodie intérieure' so frequently perceptible in *Du côté de chez Swann* and, when Marcel still had hope, often also in *La Prisonnière* and in *Albertine disparue*. The quality of the present narrative is rather that of *Le côté de Guermantes* and of *Sodome et Gomorrhe*, reflecting a mind directed outwards, the intelligent, ruthless, analytic mind of Proust the satirist and critic of contemporary manners and morals. Still, even in his most La Rochefoucauld and Saint-Simon vein, Proust can never halt the restless activity of his imagination. Touched by this splendid alchemy, certain features of a human landscape which we had otherwise scarcely borne to contemplate, are invested with a sinister and fascinating beauty, though their intrinsic reality remains unaltered. Playing upon the spectacle of a great city at war, the Proustian imagination creates another kind of beauty, the unreal loveliness of an Oriental fairy-tale, a dream city where the infinite space reaching from pavement to firmament is sectioned by moving shafts of lights ranging through all the hues of an Arabian Night from blue to indigo, from violet to amber and from amber to a sublunary, phosphorescent green. And though Marcel resolutely tries to rivet his attention on present impressions, to live as all of us do in wartime, in the actual moment, he cannot prevent the intermittent, backward thrusting of memory, that involuntary expansion of the consciousness we call remembering. Every novel sensation, in order to be understood by the intelligence, implies a necessary comparison with the past, an inevitable reference to history, even though history never in reality repeats itself. So Marcel's narrative spirals backwards to catch in the noose of a sudden reflection, the recollections of his conversations long ago at Doncières with Robert and his charming young brother officers. In this and other subtle ways Proust contrives to bring together within the focus of *Le temps retrouvé*, in something resembling Bergson's duration where past and present meet and interfuse, the surviving characters of his novel, the Verdurins, Brichot, Cottard, Ski, Norpois, Oriane and the Guermantes, Gilberte and Odette, Morel and Charlus.

The first chapter of *Le temps retrouvé* opens with one of Proust's incomparable 'transpositions': it is a miniature, executed in the best Elstir manner. Treasure it, however, and lay it away with its perfume of lilacs and roses beside that other equally lovely memory-image of the little 'raidillon' humming with the scent of may blossoms. For this is destined to be your last impression, as it is Marcel's, of the ideal beauty materialized in the names, Combray and Tansonville. In a memorable page, the greatest French stylist of our age lends actuality and permanence to an experience everyone will recognize who has ever wakened on a fine morning in the country. I mean that delicious confusion of nature and domestic art which mischievous, rioting Spring creates in an old house like Gilberte's by the simple device of abolishing man's absurd lines of demarcation, by allowing the garden to invade rooms pretentiously decorated with roses, apple-blossoms and ridiculous, perching birds.

Toute la journée, dans cette demeure de Tansonville un peu trop campagne qui n'avait l'air que d'un lieu de sieste entre deux promenades ou pendant l'averse, une de ces demeures où chaque salon a l'air d'un cabinet de verdure et où sur la tenture des chambres, les roses du jardin dans l'une, les oiseaux des arbres dans l'autre, vous ont rejoints et vous tiennent compagnie — isolés du moins — car c'étaient de vieilles tentures où chaque rose était assez séparée pour qu'on eût pu si elle avait été vivante, la cueillir, chaque oiseau le mettre en cage et l'apprivoiser, sans rien de ces grandes décorations des chambres d'aujourd'hui où sur un fond d'argent tous les pommiers de Normandie sont venus se profiler en style japonais, pour halluciner les heures que vous passez au lit, toute la journée je la passais dans ma chambre qui donnait sur les belles verdures du parc et des lilas de l'entrée, sur les feuilles vertes des grands arbres au bord de l'eau, étincelants de soleil et la forêt de Méséglise.[1]

[All day long, at Tansonville, in that slightly over-countrified house which gave the impression of being merely a place for a nap between two walks or during a sudden downpour, one of those dwellings where every sitting-room looks like a rustic arbour, and where, on the wall-paper, the garden-roses in one of the rooms, the tree-birds in the other, have overtaken you and keep you company —some stray ones at any rate—for it was old-fashioned wall-paper where every rose was sufficiently detached for you to have been able, had it been real, to pluck it, and each bird for you to put it in a cage and tame it, with none of those showy decorative patterns one gets in rooms nowadays where, against a silver background, all the apple-trees in Normandy, silhouetted in the Japanese manner, have come along to hallucinate the hours you spend in bed, all day long I stayed in my room which looked out upon the beautiful verdure of the park and the lilacs at the entrance, upon the green leaves of the tall trees sparkling in the sunshine at the water's edge and upon the forest of Méséglise.]

Marcel now tells us of the immense change that has occurred in Saint-Loup since the old days at Balbec and Doncières when the tantrums of the actress Rachel nearly drove him out of his mind with jealousy and despair. In his place we observe a

[1] *TR.* I, 7.

stranger. Although physically he has altered little, resembling more than ever the restless, alert and gold-crested bird of Marcel's early impressions, Saint-Loup's character has undergone a sinister and fundamental transformation. This can best be expressed in the brutal statement that Morel now occupies in his mind the place formerly occupied by Rachel and which belongs to his wife, Gilberte. Marcel's observations reveal how deeply seated is Robert's terrible vice. Gone is the old spontaneous affection, the direct and charming frankness of speech and gesture. Robert, as his old friend is obliged to admit with sorrowful reluctance, is now a hypocrite and a liar. Moreover, when Gilberte uncovers his falsehoods, her husband is subject to hysterical fits of theatrical self-abasement or maudlin protestations of tenderness. For the nephew, as Marcel shrewdly notes, has inherited not only his uncle's vice but also the baron's methods of camouflage so that Gilberte is constantly made unhappy by Robert's apparent infidelities and by the public nature of his assignations with women. Marcel is particularly repelled by this aspect of his friend's hypocrisy and it hurts him to see poor Gilberte painted like Rachel, imitating the latter's flamboyant mode of dress in a pathetic effort to recapture her husband's love.

Now, although Proust has always taken considerable trouble to emphasize, in his novel, the fallibility of the average observer's perceptions, he confronts us here with a complete and fundamental transformation of character which cannot be attributed to the obtuseness of Marcel or of the reader. In the space of a few years Hyperion becomes a satyr—even worse, a sodomite. Once again, in order to appreciate what is new in any novelty, the best way is to consult history. Proust, it will be seen, is breaking with a tradition respected by every French novelist from Mme de La Fayette to Flaubert. This tradition, which derives from a fixed belief in the unity of the individual self or personality, rules that the novelist, in exposing a character, must always reflect that unity. He may depict a character as a series of psychological states which are evoked, only very gradually, by certain situations or circumstances. Or, on the other hand, having exposed the dominant traits or passions which essentially compose a character, he may then proceed like Balzac or Stendhal to demonstrate the repercussions produced by a dominating personality on its environment. Again, as in the case of Mme de La Fayette, the novelist may reveal the terrific force exerted by the passion of love in its efforts to transform a personality, for instance, to change a married woman of high principles into an adulteress. But even if this had happened to the princesse de Clèves, such a momentary lapse does not constitute a revolution equivalent to that imagined by Proust since, obviously, if Mme de La Fayette's heroine had succumbed to temptation she would have experienced bitter remorse. The real unity of her character would not have been destroyed. To grasp the extent of Proust's departure from tradition we should have to picture a princesse de Clèves inexplicably transformed into a cynical wanton, Grandet into a dissipated spendthrift, Emma Bovary into a Mme Arnoux or Julien Sorel into an abbé Constantin. That life offers surprises resembling that which now confronts Marcel is beyond dispute. Most of us who have lived any length of time can cite examples. The writer can recall the shock he experienced after an interval of many years on discovering that a person known in his youth as the very soul of generosity, open-handed to a fault, had changed into a regular Harpagon. But there was a reason for this transformation. In middle-age, yielding to a natural impulse, this man had stood guarantor for a relative by marriage who went bankrupt for a very large sum. Reduced to something like penury, obliged at fifty-five to start afresh, the benefactor underwent a complete change. His character was utterly transformed by the shock of this experience. Forced to observe the strictest economy in little things, the habit of saving degenerated into avarice.

Proust, however, indicates no such turning-point in the psychological evolution of Saint-Loup. Wise after the event, the reader can no doubt turn back to that extraordinary conversation overheard by Marcel between Robert and one of the Guermantes flunkeys. But this is only illuminating in retrospect. At the time, all Marcel could possibly have learned was that Saint-Loup possessed an unexpected capacity for idle malice. Bad enough, certainly, yet hardly a symptom of the integral change we now observe in Robert. Proust talks of Saint-Loup's *mal héréditaire* and from a former allusion to Kotzebue's comedy *Onkel und Neffe*, he clearly believed that nephews tend more readily to inherit their uncle's rather than their parents' qualities or defects. One is reluctantly obliged, therefore, to conclude that this is his sole explanation of Saint-Loup's metamorphosis. Sexual inversion, it seems, is a hereditary disease, the insidious effects of which may be delayed for many years. That Proust held this opinion is clear from other examples which occur in his final volume. Such is the theory which, according to the critic, Alain, was originally advanced by Lombroso, but has been refuted by medical science. Alain, it will be recalled, takes Proust severely to task for accepting such a crazy doctrine which leaves, he says, an ugly stain on the novel. No one will disagree nowadays with Alain on Lombroso. On the other hand, it is often very tempting for a novelist to mistake a new and convincing theory for a scientific law. I suggest, also, that in this case the temptation was unusually strong. Proust, as we have frequently observed in his method of exposing a character, tries always to show up the weakness of the empirical psychologists of the Taine school, who claimed to be able to discover the real unity of a personality by piecing together certain psychological states, as if such incomplete, external notations could ever reveal the essence of a mobile and constantly altering *moi*. That is why Proust admired and to some extent imitated Dostoevski's mode of reflecting character. Remember that conversation between Marcel and Albertine where the former compares the great novelist to the painter Elstir since both, instead of presenting things in their logical order, beginning, that is to say, with the cause, show us first of all the effect, the illusion that strikes us. The behaviour of Dostoevski's characters, he explains to Albertine, is as deceptive as the impressions produced by Elstir's paintings, where the sea appears to be in the sky. In the Russian's novels we are astonished to note that a man we had thought of as a cunning rascal is fundamentally an excellent fellow and vice-versa. And this is precisely how Proust now presents Saint-Loup. Only, since he was a French and not a Slav novelist, Proust sought to bridge the gap between the real and the unreal with Lombroso's theory of hereditary inversion. But to-day, who believes in the existence of hereditary inversion? So the bridge collapses and for most readers, Saint-Loup's transformation will remain, I fear, an enigma possessing the hallucinatory quality of certain nightmares where 'fair is foul', where those one holds dearest may speak and act in the most appalling manner.

It is evident from Marcel's comments on his own actual, objective interpretation of Albertine's personality that Proust, in the first chapter of *Le temps retrouvé*, was exercised by this problem of the novelist's approach to character. Inspired now only by a mechanical curiosity, Marcel begins to reconsider certain of Albertine's actions and conversations in a new light. Gilberte, unlike her husband, cannot keep off the topic of inversion, which gives her visitor an opportunity of interjecting a casual question about Albertine. The latter, says Gilberte, was completely innocent of such tastes. On the other hand, Marcel distinctly remembers a phrase dropped by Albertine in the early days of their intimacy, concerning her 'demi-rapports' with Gilberte. A new explanation occurs to him. What if Albertine, then very young, was really guiltless but merely wanted to appear sophisticated in the eyes of a man of the world? Another idea comes into his mind, evoked by his new impression of Saint-Loup. Quite probably, the latter, misled by Gilberte's conversation as he had been by Albertine's, married her on that account, 'espérant des plaisirs qu'il n'avait pas dû trouver chez lui puisqu'il les prenait ailleurs'.[1] Such, concludes Marcel, is the over-simplified diagnosis of Albertine's personality which now presents itself, 'maintenant que je ne voyais plus cette aventure que du dehors'.[1] Proust's inference is clear. In order to seize the essential reality of a personality, the novelist's intelligence must be reinforced by intuition, by what Bergson would call 'une espèce d'auscultation spirituelle'. That is the secret of every great artist. Marcel, however, does not at this stage consider the positive aspect of this problem.

We are now coming to an incident which suggests certain comments on the narrative form adopted by Proust and handed

[1] *TR.* I, 21.

down to him by a long line of distinguished novelists including Lesage, Prévost, Marivaux, Chateaubriand and Fromentin. It is worth noting, by the way, that in employing the 'récit personnel' Proust revived a narrative technique which had been rejected by the great nineteenth-century masters, Balzac, Stendhal, Flaubert and Zola. Proust did not merely revive this form: he exploited it in such a way as to reveal its surprising virtualities because, although it is true that the novelist who relates his story in the first person singular gives the reader thereby a sense of immediate contact with the narrator, it is equally true that very often this impression rests upon an illusion. Gil Blas, for example, can talk for hours about his adventures without ever admitting us into the intimacy of his sentiments or thoughts, whilst Marivaux's charming Marianne, who never tires of analysing her perceptions and emotions, is really a past-mistress in the art of psychological 'strip-tease'. By way of contrast, turn to the 'je' of Chateaubriand's René or of Fromentin's Dominique. One is immediately transported to an immensely deeper level of the narrator's consciousness. Proust uses the 'récit personnel', it seems to me, in a new and remarkable fashion. Marcel's narrative reveals all the levels of his consciousness from its surface contact with the external world down into those profound regions of the self where the unconscious mysteriously glides into the shifting zone illuminated by memory and intelligence. But the point I should like to emphasize is that the 'je' of Marcel refracts not a vertical, geological section of Marcel's character, not a stratification, but that continuous interfusion of various states of soul which alone can reflect the reality of a personality. No other French novelist I have read has ever employed the 'récit personnel' in such a way. Even Fromentin, though his gamut is less restricted than Chateaubriand's, is not to be compared in this respect with Proust.

Nevertheless, there are moments when the 'récit personnel' technique is a source of embarrassment to the novelist, as for example when he wants to acquaint his reader with aspects of his characters which could not possibly have come within the personal experience of the narrator. Under the old regime, it was often arranged that the latter should light upon an escritoire

or strong-box crammed with interesting memoirs. Proust
employs much the same device in order to tell us about the early
history of the Verdurins though, by the way, we are never really
told how Marcel knows about the details of Swann's love for
Odette. However, to return to the Verdurins, we should picture
Marcel at Tansonville reading himself to sleep with an unpublished volume of the Goncourts' *Journal* borrowed from his
hostess. Oddly enough, it contains an account of the writer's
relations with the Verdurins when their *salon* was in the Quai
Conti. Verdurin, we gather from Proust's brilliant and sometimes wicked *pastiche* of Goncourt, had been at one time art
critic of the *Revue des Deux Mondes,* and is the author of a
remarkable study of Whistler. Since his marriage, however,
with the Madeleine of Fromentin's famous novel, Verdurin has
given up writing, though possibly his addiction to morphia
might explain this renunciation. In any case Verdurin, the
former intimate of famous artists and authors, is now eclipsed
by his wife's rising prestige and dismissed by her friends as an
amiable philistine or at best a harmless dilettante without a line
of print to his name.

Thanks to this ingenious variant of a technical cliché, we are
able to catch a glimpse of other early examples of Proustian
characters. Brichot with shaven upper lip and butler's side-
burns infuriates Goncourt by his silence in regard to the latter's
work, thus maintaining the typical attitude of the *sorbonnard* to
contemporary literature. Here, too, is a Pole whose name
Goncourt cannot quite catch, though we know it is the princesse
Sherbatoff. According to Cottard, her exile in France is linked
with the mysterious story of an attempted assassination. The
princess apparently shot at and missed an Archduke. Cottard
strikes Goncourt as a man of remarkable intelligence and so
does the princess, maybe because she asserts that no Polish
girl would ever consent to give her hand to a man who was not
a passionate admirer of *La Faustin.* The princess is obviously
a lady of acute penetration, very different, for example, from
Brichot. Here also is an early Swann, admiring his hostess'
pearls once owned, he insists, by Mme de La Fayette, according
to a portrait in the collection of the duc de Guermantes.

Goncourt remembers the duke as a charming little boy called Basin, the favourite nephew of Mme de Beausergent, sister of the marquise de Villeparisis.

But the most arresting figure in these animated pages is Mme Verdurin herself, portrayed as she was just after her rupture with Elstir, familiarly known as Monsieur Tiche, the artist whose divine flower-paintings owed so much to her sensitive appreciation of natural beauty. Here Proust is completing a picture which we have already noted in its unfinished state. Now, with a few deft touches he deepens the impression suggested in the La Raspelière version. Listen to Mme Verdurin as she tells Goncourt of her early association with Elstir:

Je lui apprenais à disposer ses fleurs, au commencement il ne pouvait pas en venir au bout. Il n'a jamais su faire un bouquet. Il n'avait pas de goût naturel, il fallait que je lui dise: 'Non, ne peignez pas cela, cela n'en vaut pas la peine, peignez ceci. Ah! s'il nous avait écoutés aussi pour l'arrangement de sa vie comme pour l'arrangement de ses fleurs et s'il n'avait pas fait ce sale mariage!' Et brusquement, les yeux enfiévrés par l'absorption d'une rêverie tournée vers le passé, avec le nerveux taquinage, dans l'allongement maniaque de ses phalanges, du floche des manches de son corsage, c'est, dans le contournement de sa pose endolorie, comme un admirable tableau qui n'a je crois jamais été peint, et où se lirait toute la révolte contenue, toutes les susceptibilités rageuses d'une amie outragée dans les délicatesses, dans la pudeur de la femme....

Here, indeed, we have one of those imitations of which Voltaire used to say that they reveal how the original should have been written.

Also in this Mme Verdurin we have already the professional lion huntress whom Marcel knew, the tyrannical and possessive *salonnière*, brutally intolerant of any æsthetic doctrine conflicting with her own. Yet Proust gives us in his *pastiche* the impression of a Mme Verdurin whose dogmatism, although tiresome, has a real basis of expert knowledge. This is the period of her cult of painting, an informed and genuine passion. It is only when she discards it for music that one scents the odour of humbug and snobbery. On the contrary, everything in her Quai Conti *salon*, from the conversation of the hostess to the table appointments so ravishingly described by 'Goncourt', suggests a Mme Verdurin who perceives nuances of colour and elegance of form with the eye of a born artist, lacking only the artist's power to express her vision. At last we fully understand why Elstir's desertion shook her so profoundly.

The Goncourt *pastiche*, although illuminating a fragment of of 'pre-Marcellan' history, was not solely designed for this reason. In the closing pages of the first chapter of *Le temps retrouvé* we discover its true *raison d'être*, which is to illustrate the supreme phase of Marcel's disillusionment and allow Proust to suggest a way out of his spiritual impasse.

The *Journal* revives Marcel's dormant misgivings about the value of literature. It describes people he has dined with on many occasions, individuals devoid of the smallest literary interest yet who undoubtedly impressed Goncourt with their intelligence and exquisite taste. Literature, obviously, does not always reflect the truth of life since it can invest vulgar non-entities like the Verdurins with an illusory prestige. As a humble layman Marcel hesitates to elaborate his criticisms which derive, it would seem, from an heretical conviction that art is simply a beautiful lie, that the world portrayed in the artist's vision is a figment of his imagination designed to compensate us for the shortcomings of the actual universe in which we are doomed to live. Nowhere does Marcel explicitly put forward these views which, it will be recalled, form the substance of F. Paulhan's *Le mensonge de l'art*, a work no doubt well known to Proust. They are, nevertheless, most certainly implied in the passage reflecting the disillusionment inspired in Marcel by the 'Goncourt' *Journal*. But Proust does not of course present Marcel at this point as a militant heretic in revolt against an established faith and defiantly proclaiming the superiority of a new gospel. That phase in the history of Marcel's vocation is reserved for the final volume of *Le temps retrouvé*.

Meanwhile we see a tired and very sick man, about to enter a nursing-home for a long course of treatment. He derives, if anything, a kind of solace from the thought that since art is not the fine and precious thing he had pictured, illness will deprive him of less than he had feared. This situation Proust exploits in order to express with an air of diffidence that will deceive nobody, his own views on the problem of the artist's approach to reality. Highly suggestive, his observations are, however, tantalizingly incomplete and need some sort of glossary, if we are to grasp their relationship to the author's other pronouncements on the art of the novel. Marcel, who is unable to reconcile Goncourt's reconstruction of the Verdurin group with his own impressions is ready to admit ruefully that probably these are inaccurate. On the other hand, he knows that he is not totally devoid of perception, though his faculty of observation operates very differently from that of Goncourt. It functions most actively, for instance, when his attention is arrested by the sudden discovery of an unexpected identity between objects or persons that have apparently nothing in common. Thus, in a *salon*, Marcel automatically misses the hundred picturesque external traits which make the *Journal* such attractive reading. Much less interested in what people are saying than in the gestures and intonations accompanying their words, he tends always to probe beneath the surface in search of concealed realities. To borrow his own image, Marcel's mode of observation is a kind of radiography, resulting very often in pictures completely unlike the clearly defined snapshots of the Goncourt school of photography. Disconcerting, often repellent, they lack the charm of the Goncourtian portraits and in fact would be dismissed by most connoisseurs as inartistic though they capture essential truths that escape the camera of the professional Realist. As I have said, Marcel very modestly refrains from putting these criticisms into words but they are certainly implied in this illuminating account of how, by contrast with Goncourt, he looks at life.

Having disarmingly taken us into his confidence, Marcel humbly concludes that 'Goncourt savait écouter comme il savait voir, je ne le savais pas'.[1] He is still, it seems, the ugly duckling of the fairy-tale, unconscious of the glorious transformation that is to come, though not for many years. In the meantime, until his clinic is finally shut down for lack of staff in 1916, Marcel lives far from Paris, cut off from society, having, moreover, renounced all idea of ever becoming a distinguished man of

[1] *TR.* I, 40.

letters. Only once, in 1914, does he revisit the capital. It is to attend an Army Medical Board which rejects him, like Proust, as unfit for military service or for national work of any kind.

Before drifting into this æsthetic *acedia*, Marcel makes a brief attempt to understand his own divergence from the currently accepted standards of literary taste and mentions not for the first time a trait which he obviously regards as fundamental and, if not unique, at least highly original.

Il y avait en moi [he says] un personnage qui savait plus ou moins bien regarder mais c'était un personnage intermittent, ne reprenant vie que quand se manifestait quelque essence générale, commune à plusieurs choses, qui faisait sa nourriture et sa joie. Alors le personnage regardait et écoutait, mais à une certaine profondeur seulement, de sorte que l'observation n'en profitait pas. Comme un géomètre qui, dépouillant les choses de leurs qualités sensibles ne voit que leur substratum linéaire, ce que racontaient les gens m'échappait, car ce qui m'intéressait, c'était non ce qu'ils voulaient dire, mais la manière dont ils le disaient, en tant qu'elle était révélatrice de leur caractère ou de leurs ridicules; ou plutôt c'était un objet qui avait toujours été plus particulièrement le but de ma recherche parce qu'il me donnait un plaisir spécifique, le point qui était commun à un être et à un autre.[1]

Here Marcel is repeating, more or less, what he told us in *La Prisonnière*[2] about his individual outlook on life. There, it will be recalled, he said that when illness should one day destroy the various 'personnages' or selves composing the individual called Marcel, the very last to survive would be 'un certain philosophe qui n'est heureux que quand il a découvert entre deux œuvres, entre deux sensations, une partie commune'.

Now, the most common of all human activities is the construction of general ideas based on the recognition of identities or resemblances so that, in this loose sense, everyone may claim to be a *philosophe*. Clearly, therefore, Marcel's remarks must hold a deeper meaning. The observer, in this case, is the artist, more particularly the novelist, whose function is to create men and women sufficiently individual to astonish us, yet resembling us sufficiently to arouse our interest, sympathy or perhaps our revulsion. Is Proust simply restating the seventeenth-century French conception of art, the ideal of a literature

[1] *TR.* I, 36.   [2] *P.* I, 13.

which tended towards the universal and was, on the whole, little interested in material realities since these are changeable and blur our vision of the great, fundamental human traits, common to men of every race or epoch? I hardly think so. Otherwise, why does he imply that Marcel's flair for identities represents a new and fruitful approach to reality by the artist? The novelty of his attitude, if it is novel, must lie elsewhere. Perhaps a closer scrutiny of Marcel's language may furnish a clue.

In the passage just quoted, Proust compares Marcel's intermittently observing self to a surveyor who is interested, not in the material qualities of things but primarily in their 'linear substratum'. In another context, he likens him to a surgeon who perceives in the polished surface of a woman's abdomen only the underlying cancer which is destroying her. And again, in the same passage, he attributes to Marcel the remark: 'J'avais beau dîner en ville, je ne voyais pas les convives, parce que quand je croyais les regarder je les radiographiais.'[1] The idea suggested in every case is that of depth. Marcel insists that persons or things viewed or 'radiographed' in this way by the artist will appear to us strange and unreal because his interpretation or picture omits all the external features by which the ordinary observer would recognize the original. So far, Proust is perfectly clear. What is less easy to grasp is the connection between these remarks and Marcel's theory of identities, the obsession for discovering hidden resemblances between individuals or things. For it is only when such a manifestation strikes his consciousness, only when the objects or things of his experience present such resemblances that his peculiar faculty of observation begins to function. Unfortunately, too, Proust offers us but one concrete example of what occurs when Marcel's consciousness, which had hitherto been in a state of 'total engourdissement spirituel', is suddenly awakened. It is when he perceives, behind his surface impressions of Mme Verdurin's *salon* as he perceived it at different times and places, the something common to all of them, 'l'identité du salon Verdurin...située à mi-profondeur, au delà de l'apparence elle-même dans une zone un peu plus en retrait'.[1] I think, however, we can now seize the tenuous

[1] *TR.* I, 37.

guiding thread linking Marcel's theory of identities with what might be called his theory of radiographic observation. What Marcel is now describing is a mode of perception closely resembling that which Bergson attributes to the great artist in whose mind impressions of the external world of things and individuals have penetrated so deeply that he is conscious of qualitative resemblances or identities invisible to the more superficial observer who sees only a picturesque variety of heterogeneous elements. This view is confirmed in the following passage: 'Il en résultait,' he says of his 'radiographic' notations, 'qu'en réunissant toutes les remarques que j'avais pu faire dans un dîner sur les convives, le dessin des lignes tracées par moi figurait un ensemble de lois psychologiques où l'intérêt propre qu'avait eu dans ses discours un convive ne tenait presque aucune place.'[1] He does not know and will not know until he has found his vocation that it is such impressions communicated through the medium of the writer's individual style, which constitute the greatness of a work of art, precisely because they interpret a vision of the world infinitely more true and real than any collection of Goncourtian snapshots. It is significant that Marcel should mention the elusive something common to all his impressions of the Verdurin *salon*, irrespective of time or space or as he puts it, 'dans divers lieus et divers temps'. Brichot, it will be recalled, was vaguely conscious of a similar qualitative identity but lacked the artist's power to communicate its unique and individual quality. Later, in the second volume of *Le temps perdu*, Marcel will realize the very special and precious quality of such resemblances when they are seized, not just 'à mi-profondeur' but through the modality of the involuntary memory, in the very depths of his being, in the unconscious. But for that priceless invention, art, they would never be revealed to us so that, like Marcel at Tansonville, we should find life a barren and joyless experience. At times, indeed, he had felt intuitively that the artist possessed this miraculous power of surprising and revealing the inner harmony beneath the apparent discord of everyday existence, for example, when he listened to Vinteuil's septet. But now Marcel has

[1] *TR.* I, 37.

temporarily lost his faith in art which seems, like love, another illusion.

Nothing is easier to create or so hard to kill as a legend. That is why it is so difficult to write a true history of literature. The legend initiated by Proust's early critics of a wealthy dilettante obsessed by an almost hysterical cult of the aristocracy will persist, it is to be feared, as long as the fiction of a 'tendre' Racine; of a Voltaire who championed the downtrodden masses against royal tyranny and a Marivaux who wrote ethereal and unreal comedies. Of course, as Voltaire used to say, there is always a reason for every stupidity. In Proust's case it can be traced to the early Combray volumes of his novel, which reflect so exquisitely Marcel's adolescent belief in the unique, mysterious beauty of feudalism, materialized in the amaranth name of Guermantes and incarnated in the lovely Oriane de Guermantes. The slow disintegration of this belief is related in the chapters describing the young man's first actual contacts with the Faubourg Saint-Germain. As the narrative unfolds, one observes his progressive and deepening contempt for the selfishness, stupidity and frivolity which characterize, with rare exceptions, the members of that exclusive caste. What Marcel shows us, however, is not a fixed unchanging entity but a society in continuous evolution, static and homogeneous only to the eye of the superficial observer who fails to perceive the incessant re-creation due to the operation of an inner principle. I allude to that tendency to *déclassement* so characteristic of every old aristocracy. Before the first World War, as Proust reveals, this process was temporarily arrested by the Dreyfus Affair which revived the prestige of the French nobility. But the Affair is now over. It has become history, that is to say, has passed outside the zone of the national consciousness.

The chapter entitled 'Monsieur Charlus en temps de guerre' reveals the action of a corrosive and satirical mind brought to bear upon the fashionable coterie which dominated the Parisian scene from 1916 until 1918, a society where political power and wealth exert a greater influence than caste. Its reigning queen is no longer the duchesse de Guermantes but Mme Verdurin, whose chief ally is Albertine's aunt, Mme Bontemps. Gone for ever is the epoch when a Charlus, despite his sinister, unmentioned vice, was able to subjugate the most recalcitrant of *salonnières* by the threat of social excommunication. Charlus himself is now outside the pale, a victim of that eternal *devenir* which is life's very essence. The creation of the universe, as Marcel once remarked to him, did not take place once and for all: it is being re-enacted at every moment. Now, in the light of this typically Bergsonian principle, he reviews the smaller world of the Faubourg Saint-Germain from which he has been separated for so many years.

Proust tells us, it is true, that Marcel revisited Paris in the autumn of 1914, for a sojourn of two months. But not until 1916 did he actually resume contact with the people and scenes of his pre-war existence. Why, then, does Proust go out of his way to intercalate the 1914 episode in Marcel's narrative of the period from 1916 to the Armistice? First of all, presumably, he felt it necessary to define Marcel's own situation before launching him upon a narrative where the question of patriotism and other aspects of the individual's attitude to his country in time of war will occupy an important place. Marcel, we are again discreetly reminded, is a *réformé*, quite unfit for any type of national service, and Proust implies that during those two months in Paris, the invalid did everything possible to secure war employment but was sent back to his clinic for treatment. He returned, in 1916, uncured.

In the autumn of 1914, he saw Robert and his other old school comrade, Bloch. Marcel tells us that his reunion with Saint-Loup, though brief, served to mitigate the painful impressions of Tansonville and to bring back memories of the friend he knew at Balbec and Doncières. This is peculiarly evident in the account of Robert's attitude towards the war which is in striking contrast to Bloch's noisy chauvinism. The latter, convinced that his myopia is a sure guarantee of exemption from military service, is now a rampant militarist. Saint-Loup, on the other hand, though privately moving heaven and earth to get back to the army as a fighting soldier, deliberately shocks his acquaintances by flatly announcing that every fit man, including himself, who is not in uniform is quite simply afraid for his hide. 'Et moi, si je ne reprends pas service, c'est tout bonnement par peur, na!' An ardent patriot, he is incapable, however, of discussing his profound love of France, inspired, notes Marcel, by the same *délicatesse morale* which kept his mother silent about her filial tenderness. She would have gladly given her life for her own mother yet would rather have suffered a hundred deaths than talk about her immense love. It is typical also of the Guermantes in Saint-Loup never to refer to the Kaiser as Guillaume but always as l'Empereur Guillaume, a habit that exasperates Bloch. 'C'est ça, tu as la frousse, déjà tu te mets à plat ventre devant lui! Ah! ça nous fera de beaux soldats à la frontière, ils lècheront les bottes des Boches. Vous êtes des galonnés qui savez parader dans un carrousel. Un point c'est tout.'[1] For Bloch, in spite of his defective eyesight, has now been roped in by a sceptical Medical Board as a category B soldier. Consequently, he is now a confirmed anti-militarist. Marcel, whilst admiring Robert's *savoir-vivre* shrewdly points out, however, that it arises from certain serious intellectual limitations. 'Celui qui ne sait pas les rejeter reste un homme du monde.' Robert obtains a commission in the infantry and goes to the front whilst Gilberte, to escape the air-raids, sets out for Tansonville with her little daughter, only to find it in enemy hands. In a letter to Marcel she is full of praise for the correct manners of the German staff-officers billeted in her house though he thinks that her enthusiasm may be due to the 'esprit des Guermantes' who are of Bavarian descent, or again, perhaps to Gilberte's ancestral Jewish internationalism. Some months later, she writes from recaptured Combray in quite a different vein. Having completely forgotten why she really left Paris, her departure from Combray, viewed in retrospect, is presented by Gilberte in heroic colours. She now figures, to Marcel's amusement, as the châtelaine of French tradition, ignoring the protests of her friends, rushing to defend her 'cher Tansonville' from the depredations of the barbarians.

Proust does not of course attempt to follow the changing fortunes of the war, though from time to time he opens up the perspective so as to reveal, by way of contrast, the real France,

[1] *TR.* I, 69.

the France of the millions of *poilus* whose epic bravery, reflected in Saint-Loup's letters, fills Marcel's heart with deep humility and pride. This picture is always in the background of his mind as he considers the various reactions to the war of the characters we have come to know so well. For all of them are here, except Albertine, who seldom enters Marcel's thoughts. When he recalls her it is because of Andrée's husband, Octave, whose projected marriage with Albertine was the cause of the latter's sudden flight. Sometimes, too, in this unfamiliar Paris, on wintry nights in streets as quiet as those of Combray, wind-swept and chilly like Balbec in the late autumn, he wishes Albertine could walk by his side, sharing his wonder at the transformation effected by the war. Everyone who has seen the wild flowers invade the London soil from which they had been so long exiled by man will recognize in the following passage how exquisitely Proust interprets that swift and mysterious process by which Nature, slinking in the wake of war, reasserts her primeval rights.

Hélas, j'étais seul et je me faisais l'effet d'aller faire une visite de voisin à la campagne, de ces visites comme Swann venait nous en faire après le dîner, sans rencontrer plus de passants dans l'obscurité de Tansonville, par ce petit chemin de halage, jusqu'à la rue du Saint-Esprit, que je n'en rencontrais maintenant dans les rues devenues de sinueux chemins rustiques de la rue Clotilde à la rue Bonaparte. D'ailleurs, comme ces fragments de paysage que le temps qu'il fait modifie n'étaient plus contrariés par un cadre devenu nuisible, les soirs où le vent chassait un grain glacial, je me croyais bien plus au bord de la mer furieuse dont j'avais jadis tant rêvé que je ne m'y étais senti à Balbec; et même d'autres éléments de nature qui n'existaient pas jusque-là à Paris faisaient croire qu'on venait, descendant du train, d'arriver pour les vacances en pleine campagne: par exemple le contraste de lumière et d'ombre qu'on avait à côté de soi par terre les soirs de clair de lune. Celui-ci donnait de ces effets que les villes ne connaissent pas, même en plein hiver; ses rayons s'étalaient sur la neige qu'aucun travailleur ne déblayait plus, boulevard Haussmann, comme ils eussent fait sur un glacier des Alpes. Les silhouettes des arbres se reflétaient nettes et pures sur cette neige d'or bleuté, avec la délicatesse qu'elles ont dans certaines peintures japonaises ou dans certains fonds de Raphaël; elles étaient allongées à terre au pied de l'arbre lui-même, comme on les voit souvent dans la nature au soleil couchant quand celui-ci inonde et rend réfléchissantes les prairies où des arbres s'élèvent à intervalles réguliers.[1]

[Alas! I was alone and felt as if I was about to pay a neighbourly call in the country, the sort of call Swann used to pay us, after dinner, without meeting any more passers-by in the darkness of Tansonville, on his way along that little towing-path as far as the rue de l'Esprit, than I now encountered in the streets, which had become winding country lanes, linking up the rue Clotilde with the rue Bonaparte. Besides, as those fragments of landscape which change their appearance according to the prevailing weather were now freed of the setting that had irked them, on the evenings when the wind whipped past in icy squalls, I had a much more lively impression of being on the shore of that stormy sea I had so often dreamed of, than I had ever actually felt at Balbec; other natural elements, even, which had hitherto never existed in Paris gave one the illusion of having just alighted from the train, for the holidays, right in the heart of the country: for instance, the contrast of light and shade on the ground, beside one, on moonlit evenings. Moonlight produced those effects unknown to towns, even in the depths of winter; its rays displayed themselves on the snow, now no longer cleared away by any crossing-sweeper, in the Boulevard Haussmann, as they would have done on an Alpine glacier. The silhouettes of the trees were reflected in their sharp purity on that snow of blued gold, with the delicacy they reveal in certain Japanese paintings or in certain Raphael backgrounds; they lay stretched out on the ground at the foot of the tree itself, as they are often to be seen in nature when the setting sun floods and makes mirrors of the fields where trees rise up at regular intervals.]

Who has not remarked, sententiously and often, that war brings out the best and the worst in human nature? One of the great services rendered by genius to humanity is to refurbish such truisms and to show us that they are still truths. With the obvious aspects of this particular verity Proust is not directly concerned, knowing that others are better placed than he to witness and record the more brutal manifestations of human nature in times of war. There are, however, other less spectacular human traits which attain their complete and poisonous ripeness in war, and to these Proust now applies his original talents of analysis and observation. Let us watch, first of all, the activities of Mme Verdurin. She is no longer the High Priestess

[1] *TR.* I, 61–2.

of Music, no longer the hostess of La Raspelière whose passion for septets and quartets, for Debussy and Vinteuil, used to do incredible things to her blood pressure. The Verdurin *salon* is now installed in a luxury hotel, because of the fuel shortage. Here the only music is the sharp trilling of the telephone and of the voices at that invisible, mysterious other end which is not exactly G.H.Q. but one of those 'absolutely reliable sources' indirectly connected with the fount of all military knowledge. Crowded into this suite or into the Verdurin private dining-room, with periodic seepages into the hotel restaurant, you can observe the veterans of the 'clan' and their attendant satellites. Every nation at war has to contend with such pests, the rich, fashionable idlers whose insatiable vanity, whose incredible stupidity, hypocrisy and impudence generate an atmosphere of false and sensational rumours, of dangerous and irresponsible political intrigue. For the Verdurins of life, war is merely another social event, on a grander scale of course than a visit from a foreign royalty or a ball at the Guermantes' yet, essentially, an occasion to be avidly seized upon and capitalized in the interests of social prestige. Drones in the threatened hive, too stupid even to realize that its existence is in deadly peril, they fill the air with their clamorous hum, distracting and impeding the serious, active defenders. Wealthy, therefore politically influential, they pester generals and ministers with their requests for inside information or special privileges. Thus a Mme Verdurin, through the good offices of Dr Cottard, now arrayed in a queer uniform resembling that of a Haitian admiral, is in the virtually unique position of being able to munch a buttery pre-war *croissant* whilst gloating with starting eyes at the news of the sinking of the *Lusitania*. Awaiting her in the street outside is a glittering limousine chauffeured by a eupeptic individual in uniform who ought to be in the trenches. This, again, Mme Verdurin owes to her ruthless persistence or to the complaisance of her influential friends. The most bosom of these is now Mme Bontemps whose husband, the ex-Dreyfusard, holds an important post in one of the ministries. As Proust remarks with disillusioned perspicacity, all the old *canailles* of the political racket come back to power in wartime simply because no others are available possessing the necessary craft. They can always count, moreover, on the ephemeral character of the public memory and on the fundamental property of all existence, which is change. Bontemps, we are told, used to be considered an enemy of France when all Dreyfusards were equated with anti-patriots. But this appellation was replaced by that of 'opponent to the Three Years Conscription Law' so that, automatically, Bontemps became a patriot before the war and as such is now remembered. Novelties, Marcel observes truly, only appear detestable so long as they are not assimilated and surrounded by a mass of reassuring elements, only until, like Dreyfusism, they become integrated in the category of ordinary, respectable things.

These elegant gangs or coteries, which ceaselessly undermine the national effort, always operate behind an impregnable façade of 'good works', charity balls, garden-parties, fêtes, benefit performances, all of which for the Odettes and Mme Verdurins are simply excuses for gratifying their normal lusts for publicity and sensation. They have, naturally, their accredited press and a special jargon, which afford Proust immeasurable and sardonic delight. With little surprise we learn that Norpois, the veteran diplomat, is now an unchallenged authority on the European situation. More astonishing is the meteoric ascent to fame of Legrandin. The comments of Charlus on the style of Norpois and Brichot are a joy to read, with their exquisite blend of satire and erudition. The pompous clichés spawned in wartime by a well-known type of journalist are here mercilessly exposed to ridicule and expertly analysed so as to reveal the writer's fundamental ignorance of the French language and of its nuances. Brichot has another, very different critic. It is Mme Verdurin, who is jealous of the lustre now surrounding one of the oldest and therefore most despised members of her clan. Yet one divines that what she really finds intolerable is that Brichot, like Elstir, owes his fame to his own talents, unaided by the guidance of his Egeria. So the myopic professor is held up as a butt to all the habitués of her daily gatherings. Such is the penalty reserved for sacrilege. Only Mme Verdurin may speak in the name of France. I fancy that this is really why she hounds poor

Brichot into replacing his 'je' by the impersonal 'on', which she regards, one feels, as little better since it is an insufferable rival to her own imperial 'nous'. Despite her scornful public glosses on Brichot's articles these represent in Mme Verdurin's view a disloyal and perfidious encroachment on her supreme authority. On the other hand, it is still with an unshaken sense of assurance that in response to the eager questions of her neophytes she replies: 'Hé bien, voici, nous exigeons du roi de Grèce qu'il se retire du Péloponèse. . . .Nous lui envoyons. . .' and so on.

When Proust tries to understand the callous indifference and selfishness of the Verdurin breed it seems to him to derive not so much from absolute viciousness or stupidity as from lack of imagination. He himself thinks of France and of Germany as two immense aggregations of cells, giants involved in a mighty conflict where every stroke, however, is determined by tactical or strategic rules. But the direct shock of the conflict is experienced only by the cells on the periphery of these great organisms, by the cells which are continually being destroyed and renewed. The more remote ones, like the Verdurins, go on with their normal existence and, being devoid of real intelligence, therefore blind, cannot realize the imminence of the danger which daily threatens them. True, the Verdurins, since they control a political *salon* where the military situation is endlessly discussed, must be aware of the frightful losses at the front, of the whole regiments swallowed up day after day in the holocaust. In fact, they do sometimes think of these things. But, as Marcel acidly remarks: 'Une opération inverse multiplie à tel point ce qui concerne notre bien-être et divise par un chiffre tellement formidable ce qui ne le concerne pas, que la mort de millions d'inconnus nous chatouille à peine et presque moins désagréablement qu'un courant d'air.'[1]

Happily, as a corrective to this La Rochefoucauld temper, Marcel has Saint-Loup's letters from the front and, eventually, a visit from Robert, on leave. In his sensitive description of this reunion, Proust expresses a state of soul which countless thousands have experienced, though its rare quality has seldom been so directly revealed in words. I mean the sentiments of

[1] *TR.* I, 108.

timidity, of gratitude, of almost superstitious awe produced on his friends behind the lines by the soldier just back from the front line. It seems to Marcel as if he were talking to one doomed by a mortal disease, yet able to behave in every respect like a normal and well man. Robert is a visitor from another world, the unreal world of death. Everything he says, projected against this background of the supernatural, impresses Marcel by its strange insignificance.

Car il est extraordinaire [he notes] à quel point chez les rescapés du front que sont les permissionaires parmi les vivants, ou chez les morts qu'un médium hypnotise ou évoque, le seul effet d'un contact avec le mystère soit d'accroître s'il est possible l'insignifiance des propos. Tel j'abordai Robert qui avait encore au front une cicatrice plus auguste et plus mystérieuse pour moi que l'empreinte laissée sur la terre par le pied d'un géant.[1]

Yet, as I quote these lines, it is with the terrible misgiving that perhaps the emotion which they so beautifully interpret may already be losing its human and universal actuality. War, as we have learned since 1916, is tending more and more to abolish the frontier that used to separate the soldier from the civilian and to cast over all the shadow of death. In the first World War, despite occasional air-raids, the Parisian was still intensely conscious of being divided by an immense gulf from his comrade in that mysterious and fearful zone, the front line.

In this young officer home on leave, Marcel rediscovers the Saint-Loup of Doncières, agile, vivacious like some rare, yellow-crested bird about to take wing. Here is the friend whose intelligent and eager disquisitions on the art of war used to hold him entranced for hours on end. And one can guess that Marcel is for Robert still the imaginative and brilliant intellectual whose psychological theories never failed to excite his admiration. Listening to Saint-Loup's vivid account of life in the trenches, to his stories of magnificent courage and self-sacrifice, Marcel is immensely reassured. They show him in its true perspective France, the eternal spirit of France and the profound love she inspires in her children. The Saint-Loup of Tansonville is almost expunged from his memory. But only for

[1] *TR.* I, 86.

a time, unfortunately, because this is not to be his last impression of Robert.

Proust now begins to paint a scene which might be entitled 'Promenade d'une nuit d'été' though it culminates in an experience not unlike a nightmare. On the way to call at the Verdurins, distracted by the glory of a turquoise sky freezing into the glacier blue of advancing dusk, Marcel finds himself involved in a labyrinth of narrow streets and then, to his surprise, in the crowds that throng the boulevards; jostled by troops of all the Allies, amongst them Hindus and Africans, whose dark skins and exotic uniforms create the illusion of an Oriental city planted in the heart of Paris. Suddenly he descries, emerging from the shadows into the pools of diffused light cast by the blued street-lamps, a strange and repulsive individual hurrying in the wake of two Zouaves. Tall, yet gross of body, mauve complexioned, he is wearing a conspiratorial soft black hat and a flowing cloak. Vaguely he reminds Marcel of some actor or painter notorious for his perverted habits. It is the baron de Charlus, obviously surprised, to judge from his affected nonchalance, in some dubious and secret occupation. Thus Proust with a conscious eye for the appropriate theatrical effect prepares the stage for the reappearance of Palamède de Charlus, justifying the promise held out in the title of this chapter. And Marcel abandons his projected visit to the Verdurins in order to tell us about the opinions and pleasures of Charlus. War or no war, a Charlus continues to indulge his vices, just as a Mme Verdurin continues to receive.

There are occasions, I have said, when Proust unconsciously reproduces the very accents of Marivaux. Note, for instance, the tone of this passage where Marcel tries to distinguish between the 'petite personnalité primitive' of Charlus and the personality created by his besetting vice.

M. de Charlus était arrivé aussi loin qu'il était possible de soi-même, ou plutôt il était lui-même si parfaitement masqué par ce qu'il était devenu et qui n'appartenait à lui seul mais à beaucoup d'autres invertis qu'à la première minute je l'avais pris pour un autre d'entre eux, derrière ces zouaves, en plein boulevard, pour un autre d'entre eux qui n'était pas M. de Charlus, qui n'était pas un grand seigneur, qui n'était pas un homme d'imagination et d'esprit et qui n'avait pour toute ressemblance avec le baron que cet air commun à eux tous, et qui maintenant chez lui, au moins avant qu'on se fût appliqué à bien regarder, couvrait tout.[1]

In the next fifty pages of Marcel's narrative our attention is directed not to the 'inverti' but to the Charlus whose views on the war afford Proust an opportunity for considering, from a new angle, the question of patriotism.

As a preliminary, however, he reveals the great change that has occurred in the baron's social position and, even more interesting, the suite of false premisses by which the enemies of Charlus have arrived at their more or less accurate conclusions regarding his attitude to the war. Mme Verdurin, who has not forgotten the incidents which closed the Morel recital, broadcasts the rumour that the baron is a German spy. The facts are, of course, irrefutable. La Raspelière overlooks a bay and was obviously a perfect site for a submarine base. This explains the eagerness of Charlus to attend her Wednesday dinners and also why he arrived so often by a different train and would never stay the night, preferring Doncières, a military garrison. A good deal of history, Proust appears to suggest, is written according to this method—Bergson's 'mirage du présent dans le passé'. The same convincing logic attributes the baron's social isolation to his evil reputation though the fact is that Charlus, whose megalomania has embroiled him with most of his relatives and friends, rejects all their attempts at a reconciliation.

Morel, whose talent for the more scabrous forms of journalism was formerly exploited by the baron against his enemies, now discovers in the Bavarian origins of Charlus a new and fruitful subject. To the delight of Mme Verdurin the latter now figures in the violinist's malicious anecdotes under various facetious sobriquets: *Frau von der Bosch, Oncle d'Amérique et Tante de Francfort, Gaillard d'arrière*, etc. Proust, I think, has an ulterior and ironical purpose in serving up these gossipy details. Do they not illustrate, once again, the very complex nature of the concepts we apply so lightly to certain objects of our experience, without ever stopping to consider whether their application is

[1] *TR.* 1, 96.

really valid? Take, for instance, the Morel-Charlus situation. The violinist, no doubt, is upholding the cause of patriotism and of morality in exposing the baron's inversion and pro-Germanism. But as Marcel points out, he is really guilty of the blackest ingratitude and hypocrisy. In the first place, Morel is an invert himself and does not see the baron as a vicious monster. Indeed, his last impression of Charlus before their quarrel was of an extraordinarily intelligent and generous benefactor, endowed with profound sensibility and with a delicate sense of honour. Thus, remarks Marcel, whilst writing his terrible articles, Morel was really, in his inmost thoughts, attacking not the vices but the virtues of Charlus. He is also a hypocrite in posing as the champion of patriotism. Although feigning the greatest eagerness to get to the front, to the great distress of Mme Verdurin, all he has to do is to resign his snug civilian billet at the Press Bureau and rejoin his regiment. For Morel is, quite simply, a deserter.

Charlus is not, of course, a German agent but he is absolutely devoid of patriotism. Yet, as is suggested by Proust's careful analysis of the baron's state of mind in these war years, patriotism and anti-patriotism are concepts which we are prone to apply to things that are separated by essential qualitative differences and cannot in reality be included in the same general category. Mme Verdurin is anti-patriotic through lack of imagination and from the selfish desire to pursue her social activities despite the war. Likewise, Charlus refuses to allow the war to interfere with his more ignoble and sinister pleasures. But here the resemblance stops, because we must move to another plane of observation if we are to understand the unpatriotism of Charlus. The baron is a highly intelligent artist and, moreover, an invert. As an artist, Proust implies, he views the titanic struggle between France and Germany in a spirit of almost complete detachment. Unlike Marcel and millions of other Frenchmen, he is a spectator, not an actor passionately interested in the cause of France. But he is a spectator living in France and, therefore, Proust argues, everything is bound to incline his sympathies towards Germany. The views put forward in defence of this Proustian thesis are subtle though very debatable. In every belligerent country, says Marcel, the national cause is upheld by innumerable fools who deafen us with their passionate and idiotic arguments. Now these would have produced in Charlus, had he been domiciled in Germany, the same reactions which Marcel now observes and comments upon in the course of his nocturnal promenade on the Parisian boulevards. Irritated by the dogmatism and stupid optimism and by what he regards as the obtuseness of the French armchair critics, the baron takes a malevolent pleasure in exploding their fallacies. His behaviour is not entirely due to intellectual causes because Charlus, though intelligent, is also governed by an instinctive and profound pity for the unfortunate. So, if a criminal has been convicted and justly punished the baron can scarcely bear to think of the wretched man's sufferings, whilst all his fury is reserved for the latter's judges, his executioner, and the stupid, gloating mob who rejoice that justice has been done. And now, even if better informed than most Frenchmen of Germany's military strength, Charlus also knows that she will eventually be forced to surrender because of the British blockade, from fear of starvation. Therefore, all his compassion goes out to the victims of a nation, Great Britain, which he admires in some respects yet suspects of cant despite all her protestations of justice, honour and fair play. But his motives are even more complex because at times this natural sensibility is displaced by the sadism of the homosexual. In such moments, Charlus is capable of deriving a cruel pleasure from the pictures conjured up by his perverted imagination. Here Proust's exposition becomes very complicated. What he is now attempting to interpret is the conflict reflected in the Germanophilia of Charlus between two dominating elements in the latter's character: his fundamental kindness on the one hand and, on the other, the sadism arising from his 'charlisme'. Bluntly expressed, Proust's meaning is that the pervert visualizes the object of his abnormal affection as 'un délicieux bourreau'. But the imagination of Charlus the homosexual can only picture the marmoreal Anglo-Saxons in this role, certainly not the ill-favoured Teutons. And when his other self reasserts itself, he becomes once more the kind, compassionate Charlus who is shocked to think that such cruel thoughts could ever have

entered his mind. 'Il eût cru en prenant partie contre les Alle-
mands', explains Marcel, 'agir comme il n'agissait que dans ses
heures de volupté, c'est à dire en sens contraire à sa nature pitoy-
able, c'est à dire enflammée pour le mal séduisant, et écrasant la
vertueuse laideur.'[1] Chance, we know, has on several occasions
pandered to Marcel's insatiable desire to penetrate the veil
which conceals the dark, mysterious regions of the human
soul. Once again, that very evening, Chance will perform a
similar office and reveal the spectacle of a Charlus surprised in
one of his 'heures de volupté'.

In spite of the external traits and mannerisms which loudly
advertise his generic vice, the Charlus who now strolls with
Marcel along the boulevards is really the megalomaniac whom
we have so often observed at the Guermantes, in Mme Verdurin's
salon at La Raspelière and in the little Balbec train, the Charlus
whose interminable conversations or rather monologues are
vastly entertaining and sometimes profoundly instructive. One
can imagine the satiric verve with which he proceeds to demolish
the arguments of Brichot and Norpois. Convinced militarists
during the Dreyfus Affair, now of course passionate admirers of
the French army, they employ, however, the language of anti-
militarism to attack the German cult of militarism, and in every
new article ridicule their enemies because of their elementary
lack of psychology. And the classic Brichot, whose lectures
used to be regular diatribes against the æsthetic pretensions of
the modernists, Zola and the Goncourts, now tells an admiring
public that Thermopylae and Austerlitz were skirmishes compared to the stupendous battles waging at their very gates.
These and many other flagrant contradictions are excellent
targets for the baron's satire. Their exposure, as I said, cost
him little effort precisely because not being a patriot, he can
apply the methods of rational criticism to the analysis of
opinions which, nevertheless, spring from something that is
inaccessible even to the intelligence of Charlus; from a profound
and religious faith in the greatness of France and the justice of
her cause. The baron argues more subtly when he reminds
Marcel of his theory that the world exists only thanks to a process

[1] *TR.* I, 114.

of perpetual re-creation. This, he asserts, applies also to the war, which is really being declared afresh every morning. Therefore he who insists on continuing it is as guilty as the nation that began hostilities, guiltier perhaps, since the latter could not foresee all the horrors of war. The revolutions of the wheel of destiny, he remarks, are unpredictable. Exploiting this theme ingeniously in the interests of his Germanophilia, the baron hints darkly at the dangers latent in a prolonged war, the emergence, perhaps, of a change of regime. For every novelty, however alarming to contemplate, is realizable once it has been realized, like the separation of Church and State, the rehabilitation of Dreyfus, the appointment of Piquart as Minister of War. The nationalism of the anti-Dreyfusards has been transformed in fifteen years into anti-militarism, since their averred object in this war is to destroy Prussian militarism. At the height of the Dreyfus Affair, every artist was regarded as a bad patriot because every civilization which was not bellicose was then considered decadent. Now, Charlus points out, the same French nationalists try to prove from history that the arts and *la galanterie* were never suffered to flourish in a warrior civilization though, as a matter of fact, the cult of women was never so intense as in the Middle Ages, when knighthood, or militarism, was in full flower. Here is the familiar Charlus, whose eloquent dialectic reminds us so frequently of Diderot or of Anatole France's immortal Coignard. His opinions, too, present a similar blend of profound originality and amusing paradox. The analogy disappears, however, the moment the baron drags in his pet obsession. Then, as Marcel observes, he ceases to be a man of sense and utters absurdities. Of this aspect we are reminded by the presence of certain dubious individuals dimly perceived in the shadows, trailing in the wake of Charlus. Having shaken off these hangers-on the baron continues his peripatetic and defeatist lecture in a high-pitched voice, greatly amused at Marcel's ill-concealed embarrassment, hugely enjoying the indignation of the passers-by, who pause to stare at this extraordinary figure.

Je le fis remarquer à M. de Charlus sans réussir qu'à exciter son hilarité. 'Avouez que ce serait bien drôle,' dit-il. 'Après tout,' ajouta-t-il, 'on ne sait jamais, chacun de nous risque chaque soir d'être le fait divers du lendemain. En somme, pourquoi ne serais-je pas fusillé dans les fossés de Vincennes? La même chose est bien arrivée à mon grand-oncle le duc d'Enghien. La soif du sang noble affole une certaine populace qui en cela se montre plus raffinée que les lions. Vous savez que pour ces animaux il suffirait pour qu'ils se jetassent sur elle que Mme Verdurin eût une écorchure sur son nez. Sur ce que dans ma jeunesse on eût appelé son pif!' Et il se mit à rire à gorge déployée comme si nous avions été seuls dans un salon.[1]

Rather abruptly, to Marcel's relief, the talk switches over from defeatism to Morel, and simultaneously, one becomes aware of a change in the tone of the narrative. This sensation is enhanced when Marcel, spiralling out into the future, beyond the baron's lifetime, presents what virtually amounts to a synthesis of his views on the Morel-Charlus relationship. Four incidents are thus telescoped, of which the cumulative effect is to focus our attention on 'le côté presque fou' of the baron de Charlus. The latter, as Marcel observes during their nocturnal promenade, whilst alluding to his rupture with the violinist in objective and measured terms, is obviously labouring under a profound agitation. This, it later transpires, was the result of a chance encounter between Morel and Charlus, in which the former scornfully rejected the baron's offer of a reconciliation. Charlus, infuriated by the violinist's mockery, went away threatening revenge. Two years later, Marcel attempted mediation and suggested that Morel, as the younger man, ought to call on the baron. To his astonishment, Morel not only refused vehemently but confessed that he lived in a state of abject terror of Charlus. That his fears were really justified was afterwards amply borne out by a letter written by the baron just before his death to Marcel. In language reflecting a confused blend of megalomania and mysticism, Charlus disclosed that if Morel had come to see him the latter would infallibly have been murdered. From this terrible crime, writes Charlus, he was preserved, but only through the blessed intercession of his patron saint, the Archangel Michael, who inspired in the violinist that divine prudence which saved his life.

[1] *TR.* I, 142.

We may now revert to the 'promenade d'une nuit d'été', to Marcel's nocturnal meanderings which curiously imitate the illusively aimless pattern of his narrative. Remember that Proust, the least artless of narrators, has always a definite purpose in his apparent digressions. From the outset of this chapter he has been planning what might be described as an assault on the reader's credulity, that is, his intelligence. Now an assault necessitates, if I may borrow a military expression, a preliminary 'softening of the terrain', especially where, as in this case, the experiences Marcel is about to recount are of a highly unusual nature. Indeed, he discreetly insinuates, their appropriate context would perhaps be some *Arabian Nights'* tale but certainly not twentieth-century Paris in wartime. And, if we view his narrative in retrospect, it will be observed that for some time Proust has been creating, in a series of unobtrusive and suggestive touches, an atmosphere charged with the mysterious, unreal quality of an Oriental nocturne. The allusion to the baron's 'côté presque fou' heightens this impression, whilst his valedictory remarks to Marcel on the boulevard form a contributory element of this setting. As he takes leave of his companion, Charlus dwells with a certain devilish and macabre enjoyment upon the image of a Paris suddenly leaping into flames, disappearing under a dreadful rain of fire from Heaven, another Pompeii or Sodom destroyed by the avenging and righteous wrath of God. With similar intent, Proust slips in the posthumous revelations contained in the letter to Marcel, picturing a Charlus whose supreme utterances disclose the retrospective vision of a luminous intellect darkly streaked with insanity.

This exercise in hypnotism, then, is the prelude to the author's assault on our credulity, though perhaps the epithet is misleading since Proust, by his preliminary softening of the terrain normally defended by our intelligence, achieves his objective without having encountered any resistance. Lulled by the spells woven by a subtle and persuasive narrator, transported by a sort of necromancy into a region where the familiar boundaries erected by Time and Space no longer exist, if Marcel were to inform us that he had just seen a full-grown python sliding across the Place de la Concorde, in broad daylight, we should accept his statement without the slightest demur, indeed, with an eager and naïve interest. And it so happens that, although no pythons come into Marcel's story, the incidents he is about to relate are situated well outside the zone of habitual experience. Interesting as they are, however, both in themselves and for the illumination they shed upon the profundities of the Charlusian soul, the manner of their presentation is even more fascinating.

Perhaps, in this connection, we might pause once again to consider briefly the originality of the Proustian narrative and its astonishing complexity. Every great novel represents a successful act of intrusion by the novelist into his reader's intellectual privacy. Moreover, if the intruder is an artist of genius, he brings about a durable alteration in the reader's habitual modes of perception and of reflection. A great writer, through the medium of a particular narrative-form, which is the sound-track or language-track of his mind, effects an expansion of the reader's normal zone of consciousness. He really imposes upon the latter his own individual way of seeing life. This is indisputable because no one can honestly maintain that, after having read a great novel, for instance, *Manon Lescaut* or *Les Illusions perdues* or *A la recherche du temps perdu*, his former attitude to human nature has not been fundamentally enlarged and deepened. Here, of course, I am giving to the expression 'narrative-form' its largest and truest connotation. It is the art of communicating experiences seized at various levels of the narrator's consciousness, in Proust's case, from the subconscious perceptions of the Marcel of Combray or of *Le temps retrouvé* down to the more superficial impressions he gleaned in the *salons* of the Guermantes and of the Verdurins. Always, however, the art of successful narration implies the ability of the artist to effect a penetration and alteration of the reader's normal receptivity, of his usual consciousness. Sometimes, it is true, even a very great novelist may fail to achieve this object and that is not surprising. Ideally, the perfect narrative should record and transmit the most delicate vibrations of the artist's individual consciousness: it should be a sound-track of the melody of his inmost life. And this, *par excellence*, is of course the function of great poetry rather than of the novel. Yet, very often, the Proustian narrative, as we have observed, contrives to transmit the original and delicate quality of the impressions captured by the incredibly sensitive antennae of the author's consciousness. In such moments, the genius of the novelist resembles that of a great poet.

But, in the section of *Le temps retrouvé* which we are now considering, the experiences about to be narrated by Marcel are not of this texture. Material facts, they possess also the unreal quality of sensations and impressions perceived usually in nightmares and such is exactly the ambiency in which they are projected. After leaving Charlus, the narrator becomes entangled in a lacery of dark streets where all the shops and cafés are 'closed for the duration'. Tired and thirsty, he suddenly notices a small hotel where, to judge from the hum of voices and the light filtering through the shuttered windows, the proprietor must be doing a flourishing trade, though in what, it is hard to guess. As Marcel stands, hesitating as to whether he should enter, a young officer emerges, swiftly gliding into the shadows. Something about his appearance or rather, the ubiquitous, lizard-like manner of his exit, recalls the image of Saint-Loup, and by association a recent espionage *affaire* in which Robert had been quite absurdly involved, merely because his name had been noted in a certain letter seized on a captured German officer. The idea of espionage, however, is now connected in Marcel's mind with this odd hotel and, inquisitively, he mounts the short staircase leading to the vestibule. Soldiers of various units, meanwhile, pass in and out, thus giving substance to his nebulous conjectures. Unperceived, he is able to look into a kind of reception office where a few *poilus* and two workmen can be overheard discussing the war. Their conversation is typical of the Parisian *peuple*, consisting that is to say of sententious banalities, drawn from an inexhaustible fund of maudlin sensibility and unlimited credulity.

Abruptly, Marcel is jolted out of his indifference by the following casually uttered remarks:

'C'est épatant, le patron qui ne revient pas, dame, à cette heure-ci je ne sais pas trop où il trouvera des chaînes.' 'Mais puisque l'autre est déjà attaché.' 'Il est attaché bien sûr, il est attaché et il ne l'est pas, moi je serais attaché comme ça que je pourrais me détacher.' 'Mais le cadenas est fermé.' 'C'est entendu qu'il est fermé, mais ça peut s'ouvrir à la rigueur. Ce qu'il y a c'est que les chaînes ne sont pas assez longues. Tu vas m'expliquer à moi ce que c'est, j'y ai tapé dessus hier pendant toute la nuit que le sang m'en coulait sur les mains.' 'C'est toi qui tapera ce soir.' 'Non, c'est pas moi, c'est Maurice....'[1]

Maurice is clearly the brawny sailor whom Marcel had noticed, on his arrival, being shown to one of the upstairs rooms. Obviously there is no question of espionage: a terrible and brutal crime is about to be committed. Having excited our fearful curiosity, Marcel goes on to narrate, exasperatingly, the rest of the conversation, reproducing with admirable fidelity the tone and sentiments of the *parigot*. But now the *patron* enters sweating and grumbling under a load of heavy chains. Marcel, whom he eyes with distrust, explains his presence and is given a room from which, having quickly finished his much needed drink, he creeps stealthily upstairs to the top floor only to be frozen in his tracks by the sound of pitiful groans and cries for mercy. Moving cautiously forwards, he listens with his ear against the door whence issue ominous thudding noises as if someone were being lashed with a knout. Exercising his talent for eavesdropping, Marcel discovers in the wall a small uncurtained square of glass.

Alors je m'aperçus qu'il y avait dans cette chambre un œil de bœuf latéral dont on avait oublié de tirer le rideau; cheminant à pas de loup dans l'ombre, je me glissai jusqu'à cet œil de bœuf, et là, enchaîné sur un lit comme Prométhée sur son rocher, recevant les coups d'un martinet en effet planté de clous que lui infligeait Maurice, je vis, déjà tout en sang et couvert d'ecchymoses qui prouvaient que le supplice n'avait pas lieu pour la première fois, je vis devant moi M. de Charlus. Tout d'un coup la porte s'ouvrit et quelqu'un entra qui heureusement ne me vit pas, c'était Jupien.[2]

These incidents are deliberately presented *à la* Dostoevski, for it will be recalled that Proust admired the Russian's trick of shocking his reader's intelligence by confronting him first with the irrational aspect of things and people, reserving the logical or rational explanation for later in the narrative. This technical

[1] *TR.* I, 160–1.   [2] *TR.* I, 165.

device, which of course is now a cliché with authors of 'thrillers', is not used by Proust, however, for its sensation value. It serves the very necessary purpose of distracting our attention from the intrinsic queerness of the incidents themselves. The reader, whose critical intelligence, as I observed, has already been disarmed by the prevailing atmosphere created by Proust, is naïvely relieved to find that there is a concrete reason for the mysterious chains, the stifled screams and ejaculations from the shrouded torture-chamber. After all, it is only Charlus grati-fying his sadistic tastes! What we do not stop to reflect upon is the fundamental improbability of the whole episode and of its constituent elements. All that, as the French would say, 'passe comme une lettre à la poste'. Yet could anything be more reminiscent of an *Arabian Nights'* tale than this story of Marcel's nocturnal adventures? He passes abruptly via the staircase of a shabby twentieth-century Paris hotel into a profane temple dedicated to the cult of Sodom in all its hideous variants and by a strange coincidence its High Priests turn out to be Charlus and Jupien, assisted by a cohort of acolytes who represent Frenchmen of every imaginable class and profession. Petty thieves from Belleville rub shoulders here with senators, wealthy *gigolos*, officers, foreign attachés, *poilus* on leave, lift-boys, workmen and dukes. Marcel observes even that rarest of all phenomena, an infamous *abbé*. This establishment, he learns from the disconcerted Jupien, is owned by the baron, one of whose levees he is allowed to witness, thanks to a little moral blackmail. Following his usual practice, Proust rapidly switches our attention to the ridiculous aspect of these scenes. Yet whilst undoubtedly he extracts farcical comedy of a sort from the spectacle of Jupien's frantic efforts to persuade Charlus that these oafish butcher's boys, milk-roundsmen and corner-loafers are blood-stained apaches, nothing can really leaven the essential bestiality of this Proustian image of human degeneracy.

Proust's immediate object was to reveal through this extra-ordinary episode, the penultimate stage of the baron's vice. But as always with Proust the notation of external impressions is merely a prelude to an exploration in depth. Here, for example, what interests him is not so much the behaviour of Charlus and his retinue of perverts, as the psychological truths to be discerned beneath their actions. Marcel is particularly impressed by the rapidity with which the individual, once his actions assume the form of habits, ceases to be conscious of their abnormality. Charlus and Jupien, he notes, have long acquired the habit, by no means confined to homosexuals, of separating morality from a whole category of vicious actions, the commission of which, originally, must have given rise to acute remorse. Even more striking is the apparent contradiction produced by this divorce between morality and conduct. Homosexuality, as Marcel observes in the case of the young men who frequent this establishment, does not necessarily exclude courage, patriotism, the spirit of self-sacrifice and the less spectacular virtues of kindness and sensibility. Jupien, who frankly admits that for nothing in the world would he give up his odious profession, possesses the most exquisite sensibility and though largely self-educated, continually delights Marcel, as he did Marcel's grandmother, by the perfection of his language and the rare good sense of his remarks. There is, Proust implies, nothing anomalous in such cases. It is only because we observe men superficially that we imagine their whole personality to be involved in the besetting vice which is reflected in certain aspects of their behaviour. Often, however, other elements of their *moi* develop independently and unimpeded. That is exemplified in the *poilus* and workmen whose conversation is retailed by Marcel. Because of lack of a proper upbringing, or from a desire to earn easy money, they have drifted into their present habits but chiefly because they are tainted by the vice that is the source of all others, the lack of will power. What of Charlus? One might have supposed that in the case of this megalomaniac, a sentiment of personal dignity would have enabled him to resist the lure of degrading pleasures. Possibly, however, the sadism of a Charlus, his crazy penchant for chains, leg-irons and whips studded with nails is obscurely associated with a certain ideal of virility and also with a disordered medieval imagination hallucinated by thoughts of dungeons, racks and other barbarous instruments of torture.

En somme [thinks Marcel] son désir d'être enchaîné, d'être frappé trahissait dans sa laideur un rêve aussi poétique que chez d'autres le désir d'aller à Venise ou d'entretenir des danseuses. Et M. de Charlus tenait tellement à ce que ce rêve lui donnât l'illusion de la réalité, que Jupien dut vendre le lit de bois qui était dans la chambre 43 et le remplacer par un lit de fer qui allait mieux avec les chaînes.[1]

With no regret we follow Marcel out of this Sodomites' Cave through a barking air-raid into the purer atmosphere of his apartment. Saint-Loup, he learns, has been and gone, leaving his old servant searching for a *croix de guerre* which has been dropped somewhere. Marcel could tell him where to find this decoration, which one of Jupien's minions picked up from the hotel floor.

In lighter vein, Proust reflects once again, but in the conversation between Françoise and his old butler, the attitude of the French common people to the war. This *maître d'hôtel* is one of the numerous minor characters who flit across the pages of Proust's vast novel, lingering just long enough to arouse a smile or a laugh. One would like to linger also just long enough, if that were not impossible in these pulpless times, to comment on their diverse comicalities and reveal how much *A la recherche du temps perdu* owes to their collective sanity and joyous presence. I seem to remember someone very like this very *maître d'hôtel* in the early Combray pages at the same game of baiting Françoise, who rarely fails to respond in the desired manner to spine-chilling tales of imminent national disaster or equally horrific and garbled versions of current affairs. The Dreyfus trial and the expulsion of the nuns, it can be imagined, furnished the *maître d'hôtel* with magnificent opportunities, but the war is a perfect godsend. Listen to him enlarging on the Germans and what they will do when they reach Paris:

'Ils ne se pressent pas, c'est entendu, ils attendent que la poire soit mûre, mais ce jour-là, pas de pitié!' 'Seigneur, Vierge Marie,' s'écriait Françoise, 'ça ne leur suffit pas d'avoir conquéri la pauvre Belgique. Elle a assez souffert celle-là au moment de son envahition.' 'La Belgique, Françoise, mais ce qu'ils ont fait en Belgique ne sera rien à côté.'[2]

[1] *TR.* I, 200.   [2] *TR.* I, 202.

The *maître d'hôtel* is a type perhaps more common in France, where his name is legion, than in our country. Perhaps he is the inevitable product of a regime which made it rather too easy to found a newspaper and was, therefore, inundated with ephemeral *journaux de concierge*. Marcel's butler exactly reflects the mentality catered for by this gutter press and never fails to con his newspaper every evening with gloomy distrust of the powers that be, suspecting always 'le bourrage de crâne'. So Françoise, listening with pleasant horror to his private interpretation of the official communiqué, fills the house with her *Sainte-Marie des Anges!* and *Ah! Marie, Mère de Dieu!*, convinced that the Hun is at the gate or that the war will last another thirty years. Oddly enough, however, the *maître d'hôtel*, for all his pessimism, is no defeatist, but a good Frenchman who would be amazed and furious if you questioned his patriotism. But he simply cannot resist the delicious pleasure of teasing the gullible Françoise. Had she been less simple, Marcel's old servant could have quickly silenced and disconcerted her tormentor either by laughing in his face or, more effectively, by capping his lugubrious predictions with others still more lugubrious. The truth, one suspects, is that Françoise derives a secret enjoyment from being scared, like the man in Grimm's fairy-tale. A typical peasant, she is only really happy when surrounded by images of death and dramatic calamity. Naïvely credulous in some respects, she is often astonishingly hard to deceive, as Marcel discovered to his annoyance during Albertine's sojourn. The native intuition of Françoise, reinforced by her intense curiosity and by an instinctive detestation of Albertine, enabled her to penetrate with the greatest ease all Marcel's subterfuges and secrets. To Proust, the psychology of this old peasant woman is a constant source of interest and amusement, precisely because her conduct is determined more often by intuition than by acquired rational habits of thought. One trait in Françoise which he often illustrates is the disconcerting streak of cruel curiosity which throws into sharp relief the crystal purity of her natural sensibility and kindness. It shocked and astonished him first at Combray, when he discovered Françoise meditatively slaughtering a chicken, her lips compressed with annoyance, cursing it for 'une sale bête'! In profound distress, quite unable to reconcile the conflicting images of Françoise, the small boy used to creep upstairs to his room, sobbing bitterly. Since then, he has observed many variants of this psychological enigma which he has learned, however, to contemplate without emotion, though never without interest.

As Marcel is about to leave for his new clinic, the news arrives of Saint-Loup's death in action. He was killed in a raid, covering the retreat of his men. Proust, with his exquisite tact, interprets Marcel's sorrow in words deliberately chosen for their transparency, their qualities of serenity and restraint. Once again, Marcel reviews his past, watching the memory-pictures of his dead friend merge to form a complete and definitive image. Because his memories are so few and so widely spaced, Marcel's sense of loss, as Proust sensitively observes, is more intense than if he and Robert had seen each other every day. He suggests that the habit of daily intercourse narrows the margin reserved for the play of one's imagination. There is always, to quote Proust, in our relations with the friends we rarely see, 'l'illusion de la possibilité d'une affection plus grande dont les circonstances seules nous auraient frustré'.[1]

In this account of Saint-Loup's death and of Marcel's sad reflections, Proust writes with the incomparable simplicity of the great French masters. The narrative establishes an immediate community of sentiment and thought between author and reader. Saint-Loup's 'effacement de soi', the dominant trait in Marcel's memory of him, is reflected in the beautiful austerity of Proust's language, in the slow march of its grave, sculptured phrases. No one who has mourned the untimely death of a beloved friend can fail to recognize here the ideal expression of his own unuttered sadness.

Pendant plusieurs jours je restai enfermé dans ma chambre pensant à lui. Je me rappelais son arrivée, la première fois à Balbec, quand en lainages blanchâtres, avec ses yeux verdâtres et bougeants comme la mer, il avait traversé le hall attenant à la grande salle à manger dont les vitrages donnaient sur la mer. Je me rappelais l'être si spécial qu'il m'avait paru être alors, l'être dont c'avait été un si grand souhait

[1] *TR.* I, 210.

de ma part d'être l'ami. Ce souhait s'était réalisé au-delà de ce que j'aurais jamais pu croire, sans me donner pourtant presque aucun plaisir alors, et ensuite je m'étais rendu compte de tous les grands mérites et d'autres choses encore que cachait cette apparence élégante. Tout cela, le bon comme le mauvais, il l'avait donné sans compter, tous les jours, et le dernier, en allant attaquer une tranchée, par générosité, par mise au service des autres de tout ce qu'il possédait, comme il avait un soir couru sur les canapés du restaurant, pour ne pas me déranger.[1]

[During several days I remained shut up in my room thinking of him. I remembered his arrival, that first time, at Balbec when in light-coloured flannels, with his greenish eyes restless as the sea, he strode across the hall adjoining the large restaurant with its windows overlooking the ocean. I remembered what a unique creature he had then seemed to me to be, a creature whose friend it was my very great desire to become. That desire had been fulfilled beyond anything I could have believed possible, affording me, however, scarcely any pleasure at the time, though afterwards I had realized all the fine qualities, and other things besides, hidden behind that elegant façade. All this, the good as well as the bad, he had given of lavishly, day after day, and so, too, on the last day of all when he set out to raid a trench, out of sheer generosity, from the impulse to place all he owned at the service of others, just as he had, one evening, run along the backs of the sofas in the restaurant, so as not to disturb me.]

Note the recurrence of Proust's favourite symbol in the allusion to Saint-Loup 'avec ses yeux verdâtres et bougeants comme la mer' and later, on the next page, in Marcel's image of an Albertine 'indifférente à tous, et marine, comme une mouette'. Both, it would seem, are linked symbolically in Marcel's thoughts and yet the paths of their destinies scarcely touched. Behind Marcel's earliest images of Saint-Loup and Albertine, sweeping backwards, as it were, into the eternity that has engulfed friend and mistress, there lies the sea, the ever changing, mysterious and immemorial sea. In Robert's soul, as in Albertine's, a dark secret lay hidden. But if this knowledge causes Marcel deep pain, the reflection which distresses him most profoundly is that Robert and Albertine died so young, before him, they who were always so touchingly

[1] *TR.* I, 209.

anxious about his health and revealed their solicitude in a hundred trivial, unforgettable actions. The sure intuition which distinguishes genius from talent carries Proust unerringly to that spiritual plane from which alone it is fitting to survey the life of a dead comrade. In the perspective now disclosed to Marcel what stand out clearly are the noble and lovable qualities of Saint-Loup, the attributes which the latter's friend, to his eternal regret, had taken for granted, so blind to their uniqueness. These he will now remember, however, so long as memory endures. The rest he thinks of without blame or revulsion but only with pity and bewilderment.

The apartment resounds with the lamentations of Françoise sincerely bewailing Robert's death and his mother's loss, yet in the midst of her grief, dwelling with cruel pleasure on the macabre pictures conjured up by her imagination.

'Pauvre dame!' disait-elle en pensant à Mme de Marsantes, 'qu'est-ce qu'elle a dû pleurer quand elle a appris la mort de son garçon! Si encore elle avait pu le revoir, mais il vaut peut-être mieux qu'elle n'ait pas pu, parce qu'il avait le nez coupé en deux, il était tout dévisagé.' Et les yeux de Françoise se remplissaient de larmes mais à travers lesquelles perçait la curiosité cruelle de la paysanne. Sans doute Françoise plaignait la douleur de Mme de Marsantes de tout son cœur, mais elle regrettait de ne pas connaître la forme que cette douleur avait prise et de ne pouvoir s'en donner le spectacle de l'affliction.[1]

It is typical also of Françoise that in the rare moments when Marcel reveals his grief, her own tears instantly vanish. Like so many individuals, Françoise cannot bear the exhibition of emotion in others. To Marcel's surprise, the duchesse de Guermantes is genuinely distressed by her nephew's death and mourns him for a whole week, which is, he observes sardonically, remarkable for the Faubourg Saint-Germain. Saint-Loup's death has repercussions on the lives of Morel and Charlus. Robert's efforts to find the violinist's address lead directly to the discovery by the general commanding his unit that Morel is a deserter. He is saved from the punishment meted out to deserters in time of war, however, by the fact that Saint-Loup,

[1] *TR.* I, 211.

his friend, had died a hero's death. But, meanwhile, convinced that he had been denounced to the authorities by the baron, Morel insisted on making certain revelations to the police, claiming that he had been led astray by the evil influence of Charlus and M. d'Argencourt. They are arrested, though shortly afterwards released. Out of deference to the memory of Saint-Loup, Morel's divisional commander waives a court-martial and sends him to the front where the violinist earns, as a reward for his bravery, the Cross of the Legion of Honour which Charlus had once tried to obtain for him. The chapter closes with a bitter and disillusioned commentary on the French political scene after the elections of 1919.

Proust's final chapter, entitled, 'Matinée chez la Princesse de Guermantes', narrates the illuminating experience by which Marcel recovers his faith in the reality of art and, with the discovery of his true vocation, knows that his long search for *le temps perdu* is now virtually ended. At the eleventh hour, when his wearied and baffled intelligence advises him to resign a hopeless quest, the door leading to the magic cave is opened, dramatically, by a more potent agency. The treasure lies there, in the chamber, ready for the taking. Marcel's despair vanishes in that moment along with all his doubts, now replaced by an ineffable sense of joy and creative power. But we must go back to that point in his narrative where it reflects a very different state of soul, the profound and ultimate depths of his spiritual distress.

Marcel, having undergone a long but useless course of treatment in his new clinic, returns by train to Paris, brooding sadly on that absence of literary talent which had troubled him before the war, at Tansonville. More depressing still is the thought which also dates back to this period, that art is an empty lie, that the ideal in which he had himself believed despite his own lack of artistic gifts, is a non-existent ideal. As once long ago, on his memorable first journey to Balbec, his train stops in the open country, beside a screen of trees plunged half-way up the trunk, in cool shadow, the leafage in brilliant sunlight. In an apostrophe couched in language so direct and simple as to fringe upon the naïve, Proust interprets the sense of impotence that invades Marcel with his realization that although he can perceive natural beauty with the eye of a painter, he cannot feel it with an artist's soul. Automatically, he notes the play of light and shadow, the splashes of orange and gold thrown by the setting sun on the windows of one cottage, the transfiguration of another into a strange, rose-coloured substance. But this beauty leaves him cold and indifferent, arousing no spark of pleasure, as if, he says, he were politely showing a rather bored companion round his garden.

At his flat in Paris he finds, amongst a heap of cards, two invitations, one to a matinée at the Prince de Guermantes', now married to Mme Verdurin or rather, because of a second marriage, the widowed duchesse de Duras. The other is from La Berma, the famous actress, to a party in honour of her daughter. As there is no reason now why he should renounce the pleasures of society, such as they are, Marcel drives off next afternoon to the Avenue du Bois where the prince has built a new residence, through the familiar streets of his childhood along which Françoise used to take him to play with Gilberte in the Champs Elysées. They are badly paved nowadays, but Marcel is suddenly conscious of a sensation of extreme smoothness as if his car were moving up the sanded avenue of a park:

Matériellement il n'en était rien, mais je sentais tout à coup la suppression des obstacles extérieurs comme s'il n'y avait plus eu pour moi d'effort d'adaptation ou d'attention tels que nous en faisons même sans nous en rendre compte devant les choses nouvelles.[1]

Like an aviator who has been taxiing along the runway, to borrow Marcel's own image, he slowly takes off for the silent heights of memory. In this environment, he is invaded by a sweet melancholy, the cause of which it is difficult, however, to recognize, because the past through which he is moving is made up of so many different pasts, of states of soul associated now with Gilberte, now with La Berma or again, with Albertine or Andrée. Plunged in these reveries, he alights from his car to walk in the Champs Elysées, not wanting to hear the whole of the concert at the Guermantes'. Another car draws up, nearby. Inside, propped up against the cushions, is the bent figure of the

---

[1] *TR.* I, 225.

baron de Charlus or rather, what Time and an inveterate vice have left of the baron de Charlus. The Proustian imagination, playing on this hideous spectacle, illuminates the poetry which the mind of a great artist can extract from the crudest material.

C'était, à côté de Jupien qui se multipliait pour lui, M. de Charlus convalescent d'une attaque d'apoplexie que j'avais ignorée (on m'avait dit seulement qu'il avait perdu la vue; or il ne s'était agi que de troubles passagers, car il voyait de nouveau fort clair) et qui, à moins que jusque-là il se fût teint et qu'on lui eût interdit de continuer à en prendre la fatigue, avait plutôt comme en une sorte de précipité chimique rendu visible et brillant tout le métal dont étaient saturées et que lançaient comme autant de geysers les mèches maintenant de pur argent de sa chevelure et de sa barbe, cependant qu'elle avait imposé au vieux prince déchu la majesté shakespearienne d'un roi Léar. Les yeux n'étaient pas restés en dehors de cette convulsion totale, de cette altération métallurgique de la tête. Mais par un phénomène inverse, ils avaient perdu tout leur éclat. Mais le plus émouvant est qu'on sentait que la vie physique et même intellectuelle de M. de Charlus survivait à l'orgeuil aristocratique qu'on avait pu croire un moment faire corps avec elles. Ainsi à ce moment, se rendant sans doute aussi chez le prince de Guermantes, passa en victoria, Madame de Sainte-Euverte, que le baron jadis ne trouvait assez chic pour lui. Jupien qui prenait soin de lui comme d'un enfant lui souffla à l'oreille que c'était une personne de connaissance, Mme de Sainte-Euverte. Et aussitôt, avec une peine infinie, et toute l'application d'un malade qui veut se montrer capable de tous les mouvements qui lui sont encore difficiles, M. de Charlus se découvrit, s'inclina et salua Mme de Sainte-Euverte avec le même respect que si elle avait été la Reine de France.[1]

[It was, seated next to Jupien who waited on him hand and foot, M. de Charlus, recovering from an attack of apoplexy that I had not heard about (all I had been told was that he had lost his eyesight; actually, it had been no more than a temporary loss of vision for he could now see quite well), and which, unless he had hitherto dyed his hair and been forbidden to tire himself by continuing, had, as it were, by a sort of chemical precipitation, rendered visible and brilliant the metallic substance which impregnated and spouted forth, like so many geysers, from the now pure silver locks of his hair and beard; whilst it had conferred upon the aged, fallen prince the Shakespearian majesty of a King Lear. The eyes had not escaped the influence of this total convulsion, this metallurgical alteration of the head. Most touching of all was one's feeling that, as a result, the physical life and even the intellectual existence of M. de Charlus survived the seigneurial arrogance which one had once imagined to be inseparable from them. Thus, at this moment, there passed by, in a victoria, Madame de Sainte-Euverte, whom formerly the Baron had not considered elegant enough for his taste. Jupien, who tended him like a child, whispered in his ear that it was someone he knew, Mme de Sainte-Euverte. And, immediately, with infinite pains and all the studied care of an invalid who wants to show that he is capable of all the movements that he still finds difficult to perform, M. de Charlus uncovered, bowed and greeted Mme de Sainte-Euverte with the same respect he might have shown if she had been the Queen of France.]

Here is the Charlus of the ultimate phase, stripped of the insane megalomania which was the dynamic, fundamental element in his personality. The symbol of his tragic disintegration is the act just described by Marcel, the baron's humble obeisance to Mme de Sainte-Euverte. Its profound significance will be immediately visible to the reader who casts his mind back to the scene that took place at the last great reception given by the Prince de Guermantes. For Proust, clearly, this is the real tragedy of Charlus, this spectacle of Lucifer shorn of his pride, of 'le beau parleur' smitten by paralysis of that organ with which he used to terrorize the Faubourg Saint-Germain. And because his intelligence is still intact, Charlus is condemned by a refinement of torture to the consciousness of his disintegration. Spiritually, Proust surely implies, Charlus is already dead. For, with the eclipse of his *morgue*, his stupendous pride and *libido dominandi*, little now remains to counterbalance and impede the swift invasion of the spirit by the forces of materialism, the unnatural lusts of the moribund homosexual. These, one gathers from Jupien's revelations, the baron still attempts to satisfy, even when temporarily blinded by paralysis, with a kind of dreadful and bestial automatism. Charlus, in the eyes of this enigmatic and sinister catamite, is simply a 'grand enfant' whose every movement has to be closely supervised, lest he yield to the impulses of his natural goodness and of a passion which Jupien has long ceased to regard as unnatural. With this revelation, Proust's sombre and tragic picture is complete.

Chapter XI

LE TEMPS RETROUVÉ (continued)

W E may now observe the trend and quality of Marcel's inner perceptions as he leaves his car to walk towards the Avenue du Bois. To some extent the lively if frivolous pleasure aroused by thoughts of the reception offsets his discouragement of the previous day, when he was compelled to recognize the mechanical and joyless quality of the impressions inspired in him by the spectacle of natural beauty. To describe such impressions, he implies, to reproduce these *instantanés* or snapshots taken by the intelligence, is an effortless and sterile exercise, for which one need not have the talents of a true artist. Thinking of Combray, of Bergotte, he recalls how that great writer once tried to console him by pointing out that one may be an invalid and yet possess, after all, the joys of the mind. Bergotte, however, was mistaken. What connection is there between the joys of the intelligence and the uninspired, although lucid, notations of the clairvoyant reasoning mind? Suddenly, however, Marcel experiences a marvellous inner transformation. His doubts, his discouragement and sadness vanish in a flash, replaced by an overpowering sentiment of joy and of creative strength. With the revelation that art is his predestined vocation, Marcel recovers his belief in the reality of art. At last, too, he realizes that his long search for 'le temps perdu' is virtually ended because a gate which had resisted all the assaults of his intelligence now swings open, dramatically, in obedience to a more powerful agency. The past, the true past locked in the regions of his unconscious, is marvellously and unexpectedly released in a suite of gloriously resurrected memory-images, by a series of fortuitous sensations. Let us now examine an experience which, at first sight, appears comparable in the domain of art to what, in the history of a saint, would be described as a mystic illumination of the soul. Yet it would be prudent to hesitate before allowing this initial

and superficial impression to crystallize into a definitive conviction or attitude. Otherwise we should form a strangely distorted
conception of Proust's art and personality. I propose, therefore,
to scrutinize this extremely important section of *A la recherche du
temps perdu* in the attempt to find out what significance Proust
himself attaches to Marcel's unusual experience, bearing in mind
the fact that there are many odd psychological experiences
which are neither mysterious, mystic nor, on the other hand,
to be vaguely dismissed as morbid emotional states.

Marcel, on entering the courtyard of the Guermantes' residence, steps back to avoid being run down by a car. In doing so,
he finds himself tottering, in an effort to regain his balance, on
two uneven flagstones. Instantly, he is invaded by an overpowering sense of joy, of liberation from all anxiety about the
future, and from all intellectual doubts and misgivings. It is the
same sentiment of utter happiness vouchsafed to him at different
times in his life by sensations to which he has frequently alluded
and which, it once seemed to him, were somehow condensed or
synthesized in the music of Vinteuil. He mentions, for example,
the trees at Balbec, which implored him desperately never to
forget them; the memorable incident of the steeples of Martinville; the taste of the famous 'petite madeleine' dipped in tea.
Then, unfortunately, he did not stop to explore the profound
causes of that sense of perfect felicity common to all these
experiences, which differed only materially, in the character
of the images evoked, but never in their intrinsic quality. Now
as he stands in the courtyard, balancing on the uneven stones, this
sense of absolute joy is accompanied by other impressions, of
azure blue, delicious coolness and dazzling light. Once again, as
when he tasted the madeleine, he tries anxiously to seize the
memories suggested by his vision, to penetrate the secret of the
happiness which it so tantalizingly holds up before his mind. At
last, the enigma is solved. It is Venice, not the Venice of his
conscious recollections composed of the snapshots recorded by
his voluntary memory, but the Venice really perceived and lived
by his deepest consciousness and once before in like fashion
resurrected for him as he stood on the uneven flagstones of the
baptistery of St Mark's, with the entire context of attendant

sensations constituting that glorious fragment of 'le temps perdu', of his real, forgotten past.

But why, Marcel asks himself, did these images of Venice and Combray, so alike in the modality of their revelation, confer upon him that same sense of joy, 'pareille à une certitude et suffisante sans autres preuves à me rendre la mort indifférente'? Concentrating on this problem he enters the hôtel de Guermantes, and waits in a small library until the music is over. The incentive to pursue his introspection is provided by a fresh experience. A footman, in a clumsy effort not to disturb the musicians, unguardedly clinks a spoon against a plate and, once again, Marcel is flooded by a wave of sheer happiness. The sensations, though superficially different, resemble those of the Venetian resurrection in that they are sensations of summer warmth, mingled, however, with a perfume of wood-smoke and of cool forest glades. The clink of the spoon, analogous to that of a plate-layer's hammer on the wheel of a stationary train, evokes in Marcel the fleeting illusion that he is again in a railway compartment in the open country. Before his eyes is the identical screen of trees he had found it so wearisome to describe the day before, but which now communicate the secret of their beauty. As if fate, Proust suggests disarmingly, had determined on this particular afternoon in order to accelerate the process of Marcel's illumination, a servant brings him a glass of orangeade and a napkin which, as it touches his lips, releases another azure vision. This time it is the blue of the sea at Balbec. At the touch of some necromancer's hand, the Guermantes library recedes to make way for the restaurant of the Grand Hôtel de Balbec with its tall windows open to the beach and the ocean. For the napkin Marcel holds to his lips possesses the identical starched slippery feel of the towel he tried to dry himself with on his first day at Balbec. In Proust's words, 'elle [la serviette] déployait dans ses plis et dans ses cassures, le plumage d'un océan vert et bleue comme la queue d'un paon'. A complete instant of his former life which Marcel had been prevented from enjoying at Balbec perhaps because he was tired or sad, is now restored to him in the plenitude of its original spirituality, dredged of all the imperfections which are inherent in all external perceptions.

Now Marcel is resolved to explore the nature of these and other experiences, all of which fill him with an identical sensation of felicity, and if possible he will extract their hidden significance. One thing is quite certain. There is no essential connection between the images evoked by the sensation of the unevenness of the flagstones, the starched glossiness of the napkin, or the taste of the madeleine on the one hand, and on the other the recollections of Venice, Combray and Balbec recovered by his voluntary memory. The former, as Proust explains, are memories of *real*, the latter, of factitious or superficial impressions of life. That is why, so often, if we try to recall our past by the aid of our uniform or voluntary memory, life can seem so very drab though at certain moments it may strike us as so very beautiful. How can it seem otherwise, since we are basing our opinion on a facsimile of life, not on the real thing? In a beautiful passage, Proust orchestrates this idea in order to emphasize the basic and qualitative difference which separates these memories lifted miraculously out of the subconscious by a fortuitous identity of sensation from the superficial notations of the intelligence, which can be so easily recovered by a mechanical act of remembering. At every moment of our life, he explains, our slightest word or most trifling gesture captured the reflection of things with which they had no logical connection, things discounted by our intelligence as useless for the ordinary purposes of living and of action. Yet the word and the gesture were enclosed, as in a vase, in such 'useless' things; for example, in the flush of an evening sky reflected on the rose-tapestried wall of the restaurant at Rivebelle where Marcel used to dine with Saint-Loup, or again, perhaps, in the blue spirals of a summer sea in the morning at Balbec. As the years slip away, our *moi*, our personality is in the process of constant change but these various climates and temperatures of our soul are preserved, Marcel thinks, in a thousand urns 'disposés sur toute la hauteur de nos années'.[1] Sometimes, as we have just observed, one of these vases is accidentally unsealed and the original perfume of its contents is offered to our sensibility, intact and uncontaminated by the influence of our present state of soul.

[1] *TR.* II, 12.

Oui, si le souvenir grâce à l'oubli n'a pu contracter aucun lien, jeter aucun chaînon entre lui et la minute présente, s'il est resté à sa place, à sa date, s'il a gardé ses distances, son isolement dans le creux d'une vallée, ou à la pointe d'un sommet, il nous fait tout à coup respirer un air nouveau, précisément parce que c'est un air qu'on a respiré déjà, car les vrais paradis sont des paradis qu'on a perdus.[1]

Marcel's vocation, his function as an artist is now defined. It is to communicate in his work of art the quality of such moments of intensely lived existence. But, since every group of subconscious memories possesses its own peculiar quality, the mode of its expression, the material texture of the style selected for its interpretation will have to be different in every case. This is the idea so perfectly conveyed in the following words:

Car j'en devrais exécuter les parties successives dans une matière en quelque sorte différente. Elle serait bien différente, celle qui conviendrait aux souvenirs de matins au bord de la mer, de celle d'après-midis à Venise, une matière distincte, nouvelle, d'une transparence, d'une sonorité spéciale, compacte, fraîchissante et rose, et différente encore si je voulais décrire les soirs de Rivebelle où dans la salle à manger ouverte sur le jardin, la chaleur commençait à se décomposer, à retomber, à se déposer, où une dernière lueur éclairait encore les roses sur les murs du restaurant, tandis que les dernières aquarelles du jour étaient encore visibles au ciel.[2]

Marcel, however, does not linger over these considerations, which, he implies, will present no difficulties. For he now possesses a serene confidence in his own creative powers. What still eludes him is the solution to a problem hitherto never really explored. What is the cause of this felicity, which he has again experienced not once, but three times in rapid succession? These happy impressions all have one characteristic, which we must carefully note since it is obviously of vital importance to Proust. They are experienced by Marcel simultaneously in the past and in the actual moment. A remarkable effect is produced by this analogy of sensations; by the similarity between the clink of the spoon and that of the plate-layer's hammer; by the similar unevenness of the flagstones at St Mark's and in the Guermantes' courtyard; by the starched glossiness common to the Balbec hotel towel and the napkin Marcel is now holding.

[1] *TR.* II, 13.   [2] *TR.* II, 13-14.

The past invades the present with such a force of illusion that, for a fleeting instant, he does not know whether he is in the past or present, in the compartment of a train halted in the open country, in Balbec, in Venice or in the library of the Prince de Guermantes' town house. He is transformed into another being who is neither the Marcel of the past nor of the present but someone for whom the divisions established by the intelligence between past, present and future no longer exist, a creature able to enjoy these impressions in their extratemporality, in what they have in common with former days and the actual moment. This new Marcel, for a brief spell, is outside Time and is conscious of life as it is, outside Time and Space. He possesses the marvellous power of enjoying the reality, the very essence of things. Proust insists, however, on the brief duration of this illusion. It is necessarily brief, otherwise, we are told, the vertigo which accompanied Marcel's experience might have quickly been transformed into unconsciousness. According to Proust, such resurrections of the past are so complete that Marcel no longer sees the objects of his actual environment, but in their stead the railway-cutting with its screen of sunlit trees or else the beach at Balbec and the rising tide.

Elles forcent nos narines à respirer l'air de lieux pourtant si lointains, notre volonté à choisir entre les divers projets qu'ils nous proposent, notre personne toute entière à se croire entourée par eux, ou du moins à trébucher entre eux et les lieux présents dans l'étourdissement d'une incertitude pareille à celle qu'on éprouve parfois devant une vision ineffable, au moment de s'endormir.[1]

But Proust suggests that perhaps what is resurrected in such psychological experiences is something even rarer than a moment of truly lived past: 'Beaucoup plus, peut-être, quelque chose qui, commun à la fois au passé et au présent, est beaucoup plus essentiel qu'eux deux.'[2] Here is the ingenious explanation devised by Proust in support of his conjecture. Marcel tells us that if so often in his life, actual reality had disappointed him, it was because at the moment of his perceiving it, he could not bring into play his imagination, 'mon seul organe pour jouir de la beauté'. Now, however, the effect of this harsh law has just

---

[1] *TR.* II, 19. [2] *TR.* II, 15.

been suspended or neutralized. Thanks to a marvellous expedient of nature, on three successive occasions, Marcel has been able to extract the beauty from a sensation with his imagination, and *simultaneously* to perceive it directly with his senses of vision, hearing and smell. To employ a homely phrase, he is apparently able for once to have his cake and eat it. Normally, if I interpret Proust faithfully, an actual perception has to wait until it has ceased to be actual and has become a memory before we really appreciate its intrinsic reality and beauty. On the other hand, what Marcel calls 'les rêves de l'imagination' do not carry with them the idea of existence. Yet this idea is aroused in him by the shock to his senses that occurs when he is enabled, by the 'miracle d'une analogie', to experience a sensation at once in the present and in the past, outside Time or, as the invisible Bergson who is looking at us over Proust's shoulder, might interject: *sub specie durationis*. Thanks to this marvellous expedient or subterfuge, it would seem, Marcel can seize, isolate and immobilize in a brief flash of new consciousness, something which is never apprehended by the mind—a fragment of Time in its pure state. When, suffused by an overpowering joy, he heard the sound common to the spoon clinking on the plate and to the hammer tapping on the wheel, just as when he felt the unevenness common to the flagstones of St Mark's and to the courtyard of the Guermantes' residence, says Marcel, a being was resurrected within him whose spiritual nourishment is the essence of things.

Il languit dans l'observation du présent où les sens ne peuvent la lui apporter [i.e. l'essence des choses], dans la considération d'un passé que l'intelligence lui dessèche, dans l'attente d'un avenir que la volonté construit avec des fragments du présent et du passé auxquels elle retire encore de leur réalité ne conservant d'eux que ce qui convient à la fin utilitaire, étroitement humaine qu'elle leur assigne. Mais qu'un bruit, qu'une odeur, déjà entendu et respirée jadis le soient de nouveau, à la fois dans le présent et dans le passé, réels sans être actuels, idéaux sans être abstraits, aussitôt l'essence permanente et habituellement cachée des choses se trouve libérée et notre vrai moi qui parfois depuis longtemps semblait mort, mais ne l'était pas autrement, s'éveille, s'anime en recevant la céleste nourriture qui lui est apportée.[1]

[1] *TR.* II, 16.

[It languishes in the observation of the present from which the senses cannot procure for it the essence of things, in the contemplation of a past which is desiccated for it by the intelligence, in the expectation of a future constructed by the will out of fragments of the present and past from which it extracts still more of their reality, keeping only that part which suits the utilitarian human purpose it assigns to them. But let a sound, a scent, already heard and inhaled, be heard and inhaled anew, simultaneously in the past and in the present, real without being actual, ideal without being abstract, then, immediately, the permanent and habitually concealed essence of things is liberated and our true self which, sometimes, had seemed long since dead, but was not so in other ways, awakes and revives on receiving the celestial nourishment which is brought to it.]

With a persistence which seems to conceal a certain anxiety, Proust focuses our attention on the uniqueness of these reminiscences and on the extreme brevity of the 'trompe l'œil' which represented so vividly to Marcel's consciousness these recovered fragments of 'le temps perdu'; nay, of pure Time or *durée*. They are not to be compared, he repeats, with the images resuscitated by the voluntary memory. No doubt the Marcel who so frequently catalogues in this way the pictures made by the memory of his intelligence derives a certain selfish pleasure from his idle, comparative survey of various past sensations. But this pleasure, Proust would emphasize, is not comparable with the joy experienced by Marcel during the resurrections we have just described. Even more important is the fundamental difference in the two psychological states; between that of the Marcel contemplating the past through his intelligence and that other reborn Marcel confronted by memories of an entirely different order since they are extra-temporal. In picturing the Marcel of the first attitude, Proust stresses forcibly his 'plaisir égoiste', the naïve complacency of the intellectual who, it is inferred, thinks he is reliving his past in memory when all that he is doing is to 'combiner entre eux des éléments homogènes'. I will return in a moment to this significant phrase. The other Marcel, on the contrary, has no such illusion because, instead of being flatteringly conscious of his ego, he was ready to doubt its actual reality. The intelligent self, Proust appears to mean—the mind directed towards effective action—was wholly replaced by a deeper self whose preoccupation is with the 'essence of things', with the true reality of life and the images reflecting that reality. These, Proust insists, could never be resuscitated by the voluntary memory, which merely combines or arranges 'des éléments homogènes'. Here, I am certain, we have a distorted echo or Proustian variant of a Bergsonian original. In his article 'L'effort intellectuel',[1] Bergson notes that when we allow our memory to wander, idly, associating one image with another, we are really moving horizontally on a single plane. In such a case, he goes on: 'les images sont homogènes entre elles, mais représentatives d'objets différents.' Now this is exactly the process just described by Proust as characteristic of the voluntary memory. But it will be observed that he ceases to paraphrase Bergson when the latter tells us what happens when we stop day-dreaming and really try to remember; that is, when we pull ourselves together, descending vertically through various planes of consciousness in search of a recollection. This operation 'en intensité et en profondeur' is also characteristic of the voluntary memory, the memory of the intelligence, but Proust ignores the fact, concentrating solely for the time being on what Bergson calls the operation 'en extension et en superficie'. The reason, of course, is that Proust is eager to discredit the intelligence and its recollections so as to emphasize the superior value of the unconscious and its reminiscences.

It may be opportune, here, to examine the unusual psychological experiences which enabled Marcel to recover, intact, with their original, emotional content, certain fragments of his truly lived past, of 'le temps perdu', perhaps even, he says, 'des fragments d'existence soustraits au temps'. He has not the slightest doubt about their authenticity. The joy which accompanies their discovery, 'cette joie extra-temporelle', like the fortuitous, inevitable mode of their happening, convinces him that the past which was resurrected is the real past. I do not think that any useful purpose will be served by dismissing these experiences as the invention of a highly imaginative novelist. Quite evidently, Proust attached supreme importance to such involuntary resurrections of the unconscious. There is no mistaking the fervour of the conviction reflected in the following lines:

Je n'avais pas été chercher les deux pavés de la cour où j'avais buté. Mais justement la façon fortuite, inévitable, dont la sensation avait été rencontrée, contrôlait la verité d'un passé qu'elle ressuscitait, des images qu'elle déclanchait, puisque nous sentons son effort pour remonter vers la lumière, que nous sentons la joie du réel retrouvé. Elle est le contrôle de la vérité de tout le tableau, fait d'impressions contemporaines qu'elle ramène à sa suite, avec cette infaillible proportion de lumière et d'ombre, de relief et d'omission, de souvenir et d'oubli, que la mémoire ou l'observation conscientes ignoreront toujours.[1]

Marcel's experience is no more incredible than the curious psychological experience so brilliantly analysed and explained by Bergson in his article, 'Le souvenir du présent ou la fausse reconnaissance': the sudden conviction that everything we are actually seeing or hearing has happened before in minutest detail. The two experiences have, indeed, certain resemblances which on closer scrutiny will be found to be superficial. Marcel's illusion is not identical with the phenomenon of 'le déjà vu' studied by Bergson, where the essential characteristic is the evocation of a memory situated not in the past but, paradoxical as this may sound, in the present. It is a memory of the present. On the other hand, I am inclined to think that both illusions spring from the same cause, from a temporary relaxation of the mind's habitual tension; from an interruption in the rhythm of our consciousness. Bergson's explanation of 'false recognition' or 'le déjà vu' might be summarized as follows. The *élan* of normal consciousness reflects the continuous forward movement of life itself. Our everyday consciousness is focused on the present or immediate future. This tension or 'general attention to life' prevents a coincidence or fusion of our perceptions and the memories of perceptions, the creation or development of which is a simultaneous process. The present, according to Bergson, is being duplicated at every moment in two symmetrical fountains, so to speak, one of which (the perception) leaps towards the future whilst the other (the memory of what is perceived) falls back towards the past

[1] *TR.* ii, 25.

into the unconscious, since obviously our practical consciousness has no interest in the memory of things when it holds the things themselves. But picture a mind temporarily halted in its normal *élan*, a halt in the stream of consciousness, a momentary distraction or inattention to life. What then occurs is reflected in the illusion of 'le déjà vu': the recollection catches up with the perception and coincides with it. We remember and perceive simultaneously. Our mind has a memory of the present and for a few instants, recognition and cognition of the present are coexistent.

Now turn back to the passage where Marcel refers to that marvellous expedient of nature which allows him simultaneously to imagine and perceive certain analogous or identical sensations. Have we not here a typically Proustian rearrangement of Bergson's idea? It is true that Marcel is speaking of 'l'imagination' not of 'le souvenir'. But he uses the former word only in a very loose sense and, beyond doubt, the representations in question are reminiscences. They are not fabricated. Although he insists that these impressions are common to the past and to the present, generating by their fusion something perhaps extra-temporal in quality, nevertheless, in so far as they do belong to the past it is to a very definitely localized past. Marcel's illusion is not that he has been in the library at Guermentes' before and that everything he hears and sees in this environment has occurred before; that, for example, at some vague period in his past the same flunkey had given him this identical glass of orangeade and napkin and had asked him to wait until the concert should stop before entering the great *salon*. On the contrary, the feel of the napkin produces the illusion that the restaurant of the Grand Hôtel, the sea, the beach are quietly invading and replacing the library at the Guermantes', though this hallucination is indeed of brief duration. Marcel's actual environment vacillates and disappears but quickly reasserts its existence whilst he vainly tries to understand the cause of his ecstasy.

Marcel's illusion, although it is not that of 'le déjà vu', derives from the same cause—a brief yet total inattention to life, or as Bergson would say, from a breakdown in the delicate control mechanism which, in our normal waking state, prevents

the indiscriminate admission of our memories into our consciousness, admitting only those which the latter considers useful for
the sake of the illumination they may be able to throw upon our
immediate or future action. The most striking example of such
a breakdown is to be observed in the behaviour of the mind
when we are asleep and dreaming. A swarm of subconscious
memories then rush upwards into the zone lit by our consciousness. Now, it will be recalled that Marcel himself likens his
illusions to the ineffable visions which come to us sometimes
when we are about to fall asleep: and it is, therefore, rather
tempting to dismiss them as the fantasies of a waking dream.
Proust, I am certain, would have violently repudiated this explanation with its implied suggestion that Marcel's reminiscences,
like those of a dream, are probably memories of insignificant
happenings unperceived by the everyday practical consciousness.
He would be perfectly right, because they do not, in fact, bear
any resemblance to the unreal memories actualized in one's
dream sensations. No, Marcel's illusions arise from something
much deeper than the passing distraction of the mind which
all of us experience when we day-dream. Time and again, Proust
has materialized, in words of unparalleled beauty, the images
evoked at such moments by Marcel's errant mind. But here we
are confronted by something quite different, by visions such as
are beheld by a great artist in a brief instant of total detachment
from any preoccupation with the ordinary necessities of life and
action. Similar moments and visions had occurred before at
various times in Marcel's life, pointing the way to his true
vocation. Yet until the occurrence of this triple vision with its
urgent and supreme appeal, he had always failed to grasp the
significance of their revelations. Always Marcel had turned
away to follow the habitual trend of his consciousness, seeking
in its direct, superficial contacts with the external world of
action, the so-called 'joys of the intelligence'. But why, at the
eleventh hour, is he suddenly enlightened? I do not think we
need seek an explanation in any mystic force, but rather,
perhaps, in Marcel's psychological state on the eve of his
self-realization. An incurable invalid, no longer believing in
himself or in art, on the point of resuming his barren existence

as a *mondain*, nothing really attaches him to life. Even if destiny, he tells us, were to grant him another hundred years, he cannot see what interest there could be in such an extension of his existence.[1] This state of detachment from life, of complete incuriosity in regard to the everyday business of living seems to me a natural prelude to another state which it closely resembles. I mean the artist's attitude to life minus, however, the artist's joyous sense of creative power. Recurring at this crucial phase in Marcel's psychological existence with all the force of a triple impact, these 'resurrections' which had hitherto proved unavailing, now achieve their purpose. No psychological state is ever permanent: change is the essential characteristic of our psychological life. Nothing, of course, can transform Marcel into a great artist unless he is a born artist. But he *is* a born artist and now, for the first time, is conscious of his vocation. His sense of detachment from the positive, material aspects of life no longer inspires him with hopelessness since it is, in fact, an indispensable and natural preliminary to the creation of great art. For what is the artist but a man whose senses or consciousness function disinterestedly, who perceives the universe just for the joy of perceiving, who remembers just for the sheer pleasure of remembering, without any thought of effective action? This, it would seem, is Marcel's new way of contemplating life. Having contemplated, if only for a few swift instants, 'l'essence des choses' he can no longer be content with the superficial impressions seized by a purely forward-looking mind obsessed by the need for immediate action and direct material enjoyment.

In defending such an attitude, Proust was bound to expose himself to the shafts of the intellectuals. Yet I wonder whether their quarrel with Proust is not really 'une querelle de mots', for although convinced that no great novel can be made only with the data supplied by the novelist's critical intelligence, he always regarded himself as an intellectual. Certainly, on the other hand, if we accept the connotation given by M. Benda and his disciples to the term 'intellectual', Proust was an anti-intellectual. But I am equally sure that he would not have appreciated the

[1] *TR.* I, 236.

mansuetude which oozes from the following lines: 'L'œuvre de Proust', according to M. Benda, 'est parfaitement bien une observation sur la vie, sur les mœurs, sur certains mécanismes psychologiques; elle est parfaitement bien critique; mais Proust ne veut pas qu'elle soit cela, et toutes ses déclarations sur son œuvre protestent qu'il n'y a jamais voulu mettre que lui-même, qu'elle ne relève que de la méthode artistique en ce qu'elle est celle du poète, et n'a rien à voir avec une méthode objective, soi-disant scientifique, pour laquelle il n'a que du mépris.'[1] Clearly, Proust and M. Benda talk different languages. The verbal currency they use is stamped with the same effigy, but each attaches to it a quite different value. Proust, as an artist, is obviously not directly concerned with metaphysics. Nevertheless, if we may judge by the trend of Marcel's reflections on the function of the artist, he would agree with Bergson's view that true intellection is something more than an exercise of the analysing intelligence. He might, perhaps, have replied to M. Benda that the mind has another faculty which is, consequently, also intellectual; that *A la recherche du temps perdu*, like every great work of art, reflects a vision of life much more direct and real than the 'jugement sur la vie' which, for the latter, is the only criterion of greatness in a novel. It is this conception of the novelist's art, I feel, which Marcel now expounds and which, I have tried to show, Proust has so frequently realized in his novel.

In addition to the resurrections of his unconscious memory Marcel recalls other equally obscure impressions which on various occasions, had also challenged his attention because they offered the promise of new sensations or truths. Sometimes, indeed, he did stop to contemplate these fugitive images. But clearly, his mind, restive under this attempt to distract it from its habitual direction, impatiently broke off its vain introspective efforts to pursue these impressions in their swift downwards progress into the unconscious. Instead of seeking the substance Marcel remained satisfied with the shadow; fixing his perception, for example, on the cloud, the steeple, the flower, the pebble which had so persistently invited his attention though, as

[1] M. Benda in *Confluences*, No. 3 (April 1945).

he now knows, they were only the external and material signs of spiritual truths. This was the message his instinct had tried to convey: the summons to fulfil his vocation as an artist, and decipher the thoughts materialized in such impressions, whether they assumed the form of sensations resurrected by the involuntary memory from the unconscious or of new ones, for example, like those evoked by the steeples of Martinville. Now, according to Proust, this task is beyond the powers of our everyday intelligence, whose function is to collect general truths, superficial realities of the type so indispensable to our social existence. We must learn, he implies, a new way of thinking if we are to discover the ideas or psychological laws underlying the mass of impressions which reality is quietly and constantly imprinting deep down in our minds, unperceived by normal consciousness. Bergson would call it intuition. Proust describes it as interpretation, as opposed, I presume, to mere transcription. To quote Marcel's words:

il fallait tâcher d'interpréter les sensations comme les signes d'autant de lois et d'idées, en essayant de penser, c'est à dire de faire sortir de la pénombre ce que j'avais senti, de le convertir en un équivalent spirituel. Or, ce moyen qui me paraissait le seul, qu'était-ce autre chose que faire une œuvre d'art?[1]

Proust means, surely, that creative art involves something more than an intelligent view of things. The intelligence does not create: it arranges things into useful categories or general ideas. Creative thinking, on the other hand, is intuitive thinking which is not, however, supra-intellectual. It necessitates, nevertheless, a departure from our everyday habits of perception and thought. Theoretically, intuition is the immediate and integral contact of our consciousness with the objects of its perception. But Proust, who is an artist and not a metaphysician, has no such absolute aspirations although, as we have noted, Marcel has just experienced something closely akin to a flash of complete intuition. What Proust wants to emphasize, probably, is that the distinctive characteristic of the creative artist is, above all, the recognition that the intelligence does not penetrate deeply enough to follow the exact contours of reality. The reality of

[1] *TR.* ii, 24.

life resides in its indivisible continuity and change. Our intelligence takes snapshots of this flux, pieces together these inanimate cut-outs which are easily reassembled and holds up the resulting mosaic as a genuine representation of life itself. The artist, who knows that such a reconstruction is but a facsimile of reality, forces his mind to look backwards and down into itself so as to penetrate beyond the lucid yet sterile impressions adhering to its surface. Such, indeed, is the function of the creative or artistic mind whose consciousness is larger and more profound than that of the intellectual. And for Proust, the true objective of the creative artist, of the novelist, is not, *pace* M. Benda, to arrive at a critical judgement on life but to enter by sympathy into the uninterrupted rhythm of existence and so, intuitively, to know its reality. Like every great artist Proust knew, of course, how difficult it is to force the mind out of its usual rut and to explore the regions of its own unconscious. No wonder that so many writers shirk the effort, seizing on any excuse to salve their artistic conscience. It is so easy, observes Marcel, to persuade oneself for instance that one's first duty as a writer is to assure the triumph of justice or to reform the national morals. There are many plausible reasons for avoiding a difficult task.

Perhaps if we follow the train of Marcel's reflections, we may arrive at a more concrete impression of Proust's artistic doctrine. For, although Marcel has found his vocation, the work of art which we know as *A la recherche du temps perdu* has yet to be written. On one matter, Proust is quite intransigent. He holds the unshakable belief that the only authentic record of an individual's life is that which is deposited in his unconscious. This, although he admits that it cannot always be utilized, is the novelist's most precious document, the true book of his life. No doubt, for the critical or scientific observer, this 'livre intérieur' will always remain a closed book, a 'grimoire' or meaningless jumble of cabbalistic scribbles. Yet, in order to interpret the reality of human existence, the artist must learn how to decipher these scribbles, since they are the material traces or impressions of ideas directly and profoundly graven on our inmost being by life itself.

Ce livre, le plus pénible de tous à déchiffrer, est aussi le seul que nous ait dicté la réalité, le seul dont 'l'impression' ait été faite en nous par la réalité même. De quelque idée laissée en nous par la vie qu'il s'agisse, sa figure matérielle, trace de l'impression qu'elle nous a faite, est encore le gage de sa vérité nécessaire. Les idées formées par l'intelligence pure n'ont qu'une vérité logique, une vérité possible, leur élection est arbitraire. Le livre aux caractères figurés non tracés par nous est notre seul livre. Non que les idées que nous formons ne puissent être justes logiquement, mais nous ne savons pas si elles sont vraies. Seule l'impression, si chétive qu'en semble la matière, si invraisemblable la trace, est un critérium de vérité et à cause de cela mérite seule d'être appréhendé par l'esprit car elle est seule capable, s'il sait en dégager cette vérité, de l'amener à une plus grande perfection et de lui donner une pure joie. L'impression est pour l'écrivain ce qu'est l'expérimentation pour le savant avec cette dif-férence que chez le savant, le travail de l'intelligence précède et chez l'écrivain vient après.[1]

[This book, the most painful of all to decipher, is also the only one that was dictated to us by reality, the only one of which the 'impress' was made on us by reality itself. No matter what be the idea left upon us by life, its material shape, the trace of the impression it made on us, is still the token of its necessary truth. The ideas formed by the pure intelligence have only a logical truth, a possible truth, their election is an arbitrary matter. The book with the figured characters, not traced by us, is our only book. Not that the ideas which we form may not be logically accurate, but we do not know whether they are true. Only the impression, however flimsy it may seem materially, however improbable its outline, is a criterion of truth and because of that is alone worthy of being apprehended by the mind, for it alone is capable, if the mind can extract that truth, of bringing it to greater perfection and of yielding it a flawless joy. The impression is, for the writer, what experimentation is for the scientist, with this difference, that in the case of the scientist the work of the intelligence precedes and in that of the writer comes after.]

I would invite the reader to meditate on the first sentence of this extract because here, it seems, Proust refutes in advance any suggestion that the artistic method, the approach to reality which he demands of the creative artist, implies the possession of any mysterious or extra-intellectual faculty. If we retain his metaphor, 'le livre intérieur' contains the material to be de-ciphered or interpreted by the novelist, and all that Proust asks

[1] TR. II, 26.

of the latter is an effort familiar to every scholar. Bergson describes it as the attempt, often painful, which the scholar makes to place himself suddenly at the heart of his subject, seeking, if possible, that impulsion or incitement which, once discovered, will launch his mind on a route where it will be able to obtain a clear vision, not only of the materials he has amassed but of other even richer facts. Now turn to Marcel's reflections and note these significant words:

Ce que nous n'avons pas eu à déchiffrer, à éclaircir par notre effort personnel, ce qui était clair avant nous, n'est pas à nous. Ne vient de nous-même que ce que nous tirons de l'obscurité qui est en nous et que ne connaissent pas les autres. Et comme l'art recompose exactement la vie, autour de ces vérités qu'on a atteintes en soi-même flotte une atmosphère de poésie, la douceur d'un mystère qui n'est que la pénombre que nous avons traversée.

As Bergson once remarked, 'il y a deux espèces de clarté'. And, unfortunately for Proust, the perceptions of the artist, of the intuitive mind, will always seem obscure to those of his readers who prefer the 'clear and distinct' perceptions of Cartesianism. Bergsonians, on the other hand, will have had no difficulty in understanding the introspective process which Marcel has just described, especially if they recall what Bergson says about the 'fringe' of nebulosity which surrounds the luminous core of the intelligence; affirming by its presence that the part of our existence so clearly and distinctly perceived by our intelligence is not the essential, not the most profoundly felt or lived part. Obviously, this Bergsonian 'fringe' is Proust's 'pénombre' which, says Marcel, must be penetrated if we would seek reality. This demands, of course, a reversal of the normal direction of the mind, an orientation inwards and that, in turn, implies an enlargement of our mental horizon. Yet, he suggests, such an effort is gloriously rewarded, for in that descent into the unconscious, the artist obtains a wonderful vision, an ineffable sensation of inner harmony. So, I believe, we must interpret his reflections. At the same time, I readily understand the reaction of the traditional intellectuals to such ideas, a reaction which is liable to express itself in many forms

[1] *TR.* ii, 27.

ranging from Voltairian mockery to the indulgence of Alain and M. Benda, who regard Proust, apparently, as a remarkably intelligent and observant novelist who was regrettably obsessed, however, with the crazy idea that in addition to a psychology of the conscious there is also a psychology of the unconscious.

I do not quite know which is less illuminating, this 'ce qui n'est pas clair n'est pas français' approach to Proust or the attitude of mind of those fervent worshippers who view him as a mystic ripe for canonization. Surely, between these two extremes, must lie another way. This I will now try to discover in my attempt to extract and interpret the Proustian doctrine of art contained in Marcel's reflections.

We must not forget that at this moment, Marcel is inspired by the fervour of a convert so that we need not be astonished to observe a gradual change in the tenor of his thoughts when he begins to realize that it is one thing to be inspired by religious faith and quite another and more difficult enterprise to translate faith into good works. This does not in the least, however, shake his conviction that the only art worthy of the name is that which can find some way of discovering and expressing our true experience of life, such as we felt it in the depths of our sensibility, not as we thought or conceived it with our surface intelligence. Such is the basic tenet of the creed now so richly illustrated and subtly expounded by Proust.

The artist is not free to choose the work of art. Virtually, it exists within him as a record, a 'livre intérieur' which must be interpreted by the artist. No one can help him in his task of decipherment which is, in fact, artistic creation. In discovering his true self, the real past which is so different from anything he ever believed, the artist is exercising his predestined vocation. He is realizing himself in art. Marcel is now telling us the conclusions, the precious truths he has learned from the memories resurrected by chance from his unconscious. Through art, he means, this marvellous expedient of nature can be imitated and perfected. By learning to distrust the superficial perceptions and memories of his intelligence, and not to look for reality in external appearances, the novelist is really learning how to recompose life, to discover the original quality of the sensations with which his memories coincided but from which they have diverged. However much he may be tempted, he must never swerve from this task or allow himself to be troubled by slogans or theories of art. Now Proust turns to attack certain of his literary *bêtes-noires*, the advocates of popular art, of national art, the writers who talk glibly of 'intellectual values', the demagogues who summon the artist to emerge from his ivory tower, above all, the so-called 'realism' of the Naturalists for whom a novel is a kind of cinema film of life. To illustrate, by contrast, the absurdity of their false conception of art, Proust introduces a charming incident. Marcel, who is still waiting in the Guermantes' library, turns to inspect some of the Prince's celebrated first editions. The first that comes to hand is George Sand's *François le Champi*, which arouses an impression apparently quite out of tune with his immediate thoughts. But suddenly, out of the past there arises from his deepest consciousness the memory of another impression replete with tender recollections of that night, long ago at Combray, when his mother, immolating her sense of duty to her immense maternal love, distressed at the little boy's tears, read to him aloud from *François le Champi*. As Marcel's eyes rest on the magic title, that small boy is resurrected from the past, that self who really knows the book and alone has the right to read the name, *François le Champi*. It is he who now comes forward, taking the place of the other Marcel and spells out the title once again,

avec la même impression du temps qu'il faisait dans le jardin, les mêmes rêves qu'il formait alors sur les pays et sur la vie, la même angoisse du lendemain. Que je revoie une chose d'un autre temps, c'est un autre jeune homme qui se lèvera. Et ma personne d'aujourd'hui n'est qu'une carrière abandonnée qui croit que tout ce qu'elle contient est pareil et monotone mais d'où chaque souvenir, comme un sculpteur de Grèce, tire des statues innombrables.[1]

Whilst we are still, like Marcel himself, under the spell cast over our humdrum, reasoning intelligence by these fortuitous and illuminating revelations, culminating in the enchanting *François le Champi* scene, Proust makes a supreme attempt to define the ideal which must be the objective of every true artist.

[1] *TR.* II, 34.

GP

33

It is clear from Marcel's experiences, that things we have seen once and now see again after many years often have the power to resurrect, with the mood in which we first beheld them, the images once caught in the mind's original field of vision. That, Proust explains, is because objects, when perceived by us, are transmuted into something immaterial, of the same spiritual quality as our thoughts and emotions of that bygone moment, with which indeed they become completely interfused. Here is one of two passages where he plays upon this theme until its melody drifts into our consciousness.

Une image offerte par la vie, nous apporte en réalité à ce moment-là des sensations multiples et différentes. La vue par exemple de la couverture d'un livre déjà lu a tissé dans les caractères de son titre les rayons de la lune d'une lointaine nuit d'été. Le goût du café au lait matinal nous apporte cette vague espérance d'un beau temps qui jadis si souvent pendant que nous le buvions dans un bol de porcelaine blanche, crémeuse et plissée qui semblait du lait durci, se mit à nous sourire dans la claire incertitude du petit jour. Une heure n'est pas qu'une heure, c'est un vase rempli de parfums, de sons, de projets et de climats.[1]

[An image presented by life really brings to us in that instant multiple and varied sensations. The sight, for instance, of the cover of a book once read has woven into the characters of its title the moon-beams of some distant summer night. The taste of our morning coffee brings us that vague hope of a fine day which formerly, when we used to drink it from a bowl of white, creamy porcelain, wrinkled like curdled milk, began to smile at us in the faltering brightness of dawn. An hour is not just an hour, it is a vase filled with perfumes, with sounds, with projects and with climates.]

The version I have just quoted is a revision of an earlier one, but in both the author's motive is the same. It is to accentuate the original quality that distinguishes his conception of realistic art from the 'réalisme' of the Zolaists.

Before we allow ourselves to be swept along by Marcel's narrative into a path diverging somewhat from the well-beaten track of simple logic, it might be wise to pause and take our bearings. The objective towards which Proust is leading us is, I think, already visible. The artist must find some way of

<hr>

[1] *TR.* ii, 39.

discovering and expressing the original and real impressions made upon him by life, since they alone contain the essence or reality of existence. But how does he recover them? Proust tells us that they are retained in things, or rather that they can be released when a sensation evoked by an object in actual contact with our senses coincides with a former, analogous sensation, though perhaps aroused by a different object. Thus, fortuitously our soul is invaded by a swarm of reminiscences. A state of soul which we know for the first time, a fragment of our life as we had really lived it, is experienced by us. Moreover, it is experienced simultaneously in what is conventionally but quite unrealistically termed the 'past' and 'present'. In fact, all these impressions are extra-temporal. So far, so good. The novelist's true function is to re-create through memory his real impressions: 'L'art recompose exactement la vie.' How does he do this? Must he always depend on chance, in other words, on the caprice of Nature in order to recapture 'le temps perdu', his truly lived past? We recall, for instance, Marcel's hopeless attempts at Tansonville to evoke such reminiscences by an act of voluntary remembering when he saw once again the objects of his child-hood's environment. Marcel's reply at this stage—for he has not yet begun to create his work of art—is that, indeed, his Tansonville experiment was doomed to failure. The extra-temporal impressions evoked by an essential quality common to the sensations of the past and of the present are fortuitously released. Yet, Marcel, as we shall observe, whilst never relinquishing this conviction, will gradually find himself obliged to regard it as an ideal, a guiding principle never capable of being wholly realized, but which must always be in the forefront of the artist's mind because it illuminates the work of art.

Now, perhaps, we may return to the narrative with some assurance of being able to follow its complexities, and with the aid of Bergson, to grasp its implications. The Zolaists, with their so-called 'réalisme' and their 'art vécu' annoy Proust considerably. He regards their 'littérature de notations' as a valueless inventory of trivialities, of inaccurate impressions which leave out everything that really constitutes experience. Proust can imagine nothing more joyless than such 'réalisme',

nothing more remote from real life since it interrupts all
communication between our present self and its past. Literature
is not a documentary newsreel. What then, is the reality which
the novelist must seek and how can it be communicated?

Ce que nous appelons la réalité [says Proust] est un certain rapport
entre ces sensations et ces souvenirs qui nous entourent simultanément
— rapport que supprime une simple vision cinématographique, laquelle
s'éloigne par là d'autant plus du vrai qu'elle prétend se borner à
lui — rapport unique que l'écrivain doit retrouver pour en enchaîner
à jamais dans sa phrase les deux termes différents. On peut faire se
succéder indéfiniment dans une description les objets qui figuraient
dans le lieu décrit, la vérité ne commencera qu'au moment où l'écrivain
prendra deux objets différents, posera leur rapport, analogue dans le
monde de l'art à celui qu'est le rapport unique de la loi causale, dans
le monde de la science et les enfermera dans les anneaux d'un beau
style, ou même, ainsi que la vie, quand en rapprochant une qualité
commune à deux sensations, il dégagera leur essence en les réunissant
l'une et l'autre pour les soustraire aux contingences du temps, dans
une métaphore, et les enchaînera par le lien indescriptible d'une
alliance de mots.[1]

[What we call reality is a certain relationship between those
sensations and those memories that simultaneously envelop us—a
relationship abolished by a mere cinematographic vision, which
thereby diverges from the truth all the more since it professes to
confine itself to the truth—a unique relationship which the writer
must discover so as to link together for ever in his phrase its two
different terms. One may, in a description, make the objects that
figured in the place described succeed each other indefinitely, the
truth will only begin to appear at the moment when the writer takes
two different objects, fixes their relationship analogous in the world
of art to that unique relationship, the law of causality, in the world
of science and encloses them in the inevitable linkage of a fine style,
or even, just like life, when in bringing together qualities common to
two sensations, he releases their essence by uniting both, so as to abstract them from the contingencies of time, in a metaphor, and chains
them together by the indefinable nexus of an alliance of words.]

The general sense of this passage I have already explained,
but if we consider its implications it will be seen to contain
distinct reminiscences of Bergson. The novelist, Proust suggests,

must express the real nature of the self and, therefore, forge a narrative style which shall render visible the surprising inter-fusion of sensations and memories that compose the real self, the fundamental *moi*. Indeed, it is this mutual penetration which constitutes the essence or reality of our inner life. The fallacy of the Realists, he implies, lies in the supposition that these diverse impressions can be communicated in a historical, des-criptive narrative, as if they were a logical sequence of immobile and simple psychological states. But it is false to assume that our real impressions exist in a homogeneous milieu, succeeding each other according to the law of cause and effect, in space-time. It is clear from Marcel's experiences that the elements constituting this mass of interfused sensations and memories, our real life, are not associated in such a logical manner. In this illogical inner world, the effect does not immediately follow its cause: conventional Time which is actually Space, has no authority here. The factitious divisions made by our intel-ligence in duration, in real Time, are completely ignored. No, our real memories and sensations are linked by a special, unique, qualitative 'rapport' or resemblance. This is the common essence, the reality, which the novelist must discover and explore with his intelligence. Its material trace may be quite insig-nificant, like the similarity of 'feel' in the Guermantes' napkin and the Balbec hotel towel; the similar unevenness of the flagstones at St Mark's and the Guermantes' courtyard. What matters to the artist is the qualitative 'rapport' they exteriorize, the essential quality of the impressions they engender. These are the precious materials of his work of art although, unfor-tunately, as Proust has to admit, they are rare and must be supplemented by the less valuable impressions, by the truths directly obtained by the intelligence from the external reality of everyday life. These are not to be despised,

car elles pourraient enchasser d'une matière moins pure mais encore pénétrée d'esprit ces impressions que nous apportent hors du temps l'essence commune aux sensations du passé et du présent, mais qui, plus précieuses, sont aussi trop rares pour que l'œuvre d'art puisse être composée seulement avec elles.[1]

[1] *TR.* ii, 53.

Nothing could well be more unjust and liable to distort our vision of Proust's art than to interpret this admission as a renunciation of the artist's ideals. One may dismiss, of course, the suggestion that Proust, in a belated attempt to 'save face', inserted this phrase in order to disguise the fact that he was guilty of a flagrant breach of contract, his failure, in short, to deliver that novel entirely based on the unconscious which he was supposed to have promised his readers. The truth is, of course, very different. Proust never relinquished the conviction —which is also Bergson's—that if we would know the real nature of our own life or of life in general we must start off by recognizing that the impressions obtained by our workaday intelligence compose, in their ensemble, an inaccurate picture of real existence. Nature, life itself, suggested this truth to Marcel. It is not surprising, therefore, to find him attaching very great importance to those reminiscences which are resurrected, not by an effort of his will, but spontaneously, by an act of Nature. On the other hand, we have only to follow the course of his reflections to see that, whilst prizing these unique experiences, for their intrinsic value, he sees in them only 'un commencement d'art'. From them, as an artist on the eve of creation, Marcel has learned a valuable and fundamental truth. It is that beneath the superficial, material impressions made on his senses by things and people are to be found, at a deeper level, the real, though immaterial impressions that escaped the attention of his intelligence. On this account, they have not been recorded in the book of his practical or useful memories. Nevertheless, they have penetrated Marcel's sensibility and imprinted themselves in another book 'le livre intérieur'. This is a fact proved by his personal experience. Such vital impressions arise spontaneously from time to time into the zone lighted by one's immediate consciousness; not only in dreams where they appear in a distorted form, but also during the waking state, in their original and true guise.

Marcel has found his vocation. In other words, his being is now oriented towards the objective for which it was predestined by Nature. That objective is the creation of the work of art which, for Proust, is an act of inward vision and of interpretation.

Marcel is armed for his difficult task by the knowledge that underneath external reality is the inner reality, life itself. To create the work of art, he must obtain and exteriorize in language a vision of this marvellous world within himself, its rich, indivisible continuity of interfused perceptions, sensations, emotions and ideas. By an effort of intuition, by distracting his mind from its normal preoccupations, forcing it to look backwards and downwards and to ignore its own superficial impressions, the great novelist obtains a true vision which he reveals to us in words chosen for their qualities of transparency and reflectiveness. But surely this is a purely subjective vision, merely, as M. Benda would say, 'une affirmation de la sensibilité de l'auteur...une œuvre poétique'. What about 'la méthode objective' which alone, if we accept the opinion of M. Benda and his disciples, can produce great novels? Proust would reply, to judge from the tenor of Marcel's reflections, that the artist's first business is to know himself. Then, having learned to distinguish between his true self and the other, unreal, external or social self, he will be better equipped to decipher or translate the impressions made upon him by the words, gestures or actions of other individuals. A great novel, Proust would say, is neither the product of a subjective nor of an objective mind because, with his supreme good sense, he knows that such antinomies are artificial concepts. They have no existence in fact. The first indispensable step towards an understanding of *A la recherche du temps perdu* is to get rid of such misconceptions. For Proust it is an axiom that all true reality is subjective, which is only another way of saying, after all, that the only person we have a chance of *really* knowing is ourself. Few possess the courage, however, to face such an ordeal. But the artist must perform this experiment on himself: in no other way can he acquire a method of approach to human nature and a knowledge of the laws governing human psychology. Only then is he properly equipped to observe and interpret the behaviour of the men and women whose lives impinge upon and mingle with his own. As a result of this method, no doubt, the novelist will often disconcert a public accustomed to a more 'logical' or conventional representation of life. Perhaps also, he may not always succeed in expressing the essential reality which he discovers within himself. Yet, as Proust remarks, we can at least learn something from his failures, whereas there is nothing to be learned from the successes of 'le réalisme'.

Nowhere else does the articulation of Proust's thought so closely follow Bergson's as in these reflections on the nature and purpose of great art. For both writers, art is essentially a reorientation of the mind, accompanied by an intensification of its power to receive impressions. This is surely what Proust means by 'le pouvoir réfléchissant' of the novelist.[1] The objects that produce impressions may be trivial or noble but what really makes great art is the depth of their penetration into the artist's consciousness and the latter's ability to interpret and exteriorize them in the work of art. Bergson saw, even in the greatest art, only a partial realization of that 'integral experience', that metaphysical intuition of reality which is the supreme objective of all his philosophic thinking. For Bergson the existence of great art was important but chiefly as proving that it is, in fact, possible to think intuitively, to break with the habitual, practical course of one's thought and so 'ressaisir la vie intérieure, au-dessous de la juxtaposition que nous effectuons de nos états dans un temps spatialisé'.[2] Proust, in the following passage, as in so many others, restates and elaborates Bergson's idea which forms, indeed, the basis of the Proustian conception of art.

La grandeur de l'art véritable, au contraire, de celui que M. de Norpois eût appelé un jeu de dilettante, c'était de retrouver, de ressaisir, de nous faire connaître cette réalite loin de laquelle nous vivons, de laquelle nous nous écartons de plus en plus au fur et à mesure que prend plus d'épaisseur et d'imperméabilité la connaissance conventionnelle que nous lui substituons, cette réalité que nous risquerions fort de mourir sans l'avoir connue, et qui est tout simplement notre vie, la vraie vie, la vie enfin découverte et éclaircie, la seule vie par conséquent réellement vécue, cette vie qui en un sens, habite à chaque instant chez tous les hommes aussi bien que chez l'artiste. Mais ils ne la voient pas, parce qu'ils ne cherchent pas à l'éclaircir. Et ainsi leur passé est encombré d'innombrables clichés qui restent inutiles parce que l'intelligence ne les a pas 'développés'. Ressaisir notre vie; et

---

[1] *JF.* i, 117.   [2] *La pensée et le mouvant*, p. 88.

aussi la vie des autres; car le style pour l'écrivain aussi bien que pour le peintre est une question non de technique, mais de vision. Il est la révélation qui serait impossible par des moyens directs et conscients de la différence qualitative qu'il y a dans la façon dont nous apparaît le monde, différence qui, s'il n'y avait pas l'art, resterait le secret éternel de chacun.[1]

[The greatness of true art, of the art which M. de Norpois would have described as the pastime of a dilettante, was to rediscover, to recapture, to make known to us that reality so distant from our everyday existence, and from which we stray ever farther according to the increasing solidity and impermeability of the conventional knowledge which we substitute for it, that reality which we run a serious risk of never knowing before we die, and which is nothing more or less than our life, our real life, life finally discovered and illuminated, that life which, in a sense, is present at every moment in all men as well as in the artist. But they do not see it because they make no effort to illuminate it. And so their past is cluttered up with innumerable negatives which remain useless because the intelligence has not 'developed' them. To recapture our life, and also the life of others; because style, for the writer as well as for the painter, is a matter not of technique but of vision. It is the revelation, which would be impossible by direct or conscious means, of the qualitative difference there is in the way the world presents itself to us, a difference which, but for the existence of art, would remain the eternal secret of each individual.]

When Proust sets out to define the artist's task, the method by which alone it is possible to seize the inner reality of existence, the basic pattern of his thought again coincides with that of Bergson. It is fascinating, however, to watch the subtle transformation effected on this ground design by Proust's rich and ingenious embroidery. The function of the artist is really that of a translator or interpreter. Beneath matter, experience, words, there is 'something different', a significance hidden from the ordinary man whose normal state of mind is always a state of tension, keyed for action. We live, as Proust remarks after Bergson, 'détournés de nous-même'. Artistic creation involves a complete reversal of this attitude of mind. The artist must patiently undo the work achieved by our intelligence, by our *amour-propre*, our passions and habits which are continually hiding our real impressions from ourselves in the practical

[1] *TR.* ii, 48.

interest of what we erroneously call living. Creative art, therefore, is essentially a 'retour aux profondeurs' which, as Marcel
also realizes, will be a painful, if salutary operation, involving
the sacrifice of all the comforting illusions with which *amour-
propre* has camouflaged his real sentimental life. He must
ruthlessly tear down this shimmering, meretricious veil and
look at the true picture of his love experience. Not that Marcel's
experience, in these hours of love, has been fundamentally
different from that of other men. Proust never claims that it is
this which distinguishes the artist from other men, an important
point ignored by critics who seek to depreciate his novel by
suggesting that it reflects an experience so unique, so personal
as to have merely an æsthetic value and is but the affirmation
in beautiful language of Proust's sensibility. On the contrary,
Proust cherishes no Romantic illusions about the uniqueness
of Marcel's experiences: they are essentially those of the
ordinary man. The great difference, however, is that Marcel is
an artist and can interpret his experiences. Proust illustrates
this difference in a simile borrowed from Bergson:

> On éprouve, mais ce qu'on a éprouvé est pareil à certains clichés qui
> ne montrent que du noir tant qu'on ne les a pas mis près d'une lampe,
> et qu'eux aussi il faut regarder à l'envers: on ne sait pas ce que c'est
> tant qu'on ne l'a pas approché de l'intelligence. Alors seulement quand
> elle l'a éclairé, quand elle l'a intellectualisé, on distingue, et avec quelle
> peine, la figure de ce qu'on a senti.[1]

In Bergson's *La perception du changement* you will find the same
conception of the artist's function. The poet or novelist, he
says, who expresses a state of soul does not wholly create it. The
poem or novel gradually reveals nuances of thought and emotion
which have long existed as part of our own inner life yet, but
for the revelation of art, would ever have remained invisible,
'telle l'image photographique qui n'a pas été plongée encore
dans le bain où elle se révélera'.

I would draw attention here to the special connotation given
by Proust to the terms *intelligence* and *intellectualiser*. Marcel
is speaking of the artist's intelligence which is the critical
or reasoning intelligence reinforced by intuition, therefore

[1] *TR.* II, 50.

diverted from its habitual direction. His implication, obviously, is that he never knew the true nature of the impressions or sensations made upon him by Gilberte, Mme de Guermantes or Albertine because the reasoning intelligence, which is so indispensable for the ordinary purposes of life, cannot possibly illuminate or 'intellectualize' an experience so deeply sited in the obscure regions of the soul. Now, however, even although it involves the destruction of many illusions, the painful sloughing of the protective covering devised by his instinct for self-preservation, Marcel is resolved to discover, and in so far as is possible, to reconstruct his true past and his real self, 'le moi fondamental'. Only in so far as is possible, because although Marcel still believes that there must be a plane where art and reality exactly coincide, he is also compelled to admit that the artist, the individual craftsman, has to work on another plane where brass tacks are more plentiful than golden nails. In other words, whilst the Proustian conception of art may be identified up to a certain point with Bergson's intuitionism, beyond that point the novelist and the philosopher part company. It is tempting, under the spell of Marcel's narrative, to ignore the existence of this limitation imposed on the novelist by the nature of his art and of his medium, language, which is intrinsically symbolic. Yet, as Proust himself remarks in a totally different context, intentions do not count in art; only the work of art itself. In *A la recherche du temps perdu* he has created a work of art which affords a closer view of reality than any other French novel I have read. But it is not the realization by a novelist of Bergson's metaphysics of intuition.

There can be few examples, surely, in any literature, of a novelist so intensely aware of his own creative processes, of his aims and the obstacles in the way of their fulfilment. As Proust, in his disarmingly communicative narrative, enlarges on these matters one begins to perceive, in retrospect, the full significance of the incidents so minutely described in the opening pages of this chapter. We know that Nature, through her spontaneous resurrections of 'le temps perdu', has shown Marcel truths of inestimable value to the artist. One feels, however, that only now is he beginning to grasp a basic truth contained in these manifestations. It is the function of art, no doubt, to re-create Nature: 'l'art recompose exactement la vie.' But the artist must not hold the illusion that his creative acts can ever possess the spontaneous, effortless quality of natural creation. A consciousness of this truth, I think, is progressively reflected in this closing volume. Note, for example, how Marcel, now that he is about to create his work of art, dwells on the thought that great art is perhaps never realized except at the cost of intense spiritual travail and suffering. This idea, of course, has long haunted the imagination of the Romantic artist. What is interesting to observe is the process by which Proust, who is not a Romantic, allows it to colour his reflections on art.

In order to create his work of art, the writer must re-read the book of his life and establish the original text, a task fraught with pain and disillusionment. Proust does not deny the existence of another, happier phase in artistic creation when the artist, having discovered the authentic text, proceeds to his commentary, expressing in the form of general ideas the permanent, universal truths extracted as a result of his studies. But the really difficult task is to decode this 'livre intérieur', to review one's whole past in a spirit of ruthless honesty, looking for the original writing in the palimpsest, discarding all those words, actions and gestures which, in the aggregate, compose the attractive, yet meretricious record of one's life and personality. Confronted by this labour, Marcel knows that he will need great courage as well as skill and integrity. After all, the fabric of what we naïvely call our happiness is largely made up of all these sham realities with which, at every moment, the individual deludes himself and other people. He does not often lie deliberately. It is simply because, preoccupied with the absorbing business of living for action and for the excitement and pleasure of the actual hour he rarely pauses to ask what life really means to him. Every impression made upon us by an object, Proust truly observes, is twofold. One part is sheathed in the object itself, the other within ourself. But it is only the external unimportant part of the impression, visible to all, that we trouble to communicate: the other we ignore, so that it is never known to us or to others. Vaguely, we dismiss it as inexpressible because of our constitutional, and in Proust's view, our unforgivable intellectual laziness. He does not specifically name this common malady of the human spirit, but his merciless analysis of its symptoms makes any such formal diagnosis superfluous. One recalls at this point what La Rochefoucauld says in his *Maximes* about 'la paresse', the most insidious and malignant, he thought, of all the human passions. But he attacks 'la paresse' for reasons diametrically opposed to those adumbrated by Proust. Intellectual laziness, for the seventeenth-century moralist, is a curse because the victim of this 'béatitude de l'âme' neglects his social duties and ceases to be a man of action. Proust, on the contrary, would maintain that the life of action, precisely by fostering a superficial illusion of beatitude, distracts us from the most important affair in life which is to know the reality of life itself. Was it not this disease, more baneful than any physical malady, which so long prevented Marcel from discovering his vocation? Now that it is out of his system, he can observe how noxious and pervasive are its effects. Even when we deliberately seek impressions, for instance in the contemplation of artistic or natural beauty, our incurable intellectual sloth, our cowardly fear of introspection exerts its influence. It may be a symphony or a poem or some ancient church that leaves its special original impression on our consciousness: yet always, instead of turning our mind inwards in an effort to perceive the real, individual quality of the impression, we are content to look only at its external trace and it is this we try to express, probably by incoherent, meaningless superlatives of admiration or by frantic hand-clappings. Quite probably, too, still escaping our stern and clear duty, we go again and again to hear the symphony, to see the church or else re-read the poem until we know everything about them except what really matters—the impression they made upon our soul. Few can read without a sense of discomfort, perhaps of shame, these pages where Proust ruthlessly exposes the shallowness of what so often passes for a knowledge of the arts, for erudition: 'cette fuite, loin de notre propre vie que nous n'avons pas le courage de regarder';[1] the sad or perhaps ridiculous sterility of the self-styled connoisseurs; the futility of the literary schools or chapels with their ephemeral, bumbling slogans; the false scales of the critics who assess a work of art by the 'intellectual' or moral pretensions of its subject.

Marcel, as he turns away from this spectacle, can see his own course more clearly defined: 'les vrais livres doivent être les enfants non du grand jour et de la causerie mais de l'obscurité et du silence.'[2] Proust does not mean that the novelist should be a recluse, a dreamer. For although Marcel will always regard as unique the impressions fortuitously resurrected by the modality of the involuntary memory, he recognizes that the bulk of his raw material consists of impressions obtained in the ordinary process of social existence, in his contacts with other people, during his hours of love, of sorrow, of frivolous pleasure. Unknown to himself, life was busy inscribing these impressions in his 'livre intérieur' which he must scrutinize and decode. This is the work that must be carried out in solitude, in that grim yet inevitable conversation with himself, that private interview between the artist and the man when all subterfuges and illusions are tacitly laid aside and nothing counts but reality. So we must envisage Marcel's present state of mind. The time has come to practise his vocation, a solemn hour for every man, whatever his calling. For none, however, more solemn than for the artist because, as I think Proust implies, his is not a vocation where success is measured by progress beyond a point attained by his predecessors. The greatest writers create in the knowledge that recognition of their genius will only come after death. One thing, above all, is certain and it is symbolized in Marcel's analogy between the soul of the artist and the grain of wheat. The grain stores up its rich substance that will nourish the plant but dies itself so that the plant may live and flourish. It is so with the artist whose life, with its memories of sorrows and joys, composes a reserve similar to the albumen secreted in the embryo of the grain of wheat.

Ainsi toute ma vie [reflects Marcel] jusqu'a ce jour aurait pu et n'aurait pas pu être résumée sous ce titre: Une vocation. Elle ne l'aurait pas pu en ce sens que la littérature n'avait joué aucun rôle dans ma vie. Elle l'aurait pu en ce que cette vie, les souvenirs de ses tristesses, de ses joies, formaient une réserve pareille à cet albumen qui est logé dans l'ovule des plantes et dans lequel celui-ci puise sa nourriture pour se transformer en graine, en ce temps où on ignore encore que l'embryon d'une plante se développe, lequel est pourtant le lieu de phénomènes chimiques et respiratoires secrets mais très actifs. Ainsi ma vie était en rapport avec ce qui amènerait sa maturation.[1]

But Marcel's analogy is true only in the sense that the artist is resigned to the fact that posterity will never know, perhaps never care to know, the extent of his personal sacrifice, of his self-immolation. We would be completely wrong to pursue it further and compare the unconscious creative processes of nature with those of art. The opposite is true since the dominant theme of Marcel's reflections is that creation, for the artist, necessarily involves suffering. But in one respect, as Marcel discovers, nature has been preparing the way for art. During the fallow and apparently wasted years, the instinct to whose voice he refused to listen had been equipping him for his destined task. Influenced by that 'sentiment du général' which is characteristic of the artist's outlook on life, Marcel had always unconsciously recorded the gestures, accents, words, dismissed by his intelligence as trivial yet which really interpreted the personality of the individuals whose conversation he ignored. Intuitively, he had always recognized the importance to the future novelist of such apparently meaningless signs. We who have read *A la recherche du temps perdu* recognize, for our part, the admirable fidelity with which Marcel observed the precepts contained in the following lines.

Par de tels accents, par de tels jeux de la physionomie, par de tels mouvements d'épaules, eussent-ils été vus dans sa plus lointaine enfance, la vie des autres est représentée en lui et quand plus tard il écrira, elle lui servira à recréer la réalité soit en composant un mouvement d'épaules commun à beaucoup, vrai comme s'il était noté sur le cahier d'un anatomiste, mais gravé ici pour exprimer une vérité psychologique, soit en emmanchant sur ce mouvement d'épaules un mouvement de cou fait par un autre, chacun ayant donné son instant de pose.[2]

It is, however, more difficult and intensely more painful for the artist to seek the element of universal truth, the psychological

[1] *TR.* II, 54.   [2] *TR.* II, 55–6.

law implicit in his own passions. Yet such is the indispensable condition of great art. In Marcel's case, it will mean the resurrection of sorrows long vanished into oblivion. He will have to re-live, in its complete and original reality, that fragment of his life which linked him to the beloved grandmother whose sufferings he regarded with such indifference, whose loss he had so easily banished from memory. He must reopen also that chapter of his life entitled *Albertine*, read it again, but this time with scrupulous honesty, and in the same spirit write his commentary so that others who never knew the real Albertine will be able to annex his love and superimpose it upon their own love for some very different woman. Yet does not the artist, on the other hand, by the very act of extracting 'la belle généralité' from his own sufferings achieve thereby a certain tranquillity of soul? Proust would admit that this is, to some degree, undeniable. But he also points out that the life of an artist does not end with the completion of one work of art. The original cause of his sufferings, as in the case of Marcel's unhappy love for Albertine, still persists and will lead him into other tragic liaisons. There is never, he grimly hints, any fear that the supply of these 'grands chagrins utiles' will ever run short. Life is very generous in this respect. Only, they do not last long, so that the writer must hasten to explore their action upon himself lest death arrest his researches. The Proustian imagination, fascinated by this idea, launches upon one of its rare stratospheric flights.

Le chagrin finit par tuer. A chaque nouvelle peine trop forte, nous sentons une veine de plus qui saille et développe sa sinuosité mortelle au long de notre tempe, sous nos yeux. Et c'est ainsi que peu à peu se font ces terribles figures ravagées, du vieux Rembrandt, du vieux Beethoven de qui tout le monde se moquait. Et ce ne serait rien que les poches des yeux et les rides du front s'il n'y avait la souffrance du cœur. Mais puisque les forces peuvent se changer en d'autres forces, puisque l'ardeur qui dure devient lumière et que l'électricité de la foudre peut photographier, puisque notre sourde douleur au cœur peut élever au-dessus d'elle comme un pavillon — la permanence visible d'une image à chaque chagrin — acceptons le mal physique qu'il nous donne pour la connaissance spirituelle qu'il nous apporte; laissons se désagréger notre corps, puisque chaque nouvelle parcelle qui s'en détache, vient, cette fois lumineuse et lisible, pour la compléter au prix de souffrances dont d'autres plus doués n'ont pas besoin, pour la rendre plus solide au fur et à mesure que les émotions effritent notre vie, s'ajouter à notre œuvre. Les idées sont des succédanés des chagrins; au moment où ceux-ci se changent en idées, ils perdent une partie de leur action nocive sur notre cœur, et même au premier instant, la transformation elle-même dégage subitement de la joie.[1]

[In the end, grief kills. With every new and intense affliction, we feel one more vein jutting forth and tracing its sinuous, deadly path along our temple, under our eyes. And thus are formed those terrible ravaged faces, of the aged Rembrandt, of the aged Beethoven, whom everyone jeered at. And the pouches under the eyes and the wrinkles on the brow would not matter were it not for the suffering in the heart. But since forces change into other forces, since continuous heat becomes light and the electricity from the lightning-flash can photograph, since the dull pain in our heart can hoist, as it were, its own flag—the visible permanence of an image at each fresh grief—let us accept the physical hurt inflicted on us for the sake of the spiritual knowledge which it brings us; let our body disintegrate since each fresh particle that crumbles away from it is there, luminous and readable now, ready to be added to our work in order to complete it at the cost of sufferings which others more gifted do not need, in order to render it stronger and more enduring whilst our emotions are gradually wearing away our life. Ideas are substitutes for afflictions; at the moment when the latter change into ideas, they lose part of their noxious effect on our heart, and even at the first instant, the very process of transformation suddenly releases joy.]

In this final review of the ideas which are to determine the form and substance of Marcel's novel, Proust inserts an explanation closely resembling an apology. 'De ma vie passée, je compris', says Marcel, 'que les moindres épisodes avaient concouru à me donner la leçon d'idéalisme dont j'allais profiter aujourd'hui.'[1] He has learned, in brief, that matter, in itself, is unimportant since it can so easily be transformed by thought, by the idea we form of an object. There is no need to search for illustrations of this psychological fact: they are to be found in every chapter of *A la recherche du temps perdu*. Idealism, for Proust, is the radioactive element in love, whether it is Swann's love for Odette, Marcel's 'désir moral' for Albertine, or the impure passion of Charlus for the violinist Morel. Now we

---

[1] *TR.* II, 63.

come to the motive underlying Proust's allusion to idealism, the astonishing powers of which, he claims, are nowhere so completely demonstrated as in 'le phénomène si mal compris, si inutilement blâmé, de l'inversion sexuelle'.[1] It is no doubt remarkable, Proust suggests, to witness that obliteration of reality by the idea, which occurs when a man falls in love with an ugly woman. But what could be more profoundly illuminating than the spectacle of a *grand seigneur* infatuated by a bus-driver?

In fact, Proust now displaces Marcel, and takes over the narrative, appealing directly to the reader not to be shocked or puzzled by the pages of his novel devoted to the analysis and interpretation of homosexuality. Observe, however, his reasons. A novel is a kind of optical instrument presented by the novelist to the reader so that the latter may discern for himself something which, but for the artist, he might not have noticed. No one will disagree with this definition, which is a Proustian transposition of Bergson's admirable observations on the function of the artist. Now, although Proust rightly argues that the reader judges of the truth of a novel by the recognition within himself of the psychological states portrayed by the writer, he is obviously aware that in *A la recherche du temps perdu* there is a great deal that the reader may not or will not recognize. But Proust is not very much worried about the reader who may be shocked by Charlus and Morel. His real concern is that the reader who honestly looks into his own mind, in the light of the novelist's larger vision of human nature, may find it quite impossible to discover even the virtual existence within himself of emotions and thoughts which, if allowed to crystallize, would resemble those attributed by Proust to his two perverts. All Proust can do in such a case is to hold up another, more powerful glass and say: 'Regardez vous-même si vous voyez mieux avec ce verre-ci, avec celui-là, avec cet autre.' In plain language, he tells us to go back and read his novel more attentively.

If we place this passage in its true perspective, however, it will be seen, I think, that Proust found it essential to devote a considerable part of his novel to the subject of inversion in

[1] *TR.* ii, 69.

---

order to complete the great fresco illustrating the theme of idealism, which is nowhere more directly reflected, he believed, than in the passion of love. In his novel, Proust reveals every aspect of love, even the most abnormal manifestations of this passion. And for the same reason he allots an important place in his scheme to jealousy, the immense potentialities of which are vividly revealed in the hallucinations of Marcel and Swann. For jealousy also reflects the transforming force exercised on matter by the idea. Proust's design seems to me defective because its proportions do not correspond to those of the larger design of life itself. Is it really true, I wonder, that the best way to demonstrate the force of a psychological law, in this case the transforming power of idealism, is to select one of its most unusual manifestations, sexual inversion? Marcel's line of reasoning might lead, I fear, to the strangest conclusions, for instance, that the law of gravity is only convincingly proved, not by Newton's apple, but by the crash of an elephant from the roof of a skyscraper into the street below.

Our mind is constantly projecting itself on matter and the resulting image is what we call reality. We only think, however, that we see things in themselves: an illusion due to our habit of inaccurate perception. Now if, as Bergson remarked, we were endowed with absolutely pure perception, we should perceive things in themselves. As it is, owing to the immense contribution furnished by memory, our perceptions are largely subjective. On the other hand, every perception of the external has its roots in an instantaneous and real perception, if we could only seize it at that stage. This is precisely the task confronting the philosopher. Proust, it would seem, regarded it as an ideal of the artist whose function is *par excellence*, to obtain by a clarification of his own perceptions an objective vision of existence. The work of art is a vision in which the spectator may behold in turn a less subjective, more intuitive vision of himself and the universe. Bergson, despite his great admiration for the artist, was convinced that the latter can never give us an integral vision of the real. This splendid role he reserved for the metaphysician.

In this fashion, I interpret Marcel's present reflections, particularly the following thoughts:

Je m'étais rendu compte que seule la perception grossière et erronnée place tout dans l'objet, quand tout est dans l'esprit; j'avais perdu ma grand'mère en réalité bien des mois après l'avoir perdue en fait, j'avais vu les personnes varier d'aspect selon l'idée que moi ou d'autres s'en faisaient, une seule être plusieurs selon les personnes qui la voyaient (tels les divers Swann du début de cet ouvrage, suivant ceux qui le rencontraient; la princesse de Luxembourg suivant qu'elle était vue par le premier président ou par moi), même pour une seule au cours des années (les variations du nom de Guermantes, et les divers Swann pour moi). J'avais vu l'amour placer dans une personne ce qui n'est que dans la personne qui aime. Je m'en étais d'autant mieux rendu compte que j'avais fait varier et s'étendre à l'extrémité la distance entre la réalité objective et l'amour (Rachel pour Saint-Loup et pour moi, Albertine pour moi et Saint-Loup, Morel ou le conducteur d'omnibus pour Charlus et d'autres personnes).[1]

[I had realized that it is only crude and erroneous perception which situates everything in the object when everything is in the mind; I had lost my grandmother in reality many months after having lost her in fact, I had seen persons vary in appearance according to the idea formed of them by myself and others, a single person become several according to whoever saw him (like the different Swanns at the beginning of this work, according to those who met him; the Princess of Luxembourg according to whether she was seen by the High-Court Judge or by me), even for a single person in the course of years (the variations of the name Guermantes, and the different Swanns for me). I had seen love situate in a person what is merely in the person who loves. I had realized it all the more clearly because I had varied and extended to the extreme limit the distance between objective reality and love (Rachel for Saint-Loup and for me, Albertine for me and Saint-Loup, Morel or the omnibus-driver for Charlus and other persons).]

And, having read the novel Marcel is about to write, viewing his completed work of art in the light of his present meditations, we are in a better position to appreciate its originality and greatness. Every great work of art destroys a few more of the illusions which compose in the ensemble our ignorance of life. Proust launched a destructive attack on an illusion which most of us wrongly regard as the indispensable condition of the happy life: the illusion that the world visible to our everyday consciousness is objective and real and, with all its defects, is the best of all possible worlds. Happy ignorance? Necessary

[1] *TR.* ii, 72.

ignorance? Ignorance, for the artist, as for the philosopher and scientist, is never a happy state. To regard it as necessary is a blasphemous and cowardly negation of man's finest attribute; of what essentially distinguishes man from all other sentient beings: the will to know.

I have always imagined, perhaps naïvely, that the most tormenting of all the problems confronting a novelist must be the choice of a suitable closing scene. My commiseration does not of course extend to those confectioners of fiction who inform us coyly that the ending 'just wrote itself', three words which read in their Latin translation, *desinit in piscem*. No, my sympathy is reserved for the masters, especially for Proust, because his novel, unlike those of his predecessors, does not follow the traditional pattern of drama, with a clear-cut exposition, crisis, peripeteia and dénouement. Genius, however, always finds a simple and original solution to every problem. So did Proust when he entrusted all the arrangements for his final tableau to that experienced producer and incomparable scenic artist: Time.

The concert over, Marcel is ushered from the library into the great *salon*, there to be confronted by an extraordinary spectacle, though, as it gradually transpires, no one else appears to find it extraordinary. It is a masquerade where all the 'effects', down to the minutest detail, have been patiently elaborated and brilliantly realized by Proust's appointed impresario: Time. The general illusion which he has obviously aimed to create is that of Old Age, and so wonderfully trained are the actors and actresses, so perfect in their acting and make-up, that at first the bewildered Marcel finds it extremely hard to recognize their real identities. Most of them, however, he has known for years. The affable gentleman with whom he is now shaking hands is the prince de Guermantes, but amazingly disguised as a venerable *grand seigneur* with silvery, flowing beard and dragging gait. Beside him is Marcel's old enemy, M. d'Argencourt, undoubtedly the hit of the show, with his incredibly lifelike impersonation of an old *gaga* with one foot in the grave, who might have stepped straight out of a farce by Regnard or Labiche. Gradually, as he moves amongst the guests, he manages to penetrate nearly all their disguises though some completely baffle him. Greeted by a stout, elderly woman who seems to know him well, Marcel hesitates, smiling, before saluting her as Mme de Forcheville, his grand-uncle Adolphe's lady in pink, the Odette with whom Swann was once so madly in love. But it is her daughter Gilberte, though Odette is also here, yet unrecognizable because she has not changed.

Odette is not by any means the only one to defy Time. Indeed, the general conclusion to be drawn from Proust's fascinating description of this pageant staged by Time is that in contrast with the docility of the men, the feminine members of the cast are a continual nuisance to the producer by the diabolic ingenuity with which they evade his orders. This does not escape the watchful eye of Marcel, who appears to derive a malicious pleasure from Time's discomfiture. Who else could have satirized so wickedly, in the following parody of *Salammbô*, the agelessness of the duchesse de Guermantes.

> . . .je venais de la voir, passant entre une double haie de curieux qui, sans se rendre compte des merveilleux artifices de toilette et d'esthétique qui agissaient sur eux, émus devant cette tête rousse, ce corps saumoné émergeant à peine de ses ailerons de dentelle noire, et étranglé de joyaux, le regardaient, dans la sinuosité héréditaire de ses lignes, comme ils eussent fait de quelque vieux poisson sacré, chargé de pierreries, en lequel s'incarnait le Génie protecteur de la famille Guermantes.[1]

When Proust is on this subject, his style is quite inimitable and one's only embarrassment is that of choice. Lack of space makes it impossible, unfortunately, to quote his two brilliant pages on the princesse de Nissau, so I must be content to reproduce these extracts:

> Une dame sortit, car elle avait d'autres matinées et devait aller goûter avec deux reines. C'était cette grande cocotte du monde que j'avais connue autrefois, la princesse de Nissau. Mis à part le fait que sa taille avait diminué — ce qui lui donnait l'air par sa tête située à une bien moindre hauteur qu'elle n'était autrefois, d'avoir ce qu'on appelle 'un pied dans la tombe' — on aurait à peine pu dire qu'elle avait vieilli. Elle restait une Marie-Antoinette au nez autrichien, au regard délicieux, conservée, embaumée grâce à mille fards adorablement unis qui lui faisaient une figure lilas. Il flottait sur elle cette

expression confuse et tendre d'être obligée de partir, de promettre
tendrement de revenir, de s'esquiver discrètement, qui tenait à la
foule des réunions d'élite où on l'attendait. Née presque sur les
marches d'un trône, mariée trois fois, entretenue longtemps et riche-
ment par de grands banquiers, sans compter les mille fantaisies qu'elle
s'était offertes, elle portait légèrement comme ses yeux admirables et
ronds, comme sa figure fardée et comme sa robe mauve, les souvenirs
un peu embrouillés de ce passé innombrable.... Puis m'ayant quitté,
elle se mit à trotter vers la porte, pour qu'on ne se dérangeât pas pour
elle, pour me montrer que si elle n'avait pas causé avec moi, c'est
qu'elle était pressée pour rattraper la minute perdue à me serrer la
main afin d'être exacte chez la reine d'Espagne qui devait goûter seule
avec elle. Même près de la porte je crus qu'elle allait prendre le pas
de course. Elle courait en effet à son tombeau.[1]

[A lady went out, for she had other afternoon engagements and
was due to take tea with two queens. It was that famous Society
cocotte I once used to know, Princess de Nissau. Apart from the fact
that she had grown slimmer—which, with her head situated at a much
lower altitude than formerly, made her look as though she had, as they
say, 'one foot in the grave'—you could hardly have said that she
had aged. She was still a Marie-Antoinette, with her Austrian nose,
delightful to look at, preserved, embalmed thanks to a thousand
adorably blended cosmetics which gave her a lilac complexion. There
hovered over her face that confused, appealing expression of being
sorry to have to leave, of promising tenderly to come back, of slipping
away discreetly, which came from the swarm of exclusive gatherings
where her presence was expected. Born almost on the steps of a
throne, married three times, long and lavishly maintained by big
bankers, not to speak of the thousands of fancies to which she had
treated herself, she wore lightly, like her admirable and round eyes,
like her make-up and like her mauve dress, the somewhat muddled
recollections of that innumerable past.... Then, having left me, she
began to trot towards the door, so that no one should put himself
about because of her, to show me that if she had not stopped for a chat
with me, it was because she was in a hurry to catch up the minute lost
in shaking hands and arrive punctually at the residence of the Queen
of Spain who was to take tea alone with her. Even near the door
I thought she was going to break into a run. She was, in fact, running
to her grave.]

  Style, Proust once remarked, is, for the writer as for the
painter, a question, not of technique, but of vision. This truth is

[1] *TR.* ii, 167-8.

demonstrated everywhere of course in his novel, yet nowhere
more convincingly than in the pages inspired by Marcel's
reflections on Time. That is because no one has ever observed
like Proust the hundred ways in which Time, of which one is
usually conscious only as a colourless and bodiless entity or
concept, is, nevertheless, constantly being materialized or refracted in ourselves and in the persons and things composing
our universe. It is this idea of Time, Marcel tells us, which
will determine the shape of his work of art.

Cette dimension du Temps que j'avais jadis pressentie dans l'église
de Combray, je tâcherais de la rendre continuellement sensible dans
une transcription du monde qui serait précisément bien différente de
celle que nous donnent nos sens mensongers.[1]

What does Proust mean, in this context, by 'le Temps'? Is
it real Time, Bergson's 'la durée', or clock-Time, the abstract,
mathematical Time which the latter contemptuously dismisses
as a mere fourth dimension of Space? Quite obviously, it is the
latter, the Time which Marcel tells us has been rendered visible
to him by the reception at the Guermantes, and which he proposes to render visible to us in his novel. Otherwise, how are
we to interpret his profound anxiety when, on entering the
salon, he observes the incompatibility between the idea of a
destructive Time, that is, of Time which is counted in days and
years, and his former idea of a real Time which is not quanti-
tative but qualitative?

Mais une raison plus grave expliquait mon angoisse; je découvrais
cette action destructrice du temps, au moment où je voulais entre-
prendre de rendre claire, d'intellectualiser dans une œuvre d'art des
réalités extra-temporelles.[2]

But as we have learned from the passage I have quoted, which
appears at the very end of *Le temps retrouvé*, Marcel was
apparently obliged to abandon his original ambition or at least
to resort to a compromise.

As the afternoon draws to a close, Marcel, after reflecting
upon the variety of sites or places of his existence refracted in the
spectrum of Time, of Time as he sees it exteriorized in this

[1] *TR.* ii, 256.   [2] *TR.* ii, 98.

reunion of old friends, arrives at two conclusions. In narrating
the history of his life, he must jettison the traditional 'plane'
psychology of so-called realism and substitute what he calls
a sort of psychology in Space. Only in this way can he succeed in
portraying 'cette grande dimension du Temps suivant laquelle
la vie se réalise'.[1] This does not mean, however, that he has
renounced his belief that the only real impressions of his
existence are those precious extra-temporal, fragments resurrected by his unconscious memory. He still shares Bergson's
conviction that whilst it is necessary, owing to the exigencies of
social existence, that we should think of Time as measurable
like Space, real life, our inner life, is an indivisible continuity.
Whilst never losing his faith in the uniqueness of his 'résurrections de la mémoire' or in the hope that the artist will eventually
find a way of expressing real Time, Marcel is evidently compelled to admit that such intuitive revelations are of brief
duration and are moreover involuntary or fortuitous. Besides,
the public to whom the artist must communicate his intuitive
vision of life as it evolves in real Time, is a public accustomed
by habit and by necessity, to eliminate real Time from its
consciousness. This, I think, is implied in his decision to set
out in bold relief the notion of Time—that is to say, mathematical
Time—which is usually invisible, yet incorporated or realized
in himself and in all the people whose lives have helped to
compose the design of his own life. But this aspect of the work
of art, Proust infers, will never possess the unique quality of
Marcel's 'résurrections de la mémoire' though, by contrast, they
will shine out with enhanced beauty.

Proust speaks with the humility of the truly great artist for
whom creation must always be an act of faith, the hopeful
striving to achieve an inner ideal. What others regard as success
will always seem to him to fall short of perfection. And when, as
in the case of Proust, an artist makes us the confidants of his
secret aspirations, it is surely unjust and ungrateful to ignore his
positive achievement under the pretext that he has failed to
attain his confessed objective. Therefore, in this matter of
Proust and Time, even if he has not discovered a miraculous

[1] *TR.* II, 238.

way of communicating life *sub specie durationis*, do not let us forget the genius of the novelist who has revealed the hundreds of subtle modes by which the idea of Time permeates and influences our lives. Proust illustrates the secret activities of Time everywhere in his novel. But for a mass revelation nothing can parallel this final scene where all the surviving characters of *A la recherche du temps perdu* are illuminated in the searchlight of Time. A terrain that had appeared smooth and uniform is brilliantly projected in sharp relief, displaying a landscape of singular variety.

Marcel, a sympathetic yet amused spectator of Time's stubborn conflict with the duchesse de Guermantes is suddenly transformed into one of the actors in this masquerade. Oriane's greeting: 'Quelle joie de vous revoir, mon plus vieil ami!' is like the blast of the last trump. A new and startling image which nothing can henceforth obliterate is reflected in her words, the image of an elderly gentleman. Just in case he might be tempted to elude this vision, fresh reminders surge up from every quarter. The young officer whom Marcel had thought of as a possible comrade, a successor to Saint-Loup, and who was prevented from attending the reception, sends a deferential little note signed 'Votre petit ami', the kind of note Marcel used to write to his seniors by many years. A charming girl invites him to dine at a restaurant and he accepts with the punctilious reservation: 'si vous ne trouvez pas compromettant de venir dîner seul avec un jeune homme'. The laughter evoked by his involuntary remark rather piques Marcel until he remembers that Time has just cracked another joke at his expense. And his morale is hardly uplifted by the numerous solicitous inquiries about his health coupled with the friendly assurances that at his age he need not worry about influenza which is dangerous only for young persons.

Bloch is here, also, though his name has been changed to Jacques du Rozier. Changed in appearance as in manner, he reveals no trace of the individual we met long ago in Mme de Villeparisis' *salon*. Tailored by Savile Row, impassive and monocled, the Bloch who used to embark on long journeys in response to invitations never meant to be accepted, now looks upon his appearances in the Faubourg Saint-Germain as tiresome duties. Something of his juvenile curiosity, however, is revived by this meeting with Marcel who finds himself replying to Bloch's questions exactly in the manner of Swann and Charlus when they used to unravel for his instruction the tangled web of genealogy. Morel stops to exchange a few civilities, a completely altered Morel who is known to society, not as the former protégé of Charlus, but as the witness in a recent famous trial when his evidence sent the accused to jail and impressed the judge and counsel by its high moral tone. Marcel, renewing contacts after many years with one after another of the people he used to know, is reminded by their presence of those whom he will never see again. So the past mingles with the present to form a strangely complicated design. And yet, he reflects, although destiny brought him into touch with each of these individuals, it was always in circumstances that interposed a veil between his mind and their true individuality. Vamping a Bergsonian idea, Marcel observes that between ourselves and others there is a 'liséré de contingences' which prevents an absolute coincidence of our mind and reality. Therefore, although the life of another may seem to follow the course of our own, this is always an illusion. 'Nos vies parallèles ressemblent aux bords de ces allées où de distance en distance des vases de fleurs sont placés symétriquement mais non en face les uns des autres.'[1] Proust does not enlarge on this thought. Had he done so it would have been, no doubt, to point out how greatly life is saddened and complicated by our refusal to face the truth symbolized in Marcel's image. He himself now knows, too late, that much of his own unhappiness derived from no other cause. No two persons have the same way of remembering experience or of receiving impressions from life: a very obvious fact, of course, yet one which few of us ever really apprehend. As a result, we live in a perpetual state of astonishment. Thus Marcel is surprised to observe the affability shown by Legrandin to Bloch whom he formerly regarded with unmitigated contempt. And the duc de Villemandois, whose persistently insulting attitude to Marcel and the latter's natural reaction had made them tacit enemies, now evinces a genuine and cordial

[1] *TR.* II, 161.

desire to renew his acquaintance. This remarkable *volte-face* is not to be explained by the changed social position of Marcel, nor in the case of Legrandin by the fact that Bloch is now a distinguished writer. The true reason is that in the memories of Villemandois and of Legrandin they exist only as fragmentary, not as uniform images. Marcel, for Villemandois, is simply a person he vaguely connects with the society who frequented his aunt's *salon*. Probably, too, there was no resemblance between the impressions made on his mind by Marcel's truculence and the effect which the latter naïvely believed he had produced.

Proust was always vastly intrigued by the *terra incognita* which separates one individual from another and that is why he attaches so much importance to the idea of Time. With remarkable thoroughness Marcel now scrutinizes the bodies and minds of his old friends and enemies, observing the destructive effects of age until, by dint of comparing his actual perceptions with the images lodged in memory, he sees these individuals in volume, stereoscoped, as it were, in Time. Sometimes it would seem, however, that this fourth dimension is absent; that nothing remains, for example, to connect a certain hard-eyed, fleshy politician with the former school comrade whose name he bears. Suddenly the politician, tickled by one of Marcel's remarks, utters a crazy hoot of laughter and magically the missing plane slides into place and the personality stands out in volume, casting a shadow into the past. These people exteriorize Time, lending substance and colour to what is normally invisible, colourless, immaterial. In the alterations due to the passage of years, they reflect not only the movement and change of the universe but also reveal to Marcel the solidarity of his past and actual perceptions. Viewed in the perspective of Time, his relationships with all these men and women become more clearly visible and the *terra incognita* loses some of its mystery. Clearer, too, is the huge and intricate chart of Marcel's existence, the course of which now can be seen as a network of tiny, interconnected rivulets, hitherto unsuspected because they had been forgotten or, more often, never consciously perceived. Here, also, is the design of his work of art though there are many lacunae, missing strands which memory is powerless to re-create. Nevertheless, as he talks with the duchesse de Guermantes, Bloch, Gilberte and Odette, observing them in Time, the pattern of his existence begins to acquire, under the re-creative influence of memory, a dynamic force of proliferation. Gilberte was the little girl who once looked at Marcel through a flowering hawthorn hedge and the man behind her with the protruding eyes was, according to Combray gossip, Odette's lover. But he must have been the Charlus of the Grand Hôtel at Balbec, the nephew of Mme de Villeparisis. And Gilberte's mother, Odette, was the Miss Sacripant of Elstir's portrait, the 'dame en rose' he met in grand-uncle Adolphe's flat, the Mme de Crécy who married Swann and, strange to say, who is Jupien's cousin. Charles Swann was the family friend who used to drop in on summer evenings at Combray: Marcel can still hear the tinkling of the bell that announced his arrival. This was the same Charles Swann whom his aunts spoke of humorously as a flighty young fellow with no social position, though the duchesse de Guermantes knew him only as the Swann of the Jockey Club and the intimate of the Prince of Wales. What does Marcel know of Oriane herself? In his memory there are so many different images of the duchesse de Guermantes: at the marriage of Dr Percepied's niece; in Mme de Villeparisis' *salon*; in the quiet streets of the Faubourg Saint-Germain; at the gala matinée in the Opéra-Comique. There are so many fragmented images. Now Gilberte is talking of Robert. Another vision surges up, revealing a suite of other fragmentary impressions: Balbec; Rivebelle; Doncières; his Paris flat on the evening he wept over the frustrated love affair with Mme de Stermaria whom he has never met. The design grows in complexity as the past actualizes itself in the present, foreshadowing the pattern of the future when Gilberte brings forward her daughter, now sixteen, in whom the past lives on —Marcel's past with Robert.

Ce nez charmant, légèrement avancé en forme de bec, avait la courbe, non point de celui de Swann mais de celui de Saint-Loup. L'âme de ce Guermantes s'était évanouie; mais la charmante tête aux yeux perçants de l'oiseau envolé, était venue se poser sur les épaules de Mlle de Saint-Loup, ce qui faisait longuement rêver ceux qui avaient connu son père. Je la trouvais bien belle: pleine encore d'espérances. Riante, formée des années mêmes que j'avais perdues, elle ressemblait à ma jeunesse.[1]

In these pages where Time is accorded the ceremonial honours of an apotheosis, there is hardly a line which does not brilliantly illustrate the Proustian maxim that style is essentially a question of vision; that the artist sees the universe in a certain way and communicates through his style the unique quality of his vision. Now, what Marcel sees at this Guermantes' *matinée* is not a vision of the past but of something which he tells us is much more precious: it is a vision of the relationship linking past and present, of past and present interfused. Therefore, Proust does not stress the *eheu! fugaces* aspect of the Time idea, though many passages reveal how exquisitely sensitive he was to the poignant quality of the emotions which invade our consciousness when we contrast the drabness of actuality with the fragrant beauty of our memories and allow our thoughts to linger on that which used to be when we were young and gay and full of hope. And even towards the close of Marcel's narrative when certain disturbing physical symptoms flash out their warning message there is no suggestion of self-pity or regret, though from time to time we can hear the plangent chords of distant and funereal music. Proust, as if to belie La Rochefoucauld's maxim: 'Le soleil et la mort ne peuvent se regarder fixement', gazes unflinchingly at death with a serenity resembling that of Odette whom we now observe in the Guermantes' *salon*, holding in her cool and indomitable eyes the yellow, leonine stare of her last lover, Basin de Guermantes.

Proust is seldom flippant and never morbid on the subject of death. Occasionally, as we have noted, he appears to share Bergson's view that the soul probably survives the disintegration of the body; or that, at any rate, in the actual state of our knowledge concerning this problem of immortality, the onus of proof now rests with the materialists. Quite definitely, however, he refuses to believe that the soul, even if it does survive, can preserve a memory of its earthly past. Indeed, this is Marcel's supreme consolation when he considers how quickly the dead

[1] *TR.* ii, 239.

cease to exist in our hearts and, nevertheless, live on in our memory, though the mode of their survival is perhaps more terrible than complete oblivion. This thought is born of a casual remark uttered by the duchesse de Guermantes with whom Marcel is exchanging reminiscences. She recalls the evening of the fancy-dress ball and Marcel's refusal to accompany them because of an appointment with a girl at his flat, a naïve admission which greatly amused the duke. The girl was Albertine, whom he has long forgotten and ceased to love.

C'est que longtemps après que les pauvres morts sont sortis de nos cœurs, leur poussière indifférente continue à être mêlée, à servir d'alliage, aux circonstances du passé. Et sans plus les aimer il arrive qu'en évoquant une chambre, une allée, un chemin, où ils furent à une certaine heure, nous sommes obligés, pour que la place qu'ils occupaient soit remplie, de faire allusion à eux, même sans les regretter, même sans les nommer, même sans permettre qu'on les identifie. (Mme de Guermantes n'identifiait guère la jeune fille qui devait venir ce soir-là, n'avait jamais su son nom, et n'en parlait qu'à cause de la bizarrerie de l'heure et de la circonstance.) Telles sont les formes dernières et peu enviables de la survivance.[1]

Out of Marcel's spiritual renaissance there emerges the apprehension of imminent death, an emotion he had never thought to experience again. For Proust, clearly, this was inevitable because the love of art implies an utter surrender of the self. By a curious extension of the Bergson concept of life as eternal re-creation, Proust explains the mechanism by which Marcel's fear of death was resurrected. Every time he fell in love, the thought of death appalled him: it was intolerable to reflect that the being who loved Gilberte or Albertine should ever cease to exist. Yet the self who loved Gilberte died in order to make way for a new self who existed solely for Albertine yet also died, again to be survived by another self, another Marcel who now experiences no suffering. Therefore, concluded Marcel, there was no need to be terrified of the idea of death. But now that he is in love with a new mistress, art, without whom life is inconceivable, the old dread returns in a new form: the work of art awaits creation. An accident, a malady entailing loss of memory, the slightest damage to the protective casing of that frail embryo may cause its sudden destruction. And something occurs to prove that this is no foolish anxiety. One evening, on his way to a social function, Marcel nearly falls down three times on the stairs. Two hours later, on his return, he is discovered in a state of mental 'black-out', accompanied by the terrible feeling that he no longer possesses any thought, memory or even existence. And so far not one line of his book has been written. Small wonder, then, if the idea of death has now become an obsession, disputing for mastery in his consciousness with the idea of Time.

Proust does not contemplate Death or his associate and usher, Time, with mystic awe, but with an interested apprehension. Like Marcel at the Guermantes', he observes their inseparable activities with the enlightened deference of an artist contemplating the work of a master. Old age impresses him as more terrible than death because it is so often accompanied by loneliness, pain, neglect and sometimes by cruelty. When Marcel considers the fate of very old people it is with unbearable sadness. They seem to inhabit, in the precincts of the cemetery, a closed city where the lamps are always shining dimly in a perennial mist. The emotion symbolized in Marcel's image discreetly permeates this final chapter of *A la recherche du temps perdu* and achieves at times a diamantine and immortal crystallization. I am thinking, particularly, of the episode where the famous tragedienne, La Berma, is revealed, off-stage, but in the greatest part she ever played. And with this last impression of Proust I will conclude my attempt to interpret his great work of art.

In the flower-paintings of certain Flemish masters one can sometimes espy in a dewdrop the reflection of a window looking out upon a distant landscape. In much the same fashion, Proust captures in this miniature pendant to Balzac's *Le Père Goriot*, a fragment of Marcel's existence; nay, of an epoch. At the Guermantes' matinée, the centre of attraction is Rachel, the former mistress of Saint-Loup, once known to Marcel as 'Rachel quand du Seigneur'. She has just been reciting the poetry of La Fontaine, to the approving murmurs of an audience schooled by the duchesse de Guermantes, according to whom Rachel is the most talented of living French actresses. Oriane has obviously forgotten that remote and very different recital which took place in her own *salon*. Meanwhile, in another quarter of Paris, La Berma is also holding a reception, in honour of her adored, ungrateful daughter and her despised son-in-law. Here is the idol of Marcel's adolescence, the actress whose marvellous interpretation of Racine's *Phèdre* first taught him the meaning of creative art. Now she is old and tortured by an incurable disease. Yet, in order to satisfy her daughter's craving for elegance and luxury, she continues to appear on the stage. The hour appointed for the reception is long past but, except for a solitary young man, there are no guests. Soon he departs for the Guermantes', sullenly envied by La Berma's daughter who would sacrifice almost anything and, indeed, sacrifices her mother's prestige, in order to be introduced by Rachel to the society of the Faubourg Saint-Germain. No sooner has La Berma sadly retired to her room than the young couple furtively drive off to the house in the Avenue du Bois and, though uninvited, succeed finally by their abject importunings in being admitted to the presence of Rachel. By this act the daughter effectively kills her mother, for she ruins her social position, exposing her to the ruthless mockery of a woman whom La Berma had never deigned to recognize as an actress, much less as a rival. Style, for Proust, is the revelation, impossible by direct or conscious means, of that immaterial something which is the quality of the artist's unique vision. In the course of this study many passages have been quoted which perfectly realize his noble conception of the supreme function of language. Here is a final illustration. It is the passage where this incomparable stylist communicates Marcel's impressions of the doomed tragedienne as she is about to enter that closed city which houses the very old whom no one loves any more.

Quand la Berma vit l'heure passer et comprit que tout le monde la lâchait elle fit servir le goûter et on s'assit autour de la table mais comme pour un repas funéraire. Rien dans la figure de la Berma ne rappelait plus celle dont la photographie m'avait, un soir de mi-carême, tant troublé. La Berma avait la mort sur le visage. Cette fois c'était bien d'un marbre de l'Erechtéion qu'elle avait l'air. Ses artères durcies étant déjà à demi pétrifiées, on voyait de longs rubans sculpturaux parcourir les joues, avec une rigidité minérale. Les yeux mourants vivaient relativement par contraste avec ce terrible masque ossifié et brillaient faiblement comme un serpent endormi au milieu des pierres. Cependant, le jeune homme qui s'était mis à table par politesse regardait sans cesse l'heure, attiré qu'il était par la brillante fête chez les Guermantes. La Berma n'avait pas un mot de reproche à l'adresse des amis qui l'avaient lâchée et qui espéraient naïvement qu'elle ignorerait qu'ils étaient allés chez les Guermantes. Elle murmura seulement: 'Une Rachel donnant une fête chez la princesse de Guermantes, il faut venir à Paris pour voir de ces choses-là.' Et elle mangeait silencieusement et avec lenteur solennelle, des gâteaux défendus, ayant l'air d'obéir à des rites funèbres.[1]

[When La Berma saw the hour pass and knew that everybody was deserting her, she had tea brought in and they sat down round the table but as if for a funeral repast. Nothing now in La Berma's face recalled the woman whose photograph, one evening in mid-Lent, had so profoundly disturbed me. To use a popular expression, La Berma had death on her face. This time she did indeed look like one of the marbles from the Erechtheion. Her hardened arteries being already half petrified, one saw long sculptural ribbons running across her cheeks, with a mineral rigidity. The dying eyes were relatively alive by contrast with that terrible ossified mask and glittered faintly like a snake asleep amongst the stones. However, the young man who had sat down to table out of politeness kept constantly looking at the time, attracted as he was by the brilliant fête at the Guermantes'. La Berma had not one word of reproach for the friends who had let her down and who naïvely hoped she would not know they had gone to the Guermantes'. Only, she murmured: 'A Rachel giving a party at the house of the princesse de Guermantes, you have to come to Paris to see things like that.' And she partook silently and with solemn deliberation of the forbidden cakes, as if she were observing some funeral rite.]

[1] *TR.* II, 191-2.